Legal Discourses

Marcus Galdia

Legal Discourses

PL ACADEMIC RESEARCH

Bibliographic Information published by the Deutsche Nationalbibliothek
The Deutsche Nationalbibliothek lists this publication in the Deutsche Nationalbibliografie; detailed bibliographic data is available in the internet at http://dnb.d-nb.de.

Library of Congress Cataloging-in-Publication Data
Galdia, Marcus, 1961- author.
Legal discourses / Marcus Galdia.
p. cm.
ISBN 978-3-631-65590-0
1. Semantics (Law) 2. Law—Language. 3. Law—Philosophy. I. Title.
K213.G355 2014
340'.14—dc23
2014022565

ISBN 978-3-631-65590-0 (Print)
E-ISBN 978-3-653-04812-4 (E-Book)
DOI 10.3726/978-3-653-04812-4

PL Academic Research is an Imprint of Peter Lang GmbH.

Peter Lang – Frankfurt am Main · Bern · Bruxelles · New York · Oxford · Warszawa · Wien

This publication has been peer reviewed.

www.peterlang.com

Contents in Brief

Detailed Contents

Preface

In this book, law is approached from the legal-linguistic perspective. Its aim is to clarify the processes in which the meaning of law emerges in legal discourses. Specifically, professional and non-professional discourses about law are analyzed here in order to enable the understanding of law as a discursive practice. With this aim in mind, the book identifies and subsequently focuses upon the epistemological consequences of the discursiveness of law. They are reflected in the analysis of the emergence of the conceptual basis of law and the formation of its argumentation as amalgams of legal signs that form legal discourses. Other relevant legal-linguistic operations such as legal interpretation or legal translation are scrutinized in terms of their theoretical prerequisites and their practical consequences as discursive practices. Their analysis also shows the potential and the limits of law as a social and as a linguistic phenomenon that is determined by its discursiveness. Finally, the book demonstrates how the discursiveness as the distinctive feature of law establishes the connection between law and other social sciences. This specific connection is narrative because law communicates messages. Legal messages may have different logical and textual structures; they may be perceived as rules, principles, provisions, decisions and others. They can be characterized more precisely as legal speech acts of justification, description of facts and so on. Meanwhile, their common characteristic feature is the fact that they are expressed linguistically and that they emerge and are applied in meaningful textual forms. Therefore, textuality and narrativity of legal texts as well as of texts related to law are scrutinized here in order to make plain the material consequences of discursiveness in law. Narrative forms, legal terminology, and textual parameters display and materialize the structure of law as a discursive phenomenon. As a result, the emergence of law in power structures, its application in legal-linguistic operations, its rationality as a social mechanism and the fundamentals of the legal profession can be better grasped in the legal-linguistic perspective. Last but not least, speaking about law as a social activity emerges towards the background of all these discourses, their narratives, and legal speech acts used in legal-linguistic operations. This book therefore concerns mainly speaking about law. This speaking about law is not just talking or saying something or saying whatever. Therefore, many pages are spent here on describing some of the characteristic features of this speaking. People speak about law on different levels of professionalism and personal involvement. Some people may argue that 'freeholds cannot be put in abeyance' while others will pretend that 'U.S. Supreme Court justices are simply out of touch'. Traditional legal theory strictly divides this speaking about law into two. It distinguishes between professional legal discourses that interest it and other non-professional discourse that it neglects. This strict division may however be premature because social discourse has a more permeable structure. Juridical institutions function within such open and permeable discursive structures and they also benefit from them. Therefore, the legal discourse that is constitutive of the emergence of meaning in law has to integrate this diversity of speaking about law. The legal discourse that represents all this speaking integrates discourses in juridical institutions as well as discourses that take place outside this particular institutional setting. This circumstance also justifies the title of this book that refers to this not fully explored and clarified dichotomy. As mentioned, this dichotomy is strict only in theory; in social practice registers and roles often change and intertwine. Judges deal with law within their professional activity, they deal with law when they discuss legal problems with their guests at birthday parties, and they deal with law when they read detective stories in their leisure time. They and their interlocutors appear in these different discourses in different social roles where they practice different linguistic registers. Therefore, it seems worthwhile to focus on interconnections between these discursive situations that are gaining momentum in the modernizing and globalizing world. To see judges exclusively in their professional settings or to portray jurists exclusively in their action as professionals of law might impoverish our knowledge of contemporary law. Traditional legal theory rarely enquired into non-professional discourses about law in their relation to strictly professional discourses. Meanwhile, social circumstances under which different types of legal discourses come about are multiple. A more integrative perspective that is adopted in this book tries to cover this multitude of constellations in which language is used in situations connected with law. Finally, the stress upon the discourse as the biggest structuring unit in legally relevant social interactions in which meaning emerges in law prevents the analyzed material from fragmentation. Elements of the legal discourse, even if sometimes analyzed in isolation, are interwoven in overarching structures and become truly meaningful and operative in law only within these structures. Therefore, saying something in a legally relevant context means participating in a broader process of emergence of meaning in law. Such processes are not only 'broader', they are also 'complex'. The consequence of this speaking in broader contexts and towards complex backgrounds is a relatively complicated methodology that aims at explaining the language use in law. After all, complex phenomena require complex theories and the challenge concealed in the complexity of things turns legal-linguistic research into a fascinating life-long adventure. In fact, since Aristotle no other human activity has proven to be more noble and edifying than philosophical research. The methodological complexity of this essay should therefore not be perceived as a disadvantage.

Legal discourses relate to legal language. In my previous monograph *Legal Linguistics*, which was published in 2009, I mainly dealt with the description of the legal language and with the task of structuring the field of legal linguistics as a scientific discipline. *Legal Linguistics* as a general introduction into the field starts with the most fundamental question of this branch of knowledge, i.e. how law is created and applied with linguistic means. In breaking down this vast question, I identified the linguistically relevant aspects of language use, especially its terminology, and I scrutinized the most significant legal-linguistic operations such as the legal argumentation, the legal interpretation, and the legal translation. I aimed at showing the linguistic strategies that are most instrumental in the development of professionally convincing legal argumentation, primarily around terminological units. Meanwhile, also the problem of emergence of meaning in law is treated there and the relation of professional legal language and ordinary language is recognized as crucial to the development of the future law. Issues of the textuality of law and its narrativity play already an important role in *Legal Linguistics* although they are treated there rather as mere samples of legal-linguistic use of words in speech acts. Meanwhile, all named problems dealt with in *Legal Linguistics* constitute the legal linguistics as a field of academic studies. Therefore, I refer to them regularly here within the framework of legal discursiveness. All of them are relevant to legal discourses; yet they are as particular examples of the use of language in law better integrated within the research into the possible structure of the field. My *Legal Linguistics* is in my view best understood when positioned in the middle of this book, so to say between its lines. It provides comments and materials to many rather theoretical questions that seem to me unavoidable at this stage of development of the legal-linguistic research. In this book I stress the theoretical prerequisites and the practical consequences of the research into the legal language. I focus on legal discourses because they best represent the speaking about law. Legal discourses automatically and inherently reflect all problems of the legal language and help discover some others. Yet, finally they also explain law and therefore dealing with them on many pages is a rewarding task.

Monaco, April 2014

Acknowledgments

My systematic interest in legal-linguistic questions goes back to courses delivered by Professor Edeltraud Bülow at the University of Münster. I benefited from Prof. Bülow's teaching to an extent that is identifiable in every other line I write down on law and language. For all this I remain in her debt. Equally, I wish to thank Professor Heikki E.S. Mattila (Helsinki) for his support in my legal-linguistic undertakings. Never would I have got involved in the preparation for publication of my disparate notes on legal-linguistic issues without his encouragement and advice. Likewise, Professor Jaakko Husa from the University of Lapland in Rovaniemi and Dr. Aleksandra Matulewska from the Adam Mickiewicz University in Poznań were in their reviews of my previous book very helpful in identifying critical points in my *Legal Linguistics* that are at least partly elucidated in this work. Courses on Legal Linguistics and Comparative Law that I gave in 2011, 2013 and 2014 at the Riga Graduate School of Law (RGSL) helped me to address legal-linguistic issues from a perspective that can be interesting also for students. I would like to thank Ms Irēna Lapsa, Mr Christopher Goddard, and Mr Antonio Liaci from RGSL for their interest in my research as well as for their support and words of encouragement. Some students in Riga responded with unexpected interest to my views upon law and language. This circumstance is particularly inspiring because my rather cumbersome methodological approach may easily surprise the neophyte. Meanwhile, I was not less surprised when I first heard of legal linguistics and its method more than thirty years ago. Interest in the matter helps overcome initial confusion and students eager to learn unusual matters gave a new impetus to my writings. Many of the issues discussed in the book were also introduced into my law courses at the International University of Monaco (IUM) and they were patiently received by students. I tried to include in this book remarks and experience from these courses that covered different aspects of law. Particular thanks for feedback on my legal-linguistic experiments go therefore to my IUM students. Ms Susan Eklöw, Head of the Library and Research Services at IUM, was helpful in ordering books needed for this research. Professor Grażyna Maria Mirecka of IUM generously advised me on the use of computer technology that I will apparently never be able to grasp satisfactorily and use independently. My thoughts on legal translation that are exposed in one of the chapters of this book were presented and discussed in January 2012 with the staff of the Directorate-General for Translation of the European Commission in Brussels and with the translators at the Court of Justice of the European Union in Luxembourg. I would like to thank Mr. Ingemar Svartvik (Brussels) for initiating and facilitating this exchange.

The author

Introductory remarks

Legal-linguistic perspective

Law emerges as a social and as a linguistic practice in an area that is situated beyond the boundaries of the legal science. It is shaped by conceptions of right and wrong in society that are materialized in social discursive practices. Law that is shaped in these discursive practices is the object of the legal science. Jurists scrutinize this law and apply it in multiple legal-linguistic operations. Interestingly, though, most jurists join in the analysis of law at a relatively late stage. Some other jurists who deal with the fundamental research into law transgress this self-imposed boundary and concentrate on earlier stages of the emergence of law. What is more, they proceed from different perspectives. One of these perspectives is based on legal linguistics and this book deals almost exclusively with this perspective. The legal-linguistic perspective is favored in this book and the chapters that will follow provide reasons for this preference. In fact, legal linguistics discovers and scrutinizes legal-linguistic operations. It clarifies the way in which language is used in law in broader contexts that include institutions and other power structures. In these numerous institutional contexts where people communicate while using speech acts the meaning of law is constituted. Legal linguistics describes this still largely unclear field. As said, the context of emergence and understanding of law is broad. Written sources such as statutes and court precedents and orally transferred exchanges among legal professionals and non-professionals about the appropriate understanding of law form oceans of material linguistic testimony about shaping and applying law. Judgments, scholarly writings, daily talk, detective stories, and similar artifacts enable us to access the relevant mind-sets of legal professionals and of non-professionals alike. After all, jurists are human beings and their perception of law is rooted in all aspects of visual and non-visual sign systems that constitute law in its institutional sense. Also citizens at large reflect upon legal problems that are formed around their unprofessional linguistic frameworks of reference. As actors in legal discourses they are not less important than are the legal professionals because they are the princes of law, the sovereigns who shape the law. Citizens at large are less skilled in the art of participation in legal discourses than are professionals. Regularly, their interest in law is limited to the content of law. They also tend to underestimate the discursive character of law and approach law as if it were a matter of fact. Due to this fundamental misunderstanding they are therefore less efficient in processes of shaping and understanding of law. Their specific approach to law marks also the traditional divide between the discourses about law as open discourses and the discourses in law where only professionals become engaged in strictly institutionalized professional exchanges about law. The legal-linguistic approach aims at describing all these discourses because the understanding of law depends on their knowledge.

Discursiveness of law

Law, as mentioned, is a discursive practice. Discursiveness, in fact, is its main characteristic feature. Therefore, one could argue that jurists are specialists in professional, institutionalized discursive practices that constitute law in numerous speech acts structured around social institutions, legal and others, related to law. Some of them, like politics, are areas that are so close to law that some tend to confuse both. Some other areas such as history or literature are less closely related to law and legal discourses that are practiced within their boundaries lead often to frictions when confronted with law in its proper institutional sense. Meanwhile, law that is shaped in multiple legal discourses cannot be understood when its scrutiny is limited to professional discourses that display statutory language and court decisions alone. The epistemological perspective upon law has to be broadened and include all operational discursive contexts of law. The practical spheres where these discourses take place must be identified and integrated. Some interdisciplinary perspectives upon law already integrate discursive spheres relevant to law. Interdisciplinary branches of knowledge such as Law and Literature, Law and Economics, Law and Politics or Law and Visual Arts Studies illustrate the range of topics relevant to legal discourses that must be taken into consideration in an enterprise that aims at understanding law. Next to these interdisciplinary undertakings, legal linguistics also addresses the challenges in describing and understanding law in a broader epistemological context. It posits that law can be approached efficiently through the scrutiny of its language. It is therefore based on a relatively simple thought as it assumes that law, being a linguistic phenomenon, should be primarily scrutinized as such. This approach imposes itself because it refers to the material part of law, to the elements of social reality that are construed as law and which can be read or heard as language. Such an approach has also the advantage that it reduces the risk of drifting into metaphysics because the object that is canvassed in legal-linguistic studies is originally and materially present in its linguistic dress. It is also methodologically safe because no one can seriously deny the linguistic nature of law. However, law as an object of studies cannot be simply measured and weighed. Therefore, every start that takes language as the main point of scrutiny includes the evident risk in taking further steps. Everyone who treats law in a broader intellectual context will sooner or later be asked how he can actually know all that he so boldly asserts. Therefore, also the legal-linguistic approach has to prepare its own defense strategy. Defense of the legal-linguistic approach to law is not always easy. Some basic operations in law such as legal argumentation or legal interpretation cannot be materialized in a form that would convince the skeptic as a proof of the exclusively correct apprehension of law. But this risk in the defense strategy can be turned into the strength of the whole approach. While the legal linguistics opens our eyes to law, it also achieves more than only let us see the law. It provides the theoretical tools for dealing with law in a broader setting that surpasses the boundaries of positivist attempts at dealing with law. These positivist perspectives upon law that are hostile to legal linguistics reduce the legal science to an enterprise collecting allegedly right assumptions about the meaning of legal rules. Meanwhile, legal linguistics is more advanced than skeptical and critical minds assume because it is apt to demonstrate the multiple facets of law that some others simplify all too eagerly. It attempts, and it is also able to show how meaning emerges in law. Many other approaches to law limit their efforts to showing the results of the struggle for meaning in law. These approaches are not sufficient because the results as such are much more evident than the processes in which they come about. And exactly these processes, and not their mere results, enable the understanding of law. Finally, by pretending to do a lot legal linguistics is actually doing much less. It deals predominantly with the theoretical prerequisites and the practical consequences of the discursiveness of law. Its domain is the set of legal-linguistic operations that form the legal discourses. As a result, it shows law as a social phenomenon where power is exercised with linguistic means. Legal linguistics scrutinizes the linguistic forms of this exercise of power that are, as mentioned, discourses. Finally, while describing the discursiveness of law, legal linguistics also shows the limits of law. Therefore, it is actually not doing much because it constantly deals with one feature of law; it focuses upon its discursiveness. Meanwhile, the discursiveness as a structural feature links law to other social sciences. Thus, with the assistance of the legal-linguistic approach law becomes fully integrated into social sciences. By incorporating law into social sciences, the limits of the positivist legal doctrine that opposes this integration are irreversibly overcome. One can scarcely hope to accomplish more in a social science, especially when one is doing so little.

Structure of Legal Discourses

As to its structure, the book consists of nine interrelated parts divided into smaller interdependent paragraphs. The argument of this book is developed in concentric circles. This means that the structurally relevant features of the legal discourse are treated one by one, in nine parts. However, as all of them are interrelated, every part focuses on one of them in the context of other characteristic discursive features. The legal-linguistic point of departure imposes this contextual treatment of discursive features due to the complexity of the legal language that emerges in different social settings. In fact, the first part produces an amalgam of disparate speech acts that create the legal language. To cope with these particularities some more theoretical concepts and frames of reference seem to be necessary in order to avoid an unstructured assembly of speech acts that could be identified and classified ad infinitum. The following part concentrates therefore on legal ontology and legal epistemology and it discovers the discursiveness of law as its main legal-linguistic characteristics. The part on discursiveness, that limits the risk of drifting into an ocean of discursive particularities, helps us to structure the argument, yet it also shows that the legal discourse needs a more advanced perspective for its description. This perspective is found in legal semiotics that allows describing the legal discourse in terms of its main legal-linguistic operations. Thus, the description of the legal discourses approaches again the level of particularities. Yet, rational argumentation that permeates legal speech acts and all legal-linguistic operations, which are identified in the semiotic perspective, establishes again the link to the general, theoretical platform of legal-linguistic analysis. Therefore, a part on rationality and argumentation follows immediately upon the description of semiotic characteristics of the legal discourse as a result of the discursiveness of law. This part shows legal language in its most abstract form that manifests legal-linguistic regularities that should not remain without consequences for the legal science. These legal-linguistic regularities justify the claim for the linguistic turn in law that would finally enable to re-write law from the legal-linguistic perspective. Before, however, the law in force is re-written in line with the postulates accumulated in the previous parts (and this will not happen in this book) another part is devoted to existing ways and moods of stating and creating law in terms of its narrativity. Legal narrativity, that is the material component of legal discursiveness, is treated at a relatively late stage in this book because discursiveness seems to be not only primary in conceptual terms but also rather badly known and rarely researched. Narrativity, in turn, dominates professional and non-professional legal discourses because for most speakers discourses are mainly about something.

Those speakers are actually not really wrong and the part on legal narrativity also shows the complexity of narrative structures that are relevant to legal discourses. Argumentative features underlie whatever narrative structure in law and it can therefore be posited that they are its ubiquitous characteristic feature. This is the reason why a part on ubiquitous argumentation in law follows upon the part on legal narrativity. The ubiquitous legal argumentation enables to treat law also practically in terms of the ongoing globalization process. It may be expected that a new language of law will emerge in the course of this process. Some discursive features of this future language are today present in the theory of legal translation that is one of the pillars of the legal-linguistic globalization research. Legal translation as a branch of knowledge is particularly helpful at this point of the argument that is mainly future-oriented. The legal translation as one of the most conservative and also meticulously researched branches of legal linguistics stabilizes the vista upon the future legal language. This practically relevant part shows also that legal linguistics is not only a theory of law but also a mechanism of its application, locally and globally. At this point also the legal discourse is finally identified and characterized, both theoretically and practically. It is the moment when the book can end. Yet before it ends, some perspectives upon the future of legal discourses are sketched that propose to the reader a choice between an optimistic and a pessimistic narrative about the law of the immediate and the more remote future. The author can withdraw from the book at this stage as the choice between the narratives and their further development belongs to all readers who as citizens are the authors of law and as sovereigns of law they are responsible for the planet where they dwell.

Part 1: Legal-Linguistic Points of Departure

1.1 Some fundamental questions

Legal linguistics argues and also proves that the emergence of meaning in law is the fundamental question of the legal science. Therefore, when dealing with law and with the multiple problems that it causes in its linguistic formulation and in its application, it persistently focuses on the issue of meaning. In contrast, mainstream legal theory and legal doctrine deal with many issues other than the emergence of meaning in law. From the legal-linguistic perspective it is however vain to deal with whatever legal problems when the fundamental question that regards meaning is omitted. Unfortunately, this occurs regularly in the legal research and in the legal education. Legal linguistics provides a methodological remedy for this sort of perspectival distortions in enquires into law. It develops a set of methodological questions about law that integrates many legal problems that were hitherto discussed as issues of legal doctrine. Furthermore, it repositions these questions in a way that makes legal research and legal education possible in the perspective that is central to legal linguistics. The book that follows tries to demonstrate how this task could be practically accomplished. Meanwhile, it goes also without saying that achievements of the mainstream legal theory, legal philosophy or legal sociology that deal with related or analogous issues must be integrated into the legal-linguistic perspective. Legal-linguistic research that falls behind the state of the art documented in these sister disciplines would not be worth its name. The interest in distinctive features of law, in power structures, and in the scope and methods of legal regulation that steers the research in the sister disciplines of legal linguistics has to be admitted as a benchmark for measuring its usefulness. Legal linguistics can be taken seriously and convince even its opponents only when it provides results that can at least compete with, if not surpass, the knowledge accumulated in its sister disciplines. Within these disciplines one can identify at least some schools or scholars who scrutinize law from perspectives that are close to legal linguistics. These perspectives will be stressed in the following chapters to the deplorable, yet unavoidable neglect of many other views that are valuable to the study of law while remaining indirectly connected with our topic. The selective approach to existing views, opinions and theories about law is methodologically essential because legal linguistics does not aim at integrating all interesting theories about law. Central to the legal-linguistic perspective are language and discourse, other legally relevant aspects of law interest it less. In fact, the legal-linguistic perspective primarily focuses on language and discourse in the hope that through their scrutiny law will be understood more fully, if not completely.

1.2 Meaning and discourses in law

The relevance of meaning emergence in the area of law is not an extraordinary or surprising question. In all other social sciences, and foremost in linguistics, emergence of meaning is central to the formation of their conceptual frames of reference. Also in these branches of knowledge scholars deal with many other issues than meaning. Meanwhile, their efforts would be of secondary importance would they not be directed towards elucidation of this fundamental question. Legal linguistics teaches us also that meaning in law does not simply emerge in a void space. It appears in social interactions that can be called legal discourses. Identifying legal discourses, tracing their modes of appearance and their effectiveness are the steps dictated by the legal-linguistic approach. Significantly, Peter L. Berger (1963: 40) characterized the general situation of the use of language in law with following words: "Almost any human activity can, at one time or another, fall within the province of the lawyer. This, indeed, is the fascination of the law. Again, we will find here a very special procedure of abstraction. From the immense wealth and variety of human deportment the lawyer selects those aspects that are pertinent (or, as they would say, 'material') to his very particular frame of reference. As anyone who has ever been involved in a lawsuit well knows, the criterion of what is legally relevant or irrelevant will often greatly surprise the principals in the case in question." Berger aptly identified the general, abstract way of legal reasoning within the frame of reference that is imposed by the legal doctrine. He furthermore stressed that this frame of reference is specific due to a particular use of language. Certain aspects of social reality are 'material' for a lawyer and this choice of 'material facts' may take non-lawyers by surprise. Legal discourses take place in this enigmatic and also controversial area where 'a very special procedure of abstraction' is applied. Berger's characterization of the general discursive situation in law could be used as a point of departure for a future-oriented vision upon law. It can however also be used as a point from which a retrospection that elucidates his view might take place. Therefore, in this chapter we will take several steps back and look behind the general situation of discourse that was sketched in these introductory lines in order to make plain how the perspective upon law that is here called legal-linguistic came about.

These steps back shall also avert the risk of falling behind the achievements of other related disciplines. In fact, Berger's analysis is not primarily legal-linguistic as it aims at explaining society, and not law. Meanwhile, while explaining the one, it also clarifies the other. It is therefore, like many other approaches that are primarily not legal-linguistic, helpful in legal linguistics. Many concepts and conceptions that were coined in other disciplines can be integrated into the legal-linguistic research that does not start or develop in a vacuum. It may also be expedient to remind that legal linguistics developed not only around or within linguistic methods and conceptions (Mattila 2013: 15–19). Its background is composed of elements of the philosophy of language and the philosophy of mind that developed within the tradition of the analytical philosophy. Moreover, linguistic pragmatics and American pragmatism that both are related to the fundamental methods and achievements of the analytical philosophy added tools and results to the emerging legal-linguistic perspective (Galdia 2009: 51). Deontic logic, legal hermeneutics, and theory of legal argumentation provided specific contributions to the legal science that have to be considered from the legal-linguistic perspective as well (cf. Aarnio 2012). When we know all this, we also know a lot about law. One could therefore argue that actually a step forwards would be better adapted to the development in the legal research than a step back that is proposed here. This would be a possible, yet not necessarily the only appropriate step. At its inception, also the analytical philosophy claimed a radical breach with the philosophical tradition of two and a half thousand years. However, further inquiries into the nature of analyzed problems showed links to other philosophical traditions that made this breach appear much less radical (Laugier/Plaud 2011: 14). Legal linguistics is in the same position. While being a relatively new and weakly institutionalized area of knowledge, it also looks back at a history of conscious emergence of concepts, conceptions and perspectives that finally condensed into a more unified field of methods and results that today can be called legal linguistics. The chapter below should therefore make plain that questions asked in legal linguistics are not coincidental and that they reflect the problems described by Berger in form of the general discursive situation.

1.3 Linguistic turn in law

Legal linguistics is a strategical intellectual undertaking. It primarily aims to accomplish the linguistic turn in law because it is well aware of the particularities of language use in law. Meanwhile, the linguistic turn is not a specific method developed for dealing with law. For philosophy, John Searle (2006) argued that its greatest achievements "over the past hundred or one hundred and twenty years have been in the philosophy of language." In the legal sciences, however, language has played a subaltern role although law has been identified as a linguistic phenomenon par excellence. Also the traditional legal theory devoted more effort to justifying or criticizing the power structures in which law has been created and applied than to its linguistic aspect of emergence and application. Theoretical works that explicitly focused on the language of law were rare and they lacked influence upon the legal science. In the way of most striking examples one could mention Eugeniusz Bautro's (1935) attempt at establishing a science called by him 'legal linguistics' and Karl Olivekrona's (1969) analysis of legal language and social reality. More recently, however, interest in the linguistic aspects of law reached the level of institutionalization within the interdisciplinary dialogue between the legal science and other disciplines. The works by D. Mellinkoff (1963), P. Tiersma (1999) and Heikki E.S. Mattila (2012, 2013) imposed on the scientific community a perspective upon law that has hitherto been perceived as an undercurrent of legal thinking. In addition, the institutionalization of legal-linguistic studies in form of university courses, master's programs, and specialized professorships paved the way towards broadening the linguistic perspective upon law. These steps cannot be perceived as an accomplishment of the linguistic turn; yet they are moves towards a paradigmatic change in legal sciences that seems unavoidable. Also the author of these lines tried to strengthen the tendency towards linguistic turn in the legal science. In *Legal Linguistics* (2009) I tried to develop the general structure for legal linguistics and I also tried to identify some of its most urgent issues for the research to come. The first step being done, I now make the second step towards implementation of claims developed under the program for the linguistic turn. All the named efforts notwithstanding, the linguistic turn in law will not be achieved without a more vigorous support and innovative contributions coming from many. Paradigmatic changes in an area of knowledge may be initiated by a few scholars; yet they bear fruits only when many others join them and support the paradigmatic move with new ideas to which they are truly committed. The contemporary tendency is rather positive, at least in terms of numbers. Also in legal sciences quantity and quality are not disconnected, and sooner or later more distinct profiles of a new legal linguistics will emerge. They will hopefully materialize and finalize the paradigmatic change in the legal sciences. By achieving this lofty goal we will also be able to explain the intricacies of the general discursive situation described by P. Berger. We will also be able to overcome the perplexity caused by the use of language in law that was legitimately perceived by Berger and many others as 'particular'.

1.4 Discursive choices and particularity of language use in law

The choice of 'legal discourse' as a focal point for this essay can be justified as a more or less automatic consequence of dealing with theoretical fundamentals of legal linguistics. Their most challenging element is the 'particularity' of the use of language in law. This particularity can be explained with the help of many philosophical approaches. The schools and tendencies in philosophy that were exploited in my *Legal Linguistics* include analytical philosophy, linguistic pragmatics, semiotics, and Michel Foucault's 'épistémologie'. All of them lead in the synthetical view upon the development of their epistemological frames of reference towards increased interest in 'discourse' and in 'discursive practices'. As a result of the theoretical analyses that were accomplished in the past, it has become evident that linguistic analysis cannot be limited to isolated terms or concepts, to speech acts or isolated signs. Therefore, it became urgent to consolidate the available knowledge with the help of broader concepts apt at integrating smaller elements of linguistic meaning constitution. 'Discourse' and 'text' were such concepts that provided for a more coherent view of the assembled samples of speech. Consequently, also in legal linguistics many researchers began to study discourses, mostly in the form of 'courtroom discourses' because these texts appealed to linguists due to their incontestable discursive nature. With good reasons one could limit the epistemological interest in the 'legal discourse' to linguistic practices, strategies and devices used by participants in courtroom discourses. For legal linguists these discourses are fascinating because they illustrate the processes of planified and spontaneous emergence of meaning in law. This interest is not new either. Already G.W.F. Hegel in his *Philosophy of Right* (1821) became interested in processes of 'administration of justice' where the 'abstract right' is invoked. An 'abstract right' has according to Hegel an 'infinite personality' and it therefore needs semantic concretization, or 'crystallization' in Hegel's language, when it is expected to be of use in the legal practice of 'administration of justice'. Hegel's philosophical approach also explains why institutionalized processes of 'administration of justice' were established with the aim in mind to make operational this sort of 'abstract right'. Likewise, J.S. Mill in *Utilitarianism* (1863) spoke about the 'useful accommodation of language' when law is applied. Contemporary research into 'courtroom discourses' shows how this task is practically accomplished. Meanwhile, reflection upon discourses in law also indicated the ubiquitous application of discursive practices in law. One can therefore make several steps ahead and include legislative discourses as well as scholarly and educational discourses in the sphere of professional legal-linguistic interest. The methodological problem of determining the range of discursive practices in legal linguistics can be reduced to the question where to stop. Some scholars assert that where professionalism in law ends there by necessity also law and related science must end. It means that as long as speakers debate about the possibility to 'put a freehold in abeyance' they use language in a professional way and it makes sense to research such use of language. G.W.F. Hegel warned against such artificial limitations to testing socially relevant speech. In the addition 135 to paragraph 215 of his *Philosophy of Right* Hegel writes: "The legal profession, possessed of a special knowledge of the law, often claims this knowledge as its monopoly and refuses to allow any layman to discuss the subject." He firmly opposed this limitation as "Law is concerned with freedom, the worthiest and holiest thing in man, the thing man must know if it is to have obligatory force to him." Hegel aptly identified the most important problem of legal discourses. Law is not only literature or talk; its essence is not the exchange of views about right and wrong in society. Law imposes and enforces behavior because it is backed by 'obligatory force' that may limit 'freedom'. In order to function in society, law needs acceptance because sheer threat with its forcible application has limits (Berger 1963: 85). Everyone has therefore an interest in speaking validly about it, not only the professionals of law. And, as a matter of fact, most people regularly speak about law; they may use different registers while addressing legal issues. Yet their eagerness or readiness to speak unites them around the subject that is called law. Hegel's remark encourages legal linguists to reformulate the initial methodological question as to where to stop into why actually stop. What is more, research into written cultural artifacts such as literary studies, research into the use of language such as linguistic pragmatics or even the mainstream legal theory teach that it is unwise to stop halfway. It seems that the proper approach to 'discourse' in law concerns the method in which its varieties are described rather than the administrative limitation of meaningful involvement in the research of discursive complexity.

1.5 Legal discourse without limits?

The discursive complexity that is represented in the legal discourse is therefore hostile to choice. Its outer limit seems to be the social practice of speaking about law. One could therefore posit that wherever people speak about law, legal linguists should be present and represent this speech in meaningful categories formed by their science. This seemingly unlimited range of involvement with legal discourses makes sense because it shows the potential and the limits of the legal science and also the limits of law. It also shows that the analysis of the legal discourse is a practical activity. Some of the following examples may be used as paradigmatic illustrations of the discursive complexity in law that is clarified by the analysis of the legal discourse. The first constellation concerns linguistic conventionalism. G.W.F. Hegel's English-language translation of his *Grundlinien der Philosophie des Rechts*, which was helpful in developing the argument of the above paragraph, regularly uses the term 'law of the land' in contradistinction to 'natural law'. The differentiation depends on the existing convention of language use in the English language that establishes the distinction between 'law' and the 'law of the land'. This usage is also productive in Art. 6 of the U.S. Constitution that says in its second section: "This Constitution and the laws of the United States which shall be made in pursuance thereof and all treaties made, or which shall be made, under the authority of the United States, shall be the supreme law of the land; and the judges shall be bound thereby, anything in the Constitution or laws of any State to the contrary notwithstanding." Legal-linguistic conventionalism is responsible for the use of 'law of the land' in both text samples. The American Constitution could have been framed linguistically in a way that would provide for the mentioned legal acts to be the 'supreme law of the federation' or the like. However, this is not the case and legal linguistics demonstrates that this choice is not a coincidence. Yet, the conventionalism in the above example is contrasted with a second paradigmatic type of the use of language in law based on legal-linguistic creativity. It leads to the coinage of the 'supreme' law of the land in the Constitution and to the emergence of 'supremacy of law' (cf. Dickinson 1927). In the quoted constitutional provision, legal-linguistic creativity is connected with other examples of legal-linguistic conventionalism, for instance through the recurrent use of the legal 'shall' in the text. Next to it, a third type of language use appears in it that is characteristic of the ordinary language. It is represented by the ordinary 'shall' of the 'laws…that shall be made' that simply refers to future legislative developments and does not impose any legal obligation like the legal 'shall'. The legal 'shall' is used later in the section in formulations such as 'shall be the supreme law of the land' or 'judges…shall be bound thereby'. The vicinity of both uses will be one of the problems of this book as it is central to every assumption about the role of ordinary language in legal discourses. Some legal-linguistic coinages such as 'due deliberate speed' have been even welcomed in the literature (Berger 1963: 103). Also 'courtroom discourses' are a particularly firm subtype within this paradigm of the use of language in law because in them both registers are intertwined. The use of language in the above types and subtypes can be accessed from the diachronic or the synchronic level of description. Diachronically, the French legal term 'haro' that refers to opposition in court action is out of use nowadays in professional legal texts. Yet it survives in ordinary language in metaphors referring to public criticism, mainly of celebrities or politicians. Legal language can also be accessed from the perspective of legal-linguistic diversity as is done, for instance, in the comparative legal linguistics by Heikki E.S. Mattila (2012, 2013). The English-language translation of Hegel's *Rechtsphilosophie* offers an example of such practice. Its English translator tried to come to terms with Hegel's philosophical language, especially when 'right' comes into question. In the addition 20, paragraph 33 he explains 'right' by 'Recht' and this by 'jus'. The text sample says: "In speaking of Right (Recht, i.e. jus) in this book, we mean not merely what is generally understood by the word, namely civil law, but also morality, ethical life, and world-history; these belong just as much to our topic, because the concept brings thoughts together into a true system." Also J.S. Mill stated rather assertively in his *Utilitarianism* (1863): "Recht, from which came right and righteous, is synonymous with law." The comparative legal linguistics is based on a method that elucidates such risky semantic transformations. In addition, reflective language use is represented in borderline situations where law regulates language use. A text sample such as: "May a state other than the state of domicile of the creditor levy a transfer tax upon intangible property, the interest in which is transferred by the death of the creditor?" will immediately be qualified as legal (sample from: A. Frank, *Double Taxation of Intangibles*, in: Marquette Law Review 1943, vol. 27, p. 95). Other texts are less explicit in terms of their belonging to the text type that is characterized as 'legal'. American court opinions concerning Miranda-rights illustrate such procedures. The Miranda-rights aim at informing suspects in criminal proceedings about their right to remain silent. This right notwithstanding, public authorities, police and other investigative agencies, tend to encourage the suspects to speak. Numerous court opinions, that will be discussed later, deal with different constellations that developed in the shadow of the constitutional right to remain silent. Another subtype of the reflective paradigm relates to the regulation of language use in the public sphere. Many countries developed abundant linguistic legislation that regulates language use in bi- or multilingual countries. By so doing, they initiated legal discourses about meaningful limits of language use in the public sphere. Furthermore, the use of language in law can be contrastive or competitive. Contrastive are legally relevant speech acts that render law in equivalent ordinary speech. Textual samples of such discourses that include the device 'Don't ask, don't tell' as a reference to legal-linguistic practices in the U.S. army or 'mooching off Medicaid' or 'milking the firm' when the application of the doctrine of 'piercing the corporate veil' is at stake are introductory examples into the debate about lay persons' reflections upon law that will be deepened on the pages that follow. Contrastive language use includes a subtype that is the ironical use of legal language. I could name a dog 'Promissory Estoppel' as I could name it 'Humpty Dumpty'. While exercising the choice and preferring the reference to the legal notion of 'promissory estoppel' I would document linguistically a reference to law and enter into a discursive practice within discourses around law. The ironic language use is not irrelevant in the legal discourse because it displays speakers' attitudes towards law. Methodically more problematic is the competitive language use in discourses about law. Competitive language use is present in narratives that illustrate fictitious law. This is the case especially in literary samples that will be regularly used in this book. There, no claim to render the law in force is ever raised, yet situations of language use come close to those really existing. A typical example of such a procedure initiates in the chapter XII of Charles Dickens's *The Pickwick Papers*. The protagonist, Mr. Pickwick lives in London, in Goswell Street. His landlady, Mrs. Bardell, a widow who lives with her only son, is described by Dickens as "the relic and sole executrix of a deceased custom-house officer." Some day Mr. Pickwick decides to employ a man-servant. He prepares Mrs. Bardell in his habitual ceremonial way for changes that this decision will bring in their lives. He questions Mrs. Bardell.: "Do you think it a much greater expense to keep two people than to keep one?", "It'll save you a good deal of trouble, won't it?" and the like. Mrs. Bardell conceives the situation in the sense of a linguistic stereotype 'à deux c'est plus facile' that, as a rule, introduces a marriage proposal. She therefore expects as a result of their exchange "a matrimonial twinkle" that pleases her. In this moment, so Dickens, "their eyes meet". Finally Mrs. Bardell "rose from her chair and without more ado flung her arms around Mr. Pickwick's neck, with a cataract of tears and a chorus of sobs." She feels formally engaged to Mr. Pickwick and Mr. Pickwick is perplexed. Their minds clearly did not meet when their eyes did and yet Mrs. Bardell later claims either wedding or compensation for the broken promise to marry her. As Mr. Pickwick does neither the one nor the other she sues him in a court and the jury decides that the half of the sum required should be hers. Mr. Pickwick, the sympathy of his friends notwithstanding, has lost in terms of law. He is a victim of his clumsiness in the use of language in legally relevant situations. He neglects to identify the linguistic situation that has a profound social dimension and perceives it as purely private, as a piece of conversation. Mrs. Bardell, however, interprets legally relevant social speech in the light most favorable to her. Finally, she dishonors herself and also pays a symbolic price for her 'sin'. In Dickens's literary world she cannot profit from her doubtful manners. The parallel world that Dickens developed in this episode allows for testing the legal language.

Therefore, several such literary samples will be used in this book as examples of legal narratives that compete with law. There, especially the use of language has been perceived as problematic. Finally, universal language use is also present in law. In a text sample that is helpful in our context Berger (1963: 36) ironically warns against sociological writings: "The sociologist who sells his wares should make sure that he clearly pronounces a caveat emptor quite early in the transaction." The legal maxim 'caveat emptor', which emerged in the Roman law, is used in an extra-legal context. It illustrates the tendency in language to unify ordinary and specialized registers. This interesting particularity is essential to legal linguistics and will be discussed more broadly later. It is not coincidental that it is mentioned here in the last place. In fact, the legal discourse develops in interrelation with other discourses. The material analyzed in this book shows this regularity. Furthermore, the legal discourse is transformed in the social discourse about necessary and appropriate legislation (cf. Vogel 2012). In the light of the above paradigms that reflect the situations of language use in law it appears as methodologically impossible to concentrate only on some of them and claim to deal with the legal discourse. The limits of the legal discourse are set by the existing types of language use in law. Therefore, our enterprise has limits, yet they are extensive. Consequently, legal linguistics must be able to integrate any speech about law.

1.6 Non-committal use of textual samples

In order to illustrate the complexity of the legal discourse numerous text samples are quoted or referred to in this book. Reference to them does not equal commitment to their messages as many of the text samples are largely useless from the point of view of our contemporary knowledge about law. Their role is to illustrate the process in which legal language develops in discourses and not the education about the law in force. It is therefore not crucial to the legal-linguistic perspective whether Plato, Aristotle, Bentham, Hegel, Marx or Hart were right in their attempts to conceptualize law and whether their approaches to law might be helpful today. Many legal theoreticians, among them R. Dworkin, never looked back but started from the state of the art that they found immediately before them. This ahistorical method does not impede progress. Yet, it does not elucidate the process in which the legal discourse emerges. It is therefore not used here. Equally, it is not relevant to determine whether an opinion about law expressed by a citizen or a group of citizens 'makes sense'. P. Berger (1963: 85) wrote about the 'reluctance to eliminate capital punishment from the American criminal law': "Violence is the ultimate foundation of any political order. The common-sense view of society senses this…" and he pointed out that the reluctance to abolish the death penalty in the U.S. "is probably based in equal measure on stupidity, superstition and the congenital bestiality that jurists share with the bulk of their fellow citizens." Such an opinion is used here as a text sample only to prove that the types of legal discourses that are mentioned here exist in the socio-linguistic practice. It could be contrasted with the bulk of U.S. Supreme Court decisions that never address the issue of 'stupidity' within the American citizenry. Methodically, all opinions about law are interesting for the legal linguist. We speak about law in the way we do because speakers before us established some discursive patterns that contemporary speakers further modify. Their speaking helps determine the discursive regularities in law that also are the issues of immediate and urgent concern in the legal-linguistic research.

1.7 Legal-linguistic method

In the above paragraphs, and especially in 1.5, textual samples have been introduced and they were presented as being typical of the legal language. Additionally, a taxonomy of these samples has been proposed and some textually relevant differences have been established among them. Identifying the text samples as relevant to legal linguistics is an undemanding task, interpreting them is a challenging undertaking. Meanwhile, the easy and the complicated tasks can be accomplished only with the help of a method, and this method, although mentioned in the above paragraphs regularly, has not been explained. Legal linguistics cannot be based only on intuition, although speakers' experience in the daily use of language matters also for a professional student of language. Speakers' experience and an idea of what rationality might be provide some help at the entry stage into the intricacies of law and language. However, the practical problem that emerges then is unsolvable with the help of some daily linguistic competence and sound views about language use. The bulk of textual samples could, when undirected by a method, grow unlimited. Not much use for science would emerge from such a compilation of linguistic examples, even if some preliminary order could be imagined to structure the collection. The problem is that the collection of linguistic samples has to make sense, and this sense in research is determined by method. In most established sciences this is not a problem because methods used there were applied regularly and by many researchers. Therefore, experience accumulated by generations of researchers can be used when methodological choices are made in these branches of knowledge. These choices are often tacit or summary as the method is regularly not a problem in established sciences such as chemistry or civil engineering. Legal linguistics is different. It develops as a new science in a struggle for the appropriate method. Guidance is needed in this undertaking and it comes from many better researched and settled disciplines, such as philosophy and linguistics. Yet, first things should be researched first. Therefore, an ontological and epistemological scrutiny of law and its language may be helpful in identifying and justifying methodological choices that are inherent in the above paragraphs. The following part will shed some more light upon the problems of the legal-linguistic method.

Part 2: Legal Epistemology and its Consequences

2.1 Legal ontology and legal epistemology

Theoretical reflection about law traditionally oscillated around two fundamental questions. The first has been asked already by the ancient Greeks and other thinkers in antiquity, the second is related to the first, yet it seems to have emerged later. The ancient Greeks confronted us with the question as to what is law. Subsequently, the question as to how we can know what law actually is has been asked as a result of a long process of research into the first question. This transformation of cognitive interests constituted a lucky turn for law and later it will become clearer that the second question is more helpful in the searching for law than is the first question. Meanwhile, the first question cannot be neglected. It reflects the original linguistic process of constitution of the theoretical discourses about law. Other, mostly practical discourses about law emerged because this first fundamental question had been asked. Therefore, helpful or cumbersome as it may be, the ontological question has accompanied jurists and all others interested in law since times immemorial in their search of law. In our time, the question as to how we actually know what law is became dominant. This shift in attention towards law has a rather practical reason. Law is for the contemporary jurist and the contemporary citizen what it means. Therefore the interest in the process in which one can acquire knowledge about the meaning that emerges in law replaced the interest in the somehow sterile question as to what law might be beyond its meaning. In sum, somebody who knows how meaning emerges in law knows and understands the law. Law as a branch of knowledge is therefore a relatively simple enterprise. This encouraging circumstance notwithstanding, some intellectual efforts are inevitable when one aims at understanding it. These intellectual efforts that relate to the knowledge and the understanding of meaning are limited to the knowledge of the language in which this meaning by necessity emerges. This is so because there is nothing more to research in law than language when one wishes to understand law. Theoretical research related to law may include other than legal-linguistic questions. Yet, as a result of such questions something else than law will be better understood, for instance power or society. Finally, all this seemingly complicated ontological scrutiny can be reduced to one situation: Knowing how meaning emerges in a situation in which language is used in law.

Hence, the epistemology of law can be expressed in form of a fundamental question: Is there a universal knowledge of law in terms of science? Or is there only a succession of rules that constitute law as a sum of the disparate legal regulation now in force? From the legal-linguistic perspective it can be maintained that reliable knowledge about law exists. It exists at least in the shape of legal linguistics that provides a method for the inquiry into law. This method is based on the mastery of legal-linguistic operations that appear in legal discourses. Also this knowledge follows from the ontology of law that is a discursive practice. Therefore, the ontological question is not without importance in the contemporary debate about law. It is however positioned differently than for instance in the Middle Ages when the ontology of law was perceived by scholars such as Thomas of Aquino as the theory of law that also included its fully fledged doctrine. Thomas of Aquino demonstrated this approach in his *Summa Theologica* where he treated the legal ontology and the legal doctrine as united in the theology practiced by his church. His approach is methodologically not unique. In earlier times, the most eminent ancient Greek philosophers, Plato and Aristotle, formatted this thinking. One can assume that the legal theory would have advanced quicker had it followed the Greek sophists and the ancient Roman jurists whose works are known from the *Corpus Iuris Civilis*. Both were closer to the legal-linguistic fundamental problem of emergence of meaning in law. The traditional Occidental legal philosophy that followed the ontological path has undeniably shown some relevant aspects of law. It frequently formulated the basic question with the help of a discursive qualifier and asked what law 'actually' is. This 'actual' law in terms of the traditional philosophy of law was apparently construed as something different from the really existing law. Otherwise, the discursive reference to law that might be something different from what it seems to be would not make sense. Today, we have given up in arts and sciences this mode of formulating basic questions. The second basic question coined in the language of the traditional philosophy of law concerned the subject matter of legal regulation. It sounded mostly like: what kind of behavior should law prohibit and what kind of behavior should it allow? It was directed towards the content of legal regulation. This type of regulation-related inquiry is even less interesting nowadays because the content and the scope of regulation follow directly from the way in which law is made. It means that they, in theoretical terms, follow from it discursively. Therefore, there is no need to deal separately with the content of appropriate regulation in law because it is not an independent element of law. In sum, law is something different from the visions offered by Plato in his *Laws* or by Thomas of Aquino in his demonstration of legal questions that reflect the interests of his religion. Both philosophers had asked questions that were subsequently evaluated in a long process of application of various epistemological tests because both had been very skilful participants in the debate about law. Jeremy Bentham in *An Introduction to the Principles of Morals and Legislation* (1789) and in *A Fragment on Government* (1776) refreshed the legal thinking in that he introduced the notion of 'happiness' into the learned discourse about law. Later, Immanuel Kant and G.W.F. Hegel in their works on the philosophy of law repositioned our intellectual interests towards the epistemological enquiry into the linguistic coinages in law. This re-adjustment of perspective was more in line with legal-linguistic problem settings although it on its face stressed reasoning rather than language use. Only the linguistic turn that was initiated by the analytic philosophers in the twentieth century provided the necessary broad conceptual basis upon which our enquiry into law could develop as an integral part of a broader discourse about knowledge and science. Thus, the scientific foundation for the development of a legal-linguistic science was formulated. It took again much time until this science – still loosely connected yet dynamically developing – could emerge and become noticed by other branches of knowledge that also deal with law. Within its own paradigm, it established the claim that our explicit knowledge about law is not sufficient.

2.2 How to approach law?

The lack of knowledge about law may enhance one's interest to know more about it. This interest is by its nature epistemological because it is directed towards acquiring knowledge that differs from daily experience and that is more complex than the knowledge we acquire and apply in daily life situations. The best way to approach the law under these circumstances is to ask what the most striking element in it is and then attack law exactly under this angle. Many people have the impression that language dominates law, that law is therefore best approached from the side of its linguistic form. Epistemological aspects of law are indeed linguistic as law is expressed in language. Linguistic facets of law cannot, therefore, be underestimated. Yet, they should not be overestimated either, as law in terms of its mechanisms and in terms of its regulation is clearly about power and not about language. Power aspects are integrated into law with linguistic means as law is based factually on power and enforced in institutionalized power structures. One might try to enquire into law while approaching these structures and the way they used to function, i.e. while neglecting the linguistic form and considering the results, the consequences of implementation of power with linguistic means. However, all these structures function in communicative situations with the help of language, unless pure physical force is implemented in them. What is more, this non-linguistic view upon law would not be able to function without language because it is bound to language in one way or another. Apparently, we cannot reach much knowledge about law without approaching its linguistic manifestation. Yet, we cannot approach law by simply looking at its linguistic manifestation. Much more work will be needed to get a glimpse of real law in the ocean of legal discourses where it floats.

2.2.1 Search for law

The practical problem with law is that it is not simply there like a pen or a cat. It is therefore not possible to take hold of it and make something of it or with it as it may be done with a pen or with a cat (within the limits of the legislation in force aimed at protecting animals, of course). A pen can be held in hand, used for writing or be broken. A cat can also be of use, at least sometimes. Yet law, before it is used, must be found. In order to find something one needs a method. This method may be extremely simple; it may, for instance, be expressed with a device: seek and you will find. Neither the pen nor the cat in our examples would be traced without the understanding and applying of the simple methodology expressed in the device. We could also avoid the problem with searching for the pen while applying a more advanced device expressed with: always put objects back at the place wherefrom you have taken them. This searching strategy would have averted our problem with the pen, but not with the cat as cats are much too mobile to enable the application of our simple and otherwise efficient device. Therefore, in order to search for the cat we need more sophisticated strategies expressed in more sophisticated methodological devices. When it comes to the search for law, it is even more complicated because law can be found only when the researcher determines the legal methodology that must be adapted to the complex object of search. With other words, to find law one has to know in advance what is law (Schmid 1946: 58). You definitely cannot find law like you find your pen that rolled too far in the drawer of your writing desk or your cat that get lost in the park in the neighborhood of your dwelling. Doubtless, for the two named searches you also need a method of the sort that was indicated above; yet this method is a rather simple technique of looking closer. School children easily cope with such tasks. They, like the adults, find the pen or the lost cat, partly because both are clearly determined in advance, so to say automatically identifiable as such. Law that is found in accordance with the methodological search is of different nature. The pragmatist finds another law than the positivist. Someone devoted to Marxian or Marxist theories of society will find another law than someone who was trained and is deeply committed to the world view founded on Thomas Aquinas' theology or the principles expressed in the Quran. This determination of perspectives upon law, that scholars call approaches, takes time; it takes even more time than the subsequent work on law, once it is successfully found. This effort may seem an unjust burden imposed upon jurists. Yet, others suffer in equal degree. A sociologist cannot simply deal with society; he must search for it, and he will find it with the help of an approach. A psychologist cannot simply deal with personality, because what is personality is determined by an approach to human psychology, and these approaches are numerous. For a linguist, the concept of language is determined by the linguistic approach to which he is committed. We could even refer to theologists such as Augustinus or Thomas of Aquino and their interest in god; they too find a god determined by their approaches. After all, approaches determine our knowledge and there is no scientific knowledge beyond our approaches. Scholars are therefore prisoners of approaches like citizens are prisoners of societies. Both can move only within the predefined limits of their cages, yet they have the choice of their cage. Therefore, also the jurist is searching for law not at large, but in a thoroughly determined cage. Once the jurist found the law, i.e. when he has determined what it is for him in the light of an approach, he can describe it. Here, the description of law varies as the approaches to law differ. For instance, the American law when it is described by a pragmatist, like the author of these lines, will differ considerably from a description undertaken by a positivist. The view upon the law of past centuries is even more risky because this law survives today solely in written documents. Therefore sophisticated methods will be needed to reconstruct the processes in which meaning might have emerged in it. Let us at this stage assume that these tasks can be solved with appropriate methods. Meanwhile, one more task remains, that of the application of law. Philosophizing about law is an inoffensive exercise unless it is limited to writing. Law that is applied is a deadly tool, literally and metaphorically. This intricacy also explains why so much effort has been invested in explaining how law is or should be applied. Application of law is connected with understanding, and understanding emerges in the process of searching for meaning. This, in brief, is the way to find the real law.

2.2.2 Encounters with law

Law can be met in different situations. First, law is present in social life as its most efficient regulative mechanism. Social reality is structured by legal norms in addition to many other types of norms that are relevant to and constitutive of society. In daily life, the efficiency of the legal norms is largely based on their persuasive force that is grounded in rationality and that convinces the persons confronted with a legal problem because of the quality of the rational argumentation. For instance, when drivers are obliged by the road code to use the right-hand side of the road, so most of them will follow the rule, mainly because they understand that road traffic must be regulated in a formal way. They will also understand that the safe use of the road is only possible when a direction of driving is formally imposed by the road code. This holds apparently true even if the choice is made rather arbitrarily between the left-hand and the right-hand side of the road. The drivers will even accept a degree of arbitrariness in the norm because they are able to grasp its finality that rationally convinces them. This regulative choice exercised by the legislator in the process of the constitution of the legal norm is accepted, although better proposals might exist that would enable us to avoid the arbitrary element in preferring right to left. As is known, legislators in some countries distinguished themselves in following a minority preference for the left-hand side traffic that is, theoretically, no less rational. This choice could be challenged with arguments that would question its appropriateness in a world dominated by the right-hand side rule. The minority preference rule might also be seen as a regulatory decision that complicates the daily life of people in a globalizing world. Therefore, the more advanced are the intellectual efforts invested in the regulation of a legal problem, the higher will be, as a rule, the efficiency and acceptance of law among those who are ready to make the intellectual effort and grasp the rationale behind the sterile letter of law. Those who are less inclined to make this effort will be convinced by other means that are no less persuasive because they include the act of enforcement of legal provisions. In fact, law's efficiency as a regulative mechanism depends also on the possibility of enforcement by the government that disposes of the monopoly on the use of force in democratic society. Law is clearly not done to threaten or compel; it is established in order to convince. Yet, its structure includes also the forcible element that is instrumental in ensuring the efficiency of legal mechanisms when linguistic persuasion fails. One should not forget that this is actually a rare situation as people follow the law in most cases. Also in road traffic most rules are followed by drivers, even if experience of driving sometimes imposes some sarcastic remarks on our mind in all discursive situations related to the travel on roads. Meanwhile, the first type of encounters with law is of intellectual nature because law is present there in the linguistic form of a rule. This rule is accompanied by a specific proposition about the meaning of a legal provision in the particular situation of its application where the driver on a narrow road has, for instance, to decide whether she actually is driving on the right-hand side of the road. This rule can also be practically observed in its application, for example, while driving in cooperation or in competition with other drivers. Law is therefore something that is in its essence beneficial to society because it, at least ideally, regulates social life in a rational way. People are mostly aware of this particular quality of law. Second, law is experienced in more dramatic situations, for instance when a wrong happens to somebody. Humans are fragile, both mentally and physically, and even if some of them dislike the reference to their most fundamental anthropological characteristic feature that is their physical frailty, this very feature is constitutive of many situations in which also law has to be applied. Some of these situations are dramatic, if not tragical, as are all situations that depend on the human condition. These situations are not particularly rare, either. A court decision, as so often, may be used to illustrate this situation that includes a legal element in a dramatic situation of life. The situation is as banal as it is tragical: A passenger on a flight is seated in the non-smoking section of the plane, yet close to the smoking section. Smoke penetrates until his seat. As he suffers from asthma, his wife asks the flight attendant to allow him to move to a seat more distant from the smoking section. This request is categorically denied, the passenger's respiratory problems increase rapidly and assistance provided by a medical doctor present on board is of no avail. The passenger dies. His widow is of the opinion that the airline is liable for her husband's death and sues therefore in a court. Finally, the U.S. Supreme Court had to decide the litigation between the airline in question, Olympic Airways and Ms Rubina Husain, the widow of the deceased Dr. Abid Hanson (cf. the Supreme Court decision 540 U.S. 644 from 2004). One cannot deny that this tragical situation implies a legal problem. Clearly the flight attendant was not helpful, yet Dr. Hanson was chronically ill and he was aware of his illness. Are airlines liable under such circumstances? And if so, how to draw the line between constellations that lead to liability and those that do not? It is obvious that airlines cannot be responsible for all negative consequences that may emerge during flights. At this point in time the search for law begins. This search for law is not an academic enterprise; it is a battle for law because it involves adverse interests. This battle has its own dramatic components, mostly because the idea of justice comes to mind when situations such as the above are invoked. Let us at this stage reduce the suspense that is misplaced in a serious analysis. Justice will triumph in this case and the U.S. Supreme Court will hold in its mentioned decision the airline liable for causing the death of its passenger. The unambiguous result in this case enables now to concentrate on the aspects of finding the law from a less emotional perspective.

2.2.3 Law apprehended

One may suppose that the communication of the mere result of the above litigation without further explanation would not satisfy most readers. They might argue that a simple reference to justice will not do in this case. They could ask whether law has been applied in this case, what does this law say and how someone may know what it means. When these questions are answered, one may legitimately suppose that an explanation of law has been provided in the sense that it had been clarified which of the two parties to the litigation was right in terms of law. To satisfy all these requirements a lot of questions will have to be answered. And it may be mentioned already at this stage that one book is not enough to answer all of them in detail. Meanwhile, many questions can be answered and they will be approached here in a specific order. To begin with, the facts as described above are not a sufficient basis for any professional analysis. They may be perceived, like media reporting, as a sort of a spotlight upon the reality that enables the reader to associate emotionally with one of the parties concerned, yet not more. To understand the legal problems of the case properly, some factual details are necessary to be known. The deceased Dr. Hanson travelled with his spouse, some other friends and family members for vacation, on a flight from San Francisco via Athens to Cairo. On his first flight, during the stopover in New York, he learned that the airline allowed smoking on international flights. As an asthma patient he was sensitive to second-hand smoke and therefore requested and also obtained a seat in the non-smoking section. The flight was unproblematic for Dr. Hanson. On his flight back home he showed at the check-in counter his physician's letter that mentioned his "history of recurrent anaphylactic reactions." After boarding, however, he discovered that his seat located in the non-smoking section was only three rows in front of the economy-class smoking section. His wife requested for the first time the flight attendant, Ms. Maria Leptourgou, to have her husband moved because of his allergy to smoke. The flight attendant refused. After another request that was again refused, the victim, Dr. Hanson, was shortly after takeoff surrounded by ambient cigarette smoke. For the third time the flight attendant refused to reseat him claiming that the plane was full. She however consented to Dr. Hanson or his spouse contacting other passengers who might be willing to switch seats. Neither Dr. Hanson nor his wife did this. In fact, there were eleven unoccupied passenger seats available, mostly however in the economy class. Neither Dr. Hanson nor his spouse had any knowledge of the free seats. As his breathing problems increased, Dr. Hanson stood up using his inhaler and walked to the front part of the airplane where more fresh air was available, but his breathing problems increased further. A medical doctor, who accompanied him, administered a shot of epinephrine, and when all this did not help, the physician started cardiopulmonary resuscitation procedures and gave him oxygen, yet in vain. Dr. Hanson died on board; no autopsy to determine the cause of his death was performed for religious reasons. In the U.S. Supreme Court decision the facts are reflected in the part of the case that relates to the application of law. The legal claim concerns liability of the carrier on an international flight for an accident that caused the death of a passenger. The legal issue that is at stake in this case concerns the application of a provision in an international treaty because the incident happened on an international flight. Legally, it could also concern the causing of wrongful death that is a tort under American law, yet the claim under an international instrument prevails over domestic law. The applicable provision of law is here Art. 17 of the Convention for the Unification of Certain Rules relating to International Carriage by Air from 1929, called in juridical practice and in the aircraft industry 'Warsaw Convention'. This Convention says in the pertinent Article 17: "The carrier shall be liable for damage sustained in the event of the death or wounding of a passenger or any other bodily injury suffered by a passenger, if the accident which caused the damage so sustained took place on board the aircraft or in the course of any of the operations of embarking or disembarking." While applying Art. 17 the court had therefore to ask whether an accident happened in this case because the airline's liability for damages comes into question only in case of an accident that took place on board an aircraft. More exactly, the legal issue is expressed in the language of the court as: "whether the 'accident' condition precedent to air carrier liability under Art. 17 is satisfied when the carrier's unusual and unexpected refusal to assist the passenger is a link in a chain of causation resulting in a passenger's pre-existing medical condition being aggravated by exposure to a normal condition in the aircraft cabin." When one looks back to the facts and reads again the text of Art. 17, doubts could come up as to the occurrence of an accident on board that might have caused Dr. Hanson's death. One could look for further assistance into the text of the Convention; yet the text does nowhere define an 'accident on board an airplane'. The court could have determined the meaning of the term 'accident' also autonomously, so to say on its own, yet a precedent case, Air France v. Saks (470 U.S. 392), dating from 1985 is there. In this precedent the question of what 'accident' under Art. 17 actually means has been determined by the Supreme Court. Meanwhile, the court willful at applying the ordinary meaning of the term 'accident' in the English language, also consulted authoritative dictionaries. It found out that the term 'accident' had in the English language at least "two plausible yet distinct definitions." According to *Webster's New World College Dictionary* 'accident' may mean: "a happening that is not… intended." This is a meaning alternative reiterated also in the *American Heritage Dictionary* that refers to the "lack of intention, chance." On the other side, the *Black's Law Dictionary* defines 'accident' as "an unusual or unexpected event," whether the result of intentional action or not, "an unusual, fortuitous, unexpected, unforeseen, or unlooked for event, happening or occurrence…and if happening wholly or partly through human agency, an event which under the circumstances is unusual and unexpected by the person to whom it happens." In Saks the court inferred from the existing definitions the meaning of 'accident' in the sense of Art. 17 of the Warsaw Convention as an "unexpected or unusual event or happening that is external to the passenger." In any case, the Saks court underscored that the 'accident' that is meant in Art. 17 refers to an "unexpected or unusual event or happening that is external to the passenger" and not to "the passenger's own internal reaction to the usual, normal, and expected operation of the aircraft." This distinction is deducted from the aim of the Convention and its Art. 17, and is as such incontestable. Clearly, the Convention cannot make the airline responsible for the fact that a passenger may die on the flight, due to his or her health situation while the plane is operated normally and when, for example, pressurization, that is a normal technical operation of an aircraft, takes place. This inference is however relatively weak in terms of its operationability in this case. It is rather obvious and it imposes itself logically. It is nearly useless as it does not concern the legal issue of the case. Likewise, all linguistic reference quoted by the court provides a lot of information about the term 'accident'. Yet this linguistic information does not allow answering the question whether an 'accident' happened here. One could express the problem of the case, as the airline sees it, in a simplified formula: No 'accident' in the sense of an event or occurrence happened here because the airline did not act. Dr. Hanson who suffered from respiratory problems died, possibly due to exposure to the ambient cigarette smoke that aggravated his known health precondition. Smoking on board was allowed and it was legal on international flights. No event that was controlled by the aircraft was abnormal, with the exception of the refusal by the cabin attendant to reseat the vulnerable passenger although airlines' guidelines provide for assistance in such cases. The 'injury producing event' was, so the airline, the ambient cigarette smoke, yet the cigarette smoke was not irregular on an international flight. Or was, as the estate of Dr. Hanson claims, the refusal to reseat Dr. Hanson the event that produced the injury and led to his death. Both interpretive varieties of 'accident' are rational. The necessity of choice, a logical and linguistic operation that enables meaning to emerge in the framework of the Art. 17 and the Convention as a whole, constitutes the link between law and language. It shows that both are inseparable. Law, that is the meaning of legal rules in their application, is operational in society exclusively under this condition of choice that is an argumentative and interpretive operation. Thus, the court has to determine on what facts the 'accident' as a controlling term will be based. All above has been already quite complicated, yet more is to come. One of the Supreme Court judges did not share the view of the majority that decided the litigation against the airline's interests. He therefore filed a dissenting opinion in which another judge partly joined. Such a step taken by a professional of law indicates a problem, as it would be difficult to claim that other judges who constituted the majority did not know the law. Does the dissenting judge know the law better than the majority? Why can he claim to know it better than the majority of his colleagues at the Supreme Court? Or could law be a subject that cannot be learned? Could it be that it cannot be mastered in a way that one would become an expert in it and other qualified jurists as experts who know the law would always join in when the right decision is taken? Can there be one right decision in litigation? And if not, what sense does it make to establish and apply law in society? These questions impose themselves under the circumstances of this case and they will be addressed later in this book in detail. Let us further complicate the situation in which the Supreme Court has to make its decision. Art. 17 of the Warsaw Convention has been originally drafted in the French language and the French text says: "Le transporteur est responsable du dommage survenu en cas de mort, de blessure ou de toute autre lésion corporelle subie par un voyageur lorsque l'accident qui a causé le dommage s'est produit à bord de l'aéronef ou au cours de toutes opérations d'embarquement et de débarquement." The Supreme Court follows in its decision the English translation of the French original that has been used by the U.S. Congress in course of the ratification procedure of the Convention in 1934. Could the French term 'accident' be interpreted differently than the English term 'accident'? The *Larousse* dictionary of the French language mentions different aspects of use of 'accident' in the French language, such as "événement malheureux, entraînant des dommages matérielles ou corporelle." 'Accident' also covers occurrences that interrupt the regular course of things, the 'vicissitudes', yet also 'accidents du travail'. Last but not least, 'accident' is a term in philosophy and in music, covering there three different meaning constellations, also in English. Overall, the dictionary might suggest that the broad semantic range of 'accident' in the French language that is mainly due to its rather general Latin antecedent 'accidens', i.e. 'what occurs', would make the decision easier for a French court. Meanwhile, as so often, the spoken French knows also the narrow use of 'accident' that is synonymous with 'catastrophe aérienne', as in 'On a annoncé à la radio un accident d'avion' that clearly refers to a crash and not to an occurrence on board a plane. Thus, the clarity that was already approaching disappears again. Somewhere, a more systematic approach to the search of meaning that goes beyond the purely lexicological analysis would be necessary. First of all, 'accident' appears in Art. 17 connected in both French and English versions with the 'operations of embarking and disembarking'. Contextually, therefore, it could very much be understood as being limited to an unexpected occurrence in the air, it is a catastrophe, as well as to all incidents of the analogous sort that might happen during the embarking and disembarking. The context might suggest this. Second, the aim of the provision might indicate a broader or a narrower understanding. One could ask: when the convention wishes to encompass occurrences during the flight and technically related operations as well as whatever other events on board, including the behavior of airline personnel, why does it not mention it explicitly? Is it the case because this broad meaning is so clearly included that it is unambiguous for jurists? The controversial treatment of the semantic question by the Supreme Court indicates the contrary. Would it then be possible to claim that the convention covers only the narrow use of the term as it is given in the French language, because otherwise it would clearly mention that this is not the case? Furthermore, the Warsaw Convention is drafted in legal language; an airplane is an 'aircraft', in French 'aéronef', the damage is 'sustained' etc. Would it not be possible to express the legislative intention more clearly, for instance by saying what is meant by it in terms of ordinary language? The semantic analysis of 'accident' both in the English and in the French language seems therefore to have a limited impact on the final decision taken by the court. In fact, would it be possible to maintain that the court assigns to the term 'accident' a juridical meaning due to its institutional privilege, i.e. that it creates meaning while making clear what a term means in law? At this point, almost surprisingly, one could have the impression that law has been found, that the focus in which law emerges has been identified. This apparent process of law finding does not take place in a vacuum. Instead, there is method in it, and this method is determined by procedure. There are participants acting in the procedure, time and space of the procedure are equally determined. The participants act; they use language while making their assertions about the valid law. There are many interested participants in this case next to the parties. An 'amicus curiae' representing the U.S. government asked the court for an opinion favorable to the estate of Dr. Hanson; another 'amicus curiae' acting for the Air Transport Association of America asked the court to support the airline. There is a timeframe: the case is argued before the Supreme Court on November 12, 2003, and decided on February 24, 2004. The decision is thus not taken immediately after the hearing of the case; it is apparently pondered and possibly also discussed controversially among the judges. The very existence of the dissenting opinion supports this assumption. In fact, this relatively simple litigation illustrates the main issues relevant to the search of law. It may be surprising, but their number and complexity resulted in many books on theoretical aspects of law. The book you hold in hand is one more attempt to cope with the complexity of intellectual operations aiming at finding the valid law. In terms of the narrative rendered and developed in the above lines the theoretical issue appeared in its daily, practical dress, reduced to the search for the device that should determine who is right in the above case. When legal cases, i.e. situations of life, are abandoned for a moment, as will be done here, the search for law appears as a much less banal intellectual activity.

2.3 Static reason or law in action?

Law that is found in the way described above is largely independent of its visible artifacts such as constitutions bound in leather with golden ornaments, systematized statutes, collections of precedents, and the like. Law as we know it today cannot cope without these artifacts; yet, it is in its nature different from them. Meanwhile, the legal artifacts are also the first source of misunderstandings in the search process of law. Some tend to assume that they found the law when they find a legal artifact. This static view upon law is actually a view upon legal artifacts that relate to law without being it. Law cannot be identified with their help alone because it is not static. These material artifacts tend therefore to volatilize, as law can change at whatever moment and an artifact that constitutes the material reference to it becomes a souvenir of law in the very moment in which the legislator amends a legal act. Legal artifacts are also therefore misleading because they often, or even mostly, represent law as it had been. Overall, the main obstacle in the search for law is this misleading materiality of law. Artifacts that can be seen impose themselves as a representation of law upon the searcher because the law, unlike them, cannot be visualized. Foremost, law is a social practice which means that it is something that is made with reference to something else, for instance a court decision that is made with reference to an act passed by the Parliament. A court decision is this something which we are searching for, because it is the application of a statute in a particular situation. This linguistically fixed application is the sign of law that we need to grasp as law. Lawyers often call these applicational circumstances of law 'cases' and describe them in form of an adversarial presentation, for instance Olympic Airways v. Husain (cf. above). Cases can be traced back to their initial sources of publication, like Glen v. Club Méditerranée that can be found while following the coded reference that follows its name, here 540 U.S. 644 (2004). Hence, Olympic Airways v. Husain stands for law, but it does not suffice to represent it, as it is still only a case. Without its interpretation as a case towards the discursive background of other related cases that are 'precedents' in a succession of juridical application acts it would remain a dead artifact. In order to understand it, we have to make it speak. It speaks to us through the means of an analysis that relates it and the reference to other cases and statutes towards the interest which we have in it at a given period of time. This procedure of searching and understanding law is rather cumbersome. Meanwhile, it also explains why it is usually not uncontroversial when we proudly proclaim that we have found the law.

As said, modern legal theory perceives law as a constantly changing phenomenon, a law in action, subject to modifications due to changes in the social discourse. When in society the focus upon discursive practices is readjusted, the law must follow suit. Yet, fundamental theoretical objections against this conception had been set up already in antiquity. Aristotle proposed a two-fold concept of law. In his *Politics* he makes frequent references to law that he perceives as a static mechanism of societal regulation. The ancient Greeks aimed at finding order amid the chaos around us and they construed order as something static. Aristotle writes in *Politics* (1287a1): "The rule of law is therefore preferable, according to the view we are stating, to that of a single citizen. In pursuance of the same view it is argued that, even if it be the better course to have individuals ruling, they should be made law-guardians or servants of the law…law trains the holders of office expressly in its own spirit, and then sets them to decide and settle those residuary issues which it cannot regulate, 'as justly as in them lies'. It also allows them to introduce any improvements which may seem to them, as the result of experience, to be better than the existing laws. He who commands that law should rule may thus be regarded as commanding that God and reason alone should rule; he who commands that a man should rule adds the character of a beast. Appetite has that character; and high spirit, too, perverts the holders of office, even when they are the best of men." For Aristotle, law is 'reason without desire'. This conception of law is opposed to a search of law that was proposed above. It illustrates a static law that some, we would call them today experts, may see and formulate because they are particularly reasonable and independent persons. Others would have to follow this law that once apprehended does not need to be changed because it corresponds with reason. And indeed, why should a reasonable law be changed under unchanged circumstances? It is true that a change under unchanged circumstances would not make much sense, yet such situations in law are rare. What is more, law for Aristotle does not even need to be written. Aristotle adds in *Politics* (1287a32): "...laws resting on unwritten custom are even more sovereign, and concerned with issues of still more sovereign importance, than written laws; and this suggests that, even if the rule of a man be safer than the rule of written law, it need not therefore be safer than the rule of unwritten law." Law, in theoretical sense, seems for Aristotle to be so stable that it even does not need to be fixed in writing. The writing requirement is not incompatible with legal-linguistic observations although requirements of legal certainty may suggest written form for statutes and precedents and whatever other legally relevant documents. Aristotle's conception of static law comes close to some constitutional provisions of contemporaneous law. Some provisions are static, i.e. they cannot be repealed or amended, as for example the Art. 1 and the Art. 20 of the German Constitution that are declared unchangeable in Art. 79 (3). Art. 1 protects the human dignity and Art. 20 declares that Germany is a federal, social, and democratic republic. Also the U.S Constitution includes in its Art. V a limitation of a static type, noticed already by H.L.A. Hart (1961: 71). This famous formulation provides in Article V for a possibility of amendments to the U.S. Constitution "Provided that no Amendment which may be made prior to the Year One thousand eight hundred and eight shall in any Manner affect the first and fourth Clauses in the Ninth Section of the first Article..." In terms of the Aristotelian concept of law, these provisions are strong law because they are based on unwritten principles that make them static, unchangeable. Other laws that are written may be changed as the experience of legislators dictates. Practically, however, they represent the majority of regulation. Yet, for Aristotle, they regulate 'residuary issues'. Meanwhile, Aristotle is in his multilayered conception of law very contemporary. He seems to have been the first thinker in the Occidental legal tradition to have insisted on rationality as a constitutive element of law. And he was right to do so. Even today confusion persists as to the appropriate action where policy and law are intertwined. Some of the legal issues may be perceived today as issues of policy. The difference between questions of policy and of law is unclear for many. In the American debate about the legality of the U.S. intervention in Iraq some have asked: Should high Bush Administration officials be prosecuted for ordering torture? Does a complaint change in quality when instead of torture some speak of 'enhanced interrogation techniques' such as sleep deprivation or water boarding? Here policy refers to law and vice versa (Dworkin 2006: 26, 156). Argumentation rooted in the Aristotelian concept of rationality is the only remedy in such cases. In fact, rationality is not the only ontological problem in law. It is however a static element of its structure. In this sense, law is static as it constantly reflects its argumentative and changing nature.

2.3.1 Existence in terms of law

Existence is one more ontological trap in law. In the litigation Glen v. Club Méditerranée, S.A. decided by U.S. Court of Appeals for the Eleventh Circuit (No. 05–12648) in 2006 the court had to clarify whether the plaintiffs were entitled to compensation due to alleged profitable use by the defendant of a beachfront property situated in Cuba. The Cuban government expropriated the plaintiffs and many others in the aftermath of the Revolution of 1959. The defendant invoked the act of state doctrine that "precludes the courts of this country from inquiring into the validity of the public acts a recognized foreign sovereign power committed within its own territory" (cf. Banco Nacional de Cuba v. Sabbatino, 376 U.S. 398, 401, 84 S.Ct. 923, 926, 1964). According to the court that referred again to a precedent, the doctrine requires that "the acts of foreign sovereigns taken within their own jurisdictions shall be deemed valid." Therefore the court dismissed the appeal. Meanwhile, the openly illegal expropriation of the plaintiffs is not recognized by this decision. However, the act of expropriation is deemed valid for the purposes of this litigation. This means that it is perceived as valid in terms of a specific procedure. Otherwise, it remains a clear violation of the principles of international law. The U.S. Helms-Burton Act (22 U.S.C. § 6081 (3) (B)) condemns such confiscations as "wrongful," yet it does not proclaim them ineffective. They have therefore a complex existence in law, being legal and illegal at the same time. Does law break with reality in that it establishes its own conceptual realm? Indeed, existence in law is specific as is specific the existence of every social phenomenon. Legal ontology is in principle conventional because we can agree on the establishment of whatever social institution provided the process of establishment is rational. Therefore, there is actually no cat in law that would correspond with the cat in nature. Our search for it was described in the preceding paragraphs as a quintessentially simple operation. It becomes more complex when we search for the cat in law as a legal entity. The cat is in terms of law either a 'chattel' or a 'res nullius' when savage. Cats may also be dogs in terms of a 'no dogs' board that, as a rule, prohibits entry into premises in company of animals and not only dogs. The existence of a cat in law can become even more complicated. Some statutes may establish further going fictions rooted in social fashion of the moment such as declaring animals not to be chattels and simultaneously declaring provisions concerning chattels to be applicable upon them in analogy. For instance, Art. 90a of the German Civil Code (BGB) says: "Tiere sind keine Sachen. Sie werden durch besondere Gesetze geschützt. Auf sie sind die für Sachen geltenden Vorschriften entsprechend anzuwenden, soweit nicht etwas anderes bestimmt ist. – Animals are not chattels. They are protected by particular laws. In all matters that concern them provisions related to chattels shall be applied in analogy, unless other provisions provide for the contrary." Our cat would have a life of a dog under such conditions and ontologists could spend volumes upon the analysis of its analogous existence. Yet not only cats suffer under misconceptions of legal ontology. For instance, in a very controversial decision Citizens United v. Federal Election Commission (130 S. Ct. 876, 2010) the U.S. Supreme Court affirmed that the First Amendment of the U.S. Constitution that protects the freedom of speech also applies to corporations. Some have claimed that the court had declared the corporations "ontologically equivalent" to human beings, "supposing corporate animacy to be a kind of human life" (Doctorow 2012: 122, 124). Meanwhile courts, including the U.S. Supreme Court, shape the law, i.e. the social reality, and they have the right to so proceed. Doctorow criticized the mentioned decision for "bringing into the American narrative the fervid life of a golem." He further contended that "...if we accept corporations on their own terms, we cannot at the same time grant them human rights. They simply lack the range of feelings or values that define what it is to be human. Humans can act against their own interests, they can feel sympathy for others, and they can be merciful. Corporations cannot act except in their own interest, they do not know compassion and will not act mercifully unless there is some public relations advantage to it. Corporations do not live and die..." (Doctorow 2012: 123). However, the problem with the 'ontological part' of the Supreme Court decision is that the corporation is not perceived there as "ontologically equivalent" to human beings as Doctorow claims. Instead, it is viewed as having the same right to protection under the First Amendment in a way of legal fiction. The U.S. Supreme Court does not claim that the corporation has the existence typical of other beings and therefore has to be protected like those beings. It creates a fiction and it clearly says this. The creative force of the legal language is rooted in the potentiality of shaping fictitious worlds that might sometimes be mistaken for 'false ontology'. Doctorow (2012: 123) is however right in his criticism of the decision that one would wish to spare Americans in the present form due to its potentially devastating consequences for democracy in America. The above examples show, at least for the time being, that the existence in law is less central to legal-linguistic research that one could have assumed. Existence in law is a creative operation and its main instrument of creation is language. Later we will see in more detail how language enables the creation of law.

2.3.2 Does the nature of things shape the law?

From the inception of the discourse about law in the Occidental world the idea of law that corresponds with the nature of things dominated the reasoning of, mostly Greek, philosophers. Plato presents in his *Laws* an idea of legislation perceived as best under the given circumstances. For Plato, it is the best legislation because it corresponds with the underlying things and their nature. Aristotle also viewed law in terms of the nature of things. This tradition of thinking about good law as one that corresponds with the nature of things is still dominant in works such as Charles de Montesquieu's *The Spirit of Laws*. Montesquieu writes in the *Preface* to his *Laws*: "I have not drawn my principles from my prejudices, but from the nature of things." The nature of things is the crucial argument that Montesquieu uses in support of whatever regulative measure that he proposes. For him, a regulative measure is appropriate, even more, it is the best solution because it corresponds with the nature of things. This way of thinking is not an Occidental specialty. D. Cao (2007: 1) refers to Yan Fu and conceptions of traditional Chinese law where 'li' was associated with the 'order of things' or 'things as they are' and 'fa' with the 'Western law' as 'human made law'. Common for these conceptions of good law is also the conviction that there is one right, i.e. best solution, to a given legal problem as a consequence of the static law. Nature can also be used to establish power structures. In *Politics* IV (chapters 14–16) Aristotle distinguishes three elements in constitutions which he calls powers, these powers being the deliberative, the executive and the judicial. The trichotomy resembles Montesquieu's distinction between the legislative, the executive and the judicial powers. Yet, as the result of his assumption that laws should be permanent not much room is left for the legislative power. The role of these powers is therefore different, especially because the ancient Greeks did not have professional jurists; and this fact narrows the gap between the deliberative and the judicial powers considerably. Thus, this nature of power structures distributes the power unevenly and the process is deemed appropriate because it is natural. This example shows the most dangerous consequence of the 'natural' argument in law because it presents conventional constructs as results of natural processes. Yet, nature should not be underestimated. Henry Fielding writes in *Tom Jones* (XII, 2): "…if we shut Nature out at the door, she will come in at the window; and that puss, though a madam, will be a mouser still." Therefore, considering natural parameters in legislation is a necessary thing, provided that these parameters are really natural and not conventional.

2.3.3 How does law operate?

Meanwhile, law rarely relies on natural parameters and prefers conceptual construction. This way of shaping law was construed as creation of fictitious worlds. Already J.S. Mill mentions in a revealing context the fiction in law as its dominating feature in his *Utilitarianism* (1863), in chapter I, General Remarks, with reference to the problem of discordance in sciences: "Were it not so, there would be no science more insufficiently made out, than algebra; which derives none of its certainty from what are commonly taught to learners as its elements, since these, as laid down by some of its most eminent teachers, are as full of fictions as English law, and of mysteries as theology." Such legal fictions are created linguistically. By way of example, let us take a situation where the creditor requires a guarantee from a third party in the event that his primary debtor defaults on his payment. The creditor may ask the secondary debtor to stand surety independently of possible claims the primary debtor might have against him. To accomplish this goal, language provides a device that can be used in such situations; it is called an 'absolute and unconditional guarantee'. Now, let us assume that the primary debtor pretends to have been victim of a fraud by his creditor and refuses to pay. Will the secondary debtor under his absolute and unconditional obligation to pay be able to refer to the defense of the primary debtor? A guarantee that is 'absolute and unconditional' must be properly drafted in order to be operational. The New York case law requires that this condition be explicitly stated in the text of the document. The document must also include language that affirms the enforceability of the guarantee under "any other circumstances which might otherwise constitute a defense." The document should furthermore avoid any explicit representations, especially those arising under the principal obligation which could give rise to defenses. These are the main conditions for the constitution of an effective speech act of an absolute and unconditional guarantee under New York law (cf. Fogelson v. Rackfay Construction Co., 300 N.Y. 334, 340, 90 N.E. 2d 881, 884 1950); Sabo v. Delman, 3 N.Y. 2d 155, 161; Danann Realty Corp. v. Harris, 5 N.Y. 2d 317, 157). This speech act requires the creation of legal terms such as 'absolute and unconditional guarantee'. These terms warrant the efficiency of speech in legally relevant contexts. Creation of such speech is rule-governed and the rules have their own ways of emergence that initiates in linguistic behavior. These multiple linguistic rules also enable the operation of law. However, it is difficult to imagine that they could exist in isolation. Attempts at overcoming this isolation methodically will be discussed in Part 3 of this book.

2.3.4 Turning the concept of law upside down

Another interesting legal-linguistic phenomenon is the jurists' interest in defining the concept of law. The enterprise fascinates even more when the analysis is undertaken in a splendid isolation from the legal practice. The first question that imposes itself is to ask why did jurists actually engage in an enterprise of an inquiry into an abstract concept of 'law' that is equally abstract as the concept of 'red'. It is connected with the question why did jurists actually get involved with concepts at all. Both questions can be answered. The positivists' belief that conceptual analysis and defining of concepts in law would made the concepts unequivocal and directly applicable without any further legal-linguistic operations such as interpretation and argumentation sharpened their interest towards concepts. The quest for legitimacy in the exercise of law caused the work on an isolated concept of law that basically meant that law is a 'thing' that you have to obey. This approach required the emergence of a law isolated from other social phenomena as otherwise the issue of unconditional obedience to laws would become difficult to defend. In fact, the interest and work on concepts reach in history, as so often, down to the ancient Greeks. The Greek philosopher Epicurus wrote in his *Letter to Herodotus*: "In the first place, Herodotus, you must understand what it is that words denote, in order that by reference to this we may be in a position to test opinions, inquiries, or problems, so that our proofs may not run on untested ad infinitum, nor the terms we use be empty of meaning. For the primary signification of every term employed must be clearly seen, and ought to need no proving; this being necessary, if we are to have something to which the point at issue or the problem or the opinion before us can be referred." In their legal thinking, the Greeks tried to grasp the concept of law in abstract terms. The Greek notion of nomos (νόμος) connotes order that is also the most ancient conception of law. Not only among the Greeks but also in other ancient cultures, law has been perceived as an order established in harmony with other superior orders, such as the heavenly order, for example. This Greek conception of law, however, is still not a concept; it is an appealing, yet a vague idea. With today's vocabulary we would almost certainly be able to qualify it as a vision of law. This vision of law that is based on order is epistemologically valuable as it explains why we still can speak about laws also in the natural sciences. For the ancient Greeks the world could be explained through observable regularities, through laws that governed everything everywhere. With this conception, which is based on underlying or overarching laws, they made the world in principle understandable, accessible to the mind. At the same time, however, some of them, at least, introduced concepts such as the 'first mover' and others made the functioning of the world dependant on divine will and a supreme lawgiver. This argumentative element in the rational description of the world complicated the development of inquisitive thought and paved the way to a thinking that in the Middle Ages became dominant in the Occident. Centuries were needed to get rid of this intellectual ballast that partly had been thrown off with the help of the linguistic analysis in philosophy. Therefore, 'nomos' in law remains a conception, and not a concept of law. Later, in the Occidental philosophical tradition J. Locke, Th. Hobbes, J. Bentham, J.S. Mill, I. Kant, and G.W.F. Hegel defined the concept of law on their own terms; yet in principle they remained within the prescriptive tradition of reasoning about law. Thus, jurists deduct from the concept of law that it commands and that it imposes social order. Interesting in it is the idea that the concept of command is implicit in law, as it is in its nature pragmatic. The English analytical jurisprudence, of which John Austin (1790–1859) was the most prominent representative, defines the law as a 'command' imposed upon an inferior by a superior. V.Tokarev (2010) proposed to modernize Austin's concept of 'command' and talk instead of 'rule'. This proposal seems to be a well-adapted term that reflects Austin's intention and the contemporary understanding of the 'sovereign command'. Another definition that comes closer to future approaches to law in the American legal realism, such as the one formulated by T.E. Holland in his *Elements of Jurisprudence* (1880) that emphasizes as characteristic for law those general rules of action that are enforced by a sovereign political authority, makes a step towards acceptability of law. Subsequently, the American legal realists defined as law any rule that society would enforce. More contemporary conceptions such as H. Kelsen's and H.L.A. Hart's are a progress within this traditional paradigm. Meanwhile, also these conceptions avoid the discursive approach to law. The limits of positivist conceptions of law became apparent in such writings. Finally, Ronald Dworkin (1977, 1999) made clear that the positivist concept of law is not helpful because it does not explain the social phenomenon law. His criticism, which is perceived by some as obsolete today and as a part of the classical debate about law, has particular importance for the reflection about law in terms of the legal discourse. Dworkin made clear that the concept of law, as it has been defined by Hart, does not consider the main characteristic feature, i.e. its discursiveness. Such a concept is much too neutral to the legal discourse to become ever operational in legal science. Legal arguments must come from somewhere as they clearly cannot come from law alone. When law becomes separated from its underlying system of societal values, it appears as a skeleton cut off from conceptions of rights and justice. It is abstract and covers some structural features of law, yet not the core of the phenomenon that is its discursiveness. Therefore, not much can be done in law with conceptions and concepts that are not deeply rooted in discursiveness.

2.4 What is the domain of Law and Language?

The above examples and remarks make clear the necessity to establish a branch of knowledge called legal linguistics that would be able to elucidate such and related questions. Yet, one branch of law-oriented inquiry cannot deal with all questions concerning law, especially when the legal discourse is construed rather broadly as is the case in this book. What would be the domain of such inquiry? Everyone dealing with legal-linguistic problems asks this fundamental question. Some perceive the general relation between the two phenomena as a sufficient answer to this intricate question. The answer may have several components; one of them refers to the interrelation of legal concepts in legal systems. To illustrate, the common law uses for civil court procedures mainly two legal actions that are called 'action for damages' and 'action for specific performance'. In the case of the breach of contract the aggrieved party is either entitled to sue for damages as is the rule in the common law jurisdictions or sue for specific performance, mostly in order to obtain a specified object. Both actions exist also in the civil law jurisdictions, also in corresponding terminological dress. Meanwhile, in the architecture of the legal practice their role is different in both jurisdictions. In the civil law jurisdictions, in case of a breach of contract the action for damages is used only when specific performance that is the dominant action in the civil law countries cannot be applied because the object does not exist any more, etc. Therefore, Law and Language concerns the area of law where linguistic architecture transgresses the realm of terminology that may be confusing because it simplifies the law. Pure terminological work does not take note of the role the adequate foreign legal concepts play in the law of another jurisdiction (cf. Coendet 2012). Therefore the comparative legal-linguistic perspective covers this interdependence of terminological constructions. Meanwhile, this work on law also shows that whatever inquiry into its linguistic substance requires more than an interdisciplinary approach. At least in such moments it becomes clear that legal linguistics is unavoidable in approaches that aim at understanding law.

2.5 Consequences of the epistemological interest in law

This chapter suggests that searching for law is best started at the linguistic level of its expression. It also shows that the linguistic level of legal expression goes beyond grammar. Linguistics is not grammar and questions of linguistic existence in law, of legal rationality or of legal argumentation such as the analysis of the 'nature of things' cannot be coped with methods that simply classify words. Evidently, it is not worthwhile to look for spelling mistakes in the Supreme Court decisions. One may spend some time on this exercise, yet law will not change even if a meticulous and elaborate collection of this sort of deficiencies would be presented. Language in law is more than correct spelling and good school grammar. It does not mean that both can be neglected (cf. Jopek-Bosiacka 2006: 73). Meanwhile, language in law, or the linguistic aspect of law, is much too serious a matter to be approached from a grammarian's perspective. The non-grammarian, epistemological approach to the legal language focuses on the shaping of conceptions and concepts of law and the larger linguistic formations such as legal speech acts or legal discourses that are characteristic of it. The interest in legal epistemology leads to a realm where language is used to shape and to defend power structures. This complex and largely intransparent process occurs in discourses. The methodological question is how to show these discourses in a way that would be theoretically justified and practically useful. Apparently, we will have to dig for the legal discourses in the societal diachrony and in the societal synchrony as discourses are not present at sight. We can use the legal archaeology to accomplish this task.

2.6 Legal archaeology

The search for law undertaken here focuses upon the way how legal language, its fundamental concepts and all linguistic mechanisms that make it operative in society are constituted. Conceptions of law and legal concepts emerge in broader contexts that must be seized in order to understand law. As an undertaking of legal linguistics our search for law is discourse-oriented, as a pragmatic legal theory it keeps an eye on power structures and the exercise of power with means of law. As a legal archaeology or legal epistemology it looks at processes in which the language of law emerges in the struggle for power in state and society. Theoretically, therefore, the point of departure in a legal-linguistic attempt to understand the law is the observation that people speak about social problems that are conceptualized as law. Prerequisites and consequences of this speaking are the domain of legal linguistics as a theory of law. Before the nature of legal linguistics as a theory of law will be explained, and this will happen late, towards the end of this book, much archaeological work and also simple digging will be done to make discourses or at least some of their parts emerge from the social practice. Social practice is the place of our field work and we dig at it wherever people speak with each other about law. This search of law is methodical in the sense explained in this chapter. Methodically determined search for law can be challenged only by serendipity. The notion 'serendipity' was introduced into the English language by Horace Walpole in 1754 in reference to a Persian fairy tale *The Three Princes of Serendip*. The three princes of Serendip, that is the Sri Lanka of today, constantly discovered things by chance without being in quest of them. The dictionary definition characterizes 'serendipity' as the occurrence and development of events by chance. This concept is methodologically interesting mainly for natural sciences where discoveries often occur by accident. Yet also in law serendipity, now known also in the French scientific terminology where it is called 'sérendipité', may become relevant, especially when newly passed legislation leads to unexpected and unpredicted consequences (cf. Andell/Bourcier 2009). Also in the legal interpretation serendipity is important, mainly in situations where statutory provisions are drafted and enacted in the belief that they are semantically crystal clear, but later cause considerable problems in their application due to unexpected semantic intricacies. Therefore, the methodical legal-linguistic searches as well as the legal-linguistic serendipity are relevant to the legal archaeology, although in different degree. In the following part, a step towards understanding one more fundamental methodological legal-linguistic notion will be taken. Discursiveness will be scrutinized and made operational in legal linguistics. Part 3 will further strengthen our initial and reiterated view that law is engendered in linguistic practices that can be approached methodically.

Part 3: Discursiveness of Law

3.1 Speaking about law

Speaking about law is different from speaking about weather or about quantum mechanics. Law does not exist beyond social discursive practices and therefore, at least theoretically, all speaking about law is rooted in its discursiveness. The discursiveness as notion means primarily that a legally relevant issue that attracts speakers' attention can be approached only with linguistic means. The fact that law is rooted in discursiveness has one fundamental consequence: it seems worthwhile to describe it from the perspective of a discourse. Several eminent scholars such as Michel Foucault, Mikhail Bakhtin, John Searle and Jürgen Habermas developed broad theoretical frameworks that can be used to identify and better understand legal discourses. All of the mentioned approaches are useful in a legal-linguistic analysis. Although they emerged in different intellectual traditions, they are not contrary but rather complementary. They will be used in the following chapter in different degrees, depending on their particular usefulness for the discussed issue. Discourse is a complex notion that is researched in most works on this topic in a reduced form that reflects the actual needs of a researcher's approach. However, some researchers such as Michel Foucault dealt also with the philosophical prerequisites of the discourse. Foucault's approach is therefore well adapted to the needs of investigating legal discursiveness.

3.1.1 Foucault as pilot

Michel Foucault constructed in his two fundamental works *Les mots et les choses* (1966) and *L'archéologie du savoir* (1969) a perspective upon social phenomena that he qualified as epistemological in the sense of a scrutiny of the conceptual architecture of knowledge. He has covered numerous areas of human experience and knowledge of which the part related to social phenomena is particularly valuable to approaches based on the scrutiny of language use. However, purely linguistic approaches to social reality need an additional theoretical fundament in order to become practically operational. John Searle offers such a conception based on philosophical theories rooted in ordinary language philosophy that can be integrated into the broad perspective determined by Foucault's conception of 'épistémologie'. The scrutiny of language use would be however partial were it reduced to history of concepts even if the enterprise is undertaken within a more advanced methodological approach such as Foucault's. The approach that is called here legal-linguistic has to reconstruct not only the conceptual structure of law but also its argumentative structure. Searle's constructionist understanding of social reality as stated in *The Construction of Social Reality* (2011/1995) reflects perfectly these needs in a critical project. The critical project aims at understanding the phenomenon 'law'. Clearly, fundamental studies of law should also help developing a better law, the law of the future. At this point, all the approaches that were adopted and linked in the enterprise aiming at understanding law are not particularly efficient. Meanwhile, law as a social phenomenon depends on society that must take the responsibility for its law. Sometimes, therefore, scientific approaches must limit their ambitions and appetites. Clearly, law reflects society in which it emerges. Society that is negligent of its democratic development will not engender any law worth notice. The legal-linguistic method present in the above approaches more or less explicitly cannot be made responsible for deficiencies in legal discourses. One of its predominant tasks is however to make such deficiencies clear.

3.1.2 Foucault and legal science

Our main pilot was not a jurist. Some critics might object to his choice as our main pilot because of lack of professional qualifications. Michel Foucault devoted most of his epistemological analyses to subjects other than law. Law as research object or teaching subject plays scarcely any role for him. This lack of attraction may surprise with an author who did not avoid political involvement, neither personally nor in his capacity as a scholar. Meanwhile, Foucault stressed the concept of power rather than the concept of law. In general, Foucault has had a strong interest in all socially relevant phenomena; his silence about law must have reasons. Apparently, the tasks of strategic circumvention of the cumbersome edifice of law and addressing the most salient problems relating to the exercise of power were more appealing to him. Moreover, the absence of any discussion about paradigmatic change in the legal science must have rendered Foucault as a non-jurist rather skeptical towards his colleagues-jurists. Indeed, law's paradigmatic multiplicity is not well visible to non-jurists. What is more, most jurists have a problem with the pluralistic legal theory as they perceive their subject and its method as a monolith. Jurists, unlike philosophers, perceive themselves simply as jurists. Sometimes, a qualification such as 'pandectist' was added in the past; yet it is a weak attribute as it describes the style of thinking rather than a scientific method. The same concerns attributes such as 'canonist' and 'romanist' as all jurists are nolens volens canonists and romanists, at least a little bit. In terms of theory all these attributes mean simply 'positivist'. Positivist views upon the subject 'law' and its method still dominate the legal studies and the daily practice of jurists. In contrast, philosophers are phenomenologists, hermeneuticians, Marxists, analytical or post-analytical philosophers and the like. At the same time they may be specialized in ethics, aesthetics, epistemology or metaphysics. Most jurists do not know any methodological diversity. They may specialize in contracts, property or criminal law. Yet this specialization is subject matter- and not method-oriented. From the very beginning of the legal science in ancient Rome jurists were mainly divided along ideological rather than methodological lines. They were in terms of contemporary political debate perceived as belonging to the right or to the left wing of the political spectrum. Dividing jurists into Sabinians and Proculians in ancient Rome is a convincing illustration of this state of affairs. Also in ancient China the legalists differed from other scholars by their belief in the efficiency of law isolated from morals as a tool of social engineering, especially in the area of penal law. Meanwhile, they made part of the traditional Chinese scholarship and followed the Confucian method of text creation and interpretation like all others. In sympathy for monolithic positivism East meets West. Later times did not change this reluctance towards any methodological debate among jurists. In the Occident, the influence of classical Roman law differed in particular epochs. Also the approach to the nature of law differed in these epochs. Yet, the positivist method that treats law as a matter of fact remained applicable in all these epochs. Needless to stress that such a simplification of the cognitive interest towards the subject 'law' could not attract a researcher such as M. Foucault for whom method largely equaled science. This is an attenuating circumstance that also allows for using the skills of a non-jurist in the area of law.

3.1.3 Foucault's approach to law and power

Michel Foucault's approach to law and power is essential to any legal-linguistic analysis because it stresses and also proves the interrelation between power and language in social structures such as law. Foucault also stressed the character of law as a social mechanism and opposed the isolationist perspective upon law. Therefore, Leonard M. Hammer (2007: 1) characterized Foucault's attitude towards law as avoiding "any notion of law or norms as maintaining an elevated position when compared to other forms of social forces and attendant developments." Clearly, law plays a role for Foucault in shaping the social reality with rules that are imposed by force. For law this structure has consequences.

Hammer (2007: 3) refers to the most basic one: “For Foucault, the state is a creation of our discourses and is not representative of a unified whole.” Therefore power will be present in the discourse whenever there is law in an organized social structure. When the legal linguist approaches law from the perspective of language she must keep in mind this characteristic feature of law that is simultaneously a product of linguistic and of social processes that are steered by power structures. Therefore, Foucault’s approach is also a benchmark that measures all legal-linguistic attempts at understanding law from the perspective of language. It eliminates as inadequate all attempts that underestimate or exclude the element of power in the analysis of the legal discourse. Incidentally, Foucault also comes to terms with the ‘legal’ system as he does not allow for isolationist approaches to linguistic representations of the social reality. In his view, law is not a final product of power structures but rather an ongoing discursive process of its content-oriented formation. Discursive formations create “the effect of truth” (Hammer 2007: 21), yet they are never true. This is also the illustration of the discursive practices that create the link between words and things in Foucault’s theory of discourse. It explains why certain arguments dominate in some legal questions while others are absent. It proves that there is no chaos in the legal argumentation and that legal arguments are not products of spontaneous invention or intuition. They are grounded in rules that prefigure their logical structures and their contents. Furthermore, it is remote from jurists’ dream of ‘coherence in law’ and it focuses on ‘correlations’ of discursive arguments (Hammer 2007: 22) rather than on alleged systemic clarity that in parts of legal theory is called ‘coherence’. Therefore, ‘coherence’ is a term in legal discourses and not their product. A ‘legal system’ cannot engender ‘coherence’ in a social reality that is marked by antagonism inherent in power structures. For instance, in international law a question may come up whether a state actually exists (cf. Krasner 1999). In such a debate arguments can be distinguished as being ‘de facto’ or ‘de jure’ (Hammer 2007: 30), yet a coherent product of this multilayered argumentation will not emerge. As a part of the discursive practice, arguments will remain mutually exclusive and will be only better understood when classified as arguments ‘de facto’ or ‘de jure’. Some of these legal arguments will be considered while others will be omitted. The final decision about the existence of a state in question will be a choice of arguments that results from a formative discursive practice. Any further step towards constructing coherence in such evident choices would lead directly into the essentialist trap. Discourse analysis in Foucault’s terms is therefore primarily about its formation in structures defined by the exercise of power. A power structure may favor some beliefs to the detriment of others while pretending to protect the freedom of all such related beliefs. When for instance religious freedom is in question, 'belief' may acquire a significance that might be perceived as limiting its negative forms (Hammer 2007: 74). Therefore the French translation of 'belief' in Art. 18 of the UN Covenant on Civil and Political Rights (CCPR) is not 'croyance' but 'conviction' that encompasses also secular beliefs. In such a linguistic operation a fragment of the social reality is shaped with linguistic means. Hammer points even to the physical act of shaping while saying that the French representative simply changed the translation of 'belief' from 'croyance' into 'conviction' during negotiations within the UN. Also the letter by the U.S. Secretary of Education cited below (cf. 4.3.9) is an illustration of a discursive practice that can be traced back to its roots. Both examples show how social construction with linguistic means can sometimes be portrayed with amazing transparency. This is however not always the case. Therefore, also in this essay most results are achieved through the interpretation of formative elements of legal discourses. This interpretation is legal-linguistic as it results from Foucault's approach to power, law, and language that cannot be separated without causing distortions in the perspective upon society and its language.

3.2 Discourse and discursiveness

Discourse is seen by Michel Foucault as "a system of meaning...including all types of social and political practice, as well as institutions and organizations" (Howarth 1995: 115). Also M. Hajer (1995: 44) defined the discourse in the Foucauldian sense as "a specific ensemble of ideas, concepts, and categorizations that are produced, reproduced, and transformed in a particular set of practices and through which meaning is given to physical and social relations." The term 'discourse' is used in philosophy and in linguistics in different contexts with broader or narrower meaning that comes close to 'text' or 'utterance'. Ch. Baylon (1991: 235–236) has identified some of them. He included the meaning of discourse that equals 'parole' in Saussurian structural linguistics, further a unit that transcends the phrase, the assembly of rules that link phrases together, the opposed of 'utterance', yet also any utterance that presupposes a speaker and a hearer, any device that contextualizes language use. 'Discourse' was construed in the contemporary research as a synonym of 'parole' in terms of structural linguistics, as a 'transphrastic unit', i.e. a linguistic unit that transgresses the phrase, further as a message and an utterance in the general sense. Z. Harris proposed a definition that positions 'discourse' within intertwined series of sentences, L. Guespin characterized 'discourse' as an entity opposed to utterance that conditions this utterance. For L. Bloomfield (1914: 167) all interrelation of words is "primarily discursive." E. Benveniste in his *Problèmes de linguistique générale* (1966), vol. I, p. 242, stressed the structural necessity for the existence of a speaker and his interlocutor and the intention to influence the interlocutor. Finally, any linguistic entity that can be contrasted with the finite structure of language was perceived as discursive. This entity is the place where creativity can be exercised, where contextualization – also in its unexpected forms – takes place, where new values are conferred upon language. Following the Saussurian concept of 'langue' as a limited domain of the linguistic science and 'parole' as a residue of speaker's liberty, the discourse analysis in pragmatic sense concerns rather 'parole'. It concentrates on elaborating of constraints or regularities of such a discourse and envisages the way in which things are said rather than what is said (Baylon 1991: 237). These regularities can be found in the language itself, in history, ideology, habitus, mentality, and since M. Foucault's works, also in our knowledge. This expanded conception of discourse, especially in the sense introduced by Foucault, combines linguistic and extra-linguistic elements. Therefore, Foucault (1966: 102) stresses the discursiveness rather than the discourse: "Ce que nous laissent les civilisations et les peuples comme monuments de leur pensée, ce ne sont pas tellement les textes, que les vocabulaires et les syntaxes, les sons de leurs langues plutôt que les paroles qu'ils ont prononcées, moins leurs discours que ce qui les rendit possible: la discursivité de leur langage." Foucault underscores in his unique approach to discourse analysis the feature of discursiveness in linguistic practice, i.e. that something is mainly a discourse and not something else. Preliminarily, one could say in the way of example that a book is a discourse by necessity and primarily and a bridge is not a discourse although to construct it some discourse is necessary. This example makes plain in a somewhat brutal way the importance of the discursiveness as introduced into philosophical analysis by M. Foucault. When applied to law, it provides for an overarching analytical concept apt at integrating the two most significant ingredients of law, i.e. power and language.

3.2.1 Discursive contexts

The notion of context is no less ambiguous than the one of discourse. It can mean interpersonal or social context, in the French terminology 'contexte interpersonnel' and 'contexte social'. 'Context' may extend also to the physical environment and it can encompass general knowledge (Akmajian 2001: 388). Ch. Baylon (1991: 236–237) stresses that the research in the English-speaking countries favors the interpersonal context, while the French linguistic research, represented mainly by D. Maingueneau et O. Ducrot, relies more on social contexts in the tradition initiated by the writings of Mikhail Bakhtin. Also J. Derrida (2002: 236) warned against too narrow definitions of 'context' in cases where: "One is acceding to the place where the always necessary context of the performative operation (a context that is, like every convention, an institutional context) can no longer be saturated, delimited, fully determined." Finally, context has also been defined in contradistinction to co-text, as in L. Valeika and J. Buitkiene (2003: 58): "The context is the very situation in which a linguistic unit occurs, while the co-text is the linguistic environment of a linguistic unit." It has been also claimed that the context should not be specified in advance but rather discovered in a pragmatic analysis (cf. Levinson 1983: 22). For the legal linguistics a broad notion of context is needed due to the involvement of institutionalized and non-institutionalized elements that compete or coexist in legal discourses. In law, the context is mostly institutional as far as the application of law is concerned. Scholarly research into law might be the only exception to the institutionalization prerequisite provided that law is interpreted there independently within the free doctrinal or academic discourse. Place and time are not less essential although juridical validity of application and interpretation of law that is included in these two elements is integrated into the institutionalization prerequisite. Finally, 'context' may be perceived broadly as in this book where not only the professional legal discourse but also non-professional discourses about law are taken into consideration. This broad conceptualization of 'context' appears necessary because every professional or non-professional argument in the legal discourse is rooted in discursive contexts. As a result of this mechanism, the meaning of law depends directly on such contextual arguments. Limiting the context of the legal discourse equals therefore automatically limiting of meaning emergence in law. In the traditional legal theory that allows exclusively certain professional arguments to be used in the discourse about the meaning of law the emerging meaning is largely predefined, or at least limited in advance to certain semantic constellations. Is the legal context defined broadly, then also the background and the consequences of this limitation become apparent. Contextual linguistic elements of legally relevant situations are for instance 'eavesdropping' or spreading or dispelling 'rumors' or 'gossip'. Novels make aware of their contextual importance for law. In F. Dostoyevsky's *Crime and Punishment* the eavesdropping by Svidrigailov (cf. part V, chapter V) plays an important role in the development of the whole plot and becomes paradigmatic for the whole non-verbal act that was researched later by others (Locke 2011). Eavesdropping may give rise to blackmailing (cf. Marx 2011) that engenders a language of its own. Wilson (2003) reports that a 19th century English courtesan

Harriet Wilson blackmailed celebrities and demanded payment of an 'exclusion fee' for not mentioning their names in her memoirs. An opposite legally relevant concept to eavesdropping is 'privacy' (cf. Warren/Brandeis 1890; Westin 1967; Moore 1983). Its accompanying linguistic phenomena are 'rumor' and 'gossip' (cf. Rosnow/Fine 1976). Marx (2011) stressed that 'eavesdropping' as a social phenomenon has anthropological and biological components that elucidate it in terms of evolutionary development. The above examples strengthen the thesis that the legal context cannot be determined once and for all. It largely depends on the interpretive approach to law.

3.2.2 Discursiveness of law

Discursiveness of law is grounded in the preconditions of whatever legal question. Legal questions emerge when there is doubt about the legality of action, undertaken or prospective, or when the action undertaken is countered by an adversary. Therefore, there cannot be any non-discursive law. This means also that there is no one right and final answer to legal questions. Otherwise the social discourse about the most appropriate law would not make much sense. The social discourse is a strategic solution to anchor the legal discourse in a broader discourse about right and wrong in society. This discourse is also the foundation of the legal discourse because the most relevant arguments about the appropriate or the best law emerge in its social setting. Historically, some smaller linguistic forms were considered as related to the issues here discussed. Discursiveness occasionally appeared in form of a 'polemic' that etymologically can be traced back to 'war' and to 'dialogues' where the parties shared the argumentation and tried to develop a better shape for it. The 'debate' is one more such related although marginal concept in the discussion of the conceptual field of legal discursiveness. This terminological differentiation is not particularly relevant when discursiveness is understood in terms favored here; it is integrating law and language. This perspective upon discursiveness is Foucauldian. M. Foucault, whose concept of discursiveness is central to the development of a notion of 'legal discourses' thought primarily about the emergence of scientific concepts within a broader social context when he developed the notion of 'discursiveness'. For Foucault (1966) science is more than a representation of knowledge. It is a practice and it is an institution. Science has the privilege to state knowledge authoritatively; it does not simply discover or describe it. Scientific or academic discourse is therefore also a social practice that is connected with power structures or that, with other words, makes part of them. The image of a scholar working in the ivory tower has been once and for all demystified by Foucault. Social practice includes application of knowledge; knowledge exists not in order to be known but in order to be applied. The application of knowledge occurs in discourses. Discourses do not represent knowledge; they shape it (Foucault 1966: 14). Consequently, subjects treated in the branches of knowledge follow discursive tendencies that shape and cause their emergence (Foucault 1966). Their subject matters, i.e. the things treated, appear in these discourses and not independently of them. In legal sciences, there is therefore no knowledge about 'contracts' or 'property', but a discursively determined way of speaking about such issues. It is possible to approach this specific way of speaking about both and about all other terms and concepts of law in a chronological perspective that shows the moments in which the perception of things changes in the discourse. Such an approach is called by Foucault 'épistémologique' and is perceived as archaeology of knowledge in contradistinction to history of thought (Foucault 1966: 13). In my *Legal Linguistics* (2009) I tried to demonstrate on examples taken from the Roman law how such 'epistemological' analysis of the emergence process of legal concepts could look like (Galdia 2009: 288–291). In his work, Foucault described the human sciences from the perspective of the breaches that appear in the discourses about things (cf. also Kuhn 1973). In these breaches new knowledge emerges and is tested. Unlike historians, Foucault was able to show the complexity of these processes in their social condition. The embeddedness of discourses in discursiveness can be illustrated on an example taken from the American (legal) history. In the course of the American Revolution the constitutional discourse in North America changed along transformations that took place in the politically determined process of reformulation of discursive topoi. As a result, 'British America' was perceived as 'United States of America', oftentimes also by persons who previously referred to 'British America' as participants in constitutional discourses there. Discursiveness prefigures here the formation of a central topos in the American discourse about independence. This somehow paradoxical process of coinage of discursive terms such as 'United States of America' can take place because the whole discourse about American (legal) independence is based on language as there is nothing more to refer to. This process also forms knowledge in a way that enabled the American revolutionaries to talk meaningfully about the existence of the 'United States of America' even before the revolutionary process was over and before it has proven successful. Meanwhile, when knowledge is formed discursively there is a risk of emergence of discursive practices that pretend to shape knowledge, yet propose science without knowledge. Such discourses can be called empty, i.e. providing only words. Empty discourses are particularly threatening to areas of knowledge such as law that is exclusively a discursive practice. Yet, empty discourses are oftentimes corrected by following discourses and give rise to new substantiated discourses. Also, any possibility of discursive digression signals the argumentative potential in a topic. As a rule, science with method emerges in such disorderly discourses as a remedy for both calamitous situations where science survives without knowledge and where knowledge declares to cope well without science.

3.2.3 Monologues as discursive prerequisites

Discourses have usually a preliminary, pre-discursive stage. Their formation may start with a monologue that is shaped in speaker's inner forum. Definitely, also the unconscious has a role to play there. Jacques Lacan in his work *De la psychose paranoïaque dans ces rapports avec la personnalité* (1936) demonstrated that the unconscious is structured like language. When this preliminary monologue that starts in the unconscious and that subsequently reaches the stage of consciousness is uttered, it enters the public sphere. In this moment it also becomes part of the public discourse. In law, apparently, this process is less monological because many discourses are formed in constant interactions. However, collectiveness of speech includes also the situation of the reflecting speaker who uses language to prepare or to test socially relevant speech acts. Some people used to speak subvocally, so to say 'as if (they) were speaking to (themselves)' (Corder 1977: 24), although people "do not normally vocalize in privacy" (Furberg 1986: 64). Yet, some people speak even aloud addressing no one else but themselves. Bliss Perry says about the poet in his classical work *A Study of Poetry* (New York, 1920, p. 107): "But whether his primary aim be the relief of his own feelings (for a man swears even when he is alone!) or the communication of his feelings to other persons, it remains true that a poet's language betrays his bodily and mental history." In terms of pragmatics, J.L. Austin (1975: 22) perceives such speaking as 'hollow': "…a performative utterance will, for example, be in a peculiar way hollow or void if said by an actor on the stage, or if introduced in a poem, or spoken in soliloquy." Psychologists spent some time on analyzing this phenomenon and they tried to imagine the reasons for this seemingly abnormal activity. They found nothing abnormal at it. Others may not see much sense in speaking to no one. Yet, speaking to oneself prepares the social discourse (cf. Eemeren/Grootendorst 2011: 14); it forges its structures and topics. Monologous forms are one of the preconditions of discursiveness – we address ourselves in these monologues as if trying out our thoughts and the linguistic strength of our arguments; we listen to their sounds. Only afterwards the thoughts enter the public sphere and are presented to others. Jacques Lacan saw this making public of private matters as the beginning of discourses. Later, Jürgen Habermas

(1988) developed a theory of communication in the public sphere that starts at the moment when discourses become effective. Effectiveness is pertinent to social discourses. As long as we speak subvocally about the necessity to abolish the death penalty or to get rid of the government whatsoever, we are not involved in a discursive practice. Yet, we also act pre-discursively. Some discursive topics come up in the discourses quasi-spontaneously, not being planned monologically in advance. They must, however, be in a way prepared conceptually, be it only subliminally. Were it not so, it would be difficult to understand why certain thoughts appear to speakers in discourses quasi-spontaneously. Discursive reasoning is opposed to intuitive cognitive processes. Thoughts develop there incrementally, step by step until composed knowledge is established. Also within dialectic approaches to reality the assumption has been expressed by G.W.F. Hegel and others that whatever view about reality is shaped within the perspective of competing theses and antitheses that merge thus forming a synthesis. These synthetic processes also form the background of the subject-matter oriented approaches to discourses that are viewed as explicitly legal. In such approaches to legal discourses the stage of their mental composition is omitted. Yet, it should not. Meanwhile, every model or conceptualization of a socially relevant area in our mind also simplifies; the model psychology calls it 'framing effect'. Contemporary research treats the mentioned problems under the topic 'self-argumentation' (Paglieri/Castelfranchi 2009). Self-argumentation is perceived as a function of internal discourse. This function has been for long rather neglected in the research and therefore not much can be said about it. Meanwhile, it is important to stress that argumentation does not exclusively concern the discourse with others. It apparently takes place in the inner forum of the argumenting subject as well. Its role in the process of shaping public discourses is unclear because the question whether discourse creation is primarily rooted in the individual or in the collective practice remains open. It seems that both aspects of discourse emergence would have to be thought together in order to understand the formation of discursive contents and procedures.

3.2.4 Other discursive prerequisites

Most generally, discursiveness presupposes the existence of one world in which conscious speakers can meaningfully communicate (Searle 2011: 7). The most relevant communication about this one world will be verbal and it is thinkable only when the speaking subjects share their intentionality, and not only words and rules for the combination of words. They must be able to share their beliefs, desires or intentions. Otherwise, they would have nothing in common to talk about (cf. McGuinness 1991: 18). Thus, collective intentionality is one another prerequisite of discursiveness (Searle 2011: 33). Furthermore, discursiveness as a linguistic phenomenon presupposes a specific set of signs that are used to represent meaning. This set of signs is the natural language of discourses. As the discursiveness that interests here relates to social phenomena, the utterances, i.e. speech acts that constitute it, will not be accepted per se in socially relevant discourses. In such discourses it is crucial to know whether something that is asserted is right or wrong. The linguistic signs that constitute the language and engender meaning will be therefore exposed to tests. These tests are known as argumentative and interpretive linguistic practices. They will include procedures for distinguishing true and false, procedures for distinguishing valid and void as well as probable and improbable, rational and irrational, and numerous other such procedures. These tests will be applicable both upon rules and upon conventions (Searle 2011: 38). Principles will be used in them as tools for testing the content of speech acts. Principles and other testing criteria will be set up in procedures that are institutional. Meaning that will emerge as result of tests will be related to social facts and be valid under the condition of its institutional setting. Rationality tests dominate the discussion at this point. Recently, however, Christian Plantin (2011) broadened the discursive perspective by explicitly introducing emotions into the discourse analysis. According to Plantin the discourse is an amalgam of rational and emotional arguments. Therefore, it cannot be perceived in the dichotomy of the rational on the one side and the emotional on the other. Until now, in the legal discourse the emotional component has been observed, yet not incorporated into the method of analysis. Plantin is definitely right in positing that a discourse about values cannot be unemotional and that emotions are inseparable from other more rational components. His approach termed as 'argumentative construction of emotions' should be incorporated into the method of legal discourse analysis. Interestingly, experienced classical legal writers such as Ch. de Montesquieu used surprising emotional arguments in their writings about law. Montesquieu says in the *Advertisement* to *The Spirit of Laws* about the 'politically virtuous man': "He is the man who loves the law of his country, and who is actuated by the love of those laws." Reference to 'love' in legal contexts is rare nowadays. Meanwhile, a Chinese collection of legislative acts for students edited 2006 by the Law Press China proclaims on the book cover (in the English language): "I love the law/I know the law." Other emotional moments in legal texts are of stylistic nature. For instance, Mattila (2013: 123) showed that archaism and solemnity are present in modern legal texts and that the "requirement of gravity" is respected by many legislators. Kubánek and Klabal (2012: 14) demonstrated that the new Czech civil code that became effective on January 1, 2014 has been deliberately drafted in terms that are perceived as archaic by some speakers because such language may accommodate expectations of many citizens. In historical times, in the Byzantine tradition, Emperor Justinian addressed his *Institutiones* to the 'youth eager to acquire knowledge about laws' ("cupidae Legum juventuti"). Such examples are numerous in an area that has been traditionally perceived as unemotional. These, in short, are the prerequisites for discursive practices in which communication about law in the one physical and mental world shared by the speakers will take place.

3.3 Discursiveness and discourse analysis

For law the main consequence of its discursiveness is that it has to be analyzed as a discursive practice. Discourse analysis regularly starts with narratives that represent discursive practices. Narratives structure the discourse and provide for clarity and stability in it (Gottweis 1998: 3). Discourse analysis shows how meaning is constructed discursively in these material representations, i.e. how is language used in them to engender meaning. Understanding the meaning constitution has several prerequisites. Historically, already the hermeneutic approach to language understanding that stressed the circularity of understanding processes and the structuralist conception of language challenged the traditional philosophical conception of understanding meaning in linguistic expressions. F. de Saussure is known to have introduced the structure of a linguistic sign composed of a signified, for instance 'cat' or 'law', and the signifier that can be described as sound emission /kæt/ or /lo:/. The discursive meaning is independent of the material world where there are cats or a social practice where law may be traced in socially relevant contexts. Saussure described therefore the link between the signified and the signifier as arbitrary because the concepts could be linked to other sound emissions equally well (Saussure 1967: 66–68). Understanding of meaning is therefore for Ferdinand de Saussure understanding of both the signifier and the signified that are inseparably linked like two sides of a coin while remaining arbitrarily related to each other. With this apparent paradox in mind, M. Foucault made the next step and linked the linguistic sign to the reality that it represents. For Foucault discourse has no actual meaning (Hammer 2007: 64) but provides a matrix for the formation of meaning. Foucault sees the discourse in its relation to knowledge as a reflection of knowledge. Discourse is therefore semantically amorphous as it provides for the possibility to constitute meaning in a social practice. This result is in line with the legal-linguistic approach to meaning. Also there meaning is understood as emerging in complex argumentative structures where language and power interact. In fact, meaning in law emerges neither linguistically nor legally; it manifests itself as a result of legal-linguistic discursive practices. Dworkinian constructive interpretation is one such mechanism that illustrates the procedure (Galdia 2009: 207). This operation has been for the structuralist Saussure rather negligible under his conception of language. The "struggle for meaning" (Laclau/Mouffe 1985) results from this trichotomy that is not contingent because it is engendered in a historical context (cf. Derrida 1974 in Clegg 1989: 151). Moreover, in written texts the hermeneutic circle must be added to the epistemological matrix as an indispensable requirement because in law a process of reading is regularly involved in meaning constitution. M. Foucault (1966: 44) aptly determined the relation between hermeneutics and semiotics in that he distributed the tasks between both: "Appelons herméneutique l'ensemble des connaissances et des techniques qui permettent de faire parler les signes et de découvrir leur sens; appelons sémiologie l'ensemble des connaissances et des techniques qui permettent de distinguer où sont les signes, de définir ce qui les institue comme signes, de connaître leurs liens et les lois de leur enchaînement…". Furthermore, reading is not value-free or neutral; it takes place towards ethical convictions that shape the reading act. Finally, introducing the interpreter into the main semiotic framework made the process less abstract and helped explaining how people and not only philosophers understand linguistic expressions. The triade composed of signifying, signified and interpreter in his historical context provides the matrix for the description of the way how meaning is constituted in contexts and why it is exposed to change. Scholars such as Robert Brandom (2000) developed detailed theories about meaning constitution. There, meaning is constituted in interpretive strategies that are developed to convince others about the appropriateness of the interpretive propositions.

3.3.1 'Différance' in law

One of the consequences of the reflected divide into legal norms and others may be, as said, a newly structured discourse that attempts at integrating the formalistically split levels of speech and action into a broader unit. The legal discourse of the 'différance' used by Jacques Derrida, François Lyotard or G. Spencer-Brown makes clear the difference between the positivist discourse about law as a discourse about facts and a reflection that focuses on the interplay between facts and norms that constantly change shape in the legal discourse. The constitution of meaning in legal discourses of this type shows the dynamic of law in application, i.e. its social existence. It includes one more fundamental element, the attitudes to forms and contents in law. These concepts were largely neglected in the traditional legal theory. Meanwhile, our approach to law, the angle from which we view it, is decisive for whatever discussion about the emergence of meaning in law. This angle or perspective controls the emergence of relevant arguments in the legal discourse. It is therefore one of the most salient elements of the legal context. It includes such fundamental, yet rarely mentioned attitudes to law as 'taking law seriously' or 'neglecting law' in one's biographical project. Often the 'reliance upon the law' as social mechanism has been quoted as one more attitudinal example. Finally, 'différance' shows law's real face. For legal texts the approach of 'différance' has one more consequence in that it annihilates the alleged unity of text and discourse in law. Jurists, especially the positivists, tend to perceive legal texts and legal discourses in a harmonious form that resembles sacred texts commented by theologists. Splits, inconsequences, breaches, chasms, tilts and some other figures typical of legal argumentation are perceived there as intrusions into the harmonious sphere of law as it ought to be. Meanwhile, law as the discourse of 'différance' manifests itself in breaches, fragments, splits and tilts. It may be an unpleasant experience for all citizens who participate in acts of application of law of this kind. Meanwhile, it is worthwhile to remember that legal discourses are not religious ceremonies or artistic events. They are not philosophical symposions, neither are they exercises in legal rhetoric. They take place towards the background of numerous discursive forms that influence them without making part of them. The legal discourses cannot influence the emergence of such surrounding discourses, yet the 'différance' helps trace the borderline between legal and other discursive practices.

3.3.2 Discursive law in discursive societies

We have reached a point in our investigation where we cannot have any doubts that law is a discursive social practice. Nevertheless, let us reiterate that law is in its essence discursive because it cannot emerge without discourses about its content, past, present, or future. It is a social discursive practice because a monological law is at best a prolog to an effective discourse about the content of law that will always be social at the end, as it presupposes at least two participants. Daniel Defoe's literary hero, Robinson does not need any law on his island. In Defoe's novel he will rarely get involved in inner monologues about whatever reasoning pertaining to possible contents of legal claims. We therefore agree that law is a social discursive practice, and to those who do not feel at ease with this result we can only say that this conclusion is value-free and that it does not presuppose anyone's commitment to the idea of law as a social discourse. Law consists of discourses almost like rain consists of drops of water. In this case a publicly expressed support for such a rain structure would surprise as a largely unneeded, irrelevant statement. Meanwhile, in the background of most reservations against the discursive character of law there are attempts at formalizing the law. All of them, as they had been only attempts, failed until now (Galdia 2009: 63). One could say they failed because law is a discursive social practice and therefore it cannot be formalized. This is also what we think, and we do not say that it is good that it is like that. Aspects of law are certainly formalizable, yet law in its essence cannot be subjected to formal operations, unless one is willing to change the concept of law. To make it clear, our law, i.e. the law as we know it since the Roman times, is not in its essence formalizable. Yet, other thinkable types of law may be well adaptable to formal requirements. Let this be a consolation to all those who have hard time accepting law as it appears today. Should such alternative conceptions some day become law, we would have to deal with another type of law and all or most of our legal theory would become obsolete. Yet, these times are not in sight.

3.3.3 Ideally discursive societies

More complicated is the concept of discursive societies. Law is definitely discursive, as there is nothing more in it as words lined up in more complex forms that are called 'speech acts'. In society, however, many things happen, some are verbal, and others are not. People wage wars or eat ice cream; both are actions that oscillate on different levels of complexity, and they are not discursive as far as we focus on the mere struggle as physical confrontation or the consumption of frozen flavored cream. They are clearly social practices; yet their rules are not known in equal degree. All of us know how to eat ice cream, only some master the technique used in modern wars. Many social practices are discursive; take for instance a telephone conversation. Society, when it is seen towards the background of such examples, appears as an amalgam of discursive practices and of non-discursive practices. Why then should we speak about discursive societies? There is at least one reason for this experiment. Ideally, modern societies might develop cultures that are exclusively discursive. It means that bridges would not be constructed in them, yet the fact of the existence of bridges in the given society would be affirmed linguistically in institutional procedures that legitimize these affirmative utterances. No such society exists as of now, and would it exist it would initiate with the setting up of a purely discursive societal form of being the beginning of its own end. Modern societies are, however, dominated by discursive practices. Again, we do not determine whether this state of affairs is satisfactory. We only conclude that the dominant communicational form in modern societies is discursive, i.e. some people speak to some other people and while so doing they make things happen. To express it with other words, they do not make anything more than speaking while doing these things. J.L. Austin (1975) concentrated on some such actions and perceived them as rather exceptional. Meanwhile, in a discursively dominated society such practices prevail, in discursive societies there would exist exclusively discursive practices. Hence, a discursive society requires an advanced linguistic culture. For societies that are not exclusively discursive some other material contexts are relevant. Typically, democracy and not tyranny or arbitrary rules based on physical violence provide a more propitious ground for the development of such a mixed culture. For Europe, written documents such as the *Universal Declaration of the Rights of Man and Citizen* and for the U.S. *The Federalist* mark the beginning points of emergence of such a discursive culture. They will be analyzed later in more detail.

3.3.4 Non-discursive areas of social action

The difference between discursive and non-discursive practices is an observable matter of fact. Yet the difference between both aspects of practice is less salient than could be expected because social practices are inter-related. A non-discursive practice is for instance the construction of a bridge. It is a technical and a practical aim-oriented activity. Meanwhile, the linguistic act of determining whether an object actually is a bridge is a discursive practice related to a non-discursive practice. Also an isolated semantic inquiry 'What is a bridge?' is a linguistic (discursive) practice. In this case, one could even risk answering the question in terms of a discursive practice without reference to the non-discursive elements of bridge construction. However, the entirety of discourses about bridges is in one way or another connected with the discourse of architecture related to bridges. There, architectural discourse is rendered in the formalized language of mathematics that enables bridges to stand. Therefore, in the general discourse about bridges both practices are at least interrelated. The distinction between discursive and non-discursive practices is important. Non-observance of differences between discursive practices leads to disturbance in societies, especially in the case where non-discursive practices are replaced by discursive practices. Such societies will not satisfy the citizens who happened to live there. Meanwhile, the mere fact that both types of practices can be exchanged signals that the difference is somehow problematic. For instance, political discourses make use of this structural weakness of discourse constitution. Political discourses that aim at setting discursive parameters for federatory speech are typical discursive practices that generate language use. They display greater inventiveness in relation to social facts. Their authors dare to argue: 'There is no inflation. There is no economic crisis. The crisis is over; happy days are here again.' It seems not to matter that social facts prove the contrary of these optimistic statements. Political discourse turns non-discursive reality into discursive practice. Assertions can be made there in contradiction to the most elementary knowledge about social reality. Words in those discourses are believed to become things by repetition, as in the example of mantras. Some methods of persuasion or hypnosis are also based on this conviction. For instance, the famous French 'méthode Coué' consists of an autosuggestive practice of repeating a phrase: "Tous les jours, à touts points de vue, je vais de mieux en mieux." Famous songs used the same approach: "Happy Days Are Here Again!" by Milton Hager and also its French version "Qu'est qu'on attend pour être heureux?" are based on this simple pragmatic device of language use. These approaches are metaphysical because they deny the existence of non-linguistic prerequisites for things and events. They pretend that health, happiness, or well-being are discursive matters. Yet, this is clearly not the case.

Law may display some quintessentially non-discursive actions such as the execution of a capital punishment verdict. Although the physical act of execution as such may be non-verbal, it is connected with the use of words. T. Capote, who witnessed the execution of the Clutter family murderers on April 14, 1965 in Kansas, described the execution of Hickock in his novel *In Cold Blood*: "Accompanied by six guards and a prayer-murmuring chaplain, he entered the death place handcuffed and wearing an ugly harness of leather straps that bound his arms to his torso. At the foot of the gallows the warden read to him the official order of execution, a two-page document…As is customary, the warden, having finished his recitation, asked the condemned man whether he had any last statement to make." Hickock made his statement. Then he said politely to the present police agents: "Nice to see you." Further prayers were recited when Hickock was mounting the scaffold steps, apparently to save time, as the execution of his accomplice, Smith, had to follow next. Capote writes: 'The Lord giveth, the Lord taketh away. Blessed is the name of the Lord', the chaplain intoned,…and as a delicate black mask was tied round the prisoner's eyes 'May the Lord have mercy on your soul.' The trap door opened, and Hickock hung for all to see a full twenty minutes before the prison doctor at last said, 'I pronounce this man dead.'…While waiting for the second execution, a reporter and a guard conversed. The reporter said, 'This is your first hanging?'…" The scenery that may be perceived as described by Capote with much veracity is extremely discursive and the doctor's pronouncement plays a role of a legal performative in it. The absence of his pronouncement would definitely not make Hickock resuscitate, as the omission to read the order of execution to the condemned would not make the physical act of hanging less efficient. Further, the possibility to make a last statement remains a procedural formality and Hickock, possibly not prepared for this eventuality, says banally: "I just want to say I hold no hard feelings. You people are sending me to a better world than this ever was,...". After this short statement Hickock greeted the police officers, as mentioned above. Symbolically expressive are also facts that preceded Hickock's execution, at least as rendered by Capote: Hickock is proposed to order his last meal. He chooses shrimp, French fries, garlic bread, ice cream and strawberries with whipped cream. Capote, mindful of the symbolic character of this choice, spells the menu distinctively: "Shrimp. French fries. Garlic bread. Ice cream and strawberries and whipped cream." Law, although so often oblivious of main traits of humanity, tends sometimes to stress its anthropological component symbolically. Also post-execution linguistic practices are specific. After the execution the Kansas City *Star* reported: "Die on Rope for Bloody Crime...Richard Eugene Hickock and Perry Edward Smith, partners in crime, died on the gallows at the state prison early today for one of the bloodiest murders in Kansas criminal annals. Hickock, 33 years old, died first, at 12:41 A.M.; Smith, 36, died at 1:19..." Significantly, the time of the execution is reported and this time indication seems to correspond with the prison doctor's pronouncements. For the executed, one might assume, the life ended at the start of the execution and not twenty minutes later when they were pronounced dead. Also the order in which the execution proceeded is reported by the newspaper as if it were imposed by law. Capote mentions that the order of execution has been suggested by the condemned themselves who preferred the alphabetical order although they had also the opportunity to "draw straws to see who dropped first." Incidentally, though, the short dialogue between the guard and the reporter illustrates one more fundamental legal-linguistic regularity. People have the tendency to speak in the most awkward situations and they make use of their capacity to develop and to use language as an anthropological constant practically everywhere. Indeed, people are people because they speak. This anthropological constant seems also to explain Hickock's interest in making his banal statement that evokes his tragical and miserable life philosophy. Therefore, when we are said that language is a social institution we are also revealed a more fundamental truth: who does not speak does not belong to society. In Capote's scenery everyone tries to speak and some of the speakers even develop discursive practices. The sequence that takes place between the guard and the reporter is significant in this sense. There is no social convention for this sort of dialogues; people are usually embarrassed to say something in a setting that is described above and they surely do not learn at school what one has to say in such situations. Hickock's polite greeting of the police agents who enabled his condemnation is one more such innovative procedure for speaking in situations where there is no reported convention for appropriate language use. In fact, it is doubtful whether someone could assume that it is appropriate to greet people who assist at one's execution. Hickock nevertheless did so assume and by so doing he showed that he was much more human than the justice system had assumed of him. Meanwhile, society sanctions the acts of bringing to death of such clumsy and miserable people. In some respects, however, many of them appear to be more human than society in that they are not ready to give up their faculty of speech. This faculty of speech connects them with society and this is also society that brutally cuts this last link. It follows from the above that Hickock should not have been executed. This holds true also for Smith whose case is not included as it leads to the same legal-linguistically relevant results. Discursive elements were also manifestly present during the execution of Elena and Nicolae Ceauşescu in Romania in 1989 and of Saddam Hussein in Iraq in 2006, as can be seen from records that are available online. In fact, even if a phenomenon such as the execution is described in terms of its non-discursive components, its discursiveness can as a rule be inferred from the context. This holds true even for historical events. For instance, R. Holinshed reports in the first volume of his *Chronicles (of) England, Scotland, and Ireland* (1807, p. 314) that under King Henry VIII seventy-two thousand thieves were hanged in England. Furthermore, while speaking about the Victorian age, J. Symons (1975: 46) argued that: "11,000 murders were committed in Britain every year during the early part of the century..." The historical accuracy of the published data notwithstanding, the discursiveness of law appears under such circumstances as a marginal aspect of history. In circumstances where sheer power or violence rule, also the importance of attempts to broaden the scope of epistemological analysis such as those represented by the legal-linguistic perspective may appear vain. Yet also the sense in acquisition of knowledge has its limits. While knowledge is power, there are also other types of power that may sometimes prevail over more civilized versions of power. No other remedy against this corruptive phenomenon is known as continuous acquisition of knowledge. Knowledge therefore is acquired also in situations in which it cannot help.

3.4 Discursiveness and creativity

Hickock's speaking in a situation where there is no convention for the use of language is an example of a creative practice that speakers seem to master perfectly. They are, like Hickock, able to make use of creative linguistic devices in situations that are critical to them. 'Critical' or 'borderline situations' extend up to the level of the threat to one's life, when life, like in Hickock's case hangs by a thread. Also monologues take place in such situations, in "moments of great courage" when the speaker thinks about his own death or the "ultimate extinction" of one's family (Searle 1999: 48). Regularly, however, creative practice takes place under less dramatic circumstances (cf. Vlachopoulos 2011). Creativity is therefore a surprising phenomenon because it concerns the most serious and the least serious circumstances in life. The American author, Samuel Langhorne Clemens, known as Mark Twain, invented his literary pseudonym while observing fishermen who 'marked a twain'. In so doing, he was not only ingenious, he was also quick. Creativity in law is less spontaneous, yet it lacks the gravity of nuclear physics. Legal doctrine is constructed as a cascade of legal notions. For instance, 'contract' as legal notion is conceptually rooted in another legal notion that is called 'agreement' (Black 2012). In torts, a cause that may lead to liability may be classified as 'proximate' or 'remote'. This example includes also a moment of visualization as thinking in images must accompany this sort of conceptual inventions. A new tort can be created and it may be called 'tortious interference of contract'. More contemporary notional coinages such as 'animal welfare' (Vels 2004) or 'war on terror' (Duffy 2012) appear not only within a restricted semantic field. 'Animal welfare' is used in connection with 'unnecessary suffering' (Vels 2004); 'war on terror' is connected with 'extraordinary rendition' and 'detention' (Londras 2011). 'Detention' collocates with 'immigration detention' (Wilsher 2011). Interestingly, both Duffy and Londras apostrophized the term 'war on terror' as it is done also in this text, apparently with the intention to mark the distance of the academic community towards this sort of manipulative linguistic creation. Other recent creations such as 'prisoner abuse' correspond with the more traditional 'enemy prisoner' (cf. Forsythe 2011). New creations engender sub-classes of notions as in the case of 'shipping interdiction' (cf. Guilfoyle 2011). For 'shipping interdiction' the sub-class may include 'stopping, searching, and arresting foreign flag vessels and crew on the high seas'. Guilfoyle describes the application of these notions to situations such as piracy, slavery, drug smuggling, fisheries management, migrant smuggling, and proliferation of weapons of mass destruction or maritime terrorism. Some samples of legal-linguistic creation are well documented. For instance, the British politician, Sir James Dalhousie

(1812–1860), Governor of India of his time, is remembered as the creator of the 'doctrine of lapse'. This doctrine established as a principle of law that territories of India that had no immediate heir became British by the mere operation of law. The doctrine is based on a common law principle that 'lapsed legacies fall into the residuary estate'. It is enough to skillfully define this 'residuary estate' and the acquisition of property is perfect. Dalhousie's 'brilliant' idea may have induced some people such as Sir Alexander Arbuthnot to admiratively describe Dalhousie as "one of the greatest rulers, if not the greatest ruler, that India has known." In fact, the idea that underlies the doctrine is relatively simple: as soon as a territory becomes free, it is ours. The legal creation is based here on arrogance, assertiveness, and brutal expansionism. It may leave room for some admiration because ethical principles would hinder most people, yet not Earle of Dalhousie, to set up such arbitrary rules for acquisition of property in foreign countries. His admirers stressed that India owes him its railways network and its telegraph service. They praised him for having "found leisure to introduce many internal reforms in India," which apparently also include the invention of the 'doctrine of lapse'. The admiration of his person seems to have been caused by 'his power of debate that soon won him office'. The Dalhousie-case shows the deceptive limits of language use in law but also its creative potential. In fact, all above examples demonstrate that creativity in law is discursive.

3.4.1 Diversity of legal discourses

Diversity of discourses in law corresponds with the methodological diversity of their treatment. Their main common point, however, is the attempt to show the language in its different manifestations within legal contexts. The consequence of such a generous research license is that many heterogeneous analyses of language used in legal contexts can be perceived as methodologically discursive. They have to be diverse as are diverse the communicational practices in society. Some such practices such as sentencing or writing court opinions are well known and regularly covered in the legal-linguistic research. Others, such as lobbying are difficult to embrace methodologically as reliable data about language use in lobbying practices is available at best in a reduced form, if at all. Meanwhile, lobbying as legal-discursive practice is relevant both to law and to legal linguistics. Laws are expected to be drafted in the general interest. Meanwhile, lobbying either narrows down a proposed legislative act or tries to initiate legislative projects with the aim to favor a social group. It is a good illustration of the amalgamation of language and power, and it is definitely not a coincidence that linguistic data needed to research this phenomenon more closely are restricted.

Therefore, the common and the less common discursive practices in law represent legal-linguistic devices within the discursive diversity that should be dealt with by legal linguists with equal interest. There is no need to limit this diversity as has been sometimes the case in the mainstream legal theory. This diversity of discourses explains the multitude of methods that have been developed in order to cope with the diversity of discursive types. These methodological approaches to legal discourses are either general or particular. General approaches tend to describe the legal discourse in terms of the mainstream (legal) or social theory. Many researchers, such as J. Habermas (1988; 1992; 1996), R. Alexy (1986; 1995), and A. Aarnio (1987; 1989) proposed such theoretical foundations for social or legal discourses. Particular approaches are based on the conviction that linguistic details matter. Therefore, they provide for a multitude of meticulous observations based on particular, i.e. singular communicative situations that they subsequently may generalize or not (Weisberg 1992; Galdia 2009). These particular approaches include conversational analysis (especially of language used in court hearings) and interpretations of singular speech acts in order to understand them (Gotti 2008; Anesa 2009). Generalists have the ambition to understand the discourse as an abstract act of speech in its social settings. Particularists prove that the generalists' approach is practically relevant. Both approaches are therefore complementary, as no particular discourse exists without the general discourse and vice versa. Most analyses in both approaches concentrate on procedures. In this book, in an approach that integrates the human dimension of law, aspects of contents transferred in law are equally significant as are the communicative procedures in which language is used in legally relevant contexts. This idea is derivative of J. Habermas' attempts to reach valuable goals in society within communicative practices that in abstraction may engender whatever results, wishful as well as detrimental.

3.4.2 Divide between professional and non-professional discourses

This divide has been introduced by certain professionals. Non-professionals do not feel bound by the imposed limits and develop their own free discourses that occasionally may disappoint professionals. Some legal scholars characterized the limitations imposed upon professional legal discourses by institutions, especially by the supreme courts (Alexy 1983: 340). They insisted on the development of legal argumentation within these limits and perceived only this kind of argumentation as truly professional. This approach may take by surprise as rarely a profession accepts limits imposed upon its work by a formally composed institution distinct from them. Some jurists may suffer from civil immaturity caused by one's own fault mentioned already by Immanuel Kant as "selbstverschuldete Unmündigkeit." Kant equally advised to overcome this self-imposed restriction to reasoning. Therefore, it may be that in parts of the legal theory those institutional limitations have been accepted all too easily. Yet, there is no doubt that these limits exist. The question that has to be asked is whether they could be overcome. It seems that imposing limits on discursive mechanisms in a democratic society is a counter-productive measure. Law in a democratic society is a vision, an ongoing project. Limiting it means limiting the development of the democratic society. Counter-tendencies to the restrictive approach exist as well. Legal discourse has been practiced as an open discourse by the judge Benjamin Cardozo in the U.S. (cf. Posner 1990: 20–32) or by the Freirechtsschule in Germany (cf. Siltala 2011: 3). Dealing with the professional legal discourse is a task to be addressed by legal scholarship. Limiting this scholarship to argumentation approved by some formally competent institutions that themselves are not even academic does not seem to be justified. Already K.F. von Savigny conceived law in its scientific form as 'wissenschaftliches Recht'. In order to remain or become scientific, the law must develop exclusively under constraints of rationality. This is also one of the reasons while in this book legal discourses are treated rather broadly and actually whatever discourse with reference to law is taken into consideration. This does not mean that there is no scale of relevance between different discursive contributions. Some of them like academic discourses are particularly interesting (especially for the academia).

3.4.3 Academic discourse

Academic discourse developed in interdependence with power structures. Already in ancient Greece 'academic' institutions participated in processes where state ideology has been shaped. In more contemporary terminology both Plato's and Aristotle's schools could be perceived as think tanks where policies and ideologies for the ruling class were developed. Also in ancient China educational institutions developed in close connection with power structures. Yet, next to the mentioned activities also theoretical reflection has been cherished in these institutions. It brought results which are useful even more than two thousand years later. In subsequent epochs the institutional embeddedness of academic institutions did not change radically and therefore academic discourse develops until today in interrelation with the dominant political and social discourses (cf. Greimas 1977: 108). The academic legal discourse is more than other branches of the academia linked to power structures due to its very substance that is power exercised in these structures with the help of law. Both main currents of the academic legal discourse, i.e. the affirmative and the critical discourse, reflect therefore in their conceptual bases the close relation that legal academia entertains with power structures. Illustrative of affirmative discourse is the following text sample: "The American Constitution is, so far I can see, the most wonderful work ever struck off at a given time by the brain and purpose of man," as stated by William E. Gladstone in his essay *Kin Beyond Sea*, published on July 26, 1878 in *The North American Review*. Critical discourse, in turn, may be characterized as a type of reflection upon law that is practiced in this book. Meanwhile, an appraisal of the position that legal linguistics maintains in the discursive context of academia and power seems not to be feasible today because the legal-linguistic research has a relatively limited output compared with the mainstream legal research. Its relation to the dominant political and social discourses is however visible in research contributions that directly concern the functioning of political and social institutions such as supreme courts or the institutions of the European Union. Therefore, at least in general, the legal-linguistic discourse has been mainly shaped by purely theoretical discursive formations that included such non-ideological concepts as discursiveness. Essential to our non-ideological view upon discursiveness is – next to the epistemological perspective – the analytical philosophy and its further developments (cf. Mead 1934; Searle 2011). It has its origin in the works of Bertrand Russell and in the Vienna Circle for which Rudolf Carnap's and Ludwig Wittgenstein's works have been emblematic. Their main idea had been that philosophical problems, unresolved issues in ethics or logic were caused by incorrect formulations, i.e. by inappropriate use of language. It was therefore recommended to transform the philosophical discourse into well-formed statements in which philosophical problems would dissolve when the statements were aptly framed. This aptitude to reformulate the discourse came from the human ability to think and act rationally. Whenever this ability is neglected in thinking or acting, philosophical problems emerge. Overall, in terms of philosophy, the analytical philosophy focused in its initial phase on aspects of dialectics (forms and fragments of discourses) and it transformed ontology into linguistic analysis. Later on, it became explicitly pragmatic. Pragmatics, for its part, shows that many pragmatic rules of language use that are relevant to its understanding are distant from predicate or propositional logic. The implicit, shared background knowledge, solutions to ambiguities and paradoxes in contexts are difficult to integrate into formal-logical approaches due to the complex nature of contexts. They also showed that the total formalization of language is impossible; however they do not contradict any attempts towards modeling of linguistic operations. Central to these discourses remain the notions of rationality and reasoning.

3.4.4 Didactic discourse

Speaking about law includes also the way in which professionals, mostly teachers of law, address interested laymen or the youth studying law. Laypersons are mostly approached from the factual and emotional perspective; the so-called technicalities of law are presented to them as mysterious or esoteric. In educational institutions law has been traditionally taught in terms of positivism, i.e. as a matter of fact. The traditional legal research has been dominated by a host of particular positivist theories and therefore remained inaccessible to other social sciences. It seems that the requirements of acceptability of law in society have not been strengthened by this type of discourses. The didactic discourse creates structures such as 'This case arouse when...' for the introduction into the analysis of a court opinion in class. It recreates working definitions for purposes of modernized spoken language, as for 'torts' that is 'a branch of law focusing on behavior that violates recognized legal standards and causes harm to another person'. In class talk, the plaintiff 'experienced harm' or the defendant 'exercised reasonable care' and 'no controlling precedent' may exist about a relevant detail of the 'tortfeasor's action', the state law being 'inconclusive'. This language imposes speech structures upon students that emerge gradually in their own language, passing by a stage where levels of speech are mixed. This phenomenon of the unstable language that consists of elements of professional and non-professional language is an interesting feature of the legal language, both in its oral and its written variety. It is however badly researched, if at all. The didactic discourse is traditionally a hierarchical discourse. It includes anaphorically overloaded speech, which is typical of legalese, such as: "The student will choose a focused topic with Professor M. and then the student must locate on his or her own an outside promoter in the area to assist the student in qualifying the student's topic, generated research, outline and drafts." The hierarchical didactic discourse displays the positivist structure of educational law, where an educational institution, like army and prison, is viewed to be by its nature not a democratic institution (cf. White 2010: 793). Another characteristic feature of the didactic discourse is that law like medicine is primarily a practical activity and therefore teaching law in isolation from practice is very challenging. Furthermore, the undetermined academic status of the legal doctrine turns the teaching of law into a slippery enterprise. Teachers of legal doctrine must accept the risk that they may profess knowledge that is not a science. Legal theory enjoys like other philosophical disciplines an uncontested academic status, yet it is not particularly influential in law schools. Legal linguistics as a part of legal theory has been until now not more influential than has been the mainstream legal theory. Therefore, the didactic discourse in law is mainly developed around issues relevant to the legal doctrine and in accordance with its specific methodology.

3.4.5 Relative independence of non-professional discourse

The non-professional discourse does not follow the doctrinal structure of law. It may occasionally make use of formal legal terminology; this however frequently includes the change of meaning. Its independence is limited because the legal terminology imposes its framework, even if the doctrine as such cannot be forced upon the non-professional discourse because it is esoteric and would have to be studied before it can be used. People will always say: 'I buy a ticket' without any reference to the underlying contract for transport or for other services that are embodied in the ticket. That tickets are worthless is however clear to every 'buyer'. It would otherwise be incomprehensible why most tickets end up in waste bins after the underlying contracts have been performed. Rarely a cinema ticket it put up after a film has been viewed, because it has no value other than a souvenir. The film may have had some value and this may be the reason for some people to collect tickets. Examples of independent non-professional use of language relevant to law are legion. Terms such as 'foreign' and 'alien' enterprise in U.S. corporation law are perceived by some speakers in reversed order, as some apparently construe the adjective 'foreign' as being stronger that the adjective 'alien'. 'Possession' and 'ownership' are frequently used as synonyms by laypersons. 'Obligated' and 'obliged' are differentiated although the legal language uses them mostly as synonyms. In terms of legal linguistics this dichotomy marks discursive inappropriateness of linguistic coinages. A term can be perceived as discursively inappropriate when it does not support the discourse. The communication is disturbed by such terms. The discursive inappropriateness of complex legal and economical concepts such as 'property' that are also used in the ordinary language became evident in the recent financial crisis and in the proceedings of foreclosures that followed in the U.S. A typical media narrative referring to these circumstances might read as follows: John and Ann Smith are a young couple with two small children. Within the past four years they stretched themselves financially in the course of acquiring and furnishing their first home and starting their family. Recently, John was laid off from his job and Ann was then injured in an automobile accident and had to stop working. John's unemployment benefit is insufficient to provide for the ordinary family expenses, much less meet the heavy financial obligations the family has taken on. The bank has filed a notice of intent to foreclose the mortgage on their home. This typical media narrative may appear as naïve or even cynical, and in fact it is both. In such textual surroundings usually also John's and Ann's property right is invoked in the linguistically appealing and illustrative form of the bank taking their property away from them, also more dramatically referred to as 'taking their house away from them'. Clearly, the ordinary, the economical and the legal property concepts do not correspond narratively, and the concept of property in daily language matches the reality of foreclosure even less. This disparity may be caused by the post-modern tolerant attitude in society towards debt accumulation and understanding for debtors saddled with debt beyond their ability to repay them. Linguistically, such attitudes will manifest themselves in the reduction of stigma towards those who suffered 'severe economic dislocations' which means that they have no money. As can be seen from the above examples, it is difficult to analyze such disparate discourses in a coherent way because the methodology for a more stringent analysis actually does not exist.

3.5 Discursive contents

It may be occasionally difficult to distinguish the eminent domain in a specific legal discourse. In most cases the institutional setting, i.e. the fact that the discourse takes place in a court of law signals that we have to do with a legal discourse. It is then necessary to determine what the discourse is about. To accomplish this task the interpretation from the professional's perspective is required. Formal approaches to this question are less productive. Nevertheless, it seems to be possible to determine also this issue because legal discourses clearly have contents, they must be about something. Let us look at a less convincing example. In City of Everett v. Estate of Sumstad et al. (cf. Supreme Court of Washington, 631 P.2d 366, 1981 Wash. Lexis 1139) discursive core terms have been determined formally by the editor of the published decision. They include: "safe, engine, auction, locked, summary judgment, unknown, auctioneer, scrap metal, manifestation, compartment, locksmith, opened, containers, outward, inner door, purchaser, inside, aircraft engines, consensual, buyer, mutual assent, unexpressed, manifest, and seller." Is the discourse in City of Everett really about these issues? The text of the court opinion clearly includes the named nouns and other parts of speech. Yet, doubts are in place when the list of terms should be used as a characterization of the legal discourse in City of Everett. This sample shows that unresolved methodological problems in legal science lead to pseudo-formalizations that engender useless results. Nowadays, their number is increasing due to generous storing potentials that the information technology made possible. Mechanistic approaches to legal language are however rare. Some more sophisticated although not less fallacious views will be discussed below.

3.6 Hostile winds cannot prevent discourses

Many jurists and possibly also some linguists adopt a critical stance to books such as ours. They will usually criticize the risky methodology that in their view consists in combining things that are regularly kept apart. They will refer to lack of competence and lack of reference to accepted authorities in such books as often no source will be there that would support facts relevant to the fundamental legal-linguistic research. It seems that only the reference to legal practice is an argument that could contradict this sort of criticism. Also therefore one may mention here again the role of discursiveness in law that has been established beyond any doubt by people more competent than the writer of these lines. Meanwhile, it is also worthwhile to invoke the non-discursive approaches to law in order to better understand the disastrous consequences that such theoretical views produce in an eminently practical field such as law. Several approaches to law are clearly contradictory to the view upon law that is presented in this book. Positivist approaches which claim that legal meaning is pre-determined in legal texts, essentialist views, and approaches that lead to reification of language use in law still exist in academic research. They will be discussed in what follows. It is equally beneficial to retrace the way of their emergence in the history of thought and to identify the point in time where they have been weakened by explicit anti-metaphysical argumentation. In so doing, we remain committed to Foucault's 'epistemological' account of the emergence of meaning that becomes knowledge. While discussing such issues one may also try to imagine argumentative strategies that emerge in societies that are dominated by such views.

3.6.1 Largely non-discursive valuable approaches to law

Next to the mentioned hostile approaches to legal discursiveness there exist also some valuable perspectives upon social sciences including law that stress other than discursive features of law. Among them the autopoietic approach of H. Maturana and F.J.Varela (1980) and parts of N. Luhmann's writings (1993) as well as the systemic approaches of Carlos Alchurón and Eugenio Bulygin (1971) or Ota Weinberger (1979) should be mentioned. Cognitive sciences are also sometimes ambiguous in their relation to the discursiveness of law, especially when they characterize the human mind as a computing structure: "thinking is a kind of computation," so Steven Pinker (1997: 21). Such approaches may permit discourses in law, yet they will be of different nature than those discussed here. In physics, particularly the fractal geometry (Bejan 2012: 10) and the constructal law developed by Adrian Bejan (2012) interpret law as a social phenomenon governed by physical laws. The idea of constructal law is based on evolution as a physical process of change occurring in time. This change cannot be influenced by human factors because these factors are shaped by physical processes. A. Bejan (2012: 236) perceives even the rule of law as prefigured in nature as it is in his view better suited to master the flows in society that are improved in the process of evolution: "The rule of law – waiting patiently in line, as opposed to triggering a stampede at the gate – is culture. Those who possess it travel far, which is the opposite of being taken to the morgue." The named approaches to law are predominantly non-discursive as they maintain that law is based on mechanisms that are found in nature and can be expressed in the formalized language of mathematics. They do not, however, exclude discursiveness totally, because they admit varieties of evolutionary developments that are not steered by nature as long as they do not contradict the general tendencies of physical laws. Future developments in science will show the relevance of these approaches that may become, in one way or another, integrated into naturalized conceptions of social sciences.

3.6.2 Discursiveness and meaning determination

Discursiveness has at least one serious adversary that is the idea of determinate meaning in language (and also in law). 'Determinate' means in the sense of analytical philosophy that the meaning can be unequivocally proven. Meanwhile, language engenders meaning in that it shapes our view upon the world, it clearly does not simply mirror the world (Fischer/Forester 1993: 1). Language is never neutral; language in law manifests itself as a discursive conception of power. As meaning emerges according to R. Brandom (2000) in an interaction, so do also opinions about law. The meaning alternatives attributed in them are successively understood; they are gathered into a whole by the process called 'discourse' (Innis 1985: 102). The sense of law is constituted in a discourse. This discourse can be situated between polemic and dialogue, where the interaction takes place with changing majorities – like the rule of a minority government. According to Searle (1999: 4) L. Wittgenstein had shown that our discourse consists of series of mutually translatable and incommensurable language games. We are not engaged in one big language game, in which there are universal standards of rationality and where everything is intelligible to everybody. The discourses are formed of series of smaller language games, each with its own inner standards of intelligibility. Also, W. Quine is supposed by many – so Searle (1999: 11) – to have refuted the view that the words of our language have determinate meaning. All these views constitute a challenge to the legal doctrine because there the language of law is perceived as determined or mechanically determinable. Legal-linguistic operations are misconstrued in the traditional approaches to law as devices that decode this pre-determined meaning. No procedure could be more misleading than the deterministic approach to legal language.

3.6.3 Purists' and essentialists' views upon legal language

Views about the concept of law differ and this book does not necessarily show this difference as it proposes a conception based mainly on philosophical and linguistic pragmatics. Some other concepts of law can be termed as essentialist and positivist as they perceive law as a thing, as a matter of fact. Law for them will be 'natural' or 'true'. Purists stress the conceptual clarity, exactness and the purity of the legal language. They regularly stress the necessity to avoid foreign borrowings in the legal language. These conceptions are not really a challenge to a pragmatic concept of law and legal linguistics as they simply underestimate that law is a discursive practice and not an object that can be described, measured and weighed like a stone. With a passion typical of geologists, purists and essentialists will engage in an isolated process of discovery of legal semantics that they, as a rule, will be able to accomplish on their own terms. As a result of such an enterprise, law will emerge as a clearly described set of well defined rules, only that this result will be an individual conception of law, a profoundly 'private law'. Already G.W.F. Hegel mentioned 1821 in the famous paragraph 140 of his *Philosophy of Right*: "Such a law is degraded to a mere external letter, in fact to an empty word, if it is only my conviction which makes it a law and invests it with obligatory force." Positivists of this sort are on the way towards their 'private law' and such a law is unthinkable. Reasons for this assertion are easily predictable: law is a social phenomenon and this fact may sometimes be perceived as an irritating circumstance because one cannot simply write one's own law as such an entity is a contradiction in terms. Law, as has been shown, emerges in discursive practices because – as a social phenomenon – it is rooted in the principle of discursiveness. Discursiveness of law is not simply an idea, one of many thinkable conceptions of law. Discursiveness determines law and it also excludes attempts at describing it without recourse to this fundamental principle. This methodological restriction does not concern uniquely law. Geology, for instance, excludes poetical description of stones as valid results of geological research, and rightly so. Legal science should not be more tolerant. Therefore, essentialist and puristic views – that will not advance the conception of law – equally belong to the extreme discourse about law or language, or about both. Further conclusions impose themselves rather automatically.

3.6.4 Essentialism and legal discourses

The battle against essentialism in law and beyond it is as urgent as it is hopeless. In large segments of society the existence of legal and other terms or concepts with pre-defined contents is taken for granted (cf. Janicki 2006). Anti-essentialism tries to make plain that terms and concepts as linguistic creations are by necessity not fully clear and that definitions cannot clearly and adequately reflect physical, social, or mental reality; they will remain circular in relation to word meaning (Kopytko 2002). G.W.F. Hegel, whose *Philosophy of Right* was already used as an argument against positivists' approaches to law, reiterated in the *Introduction* to his work the Latin legal maxim 'omnis definitio in jure civili periculosa'. Hegel continues: "In fact, the more disconnected and inherently contradictory are the provisions giving determinate character to a right, the less are any definitions in its field possible, for definitions should be stated in universal terms, while to use these immediately exposes in all its nakedness what contradicts them – the wrong in this instance." More contemporary criticism on essentialism may be traced back to Paul K. Feyerabend's postmodern thought or to Karl Popper's rejection of Aristotelian essentialist thinking. The second approach to anti-essentialism is represented in numerous works by Karol Janicki (2002; 2006; 2010) as well as in many works developed within social constructionism. Among John Searle's works *The Construction of Social Reality* (1995) and *Freedom and Neurobiology: Reflections on Free Will, Language and Political Power* (2007) are particularly relevant to any inquiry into problems of legal discursiveness. All too often legal terms and notions are perceived as largely interchangeable and in their 'essence' clear. What is more, they are viewed and lexicalized as entities that exist like natural features, like for example the blue color of someone's eyes. In terms of the structure of the legal discourse the ontology of law is fundamental to any reasoning that is undertaken under this heading. This is so because a legal term such as 'contract' has another mode of existence than 'blue eyes', yet this difference is not made by an essentialist. The ontological difference that is shown in this example manifests that both theoretical and practical legal reasoning depend on the ontology of law as a subject of professional and non-professional discourses. When, for instance, it is assumed by some discourse participants that 'family' is 'essentially' constituted of a man and a woman and their biological progeny, it will be difficult if not impossible to introduce convincingly and productively the notion of 'same-sex marriage' into this discourse. Kerber (2012: 90) writes about the argumentative deadlock in such a discourse: "Against the claim that the definition of marriage is fixed and unchanging, supporters of change have argued that marriage is and always has been an evolving institution, and that marriage retains its relevance to modern society not by stasis but by change." Meanwhile, for an essentialist who believes that her definition of marriage reflects a pre-existing entity, it is rationally unacceptable to become involved in any discourse concerning the topic of 'same-sex marriage'. On the essentialist view, the 'same-sex marriage' or its French version of a 'mariage pour tous' is simply absurd. And the essentialist position seems to such a speaker rational because it is based on a fundamental ontology that for her equals essentialism. The essentialist's problem is that she is unable to recognize the methodological fallacy in her approach to ontology. Indeed, the essentialist ontology "engenders a very unrewarding set of beliefs," and as its result, language users attribute to words an importance that they do not have (Janicki 2002). In fact, language, both in law and beyond it, does not transfer any essence of things to which it verbally relates. It does not force us to believe that 'family' by the nature of things consists of a bond between a man and a woman. Conventionally, at a certain period of time, this may be so. Yet the linguistic convention of use can change. This possibility of change notwithstanding, the essentialist remains the guardian of an alleged semantic stability that is an extra-linguistic, and above all, a false belief. Intolerance, belief in one's infallibility, dogmatism, assertiveness and the even more ignoble readiness to resort to linguistic manipulation regularly accompany an essentialist when she becomes involved in a discursive practice. Essentialism as a philosophical doctrine is the nightmare of discursive practices and a tragedy for societies where it gives the tone. Discourses with essentialists are unavailing; societies where they exercise power regularly regress. Therefore, the issue of essentialism in law and around it is of primordial importance for every methodological analysis of the legal discourse because it concerns the very nature of this discourse. In fact, many pages were spent in this book on showing that the legal discourse is rooted in discursiveness as the most salient ontological feature of law. It is therefore possible to state safely that law is a discursive practice that emerges and that is applied in institutionalized linguistic practices where meaning comes about as a social construct. No reference to whatever pre-existing entities is necessary or even possible in such an argumentative setting. Janicki (2002) rightly stresses in this context the role of language awareness as a method that could alleviate problems with understanding of linguistic utterances in society. When language is construed appropriately, it protects its users against essentialist pitfalls. It enables a rational debate about legal issues that due to the discursive nature of the phenomenon 'law' can be solely linguistically and socially defined. This means that they also can be re-defined at any moment in relevant social practices such as legal and other discourses. Is the discursiveness of law not accepted or not reflected in the fundamentals of the discursive practice, then no rational results can be expected from it. Furthermore, the language awareness protects against instrumentalization of language use in terms of political correctness, against the manipulative use that is concealed in incomprehensive language and against authoritarian argumentation (cf. Janicki 2002). Finally, language awareness includes also the discursive competence that is necessary for dealing with misunderstandings, imprecision, and fuzziness in language use (Janicki 2002). It enables the language user, also the jurist, to become consciously creative in his use of language, including the metaphorical use of language that most jurists fear more than hell fire.

However, the public discourse prefers rather essentialist commitments, for example in public statements of judges who, as a rule, stress that 'their task is to apply the law.' The political and the legal discourses commingle in situations where judges are directly elected by citizens, as is the case in the United States (Gibson 2012 b). Campaigning for judicial posts is by necessity dominated by political arguments and also by formal, positivist declarations of commitment to legality. The argumentation used by candidates in hearings before representative forums, for instance in cases of U.S. Supreme Court justices, is even more formal and assertive. In the confirmation hearings on their nominations before the U.S. Senate Committee on the Judiciary the candidates Sonia Sotomayor and John J. Roberts jr. expressed strictly essentialist views about the methodology of their professional work (Greenhouse 2012: 74). S. Sotomayor told in her statement: "In each case I have heard, I have applied the law to the facts at hand." The future Chief Justice Roberts declared: "Judges are like umpires. Umpires don't make the rules, they apply them." He also added: "…the role of the Court is to serve as a neutral and detached umpire when it enforces the fundamental guarantees of our Constitution" (Stone 2013: 36). Greenhouse (2012: 74) assumes that the senators insisted on "value-free formulations" that would endorse "the myth of legality" traditionally cherished in juridical and political institutions. Such scaring essentialism has long roots. R. Waldo Emerson wrote 1836 in his *Nature – Origin, Growth, Meaning*, that is still read uncritically in many American schools, in Chapter IV that is entitled *Language*: "A third use which Nature subserves to man is that of Language. Nature is the vehicle of thought, and in a simple, double, and threefold degree. 1. Words are signs of natural facts. 2. Particular natural facts are symbols of particular spiritual facts. 3. Nature is the symbol of spirit. … Every word which is used to express a moral or intellectual fact, if traced to its root, is found to be borrowed from some material appearance…Because of the radical correspondence between the visible things and human thoughts, savages, who have only what is necessary, converse in figures…The immediate dependence of language upon nature, this conversion of an outward phenomenon into a type of somewhat in human life, never loses its power to affect us." Emerson's concept of language is a vision, a language Emerson would prefer as he assumes that nature works like pure mechanics. No discursive and open structure such as our language with its simple and complex speech acts that depend on interpretation fits into such a vision.

3.6.5 Reification of legal language

Anti-essentialist views are directed against the reification of linguistic entities, also in their abstract form (Mulder/Rastall 2005). According to Mulder and Rastall, not only words of a language but also the linguistic theories have to be perceived as "explanatory constructs without existential claims." What really exists, is the speech actually produced that must be distinguished from a belief that it represents things expressed in it. Meaning exists only in actual speech acts (Rastall 2006). We can therefore speak about a contract without believing that beyond the speech, actual or potential, there exists a general idea of a 'model contract' that underlies our speaking about it. Meanwhile, something clearly exists, because otherwise no meaningful communication would be possible. However, this something is not a pre-defined object but rather fragmentary convictions and beliefs that make parts of other discourses. Lakoff (1987) described communication as a process where individuals lump similar concepts together based on personal experience. In daily life this procedure of categorization and simplification may suffice. In complex professional settings, communication will be more formalized, yet not fundamentally different. It would therefore not be particularly helpful to assume that judges – or jurists in general – communicate strictly professionally and lay persons communicate strictly informally. Discourses, both professional and non-professional, are structured as amalgams of speech acts where professional and non-professional features intertwine. Formerly represented views that tried to capture the essence of things in words and in laws often focused on etymology (cf. Dasgupta/Singh/Ford 2000). Against all beliefs of the ancients, etymology shows only the linguistic origin of a word, it accounts of a word's original meaning. It does not reveal any general semantic features of a word or its 'essence', i.e. its immutable relation to extra-linguistic reality. J.S. Mill says in *Utilitarianism* about etymology: "Etymology is slight evidence of what the idea now signified is, but the very best evidence of how it sprang up." With this in mind, substantivists such as Dasgupta and others tried to offer synchronic sources for words that structuralism or purely etymological approaches could not provide. Also J.L. Austin (1956/7) remarked in *A Plea for Excuses*: "a word never – well, hardly ever, – shakes off its etymology and its formation. In spite of all changes in and extensions of and additions to its meanings, and indeed rather pervading and governing these, there will still persist the old idea. In an 'accident' something befalls; by 'mistake' you take the wrong one: in 'error' you stray: when you act 'deliberately' you act after weighing it up (not after thinking out ways and means)." Indeed, it goes without saying that our words, in law and beyond it, come from somewhere and that they also change their meaning. Therefore a purely etymological approach would not do in law. Lexical units are clearly interrelated, and have their inner motivation that can be elucidated. It is definitely good to know that the Latin term 'iustitia' comes from 'ius stitium', i.e. the cessation of claims or that 'publicum' as a hybrid term is derived from both 'pubes' and 'populus' (cf. Domingo 2010: xix, 49). Especially in law this procedure of etymological clarification is fruitful and effective as the origin of many terms is clearly documented in written sources as the above analysis of the 'doctrine of lapse' has shown. Meanwhile, motivation for the emergence of words and their interrelations is one thing; their meaning within legal discourses is another. When in the cyberlaw the discourse introduces the term 'public commons' based on the idea that information is a 'common good', then terms such as 'internet commons' and 'sustainable commons' will follow suit, and this is not a coincidence (cf. Benkler 2011: 154; Gabstone 2013). The linguistic substance provides some material, yet the discourse supplies the decisive rest. Discourse will therefore always control the substantivist input because it steers motivations behind words. The motivation and the interrelation of words are productive devices in the sense that no rigid semantics of the words in law and beyond it can ever come about.

Language may also strengthen the tendency to petrify law. In Art. 71 of the Constitution of India, the heading says: "Matters relating to, or connected with, the election of the President or the Vice-President". The ability to distinguish in a conceptual textual contrast between 'matters that are connected with' and some others that are 'relating to' is typical of legal texts where difference in the language holds for difference in the matter. At another place, the 'distinction without difference' as discovered in legal discourses had been mentioned (cf. Galdia 2009: 46). Henry Fielding in his *Tom Jones* identified 'distinguishing of differences' as a general principle of discursiveness, valid not only in law. He wrote already in 1749: "By genius I would understand those powers of the mind, which are capable of penetrating into all things within our reach and knowledge, and of distinguishing their essential differences." In an ironical passage where a minor personage becomes involved in a loyalty conflict in Book VI of *Tom Jones* he also textually functionalizes the 'distinction without difference': "…Conscience, like a good lawyer, attempted to distinguish between an absolute breach of trust, as here, where the goods were delivered, and a bare concealment of what was found, as in the former case. Avarice presently treated this with ridicule, called it a distinction without difference, and absolutely insisted that when once all pretentions of honour and virtue were given up in any one instance, that there was no precedent for resorting to them upon a second occasion." In fact, many deleterious interpretive practices in law are rooted in the distinction without difference.

3.6.6 Strictly non-discursive approaches to law

We turn now to some general non-discursive conceptions of law. They are in fact not really different from approaches that were described above. Also in these approaches law is construed from a positivist, essentialist, reifying perspective. Most conceptions of law that oscillate around the idea of law as a system of rules are expressly non-discursive. The pre-determined 'legal system' that is composed of rules excludes for many representatives of such conceptions, which could be assembled under the label of positivism, the discursiveness as the constitutive element of law. Law is perceived in such conceptions as basically predetermined in the existing rules. Jurists' role is to decipher the meaning of law in cases where doubts about the content of rules persist. This approach also includes the amazing presupposition that law is in most cases, called sometimes routine cases, clear to the extent that it can be applied automatically. All such positivist conceptions are hostile to the idea that law emerges as a result of language use in discursive practices and that it is applied in legal discourses. Historically, intermediate positions such as H.L.A. Hart's attempt to come to terms with law within a largely positivist conception that is rooted in the tradition of analytical jurisprudence, help trace the erosive trends in the positivist building. In his *Concept of Law* (1961) H.L.A. Hart tried to overcome the limits of the traditional common law theory of jurisprudence based mostly on John Austin's 'imperative theory' as stated in *The Province of Jurisprudence Determined* (1832). J. Austin construed law as 'sovereign's coercive order' that was the basis for whatever particular law that followed from this fundamental rule. Hart, who was well aware of the criticism of this conception of law, expanded somewhat the notional field of Austinian jurisprudence while remaining in the legal world limited by pre-existing rules. He could not avoid mentioning the linguistic perspective in times when the linguistic turn was a general issue in academic debates both at Oxford and at Cambridge. Hart cites in a conciliatory spirit J. L. Austin's methodological commitment to "a sharpened awareness of words to sharpen our awareness of phenomena." At least programmatically, Hart (1961: vii) is committed to raising questions "which may well be said to be about the meaning of words." More often than not he also makes use of some linguistic inquiry when dealing with particular questions of legal semantics. However, this occurs mostly in rather marginal cases when he e.g. distinguishes between 'being obliged' and 'having an obligation' or encourages investigation into "the words 'must', 'should' and 'ought to'" (Hart 1961: 9, 10). For Hart, such small linguistic analyses strengthen the conception of law as a system of rules rather than the linguistic conception of law. His courageous 'varieties of imperatives' in the chapter on laws, commands and orders (Hart 1961: 18–20) will be later dressed in a rigid corset of rules that is a methodological step back. Meanwhile, Hart may be held as taking an intermediary position because he explicitly refers to linguistic approaches to law albeit with the intention to expand the traditional positivist vista upon law. He is committed to develop the 'concept of law' that is also the 'nature of law'. After having introduced his famous concepts of 'primary and secondary rules' Hart (1961: 208) claims: "Though the idea of the union of primary and secondary rules has these virtues, and though it would accord with usage to treat the existence of this characteristic union of rules as a sufficient condition for the application of the expression 'legal system', we have not claimed that the word 'law' must be defined in its terms. It is because we make no such claim to identify or regulate in this way the use of words like 'law' or 'legal', that this book is offered as an elucidation of the *concept* of law, rather than a definition of 'law' which might naturally be expected to provide a rule or rules for the use of these expressions." Like in many other places in his book, Hart does not really feel at ease with positivism even if he by whatever reasons favors this conception textually, if not politically. Hart's concept of law remains problematic because it develops an analysis of law as if 'law' were not a socially constructed phenomenon. His 'concept of law' seems to have a purely logical ontology, i.e. being an amalgam of rules of different quality. Meanwhile, in a sideline narrative Hart (1961: 78–79) even includes explicitly discursive elements: "...we have already seen in Chapter III the need, if we are to do justice to the complexity of a legal system, to discriminate between two different though related types. Under rules of the one type, which may well be considered the basic or primary type, human beings are required to do or abstain from certain actions, whether they wish to or not. Rules of the other type are in a sense parasitic upon or secondary to the first; for they provide that human beings may by doing or saying certain things introduce new rules of the primary type, extinguish or modify old ones, or in various ways determine their incidence or control their operations." Thus, Hart was aware of the circumstance that law is made with words; yet he was not ready to draw consequences from this fundamental discovery for his approach to law. Furthermore, he was not ready to rethink his vision of law in the light of the linguistic theory developed by J. L. Austin whose work he knew and to some extent even incorporated into his approach. Oscillating between positivism and its criticism, H.L.A. Hart's 'concept of law' remains an interesting example of an approach to law that is oriented backwards yet considers also the potential that allows the expansion of the now overcome positivist view. Ronald Dworkin in *Taking Rights Seriously* (1977) made this mediating position plain and developed the aspects of Hart's conception that were tolerated by Hart as the conceptual potential of his 'concept of law' without really making a part of it. Later on, R. Dworkin especially in his *Law's Empire* (1986), A. Aarnio at least in his *The Rational as Reasonable* (1987) and others have aptly shown that compromises with the past such as Hart's cannot last. The way to the discursive conception of law was thus broken through and the analysis of legal reasoning from a more or less explicitly stressed linguistic perspective set on.

3.7 Discourses and theories

When law is perceived as a discursive practice, it is approached and addressed theoretically. Our knowledge that law emerges in discourses establishes a sufficiently sturdy basis for a theory of law. This theory of law is linguistic because discourses are linguistic phenomena and they also are the most distinctive feature of law. This does not mean that law as a phenomenon is purely linguistic; it only underscores the extraordinary importance of the linguistic element in it. Next to scientistic approaches to law that start with academic, scholastic, and positivist perspectives via structuralist and socially critical positions and that end with post-modernist deconstruction there is still room for other more spontaneous opinions. They start with mythology, and reach poetry and drama while passing by the novel. Law is not only an object of academic research; it is, unlike other subjects such as nuclear physics or mathematical astronomy, not protected by a formal language that bars access to non-specialists. All of these texts display different levels of rationality. All of them have a message to communicate about law. One can assume that law developed only because of the multitude and diversity of views upon it that constantly give rise to new legal narratives that generalize experience. Therefore, it pays to deal with the discourse in a theoretical way, also in legal linguistics.

3.7.1 Legal discursiveness 'more geometrico'

Law understood as discursive practice has been sometimes perceived as a type of discourse that could or even should be formalized. In parallel, mathematics has also been understood as a discourse with strictly determined objectives such as 'demonstration', 'understanding', 'applying', 'solution' etc. This specific discourse, when construed axiomatically, imposes constraints on the speakers' freedom of speech. These constraints can be understood as linguistic operations that guarantee the rationality of the discourse. The constraints reduce the speech to a set of speech acts – like the above mentioned, i.e. 'demonstration' or 'applying'; they are based on an axiomatic 'life' form. Euclid's *Elements* are a typical example of such a linguistic operation. In book I, definition 1 Euclid posits: "A point is that which has no part." Aristotle, who did not write any treatises on mathematics, would probably have explained why mathematics might or might not start with the definition of the point. For Euclid such explanation is contrary to the mathematical language that is axiomatic in essence. Meanwhile, Aristotle commented upon the problem of defining lines and points in the first book of his *Metaphysics* (992a): "When we wish to reduce substances to their principles, we state that lines come from the short and long (i.e. from a kind of small and great), and the plane from the broad and narrow, and body from deep and shallow. Yet how then can either the plane contain a line, or the solid a line or a plane? For the broad and narrow is a different class from the deep and shallow. Therefore, just as number is not present in these, because the many and few are different from these, evidently no other of the higher classes will be present in the lower. But again the broad is not a genus which includes the deep, for then the solid would have been a species of plane. Further, from what principle will the presence of the points in the line be derived? Plato even used to object to this class of things as being a geometrical fiction. He gave the name of principle of the line – and this is often posited – to the indivisible lines. Yet these must have a limit; therefore the argument from which the existence of the line follows proves also the existence of the point." Aristotle's comment is only a digression upon the ontological and epistemological status of lines and points. Yet, compared with Euclid's axiomatic approach to geometrical expression Aristotle's digression is much more explicit. It proves also that it is possible to speak about mathematical problems explicitly, notwithstanding the formalized expression that mathematicians adapted for their professional needs. Levels of explicitness in speech are not only relevant to geometry. They matter equally in the area of law. The Aristotelian approach to explicitness, though illustrated in the above sample only with a digression, proves the possibility of explicit speech that is one of the main concerns of this essay.

Yet, generally, mathematics does not use the Aristotelian approach and prefers hermetically closed and formalized language. Mathematical speech acts such as counting or measuring use numbers like words that differ like words of ordinary language differ. Words may belong to different speech act types that tend to be reversible, such as factoring and developing or differentiation and integration. Particular discourses typical of mathematics are formed around leading speech acts as those mentioned above and many others. Formalized discourses in mathematics are construed as sets of statements that are expressed in a framework which by definition excludes any contradiction. Therefore, some qualified them as particular discourses in opposition to absolute discourses because they aim at coherence and not truth. Recently, Gillian Beer (2014: 61) identified in Virginia Woolf's novel *The Waves* (1931) a type of meaning without language: "There is a square; there is an oblong. The players take the square and place it upon the oblong. They place it very accurately; they make a perfect dwelling-place. Very little is left outside…Wander no more, I say; this is the end. The oblong has been set upon the square; the spiral is on the top." This "absolute geometry of meaning without language" is present also in Woolf's reflection upon the sign 'zero': "Look, the loop of the figure is beginning to fill with time; it holds the world in it. I begin to draw a figure and the world is looped in it, and I myself am outside the loop; which I now join – so – and seal it up, and make entire, and I am outside of it,…" This 'meaning without language' is however a literary fiction; regular geometry is perfectly transformable into the formal language of mathematics and it is therefore very doubtful whether 'a perfect geometry' without language could exist as it presupposes abstract reality without interpreters. Only when nature is left unobserved, language does not need to be used, yet this ontology is poetical. It is however able to suggest us the philosophical limits of meaning. Also mathematical discourse represents only one of multiple facets of the human mind; it shows some aspects of reasoning (cf. Núñez 2008: 341). Yet, it clearly does not represent mind or reasoning as such. This relative or particular character of mathematical discursiveness limits its utility as a basis for formalization of legal discourses. It does not exclude such experiments which, even if successful, would only show some aspects of legal reasoning. Mathematics and law as disciplines definitely coincide as they are at least in the Occident both been practiced since twenty five centuries. Laws were also central to both of them from their very inception. In mathematics, a law is a fundamental principle that specifies the necessary relations between the constituents in a set. 'Legal' laws in their linguistic form pretend to reach the same objective while constituting concepts (nouns, adjectives) that can also be qualified differently (morphemes, phonemes). Legal-linguistic operations function within an open space for professional arguments. Some have hoped that logic could be used as a device that would pave the way towards unifying both concepts of 'laws'. In the interface of both areas legal logic emerged as the most formal approach to law. It represents the most formal approach to law because it is closer to mathematics than any other area relevant to law. At the same time, it remains connected with law through its anchorage in its mother discipline, philosophy.

3.7.2 Legal logic

Legal logic attempts at expressing the abstract proprieties of law. Meanwhile, when so expressed, they remain very abstract (Galdia 2009: 82). In the legal discourse the controlling linguistic operations support the application of law that is something concrete. Abstraction is fascinating, yet the reverse mental operation, the concretization, dominates the work that jurists are expected to do. It remains to be seen whether through the mastering of legal abstraction – more mathematico – the reverse of the process, i.e. the concretization could be demonstrated. Inversion is a typical mathematical discursive operation; yet its applicability in law is unclear. Meaning manifests itself in concrete signification; there is no meaning beyond a concrete situation of language use. Logical rules such as the requirement of non-contradiction clearly apply in law as they apply everywhere else in the reality that we experience. A statute imposing circulation on the right-hand side of the road cannot simultaneously order to drive on the left-hand side of the road. It could be probably formulated in a way that would leave the choice to drivers, provided their choice is coordinated. It would not be illogical, although rather not advisable. Similarly, a rule imposing circulation on the right-hand side cannot be simultaneously interpreted as imposing to drive both on the right-hand and on the left-hand side of the road. Meanwhile, other formulations of the rule might invite differing interpretive proposals that would lead to mutually exclusive results. Therefore, the question whether more than a dialogue between legal logic and legal linguistics is possible remains open.

3.7.3 Discourses about matter

Different from the above discourses are discourses about the existence of physical matter in all their forms. In astronomy, it would be possible to agree – as had been imposed and practiced by institutions for centuries – that the true system is the geocentric one. Yet, such a linguistic regulation, which is a limitation of discursive practices, would not change the fact that only the heliocentric and not the geocentric model represents the physical reality in some remoteness from us. This discovery does not preclude metaphorical coinages. Metaphorical use is included in the rationality of language use; there is neither sunrise nor sunset even if we constantly speak about both. This notwithstanding, we constantly use such metaphors when we speak (Winter 2008). Immanuel Kant in his *Kritik der reinen Vernunft* (1787) perceives time as non-discursive: "Die Zeit ist kein diskursiver, oder, wie man ihn nennt, allgemeiner Begriff, sondern eine reine Form der sinnlichen Anschauung" – "time is not a discursive, or as it is called, general conception, but a pure form of the sensuous intuition" (cf. Part I, sec. II,§5 or Chapter 4, Section 4 *Von der Zeit* of the German original). Furthermore, space is for Kant "no discursive, or as we say, general conception of the relations of things, but a pure intuition" (cf. Part I, sec.I,§2). Further, medical practices are all but linguistic. A linguistically achieved agreement that a patient is in good health while in reality he is seriously sick will not change the patient's medical condition. He remains sick even if sophisticated medical wording declares him free from any disease. We could also study the language use in surgery as there is no fundamental objection to such cognitive interest. Yet, while researching textbooks on heart or brain surgery we have to be aware of the fact that brain or heart surgery is not essentially about language use. Skills in surgery can be dispensed also through factual demonstration so that not even its descriptive part is naturally discursive. However, the study may say us something when we, for instance, find out that words used in it are of Latin or Greek origin. Meanwhile, this choice of words is rather neutral to acts of brain or heart surgery where lancets and lasers dominate over words. Epiphenomenalism of language is rooted in this relation. This discovery is also relevant to law and will be discussed later.

3.7.4 Revolutions and legal discourses

Seen in the historical perspective, the legal discourse finds its limits in social revolutions that factually destroy its basis. Revolutions manifest more than other social processes the dependence of law on social discursive practices. The end of an epoch means the end of its law; new law emerges only when new society is constituted. In the meantime, there is – so to say – nothing to talk about in a way of law. The only discourse thinkable under such circumstances is the discourse about the making of the new law. The new epoch is usually also prohibitive of the use of traditional discursive forms; under changed social conditions old law cannot be publicly mentioned nor researched. The Soviet Revolution brought such a change in that it not only overthrew the old system and its law but also prohibited any public use of the old law that subsequently has fallen into oblivion. Already Aristotle mentioned in his *Politics* (1315b40): "constitutions change, as a rule, more readily into an opposite than into a cognate form." Aristotle's remark concerns a regularity that has consequences for text types in law. As a matter of fact, revolutions, such as those prepared and supported in the *Federalist*, use textual patterns that are more stable than are the forms of government. Aristotle's *Politics* renders the intent of discursive practices such as the one typical of *Federalist* in its paragraph 1260b27: "Our purpose is to consider what form of political association is best for people able so far as possible to live as they would wish. We must therefore consider not only constitutions actually in force in cities that are said to be well governed, but also other forms of constitution which people have proposed if these are thought to have merit." In respect of this methodological goal, the *Federalist* is textually a regress behind the *Politics* that adapts an inquisitive approach to the analyzed questions unlike the *Federalist* that only pretends to so proceed. The detailed analysis of this process will follow later.

3.8 Can there be a legal ethics?

The mentioned problems have also an ethical dimension. The question of ethics matters in the legal-linguistic research at least since J. Habermas's introduction of discursive ethics and J. Searle's claim that language includes a deontic element (cf. Searle 2006). Today, one may assume a general consensus in pragmatics that relates to these views. However, the legal discourse also comprises the anthropologically and philosophically founded discussion about the juridical version of ethics, called in the French language 'version juridique d'éthique'. In essence, the discussion concerns the paradoxical situation perceived by some as typical of judicial institutions (cf. Skuczyński 2013). These institutions coin a version of ethics that is reduced to their institutional needs. This limited ethics, sometimes also called 'a moral minimum' could also be named 'legal ethics'. And indeed, already the ancient Roman law has been viewed by its theorists as a social mechanism that demands only a minimum of respect for ethical rules. Legislators are expected to draft legal provisions and especially the penal statutes along this minimalistic guideline. H.L.A. Hart knew this sort of ethics. In *The Concept of Law* (1961: 7) he wrote: "Killing and the wanton use of violence are only the most obvious examples of coincidence between the prohibitions of law and morals. Further, there is one idea, that of justice which seems to unite both fields: it is both a virtue especially appropriate to law and the most legal of the virtues. We think and talk of 'justice *according* to law' and yet also of justice or injustice *of* the laws." For Hart, assertions such as 'an unjust law is not a law' show that "law and morals share a common vocabulary" (Hart 1961: 8). Other scholars, such as R.M. Hare (1952), scrutinized this common vocabulary that became better known as 'the language of morals'. Previously, the poet John Milton combined the vocabulary of law and ethics in *Paradise Lost* (book I, verses 27–32): "Say first, for Heav'n hides nothing from thy view/ Nor the deep Tract of Hell, say first what cause/ Mov'd our Grand Parents in that happy State,/Favour'd of Heav'n so highly, to fall off/ From their Creator, and transgress his Will/ For one restraint, Lords of the World besides?" Milton refers to a moral obligation rooted in obedience to a creator which should not be transgressed. Legally relevant vocabulary that he uses in his poem is related to morals as interpreted by him. Pure legal rules would not appeal to Milton. By contrast, the idea of a binding obligation that has a moral background was unknown to ancient Romans. One of the versions of the Romulus myth as stated by Titus Livius in his *Ab Urbe Condita Libri* (lib.I. cap.5, 6) invokes the establishment of an obligation by a ruler, in casu Romulus, that binds all subjects, also his brother Remus. Remus transgresses this obligation and must be punished to maintain the legal rule in force: "Ita Numitori Albana re permissa Romulum Remumque cupido cepit in iis locis, ubi expositi ubique educati erant, urbis condendae. Et supererat multitudo Albanorum Latinorumque; ad id pastores quoque accesserant, qui omnes facile spem facerent parvam Albam, parvum Lavinium prae ea urbe, quae conderetur, fore. Intervenit deinde his cogitationibus avitum malum, regni cupido, atque inde foedum certamen, coortum a satis miti principio. Quoniam gemini essent nec aetatis verecundia discrimen facere posset, ut dii, quorum tutelae ea loca essent, auguriis legerent, qui nomen novae urbi daret, qui conditam imperio regeret, Palatium Romulus, Remus Aventinum ad inaugurandum templa capiunt. Priori Remo augurium venisse fertur, sex vultures, iamque nuntiato augurio cum duplex numerus Romulo se ostendisset, utrumque regem sua multitudo consalutaverat: tempore illi praecepto, at hi numero avium regnum trahebat. Inde cum altercatione congressi certamine irarum ad caedem vertuntur; ibi in turba ictus Remus cecedit. Vulgatior fama est ludibrio fratris Remum novos transluisse muros; inde ab irato Romulo, cum verbis quoque increpitans adiecisset 'sic deinde, quiqumque alius transiliet moenia mea', interfectum. Ita solus potitus imperio Romulus; condita urbs conditoris nomine appellata." Titus Livius favors another version of the myth that acquits Romulus of responsibility for his brother's death. Meanwhile, the more popular account that he also states in his writings makes more sense in terms of norm constitution. A rule is imposed by powerful means with reference to irrational and accidental events. No attempt to establish the rule on an ethical principle is undertaken by Romulus. The imposition of power is replaced by a procedure for naming the town; as

Romulus imposes himself, the town is named after him. The name of the town – Rome – also symbolizes his power monopoly and makes it clear to all those who, despite Remus's dramatic destiny, still might not understand that Romulus is their only ruler. Roman power is not based on ethics because power is tantamount to force. The forceful Roman acquired power and he exercised it by formal laws that he claimed forcefully, when needed. Ethics was good for society that constituted itself outside power structures where the rest of civilian life took place within the unquestionable power framework established by force. Virgil made in *Aeneis* (book VI, 851–853) this lawlessness of the Roman Empire particularly clear: "…tu regere imperio populos, Romane, memento -/ haec tibi erunt artes – pacique inponere morem,/parcere subiectis et debellare superbos." Thus, the essence of the Roman Empire consists in governing according to a simple rule: the politics of appeasement has to be imposed; those who submit to the Roman rule are treated well, others are combatted. No law is needed to run such an empire. Also in more civilized circumstances, in the very city of Rome, law is received, and not agreed upon. Virgil, following the foundational myth of Rome, mentions only the law that is given to the Romans (cf. "iura dabunt" in book I, 293 and "iura dabat legesque" in book I, 507). The only evolution of such a power structure is the overthrow of rulers by force. This circumstance makes also clear why law did not play any particular role in the Roman state. Apparently, Roman law's textual remnants that make the basis for so many contemporary legal orders fascinate today more than they fascinated the ancient Romans (cf. Daube 1969). Also today numerous are states where law plays a decorative role or finds application only among the ruling families of a country. Such understanding of law comes close to the Roman practice of a state of law where law was applied selectively and irregularly notwithstanding many declarations to the contrary. In this state of affairs one could also find the intellectual basis for the quest of the legal ethics. It seems, however, that it would be easier to find the Grail than to establish exclusive principles of ethics for legal purposes.

3.8.1 Ethics of discourse

Meanwhile, legal speech acts that form discourses are not value-neutral; they transport values essential to their users. Ethics is therefore an essential element of law (Galdia 2009: 52–53). Also before Habermas's and Searle's writings ethics was present in discourses that were relevant to law in one way or another. Aristotle says in his *Politics* (1295a34, trans. E. Barker, OUP 1995): "…in the *Ethics*, we stated that the truly happy life is one of goodness lived in freedom from impediments and that goodness consists in a mean, it follows that the best way of life is one which consists in a mean, and a mean of the kind attainable by each individual." This abstract view can be contrasted with a more concrete situation. In the epoch of humanism, G. Budé wrote sarcastically in a letter to Lupset: "I might almost say we are bound to admit that this is the real end of legal training and the profession of the civil law: to make each man act with ingrained and calculated malice towards the neighbor to whom he is linked by ties of citizenship and sometimes of blood. He is always grabbing something, taking it away, extorting it, suing for it, squeezing it out, breaking it loose, gouging it away, twisting it off, snatching it, snitching it, filching it, pinching it, pilfering it, pouncing on it – partly with the tacit complicity of the laws, partly with their direct sanction, he carries off what he wants and makes it his own" (cf. G. Budé's letter dated July 31, 1517 quoted after G.M. Logan, R.M. Adams (eds.), (2002): More, *Utopia*, rev. edition, p. 112, Cambridge: Cambridge University Press). In this satirical stance there is a grain of truth. It seems that law expresses the human condition as described by Aristotle. It can also become an object of parody when it is seen from the perspective of its abuse. In modern times, discursive ethics has been taken more seriously. Meanwhile, the idea that ethical problems should be solved discursively appears regularly in the history of thought. More recently, however, Jürgen Habermas (1992) stressed in his conception of the 'Diskursethik' the mechanisms in which consensus is obtained in value-related discourses. The consensus is worthwhile to be obtained when rationality is the main test for the propositions about right and wrong. The rationality test can be efficiently applied solely under the conditions of an ideal speech situation that excludes any powerful influence upon the consensus building processes. Power positions that are obtained under such discursive conditions are truly legitimate because they are democratically and rationally founded. This type of power also corresponds with M. Foucault's conception of legitimate power. Also the academic discourse about law is connected with value choices. Knowledge claims are constructed and negotiated in value-laden discourses that demonstrate the axiological components of meaning (Giannoni 2010).

3.8.2 Avoiding participation in legal discourses

Modernity engendered a complex law that is rarely appealing to non-professionals of law as a reference for debates about its inner structure. Increasing length of court decisions and the complexity of statutory provisions do not incite citizens without legal training to enter into the discussion of details of such legal acts. The democratic participatory rights in a social discourse about the appropriate law are thus delegated to others, to those who assumingly know it better. The citizens at large often overestimate the competence of parliamentarians or jurists to deal with the subject matter of legal discourses. They do not believe that substantive legal problems must be decided democratically, as there is no other way of obtaining, it is shaping law in its material form. Lawyers and politicians do not know it better than the citizens at large whether prostitution should be legalized or penalized or whether same-sex marriages should be allowed. Participation in social discourses about the future law is unavoidable in society and the absenteeism in this type of discourse is counterproductive to democracy. Modern law can encourage citizens to take care about its shape (Mattila 2013: 51–52). Pragmatically, participation requires competence; yet it also presupposes informed and honest citizens. No wonder that under such conditions some may prefer to delegate their civic privileges to non-defined 'others'. Avoidance of participation has ethical implications. It is a choice between values to become involved in society or not to do so.

3.9 Provisional appraisal of 'results'

At this point, issues concerning discursiveness in law can be perceived as at least exhaustively addressed, if not elucidated. It has been demonstrated that discursiveness is the ontological requirement for any epistemological attempt to understand law. Law is a discourse and can be understood only as such. The task is complicated because they are many types of legal discourses. To limit the study to experts' discourses about law would impoverish the knowledge about law. However, it is difficult to develop the appropriate methodology for this task. Yet, some approaches can be avoided and this is already an epistemological progress. Positivist, essentialist, and formalist approaches to law are definitely not helpful and can be eliminated already at this relatively early stage of inquiry. It remains the task of incorporation of value-related aspects of discourse into our inquiry. The conception of 'discourse ethics' allows for such broadening of our perspective that is already very broad. No calamity can happen when it is broadened still further. We should not, however, lose sight of our main goal that is the legal discourse. We will now turn to aspects that help identify the legal discourse and also characterize some of the most relevant legal-linguistic operations that presuppose the discursiveness which has been already established with many words and examples beyond any doubt.

Part 4: Semiotics of Legal Discourse

4.1 Legal semiotics and legal discourse

Ontological and epistemological features of law that are linguistically expressed in legal-linguistic operations are reflected in the most general perspective in the legal semiotics. Many of the above mentioned problems related to the semiotic status of legal signs, reference and interpretation of legal signs, reification in legal language, use of arguments in law, narrativity and 'épistémé' can be synthesized in the theory of legal semiotics. Legal semiotics is therefore the most general theory of meaning in law. Its main challenge to the legal-linguistic perspective upon law is the question: Is discursiveness in law semiotically identifiable? Semiotical analysis of elements and operations that are typical of legal discourses may clarify this fundamental question. Some of the above examples have demonstrated that the legal discourse questions the semiotic status of signs. The debate about essentialism in law and other ontological questions show that this status is far from being clear for many jurists. Law seen from the semiotic perspective may be perceived by some jurists as burdensome rather than practically helpful. Yet, the semiotic perspective may provide more evidence for legal-linguistic hypotheses. At the first sight, however, law seen from the semiotic perspective does not look like law at all. This is the main problem that impedes the integration of this perspective into legal sciences.

Law consists of legal signs that are also the material proof of its existence. Semiotics as the science of signs discovers the way in which these signs are combined to create meaning. Therefore, after having identified discursiveness as an underlying principle that unites the legal signs, further research will be devoted to the legal discourse in which these signs create legally relevant meaning. It would not be sufficient to dwell with singular signs alone, as only in a combination that in the legal-discursive practice is the discourse, the most interesting part of their existence, namely the meaning, comes about. This meaning is both theoretically and practically the most important part of law. Doubtless, the semiotic theory of meaning originated in the elementary notion of 'sign'. F. de Saussure's approach and analysis of language is a typical example of this sort of reasoning about meaning. Meanwhile, more advanced analyses of complex texts such as literary or legal narratives show that the elementary sign is not the most appropriate basic notion in respect of this sort of texts. Even a classic such as Ch. S. Peirce (1931–60: § 2.228) did not insist upon signs being isolated as elementary structures: "A sign…is something which stands to somebody for something in some respect or capacity. It addresses somebody, that is, creates in the mind of that person an equivalent sign, or perhaps a more developed sign. That sign which it creates I call the interpretant of the first sign. The sign stands for something, its object." Peirce does not mention any limits to the complexity of the sign and rightly so. Meanwhile, in the past, especially in classical structuralism, the tendency to construe the sign in analogy to road signs, i.e. as something relatively simple has been predominant. In order to counteract this tendency, discourse as a meaningful dimension of signs has been proposed (Fontanille 1998: 19). Jean Fontanille hoped that this expanded dimension will help to cope better with meaning in texts that are not a simple amalgam of isolated elementary signs. For instance, a 'contract' cannot be meaningfully analyzed when it is based solely on two elementary signs such as 'offer' and 'acceptance'. Constitutive for this relatively simple sign in law are multiple processes in which 'the minds of the parties meet', at least in the sense of a legal metaphor. After all, actors' positions and the logic of their argumentation make their minds meet. To describe this process much more is needed than a conceptual analysis of 'offer' and of 'acceptance'. Legal speech acts used as arguments constitute the 'contract' in a discursive practice and not in isolation (cf. Schane 2012: 105). Therefore the semiotics of discourse is a useful idea that expands the traditional semiotical approaches to meaning in law as rooted in the legal sign. This approach is necessary because the analysis of isolated terms leads only to partial results and to a reductionist understanding of law. For instance, when an administrative authority introduces the term 'enhanced interrogation techniques' into its reporting practice so it is not sufficient to recognize behind this term the traditional 'torture' concealed in linguistic fumes. Law is comprehended in this case only when the prerequisites and the consequences of the use of the 'neologism' are clarified. Jan Rommerskirchen (2011: 77) stressed one more discursive aspect of law that is understandable only in the semiotic perspective. He dealt with 'precarious' communicative situations in law such as police interrogations in multicultural settings. In an example, the arrested suspect who is interrogated by police officers is asked in the course of the interrogation whether he is thirsty. He confirms and is offered a drink. Yet, he does not drink. Such communicative situations are called by J. Rommerskirchen 'precarious' because they diverge from the general scheme of communication. In terms of the speech act theory they are a challenge. The arrested suspect clearly wishes to communicate a message, but which message? It is difficult to determine the speech act because apparently the meaning of the act is hidden behind the primary superficial impression of negligence of his commitment to his own statement. Regularly, inferentialistic approaches would commit the suspect to drink when he is offered a drink that he – at least implicitly – requested. Again more than strict inferentialism is needed to come to terms with such 'precarious' communicative situations. F. Dostoyevsky perfectly anticipated this speech situation in his *Crime and Punishment* (1866). In a scene where Raskolnikov is more or less formally interrogated by the investigator Porfirij Petrovič (part III, chapter V) he is offered water, yet does not drink, although he is encouraged by the investigator to drink. His ambivalent attitude to the drink offered increases the general atmosphere of nebulous oppressiveness that permeates the whole scene. The conflict that does not emerge openly between the parties is shifted towards the non-verbal communication where conventions can be neglected in the most ambiguous way. The scene is not multicultural and it displays even a contrary phenomenon as both participants are Russian jurists. This makes it even more paradigmatic in its dramatic treatment of the verbal and non-verbal communicative elements that relate to subliminally expressed fundamental conflicts.

In legal semiotics certain issues are therefore more promising than in general semiotics. This concerns primarily semiotic operations that are undertaken on complex signs or sign clusters such as legal texts. In the legal semiotics it is more useful to analyze the semiotic operations within amalgams of complex signs than to classify legal signs according to the traditional semiotic taxonomy. This procedure goes back to Ch. S. Peirce's distinction between icons, symbols and indices and numerous other taxonomies of signs that differentiate Peirce's matrix. All this notwithstanding, law is still best studied as semiotics. Peirce himself (1958: § 8.333) makes clear our interest in general semiotics by saying: "All our thought and knowledge is by signs." This bold statement is certainly true, especially in social sciences. And it is true in life. Peirce (1963: 32) rather categorically committed himself to semiotic studies about which he wrote: "It has never been in my power to study anything, – mathematics, ethics, metaphysics, gravitation, thermodynamics, optics, chemistry, comparative anatomy, astronomy, psychology, phonetics, economics, the history of science, whist, men and women, wine, metrology, except as a study of semiotic." This statement is understandable also from the legal-linguistic perspective. The decisive question is therefore how to study law as semiotics rather than whether to study it as a semiotic phenomenon. The preceding remarks led to the conclusion that law is a discursive practice. Discursiveness in law must therefore be studied with more emphasis than other semiotic features that are definitely also present in law. In legal semiotics the interest is better directed towards the legal discourse rather than towards other features of singular legal signs. The refocusing of attention in legal semiotics from isolated signs to discourse analysis is the direct consequence of the somehow monotonous assurances in the previous chapter regarding the role that discursiveness plays in law.

4.1.1 Semiotics of discourse

Legal semiotics uses the experience of the general semiotic discourse theory. This theory begins with the idea that signs which are, as a rule, identified in isolation are actually connected. George Berkeley remarks in his *Siris* (§ 251) that "the natural connection of signs with the things signified…forms a sort of rational discourse," and is therefore "the immediate effect of an intelligent cause" (*Siris* § 254). This means that we are able to reasonably connect signs that have been previously identified as disparate. The amalgam of signs so identified will usually have a structure because it is meaningful. Likewise, René Descartes in his *Discours de la méthode* identifies the discourse as an argumentative form connected with reason; its aim is the search of truth in sciences (cf. *Discours de la méthode pour bien conduire sa raison et chercher la vérité dans les sciences*). Descartes' introductory words into his *Discours* may cause problems in other surroundings than sciences, which were for Descartes, at least in this context, natural sciences. What is more, in his writings that clearly belong to natural or to hard sciences such as *Dioptriques, Météores,* or *Géométrie* and many others he aims at manifesting how his theory works in practice, i.e. in natural sciences, while deliberately neglecting other academic disciplines such as law. It comes even worse, 1616 Descartes obtained at Poitiers a degree in law, the French 'licence en droit'. He was therefore a trained jurist, although not much of his legal studies is visible in his subsequent career. One must therefore seriously ask why he did not try to apply his discursive method upon law, a subject he had studied and graduated in. Furthermore, in his *Meditationes de prima philosophia* law is not mentioned at all. Meanwhile, law is present in the work of other thinkers who stressed rather formalization as a scientific method and not discourse and who became famous in domains other than law, for instance G. Leibnitz, at least at the margin of their academic activities. One could assume that Descartes instinctively excluded law from the application of his method as obviously situated outside the reach of his conceptual mechanics. However, the link between 'discourse' and 'reason', which he clarifies, remains useful in the context of legal discourses, even if Descartes might have opposed such application of his method. Obviously, the search for truth in law is limited to brute facts, and this might have been the reason why Descartes did not include law in the long list of academic subjects that he founded or contributed to. He mentions law and medicine in one line while sarcastically reducing them to business: "que la jurisprudence et la médicine et les autres sciences apportent des honneurs et des richesses à ceux qui les cultivent" (cf. *Discours de la méthode, Première partie*). The specific discursive truth that jurists are looking for in law would probably not pass the examination before Descartes, as law is not a formal matter and possibly therefore not interesting for Descartes, the great thinker. Meanwhile, also the opposite view is worth to be considered. Law could be perceived as even more demanding than many hard sciences because of its discursive nature. With this in mind, Descartes had been criticized by J.L. Wolzogen in his *Annotationes in Meditationes Metaphysicas Renati des Cartis* (1656) for concentrating on academically less demanding issues and avoiding the most problematic. The quote from Wolzogen's commentary on Descartes' IV Meditation is worth to be cited and analyzed even today: "Quid enim mirum, si quis v. gr. trianguli tres angulos duobus rectis, et hypothenusae quadratum laterum quadratis aequari agnoscat, demonstratione tam claram facem praeferente, ut vel dormituriens veritatem palpet? At dignoscere judicii acumine justum et injustum, honestum et turpe, magis vel minus probabile; penetrare aliorum callidissima consilia, conatus, machinationes; obviare singulari prudentia infinitis hominum technis et fraudibus; declinare provide casus non nisi probabiliter praevistos; imo, quod praecipuum est, perscrutari admirandas, et non nisi perspicacissimis oculis investigabiles divinae providentiae vias, quibus ab Orbe condito, cum majestatis suae gloriam patefacit, tum generis humani salutem curat, id demum excellentis et penetrantis judicii laudem meretur; qua laude et fructu vero semetipsos privant et magnam judicii imbecillitatem testantur ii, qui in omnibus assensum cohibent, quae evidenti et palpabili demonstratione non sunt fulta,…" Wolzogen stresses in his comment the usefullness of critical approaches to reality as decisive: while whatever question can be approached scientifically, some questions are more useful than others. What is more, not to express opinions on issues regarding justice, ethical dilemmas or fraudulent or deceiving actions of people only because no mathematical proof is available for them, equals for him the rendition of the human mind. This is the essence of Wolzogen's criticism in its part that is interesting for us today. It goes without saying that Descartes was a greater philosopher than Wolzogen and that we owe him much. Meanwhile, it is also plain that he did not approach law with the necessary understanding of the interpretive problems that law causes in application. Others have seen more sense in the legal method. For instance, the legal reasoning may have influenced a French grammarian, Claude Favre de

Vaugelas, in his *Remarques sur la langue françoise*, 1647 (cf. preface and § II, 3 and § VII, 3) towards norming of language use. In his personal case, biographers referred to the influence of Vaugelas's father who had been a jurist (Christmann 1983: 418). Unlike Descartes, Vaugelas makes use of his legal knowledge and realizes that norming is a methodological device that can be used not only in law. Also Descartes could find an appealing area for the application of his method upon law in the mechanism of norming. It is not much, because a rational discourse as the goal envisioned by philosophers means more than formal norming of language use. It would however shed some light on one of the above examples where an arrested suspect has been asked in the course of his interrogation whether he is thirsty. The question asked is not caused by the police officer's particular kindness but by the normed legal-linguistic procedure. Such questions have to be asked by interrogating policemen under the given circumstances as the procedure is obligatory; it is normed in statutory texts. It is therefore rational in its context of interrogation that is an institutional fact-finding enterprise and not an informal meeting where also drinks are offered. Also Descartes clearly stressed rationality in action as the main point of interest in communicative settings. After all, the undeniable characteristic feature of discourse is the striving for rationality. Rationality is difficult to test in the legal discourse that cannot be evaluated mathematically. However, this result does not mean that we should avoid participation in legal discourses because statements that are made there cannot be proven with mathematical rigor. Ch. S. Peirce (1931–60: § 8.322), as if in parallel to Foucauldian thought, mentioned: "Any concept is a sign, of course...But we may take a sign in so broad a sense that the interpretation of it is not a thought, but an action of experience, or we may even so enlarge the meaning of sign that its interpretant is a mere quality of feeling." The appropriation of this approach to signs would enable Descartes to deal with law as it allowed others to render the emergence of meaning in legal discourses more fully.

4.1.2 Semiotic complexity of discourse

The first step in discourse analysis is challenging and by far more complicated than the analysis of singular legal signs. The point is that discourses are discouragingly complex structures. What is more, the methodology of discourse studies is no less complex (Anesa 2009; Gotti/Williams 2010). Therefore, it seems that the most efficient way of study discourses at this stage of development of scientific techniques is to combine both the discourse and the research methodology. Foucault (1969) ventured for this approach and he proved also an amazing skill in handling both, the study of discourse and the reflection upon the method of study that he thought as a unity. Others may have more problems with such intellectual operations. Therefore, also more detailed approaches are thinkable. Akmadjan et al. (2001: 387) characterized the study of discourse as the study of units of language and language use consisting of more than a single sentence, but connected by some system of related topics. This approach, although utterly complex, has at least one advantage. It draws attention to the anthropologically essential part of discourse, i.e. to its topic and leads away from formal or formalistic interests in the structure of information that serve other than anthropologically meaningful aims. Furthermore, discourses are studied in contexts, and contexts are also composed of signs. Law includes some relatively simple sign inventories such as the often quoted road signs (cf. Studnicki 1964). Other explicitly visible or even manifestedly and legally relevant sign inventories are, for instance, public commemorations or assemblies celebrating the flag. In such more complex semiotic context, E. L. Doctorow (2012: 118/119) reflected upon the naïve version of an American master narrative: "...everything we believed about our country seemed to emanate from the American flag up on the stage. We pledged our allegiance to it. We looked at its field of colors...The expectation we had from those colors was of the beneficent intent of an elected American government, standing in service to all its citizens and working to ensure their well-being." Doctorow stressed that this basic version of the American master narrative is profoundly naïve and childish. Indeed, how could someone expect something from a 'field of colors'? Meanwhile, U.S. citizens are by law obliged to salute the flag, right hand over their hearts. The U.S. Public Law 96–344 includes the Federal Flag Code. Sec. 6 of the Flag Protection Act introduces the obligation to hold "the right hand over the heart." It also mentions the obligation to "render military salute." Therefore, soldiers salute instead of holding their right hands on their breasts. An amendment to the act allows veterans who do not wear uniforms any more to salute even in their civilian cloth. No sanctions are foreseen in the law for non-obedience, apparently due to the unclear relation between the act and the First Amendment of the U.S. Constitution that guarantees freedom of speech. Some citizens claim that the Constitution guarantees their right to refrain from symbolical gestures such as 'celebrating a flag'. The semiotic context of flag use continues. American flag does not incline, not even before the U.S. President. This rule is often not respected in celebrations abroad. Furthermore, in the context of constitution of legal signs, certain official commemorations include the presence or the reference to the constitution. For instance, in the U.S. Congress the Constitution was read on January 6, 2011 in a modernized form, with antiquated parts such as the three-fifth clause of Article 1 or the reference to the right of vote of "male inhabitants" in Fourteenth Amendment omitted. Tribe (2012: 19) criticized this practice: "Treating the Constitution as a creed to be recited in properly updated, politically correct, and perhaps theologically approved form – rather than as the inescapably flawed and invariably contested narrative of our national struggle over the fundamental commitments that define us as a people – those political leaders ignored the capacity of superseded provisions to serve as antidotes to "collective amnesia about (our) national missteps." On this view, not the U.S. Constitution but another narrative was referred to in the commemoration ceremony in the Congress. The named legally relevant contexts of sign use in law are of primary importance in processes of meaning constitution in law. They are, however, poorly integrated into legal sciences where they appear in form of anecdotes or unprofessional digressions.

4.1.3 Discourse unites language and power

In all above examples the link between law and power is evident. To render this impression theoretically operational, one has to make it explicit. M. Foucault's approach provides for such explicit account of power. For jurists, the biggest achievement of the Foucauldian notion of discourse is its overarching and integrative strength, its integrative capacity to deal with knowledge, language and power at the same time (cf. Vinnai 2010: 163). The unnecessary and disturbing split in the legal thinking sometimes oscillates around a specific variety of the legal language. This variety does not mention power and concentrates on power structures that are expressed linguistically without taking their linguistic components into consideration. This variety of legal language is overcome in Foucault's approach. Also H.L.A. Hart (1961: vii) remarked that the linguistic perspective upon law actually shows society rather than language: "...the suggestion that inquiries into the meaning of words merely throw light on words is false. Many important distinctions, which are not immediately obvious, between types of social situation or relationships may best be brought to light by an examination of the standard uses of the relevant expressions and of the way in which these depend on a social context, itself often left unstated." Finally, the discursiveness of law and the notion of legal discourse that is an off-spring of the legal discursiveness enable a more structured speaking about law. As a result of this non-essentialist speaking about law other, more advanced or more appropriate conceptions may emerge in future. As of now, it is difficult to imagine such conceptions as too much remains to be done to elucidate the on-going legal discourse in all its complexity. The complex situation in which legal signs emerge and are used in multiple legal-linguistic operations as parts of legal discourses may, however, be better understood within legal semiotics.

4.2 Non-verbal elements of legal discourses

Law has been traditionally perceived as an area of sign constitution that is predominantly verbal. Non-verbal elements of legal discourse gained momentum in the law-oriented research that in this area traditionally concentrated on the representativity of court buildings, the arrangement in court rooms, the dressing habits cultivated in judicial institutions and the like (cf. Jackson 1985; Mattila 2013: 13–14). Since the innovative semiotic analyses by U. Eco (1968/2008) the main interest was directed in this type of research to the immediately visible. Concealed, less visible parts of law, that is a social institution, were not taken into consideration. Undoubtedly, the question as to what extent the language of visual culture in law had been deciphered and explored by such research remains open (cf. Burket 2010; Asimow/Mader 2013). The results, when evaluated sweepingly, seem to suggest rather an interdependence of verbal and non-verbal signs in law with the preponderance of verbal signs. It seems also possible to assume that there is not much to be shown in law, that its visualization as a phenomenon is very limited. This result differs remarkably form the perspective established by Eco in his now already classical studies of the language of architecture that is an example of a visual sign system par excellence. In terms of methodology, the general, mostly semiotically founded research into visual discourse is relatively advanced (cf. Sandywell 2011). Unchanged remains its perspective oriented towards the visual culture of daily life, preferring the immediately visible signs. Due to the specific relation of verbal and non-verbal signs in law, methods of analysis of non-verbal signs from other areas of social life are not always directly applicable in the area of law. So are analyses of political demonstrations frequently reduced to the scrutiny of participants' physical presence. Occasionally, additional gestures such as holding hands, forming human chains or keeping candles alight are employed. *The New Yorker* reported (September 27, 2010, p. 59) that during a demonstration to support the then hostage-held and meanwhile happily liberated Israeli soldier Gilad Shalit dogs that were brought to the demonstration were wearing yellow ribbons around their collars. This outfit was meant to correspond with their owners' wearing yellow ribbons tied around their wrists. Furthermore, during demonstrations in Thailand participants were distinguished by the color of their T-shirts as was the case in remote past with the Byzantine political parties that assembled around the famous hippodrome of

Constantinople. There, color of dress had been equally distinctive. Still further and in a way of a particularly illustrative example, the magazine *Jerusalem Report* informed in its edition of December 19, 2011 that the Israeli Parliament members belonging to the Kadima party were waving black flags during a plenum vote on the new judge selection procedure on November 14, 2011, apparently as an expression of protest against the reform. As the Knesset plenary hall is kept in rather dark tones, the black flags were scarcely visible and the news magazine did not realize this circumstance in its mentioned publication that includes a photo of the scenery. Only a very imaginative reader might have tried to identify the places in the Knesset plenary hall where the black flags were actually posted. As a matter of fact, in a place predestined to speech, and a Parliament is such a place par excellence, non-verbal actions manifest a misunderstanding about the venue and its discursive function. In this particular case, they show that a chance to act politically within a linguistic argumentative practice in a legislative body was missed by the Knesset members who tried to replace it by a non-verbal exercise. Their action failed, at least partly, as they could not transfer the intention to act politically also to the citizens at large due to the limited readability of the signs in the media. Unsurprisingly, the readability of non-verbal signs is in law determined by the perspective of the third party. In Germany, in a case that concerned the Neo-Nazis, an acquittal had been reached by the defense regarding the situation in which a large group of hooligans with doubtful political sympathies formed with their colored jackets a Swastika-sign in a stadium during a football match. According to German penal law, public manifestation of fascist signs is prohibited. Meanwhile, due to doubts about the readability of the sign composed of bodies of numerous persons that was provided to the court in form of a photography, the accused hooligans were acquitted. Interpretation of non-verbal signs in the area of law that is a discursive practice is therefore meaningful in the context of their social readability.

Meanwhile, non-verbal signs may be very relevant to law. A textbook phrase says significantly: "English legal development stems from 1066 when William of Normandy gained the Crown of England by right of battle." This formulation is not uninteresting because we constantly stressed the discursive character of law, and a battle does not look like a discourse. At least, it is not fought as a discursive practice. Clearly, discourses precede it, accompany it and result from it. Yet, the non-verbal part of sign constitution can also be isolated, while at the same time the possibility of a combination with discursive practices is not excluded. Also a non-verbal sign constellation, such as the punishment by 'beheading' or 'decapitation', remains within the realm of the legal language first of all because it – as a mechanical operation – is provided a name. In the English example it has even two names, one of Germanic origin and one referring to the classical times of the ancient Romans who shared this practice of punishment with the ancient Greeks. Historical sources teach us that 'decapitation' was first incurred in England by Earl Waltheof who was beheaded upon orders by William the Conqueror in 1075. This practice of punishment ceased in England apparently in 1745 when the rebel lords were beheaded as last Englishmen in a long series of executions. The execution as such is technically not particularly difficult to invent; yet it involves discursive practices of some complexity, such as the above double naming. Furthermore, R. Weisberg (1992: 259) remarks that public hanging "was a commonplace (in England) until abolished in 1868." The Chinese writer Lu Xun in his collection of short stories *Nà Hăn* (1922) mentions that he was discouraged from becoming a medical doctor while viewing a photo which showed his fellow countrymen who enthusiastically indulged in the spectacle that a public execution seemed to offer them. In the light of this experience, any commitment to curing this sort of people appeared to him nonsensical. Other semiotically relevant aspects were mentioned here already in the context of the execution of Hickock and Smith in Kansas. One could multiply analogous examples. Historically, in Europe since the twelfth century, the punishment of tarring and feathering was applied in professional courts and also in less formal social settings. Later on, during the American Revolution, a Committee for Tarring and Feathering, which was charged with maintenance of law and order, operated in Boston (Crain 2010). As in all above examples, its activities can be understood only in discursive contexts. In sum, the legal discourse displays an interconnection of verbal and non-verbal signs with the predominance of verbal practices. This relation of predominance to the benefit of the verbal signs is, as a result, clearly related to the discursiveness of law as its constitutive element.

4.2.1 Artifacts of law

As said, legal discourse is composed of signs. In the legal discourse, law is also represented by material signs, artifacts that are more sustainable than its fragile semantic surface. Many objects such as court decisions or court seals have been created in order to make law visible. In the U.S., on some official seals the fact that the imprint is a seal is explicitly stated, in other cases it is omitted: Seal of the President of the United States, Seal of the Supreme Court Delaware, Seal of the Supreme Court of the United States, United States Court for the Federal Circuit, State of Texas, The Great Seal of the State of Nevada, and The Seal of the State of Washington. Connecticut has a seal in Latin: Sigillum Reipublicae

Connecticutensis. The official motto of the United States is Novus Ordo Seclorum. On American banknotes also the formula 'e pluribus unum' is mentioned in Latin. More recently, the fifty thousand rials banknote issued by Iran in 2007 attracted not only investors but also legal semioticians. It displays on the front the portrait of Ayatollah Khomeini and on the back the map of Iran with nuclear symbols on it. The dominating image on the backside displays the electrons in orbit around the nucleus of an atom on a map of Iran. The backside that is, unlike the Farsi-front textually held predominantly in English, includes also an ornamentally held quote in Farsi that in different available translations may be rendered as: 'Even if science is at the Pleiades, some people from the land of Persia would attain it' or 'Men from the land of Persia will attain scientific knowledge even if it is as far as the Pleiades' (which are a cluster of stars mentioned already by Homer). The banknote as a means of payment is instrumentalized here to raise claims under international law and this fact makes of it a discursive text type in law. Also names and signatures play a specific role in the legal discourse. The name of a person, first and second, is equally a legal invention. The Finnish legal scholar U. Kangas (1991) stressed its importance for structuring the relation between society and individual. Stamps have been used in China until recent times instead of signatures that were largely in use in the European countries since centuries. The Chinese preferred them to signatures because of their invariability; the hand signature was meaningless as evidence in traditional Chinese law. Therefore, work on non-verbal signs in law makes sense also within explicitly discursive approaches to law. Signs and amalgams of signs are identified in processes that were shown above. Yet, we are able not only to identify signs and to group them. We are furthermore able to interpret them meaningfully. In fact, interpretation is the most important semiotic operation on signs. In life, interpretation of signs and sign amalgams enables orientation. In terms of anthropology, orientation as a cognitive process cannot be underestimated because it equals our survival in nature. In law, interpretation is no less central. Law without interpretation would change into a frozen heap of artifacts. It would become meaningless. In the following, we will sum up some of the most relevant aspects of interpretation as a legal-linguistic operation.

4.3 Legal interpretation: Pre-interpretive remarks

Interpretation emerges wherever we encounter signs. Identifying signs and interpreting them are interrelated actions. In one of the above samples, when the arrested suspect is asked whether he is thirsty, when he confirms and is offered a drink, but does not drink it, the simultaneous identification of signs and their initial interpretation emerge as interrelated actions. No one would be interested in the situation and apprehend it, were the communicative situation not 'precarious' in the sense mentioned above. That the situation is 'precarious' is a result of interpretation. Signs are interpreted in line with rules. For instance, when a basketball player places the ball in the basket he engages in the application of rules. His making the score is visible as an act. Meanwhile his act is valid as a score and not true in the sense of the rules of basketball. The image that basketball fans admire on their TV or tablet screens may be true but it is true in the sense of seeing or viewing, not of basketball playing. Likewise, the police officer who offers a drink to the arrested suspect creates signs that are interpretable according to rules. Rules are easier interpretable in logic that uses a formal interpretive language. There, one could formulate a true statement regarding the situation with the help of Tarski's theorem: If the player places the ball in the basket, so he places the ball in the basket and this is perfectly true. This truth that seems absolute in terms of logic concerns however the seeing of an act and not the basketball playing. Should basketball rules have been violated in a way manifest to the umpire but invisible to the spectators, no score will be marked even if the player placed the ball in the basket and he as well as the viewers clearly witnessed this act. Interpretation therefore does not equal seeing or viewing. It follows rules that are not easily readable, because they are not visible. This is also the reason why Aristotle warned against overestimation of seeing or viewing things in his *Metaphysics* (982a): "sense-perception is common to all, and therefore easy and no mark of wisdom." Impressions are necessary for interpretation, yet interpretation is more than a physiological act of seeing.

As we cannot avoid the interpretation of impressions, our approach to interpretation must be based on something. This something may be conscious or unconscious. Professional interpretation as well as daily routine interpretation of singular or complex signs is rooted in both; we are often conscious about the choice of an interpretive paradigm and interpretive rules that follow from it and sometimes we are not; we take it for granted. In some extreme situations we may not even realize that we interpret linguistic messages. In law, choices may be simple. In a jurisdiction, employee or consumer protection may enjoy highest priority. Courts there will interpret laws and facts in the light most favorable to these two groups of privileged parties. In other jurisdictions, employers and real estate owners may be politically supported; courts there will interpret laws and facts accordingly. Interpretation depends on the development of discursive practices that may reflect the same texts differently. For instance, the very existence of virtually identical French and Belgian Civil Codes does not mean that like cases are solved in both jurisdictions alike and that the same provision of the code is given the same meaning. The 'interprétation belge' of the code may substantially differ from the authoritative French interpretation given by the French Cour de Cassation. Interpretation of signs depends therefore on commitments and beliefs that are usually value-laden. We cannot understand legal interpretation without being aware of this precondition.

4.3.1 Martian interpretation

The interpretive devices, mechanisms, as well as the mere emergence of paradigms and rules are better observed on fictitious examples that directly do not relate to our daily experience. Let us therefore imagine a Martian visitor to our planet. The guest is friendly received here and accompanies a Terrestrial who welcomed him first while driving a car on his way to work. The Martian realizes that on the road the Terrestrial stops any time the traffic lights turn red and re-starts any time the lights turn green. He furthermore notices that whenever the Terrestrial stops he turns on the radio and whenever he re-starts he switches off the radio. Unsurprisingly, he infers from these observations the rule that at red light cars have to stop and radios have to be switched on and at green light cars can start or keep on going and radios have to be switched off. The Martian deducts the rule with an admirable sharpness of mind. He then visits his host's working place who happens to be a surgeon in a well organized clinic. There, he notices that classical music accompanies the preparatory anaesthetic phase of surgical operations. The Martian will easily guess from this experience that classical music is composed to be used as light anaesthetic and sedative before operations. Thus, he infers from his contact with the terrestrial social reality another rule that is based on his experience with our world. All these disarming observations notwithstanding, the visitor from the red planet is simply wrong in his reading of rules that govern the terrestrial society. We have quite a lot of understanding for his reading of these rules and we should not blame him for the results attained. Yet, we cannot accept them as the right interpretation of our terrestrial social and legal rules. The reason for it is not our lack of tolerance for his sharp-minded and conclusive interpretive propositions. We have understanding for them, which means, that we can imagine that under circumstances as the above someone who does not live on earth can arrive at such conclusions while reasoning in a rational way. We, however, arrive rationally at other conclusions. We share with the Martian his observation that cars have to stop when lights turn red, yet we decline to follow the second part of his rule about the radios to be switched on and off in connection with the changing color of the traffic lights.

The reason for this is not that we are better observers than the Martian but that we possess additional contextual knowledge that enables us to infer rules from observable facts with equal rationality of concluding than is his, yet with higher quality of fit. We are in our interpretation of facts closer to rules that are binding in society than the visitor from the remote planet because we also share some beliefs and commitments in the sense introduced by J. Searle (2006). Our visitor does not know these value-related commitments and beliefs that constitute the background of our social practices. Yet, one more question remains. The Martian may realize that some drivers do not stop at red lights while others do. He may therefore modify his rule that would then say that some drivers are obliged to stop at red lights while others are not. We would again object his reading. This objection concerns the normativity of things because we know that some drivers simply abuse the rules and do not drive according to them. We as context-equipped observers also know that under certain circumstances the fire brigade or ambulances do not need to stop at red light without violating the rules of the traffic code because statutes and case law provide for exceptional rules to general rules. The Martian is however right in his reading of social rules that will mean that certain drivers stop at red light while others do not because society tolerates this sort of behavior. In this case, he is a perfect observer of social rules. We therefore end up in a paradox that the Martian actually understands better our society than we do in our formalistic normative way to recognize and interpret rules. Sometimes, shared beliefs and commitments may impede our understanding of social reality.

4.3.2 Finalist interpretation

Interpretive paradigms and interpretive rules are not disconnected from brute reality that they transform. There is some circularity in interpretation and the above examples of legal interpretation indicated such interconnection. In his anthropological and literary study *The Conquest of America* Tzvetan Todorov (1992) analyzed Columbus's letters about the discovery of West Indies and he identified a prevalent interpretive strategy in Columbus's writings that he calls finalist. He realized that Columbus had seen the discovered lands through the prism of his anterior knowledge about remote countries and the terrestrial paradise that the antique and later literature proposed to sometimes rather naïve readers. He writes: "Columbus performs a 'finalist' strategy of interpretation, in the same manner in which the Church Fathers interpreted the Bible: the ultimate meaning is given from the start (this is Christian doctrine); what is sought is the path linking the initial meaning (the apparent signification of the words of the biblical text) with the ultimate meaning." There is nothing of the modern empiricist about Columbus: the decisive argument is an argument of authority, not of experience. He knew in advance what he will find; the concrete experience was there to illustrate a truth already possessed, not to be interrogated according to pre-established rules in order to seek the truth (Todorov 1992: 17). Todorov calls this interpretive choice a hermeneutic behavior; it changes only when Columbus reflects on the beauty of surrounding nature (Todorov 1992: 17). The finalist strategy prevails however in Columbus's thinking; he is not seeking the truth, he is only interested in finding confirmation of a truth known in advance. In law, finalist interpretation is omnipresent. Finalist interpretation is an interpretive strategy that consists in proving with the help of a text an already existing assumption. This strategy is largely applied also outside legal texts, and one may actually ask whether it is interpretation at all. The fate of the finalist interpretive strategy in law is largely unexplored. For the one, an anecdote mentions the medieval jurists Bartolus and Baldus describing Baldus as seeking Bartolus's advice for the justification of a preconceived solution to a legal problem. For the other, the finalist interpretive strategy is visible also in Francisco de Vitoria's famous defense of the colonization of America. The legal arguments in favor of the colonization of America developed by Francisco de Vitoria in his *De Indis, Recenter Inventis Relectio Prior* (sec. III, pars II, no. 386) are based on the obligation of hospitality towards the newcomers. Vitoria wrote in 1539: "Sic enim apud omnes nationes habetur inhumanum sine aliqua causa hospites et peregrinos male accipere." In this view, the American Indians did not have any legal rights to refuse the colonists, as the international law of his time required from them in Vitoria's opinion that they would welcome foreigners, otherwise they would act inhumanly. Here, legal science is sophistry in the bad sense of the word, even if the requisite 'sine aliqua causa' is mentioned by Vitoria. Historically, jurists were well aware of interpretive pitfalls. At the same time, legal ideology turned interpretation into a suspected because 'political' enterprise. The same fear for interpretation led to the emergence of different strategies of linguistic securization against responsibility. For instance, the Catholic theologico-moral doctrine of 'tuziorismo', from Latin 'opinio tutior', i.e. the safest opinion, is the attempt towards rigorous legalism in interpretation. In cases of doubt between two different opinions related to moral issues the most legal opinion was to be followed. This doctrine has been adapted in law as a linguistic shield against criticism on the results of interpretation. In effect, the safest opinion had to be followed. Unsurprisingly, new interpretive results cannot be realistically expected under such a doctrine. Needless to say that the finalist interpretation does not have much in common with interpretive approaches that the contemporary legal linguistics tries to develop.

4.3.3 Oblivious interpretation

Tzvetan Todorov (1992) also described in his *Conquest of America* some hermeneutic particularities of the discoverers and conquerors. He focused on the process in which those people reflected the newly discovered world, i.e. the interpretive strategies they used to cope with the new they had seen. He maintains that finalist and systematic interpretive strategies dominated the writings of Columbus and others. Todorov (1992: 64) describes also the systematic interpretation that he also calls pre-established. He uses the example of Aztecs who linked the birthday of the child to a specified destiny fixed in advance in their horoscopes. For an astrologer or a sorcerer-fortune-teller it sufficed to determine the correlation between the birthday and the horoscope data, to establish a vision of someone's future, because to know someone's birthday is to know his fate (Todorov 1992: 63). Thus, a contextual kind of divination (Todorov 1992: 64) emerged that was meant as a basis for the rigid correlation between some predetermined data. Todorov is not satisfied with the application of these interpretive strategies under the given circumstances in the confrontation with the other; he perceives them as not modern, i.e. empirical (Todorov 1992: 23). Equally, the discovered Indians – at least at the very beginning of their new experience – did not perceive the newcomers as humans, but as gods; they were unable to recognize them as what they were, i.e. as humans equal to them despite all their superficial difference (Todorov 1992: 76). In fact, the interpretive strategies fail on both sides because the interhuman dimension is neglected in the communication. Therefore, interpretation is an act that involves the human being in its totality. For law, it has the consequence that reductive approaches to legal interpretation seem to be at least suspicious.

4.3.4 Revelation of law as interpretive device

Historically, the revelation of law as an interpretive device has been very influential. Interest in this type of interpretation came about due to a surprising assumption. In the past, many thinkers argued that law has to be either of natural or of divine origin because otherwise it would not be possible to determine the right and the wrong in it. Both labels of law can be treated as one conceptual and textual type as both presuppose that law actually exists beyond the sphere of human influence and human creation. Conceptually, this type of law is not binding on its supranatural creator. It concerns only those to whom the legal narrative is authoritatively revealed. In 1671, John Milton expressed this alleged structural feature of divine or natural law in *Samson Agonistes* (verses 307–314): "As if they would confine th'interminable,/ And tie him to his own prescript,/ Who made our Laws to bind us, not himself,/And hath full right to exempt/Whom so it pleases him by choice/From National obstriction, without taint/Of sin, or legal debt/ For with his own Laws he can best dispense." Meanwhile, Milton assumes this divine law to be also universal (verses 1053–1054): "Therefore God's universal Law/Gave to the man despotic power…" which is a free interpretation of the divine law in the Biblical context. While Milton chooses explicitly this context, he also transgresses its limits not only in the spacial perspective, as just shown, but also in the temporal perspective. In *Samson Agonistes* the divine law is functionalized anachronistically, so in verses 1425–1426: "Our God, our Law, my Nation, or my self,/The last of me or no I cannot warrant." The reference to the national state in the quoted verses and in verse 312 may have convinced English readers in the seventeenth century; within the imagery of the Old Testament it is clearly misplaced. What is more, when this law is 'our' or 'national' how could it be perceived as universal, especially by others. Milton is saved by the licentia poetica that does not impose any logical restrictions on poets. But his law is poetry. Other argumentative features of this law are structurally circular. When for example the lawfulness of self-murder is denied under either divine or natural law or both, then the opposite view is 'by its nature' "heathenish or diabolical," as rendered by H. Fielding in *Tom Jones* (VIII, 14). Divine or natural law is right because it is divine or natural, so goes the argument. Likewise, in the German classical literature J.W. von Goethe refers to the right that, as he supposes, is born with us, "das Recht, das mit uns geboren" in his F*aust*. Christopher Marlowe's *Faust* that inspired Goethe is more critical of law: "…Where is Justinian? Si una eademque res legatur duobus,/Alter rem alter valorem rei, etc./A pretty case of paltry legacies:/Exhereditare filium non potest pater nisi…/Such is the subject of the Institute,/And universal body of law: This study fits a mercenary drudge/ Who aims at nothing but external thrash!/Too servile and illiberal for me" (cf. *Faust* scene 1, 27–36). Indeed, there is no help for the natural or divine law; it has been created and remains a literary fiction. Meanwhile, narratives that transfer this law are valuable cultural artifacts (cf. Wesel 2006). They witness to the social and cultural processes in which contemporary law and its language had been shaped in the long and discontinuous course of legal history.

Religious conceptions of law represent law in terms of divine revelation. Interpretive work on law is for them work on a set of legal axioms revealed by a divinity. The character of this law as being revealed does not necessarily mean that operations on such a law would look differently. Revealed or not, law must be interpreted in order to be applied. There is no proof for the assumption that the interpretation of laws that are based on divine revelation would be less frequent or unnecessary. Jewish law has been regularly interpreted by rabbis differently (Maccoby 1989: 51, 74–80). Islamic jurisprudence is divided in several schools that differ according to the way in which they interpret the revealed law (Menski 2006: 339–344). For instance, Islamic law as revealed law refers both to the 'umma' of the believers as to the 'dhimmi', i.e to the world that is protected by Islam and the rest of the world. Domingo (2010: 20) characterizes this interrelation as follows: "For Islam, the world is divided into two parts. Those communities that live under the Pax Islamica – either because they are Islamic (umma) or because they are protected by Islam (dhimmi) in exchange for payment of jizya – from the "House of Islam" (Dar al-Islam). The other part, the "House of War" (Dar al-Harb) comprises the rest of the world. Jihad (better rendered as "holy struggle" than as "holy war," the usual translation) is the internal and external means of transforming non-Islamic lands into Dar al-Islam." The quality of law encountered under such circumstances is distinctive. In this type of law, interpretive differences will always be concealed with reference to divine intention. This may also be the reason why in the U.S. attempts to introduce reference to Christian religion into the Constitution were undertaken in the past. They also failed, as least twice. In 1947 and in 1954 the National Association of Evangelicals in vain proposed the following amendment: "The nation devoutly recognizes the authority and the law of Jesus Christ, Savior and Ruler of nations, through whom we are bestowed the blessings of Almighty God" (cf. *Time*, May 24, 1954, p. 23). Less present in the American legal discourse is the Treaty of Peace and Friendship between the United States and the Bey and Subjects of Tripoli of Barbary, signed into law by President John Adams 1797. The Treaty proclaims in its Art. 11: "As the Government of the United States of America is not, in any sense, founded on the Christian religion; as it has in itself no character of enmity against the laws, religion, or tranquillity, of Mussulmen; and, as, the said States never entered into any war, or act of hostility against any Mahometan nation, it is declared by the parties, that no pretext arising from religious opinions, shall ever produce an interruption of the harmony existing between the two countries." The text of the Treaty was authored by the American diplomat Joel Barlow. It was read in the U.S. Senate on June 7, 1797 in its entirety and unanimously approved. The text of the Treaty was published in *The Philadelphia Gazette* on June 17, 1797. The fate of this legal text is an example of asymmetric reception and discursive importance of written samples that represent law. In the tradition of the Occidental law this process began latest with the editing of the Roman law in the shape of the *Corpus Iuris Civilis*. As so often, two competing forces, continuity and discontinuity, are at work in all legal discourses that are centered on written texts. Law also owes some of its language to religion (cf. Berman 1974). Also Berger (1963: 134) refers to 'Sitz im Leben,' used for instance by K.F. von Savigny, as a term with religious connotation. For instance, I. Kant operates with this type of 'seat' when he says about the space that: "it has its seat in our faculty of cognition a priori." Meanwhile, the only identifiable structural difference between the revealed law and other types of law is the position of the legislator. In terms of argumentation, religious law enables a parallel law to emerge that under other conditions would be perceived as an act of inadmissible competition with the established positive law of the state. Active legal-linguistic operations in such revealed law will have to exclude any deliberative formation of law. They will start at a later stage, namely with the application of the revealed legal rules.

4.3.5 Constructive interpretation

Legal interpretation seems to be the most fundamental legal-semiotic, i.e. legal-linguistic operation exercised on legal signs. Therefore, numerous works have been devoted to it in the legal-linguistic research (cf. Szabó et al. 2000; Golanski 2002; Visconti 2010; Chierichetti 2010; Vinnai 2011 and others). Legal interpretation as a legal-linguistic operation is so fundamental that it has been in its fundamentality and complexity often overlooked, mostly by positivists. Occasionally, it has been treated as a play with words within interpretive canons. Such canons were usually composed of standards for grammatical, systematic, teleological or historical interpretation that – when combined – should engender unambiguous meaning of legal texts. In the course of time, some modifications were introduced into the traditional juridical canon of interpretation. Yet, its general underlying structure remained unchanged. R. Dworkin (1991) has overcome the interpretive deadlock caused in the legal sciences by the interpretive canons with his theory of constructive interpretation (cf. also Galdia 2009: 207–212). At least since Dworkin's attempt to clarify the legal interpretation its problems can be perceived as relatively well researched. Meanwhile, one thing is to understand the intricacies of legal interpretation and another thing is to propose a theory that explicitly describes them and provides guidelines for application of such discoveries in the legal practice. Overall, the recent achievements of the research into legal interpretation relate to the question of interpretive proposals about the content of law. In the light of approaches such as Dworkin's it became clear that legal signs per se do not impose any limits to the interpretation of legal texts. Therefore, no interpretive proposals about a legal text can be developed that would convince everyone by the mere nature of the undertaken operation, especially not due to the obviousness of the result. Appeals to obviousness are used as arguments in practical legal argumentation, yet obviousness cannot be readily achieved in law. Legal interpretation is therefore not directly causally efficacious as its result is never evident. Morris (1971: 461) mentions this specific causality while addressing the process of general semiosis: "A sign-situation, or a process of semiosis, is any situation in which one thing takes account of something else, which is not directly causally efficacious, through the mediation of a third something." This result looks hopeless at the first sight because legal interpretation like every other type of interpretation requires a worldview, observation and involvement in a discursive practice. There is therefore no easy-going legal interpretation. The process of semiosis that the interpreting jurist identifies and develops in a legal text (legal discourse) is much too undetermined to provide incontestable results. On the other side, the risk of arriving at arbitrary interpretive proposals within legal discourses may be perceived as worrying. Interpretive proposals of this sort are not an appealing offer because law is perceived, at least generally, as a rational and social mechanism or construct. Therefore, the interest in irrational law, within the legal sciences and beyond them, seems to be very limited. Tests or criteria for rationality of interpretive proposals about the content of law have been developed in the legal theory and in the legal linguistics (Slocum 2012). The most significant challenge to all such attempts is the necessity to determine the heuristic prerequisites of interpretive action. The stake taken in the legal interpretation, the interpreter's cognitive interest, must be determined by himself and be readable for the recipients of the interpretive proposal. Otherwise, confusion, if not arbitrariness would follow. Moreover, test criteria must be adapted to the discursiveness of law as its most fundamental feature. This has been done in numerous theoretical approaches to legal interpretation, for instance by R. Alexy (1983), A. Aarnio (1989), M. Atienza (1991; 2011) or R. Dworkin (1991).

4.3.6 Originalism as interpretive device

Originalism is an old method of text interpretation. It asks for the original meaning that the author of the text must have had in mind while writing, usually in times remote from ours. Eco (1968/2008: v) remarks about the necessity to respect the author's intention: "bisogna far dire a un autore solo ciò che voleva dire e non ciò che ci sembra dire contro le sue intenzioni..." Originalism as an interpretive device has its counterpart in reader's expectations. These expectations concern the image that the reader has about an author, for example an influential politician and legislator. Amossy (2010: 71) characterized this type of reception process of texts with reference to a descriptive model going back to the ethos of the Aristotelian rhetoric. An example may elucidate this situation. In the U.S. legal history some personalities enjoy a notoriously positive standing in the eyes of citizens and attempts at adjusting this perspective regularly fail. The person of George Washington is perceived by most U.S. Americans as positive and exemplary. Every written artifact by his hand is viewed in positive terms. For such U.S. Americans, and this means the mainstreet, his person remains virtuous, undaunted, and incorruptible. Meanwhile, historical research shows a relatively limited contribution from Washington's side to the process of immediate shaping of the American state in political processes. It could be that his role was mainly one of a good actor rather than that of a prolific playwright. The strategy adopted by Washington rarely made his points of view clearly visible and publicly known. It corresponds with the picture that the historical research has developed about his elusive personality. A note in his diary for October 24, 1774, a day he had spent in Philadelphia attending the Continental Congress, written in his characteristic style, says: "Dined with Mr. Mease and Spent the Evening at the New Tavern." Concerning the same day and the debate in the Continental Congress, the note in John Adams's *Diary* begins with following words: "In Congress, nibbling and quibbling, as usual. There is no greater mortification than to sit with half a dozen Witts, deliberating upon a Petition, Address, or Memorial. These great Witts, these subtile Criticks, these refined Genius's, these learned Lawyers, these wise Statesmen, are so fond of shewing their Parts and Powers, as to make their Consultations very tedious. Young Ned Rutledge is a perfect Bob o'Lincoln – a Swallow- a Sparrow- a Peacock- excessively vain, excessively weak, and excessively variable and unsteady-jejune, inane, and puerile. Mr. Dickinson is very modest, delicate and timid." The contribution to public discourse as testified in Adams's note is much more impressive than Washington's insipid diary entry. Any narrative about G. Washington, notwithstanding thousands of pages written by him that remain at researchers' disposal, will be limited due to the evasive character of this politician and legislator. This evasiveness and elusiveness may be characteristic of successful legislators as the historical research also shows that more engaged, more active, and more pronounced politicians and legislators than had been G. Washington finally achieved substantially and personally less than he as a player in the process of the shaping of the American republic. Therefore, originalism fails because of its underestimation of temporality of social phenomena. To illustrate further, one of the framers of the U.S. Constitution, James Madison, deals in *The Federalist* (nr. 10) purely rhetorically with the unthinkable intention 'to wish the annihilation of air'. Written in 1787, in times free from environmental concerns comparable with ours, such words were perceived as pure metaphors. None of the 'founding fathers' could imagine how close their compatriots may in future come to achieving such an absurd aim. Meanwhile, classical originalism has its textual and factual limits. These limits were challenged in the debate about the appropriate method for historical research. Yet, the debate remained inconclusive, at least as far as the above problems are concerned. Meanwhile, Brian H. Bix (2012: 154) refers to more recent versions of originalism that are called by some 'new originalism'. In these conceptions, the epistemological interest shifts from the original meaning that the constitutional drafters may have had in mind towards the 'plain meaning' of constitutional concepts in times of their introduction into the constitution. The shift does not make the originalist conception necessarily better as it remains backwards-oriented and seeks interpretive guidelines from the past. Originalists attempted to find interpretive guidelines in history, in language, and in precedent (Bennett 2012: 122–125). Such attempts are clearly essentialist because they require the belief in an underlying truth in concepts that history, language or legal precedents reveal when aptly studied. Meanwhile, these textual sources reveal at best the experience that certain people have made with concepts, conceptions, and beliefs at a certain point in time. This result does not exclude historical studies of formation of concepts or their linguistic development. Many scholars, among them also Michel Foucault, based their methods on conceptual studies in the diachronic perspective. Yet, scholars such as M. Foucault never intended to replace the ongoing discourse about meaning of socially relevant concepts with the reference to their reconstructed historical meaning. It seems that originalism in all its forms neglects the insight that interpretation as a legal-linguistic operation is a rational search for meaning. And rationality excludes all essentialist attempts in legal interpretation because they are purely metaphysical. Therefore, originalism is not an interpretive alternative to constructivist approaches to interpretation in law. It is theoretically excluded as an efficient matrix to interpret law because it does not concern law, but some other phenomena such as history of thought, psychology, legal history or anthropology.

4.3.7 Law and Economics as interpretive paradigm

Law and Economics or economical analysis of law as it is called in Continental parlance is an interpretive paradigm of law that has been recognized as such relatively recently. In fact, taking into account economical postulates is not a new strategy of legal interpretation. It seems that the innovation offered by Law and Economics has been to make this interpretive strategy explicit and controlling. Law and Economics' emergence is linked with the name of Richard Posner, judge and professor of law in Chicago. R. Posner developed his postulates mainly in the area of antitrust legislation that is closely linked to economy. Subsequently, Law and Economics' interests within the field were broadened and they encompass now all areas of law. Their success rate differs, and criticism on the methods applied in this area of research is not rare (Cutter/Ulen 2004: 506). The Law and Economics approach engendered several strong narratives that have their legal-linguistic merits. For instance, the Maggio-case decided by Justice Richard Posner displays elements of legal interpretation within the Law and Economics paradigm (cf. Northwestern National Insurance Company v. Maggio, 976 F. 2d 320, 1992). In the case, Maggio purchased a limited partnership in an enterprise involved in advanced technology and paid for it with a noninterest-bearing promissory note maturing several years later. The enterprise negotiated it to another enterprise that further negotiated it to a bank. The acquiring bank negotiated it further to another bank along with many other notes at a fifty percent discount. This bank demanded payment from Maggio when the note matured, yet he refused to pay. He invoked defenses against the limited partnership. So far the facts. In terms of law, the bank that held the promissory note claimed to have acquired it free from any defenses against former owners. Maggio contended to have been induced into the underlying transaction by fraud. This would give him a claim against the partnership, yet not against the bank, should it have acquired the note in good faith or purchased it as a part of a bulk transaction that would belong to its regular business. Justice Posner remarks to this: "The rarely litigated bulk-transfer exception identifies a narrow class of transactions where the purchaser of the (otherwise) negotiable instrument ought to be suspicious that the seller may be trying to thwart promisors' defenses and prefer one creditor over others, or committing outright fraud (the transferee might be a successor of the transferor), perhaps en route to bankruptcy. The existence of those defenses makes the promisors creditors; the wholesale transfer of their notes to a 'holder in due course' would extinguish the promisors' claims; and the fact that the transfer is not in the ordinary course of business reinforces the inference that the transfer is an attempt to extinguish creditors' claims." Meanwhile, the Supreme Court of Arizona stated in a decision reported in the judgment: "That fact alone (i.e. that a note in case was purchased at a 33 percent discount) is sufficient to alert a prospective purchaser to a possible defense." While criticizing the Supreme Court of Arizona, Posner remarks in the jargon of Law and Economics: "Alone…it is conceivable that by use of this word the Supreme Court of Arizona intended to revolutionize the law of negotiable instruments, bore a large hole in negotiability, and thereby raise transaction costs in financial markets." The dictum of the court in Arizona is made away with a bold remark: "Judicial opinions are frequently drafted in haste, with imperfect foresight, and without due regard for the possibility that words or phrases or sentences may be taken out of context and treated as doctrines." The use of a law and economics interpretive device prevents here the classical decision that would quash the summary judgment issued by the lower court. It would probably remand the case for further proceedings to find out more about the material facts, namely whether the fifty percent discount was actually granted by the seller due to known or expected defenses. As a result, the right court decision is the one that leaves transaction costs in financial markets low, a contrary decision would be in Posner's terminology 'perverse'. This is an interesting conclusion as it primarily shows how an interpretive paradigm works in law. Here, a set of economical arguments borrowed from an economical school of thought is transformed into an ideology of law. Based on this ideology, legal concepts can be filled with content and cases solved in courts of law in a specific way.

4.3.8 Establishing interpretive rules

Sometimes, discursive practices in law lead to results that may be perceived as rational although they are mutually exclusive. The results reached in them regularly show that both parties advanced reasons that may equally appeal to a rationally argumenting audience. In such cases interpretive rules are established in discourses that provide guidelines for the professional decision making. These interpretive rules emerge – sometimes in an apparent contrast with their procedural structure – as linguistic constructs. As case reference we may use the court opinion City of Everett v. Estate of Oddmund Sumstad (95 Wn. 2d 853; 631; 1981 Wash. LEXIS 1139). The story is banal: A couple of business people attended an auction and purchased there a safe for $ 50. They were told by the auctioneer that the safe's inner compartment could not be opened because the key to it was missing. After the sale, the buyers brought the safe to a locksmith who opened the inner compartment and found $ 32,207 inside it. The seller claimed the money pretending not to have sold it together with the safe. The buyers insisted on the purchase arguing that they bought what was offered to them. Rationally, one will have to admit in seller's favor that it is not particularly probable to offer for sale an object including $ 32,000 for the price of $ 50. Yet, one will also have to admit that the seller did not make any reservations during the auction while knowing and even stressing the fact that the safe was offered for sale with a locked compartment. Thus, both positions appeal because they are based on rational arguments. Meanwhile, in litigation only one party can win. Therefore, rules will be established to enable a conclusive decision in a case where pure rationality does not help. This rule is termed in American law 'objective theory of contract'.

It imposes a view upon the transaction among the parties from the position of a third person, a 'reasonable observer' who impartially tries to determine the intentions of the parties. Here, he will presumably have observed that both parties wished to sell and to buy a determined object for a determined price. He will thus infer their intentions from factual circumstances. He will not enter into the discussion whether such a transaction economically makes sense for the seller. This is not the issue, because the observer functions within a legal discourse. There, his role is to determine – in the language of the private law – the circumstances of a valid sale of objects with unknown contents. He will reasonably be able to claim that objects with unknown contents may be validly sold when the parties are conscious that they engage in a sale that includes a moment of uncertainty and they accept this uncertainty. The determination of law is a product of the interpretive rule that linguistically enables to solve the rationality deadlock. The linguistic rule of interpretation that introduces the so-called objective theory does not change the rationality status of views advanced by the parties. Meanwhile, it enables the legal decision in litigation between them.

4.3.9 Soft interpretive guidelines

Interpretive guidelines, i.e. rules for interpretation can be of formal nature, for instance the Custom's Interpretive Guidelines regarding the application of the U.S. customs regulations. They can be apparently also informal; i.e. drafted linguistically in a form that suggests informality while being formal in principle. Fluidity characterizes such texts. An example may elucidate this claim: In 2002 the No Child Left Behind Act (NCLB) entered into force in the U.S. It has been characterized by educational authorities as a landmark in education reform and described by the then-President George W. Bush as "the cornerstone of my administration." A letter of the U.S. Secretary of Education, Rod Paige, to school teachers included some informal interpretive rules (emphasis added):

The Secretary of Education
Washington D.C., 20202
September 2002

Dear Colleague:

This year began on a *wonderful note for America's 50 million school children*. When President Bush signed the No Child Left Behind Act into law on January 8, 2002, *our nation embarked on a new era in how we educate our children* and how the federal government supports elementary and secondary education. This *historic reform* gives states and school districts unprecedented flexibility in how they spend their education dollars, *in return for* setting standards for student achievement and holding students and educators accountable for results. The No Child Left Behind Act also provides more options for parents so that their children can *get the best possible education*. It also invests in teaching practices that have been demonstrated to work. In short, it aims to foster an environment in which every child can learn and succeed. It is my pleasure to provide you with this desktop reference to the No Child Left Behind Act. It offers a clear and straightforward program-by-program look at the major reforms made by the new law. I hope you will find it useful *as you implement the law*. A more complete view of the law and a more comprehensive look at the regulations and other guidance that applies to the law is available at www.nclb.gov. I want to thank you for your efforts on behalf of our young people. I wish you *success in implementing* No Child Left Behind Act, for you and your colleagues are the stewards of our children's future.

This seemingly enthusiastic congratulation letter to teachers, which is kept in an informal and slightly patronizing style, fills communicational gaps with banalities (greetings, felicitations, prospects for future success, etc) is an interpretive guideline for the NCLB. It provides a perspective upon the act that is perceived in it as "wonderful and historic." It therefore must be implemented without debate; implementation is furthermore expected to be successful. It does not allow for questioning of the principle that investment in education is coupled with a formal return mechanism. It does not step back from assuming that the addressees did not fulfill their obligations as only measures under the NCLB can provide the children the best possible education. Overall, the letter is an instruction to schools to present the NCLB in the public sphere as a success story.

4.3.10 Who can interpret?

The common law doctrine posits that the judge's task is to interpret the law. This interpreting of law comes close to the notion of application of law in the Continental European legal doctrine. In the American doctrine, the meaning of 'interpretation of law' is linked to the notion of the separation of powers. It goes like that: The U.S. Constitution establishes the Congress that makes laws. It also establishes the structure of government with the President on its top who enforces the law. Finally, it creates the federal judiciary that has the task to interpret law. The interpretation of law that is construed in this way does not prevent non-judges to express their views about the content of law. They will not be able to do it in other way than through the interpretation of statutes and precedents. Both therefore interpret law, with the difference that judges also apply law that they interpret in a valid way and non-judges do not have such privileges. The privileges of judges are therefore institutional, not qualitative and they concern the valid application of law in a process which ends with a judgment that will be enforced. The interpretation of law that is understood as a process of identification of the meaning of law is a general operation in law that is unavoidably undertaken even by a newspaper reader who reads a report about a criminal trial. In order to grasp the legal content of the report he has to interpret the law, although he usually will be doing it very summarily. Likewise, the creative element in the legal interpretation is present in the professional and in the non-professional interpretation. To understand the 'meaning of law' wants to say to create law with linguistic means towards the background of a framework of reference that includes beliefs and commitments (cf. Searle 2006). The previous paragraph on Law and Economics as an interpretive paradigm in law illustrates such a procedure. Another, more contemporary example may illustrate the procedure even better because it concerns the general interpretive paradigm. When the question arises as to the right of the U.S. citizens to bear arms, the way of finding an answer to it will be determined by the hierarchy of legal sources that functions as a principle of textual organization of law. The search for law begins with the U.S. Constitution that in its Amendment II proclaims: "A well-regulated militia being necessary to the security of a free State, the right of the people to keep and bear arms shall not be infringed." One may read in isolation from the context: "the right of the people to keep and bear arms shall not be infringed" as this formulation is evidently included in the text. Meanwhile, is this a convincing answer to the question? The isolated formulation is a part of a sentence that concerns the right of the states to entertain the militia in order to be able to sustain their rights in the union, should this action become necessary. This is an interpretation without judges. The U.S. Supreme Court created 2008 landmark law around this question in its decision District of Columbia v. Heller (128 S. Ct. 2783). The court, as so often, committed itself to an interpretive device: "In interpreting this text, we are guided by the principle that the Constitution was written to be understood by the voters; its words and phrases were used in their normal and ordinary as distinguished from technical meaning…Normal meaning may of course include an idiomatic meaning, but it excludes secret or technical meanings that would not have been known to ordinary citizens in the founding generation." It also rendered the meaning alternatives: "The two sides in this case have set out very different interpretations of the Amendment. Petitioners and today's dissenting Justices believe that it protects only the right to possess and carry a firearm in connection with militia services…Respondent argues that it protects an individual right to possess a firearm unconnected with service in militia, and to use that arm for traditionally lawful purposes, such as self-defense within the home." The court enters into the legal-linguistic analysis of the Amendment: "The Second Amendment is naturally divided in two parts: its prefatory clause and its operative clause. The former does not limit the latter grammatically, but rather announces a purpose. The Amendment could be rephrased: "Because a well regulated Militia is necessary to the security of the free State, the right of the people to keep and bear Arms shall not be infringed." For this reformulation the court referred to the 'Linguists' Brief', an expert opinion, that was provided to the court by professors of English and Linguistics. The majority, represented by Justice Scalia, did not take these linguistic comments seriously and remarked sarcastically about academic attempts to come to terms with meaning: "A purposive qualifying phrase that contradicts the word or phrase it modifies is unknown this side of the looking glass (except, apparently, in some courses on Linguistics)." Whatever interpretive proposition that contradicts the majority opinion is qualified as "a mistake" or "a faulty analysis." Only essentialist beliefs about semantics can cause such an apodictic view upon the meaning of the phrase. They are visible in the whole majority opinion and are textually characterized by an attempt at utmost precision in the sense cherished by legal positivists. Already the initial phrase: "We consider whether a District of Columbia prohibition on the possession of usable handguns in the home violates the Second Amendment to the Constitution." The phrase stresses the circumstance that the weapon in question is 'usable' although this is not especially problematic as the issue of having historical arms at home that cannot be used any more is definitely not the point in case. Furthermore, while analyzing the phrase the court assumes that: "Logic demands that there be a link between the stated purpose and the command." This may even be the case generally as meaningful speech would require such a link. The phrase in question could however equally well be an anacoluthon and then only linguistic pragmatics and not logic would be instrumental in its interpretation. The majority opinion is unable to state why it actually arrives at the result that it endorses as American constitutional law. A linguistic analysis of the II Amendment in isolation from the law cannot render any unequivocal results. Therefore, only a legal-linguistic interpretation such as the Dworkinian creative interpretation could help the court in its attempt at understanding a provision in the U.S. Constitution that should make sense in society even two hundred years after it has been enacted.

4.4 Meta-interpretive reflections

The above remarks on interpretation make clear that interpretation depends on a set of criteria that steer our observation of and reflection upon social reality. Different sets of interpretive criteria lead to different interpretive results. Interpretive criteria emerge in the process of distinguishing that is aim-oriented. With this in mind, J.L. Austin (1975: 11) remarked in a footnote concerning utterances and acts of speech: "We deliberately avoid distinguishing these, precisely because the distinction is not in point." Next to these problems the legal-linguistic interpretation as a theoretical problem includes also some interpretive mechanisms that are meta-interpretive. Such linguistic mechanisms, as for instance re-interpretation, over-interpretation, and denial of interpretation illustrate the way in which the act of interpretation is reflected upon in the interpretation itself. For legal interpretation also socio-linguistic mechanisms with an axiological component are important because they show how people make choices in strategic situations. In terms of ideology, that stresses axiological parameters in legal decision making processes, law is also perceived as an "official self-interpretation of a social group" (cf. Berger 1963: 54; Fairclough 1992). Furthermore, critics of some interpretive approaches call occasionally adversary ways of seeing meaning in texts 'eccentric interpretation'. Eccentric interpretations break with monophony that is established mostly by the affirmative or apodictic (i.e. dominant) discourse. They correspond largely with the blame related to unwelcome propositions in legal argumentation that are also framed as 'eccentric'. After all, "true understanding is a matter of viewpoint that can change in processes of rationalization" (Berger 1963: 73).

4.4.1 Re-interpretation

Interpreted law is in the course of its application frequently re-interpreted. The legal-linguistic method used there is called in the common law tradition 'overruling'. Court opinions such as Plessy v. Fergusson and Brown v. Board of Education are classical examples of the re-interpretation procedure. Both cases belong to the American landmark law (cf. Connell 2010: 946). The first of them, shortly called Plessy was decided in 1896. It concerned a complaint based on the allegation that the Fourteenth Amendment of the U.S. Constitution is violated when railways services can only be used on the basis of racial segregation even if other conditions of use might be perceived as equal. The U.S. Supreme Court based his decision on the doctrine of 'separate but equal' and held that no constitutional violation takes place under such circumstances. Later, in 1954 the same court had to decide in Brown the constitutionality of racially segregated schools that could have been perceived as being otherwise equal. The court ruled that racial segregation in schools violates the Fourteenth Amendment even if the premises in question might be technically perceived as equal. While overruling Plessy in 1954 the U.S. Supreme Court stated: "We cannot turn the clock back to 1886 when the Amendment was adopted, or even to 1896 when Plessy v. Fergusson was written. Today, education is perhaps the most important function of state and local governments…We conclude that in the field of public education the doctrine of 'separate but equal' has no place. Separate educational institutions are inherently unequal. Therefore, we hold that the plaintiffs and others similarly situated for whom actions have been brought are, by reason of the segregation complained of, deprived of the equal protection of the laws guaranteed by the Fourteenth Amendment." Thus, the overruling as a method is rooted in arguments that refer to the social evolution: times have changed and therefore the legal interpretation of a constitutional or other rule has to be adjusted to the new social status quo. The 'overruling' concerns the re-interpretation that is in line with the traditional legal methodology. It is not sufficiently explicit in use of arguments and it makes abundantly use of general arguments such as the above. Law can be also re-interpreted in terms of other approaches, such as Law and Economics or Critical Legal Studies. 'Distinguishing' is one more traditional legal-linguistic method of doctrinal non-alignment. A judge who does not wish to follow a precedent may describe differences between his case and the precedent and thus methodically avoid the application of the precedent. The avoidance method is traditionally perceived as justified in the common law methodology provided the judge explicitly makes use of it. The judge cannot simply skip the precedent that appears unsuitable in his eyes without mentioning its existence in his decision. There is, so to say, no implicit 'distinguishing'.

4.4.2 Overinterpretation

In the past, South African immigration authorities exposed foreign visitors to a form where a rubric was entitled 'race'. The British broadcaster and poet, John Arlott, wrote 'human' in the rubric. He overinterpreted the rubric's meaning in pragmatic terms. Furthermore, Mao Zedong's widow, Jiang Qing, during the trial of the so-called Gang of Four in 1980 answered the prosecutor's question whether she admits to have participated in a conspiracy: "I do not know." The prosecutor let to be entered in the trial's record: "She denies to have participated in the conspiracy." Meanwhile, the question whether this has been the sense of her words remains a pragmatic puzzle. An example of overinterpretation is also the already mentioned decision District of Columbia v. Heller (cf. 4.3.10). In the decision, the court entered into a meticulous analysis of every word in the II Amendment in the hope that the lexicological analysis will finally elucidate the meaning of the whole phrase in question. This is however a vain hope because meaning of an utterance is not an aggregate of isolated semantic units. Linguistic pragmatics teaches a lesson about such attempts at understanding language as an artificial collection of isolated words. In this sense the Supreme Court's opinion represents even linguistic under-interpretation as it underestimates the interpretive potential in speech acts. Yet, in its meticulous attempt at tracing the meaning in the II Amendment it overinterprets it in that it over-stretches its semantics (cf. Eco 1990, 2004). In language, acts of interpretation have to correspond methodologically with acts of linguistic production. In the sense of this interpretive rule, it would be deficient to scrutinize every word and punctuation in a memo that has been drafted by the writer in utmost haste. While paying too much attention to details we could in this case easily overstretch its meaning. And contrariwise, when an utterance is the result of scrupulous pondering and particularly thorough drafting equal effort should be spent on its interpretation. The wording of the II Amendment does not signal any particular commitment of its drafters to utmost precision in its expression. Rather the contrary seems to be the case and this circumstance also explains why it leads today to interpretive controversy.

4.4.3 Denial of interpretation

Nowadays, only some positivist conceptions of law may manifest the inclination towards denying or minimizing the importance of interpretation in law. Meanwhile, the anti-interpretive attitude towards language has long roots that reach until myths and beliefs of pre-scientific times. Language in this pre-rational period is reduced to magical formulas. The Greek Acontius-myth that has been described by Ovid in his *Heroides* 20, 21 illustrates such use of language. Acontius in his attempt to gain the love of Cydippe made use of a linguistic trick. He threw at Cydippe, who was sitting in the temple of Diana, an apple on which he had written: I swear by the sanctuary of Diana to marry Acontius. Cydippe unaware of the trap read aloud the words, and threw the apple away. Meanwhile, the goddess had heard her alleged vow. Due to this fact Cydippe ultimately had to marry Acontius although she had been already promised to another man. In a rational approach to language such 'vows' as the one made by Cydippe simply do not count as vows because they are made without the intention to be bound and this lack of intention is also manifest to others. Yet, the conviction that declarations can become binding even when the intention not to be bound is evident did not disappear totally from legal discourses. Yan Huang (2007: 120) refers to a legal case from Pakistan that concerned a soap opera actor and his wife who in a TV film also played the role of his wife. In the film the actor expressed the traditional Muslim formula for divorce – called in Arabic 'talaq' for 'I divorce you' – three times as prescribed by Muslim law. An ulema decree in matters Usman Peerzada and his wife Samina has been subsequently issued saying that a binding and irrevocable divorce had taken place between the spouses due to the formal recitation of the formula. In their decision the ulema disregarded as irrelevant the context of use of the formula that was well known to them and referred to the formal use of the formula as prescribed by the prophet. The case is unique in the sense that it denies the necessity of interpretation of linguistic utterances. For the ulema the language means what it means; it has its fixed inherent meaning that leads to consequences in the outer world through the mere utterance of words. While such a proceeding definitely strengthens speakers' awareness about the use of language, it is clearly inadapted as a semantic rule of interpretation because it is contrary to the very notion of language. Language, after all, is not a thing like a piece of driftwood that is simply there. Theoretically, the ulema adhere to a pre-positivistic view about language use in law because they deny any necessity to interpret utterances. Supposed further that the ulema would more formalistically, yet also more rationally, refer to the use of language in social sphere where the evidence character of performative speech acts would triumph over speaker's intention, no other result would follow. It is imaginable that in the social sphere the declarative and performative character of a speech act may require to adopt the third party perspective in viewing it. The divorce formula, when validly expressed, cannot be taken back by mutual consent of the parties; society that witnesses this process has also a word to say about the effectiveness of legally relevant speech. Also the woman involved has a right to know whether she is legally and finally divorced or not. Meanwhile, the formula expressed in a film that in terms of semiotics constitutes a secondary sign system in relation to real family life, is clearly identifiable as such and not as a fragment of real family life where real law applies. This holds especially true when viewed from the position of a third party that in this case is a TV spectator. Hence, interpretation remains unavoidable in any case and denying the right to interpret a socially and legally relevant statement goes against the spirit of law and its language.

4.5 Formalism in interpretation

Interpretation, as said, has been perceived as a risky enterprise. In terms of semiotics, there is no reason to fear interpretation as it is a natural process in which we try to understand the world. Meanwhile, already at the beginning of the development of law formal if not formalistic procedures emerged that apparently should protect against an all too inventive interpretation. On its face, formalism is a historical procedure that is perceived nowadays as overcome. The development of attitudes towards formalism has been characterized by Justice B. Cardozo in his opinion Wood v. Duff-Gordon (1917) with following, often quoted words: "The law has outgrown its primitive stage of formalism when the precise word was the sovereign talisman, and every slip was fatal. It takes a broader view today. A promise may be lacking, and yet the whole writing may be 'instinct with an obligation', imperfectly expressed." In this quote, Cardozo refers to the ancient Roman formulae that had to be pronounced by parties without fault in a court procedure. Though, formalism is not fully overcome today. An example of its vivacity is the Presidential oath, taken twice by U.S. President Barack Obama in 2009. The known background of the story witnessed by billions of TV-viewers had been an incorrectly recited presidential oath by the U.S. Supreme Court Chief Justice, John G. Roberts. The text of the Presidential oath is laid down in Article II of the U.S. Constitution: "I do solemnly swear (or affirm) that I will faithfully execute the Office of the President of the United States, and will to the best of my Ability, preserve, protect and defend the Constitution of the United States." Chief Justice Roberts, whose task was to pronounce the words of the oath, that are to be repeated by the incumbent President, instead of saying "that I will faithfully execute the office of the President of the United States," said 'faithfully' after 'President of the United States'. While repeating the oath, Obama stopped after the word 'execute' to give Roberts the chance to pronounce the text again and correctly. Yet, the Chief Justice, while repeating the text in correct order omitted the word 'execute'. After the public ceremony the White House deemed the oath validly sworn. Nevertheless, it has been repeated the following day in the White House Map Room. One might ask for rational reasons for this new ceremony. One might be equally interested in irrational motives that stand behind the decision to repeat the oath. While asked by the media why the oath swearing procedure has been repeated, President Obama answered "because it was so much fun." The second oath was not sworn on the Lincoln-Bible as the first had been, yet it had been perceived as valid nonetheless. The White House declared after the first ceremony, still on the inauguration day, that the oath will be sworn again "just to be sure." In the background of the event there were also conspiracy-theories, such as the allegation that Roberts, who belongs to a political party opposing Obama's Democrats, caused the confusion on purpose and allegations by Obama's opponents that he has not been properly sworn as President. Media (so e.g. *The Times* June 8, 2009) mentioned in this context that Obama (then a Senator) voted against the nomination of J.G. Roberts to the Supreme Court. Linguistic misgivings such as Roberts addressing Obama as 'Senator', instead of 'President' do not influence the validity of the ceremony either. Even if the constitution is perfectly ambiguous at this point as it says with regard to the incumbent: "Before he enter on the execution of his Office, he shall take the following Oath or Affirmation"-, as it does not say 'the President shall', but 'he shall', and the next antecedent to 'he' is the word 'President' in the paragraph above. There is no backing in the U.S. constitutional law for the assertion that syntactic changes introduced into a text that do not change the semantics of the utterance would matter in terms of law. Even if one would assume, as some do, that the split infinitive 'to faithfully execute' should be replaced by 'to execute faithfully', the utterance is still unambiguous for an English speaker. Finally, the context of the event clearly proves that the future President is going to swear an oath as required by Article II of the U.S. Constitution. The pragmatics of the oath heals the possible syntactic or semantic shortcomings of the procedure. The second oath was not necessary, and therefore the second ceremony should not have taken place, be it only out of formal respect for the law. Meanwhile, in the U.S. history, the Presidential oath has been sworn twice by Presidents Chester Arthur (1881) and Calvin Coolidge (1923) for similar reasons. Also 2013, U.S. President B. Obama has been sworn twice due to constitutional scheduling that helped to avoid the known problems with the repeating of the oath formula. Referring to the oath taking ceremony Obama said according to the *Times of India* of January 20, 2013: "I will be honored to again stand on the Inaugural platform and take part in this important American tradition." It remains unclear whether the split infinitive has been used purposefully in the sentence.

When contrasted with Cardozo's optimistic assessment of formalism in modern law, the Obama-case is revealing as it shows the confusion in apparently unreflected approaches to law. The effect of all this is disappointing; the mixture of magic, positivism and utilitarianism produces law that is not really law any more. Therefore, the case is also deceptive as it transfers the impression that there is no law. Yet, the law that has been overlooked is a complex social phenomenon that cannot be discarded so easily. The other thing is to deny that it has content. To deny that law displays contents is a dangerous attitude towards this complex phenomenon. Within the pragmatic approach to legal language, contents of law appear in contexts. The Presidential Oath is a typical example of such procedures. For instance, also the Constitution of India includes the expression "faithfully execute the office of the President" in its Art. 60: "Every President and every person acting as President or discharging the functions of the President shall, before entering upon his office, make and subscribe in the presence of the Chief Justice of India or, in his absence, the senior-most Judge of the Supreme Court available, an oath or affirmation in the following form, that is to say – "I, A.B., do swear in the name of God (solemnly affirm) that I will faithfully execute the office of the President (or discharge the function of President) of India and will to the best of my ability preserve, protect and defend the Constitution and the law and that I will devote myself to the service and well-being of the people of India." This sample displays textual formalism, a preference for using already texted and institutionally approved formulations. As to their contents, both formulas are poor on verifiable matter and rather symbolic. By way of contrast, the Oath of Citizenship that foreign nationals swear when granted U.S. citizenship during their swearing-in ceremony is detailed and overly ambitious: "I hereby declare, on oath, that I absolutely and entirely renounce and abjure all allegiance and fidelity to any foreign prince, potentate, state, or sovereignty of whom or which I have heretofore been a subject or citizen; that I will support and defend the Constitution and laws of the United States of America against all enemies, foreign and domestic; that I will bear true faith and allegiance to the same; that I will bear arms on behalf of the United States when required by law; that I will perform non-combatant service in the Armed Forces of the United States when required by the law; that I will perform work of national importance under civilian direction when required by the law; and that I take this obligation freely without any mental reservation or purpose of evasion; so help me God. In acknowledgment whereof I have hereunto affixed my signature." The oath includes a commitment that it had been taken 'freely without any mental reservation or purpose of evasion'. Let us imagine the impossible, namely that someone swears the oath in order to become U.S. citizen and to enjoy all privileges that are connected with this legal status, yet without paying much attention to the lofty declaration he just made. What kind of legal consequences would follow from such unwishful action? Would his mental reservation free him from tedious duties designed in the oath? In fact, law may overburden people with expectations that they regularly are not able to match to.

As has been seen, the oath as a speech act is not well integrated into legal-linguistic practices. The reason for its marginal importance in law seems to be that it originates in non-legal social practices and is better suited there. It may have had a federatory role to play as is the case with some religious oaths or the Hippocratic Oath that is sworn by physicians. The Hippocratic Oath is worthwhile a closer scrutiny. It says: "I swear by Apollo the physician, and Aesculapius, and

Health, and All-heal, and all the gods and goddesses, that, according to my ability and judgment, I will keep this Oath and this stipulation – to reckon him who taught me this Art equally dear to me as my parents, to share my substance with him, and relieve his necessities if required; to look upon his offspring, in the same footing, as my own brothers, and to teach them this art, if they shall wish to learn it, without fee or stipulation; and that by precept, lecture, and every other mode of instruction, I will impart a knowledge of the Art to my own sons, and those of my teachers, and to disciples bound by a stipulation and oath according to the law of medicine, but to none others. I will follow that system of regimen which, according to my ability and judgment, I consider for the benefit of my patients, and abstain from whatever is deleterious and mischievous. I will give no deadly medicine to any one if asked, nor suggest any such counsel; and in like moment I will not give to a woman a pessary to produce abortion. With purity and with holiness I will pass my life and practice my Art. I will not cut persons laboring under the stone, but will leave this to be done by men who are practitioners of this work. Into whatever houses I enter, I will go into them for the benefit of the sick, and will abstain from every voluntary act of mischief and corruption; and, further from the seduction of females and males, or freemen and slaves. Whatever, in connection with my professional practice or not, in connection with it, I see or hear, in the life of men, which ought not to be spoken of abroad, I will not divulge, as reckoning that all such should be kept secret. While I continue to keep this Oath unviolated, may it be granted to me to enjoy life and the practice of the art, respected by all men, in all times! But should I trespass and violate this Oath, may the reverse be my lot!" Scholars are not unanimous about the authorship of the oath. Meanwhile, the strategy behind the practice of swearing it is evident. The oath introduces an ethical element into the medical art that has been previously perceived as a simple technique. By so doing, the medical activity is transformed into a noble profession with a precise code of conduct. The rules set in the oath have often only a historical significance today and they were modified and adapted to modern exercise of the medical profession. These transformations notwithstanding, its main goal is the establishing of a corporate body, i.e. a guild, for the medical profession. Insofar, the oath as a discursive device has been very efficient because the bodies corporate that represent the medical profession exist until today. It is probable that the oath as a practice has nowadays a role that comes close to the Presidential Oath and that it approaches the symbolical. Rationalization practices in contemporary societies make such linguistic devices obsolete. This holds true especially for the Hippocratic Oath that combines in one text aspects of professional practice that are today perceived as separate. Textually, the speech act of swearing an oath oscillates between religious and ethical formulas as well as contractual stipulations. Furthermore, sanctions of non-legal nature are included in the final part of the text. Today, such an oath is simply unenforceable. This appears also to be the fate of most symbolic acts in law. In terms of law, an oath has a limited value, especially due to the inherent distrust to declarations made in legal institutions. Historically, the oath of allegiance may have had some legal importance, yet it seems that it had been used more as a political rather than as a legal device. For instance, the English king James I wrote 1609 a treatise about the importance of the oath *An Apologie for the Oath of Allegiance*. Meanwhile, the allegiance to sovereigns has been sworn as often as it has been broken. A reflex of the oath of allegiance is the act of abjuration. A famous act of abjuration has been declared 1633 by Galileo Galilei who was forced by the Catholic Church to recant his exposition of the Copernican view of the solar system. G.F.W. Hegel's English translation of his *Philosophy of Right* includes also the English language text of this abjuration: "I, Galileo, appearing in person before this court in my seventieth year, kneeling, and with my eyes on the holy Gospels which I hold in my hands, abjure, damn, and execrate with my whole heart and true belief the absurd, false, and heretical doctrine of the motion of the earth…" An act of abjuration that is sworn against one's true belief is an act of exercise of power, in casu political submission. The oath is therefore an ineffective transplant in law and it represents a burdensome and formalistic practice within the multilayered corpus of legal signs.

4.5.1 Sacrifice to the dead letter of law

Formalism as shown in the above examples cultivates the dead letter of law. Its use in the legal interpretation regularly leads to 'worse law'. Particularly instructive are cases of application of law that end up in blatant injustice. From the perspective of deciding judges they reflect the necessity to apply law 'as it is'. Judges also regularly reflect upon such results that are not acceptable from a more humane point of view. Yet, they insist on their duty to apply law and nothing more. To illustrate, the U.S. Supreme Court decided in Kauwaauhau v. Geiger (523 U.S. 57, 1998) that debt arising from medical malpractice was dischargeable in bankruptcy under 11 USCS 523 (a) (6). In this case, the plaintiff lost her right leg until knee due to negligent treatment by a physician. She won her medical malpractice suit against the physician who subsequently declared bankruptcy and contended that the claim based on his negligent conduct is discharged through his bankruptcy. The physician did not have any malpractice insurance; his salary at his new working place could not be seized by the plaintiff because of the

Supreme Court decision that affirmed the possibility of discharge in bankruptcy for negligent action of physicians. More specifically, Section 523 (a)(6) of the U.S. Bankruptcy Code provides: (a) A discharge under Section 727, 1141, 1228 (a), 1228(b), or 1328(b) of this title does not discharge an individual debtor from any debt— (6)for willful and malicious injury by debtor to another entity or to the property of another entity. The court examined the exception made in the Bankruptcy Code for 'willful and malicious injury' and found that negligent action is not encompassed by this formulation. To this effect it scrutinized even the *Black's Law Dictionary* where the word 'willful' is defined as 'voluntary' or 'intentional'. It also referred to legislative reports where the word 'willful' is defined as 'deliberate or intentional'. It entered into a syntactic analysis stating that "(T)he word "willful" in (a)(6) modifies the word "injury," indicating that nondischargeability takes a deliberate or intentional injury, not merely a deliberate or intentional act that leads to injury. Had Congress meant to exempt debts resulting from unintentionally inflicted injuries, it might have mentioned it instead of referring to "willful acts that cause injury." Or, Congress might have selected an additional word or words, i.e., "reckless" or "negligent," to modify "injury." The court did not ask whether the Congress intended to protect physicians such as the defendant from suits by their patients. It would then have come to a different result. Instead, the court defensively remarked: "Finally the Kawaauhaus maintain that, as a policy matter, malpractice judgments should be excepted from discharge, at least when the debtor acted recklessly or carried no malpractice insurance. Congress, of course, may so decide. But unless and until Congress makes such a decision, we must follow the current direction § 523 (a)(6) provides." Meanwhile, in the court decision Water, Waste and Land, Inc. dba Westec v. Lanham (955 R2d 997 1998) the Supreme Court of Colorado used the hypothetical legislative intent as an interpretive strategy. The court stated: "…We are not persuaded that the statute can bear such an interpretation. Such a construction exaggerates the plain meaning of the language in the statute. This broad interpretation would be an invitation to fraud, because it would leave the agent of a limited liability company free to mislead third parties into the belief that the agent would bear personal financial responsibility under any contract, when in fact, recovery would be limited to the assets of a limited liability company not known to the third party at the time the contract was made. This construction would open the door to sharp practices and outright fraud. We may presume that in adopting section 7-80-208 the General Assembly did not intend to create a safe harbor for deceit." The American law, as one can see from the decision, allows the courts to 'presume' the legislative intent in order to prevent blatant abuse of legal-interpretive devices. Yet, the U.S. Supreme Court did not use this argumentative mechanism to prevent the manipulation of the law by the medical doctor thus 'inviting him to continue fraudulous practice' and 'creating a safe harbor for deceit' in the sense of the argument developed in the Colorado decision. Formalism as a legal-interpretive device seems to be used in many court decisions as a mechanism of argumentative selection. The doctrinal essence of the formalistic argumentation in law is legalism. Legalism as a doctrine of application of law declares that courts in their decisions have to apply law and nothing more. It perceives this form of legal application as possible because it also presumes that legal rules are unequivocal or that they can be disambiguated to the point that makes them appear as unequivocal. Furthermore, it posits that every legal problem has only one right solution. Formalistic and legalistic arguments will be used in situations where a contrary solution to the one envisaged by the court is thinkable in terms of law, yet the court wishes to avoid it. The court will then stress that it is bound by the law in force that for the purpose of the case will be provided an unequivocal content that it, as a rule, cannot have. The role of the legal-linguistic research is to make clear that courts used interpretive mechanisms that are based on formalistic and legalistic arguments. The legal-linguistic research has furthermore the task to develop and to support interpretive mechanisms that oppose formalistic and legalistic arguments and the mechanistic application of law in the sense criticized already by B. Cardozo (1924).

4.5.2 Interpretive pragmatism in action

One of the consequences of the classical pragmatism and especially its theory of interpretation is the innovative step undertaken there towards taking into account of consequences of an action rather than the isolated semantics of utterances (Kaag 2009: 65). This approach is visible for instance in the above example that concerns Law and Economics. The appropriate meaning of an interpreted concept depends on the consequences of its use under given circumstances. In legal interpretation, this approach is rarely made explicit. Cases show how it could be made prolific in the analysis of legal notions. In a decision from 1992 by the Court of Appeal for Florida, Wells Fargo Credit Corporation v. Martin (650 So. 2d. 531, Web 1992 Fla. App. Lexis 9927) the notion of unilateral mistake has been analyzed without considering its consequences. As to the particularities of the case, Wells Fargo Credit Corp. obtained a judgment of foreclosure on a house owned by Mr. and Mrs. Clevenger. The total indebtedness stated in the judgment was $ 207,141. During the foreclosure sale that followed Wells Fargo was represented by a paralegal, who had attended more than 1,000 similar sales.

Wells Fargo's handwritten instruction sheet informed the paralegal to make one bid at $ 115,000, the tax-appraised value of the property. Because the first "1" in the number was close to the dollar sign "$", the paralegal misread the bid instruction as $ 15,000 and opened the bidding at that amount. Mr. Martin, who was attending his first judicial sale, bid $ 20,000. The county clerk gave ample time for another bid and then announced: "$20,000 going once, $20,000 going twice, sold to Harley Martin..." The paralegal screamed: "Stop, sorry I made a mistake!" Meanwhile, the certificate of sale was issued to Mr. Martin. Wells Fargo requested the court to set aside the judicial sale based on its unilateral mistake. This has not been done as the court burdened upon Wells Fargo the risk of a situation that it had controlled and perceived the mistake as avoidable. In the consequence, Mr. Martin obtained valuable real property for a grossly inadequate price. One may furthermore assume that he was aware of the erroneous offer made by the paralegal. He profited from the formalistic approach that the court of appeals has taken towards interpretation of action that in this case is based on the argument of avoidability. The court, however, did not analyze the possibility of an easy and convincing proof of the mistake by Wells Fargo and finally enriched the bidder in the name of a doubtful theory of interpretation. As a solution in terms of pragmatism one could think about an approximation of the new price which would take into account the specific situation and come more closely to the reality of the market price. More conservatively, the law permits also the rescission of some contracts concluded by mistake. Yet, such a decision could be deemed equally formalistic as the criticized court decision.

4.5.3 Judicial interpretive reference

Judges have also the task to render parties' and other participants' statements and opinions in their judgments. They also have to interpret them in the limits of the law, which means that they have to avoid the impression that they are biased towards one of the parties. In a U.S. Supreme Court decision Campbell v. Acuff-Rose Music, Inc. (510 U.S. 569, 114 S.Ct. 1164) from 1994 Justice Souter describes the impression that the court obtained from the comparison of two texts, the original lyrics of the song "Oh, Pretty Woman" composed in 1964 by R. Orbison and a parody of this song prepared by a rap music group 2 Live Crew. The judge wrote about the parody: "The words of 2 Live Crew's song then so quickly degenerate into a play on words, substituting predictable lyrics with shocking ones that derisively demonstrate how bland and banal the Orbison song seems to them." After having compared both texts, the judge describes the derived text as a speech act of parody and identifies in it a tendency to perceive the original lyrics as "bland and banal" in the perspective of the group. He also marks the distance from this opinion because the court has to remain neutral towards the quality of the text. Subsequently, the judge remarks: "The later words can be taken as a comment on the naiveté of the original of an earlier day, as a rejection of its sentiment that ignores the ugliness of street life and the debasement that it signifies." The framing strategy that shall guarantee the neutrality of interpretation is formally successful. The provisos "seems to them" and "can be taken as" mark the borderline between the perception of the court and the parodists' intention. Meanwhile, how should the court have found out that the original song may seem 'blank and banal' without having had this impression itself?

4.5.4 Fluidity and vagueness

Semiotical processes engendered not only the formalist approach to interpretation of legal signs. They brought also the contrary phenomena into legal existence. They appeared in the dress of modernity. Modernity brings along vagueness of rules that need to be learned and mastered in order to get by in modern society (Bauman 2004: 14). Fluidity of rules that modernity engenders when it "compulsively and addictively" (Bauman 2004: 30) strives to design new rules has definitely not diminished in post-modern times. Because the new rules that it compulsively and addictively engenders have no precise ends, they are constructed as elusive and delusive abstractions. Order building in modern times is not neutral and – at least according to Bauman (2004) – it is not a positive phenomenon as its first victims are the outcasts, those who do not fit into the new order and who are not needed. Order is therefore a dangerous phenomenon in law, as it may cause more damage than it brings advantages. Fluid and vague rules may provide some playground for those better adapted; yet there always will be outcasts. Modernity and its post-modern critics were not able to propose a framework for social and legal rules that would integrate society. Fluid borders of the legal discourse correspond with the fluid borders of the ordinary discourse. This discourse regularly integrates legal language or language of the public sphere. In a novel written along the principles of creative writing, *This is where I leave you*, published by Jonathan Tropper in 2009, two citations from the legal or neighboring language are used in contexts related to law. For instance, the protagonist who is facing a divorce reflects upon the ground of his divorce in striking terms: "Adultery, like any other crime, generates evidence as an inevitable by-product, like plants and oxygen or humans…" His main qualification of adultery and the analogy that follows are legal in terms of language and reasoning. This is the more surprising as a professional of law would not go that far because adultery is rarely perceived as a crime nowadays although it remains 'listed' as a criminal act in twenty-three U.S. states. In most of these states, adultery is a misdemeanor. In some other states, such as Idaho, Massachusetts, Michigan, Oklahoma, and Wisconsin, adultery is a felony, yet it is rarely prosecuted. Another personage of *This is where I leave you* refers to the ground for the divorce as: "Apparently, there was a third party involved..." while having in mind, ironically, the adultery on the part of the protagonist's wife. There is a lot of legal language in a context of the divorce that is dealt within *This is where I leave you* as an individual and not a legal problem. This circumstance does not prevent the writer from using vocabulary that belongs to the legal language. The topic, i.e. the approaching divorce procedure causes linguistic associations that include the use of legal language without any legal relevance. However, relevance is fundamental to legal texts because their social status depends on recipients' attitude to take them seriously. Therefore, the increase in fluidity and vagueness in legal texts may cause losses in the social standing of these texts. Legal discourses do not necessarily reflect this regularity of language use in law.

4.5.5 Ambivalence in legal language

Borders between ordinary and special linguistic registers seem therefore to be as fluid as are discourses that emerge around them. Ambivalence and vagueness are regularly distinguished in the legal-linguistic research (Giannoni 2010; Tiersma 2005). This is unproblematic as long as both are perceived as features of linguistic indeterminacy. Is this not the case, then the argument becomes easily circular. When it is claimed that legal language should be maximally determinate and precise towards the background of its unavoidable linguistic indeterminacy, then the legal language ends in deadlock. With this problem in mind, Cao (2004: 116) stressed constructive ambiguity in law and also distinguished between linguistic indeterminacy and legal indeterminacy. Also traditional aloofness in rendering facts or stating the law in court decisions is linguistically ambivalent to the fact that a case is solved to the detriment of one party and that in penal cases consequences for the defendant may be enormous. Medicine seems to use the same strategies of avoiding emotions in situations where the human fate is decided. This type of strategic speech marks the social status distinctively and judges seem to insist on marking their social status in judgments. Distance and stressing alleged objectivity of legal judgments that 'are as they are because law is as it is' are structuring features of judgments as text types. Textual exceptions from the rule can be found; yet, they – as so often – confirm the rule rather than contradict it. Meanwhile, in cases where judges express their personal understanding for the losing party, the idea about a possible reversal of law is never mentioned. Its underlying social mechanism is compliance with the judgment that is in all cases unquestionable for the judges.

4.6 Legal discourse and legal communication

The above remarks signal a narrow relation between the legal discourse and the legal communication. The legal discourse represents the acts of legal communication (cf. Goodrich 1987; Mattila 2013: 41). It embraces in a structured way messages that were communicated in legally relevant situations. Traditionally, specific aspects of the legal communication have been dealt within the legal rhetoric (Galdia 2009: 157). Subsequently, the discovery of broader textual structures such as legal texts and legal discourses shifted the interest in this domain towards explicitly communicational conceptions. Therefore, contemporary legal communication as research object is rooted either in the broad conception of the legal text and its components or in the parallel broad conception of the legal discourse with its constitutive elements that are the subject of this book. For instance, Mattila (2013: 41–85) discusses many such discourses under the headline of 'functions of legal language'. On the other side, in logically founded approaches to legal discourses the main stress is set upon the juridical reasoning. Language in its broader setting is analyzed there in order to infer the laws of juridical reasoning from it. This approach to legal discourses is typical of the mainstream legal theory. In linguistically founded approaches the legal discourse is the most complex structure constituted of the legal language. It is approached from the perspective of its communicative function. In general linguistics, communication is since the work of Roman Jakobson perceived as the main linguistic function (cf. Mounin 1968: 80). Legal linguists may therefore rely on it when approaching legal language. In legal language it cannot happen that a message is there, yet it lacks communicative value. Legally relevant texts are always interpretable in terms of communication because an element of intention is always included in them, be it only in the negative. This happens in semantically evasive or purposefully imprecise legal texts that are typical of the modern state under the rule of law (Engberg 2007: 76–77). Legal information is communicated with the help of argumentative speech acts. Legal argumentation is simply communication related to messages. The legally relevant message may be structured in a relatively simple way. The road signs used on the European Continent are a good example of such apparently simple structure. Round signs stand for prohibited action, triangles for danger, blue signs signal obligation or permission. The combination of shape, color and some additional distinctive elements makes the production of numerous acts of obligation or prohibition possible (cf. Droste 1972). Textbooks on semiotics offer a range of examples that illustrate these issues (cf. Nöth 1975: 59). Yet, the situation is not as simple as that. The structure of the road sign may seem simple, but only in its photographic appearance. In order to understand that a white triangle with a red margin stands for the prohibition of certain acts in traffic one has to know quite a lot about signs. It would probably be easier to write: 'No entrance' instead of deciphering the sign that conveys this meaning. A sign in general, not only a traffic sign, is arbitrary to its message. It could mean whatever, yet also what it means. Even a road sign that announces the curve and that instrumentalizes a simplified drawing of the curve is only partly symbolical and immediately readable. Interpretive skills, context and background knowledge will be still necessary to decipher the meaning hidden behind it. The communicative situation, i.e. that road signs are read in traffic necessitates the use of an abbreviated code that as such is only apparently simple. A road sign therefore transfers a message, yet it does not communicate it (Mounin 1968: 44). Communication emerges when the procedural knowledge that the recipient possesses is used in order to grasp the meaning of the transmitted message. The 'genetic information' is another such example of the transmission of a message that can become an act of communication (Mounin 1968: 44). Thus, even the most visualized signs in law do not communicate automatically. Their simple meaning is engendered in relatively complicated semiotic operations of apprehension and interpretation. Modern media and especially the internet add examples to this already disparate picture. Raadschelders (2011: 97) remarked as far as public administration is concerned that: "Informal social networking is likely to have increased exponentially with the use of Internet, iPhone, ipad, Facebook and Twitter." While informal modes of communication are normal even in public institutions such as governments, one may bear in mind that these institutions are based on formal rules and formalized relations (cf. Berring 2000; Craig 2013: 120). Therefore, communication is a very complex situation of language use in law. One could ask whether it can be treated as a speech act at all or whether it is too heterogeneous to be integrated as a working concept into the legal-linguistic research related to discursive practices.

4.6.1 Communication in law

Communicational aspects of law are placed in the center of interest of jurists since the beginning of the legal practice. Ancient Greeks paid attention to rhetorical aspects of law, ancient Romans developed a stringent legal vocabulary. Both concentrated on a function of law that is today best characterized as 'communication'. Nowadays, communicational approaches to law dominate the work of many legal linguists such as Heikki E.S. Mattila (2012, 2013), Anne Lise Kjaer and Jan Engberg. In Mattila's work the interest in the historical processes of emergence of the legal language is particularly stressed. In his approach, the emergence of legal vocabulary is integrated into the aspects of communicational theory. Thus, the scrutiny of legal vocabulary gains finality and can be analyzed from a broader perspective and in context. Notwithstanding the specifics of individual research perspectives, linguistic communication concerns mainly the functionality of discourses. In other words, the discourse functions when it communicates messages. For this, it needs an advanced variety of language because simple language or pre-linguistic imagery cannot provide information that interests others (cf. Searle 2006). In the ordinary discourse this function is unproblematic because there is usually enough language at speaker's disposal. If not, the speaker may create some language that he can propose to other speakers. In legal discourses this task is more complex, because the language that transfers messages must be created as the use of ordinary language is not perceived as sufficient in these discourses that are closely related to the exercise of power. In the pragmatically oriented legal linguistics, the question whether communication is a speech act or the condition of speech is theoretically interesting. In our context, the question would sound: is legal communication a legal-linguistic operation such as legal interpretation or legal argumentation? It would apparently be possible to construe legal communication as an overarching linguistic speech act (cf. Grabowski 1999). Yet, one could also construe it as an operative device in law that enables the emergence of legal speech acts. Communication's function would be to guarantee intersubjectivity in the process of emergence of meaning. This is essential to the legal linguistics because according to the view presented in this book there cannot be any 'private' law. Creating legal language, shaping legal information and establishing structures in which this information is communicated are the main concerns of legal communication.

4.6.2 Information in law

Discursiveness of law is directly related to the communicative function of law. In legal communication the notion of information is quite essential, yet largely undetermined. Information seems to be positioned in contrast to argumentation. Argumentation may be the more evident part of the legal discourse because legal speech acts are indirectly or directly argumentative per se. It can be therefore taken for granted that argumentative structures are inherent in the legal discourse. Meanwhile, law is undoubtedly also structured by its material elements that tend to dominate the non-professional discourses about law and are perceived there as legal information. These material elements are of narrative nature and they represent the legal regulation. Simply speaking, they say what the law is about. They are, in a way, law's most striking elements and this may also explain the interest manifested by non-professionals. They are treated in this essay as aspects of legal narrativity. Meanwhile, information in law concerns the prerequisites of validity of legal speech acts rather than the narrative aspects. Mechanisms of daily information search coincide more closely with message reception or its identification than with legal information search that is different from the message that is searched for. For instance, if we do not know the price of a newspaper that we wish to purchase we may look at the first page of a newspaper where under the newspaper's name also its price is frequently indicated: 'Price 0, 90 cents'. This price so expressed is strictly speaking data, a message that was search for. It is not information. It is obtained with the help of procedural rules that allow us to find the relevant data. In the case of the newspaper purchase the rules are relatively simple and generally known. Data indicating the price will be available somewhere on the first page, under the name of the newspaper, at its margin, at the bottom in a box, etc. Sometimes, price may be handwritten at the upper margin of the newspaper, especially when it is offered abroad. The price then will indicate the local currency that may not be explicitly stated: 'Price 0, 90' will then mean 0, 90 units of the local currency. Such data searches are daily bread of newspaper buyers and they are conducted almost intuitively. As a rule, newspaper buyers do not have problems with identifying the message that they are searching for. Should, however, in some cases problems emerge they can be easily overcome, for instance through asking the newsstand seller about the price. Thus, background knowledge, life experience, intercultural competence and other life and linguistic strategies enable the acquisition of new knowledge in form of data. Information is the process in which such data that represents new knowledge is identified. Already M. Halliday, when working on the English grammar, remarked that "information is a process of interaction between what is already known or predictable and what is new or unpredictable," as quoted by L.Valeika and J. Buitkiene (2003: 59). In law, the data or message that is searched for is more difficult to identify as shown in the introductory parts of this book. Unlike in the case of the newspaper sale, the legally relevant data is not simply and unequivocally indicated in form of a banal statement: 'Price 0, 90 cents.' It is, first of all, expressed generally, which means somewhere, for example in a law code that may include thousands of articles. It is also expressed abstractly and it may be identified by jurists or by laypersons who may provide it a specific, i.e. diverging meaning. What is more, there is no one to ask back in cases of doubt about the results of such searches for messages in law. Legal information can be therefore characterized as a complex process constituted of professional strategies of meaning identification that allow to state the law notwithstanding the complexities of the searches involved.

4.6.3 Continuity of information in law

The Information Age did not bring any particular qualitative changes into the battle for law. From the Roman times on, there is an ongoing battle between the privileged experts who know the law and those excluded from this knowledge to get access to the information that makes law. Anecdotically, this process is symbolized by the attempt to prevent the access of lower social strata to law in ancient Rome. Finally, the laws known as Twelve Tables were made public; the data about the law in force became publicly accessible. This does not solve the problem as the knowledge of law is the knowledge of the method of its application rather than access to underlying written source texts. However, the access to texts is the beginning of knowledge of law as available information. Roman law has a symbolical function to play also in this legal context. A grammar example, quoted after H. Fielding's *Tom Jones* (XII, 3): "Vir bonus est quis? Qui consulta patrum, qui leges, juraque servat" transfers values that through the use of the Latin language are perceived as belonging to the Roman law. Paradoxically, the contemporary information systems and especially websites that provide access to laws still follow the Roman track and display the statutory texts rather than the legal-linguistic method that turns them into laws. Yet, contemporary jurists are not ancient Romans. Texts of the Roman law abound in formulations that are in contrast with contemporary conceptions of law. Ulpianus in *Corpus Iuris Civilis* (CIC I.1) says about jurists: "Cuius merito quis nos sacerdotes appellant," alluding to resemblances between priesthood and legal profession. Meanwhile, modern jurists are not priests of law. They are bound by the professional obligation to submit the results of their work to tests of rationality and democracy. Therefore, it is less easy to exercise the legal profession today than is had been the case in ancient Rome. It goes however without saying that the contact with other laws is typical of law as a phenomenon. The other law as a constitutive element of the global law is omnipresent (cf. Coendet 2012). Legal culture is therefore syncretic. Voices to the contrary may uniquely concern the unwritten law or chthonic law (cf. Glenn 2010) as a presupposed early form of complex legal structures.

4.6.4 Signification in communication

Legal semiotics makes aware of the emergence of legal meaning in communicative processes. Legal meaning is formed in participative, i.e. in social processes (Cao 2004: 8). Legal signification conceived as the forming of meaningful legal signs is indifferent to private creation of law. Subjective law or private legal rules do not make much sense in a society that imposes binding procedures for the enforcement of propositions that are institutionally approved as being legally valid. This restriction to forming of signs in law which are responsible for the emergence of meaning does not mean that beliefs or opinions about the contents of law could not emerge freely. On the contrary, such beliefs or convictions are constantly produced and they are introduced into legal discourses. Paradoxically, law that is indifferent to private creation cannot develop without individual creative contribution. Meanwhile, the legal status of innovative contribution to legal discourses as legal speech acts is limited until they are not institutionally validated. Despite this institutional hindrance, it would be a misunderstanding to limit or prohibit the formulation of new propositions about the content of legal rules, even if their discursive status is often weak. This weakness is sometimes transitory, although one must admit that many alternative propositions about the content of legal rules are formulated in vain. They will never become validated by legal institutions and they will never become law. Some of them, especially those aptly stated, may remain in legal archives as testimony of turns or tilts in legal discourses. Some may be used in future in a transformed version, while others will be abandoned. Like all other discourses, also the legal discourse includes ephemeral contributions. These largely unresearched inputs into the legal debate are not well known. They form a legal discourse that has fallen into oblivion like those texts of the ancient Roman law that are lost forever. It seems that alternative propositions about the content of law, which are formed with the help of traditional arguments may be more resistant to oblivion than those that emerge spontaneously and in a critical mood. With this point in mind, Cao (2004: 3) refers to Confucianism as an ideological resource for shaping legal arguments in China, notwithstanding the historical evolutions that regularly take place in Chinese society. Moreover, arguments based on Confucian culture are present in the contemporary Chinese discourse although the detailed knowledge of the Confucian classic works remains limited in contemporary China (Cao 2004: 3). Indeed, legal culture has long roots. In China, like in the Occident, most of its elements are present in an unreflected way. European and American legal thinking is still largely Greek and Roman. Many jurists there might feel surprised by such a generalization. Yet, as a generalization this statement is illustrative of the legal reasoning in the West. In this context, Cao (2004: 4) is critical of the Asian attitude when she courageously claims: "Self-reflexive questioning in the thinking of the nature and essence of law seems recessive in these societies." Meanwhile, the self-reflective legal discourse in the West that is represented in voluminous research works is often repetitive and often also affirmative of the existing law. All in all, it is still dominated by the legal positivism. Therefore, it is unclear whether the legal discourse outside Asia is more creative than the discourse formed in the Asian legal culture that emerged around Confucian rules. In fact, as the legal discourse is finally about acquisition and maintenance of power in society, it will structurally tend towards limitation. Meanwhile, legal culture develops and survives in power structures. This circumstance explains why the legal discourse regularly appears as one-sided or dogmatic, in the West as well as in the East. All in all, only selected and approved contents about the propositions of law are historically transmitted. Transmission systems such as libraries or modern databases depend on power structures and they will not spent efforts on preserving failed discursive alternatives. The Roman *Corpus Iuris Civilis* is the most eminent example of such a transformation procedure of institutionally validated legal meaning. It has been published as a compilation of approved quotes from the classical works of the Roman jurists. The Chinese imperial legal codes testify to the same procedure in a similar way. These works emerged in institutionalized editing processes (cf. Hong 1999; Cao 2004: 17). It would be unavailing to speculate which contents might have been abandoned by the compilators of these works. Doubtless, losses in signification processes are regular, yet losses in legal discourses are peculiar. In law, no effort towards encouraging plurality of approaches in legal institutions is perceptible. One could also assume that an intellectual contribution that get lost in society could not have been particularly valuable as social input. This contention could be reduced to a formula: What is relevant to society is preserved, what seems irrelevant has been deleted. Definitely, this formula holds true for the dominating discourse. As a rule, alternatives to dominating discourses are all too eagerly forgotten or preserved in a symbolical number of copies. This is the price that has to be paid by their authors for the emergence of legal meaning in institutionalized communicative processes.

4.6.5 Creating the language of law

Creation of legal language is a rare privilege. A science fiction author, William Gibson, is credited for having coined the term 'cyberspace' in his novel *Neuromancer*. The term 'cyberspace' entered into the U.S. American legal language smoothly. It was used for instance in the court decision Gorman v. Ameritrade Holding Corp. (293 F.3d 506 D.C. Cir. 2002). The judge used it as a background concept for modern internet legislation: "Cyberspace, however, is not some mystical incantation capable of warding off the jurisdiction of courts built from bricks and mortar." Other new coinages are also used in an unproblematic way: 'donative transfers' are related to wills, 'senior citizens' may become victims of fraud, 'pre-existing conditions' may lead to the refusal of health insurance policy. Some traditional coinages such as 'property' display new semantic features in legal use. For instance, when real property is acquired with limited own capital and a large input of bank loans backed by a mortgage, the formal proprietor who is mentioned in all legal acts is the mortgage taker. Nevertheless, economically, the financial institution that provided funds for the acquisition of real property is the real owner of the estate. The procedure creates linguistically a fictitious property that often leads the involved new formal owners to the unjustified conviction that they now fulfilled their dream to the own four walls. Such formal owners also suffer a shock when they lose their so called 'property' to creditor banks. The discursive elements of property as well as the institutionalized framework of their use efficiently create property that is not really property any more. Discursively provable evidence of cases involving people who believed in this sort of property shows its detrimental influence upon biographies as has been shown above (cf. 3.4.3). Finally, however, all linguistic creation in law is constructive. R. F. Stalley (2009: xxix) refers in his *Introduction* to the English-language version of Aristotle's *Politics*, that is regularly exploited in this book, to Sir Ernest Barker's explanation of the development of the modern concept of 'constitutionalism'. Textual coinages such as "the doctrine that the law is sovereign, and that governments are the servants of the law; the lawful monarch and the tyrant who governs by his arbitrary will; the doctrine that there is a right inherent in the people, by virtue of their collective capacity of judgement, to elect their rulers and call them to account" constitute textual samples that form 'constitutionalism'. All metaphorical coinages mentioned in the above quote are recurrent in constitutional writings from Aristotle over Locke and Hobbes until Hegel and Marx in one way or another. Stalley (2009: xxx) mentions Hobbes "who describes men in a state of nature covenanting together to set up a sovereign and thus establish civil society to save their skins." He does not hesitate to use the metaphorical expression 'save one's skin' in the reference to constitutional matters. Today such metaphors may be less attractive, yet they underlie our speaking about constitutional issues and are unavoidable even in this book. Law and its doctrine clearly include metaphorical language (cf. Winter 2008), mainly because metaphors are omnipresent in language in general and there is no need to avoid them, provided one is aware of their linguistic structure and function (cf. Sperber/Wilson 2008). While being semantically implicit, metaphors mark stronger than some explicit statements pre-conceptual stages in argumentative speech acts. To illustrate this phenomenon Stalley (2009: xxxii) can be again quoted commenting on Aristotle: "We may ask whether a strong sense of community can be developed without drawing a sharp distinction between those who are and those who are not members, that is without inciting discrimination and prejudice against those who do not seem to belong." 'Those who do not seem to belong' is left without determined object in the above remark and this procedure rather stresses the fact that they do not belong to society and represents a pronounced language that avoids ambiguity while seeming to choose ambiguous formulations. Metaphoric language illustrates also the linguistic processes in which terms such as 'constitutionalism' come about. Therefore, they finally contribute to the emergence of explicit law notwithstanding the contrary impression that may suggest the contrary. Metaphorical and literal language use are interdependent because lofty coinages such as 'law is sovereign' or 'right that is inherent in the people' or down-to-earth expressions such as 'save one's skin' materialize in discursive practices and form law that is applied and re-shaped. There is no doubt that without such linguistic coinages explicit legal doctrines such as 'constitutionalism' would not emerge in social practices that are discursive.

4.6.6 Semiotics of legal discursiveness

The inquiry into semiotic aspects of legal discursiveness reinforced the initial assumptions that underlie this essay. Several findings of principal importance for legal linguistics follow from it: The structure of communicational practices in law indicates that law is a discursive practice. Legally relevant communication depends on interpretive devices that are semiotic in their nature and origin. The structure of interpretive acts in law reflects the semiotic practices of creation and interpretation of signs. Signs of law become truly meaningful when they are combined and analyzed in complex textual units such as discourses. Legal semiotics also makes clear the problems of language as a means of legal communication. Language as a code is "grossly defective," so Sperber and Wilson (2008: 85). It cannot function perfectly as a means that is coding and decoding unequivocal legal data due to the complex structure of speakers' intended meaning. This meaning clarifies only in interpretive linguistic practices that include but are not limited to disambiguation rules. Interpretation as a legal-linguistic operation can be efficient in law only when it unites legal and linguistic components in the attempt at understanding meaning in law. This is the case, for instance, in the Dworkinian constructive interpretation and also in other constructionist approaches to the legal language. Such approaches are rooted in argumentative speech that emerges discursively in attempts at finding rational solutions to legal problems.

Part 5: Legal Argumentation between Discursiveness and Rationality

5.1 Discursiveness and rationality

Discursiveness of law has consequences that have been regularly mentioned here. Legal discourses are rational linguistic and social phenomena. Research into the interrelation between discursiveness and rationality allows to answer the question as to how is meaning constituted in law. The linguistic way of expression relevant to both discursiveness and rationality is argumentative speech. Insofar, legal argumentation is the area that covers the emergence of argumentative speech and its application in legal practices as mechanisms of legal discourses. Rationality standards differ in time and space. They emerge discursively in relation to theoretical problems that are in narrative terms called topics (cf. Viehweg 1954). For the legal theory, this amalgam of problems is not really new. It has been regularly mentioned at the margin of doctrinal studies. Also the issue whether the traditional doctrine increases the rationality of the discourse belongs to this area of inquiry. The pertaining positivist attitude towards law has been characterized by Cownie (2004: 58): "Whatever they call themselves, the majority of academic lawyers occupy the middle ground between the two extremes of pure doctrinal analysis and a highly theoretical approach to the study of law. Arguably, law is a discipline in transition, with a culture where a small group still clings to a purely doctrinal approach, but a very large group (whether they describe themselves as socio-legal or not) are mixing traditional methods of analysis with analysis drawn from a range of other disciplines." Meanwhile, positivism remains the turning point of all thinking about law in academic terms even if the methodological horizons of many jurists are somehow broadened by social paradigms. The explanation for the discrepancy between the enlightened views that law cannot be perceived in positivist perspectives and the pertaining importance of positivist views may be connected with the dominant positions in academia and in administration that are still held by positivists.

5.1.1 Consequences of legal discursiveness

Incorporation of discursive approaches to law into the legal science and into other sciences has consequences. For social sciences this emphasized discursiveness opens the possibility to integrate law as research object and teaching subject. For jurists, the thinking about law in terms of demystified rationality opens ways towards developing new legal arguments that would overcome the boundaries of the traditional legal topics. For legal linguists, the research into the language of law becomes a meaningful activity because it would reach also practical and not only academic goals. Overall, law seen from the perspective of its discursiveness becomes an interesting phenomenon and the subject law would begin to interest also students. Like in all other areas of social sciences also in law limits of rationality became more and more visible as a result or foreboding of postmodernist thinking. Consciousness being placed in the center of items, which are nowadays researched, engenders more questions than it offers answers. Law does not give up the postulate of search for rationality; yet it has to admit that we cannot go beyond the rationality generally accessible to us. Neither can we neglect numerous forms of emotional argumentation that seem inevitable, yet must be controlled. In this amalgam of prerequisites and processes the modern concept of legal rationality that corresponds with social rational practices can be found and made instrumental in the application of law.

5.1.2 Rationality and freedom as fundamental concepts of legal discourses

Both topics are rarely mentioned in legal texts; rare are statutes that refer to them and legal opinions reflect only occasionally upon these fundamental issues. Instead, topics such as efficiency of law or simplicity of administration are invoked as placeholders for more advanced concepts. The U.S. Supreme Court in its decision Hertz Corp. v. Friend (130 S.Ct. 2010) mentions the logically less challenging 'simplicity' while addressing the issue of rationality: "...we place primary weight upon the need for judicial administration of a jurisdictional statute to remain as simple as possible." Reducing argumentative speech, which includes its simplification in the framework of discursive boundaries, is one such legal-linguistic operation that aims at achieving rationality in a discursive practice. In the mentioned decision, the Supreme Court became involved in an interpretive dispute about a procedural question that concerned the federal diversity jurisdiction statute. The statute says: "A corporation shall be deemed to be the citizen of any State by which it has been incorporated and of the State where it has its principal place of business." To find out the meaning of the statute that could be applied in the specific case the court uses arguments that refer to rational language use: "The word 'place' is in the singular, not the plural. The word 'principal' requires us to pick out the 'main, prominent' or 'leading' place. And the fact that the word 'place' follows the words 'State where' means that the 'place' is a place within a state. It is not the state itself. A corporation's 'nerve center', usually its main headquarters, is a single place. The public often (though not always) considers it the corporation's main place of business." The simplicity sought in the legal text is a search of rationality in the legal language. It is typical of jurists to proceed in this way when they are confronted with interpretive problems. Meanwhile, the rational legal argumentation shall engender justice as its aim. This justice has a content; it is called freedom or liberty. Not much is known about both as the legal research into both concepts in terms of their discursiveness has been neglected. The conceptual base of free action has been defined already by Aristotle. Aristotle claimed in his *Metaphysics* (book I, chapter 2, 25): "...the man is free, we say, who exists for his own sake and not for another's." Later, I. Kant added one more prerequisite for free action in the sense relevant to the constitution of discursive rights. He claimed that the freedom of a person has its limits in the freedom of another person. These requirements for free action are classical and modern law has introduced multiple modifications to the concept of free action. This notwithstanding, argumentative reference to freedom remains a constant in all discursive practices of formation and application of law.

5.2 Discursive rationality

The legal rationality is specific in the sense that mutually exclusive opinions about the content of valid or future legal norms can be expressed in it. Such statements are possible because the discourse about validity of norms is not rooted in one exclusive perspective upon normativity and its contents. The most striking example of it is the legislative decision that establishes the driving on the right-hand side of the road as a valid rule of the road code. It is evident that also the left-hand side is a valid alternative for legislative initiatives and it has been chosen by some countries. Therefore, the choice exercised does not necessarily mean that other thinkable alternatives would be less rational or non-sensical. The same holds true of semantic alternatives of valid legal norms. One of non-exclusive particularities of the legal discourse is its institutionally imposed asymmetry. For instance, in asylum seeking procedures the applicants, and not the public servants, undergo a probe in credibility that largely excludes a productive discourse that would make clear the circumstances relevant to their case (Rienzer 2011). In fact, linguistic strategies that enable an inquiry into relevant elements of an asylum case are at the disposal of the involved parties. However, the structure of the procedure set up by the bureaucracy turns the strife for overcoming intercultural problems with discursive means into a failure.

5.2.1 Free will and responsibility in legal texts and beyond

The notion of 'free will' remains a fundamental challenge to jurists in terms of rationality. Unsystematically, legally relevant human action is often positioned between determinism and arbitrariness. It means that there is, according to the beliefs underlying these positions, either no free will at all or there is unlimited freedom to act. Both positions implicitly negate law. Therefore, the discourse about free will and responsibility for action has been of fundamental importance for law as research object and as a legislative idea. Positivists among jurists adopted an intermediate, yet circular view upon the theoretical problem of free will. It might be characterized in three prongs. First, there has to be something that could be described as 'free will' because otherwise law as a formal mechanism could not work. Second, it is evident that law is institutionally applied and enforced in society. Third, therefore there must be a 'free will'. Otherwise, there could not be any jurists, at least no positivists. Many theoreticians had problems with this positivist circularity. They were equally skeptical about the postulate of arbitrariness in action and the 'suspension of moral judgment' that is implicit in this sort of argumentation (Smart 1961: 291). Finally, J. Searle (2007) proposed an intermediate solution to the problem of free will urged by the necessity to come to terms with it as the problem clearly blocks the emergence of a more coherent theory of responsibility for action in philosophy. In law, causality, liability and criminal responsibility theoretically also depend on the solution to this problem. The debate about death penalty and criminal sanctions in general is intimately related to the problem of free will. It is often overlooked in the doctrinal legal debate that prefers positivist simplification. Smart (1961: 291) invokes in this context even Marquis de Sade who provocatively wrote: "What would become of your laws, your morality, your religion, your gallows, your Paradise, your God, your Hell, if it were shown that such and such fluids, such fibres, or a certain acridity in the blood, or in the animal spirits, alone suffice to make a man the object of your punishments or your rewards?" Marquis de Sade would not be satisfied with the results provided by natural sciences as they could not prove the determinism as clearly as he might have sensed it. Predictability of human action and determinism of human action remain open to debate. In the legal practice the 'argument of choice' is preferred by courts as a lexical solution. Judges will, if need be, mention in the justification part of the court decision that 'the convicted person had the possibility to choose the right yet chose the wrong.' The problem is solved linguistically, yet it remains an intellectual challenge. The theoretical discourse about both is not willing to provide other than model-based evidence for both mentioned prerequisites for action. Jurists will have to cope with this result. One may hope that they would not adopt the positivist shortcut as a solution to an annoyingly open theoretical question in the area of law and in its surroundings.

5.2.2 Evidence

Evidence as legal problem also displays limits of legal rationality. They concern the evaluation of evidence by judges and the prediction of results that can be obtained in legal procedures (cf. Morawski 1988). A. Ross (1958: 43) wrote about the possibility of prediction that: "...it does not presuppose that we are in a position to predict with reasonable certainty the outcome of a future concrete legal case...First, the outcome will be dependent on the evidence produced and the weighing it receives...The weighing of the evidence is to such a marked extent subjective that this reason alone excludes all possibility of calculating in advance with certainty the outcome of cases in which facts are disputed. Moreover, the interpretation of legal rules...offers vital points of uncertainty. Finally, the ideas which the judge holds as to what is valid law do not constitute the only factor by which he is motivated." Evidence as a pragmatic phenomenon is linked to the fact that judges and other jurists involved in cases did not take part in the underlying events of these cases. They simply cannot know what happened. This is not a problem when parties provide to courts the same or nearly the same versions of facts. When facts provided by one party are contested by the other, only a reconstruction can help. This reconstruction of material facts of a case is undertaken with the help of witness testimony and with other means. In Regina v. Smith, the English House of Lords had to decide whether the accused who appealed the verdicts of lower courts had committed a triple murder. Smith in fact married three times, and every time shortly after his marriage his then-wife was found dead in her bathtub. Lower courts sentenced him to death for triple murder. Smith contested and referred to his particularly tragical destiny that depraved his wives of life and turned all his attempts to establish a happy family life into a fiasco, and this three times in a series. The House of Lords shared Smith's view that the series of death cases as such does not constitute a sufficient proof of his criminal guilt. Yet, the fact that Smith always looked for socially isolated spinsters as candidates for marriage, that he after the marriage ceremony left to live with them in other towns where he rented houses on the outskirts, that he finally signed life insurance policies upon the lives of his subsequent wives and after their deaths always benefited from these polices provide, when accumulated, sufficient evidence that he had committed a triple murder. Smith was hanged. Meanwhile, valuation of evidence is manifestly discursive when singular proof is not sufficient, yet cumulative evidence would suffice. Lord Wright mentions in Grant v. Australian Knitting Mills (1936): "Pieces of evidence, each by itself insufficient, may together constitute a significant whole and justify by their combined effect a conclusion." Yet, how are they combined?

5.2.3 Contradictions between words and deeds

Pragmatic linguistics insists on the correlation between words and action as a prerequisite for rational use of language. Language, however, does not prevent the appearance of utterances that are even in blatant contradiction to action. Theoretically, such constellations of language use are treated as abuse of language. An interesting case constellation consists of saying one thing, and doing another (cf. Shuy 2012; Tiersma/Solan 2012: 348–353). It is typical of deceit committed by abuse of credibility. The strategy of deceit can be followed in Dayan v. McDonald's Corp. (466 N.E. 2d 958, Ill. App. 1984). The plaintiff turned there for protection to an Illinois court against a French court decision that terminated his franchise agreement with the defendant. He claimed that under the Illinois covenant of good faith and fair dealing the franchise should have been maintained even if factual reasons may have justified its termination. Already 1970 the defendant found out serious violations of cleanliness standards in restaurants operated by the plaintiff in Paris and demanded improvement. This was promised yet the promise remained unfulfilled notwithstanding defendant's numerous interventions. Evidence has been presented to the court that grease dripping from the vents was collected in a cup, dogs were permitted in the kitchens where they defecated, insecticide was blended with chicken breading, past-dated products were not discarded, potato peelers were not cleaned, etc. The strategy of promise and its non-fulfillment was applied during fourteen years and was accompanied by lawsuits in two countries. The linguistically decisive moment is however the interpretation of the protective covenant. The plaintiff argues that all evidence notwithstanding he should be protected because the defendant may have used these circumstances in order to terminate his franchise agreements on other motives. It is imaginable that a better candidate appeared who would accept more burdensome conditions or that the defendant would wish to recapture the Paris market. Meanwhile, the court held that "where good cause exists, motive is immaterial to a determination of good faith performance." It means that even if defendant's real motives were different from those stated in the lawsuit he was entitled to terminate the franchise agreement because another motive, i.e. the violation of the franchise's cleanliness standards was proven beyond any doubt. Not only in this case the reasons for a successful action have to be material in the sense of law. That other reasons exist as well and that these reasons may be even preponderant does not matter in many cases. Law steers in such cases the formal legal reasoning that is reductive, yet also efficient. In terms of legal linguistics the reductive procedure is however not satisfactory because it does not match up linguistically to the factual complexity of the case.

Another American court decision, R.G. Group, Inc. v. Bojangles' of America (751 F. 2d 69, 1984) illustrates the situation where words and deeds fall apart. R.G. Group was interested in obtaining a franchise from Bojangles' to operate restaurants. It entered into negotiations with Bojangles' that were based on a standard form development franchise agreement. The standard agreement provided for written form of all license contracts. It said: "This Development Franchise Agreement together with all the Appendices and Exhibits annexed hereto contains the entire agreement and understanding between the parties hereto with respect to the subject matter hereof and supersedes all prior negotiations and oral understanding between the parties, if any. There are no agreements, representations, or warranties other than those set forth, provided for or referred to herein." After a meeting, the representative of R.G. Group asked the representative of Bojangles' over the telephone: "Do we have a handshake deal?" The other answered: "Yes, we have a handshake deal today and right now." However, the franchise agreement was never signed because Bojangles' franchise committee had refused to approve the application put together by R.G. Group. R.G. Group sued referring to the telephone conversation that remained uncontested by Bojangles' as to its contents. Meanwhile, Bojangles' referred to the standard agreement that provided for the written form of the license and perceived therefore the declaration made on the telephone as not binding. The court decided for Bojangles', mainly due to complex doctrinal issues connected with formalities in the application of the statute of frauds and claims under the promissory estoppel. Therefore, Bojangles' was not held liable for own words and its subsequent action. Its refusal to provide a signed franchise agreement to R.G. Group was perceived as legal under New York contract law. The court is definitely right when it mentions: "Under New York law, if parties do not intend to be bound by an agreement until it is in writing and signed, then there is no contract until that event occurs." Yet, could the parties, or the party that proposed the text of the agreement, not modify its requirement orally or wave it? This could be inferred from the negotiations between R.G. Group and Bojangles'. Discursively, both the requirements of written contract and the oral agreement coincide in the course of negotiations between the parties. Therefore, it would be important to determine the role of both contradictory components of the negotiations between them. The main contradiction exists between the standard form agreement that was the basis for the negotiation between the parties and the declaration on the phone that there is a binding contract. This contract is labeled by the parties as a 'handshake'. Pragmatically, a 'handshake' is a piece of evidence for an enforceable contract. Already the ancient Greeks spoke of the right hand (δεξιά) as synonymous with contract. Also δεξίωμα meant for them both 'handshake' and 'contract'. Since antiquity the symbolic value of the 'handshake' in social practices is higher than that of an oral declaration. This holds particularly true in case of an oral declaration that is contrary to the visible symbol of a 'handshake'. Pragmatists, such as Sperber and Wilson (2008: 86) used to speak about ostensive stimuli that manifest speakers intentions in situations where the communication is non-verbal. In R.G. Group v. Bojangles' the 'handshake' is turned into a metaphor, as no physical contact between the parties talking on the phone takes place with exception of the transmission of sound waves. Meanwhile, the 'verbal handshake' on the phone is pragmatically equivalent in its metaphoric dress to the physical handshake. Both evidence the intention to be bound by the declarations made orally. Therefore, R.G. Group v. Bojangles' is as a court decision deficient in terms of the legal-linguistic analysis of the telephone conversation between the parties. Otherwise, also as regards its result, it may be convincing as an act of application of the New York contract law because R.G. Group's claims are not limited to the 'handshake' episode. This aspect notwithstanding, the court sanctioned here a communicative situation where words and deeds fall apart and therefore, at least, as far as the 'handshake' episode is concerned, it did not propose any better law. Rationality of law was once again sacrificed to the dead letter of legal formalism.

5.2.4 Linearity of language sublated

Legal doctrine that perceives law mainly as a conceptual, i.e. a logical, yet not a linguistic construct, fails regularly in its attempts to render conceptual law linguistically. For instance, Art. 433 of the German Civil Code introduces an interrelation of rights that breaks the linearity of legal argumentation. The provision says: Art. 433 Obligations typical of sale contracts (1) The seller of a good is obliged by the sale contract to transfer the good to the buyer and to provide him ownership to the good. The seller has to provide the good free from material defects and legal objections. (2) The buyer is obliged to pay the seller the agreed price and to clear the purchased good. Since the Roman times the sale contract has been a challenge in terms of its wording because the contract actually is twofold. The sale is for the other party an acquisition, and the rights and obligations of the parties are therefore reciprocal. The ancient Romans characterized the sale contract as emptio-venditio, i.e. as a sale and as an acquisition. In this contract, the reciprocal rights and obligations are temporarily co-existent and cannot be expressed in a linear sequence of rights that would suggest a temporal sequence of acts under the sale contract. Meanwhile, textual templates that are in general use among jurists favor rather linear language. In this language, legal prerequisites follow one upon another. This linear template may also be responsible for the devaluation of the concept of emptio-venditio in the Roman law of postclassical times. In this epoch the construction of emptio-venditio lost its consensual reference and was perceived as acquisition of property in exchange of payment (cf. Dozhdev 2003: 580). Hence, a purely constructivist creation was degraded to a brute fact. The legal-linguistic background of the transformation seems evident. Many constructivist legal coinages may in their linguistic dress impede their understanding as interrelated prerequisites for validity of legal speech acts such as sale contracts. Relations of this type are called in the theory of law synallagmatic. They are theoretically well understood, yet linguistically not well rendered. For instance, the order of reciprocal acts related to transfer of ownership and payment is linguistically not clearly expressed. In many civil law systems they are described metaphorically with the German expression 'Zug um Zug'. It means that they shall occur in interrelation, yet order of acts is not determined in a 'Zug um Zug' transfer. Legal linguistics welcomes such problematic constellations, yet it would be also in charge of providing linguistic solutions to such linguistic traps in law. In this area some philosophers seem to be more efficient than legal linguists. In his *Introduction to the Science of Right* I. Kant analyzed also the synallagmatic legal relation: "…in this reciprocal relation of voluntary actions, the conception of right does not take into consideration the matter of the act of will in so far as the end which any one may have in view in willing it is concerned." The textuality of the statutory formulation that reflects a synallagmatic relation has to focus upon its form: "…it is not asked in a question of right whether any one on buying goods for his own business realizes a profit by the transaction or not; but only the form of the transaction is taken into account, in considering the relation of the mutual act of will." Hence, the language that renders this logical form has to reflect the synallagma and not the sale. No legal scholar has stated the principle of synallagmatic relations in law better than I. Kant, whose interest in law and in language had been only marginal.

5.2.5 Kant and Hegel contribute to shaping of legal discourses

Problems with language that refer to rationality and its expression in discourses have a past that witnesses to discursive processes of their formation. Among philosophers who provided fundamental contributions to the conceptual form of legal discourses are Immanuel Kant and G.W.F. Hegel. Immanuel Kant concentrated in his philosophical work upon critical prerequisites for reasoning, surprisingly also about the reasoning in and about the law. In his *Philosophy of Right* Kant, who rarely mentions language explicitly, engages in an analysis of law and ethics, their differences and affinities. He identifies legal concepts that are for him given a priori. 'Right', for instance, is such a concept that is for Kant given a priori. Although Kant does not mention language in this context, the concepts he mentions are stated in language. For Kant, language seems to be an epiphenomenon of thought; therefore he does not spent any time on dealing with it explicitly. He develops his philosophical thoughts in the tradition of his time, concentrating on knowledge acquisition and not on language in which the acquired knowledge emerges or is expressed (cf. Searle 2011: 11). Among numerous fundamental contributions that we owe to Immanuel Kant's philosophy there are also some which concern the topic of this essay. I. Kant made actually the sort of writing that is practiced here academically admissible in that he abolished dogmatic constraints in all reflection upon law. He wrote in the Preface to the first Riga-edition of his *Critique of Pure Reason* (1781): "Our age is the age of criticism, to which everything must be subjected. The sacredness of religion, and the authority of legislation, are by many regarded as grounds of exemption from the examination by this tribunal." In other words, legal discourse is not limited to affirmative and dogmatic statements about law. Instead, it is free within the limits of our reason, i.e. as a rational discourse. The Kantian modification in the structure of the legal discourse is still not generalized in the discourses in and around the law. Yet, it makes clear that only the critical legal discourse has scientific value and that other types of the legal discourse simply have different finality. Another structural feature of the legal discourse imposed by I. Kant was its explicitness that can be called Aristotelian. Kant begins his *Introduction to the Science of Right* with a passage that describes the legal science: "The Science of Right has for its object the principles of all the laws which it is possible to promulgate by external legislation. Where there is such a legislation, it becomes, in actual application to it, a system of positive right and law;...Such practical knowledge of positive right, and law, may be regarded as belonging to jurisprudence (jurisprudentia) in the original sense of the term. But the theoretical knowledge of right and law in principle, as distinguished from positive laws and empirical cases, belongs to the pure science of right (jurisscientia)... And it is from this science that the immutable principles of all positive legislation must be derived by practical jurists and lawgivers." Kant redefines in this passage and in his following remarks the postulate of discursive explicitness in legislative creation and in legal analysis. The traditional professional discourse of the legal doctrine had been dogmatic. Kant claims that whatever legal discourse must be critical when it should engender rational law. Rational principles that he is looking for are definitely not those of the legislative content because they change with time. Kantian principles are like the legal-linguistic operations unchangeable. Law's rational principles are legal-linguistic operations such as legal interpretation or legal argumentation that enable the emergence of discourses about law. Meanwhile, Kant had clearly in mind logical, and not linguistic principles. Yet, his entire philosophy is based on the presumption of the logical component of reasoning that is for him and for us by necessity linguistic. The only difference between the legal-linguistic approach and his perspective is that Kant took this natural interrelation for granted and examined the logical structure of discourse, while legal linguistics starts its inquiry with the linguistic dress of the legal discourse where logic is inherent as a prerequisite for the discursive rationality. While insisting on discursive rationality in law Kant discovered also the legal-linguistic pre-argumentative stage. Therefore, discourse about rights concerns for Kant "a right under dispute" where "there is no rights, but only one right." The legal argumentation emerges beyond particular convictions about right and wrong and it concerns the speech situation where the validity of a proposition of law must be discursively imputed to others. Kant also anticipated the façade argumentation, the 'doubtful right' and the lie as particular areas of legal-linguistic research. He recognised that a legal decision may not always display its true motives and that it can be based on expediency as well as on lies. He was open to legal-linguistic experiments and played with 'Joyecean' puns such as "to possess possession." Unlike James Joyce, however, Kant did not hold such coinages for meaningful. Unclear remains however his relation to legal constructivism. In some remarks he seems to be supportive of the idea of discursive creation of concepts in law. In the first chapter of *The Science of Right* he distinguishes between 'physical possession' as a brute fact and "a purely juridical possession of the same object." Some other concepts such as 'marriage' are however often conceived by him in essentialist terms. Last but not least, Kant introduced to the legal language terms such as 'perpetual peace' and 'ius cosmopoliticum' for global law. Finally, Kantian analysis is implicitly linguistic and the legal-linguistic analysis is explicitly linguistic. Both accept the logical structure of the legal discourse by different degrees of commitment, yet without difference in the scrutinized subject matter. This makes also plain why precursors of contemporary legal linguistics such as Eugeniusz Bautro or Karl Olivecrona relied on Kantian thought as fundamental to any linguistic inquiry into law. It is also worth mentioning that the Polish jurist Eugeniusz Bautro (1891–1961) applied Kant's philosophy as a notional matrix for his attempt to develop legal linguistics as a theory of law, (Kuźmicz 2009: 106; Schaff 1962: 367). Bautro (1935) aimed at combining linguistic and logical analysis to establish a comprehensive science that would elucidate the relations between law and language (Matulewska 2010: 109). For Bautro, the logical and the linguistic analyses of notions such as 'obligation' were essential to the understanding of law; they were a shorthand script for more complex legal-linguistic operations (cf. Galdia 2009: 115). This legal-linguistic analysis would comprise all operations with exception of the systematization of regulatory contents (Kuźmicz 2009: 102). It comes close to the conception of legal linguistics that is exposed in this book but it is also ambiguous because it could be understood as an attempt to create a 'reine Rechtslehre' in Kelsenian sense. The legal linguistics that is advocated here is anchored in forms of social life that are understood in a broader sense suggested already in the past century by L. Wittgenstein. It cannot therefore become a sterile enterprise that looks at the skeleton of law construed as an overtemporal and overspacial construct that I. Kant might have had in mind while speaking about the philosophy of law. Bautro's innovative view upon law is in parts close to the positivism of the Vienna circle as it developed in the broader surroundings of Viennese academic influence.

G.W.F. Hegel reacted with his *Philosophy of Right* (1821) primarily to I. Kant's *The Science of Right*. Hegel's work can be therefore read in comparison with Kant's treatise. Some of Hegel's results that are interesting in our context develop Kant's reasoning further and generalize some of his ideas more aptly. Hegel stresses like Kant before him the discursive nature of law. In the Preface to *The Science of Right* he argues: "It is true that the forms and rules of old logic, of definition, classification, and syllogism, which include the rules of discursive thinking, have become recognized as inadequate for speculative science; or rather their inadequacy has not been recognized; it has only been felt, and then these rules have been thrown off as if they were mere fetters in order to allow the heart, the imagination, and casual intuition to say what it pleased. And since reflection and connection of thought have after all to come on the scene as well, there is an unconscious relapse into the despised method of commonplace deduction and argumentation." For Hegel, law remains a discursive practice that is in need of a scientific method that would prevent arbitrary use of arguments in legal discourses. The primary goal of this method is the establishment of rational argumentation, in Hegel's words: "Right and ethics, and the actual world of justice and ethical life, are understood through thoughts; through thoughts that are invested with a rational form, i.e. with universality and determinacy. This form is law, and this it is which the feeling that stipulates for its own whim, the conscience that places right in subjective conviction, has reason to regard as its chief foe." In terms of regulatory content Hegel is more committed to the idea of the state than had been Kant. Domingo (2010: 171) referred to the Hegelian tendency towards 'state totality' arguing that "for Hegel, the state was totality, and its individuals found their liberty in the heart of that reality, of that effective actualization…, considered an end in itself…that completes the particularity of every individual insofar as liberty is an equally valid norm for all." The state remains for Hegel the actuality of the individual freedom: "Der Staat ist die Wirklichkeit der konkreten Freiheit." Hegel's conception of the state has been therefore often understood as endorsing the priority of state over citizens and their individual rights. Hegel was also very well aware of the fact that law is not a neutral mechanism of social organization and he explicitly mentions the "hatred of law" as one of regular attitudes towards this phenomenon. The perfect state would be able to accommodate such attitudes and to sublate them. Today, one could say that the modern state has the obligation to incorporate existing discursive practices into its mode of being. This is primarily so because the state is the result of multiple discursive practices. The previous statements would probably not acquire Hegel's endorsement. This makes also clear that both conceptions discussed here are historical and that they have their limits. They become instrumental in more contemporary approaches solely after being thoroughly re-interpreted.

English translations of Kant's and Hegel's writings on law use the term 'right' to render the German term 'Recht'. This decision of the translators is well rooted in the general understanding of the semantic difference between 'law' and 'right' in the English language. Popular discourse differentiates strictly between both as shown by Henry Fielding in his already quoted *Tom Jones*: "I myself knew a poor gentleman who was kept in a mad-house all his life by his family, and they enjoyed his estate, but it did them no good; for though the law gave it them, it was the right of another." The popular view provocatively described by H. Fielding challenges the legal theory and forces it to incorporate the distinction between 'law' and 'right' – and even 'law of right' – into the legal discourse. As can be seen from the translations of Kant's and Hegel's writings, the conceptual distinction between 'law' and 'right', which is less visible in the German language originals, remains valid as an argumentative feature in the legal discourses. It is a surprising and possibly also an unintended result of their intellectual efforts in the area of legal theory. Meanwhile, Kant's and Hegel's thoughts that were described above allow some methodological steps that are undertaken in this essay. First of all, legal discursiveness is best instrumentalized in legal-linguistic operations that strive for a better law in society. These legal-linguistic operations function meaningfully only in legal discourses that are rooted in a concept of rationality. Second, the 'rational form' of law as a feature of its 'universality' allows characterizing the positive law as a ubiquitous argumentative practice. Third, the variety of language that is used in legal discourses determines the efficiency of legal-linguistic operations as rational communicative processes. In the sense of the above lines one can therefore posit that Kant and Hegel were very influential in their description of law as a discursive phenomenon. In their philosophical conceptions of law they shaped some of the central features of contemporary legal linguistics as a theory of law.

5.3 Legal reasoning and legal logic

Legal logic attempts at describing the legal reasoning. This task is surprising and courageous at the same time. Legal reasoning is commonly depicted as a specific way in which jurists reach their conclusions when they apply statutes or precedents (cf. Savellos/Galvin 2001). It presupposes a professional way of reasoning that differs from the ordinary application of reason. Meanwhile, from the logical point of view it would be surprising to discover that a particular profession has established a way of reasoning that remarkably differs from the way other mortals shape their opinions about law or about the world in general. Traditional research has been rather favorable to the existence of legal reasoning (Engisch 2010). Changes might be introduced into this view due to the linguistic turn that stresses common life forms as a basis for understanding of speech in law and elsewhere. The topic of 'legal reasoning' remains a challenging issue for the mainstream legal theory and for the legal linguistics. Both would have to determine the role the ordinary language plays in law more specifically than it is the case today. Legal reasoning acquired a negative connotation in works such as James Boyd White's *Heracles' Bow*. In White's sense 'legal reasoning' is defined negatively as a distortion of ordinary language. R. Weisberg (1992: 304) mentions White's skepticism towards the plain English movement "because legal thinking will automatically render any system of words (even 'plain' ones) strange and unfamiliar." This view upon legal reasoning is essential to any approach to legal language as it suggests that legal reasoning is a linguistic device adopted by jurists to dissimulate meaning in law.

5.3.1 Façade-argumentation

Façade-argumentation is another device of power exercise in law that may trap the logician. Typical of a façade-decision is the discrepancy between the reasons indicated in the court opinion and the motivation that seems to have guided the judges. The legal-linguistic problem in dealing with this type of argumentation is the quality of evidence that can be provided in case of suspicions as to the character of a given court opinion. As a case reference one can use the court opinion Sutton v. Warner (12 Cal. App. 14. 4th 415, 15 Cal. Rptr. 2d 632, 1993 Cal. App. Lexis 22). The California Court of Appeal decided a lawsuit where parties agreed upon an option to buy a house. Their agreement has been oral, thus clearly violating the common law statute of frauds that provides for the written form of agreements relating to the transfer of real property. The plaintiff moved to the house, made a down payment, paid monthly mortgage installments to the defendant. He also paid taxes; he painted the interior of the house and installed a toilet and an entry lamp. However, as real estate prices changed, the defendant withdrew his promise and claimed its unenforceability due to the violation of the statute of frauds. The court, however, held that the case constellation fulfills the requirements of the 'doctrine of part performance' that balances the existing formalities under the statute of frauds when substantial improvements have been made by the promisee upon the real estate. The court assumed that it was the case here. One could however also deem the improvements as rather insignificant as also tenants used to engage in this sort of changes in the real estate they lease. It seems that the court tried to prevent that the promisor would benefit from his breach of word rather than enforce the statute of fraud literally. It does not mention this intention in its decision. Such a decision is a typical façade-decision. I. Kant in *The Science of Right* mentioned this challenging legal-linguistic mechanism that he described in *General Definitions and Divisions,* par. F (I) as rooted in pretexts: "Hence it follows, that a court of equity, for the decision of disputed questions of right, would involve a contradiction. It is only where his own property rights are concerned, and in matters in which he can decide, that a judge may or ought to give hearing to equity. Thus, if the Crown is supplicated to give an indemnity to certain persons for loss or injury sustained in its service, it may undertake the burden of doing so, although, according to strict right, the claim might be rejected on the ground of the pretext that the parties in question undertook the performance of the service occasioning the loss, at their own risk."

5.3.2 Law for logicians

The logic of law seems to be even less well researched than the language of law. Multiple constellations in law might challenge the logician. For instance, in a decision by the Dutch Supreme Court, the Hooge Raad, the question whether foreign bankruptcy legislation can be applied by Dutch courts has been decided positively (cf. Gustafsen v. Mosk HR 24.10.97, RvdW 1997, 209). However, the court states that this legislation is applicable solely when it coincides with the Dutch legislation, because otherwise it would be surprising to Dutch subjects and therefore unduly harming them. In this case, the foreign legislation is thus applicable as far as it is identical with the Dutch. Is it then applicable at all? Is it not so that in fact only Dutch legislation is applicable?

Furthermore, discursive rationality requires that no other than discursive reasons are applied in finding law. What occurs when the legislator decides to shorten the pregnancy period to seven and a half months? Can we hold against it that human pregnancy naturally takes nine months? Constructiveness in the legal language may have limits, yet its logical boundaries are not clear.

5.3.3 Law of punishment for logicians

The logic of selective punishment developed around different case constellations. For one, the U.S. penal system weakens the possibilities of recourse for the prosecution. In cases, where the jury acquits although it clearly should not, the prosecution has – unlike a party in analogous private law litigation – to accept the result. This leads to disparities that may be perceived as generating injustice, especially in cases where a principal perpetrator is acquitted and an accessory is convicted. However, the U.S. Supreme Court held in Standefer (cf. below) that symmetry of convictions is not required, even if this result may be intellectually challenging. The intellectual requisite to which the court refers is a moment of justice. Justice when understood in general terms also engenders principles that are in their essence general. It would therefore plead for the acquittal of an accessory perpetrator in case where the principal is acquitted. The general discursive rule is however modified through factual circumstances. We would, for instance, not insist upon it, would an obviously guilty principal die during the trial and therefore not be convicted. Clearly, the accessory should not benefit from such accidental circumstances. Meanwhile, the U.S. Supreme Court granted certiorari in Standefer v. U.S. (447 U.S. 10, 1980) to decide whether a defendant accused of aiding and abetting in the commission of a federal offense may be convicted after the principal has been acquitted of that offense. The defendant was indicted and condemned for making gifts to a public official, in case an Internal Revenue agent. The agent himself has been acquitted by the jury of most of the charges. The defendant therefore argued that he as an accessory to the offense cannot be convicted, while the principal perpetrator goes free. The old common law rule that is also mentioned by the court states that "an accessory follow(s), like a shadow, his principal." However, through the enactment of 18 U.S.C. 2 in 1909 the distinction between principals and accessories has been practically abolished, and it made both of them principals. Therefore, the U.S. Supreme Court viewed as unproblematic the sanction imposed upon a de facto accessory in a case where the principal has been acquitted.

5.3.4 Legal definitions

Legal definitions have been cherished by jurists as the residue of professional wisdom and reliable knowledge about law. Jurists insisted on the operation of defining in law as being particularly important because they hoped that through defining they could exclude ambiguity in the legal language (Galdia 2009: 112). These attempts have proven to be hopeless, mainly due to the structure of the natural language that aptly prevents institutionally predefined meaning to penetrate and command the body of law. Legal definitions have therefore lost their interest for the legal-linguistic research because they cannot provide what they promise. The legal-linguistic operation of defining remains however relevant because the text type of legal definition still exists and is productive in law. After all, definitions propose a notional prototype (Pinker 1999: 273) that reflects some facets of meaning. Legal definitions provide a first orientation about the possible meaning of a legal term. In terms of law, legal definitions must be general in order to be operational. They may be paraphrases: "Subject matter jurisdiction – jurisdiction over the subject matter of a lawsuit." Legal provisions may include definitions of terms mentioned in them, so in Art. 14 of the UN Convention on the International Sale of Goods (CISG): "A proposal for concluding a contract addressed to one or more specific persons constitutes an offer if it is sufficiently definite and indicates the intention of the offeror to be bound in case of acceptance. A proposal is sufficiently definite if it indicates the goods and expressly or implicitly makes provision for determining the quantity and price." Thus in the first sentence the term 'sufficiently definite proposal' is introduced and the following sentence is completely devoted to explaining the way in which the first sentence is to be construed. Meanwhile, the 'indication of the offeror to be bound' is not defined. Definitions are a broad text type in law. They may include a reductive specification of a term that is used also in the ordinary language such as: "Money – a medium of exchange authorized or adopted by a domestic or foreign government. Reference is made to Art. 1–201(24) of the UCC." They may include an element of additional information: "Precedent – a rule of law established in a court decision. Lower courts must follow the precedent established by higher courts," or examples of application: "Ordinance – law enacted by local government bodies such as cities and municipalities, counties, school districts, and water districts." They may be semantically explicative: "Exclusive jurisdiction – jurisdiction held by only one court," or institutionally explicative: "Summons – a court order directing the defendant to appear in court and answer the complaint." Explicative definitions are close to comments, e.g. Art. 2–206(1) (b) UCC provides for measures regarding an 'accommodation shipment'. Within this context, a textbook defines accommodation as "a shipment that is offered to the buyer as a replacement for the original shipment when the original shipment cannot be filled." It is however necessary to know that the accommodation is a counteroffer that the buyer is free to reject. The definition omits this critical circumstance. Some legal definitions may include elements of legal interpretation: "Assault – 1. the threat of immediate harm or offensive contact or 2. any action that arouses reasonable apprehension of imminent harm. Actual physical contact is unnecessary." Some definitions such as: 'Statute of repose' – a statute that limits the seller's liability to a certain number of years from the date when the product was first sold, describe the essence of the concept. Temporary aspects of defining are manifest in: "Offeror – the party who makes an offer. Offeree – the party to whom an offer has been made." Definitions may avoid ethically controversial issues and define concepts procedurally: 'Immoral contract' – a contract whose objective is the commission of an act that is considered immoral by society. They may proceed by semantic reduction: 'Easement' – a right to use someone else's land without owning or leasing it. Definitions around 'easement' may constitute a family: 'easement in gross' – an easement that authorizes a person who does not own adjacent land to use another's land and 'easement appurtenant' – a situation created when the owner of one piece of land is given an easement over an adjacent piece of land. They may define rare words without explaining their origin: 'replevin' – an action by a buyer or lessor to recover scarce goods wrongfully withheld by a seller or lessor. Definitions may introduce words broadly understandable for common language speakers in a narrower semantic context: 'presentment' – a demand for acceptance or payment of an instrument made upon the maker, acceptor, drawee, or other payor by or on behalf of the holder. They may concern mysterious neologisms: 'nonattainment area' – a designated geographical area that does not meet established air quality standards, or banalities: 'lawful object' – legal object. Definitions can be ironical or sarcastic. One can write in a traditional mood: statute of frauds – a state statute that requires certain types of contracts to be in writing. One can also write: statute of frauds – that unfortunate statute, the misguided application of which has been the cause of so many frauds, as formulated by V.C. Bacon in Morgan v. Worthington (1878). Already Blaise Pascal in his *New Experiments concerning the Vacuum* (1647) identified the linguistic status of 'definition' that corresponds with the discursive approach adopted in this book: "…it is evident that there is no necessary connection between the definition of a thing and the assertion of its existence, and that we can just as well define an impossible thing as a true thing." Therefore, defining as a legal-linguistic operation is the most doubtful, if not the most suspicious, of all traditional discursive practices in law. Legal definitions are a multifaceted text type in law. Strict defining is only one of their legal-linguistic functions. Their main purpose is to maintain legal discourses alive as cryptic language tends to paralyze discursive practices.

5.4 Talking like lawyers do

One of the specific features of law is that non-lawyers have pronounced views about it, like about proper upfostring of children. In this respect law clearly differs from disciplines such as nuclear physics or mathematical astronomy. Therefore, discourses in law and about law differ from discourses around the law where non-lawyers address legal issues as well as issues related to law. In numerous communicative situations these linguistic practices are intertwined. Witness testimony in courts, 'judge bashing' in the media or in political institutions, and contacts between attorneys at law and their clients mark this type of mixed discourse. Interestingly, understanding is well assured in most such situations. However, the discourse becomes less efficient when one of the parties tries to impose the rules that dominate its linguistic practices and evaluates the efficiency of the discourse exclusively from this point of view. Therefore, while linguistic understanding between professionals of law and others is in principle always possible, unilaterally imposed requirements of discursive validity may destroy the background which unites communicative practices and which enables understanding. For instance, ridiculing juridical discourse in the media with the help of samples taken out of context is illustrative of this practice. In such cases, a quote is made from a court decision and then a federatory conclusion such as 'A normal person does not speak like that' usually follows. This practice impedes attempts at understanding law and strengthens the already wide-spread impression that talking with jurists does not make sense. Also attorneys may develop linguistic strategies that aim at impressing their clients with legalese rather than explaining them the law. These strategies may occasionally correspond with clients' expectations that law is expressed in a hermetic language that they cannot understand. In such cases, paradoxically, the communicative situation is very efficient. Yet, the discourse that is structured according to such communicative strategies is irrational, notwithstanding its efficiency. Witness testimony is equally illustrative in this respect. Witnesses who do not adapt their language to institutional requirements are often not taken seriously by courts. A classical American court decision, Hollaris v. Jankowski (315 Ill. App. 154, 42 N.E. 2d 859), that has been scrutinized by Richard Weisberg (1992: 20–22), manifests this strategic tendency that makes understanding impossible. The case concerns the question whether an eight-year-old boy, Clyde Hollaris, should have been permitted to testify in a trial that concerned an event which happened when he was four years of age. The child was victim of a car accident in which he lost one leg. The judge did not exclude that a child may be witness in such a case, yet refused Hollaris's testimony. The strategy applied by the judge stroke some scholars (cf. Weisberg 1992: 22; Muller 2000) as particularly manipulative and unprofessional. This can be seen in the judge's attempt to dissimulate material facts. At the beginning of the decision the judge writes: "The complaint charges the defendants were driving a truck in an alley and carelessly and negligently drove it so as to injure the plaintiff, a boy four years of age." The age of the child is indicated, yet not the seriousness of his injury. Thus, the judge mentions that Hollaris was injured in a car accident. Yet only on the last page of his decision, and in a parenthesis, he refers to the brief of defendants' attorney who suggested that the child was placed upon the stand "solely for the emotional effect that the one-legged boy would have upon the jury." From this parenthetical remark the reader has to infer what actually happened to Clyde Hollaris. The professional duty of an impartial judge would have been to state material facts and not to avoid the reference to the main fact that makes of Hollaris's complaint a very serious suit. The case analysis makes also clear how the judge step by step prepares Hollaris's defeat. Arguments that the boy is inarticulate and slow are invoked in the decision. It is not mentioned that the boy may also have suffered under the circumstances in which he testified and which can render a victim inarticulate and emotionally perturbed, i.e. 'slow' in the language of the judge. The judge's professional deficiency could be identified in the above case with the help of legal-linguistic analysis. Legal linguistics rarely creates own terms, yet in this case it can propose the coinage 'incompetent judge' that seems to cover the situation that was analyzed.

5.4.1 Speaking in procedures

Speaking in procedures is one more device of power exercise through language. The U.S. Federal Rules of Procedure as all other acts of legislation that pertain to court procedure are an illustrative example of legal language used as device of the exercise of power. The case Weisgram v. Marley (528 U.S. 440) has been decided by the U.S. Supreme Court. The plaintiff, whose evidence to prove a product defect has been disregarded by the court as unprofessional, expected from the court a sign to provide new and more qualified evidence. Instead, the court dismissed his suit due to the lack of evidence. The plaintiff felt trapped. He expected that the court would inform him that the evidence provided by him is perceived as unconvincing and that he may consider providing the testimony by better qualified experts. The U.S. Supreme Court followed the formal rule without regard to the plaintiff's expectations that a discourse would not be terminated without explicit warning. From the point of view of an ordinary language speaker the plaintiff was entitled to such a warning. Yet, the court used institutionalized legal language within its specific procedure of use as defined by the legislation. Problematic seems in this case primarily the interrelation between rules for the use of ordinary language and rules for the use of specialized and institutionalized language. Generally, speaking in procedures may appear to linguists as a non-problem because language is always used within a set of procedural rules. However, already L. Wittgenstein insisted upon the difference between knowing rules and following them. In the light of his approach, speakers (at least native speakers of a language) master, i.e. follow perfectly rules that are necessary to use the ordinary language. Yet, most of these speakers are unable to state these rules as their knowledge of them is practical and largely unreflective. Towards this background, speaking in legal procedures is almost impossible for non-professionals of law because they had no opportunity to internalize the rules needed for efficient speech under circumstances that are unusual for most of them. Therefore, non-professionals perform badly in institutional procedures related to law. Regularly, they will avail themselves of services of professionals of law, mostly attorneys, who will speak for them. This result is disenchanting in terms of law that is perceived as a discursive practice because independent linguistic communication is one of the central elements of responsible daily action for every human being. Being deprived of the possibility to speak on one's behalf due to the lack of procedural knowledge related to institutionalized language use is questionable at least in terms of anthropology and applied linguistics. Therefore, judicial institutions appear as deficient from the position of legal linguistics that scrutinizes their activities as communicational processes.

5.4.2 Arbitrary use of language

Finally, whatever arbitrary use of language in order to mislead, misrepresent the facts or conceal the truth is a catch up for constellations of language use that are not specific enough to form a separate type of language use in power structures. The arbitrariness is the specific feature of power in language use because only the powerful can allow himself to use this risky device. A. Peczenik (1986: 7) characterized the abuse of language in legally relevant contexts: "…it is clear that there is a scope for misuse of a description to exercise power. In particular, a description of actions can legitimize power by ignoring their complexity, e.g., by ignoring interpretation, by using too general terminology, and thus ignoring the unique properties of the action…" On the other side, language – legal language included – undeniably functions under the principle of semantic indeterminacy. Meanwhile, can language in law be used in whatever way? The answer in terms of pragmatic theory is clearly no, as the use of language is limited by constraints such as commitments, backgrounds and last but not least, truthfulness. In terms of pragmatic theory, speaking a language does not make much sense without the commitment to truthfulness. All speaking against this principle of language use is characterized as abuse of language. Practically, however, this abuse is all too willingly supported and, overall, can be deemed as rather efficient in short term strategical sociolinguistic operations of acquisition and maintenance of power. An example of such successfully abusive language is documented in the court opinion Lamb v. Philip Morris, Inc. (915 F.2d 1024, 6th Cir., 1990). In this case, the defendant and members of the government of Venezuela agreed to provide the defendant privileged treatment in exchange of payments to a charity foundation. The defendant entered into an agreement with La Fundacion del Niño (the Children's Foundation). Under the terms of the agreement, the defendant was to make periodic donations to the Children's Foundation. In exchange, the defendant was to obtain price control on Venezuelan tobacco, elimination of controls on retail cigarette prices in Venezuela, tax deductions for the donations, and assurances that existing tax rates applicable to tobacco products would not be increased. The agreement was signed on behalf of the Children's Foundation by its president, the wife of the then president of Venezuela. The plaintiff argued that the agreement violates the U.S. Foreign Corrupt Practices Act (FCPA) as it "amounts to unlawful inducements designed and intended to restrain trade." Yet, as there is no private cause of action available under the FCPA, the plaintiff lost his case. The abusive and cynical creation of a 'children's foundation' in order to accept bribes proved successful in a long line of related precedents.

5.4.3 Lies as language use

People are lying notoriously, also in law. No device in the human language prevents speakers from uttering thoughts that misrepresent their true beliefs and convictions. Lying is perceived by some speakers as a communicative strategy that is close to irony. D. B. Henriques (2011) reports that she had a problem with developing her narrative about the American fraudster B. Madoff's life after two interviews with him because Madoff, sentenced to 150 years of prison, has a tendency to lie when conversing. It is therefore difficult to shape a meaningful narrative, for instance about his childhood, because the necessary technical distinction between 'true' and 'false' is impossible in his case. Pragmatically, the unmasked liar's strategic problem of language use is that when he says the truth and he has a vital interest in that others believe that he is saying the truth, he will not be believed. The ancient Greeks ironized about people's relation to truth; the *Alythia* allegory portrays the truth that is hiding in the woods because people loath it. Immanuel Kant in *The Science of Right* captured structural elements of the lie that are relevant to law. He wrote: "It is customary to designate every untruth that is spoken intentionally as such, although it may be in a frivolous manner, a lie, or falsehood (mendacium), because it may do harm, at least in so far as any one who repeats it in good faith may be made a laughing-stock of to others on account of his easy credulity. But in the juridical sense, only that untruth is called a lie which immediately infringes the right of another, such as a false allegation of a contract having been concluded, when the allegation is put forward to deprave some one of what is his (falsiloquium dolosum). This distinction of conceptions so closely allied is not without foundation; because on the occasion of a simple statement of one's thoughts, it is always free for another to take them as he may; and yet the resulting repute, that such a one is a man whose word cannot be trusted, comes so close to the opprobrium of directly calling him a liar, that the boundary-line separating what, in such a case, belongs to jurisprudence, and what is special to ethics, can hardly be otherwise drawn." In law, the situation becomes particularly worrisome when governments begin to lie. Also communication in enterprises includes language that is often manipulative and therefore not respecting the truth. Omissions of material facts in speech and writing are typical of the business language. Lies are important in law because many crimes such as fraud are committed through lying.

5.4.4 Abusing the credulity of others

Epistemologically, the question whether people in principle rather believe other people or principally rather distrust them remains open (Williams 2001). In law, the element of distrust seems to be firmly incorporated into the structures of legal argumentation. In the legal procedure, the party that asserts certain facts has to prove them when the adversary contests them. In some exceptional procedures the burden of proof is reversed, and for instance the employer has to prove that he laid off an employee on other grounds than those perceived by the law as discriminatory. The existence of mandatory credibility tests for facts and for persons strengthens the initial assumption that in legal discourses, especially in legal procedures, distrust is a constitutive element of their structure. It engenders speech acts that function within the imposed discursive structure that incorporates incredulity. The existence of credibility tests, which in law procedurally take the shape of the burden of proof, is related to the speech act of justification. Justification makes functionally sense only in broader sociolinguistic contexts where the distrust is manifest or is a formal part of the discourse, i.e. the parties cannot dispose over it freely. In a civil procedure the judge cannot simply believe the version of facts asserted by the plaintiff when the defendant contests the facts. Exceptions are thinkable and will apply when the facts asserted by the plaintiff are evident, for instance that on 9/11 an armed assault had taken place in New York. This exception is applicable due to its making part of the general knowledge that also in other social settings does not require any concrete proof to be perceived as credible. Evident knowledge is the socially evident and generally accessible knowledge. When the plaintiff asserts facts concerning a traffic accident that are contested by the defendant and the judge by chance had himself witnessed the accident as an occasional by-passer he will not be able to support the party whose version is covered by his recollection. The factual knowledge that he has acquired is not general, and therefore not evident. The burden of proof will be applied under these circumstances. In fact, there is no rule without exception and the credibility tests will be the more effective the more the facts are contested. Whatever fact or legal view can be challenged in law and it is acceptable in the procedure only unless challenged (Hart 1948). Parties will try to challenge the necessity to participate in credibility tests, especially when they may encounter problems with the formal proof in the test. The formal proof is also therefore doubtful because it does not take into consideration that the party may say the truth and be unable to formally prove it. This is especially the case when the party can prove its assertion only with the help of the adversary or a third party and these are not cooperative or even destroy the materials that might be used as evidence for its true assertion. In the American law, these problems have given rise to new torts such as 'first party spoliation of evidence' and 'third party spoliation of evidence', as discussed in Gribben v. Wal-Mart Stores, Inc. (824 N.E.2nd 349 Ind. Sup. Ct., 2005). There, the plaintiff was injured in a Wal-Mart shop. Within the discovery procedure she demanded to have the video recordings made by the camera installed in the shop accessible to the jury. Wal-Mart contended that it did not preserve the surveillance videotape and the plaintiff claimed that the evidence has been deliberately spoliated. 'Spoliation of evidence', a tort not recognized in Indiana and in some other U.S.

states, occurs when a defendant or a third party negligently or intentionally destroys or discards evidence that is relevant to a tort action against him or another party. The legal question that prohibits the approval of the spoliation of evidence as tort in some American states is that the civil procedure already regulates this type of uncooperative behavior. For instance, Indiana law that was applied in the above case includes regulation that provides remedies to parties aggrieved by spoliation of evidence. It may also deter parties who are in possession of evidence disadvantageous to their interests from engaging in such practices. Under Indiana law, it is namely well established that 'intentional first party spoliation of evidence' may be used by the court to establish an inference that the spoliated evidence was unfavorable to the party responsible, as stated by the Indiana Supreme Court in 2000 in Cahoon v. Cummings (734 N.E. 2d 535, 545).

Also the political discourse is an example of a particularly prudent recipients' strategy. Rare are recipients of political discourses, for instance listeners to political speeches, who take them literally. T. Shelby (2011: 107) while analyzing B. Obama's political agenda says about the interpretive method that he adopts: "It is generally understood that in order to be elected and stay in office, politicians often use deceit; sometimes they lie. For the purposes of this essay, I take Obama's considered public statements at face value. I assess the vision itself, a vision that many, including many racial minorities, support or find attractive. I make no claims about whether the vision is offered in good faith, about the authenticity of Obama himself, or about the extent to which his actual policy choices and political tactics square with his stated vision." This interpretive method is the last hope of an interpreter of texts. In legal linguistics, its usefulness is limited. Judicial institutions that process language have to distinguish between truth and lies, between probable and improbable, between contradiction and coherence. A judge cannot take the witness testimony or the declaration made by a party at face value. He must consider the credibility of the message and the credibility of the person who delivers the message. He has the right or even the obligation to say to a party or to a witness that despite the coherent declaration that he has heard he simply does not believe it. The professionally most advanced level of non-believing is the analysis of a statement that is proven unacceptable even if formally consistent and coherent. Legal linguistics analyzes and helps develop appropriate methods for dealing with credibility of statements (Galdia 2009: 203).

Social practices include a certain degree of incredulity towards the declarations of others as they also include a fundamental attitude of credulity to the words expressed in public. These attitudes towards the words of others are not contradictory; they are complementary because they guarantee the functionality of society as a whole. We believe in the truthfulness of some statements immediately, as we immediately do not believe in others. The tests in which this sort of evaluation takes place are largely internalized. As a rule, not much time is spent on deciding whether to believe what we are said or not. The test is a trade-off between social efficiency and equity, i.e. believing in what is true. As a result, much what is true is not believed and many lies are believed. The test is also expedient in the mentioned sense that it makes society go around even if many decisions about truth or falsity are actually wrong. On a level of individual encounters, discursive fairness is neglected because the test is a summary mechanism. Cognitive limitations of speakers and knowledge asymmetry are among the reasons for this complex attitude to a rather simple matter that is the truth. When the aggrieved party pretends to have been abused in its credulity when proposed to travel and to stay on the planet Sirius, so it is evident that untruth had been the basis of this proposal. Meanwhile, could the aggrieved party believe in the truthfulness of the proposal? Judges would tend to answer this question with no. Rationality tests are therefore not applied in an area that would be the quintessential field for their application. Lying as a speech act that in its essence pretends something different from what is believed is therefore not necessarily an abuse of other peoples' credulity because others often do not believe us. A closely related phenomenon known from the ancient times is the low expectation in the public towards truth contents in cases where statements, even if not true, are expedient. The ancient Romans put it short: Mundus vult decipi – the world wishes to be deceived. Law has adapted itself to this paradoxical situation.

Research into trust in modern societies, especially as regards internet and the 'social' networks provides arguments that stress the assumption of a discourse-specific reluctance to cope with issues of truth. Assurances of honesty or declarations of honor will not do in law. A judge cannot simply take at face value the statement of the accused who assures that he is innocent. Also in online contacts, in "computer-mediated environments" (Cheshire 2011: 49) trust cannot be simply acquired by means of assurance. For Cheshire (2011: 50), trust is relevant when risk and uncertainty exist together; trust is not simply the absence of risk and uncertainty. Communication, both online and offline, takes place in conditions that require trust because uncertainty about the reliability of information is omnipresent. As interpersonal trust develops only over time, interpersonal relations in institutionalized settings such as legal practices will rarely be based on unconditional trust. What is more, in the area of social interaction we may "trust various people in different contexts, but trust very few (if any) people in every context" (Cheshire 2011: 51). It appears that the stronger the commonalities among people involved in the discourse, the higher will be the expectancy of mutual reliability. Due to the antagonistic nature of human relations in legal settings the level of commonalities is low. Legal practices are therefore located on the fragile ground of limited trust as trusting relationships can only rarely emerge under the circumstances in which this type of communication takes place. Truth cannot be expected in them as an inherent element of legal speech acts.

5.4.5 Commercial lies

Limitations to the freedom of speech in the commercial sphere reflect the tendency among the professionals of commerce to blur the distinction between truth and lie. Lies in commercial sphere are mostly half-truths, for instance when a 'tax deferred' investment is described by a broker as 'tax-free'. Less offensive lies are known as puffery, for instance when a fast food restaurant praises its French fries as 'best in the world'. In Pizza Hut, Inc. v. Papa John's International, Inc. (227 F.3d 489, 2000) an American court of appeals had to decide whether the advertisement "Better Ingredients. Better Pizza." in a comparative advertising campaign was false advertising. As a speech act, false advertising is a lie. Lies must relate to statements of facts, otherwise Section 43(a) Lanham Act that prohibits false advertisement would not apply. In the context of this provision, general opinions such as puffery are not perceived as statements of facts. The court defines puffery as: "1) an exaggerated, blustering, and boasting statement upon which no reasonable buyer would be justified in relying; or 2) a general claim of superiority over comparable products that is so vague that it can be understood as nothing more than a mere expression of opinion." As to the qualification of puffery as lie the court quoted the legal writers Prosser and Keeton who in the fifth edition of their *Law of Torts* characterize puffing as: "a seller's privilege to lie his head off, so long as he says nothing specific, on the theory that no reasonable man would believe him, or that no reasonable man would be influenced by such talk." The court divided the advertisement slogan in two parts. First, to make a 'Better Pizza' is as an assertion a general statement of fact. Second, 'having better ingredients' is likewise a general opinion, because the assertion cannot be further quantified, as no ingredients are mentioned. Thus, the advertisement slogan appears as non-actionable under the Lanham Act. The situation is different when material proof is available, as in Kraft, Inc. v. Federal Trade Commission (970 F. 2d 311, 7th Cir., 1992). The American enterprise Kraft, Inc. brought on the U.S. market "Kraft Singles" that are process cheese food slices. Generally, individually wrapped slices of cheese and cheeselike products come in two major parts: process cheese food slices, which according to federal regulation must contain at least 51 percent natural cheese, and imitation slices, which contain little or no natural cheese. In its advertisement Kraft pretended that Kraft Singles cost more because each slice is made from 5 ounces of milk. In the broadcast version of the Singles' advertisements, a woman stated that she bought Kraft Singles for her daughter rather than "skimping" by purchasing imitation slices. She pretended that: "imitation slices use hardly any milk. But Kraft has 5 ounces per slice. Five ounces. So her bones get calcium they need to grow." The commercial also showed milk being poured into a glass that bore the label "5 oz. milk slice." The glass was then transformed into part of the label on a package of Singles. Later, Kraft added as a subscript in the television commercial: "one ¾ ounce slice has 70% of the calcium of five ounces of milk." Another commercial said: "Half of the school kids in America don't get all the calcium recommended for growing kids. That's why Kraft Singles are important." The Federal Trade Commission instituted a deceptive advertising proceeding against Kraft, Inc. under § 5 of the FTC Act. § 5 FTC Act prohibits material deceptive practices in commercials. The FTC regarded the milk equivalency claim used by Kraft as false even though Kraft actually uses 5 ounces of milk in making each Single slice because roughly 30 percent of the calcium contained in the milk is lost during the processing. With reference to this circumstance the court perceived Kraft's factual statement as deceptive. Thus, Kraft used a lie that has been determined as such in a formal, and not in a legal-linguistic procedure. From the legal-linguistic perspective, both cases that were analyzed in this paragraph are very close and it could be even posited that they represent one type of speech act. In the formal, legal procedure difference is made between quantifiable data and other vague linguistic data. In turn, ordinary language avoids this sort of distinguishing. Its mechanisms seem therefore better adapted to tracing abusive speech. Meanwhile, lies are only one of many examples of legal speech acts that display anthropological intricacies. Some of them will be discussed in the following paragraphs.

5.5 Anthropology of law

The discursive framework of reference for legal anthropology has been prefigured by Aristotle. In *Politics* (1253a2) Aristotle introduces the term 'political animal' in a phrase that can be rendered in English in the translation prepared by Ernest Barker: "…it is evident that the city belongs to the class of things that exist by nature, and that man is by nature a political animal." Numerous interpretations have been proposed to elucidate this conceptual coinage (Cooper 1990; Kullmann 1991). Aristotle writes simply and therefore probably also enigmatically: "…ότι άνδρωπος φῦσει πολιτικόν ζώον." Barker experiments with the term and writes also for 'political animal' "naturally a polis-animal." R.G. Stalley (2009: 320) comments on the term: "...this famous phrase does not mean that man naturally engages in political activity...the defining feature of humanity is not so much its political character as its rationality." Aristotle's 'political animal' is rendered in the modernized English translation as 'man is a being meant for political association' that in this linguistic interpretation paves the way towards conceptual creations such as 'political associations'. Finally, textual comparison allows the interpretation that Aristotle defines 'man' in terms of his biological inquires (cf. Stalley 2009: 321) and that he means with it that 'man' lives in society rather than alone. Characteristically also the famous passage about the human language (Aristotle, *Politics* 1253a7) follows immediately upon the definition of 'man'. Barker translates: "...man alone of the animals is furnished with the faculty of language...language serves to declare what is advantageous and what is the reverse, and it is the peculiarity of man...that he alone possesses a perception of good and evil, of the just and the unjust, and other similar qualities; and it is association in these things which makes a family and a city." Aristotle draws a conclusion from the above in *Politics* (1253a25): "Man, when perfected, is the best of animals; but if he be isolated from law and justice he is the worst of all." Already in *Politics* (1253a2) Aristotle referred to Homer's *Iliad* (IX, 63): "Clanless and lawless and hearthless is he" when speaking about the notional antonym of his 'political animal'. Finally, Aristotle's discursive framework can be reduced to a fundamental structure based on linguistic coinages such as the social character of the human being, language as a social phenomenon, intellectual capacity to distinguish between right and wrong, and the knowledge of law as a mechanism of social organization. These anthropological conceptual prerequisites also define the scope and the limits of law as a rational activity. Aristotle's framework fits perfectly the needs of legal linguistics that has to integrate these discursive constants into the general structure of legal discourse. It needs however an extension when legislative activity is in question because Aristotle systematically underestimates the constructivist feature of law and tends towards essentialist views. Meanwhile, the anthropology of law is anchored in the fact that law is made by humans for humans. Anthropological limits to legal rationality are primarily bordered on practical impossibility. Legislators, therefore, have to observe biological parameters typical of humans. For instance, a law that would reduce the duration of pregnancy to a period of seven or eight months would not be acceptable in anthropological terms. Yet, legislators also compromise with the human nature. Regulation concerning the preservatives in food products or air pollution is rather lax. Communicative aspects of law where humans speak to humans are regularly underestimated by courts and administrative agencies. This is another aspect of manifest legal anthropology. It includes the formation of law in cultures other than the Occident. Sometimes, one might argue that the formally overcome social structures still dominate the legal thinking. For instance, the Constitution of India is committed to a modern form of society. Yet, in its Art. 29 (1) it includes a formulation that may have been patterned by the caste experience: "Any section of the citizens residing in the territory of India or any part thereof having a distinct language, script or culture of its own shall have the right to conserve the same." The perception of the citizens as divided in sections must have reasons, and these reasons, which are often unreflected, come from history. The main contribution of legal anthropology to legal linguistics is however the discovery that commitments to rationality steer legal-linguistic operations. Paradoxically, legal anthropology also extensively focused on inquires into irrational elements in legally relevant contexts. Discourse coined in such contexts is a sample of legal language and it is therefore worth to be treated also in legal linguistics.

5.5.1 Friends of irrationality

Strictly rational approaches to law are challenged by culturally motivated perspectives that refer to other, less rational intellectual fundamentals. On these views, law may be based on tradition that some, for instance Glenn (2010: 4), construe as primary to reason in legally relevant contexts, mainly because tradition transports experience, i.e. best societal practices in contemporary parlance. Tradition reflects collective memory that replaces the search for appropriate law. In the argumentation based on tradition, law appears as static and its change is difficult to obtain because the main argument against it is strong; it is the assertion that 'we have always done it this way'. Meanwhile, a more inquisitive look at law makes plain that legal regulation has constantly changed and that it reflected the changes in society even if they are negated on ideological reasons. The law based on tradition is therefore a type of law that favors certain arguments that refer to its unchangeable hard core and eternal values that this law is expected to protect and to preserve (cf. Fukuda-Parr 2004). Sociologically, it functions as whatever type of law as it will have to process societal evolutions because it is law. It may then attempt at concealing argumentatively this ongoing adaptation. Also origin and legitimacy of law engendered specific argumentation that aimed at strengthening law's obligatory character. Probably, law that in some historical formations has been imposed by the political class was perceived as vulnerable. To illustrate this constellation, Herodotus in the first book of his *History* (Clio

65) refers to an account that laws passed by Lycurgus in Sparta had been delivered to him by the Pythoness in their entirety. Apparently, this reference should strengthen the legitimacy of the laws as not coming directly from a human legislator but having an origin related to divinity.

5.5.2 Magic in law

Magical use of words illustrates the first step towards public speaking, i.e. the use of language that is not planned for private communication. Magic language shall impress and engender results automatically (cf. Bülow 1986). Magical use of formulae that are often not understood by lay persons occurs frequently in law. Sometimes lay persons construe law as an area where such formulae should be applied. While in need, they will turn for legal advice and ask what they are expected to say when an event happens: 'I was mug shot on the highway while speeding – what shall I say in court?' The intention underlying the question is to obtain the liberating magical formula that should be used in court to get rid of liability. The question may thus be reformulated: 'what shall I say in the court to become acquitted?' Close to magic language is religiously connoted speech. In the perspective of legal anthropology, no significant difference has been made between religious and legal texts in the ancient times. Regarding the *Hammurabi Code* that he perceives as a sacred book, Horne (1917: 108) remarks: "Even a law code was in those days regarded as a subject for prayer, though the prayers here are chiefly coursings of whoever shall neglect or destroy the law." Finally, also superstition makes part of legal discourses. In the literature, regularly reference is made to the fact that the second and the third U.S. Presidents, John Adams and Thomas Jefferson, both died on July 4, 1826, it is on a day that commemorates the declaration of American independence.

5.5.3 Male law and Female law

Anthropological components of legal discourses pertain regularly to gender issues. In these discourses, an argumentative matrix evolves that touches upon the very essence of law. For instance, Th. Jefferson enters into a polemic with the French naturalist G. de Buffon about the female condition among America's Indians and writes in his *Notes on the State of Virginia*: "The women are submitted to unjust drudgery. This I believe is the case with every barbarous people. With such, force is law. The stronger sex therefore imposes on the weaker. It is civilization alone which replaces women in the enjoyment of their natural equality. This first teaches us to subdue to selfish passions, and to respect those rights of others which we value in others. Were we in equal barbarism, our females would be equal drudges, …" (in Query VI). Identification of strong and weak as two elements of power is linked to law that provides for 'natural equality' that does not include force. 'The other' is construed under equal legal status; barbarous in habits, yet equal under law. Discursively, Jefferson does not hesitate to call the other a few lines later 'a savage', and he can do it because in terms of the matrix he sets for a legal discourse it does not matter whether the other is 'civilized' or not, because law makes him equal notwithstanding his otherness as identified by Jefferson.

More recently, F. Héritier (2011) referred to ancient legal sources where legal positions have been traditionally termed in male perspectives that stress the female inferiority. In a Hittite code, the man cannot marry his mother-in-law or the spouse of his son or his brother. Equally, he is prohibited from marrying the daughters or the mother of the woman in question. Conversely, the prohibition to marry concerns also all the women mentioned in the named constellations; yet the Hittite code does not regulate expressly their legal position because a woman has no legal personality in its legal frame of reference. The woman is therefore not mentioned as a bearer of a prohibition not to enter into marriage with certain men, although the mirror image of the provisions clearly provides for such a prohibition. The legal text is developed along a 'valence différentielle des sexes' that is constitutive of repression that is due to gender. Roman law also displays this distorted constellation. In the Roman law, the spouse takes the place of the daughter, not of a partner in marriage – uxor filiae locus optinet. 'Female inferiority' has been also an issue for literature. J. Milton in *Samson Agonistes* refers to the alleged female argumentative inferiority (verses 903–906): "Dalila: In argument with men a woman ever/Goes by the worse, whatever be her cause./ Samson: For want of words no doubt, or lack of breath,/Witness when I was worried with thy peals." Interestingly, also Durston (2007) stressed the possible advantages that women may have enjoyed in the past due to their alleged 'argumentative weakness'.

A certain element of gender-specific behavior is present in discourses relevant to law. With this in mind, Ferreira Acuña (2011) stressed however the necessity to avoid stereotypes when approaching the discourse from the gender-perspective. She recommended to "abandonar la exaltación de las diferencias de género en el discurso, prestando igual atención a las semejanzas." Indeed, while differences exist, there exist also discursive resemblances that are no less important. When, for instance, the way of making complaints about the action of third persons is scrutinized, as done by Ferreira Acuña, so it might be that some gender-specific differences are observed, yet resemblances are more important. The speech act of complaint is characterized by attempts to accomplish solidarity with one's statement on the part of the interlocutor. Gender is according to Ferreira Acuña not relevant as far as this characteristic feature of complaint as speech act is concerned. Indeed, the main structure of the speech act will not be dependent on gender. The description of the event that underlies the complaint about the third person, the moral blame of this behavior, the indignation expressed towards the interlocutor with the expectation that he/she will join in the critical evaluation of the action may differ in terms of details. The speech act of complaint against the action of third persons will nevertheless remain constant as far as the structural features of the complaint are concerned, although the female language may be more affective and the male language more aggressive. Complaint as a speech act is independent of these features. Furthermore, temporal limits of dominant discourses are visible in the attitude towards sexual harassment of men as displayed by the U.S. court practice. In Keeton v. Flying J, Inc. a court in Kentucky dealt in 2005 with a demand for compensation for emotional distress filed by a man who suffered under his female supervisor. His female supervisor constantly harassed him by making proposals to which he did not respond. She finally terminated his employment agreement while saying: "You are not supporting me." The employer had been informed by the plaintiff about the facts, yet he only took measures that would reinstate the plaintiff in his work in another place. The court found that this action had not been a sufficient measure and decided for the plaintiff. Already in Burlington Industries, Inc v. Ellerth the U.S. Supreme Court decided in 1998 that the employer becomes liable for all disadvantages suffered by plaintiffs in harassment cases if he does not take any sufficient preventive or corrective measures after being informed about the alleged harassing behavior of a superior. The U.S. employment law broadens the discursive scope in gender related issues in that it engages also a third party that as a rule is or prefers to remain neutral in relation to this type of events that it tends to perceive as private. The Title VII of the 1964 Civil Rights Act includes a broad employment discrimination provision that prohibits discrimination based on race, color, religion, sex, and national origin. It covers employment constellations such as hiring, firing, job assignments, pay, and access to training and similar employment decisions. Unwelcome sexual advances, requests for sexual favors, and other verbal or physical conduct of a sexual nature by superior persons, for instance the refusal to go out on a date with the supervisor, co-workers and sometimes even clients can lead to claims under Title VII. Linguistically, this regulation represents an advanced practice in the discourse about anti-discrimination. Meanwhile, legal-linguistic innovation is not necessarily a progress. The paragraph below illustrates this phenomenon.

From the historical perspective, one of the most oppressive notions of the common law was the 'coverture'. Under the family law regime of coverture "wives were understood to be 'covered' under the civil identity of their husbands in much the same way as children were subject to their parents" (Kerber 2012: 91). W. Blackstone wrote in 1770 about the principle of coverture in the first volume of his *Commentaries on the Laws of England* (chapter 1, 443): "By marriage, the husband and wife are one person in law...The very being or legal existence of the woman is suspended during the marriage, or at least is incorporated and consolidated into that of the husband: under whose wing, protection, and cover, she performs every thing." Coverture has been legitimized by the claim that women are "too weak to act autonomously" (Kerber 2012: 96). The *Everyman's Encyclopaedia* commented on this implication of coverture in 1913: "In these days of agitation by certain schools of thought – fostered in England more than sixty years ago by the writing of John Stuart Mill, and expanded in more recent years in the translated dramas of Ibsen, and those of Mr. Bernard Shaw – for the complete emancipation of women from a real or imaginary male tyranny, regardless of the immutable infirmities of their physical nature, no rules of law or equity regarding the consequences of the married state, based on principles of apparently sound common sense, and framed as far as possible in accordance with the spirit of the mutual obligations imposed by the Christian religion in its conception of the married state, can cope with the movement. With the abrogation of the privileges that flowed from it to the husband comes a corresponding rejection of the benefits such state might confer on the wife. Doubtless in a highly civilized community, where pure intellect or opinion replace force as the foundation of the whole structure of society, these claims for complete independence from all real and artificial limitations of the married state may possibly come to fruition. Until that ideal is attained, even political emancipation for women, whether under coverture or not, can hardly avail anything against the normal consequences of a struggle for existence in a society where force still remains the dominant and deciding factor – a truism curiously emphasized by the violent methods adopted to attain their ends by the feminine agitators for the suffrage." Traditional family law, previously called 'law of domestic relations', "began with the principle that the husband controlled the physical body of his wife" (Kerber 2012: 91). Its roots go back to the Roman law where the wife was regarded as no more than a chattel belonging to her husband. In more modern times, Harriet Beecher Stowe's novel *Uncle Tom's Cabin; or the Life under the Lowly* – whose originality has been questioned – was regularly plagiated in the U.S. One of such copyright infringements led to a lawsuit where Harriet Beecher Stowe was represented by her husband. H. Beecher Stowe enjoyed the liberty to write sentimental novels, yet she had lived 'covered'. The result was that she alone could not sue in courts and had to be represented by her husband whose rights had been violated by the plagiates (Vaidhyanathan 2001: 202). Also her publishing contracts had to be signed by her husband. Coverture was often presented in a referential framework of apparent legal symmetry, for instance by the American jurist Tapping Reeve in his *The Law of Baron and Femme, of Parent and Child, Guardian and Ward, Master and Servant*, published in New England in 1816. The apparent symmetry of 'Baron and Femme' – that is law French for 'Lord and Woman' – is annihilated by the regime of coverture that makes the wife disappear as a legal person for the duration of her marriage, as mentioned by Blackstone. The wife was 'femme-covert', under the power or 'cover' of her husband. In the U.K., the Married Women's Property Act put 1882 an end to the coverture regime.

5.5.4 Seclusion and crocodile tears in legal discourses

Legal institutions are not particularly transparent. While court proceedings are public in most jurisdictions, many discourses take place in seclusion that is either accepted or even imposed or guaranteed by the legislation. This secrecy is sometimes taken for granted, and sometimes questioned. For the U.S., J. Toobin (2008, 2010) spoke about the secret world of the U.S. Supreme Court. Internal discourses, for instance jury deliberation or discussions among judges before they vote on a case, are rarely reported and even if reports are available the question of truthfulness of such usually partisan reports is a problem. Some sources for the structure of such discourses exist and may be used with some reward. Toobin (2010: 34) reports in the magazine *The New Yorker* a scene from the U.S. Supreme Court that concerns the public farewell to Justice John Paul Stevens: "It was also the day after Martin Ginsburg, Ruth Bader Ginsburg's husband of fifty-six years died, at their home in Washington, after a battle with cancer. Ginsburg startled her colleagues by showing up for work despite her husband's death; she wore a black velvet bow in her hair. Roberts paid a warm tribute to Marty Ginsburg, who was as jovial as his wife is reserved. As Roberts spoke, Antonin Scalia, who, with his wife, spent every New Years Eve with the Ginsburgs, wept." Surprisingly, private events are introduced into a professional setting where the most important matters of the law of the country are expected to be debated and solved. These events may apparently also move to tears those who are rarely responsive to the emotions of others. Meanwhile, anthropology of legal discourse that takes place in seclusion is as fascinating as it is limited. Many judicial institutions appear as unassailable fortresses to the citizens at large.

5.5.5 Some myths in law

Myths in law overburden the legal reasoning. In their oldest versions, Moses transfers laws that were communicated to him. Ancient myths such as the narrative about Romulus and Remus refer to ideologies that structure state and society. Romulus is primus legislator: Romulus primus iura dabat. Meanwhile, laws are constructed, not given. Possibly also therefore Ch. de Montesquieu in *Esprit des lois* deals rather with people who deal with laws. He establishes a myth that is operative even today: the division between legislative, executive and judicature. Myths tend to incorporate realistic elements into the narration, apparently to ensure or increase the acceptability of ideology or regulation that they transfer. Some legal metaphors also contributed to myth creation. The metaphor of 'clean hands' in law appears frequently, especially in the common law. Clean hands are generally commendable as a habit, and in law there are even more wishful, mostly as metaphors. Metaphors related to cleanliness are used in law as legal requirements for credibility of statements, mostly about law. 'Clean hands' are required from those who approach judicial institutions, not from those who are expected to render justice. The fundamental maxim of equity in the common law states: 'He who comes to equity must come with clean hands.' For instance, C.B. Eyre in Dering v. Earl of Winchelsea wrote in 1787: "A man must come into a court of equity with clean hands". Some manifestations of the metaphor such as the Italian 'mani pulite' refer to the action of state institutions in law. They represent non-doctrinary speaking about law.

5.6 Law as element of ethical and political discourses

Law as a subject has been regularly incorporated in discourses other than legal. It has been instrumentalized in political and ethical discourses. B. Spinoza deals with law as with an explicitly ethical and political phenomenon while discussing it passim in his *Tractatus politicus*. For Spinoza, legal issues cannot be discussed in separation from politics and legal action. Avoiding the discussion of law as an isolated phenomenon is also N. Machiavelli's choice. In fact, isolationist approaches to law, positivist and others, actually show the contrary of the intended. H. Kelsen's attempt to clean law from foreign elements that he most pronouncedly undertook in his *Reine Rechtslehre* is the most impressive achievement and a well-intentioned step towards isolating purely legal elements in law. His experiment ends up with a legal skeleton, a pyramid of legal norms structured linguistically around the basic norm (Grundnorm) as its logical bottom or visual top. One might have the feeling that this cannot be everything, that law is more than a hierarchy of rules. This separation of purely legal elements from law makes plain that there is actually not much left for law. This is a good result and it shows how right Spinoza, Machiavelli and some others had been in that they avoided the isolationist trap. Indeed, law cannot be separated from ethics and politics and this result has consequences. Such a step would guarantee the coherence of discourse where law is an element. Law schools or Continental legal faculties should follow these examples because, as of today, they favor the isolationist approach to law notwithstanding many statements to the contrary.

5.6.1 Human dimension in law

Like some of the authors quoted above, also Richard Weisberg (1992) stressed in his *Poethics*, which stands for poetic ethics, that the perspective upon law taken in Law and Literature-studies allows for an apprehension of the conditio humana that traditional legal writings exclude. He is definitely right to argue this. The legal writings, court opinions and theoretical works upon law may in their perspective be limited to so-called technical parts of law. Yet, they display the human dimension regularly, even against their express attitude taken towards the law, and maybe in such cases even most. In the American reflection about law, numerous were the critics of mechanical jurisprudence (e.g. B. Cardozo, R. Pound). Numerous were, however, also the supporters of this approach. That the human dimension is inherent in law is a feature of law itself. There is no law without human dimension. Legal writings make this feature visible. These considerations have been extended to encompass even corporations as the preamble to the *Universal Declaration of Human Rights* mentions that 'every individual and every organ of society' has to bear responsibilities under this act. In the U.S., the Alien Tort Claims Act (ATCA) institutes the cause of action against U.S. based multinational corporations when they commit torts abroad, i.e. when they violate human rights standards through their activities outside U.S. Discursively, also 'socially responsible investing' is chronologically and linguistically related to 'alien torts'. This terminological interrelation seems to be a discursive regularity; new legal terms engender other terms due to textual interconnections that are formed around semantic fields. The same discursive mechanism functions also in the ordinary language where coinages such as 'disposable diapers' and 'disposable cameras' allow the creation of 'disposable employees' in ironical speech, and possibly also beyond it. Generally, the human rights discourse is an area of law where terminological creation is abundant and it is often multilingual.

5.6.2 Human rights discourse

The human rights discourse is paradigmatic for the position of the human dimension in law. The typology of human rights discourses starts with their diachronic dimension. T. Honoré (2002) traced even 'human rights' down to the Roman jurist Ulpian. H. Joas (2011) addressed the issue of conceptualization of human rights in a philosophical perspective. In this perspective the question of material justification of the terminological coinage prevails in the analysis. Human rights are not thinkable without the creation of a legally binding concept of person and the 'sanctity' of the person. Generalization of values is the philosophical procedure in which terms of the human rights discourse emerge. Joas also demonstrates that the creation of human rights must be contrasted with the discursive practice of their application. Clearly, one thing is to find appropriate terms for the content of human rights and another thing is to implement them in discursive practices. Today, the human rights discourse displays two main problems. First, the conceptual development of human rights beyond the existing traditional canon seems to stagnate. Second, the implementation of the traditional human rights as stated in international instruments is far from being achieved. With reference to Joas one may invoke for the human rights discourse the idea of a literary law. The literary law is philosophically well founded and also admired in society, yet it does not work. Like a popular novel, it is read and it is commended, but has no bearing on the daily life of those whom it should protect. The synchronical perspective presents a more specific catalogue of human rights. Meanwhile, these contemporary human rights are not more effective than those described by Joas in the diachronical perspective. S. Moyn (2010) refers to the contemporary form of the human rights discourse that for him starts in the 70ties of the twentieth century. All other discourses including elements of general importance for the determination of the legal position between individuals and the societal forms, in which they live, have according to Moyn another structure. Sources generally perceived as fundamental to the human rights discourse such as the Levitical commands of the *Old Testament*, the Greek philosophy, the *Declaration of the Rights of Man*, or the antislavery and civil rights movements are historical forms that do not coincide with the contemporary human rights discourse. First of all, "the level of common speech," so Moyn (2010), is not reached in them; they are not widespread in the consciousness of people as it is the case nowadays due to the generalized international refusal of totalitarianism and authoritarianism. In addition, Moyn (2012) refers to the coinage of the term 'human rights' in the speeches by Franklin Delanoe Roosevelt who has had in mind a kind of welfarism rather than international human rights standards. Wilson's notion of 'self-determination' and 'anti-colonialism' were preceding the idea of human rights as internationally binding legal standards. Another discursive pattern is centered on the fundamentals of the human rights. The main topic there is: who is giving them. Also Lakoff (2008: 3) quotes as an example of metaphorical language use in constitutional law the sample: "The Founding Fathers put freedom of speech into the Constitution." The metaphors of putting or giving and taking are omnipresent in this type of human rights discourses. Their sources remain controversial, yet the political discourse transgresses the problem by avoiding it. Jacques Maritain mentioned in 1946: "We agree about the rights but on condition that no one asks us why." The 'why' of the human rights can be answered with the help of the philosophical reconstruction such as Joas's. Meanwhile, human rights as rights can become effective only in discursive practices of law (Gregg 2012). Discursive practices, values and institutions must be mobilized to transform literary human rights into rights. On paper, they cannot satisfy.

5.7 Converting words into respectable judicial discourses

Law is power expressed with linguistic means. Power, meanwhile, should be described to enable a better understanding of it. Its discursive dimension is visible in many linguistic transformations that have axiological consequences. For instance, P. Berger (1963: 54) deals with the linguistic transformation of a socially unpopular profession of the 'hangman' into a 'public servant'. Legal discourse that is close to power structures facilitates such transformations and is prone to attribute respectability to the most obnoxious people. Due to this structural ambiguity of the legal discourse, and more often than not, power is defined negatively as oppression of the weak by the powerful. This is definitely not wrong as the daily experience of millions of people provides this notion with exemplary evidence that is destiny of so many. Yet, power may also be understood more productively, as a means that normalizes or disciplines societies. M. Foucault linked both conceptions of power in his approach. He advocated for the discursive conception of power as opposed to the sovereign form of power (Dahl 1957). There, structures and agents form part of a discursive order which results from the struggle of power strategies for meaning. They are modified mutually in the course of their articulation. Also J. Habermas mentions in this context a 'herrschaftsfreier Diskurs' as an ideal discursive structure. As of now, it is easier to speak about power-dominated discourses than about non-domination. Ample linguistic material can be used for analyses of the traditional understanding of the discursive exercise of power. For the alternative project, linguistic material is missing. The following discourse around the notion of 'race' may shed some light on the evolution of discursive practices that are connected with the exercise of power.

5.7.1 Metaphor of race as power device

The metaphor of 'race' as a linguistic construct has proven fatal to societies where it has been used in law and in all discourses that relate to it. R. Kipling in his most injurious 'poem' *The White Man's Burden* captures in words the feelings of his time in relation to others: "You new-caught, sullen people,/ Half-devil and half-child." Kipling strengthened this attitude of perception of people as others. Later, S.P. Huntington amplified the otherness in *The Clash of Civilizations and the Remaking of World Order* (1998). Also G.W.F. Hegel contributed in *The Philosophy of History* to the emergence of linguistic categories that are occasionally invoked even in contemporary discourses. Hegel wrote in all earnest in the introduction to his work: "Africa proper, as far as history goes back, has remained, for all purposes of connection with the rest of the world, shut up; it is the gold-land compressed within itself – the land of childhood, which lying beyond the day of self-conscious history, is enveloped in the dark mantle of night." Rationally, civilizations or cultures cannot clash nor conflict because they are structurally interrelated. African or Asian cultures are neither structurally nor substantially separated from the culture that many perceive as European or Transatlantic. Cultures have no passports and no nationality; race and color of skin are totally irrelevant to their emergence, existence, and development. A simple story, such as the Swahili classic *Liongo Fumo,* shows how profoundly erroneous isolationist views upon culture actually are. The eldest manuscripts of *Liongo Fumo* date back to the twelfth century. They render a story that unites ethical rules, strategies of power acquisition and tribal rites. They also show that the metaphor of race is used in law as a power device.

More recently, in many U.S. legal acts 'race' has been present in a discriminatory way unto our very days. Greenville city ordinance requiring separation of the races in restaurants (Code of Greenville, 1953, § 31–8), as amended in 1958, and still in force 1960 provided that:

"It shall be unlawful for any person owning, managing or controlling any hotel, restaurant, café, eating house, boarding-house or similar establishment to furnish meals to white persons and colored persons in the same room, or at the same table, or at the same counter; provided however, that meals may be served to white persons and colored persons in the same room where separate facilities are furnished. Separate facilities shall be interpreted to mean:

(a) Separate eating utensils and separate dishes for the serving of food, all of which shall be distinctly marked by some appropriate color scheme or otherwise;
(b) Separate tables, counters or booths;
(c) A distance of at least thirty-five feet shall be maintained between the area where white and colored persons are served;
(d) The area referred to in subsection (c) above shall not be vacant but shall be occupied by the usual display counters and merchandise found in a business concern of a similar nature;
(e) A separate facility shall be maintained and used for the cleaning of eating utensils and dishes furnished the two races."

Similarly, the Code of Durham (1947), c. 13, § 42 stipulated: "In all licensed restaurants, public eating places and 'weenie shops' where persons of the white and colored races are permitted to be served with, and eat food, and are allowed to congregate, there shall be provided separate rooms for the separate accommodation of each race. The partition between such rooms shall be constructed of wood, plaster or brick or like material, and shall reach from floor to the ceiling. Any person violating this section shall, upon conviction pay a fine of ten dollars and each day's violation thereof shall constitute a separate and distinct offense." Groups of human rights activists regularly violated these provisions and challenged the local authorities. The trials of these groups of defendants have been conducted seriatim by the same judge, who reserved sentencing until all trials had been completed (Peterson v. City of Greenville Lombard, 373 U.S. 244). They mark the erosive process of using the concept of 'race' in the U.S. law. Legal-linguistic interest in this sort of texts in directed towards their excessive precision. It seems that terminological precision and casuistry engender the impression of legality in regulation. Indeed, when the legal rule appears in a meticulous linguistic dress, it may cause an unreflected impression of legality. This linguistic device is however not very efficient because it engenders only the first impression that is very easily overcome. Also vehement protests against the regulation quoted above prove its argumentative weakness. The abusive terminological precision may however appeal to those who share the ideological views that underlie this regulation. In fact, language has been since ancient times perceived as a double-edge sword; it may serve the speaker but it may also harm his interests. This ambiguity is in law a question of perspective because law displays power structures in antagonistic societies. What is harmful and what is beneficial in regulation remains therefore a question of perspective. This circumstance may even explain the very existence of rules such as those quoted above. Meanwhile, this type of excessive regulation can be maintained in society only within power structures that do not hesitate to defend it by all means. J.L. Gibson (2012a: 114) stressed one more complex mechanism of the legal discourse with racial argumentative background. According to his research, black Americans assume that they are exposed to more constraints on their political action than white citizens. While perception of political freedom regularly differs from legal guarantees of political participation that is guaranteed by laws, the negative perception index has far-going discursive implications. When black American citizens vote less frequently than others, because they perceive their action as systemically constrained, this behavior has an impact upon the exercise of other rights. For instance, when the U.S. Supreme Court guarantees the citizens the right to spend financial means without limits in an effort to influence the chances of candidates in elections, as done in the decision Citizens United (cf. 2.3.1), this right, so Gibson, "does not affect all groups, racial and otherwise, equally." Formal freedom that is guaranteed under Citizens United appears as a fiction when measured towards political realities. Analyses, such as Gibson's bring more light into the structure of the legal discourse that all too often is evaluated in formal terms.

5.7.2 Requiem for race

A requiem for ethnicity as operative notion in social sciences has been elaborated by V. Tishkov (2003). 'Race' and 'ethnicity' are also legal terms. Legal terms can be revolutionized in that they are reversed and abolished. When a term is abolished, the whole discourse that is centered on it disappears from valid usage. The new discourse that replaces it opens new perspectives for society that may or may not be useful for societal development. Among discursive approaches essentialism is the natural enemy of all such changes. The U.S. American discourse about the concept of race is still essentialist. On this view, 'race' as a concept exists in the U.S. American society because people belong to different races (cf. Holloway 2014). Conceptual creations such as 'affirmative action' or 'African American' (that replaced 'black' in the public discourse which in turn succeeded 'Negro') are all, their well-intentioned neologism notwithstanding, rooted in racial divide. The racial divide in the U.S. cannot be overcome because it is anchored in essentialist discourse. The essentialist structure of this discourse is rather complex. For instance, the U.S. Census of 1890 contained previously next to 'Negro' other related categories such as 'Mulatto', 'Quadroon' or 'Octoroon' that were taken rather seriously and were not at all interpreted as signs that 'race' as category had become obsolete. Essentialism prevented such a conclusion. Meanwhile, researchers such as D. Geary (2011: 63) stressed that the racial discourse in America evolved considerably, that it "shifted from questions of law, economics, and society…towards…culture and identity." Yet, it clearly did not surpass the 'race' as its structuring fundamental concept in the discourse which is, as said, its main weakness. U.S. President B. Obama himself in his speech known as *A More Perfect Union* which he delivered at Philadelphia on May 18, 2008 said: "It's a racial stalemate we've been stuck in for years. Contrary to the claims of some of my critics, black and white, I have never been so naïve as to believe that we can get beyond our racial divisions in a single election cycle, or with a single candidacy – particularly a candidacy as imperfect as my own." Further discursive limits became manifest, yet also neglected, when U.S. President B. Obama critically commented upon the action of the Cambridge police for arresting the Harvard professor H.L. Gates in July 2009. Gates was arrested in front of his house in Cambridge, Massachusetts. He tried to enter his house forcibly because he was missing his keys. Opponents of the presidential comments criticized the U.S. President who "(A)s defined by federalism,…should not talk about matters of state law enforcement unless some urgent federal interest compels it" (cf. Early 2011: 12). Obama acknowledged in his comments that he did not know the whole situation, yet he also added that "the police had acted stupidly" (cf. Early 2011: 11). However, in a situation with a racial background, the president had legally and discursively the choice not to react because the matter was not a federal issue or become involved because it concerned the most fundamental constitutional principles of liberty and equality. He has chosen a middle way and addressed the fundamental issue in its personal and geographical isolation; he used provisos when claiming that "not having been there and not seeing the facts" he could not say more. He nevertheless also generalized the problem claiming that "there's a long history in this country of African American and Latinos being stopped by law enforcement officers disproportionately." Discursive safety supposedly led to the inclusion of 'Latinos' into the statement that refers to a fact that, at least directly, does not concern this group of population, and under the circumstances of the statement over-generalizes it. A statement by the president in the given wording was perceived by some critics as unbalanced as "after all,…blacks and Latinos are stopped disproportionately by the police, but it is also true that they commit a hugely disproportionate share of violent crime in America – the other half of the fact that Obama's initial response seemed to elide," as mentioned by Early (2011: 12). Meanwhile, the statement should rather be understood as referring to those blacks or Latinos who are stopped disproportionately although they did not commit any crimes. Blacks and Latinos who commit crimes and are therefore stopped disproportionately were scarcely covered by Obama's protective statement. The statement as such is developed towards the background of a particular political doctrine that leads Obama's action as "he is trying to be a black president without being a black president" (Early 2011: 17). Such statements are not rare in times of fluidity of law. They also show interpretive limits in law as law that seems to say everything will finally say nothing. A requiem for race is still to be written in the U.S.

5.7.3 Problems with monarchs

Surprisingly enough, some elements of discourses about 'race' coincide with those relating to 'monarchs'. Unsurprisingly, however, this part of discourses is as political as the discourse about 'race'. Since Aristotle's enumeration of types of ruling structures the discussion about democracy cannot come to terms. The problem with Aristotle and also with Plato is that both had clearly negative views about democracy and preferred monarchy or aristocracy. These views irritated many, especially the admirers of both classics who appear in this part of their writings reactionary to modern readers. 'Monarchy' as a concept central to them is the rule by one man. Aristotle develops it around the notion of 'household' where man must dispose of everything. Household management is elevated to 'kingly rule' by semantic extension and analogy of image. It may have advantages that are mentioned even in *The Federalist*: "Energy in government requires not only a certain duration of power, but the execution of it by a single hand." This view is compatible with monarchy as a form of government. However, the American constitutional form favors the 'government by law' to the detriment of 'governments by men' in whatever way. Meanwhile, the monarch, called king, emperor, or czar is a 'sovereign'. Particularly interesting is their frequent deification that seems to form a cross-cultural element in the discourse about monarchy. In the discourse about monarchy in the Bible, divine rule is favored and kingdom rejected in favor of the rule of 'judges'. This may be the discursive starting point for the formation of notions such as 'by grace of God king of' etc. Therefore, also the 'sovereignty of people' is rooted in the concept of one man rule. It is in this sense linguistically productive. Yet, it fails because of another requisite. Monarchs have their own law. They do not follow the law that they institute: Princeps legibus solutus. This is the problem with monarchs. They are monarchs jure divino and do not fit into this world. 'Supremacy of law' is a more contemporary creation that collocates with the 'rule of law'. It shows the extent of the problem that monarchs cause, not only in legal linguistics. In fact, legal-linguistic distinctions work both ways; they create privileges and disadvantages that law perpetuates. Meanwhile, discursive mechanisms are apt at surpassing such essentialist creations.

5.8 Law as a cultural phenomenon

The answer to logical and anthropological intricacies of law seems to be law's nature as a primarily cultural phenomenon. Discursiveness of law as its main characteristic feature teaches jurists a lesson in modesty and in rationality. Jurists have to be modest in their grasping of law as law is a social phenomenon that is anchored in a very broad cultural context. Indeed, law as a cultural phenomenon is a blending of formal and informal social practices. It includes personal beliefs and political motives. Its perspective is the cultural range of language in its personal and institutional use. Topoi such as the 'melting pot' that characterizes the American society are not less important for law than constitutional terms such as 'local autonomy' or 'separation of powers'. The melting pot may have a banal origin; it refers directly to Israel Zangwill's popular play from 1908 and less directly to the metaphor of races that mixed or 'smelt' into American. This expression was used by J. Hector St. John de Crèvecoeur in his *Letters from the American Farmer*, published 1782. Crèvecoeur wrote in Letter III about the U.S. of his time: "Here individuals of all nations are melted into a new race of man, whose labors and posterity will one day cause great changes in the world." As a topos, the 'melting pot' has influenced all American constitutional law, maybe even more than the discourse around a technical term such as 'bill of attainder.' 'Melting pot' sounds less legal than 'bill of attainder', yet it is no less operative and influential in its legal consequences. Another example may show the necessity of choice that often is not mentioned in documents that it concerns. The American Constitution is centered on the term 'people'; it does not speak of Americans as a 'nation'. Meanwhile, it uses the term 'nation' in reference to 'foreign nations' and the 'law of nations.' Apparently, problems with the federal structure of the Union discouraged the drafters to use the term preferred by the French revolution and the fundamental legal acts that it engendered. Clearly, terms are used or omitted because in other discourses specific terms have been used. Therefore, it is impossible to reduce law to 'legal reasoning' or 'legal rationality' that would be the domain of the professionals of law. The institutional language that is applied within legal practices related to shaping and applying law makes use of some linguistic mechanisms that it exploits more frequently than others. Meanwhile, jurists basically think and speak as other people do, notwithstanding all their attempts to the contrary.

Part 6: Linguistic Turn in Law

6.1 Negligence of legal science

The search for law that was undertaken in the previous chapters and the results achieved during the peregrinations through legal texts and their contexts cannot remain without consequences for law. They impose a perspective upon the subject that is still an innovation in the legal science. This perspective, called sometimes with striking simplicity, yet not less pervasively 'a language perspective' (cf. Cao 2004) has its roots in areas that are close to law, i.e. in philosophy and in linguistics. Particularly in philosophy the linguistic turn had been taken very seriously as it led to methodological changes that revolutionized the subject. It also explains the shape of contemporary philosophy, even the non-analytic or the post-analytic. The linguistic turn in philosophy emerged, as some philosophers claimed, with the intention to clarify philosophical problems, open questions that for some philosophers could have been solved through linguistic analysis (Rorty 1992: 2–3). Consequently, the linguistic philosophy set out with its general hypotheses to engender a linguistic turn in philosophy as it assumed that many (if not all) philosophical problems are in reality problems of language use. It may not have solved all the problems in the way it expected. However, in that it tried to solve philosophical problems it laid the foundations for a philosophically oriented linguistics that is nowadays called linguistic pragmatics or pragmalinguistics. Linguistic pragmatics shares by its very nature numerous issues with the philosophical pragmatics. In the legal theory, the results achieved in the analytical philosophy fuelled appetites for equally spectacular results in law (Galdia 2009: 51). Meanwhile, the approach to law that emerged in line with the established methods of the analytical philosophy remains until today a side-current of theoretical debates about law. It is largely absent from the debate about the law in force, its application and its teaching. While the analytical philosophy and the tendencies of thought that emerged under its influence dominate this discipline since decades, the idea of a linguistic turn in law still did not materialize.

6.1.1 Shift towards language use

Some researchers critically remarked that the linguistic turn did not take place in law although it could have been legitimately expected to happen (Galdia 2009:

51; Slocum 2012). It has been at best reflected in some works on legal theory that, as so often, were enthusiastically received in social sciences, yet remained unnoticed in the daily debate of the legal doctrine. The reasons for this neglected reception of one of the most relevant postulates of analytical philosophy in the realm of law might be multiple. Meanwhile, it can also be assumed that jurists will have asked themselves about the possibility of application of this postulate in law. What would the linguistic turn bring them? Would it be worthwhile to reshape the discourse in the legal science and look at law from the perspective of its language? Still further, would all legal problems be solved when the legal discourse would be aptly transformed in terms of legal linguistics? For most jurists, legal problems are doctrinal problems. They are manifest, for instance, in the distinction between private and public law or when the statute of limitations is characterized as being part of the substantive and not of the procedural law. By way of example, the common law presumes that an accused person is innocent until proved guilty. This rule may be regarded as 'substantive' or 'procedural', depending on the view taken of its nature. How could here the change in perspective be of any use, would skeptical jurists ask. In fact, transforming doctrinal descriptions of law into critical legal-linguistic descriptions would constitute a progress because it would help overcome the fragmentary character of law that appears in the doctrine at best as an assembly of topoi such as those named above. More often than not, however, it appears as a listing of largely undetermined issues that are connected by tradition only. Meanwhile, such a description is not unstructured, yet its structure appears as deficient when seen from the legal-linguistic perspective. The linguistic turn in law also includes risks. The danger of the linguistic analysis of the law in force as defined by the legal doctrine is that, as its result, too much of it destroys the law that we know. The tissue of law is held together by loose discursive patterns that can easily fall apart because they consist of words. All too easily the logical analysis shows the inherent contradictions in law and annihilates more than it rescues. Therefore, sometimes the prudent approach of jurists to the project of the linguistic turn in law may seem understandable. Finally, however, it is academically not defendable.

6.1.2 Why care about language in life?

The absent, the rudimentary, and the implicit language analyses in the area of law can be contrasted with reflections upon language use in situations of daily life. In daily communication, language use has been explored by speakers on two different levels. Spoken language interested speakers mostly in terms of its immediate efficiency. Most speakers are aware of the close connection between advanced argumentative strategies and communicative situations (cf. Toulmin 1958). In daily communication, speakers make considerable efforts to use language in accordance with these requirements (cf. Jackson/Scott 1980). Yet, much less numerous are speakers who believe that they could learn from ordinary spoken language through the analysis of this language. Meanwhile, very high expectations were traditionally connected with the study of written texts. Through their study we were expected to understand the world. R. Descartes, who was clearly disappointed about such expectations, wrote in his *Discours de la méthode*: "J'ai été nourri aux lettres dès mon enfance, et parce qu'on me persuadait que, par leur moyen, on pouvait acquérir une connaissance claire et assurée de tout ce qui est utile à la vie, j'avais un extrême désir de les apprendre. Mais, sitôt que j'eus achevé tout ce cours d'études, au bout duquel on a coutume d'être reçu au rang des doctes, je changeai entièrement d'opinion." (cf. Première Partie). Descartes, therefore, developed a method for finding truth in sciences. This method helps to deal with statements such as 'The soul is immortal' or the claim in *Vedanta* that 'God is the sole real existence.' He unfortunately did not care much about other than scientific questions and he neglected issues essential to us. Meanwhile, what chance do we have to understand 'life', i.e. also law, society and the like, other than to study texts that are expressed in language? Therefore, the analysis of spoken and written language in life is not a program but a necessity for any human being. Humans differ partly because some of them expose themselves to such analytical exercises while others do not.

The origin of contemporary interest in language is connected with two scholars, J.L. Austin and L.Wittgenstein. Many linguistic and philosophical works are based on aspects of their theoretical explorations. Also this essay could not have been written without reference to basic achievements in the philosophical analysis of language that were undertaken by those two scholars and many others, whose contributions are regularly quoted in this book. However, reference to authority is a weak argument in times of generalized distrust towards meta-narratives. Theoretically, therefore, the problem whether language is in fact as essential in life as many postulate remains an open issue. Doubtless, communication is an essential form of life for the human beings. Meanwhile, also non-verbal communication exists and it seems to be extremely effective in many situations. However, meaningful communication on a higher level is possible exclusively with the help of language (Searle 2006). The more signs with a specific meaning a language has, the more efficient the communication in it will be because more differences between meanings can be made (Savigny 1983: 345). Likewise, languages are under an evolutive pressure to develop more and more signs with differing meanings (Savigny 1983: 346). In sum, language may not be the most essential thing in life, yet meaningful life without language is unthinkable.

6.1.3 Why care about language in law?

The above paragraph may contribute new arguments applicable in the legal-linguistic debate. Many jurists are clearly interested in language; yet they also pretend that they are primarily interested in law. The split made between the two phenomena is responsible for the emergence of legal positivism that as a legal theory is implicitly linguistic. Positivists' implicit interest in language makes of linguistics and of legal linguistics an area of suspicious co-operation or, at best, of co-existence with the legal science (cf. Macedo 1985: 86). The first step towards change in this relation has been accomplished in the interdisciplinary research into law and language that preceded the legal linguistics as a unified field analyzing the legal language. The existing theoretical research into the relation of law and language answers the question of what is language actually doing in law. It shows, for instance, that we accomplish perlocutionary acts when argumenting. It also shows that we are involved in interpretation of illocutionary acts when we deal with legal provisions and not with deciphering meaning that is allegedly hidden in them. A long list of such achievements could be composed on the basis of this book that regularly mentions explicit results of interdisciplinary research that challenge the positivist view upon language in law. In law, we are also regularly exposed to tests of rationality. For instance, L. Greenhouse (2012: 78) quoted a sentence from an anti-abortion platform: "The unborn child has a fundamental individual right to life which cannot be infringed." In fact, this is a postulate of a right because such a general right does not exist in the U.S. legal system, where limited 'fetal rights' are stated in the U.S. Unborn Victims of Violence Act (2004). The phrase is a typical example of discursive practices used in the area of law and is also understandable within such practices due to the interdisciplinary research into the relation of law and language. The classification of the phrase is based on a rationality test that in this example is relatively easy to accomplish. The existing research copes already very well with the analysis of such discursive contributions. When we know all this, the next step towards reformulating law in force imposes itself. This would be also the further step towards accomplishing the linguistic turn in the legal science. Yet the mentioned achievements are still remote from the finality of legal linguistics that is the reformulation of law in line with the rules of language use. Legal language is grounded in rules, or some would say in practices, conventions, i.e. neither speaker- nor situation-specific circumstances. Until now, no legal-linguistic transformation of law in force has been undertaken, not even for a small legal system. As long as a legal system is not reformulated in terms of legal linguistics, the subject will be always treated sarcastically and skeptically by mainstream jurists.

6.2 What is language?

Language is a sign system – an inventory of signs and rules that enable the emergence of meaning and its understanding. Some classical views upon language establish a hierarchy of levels that make language work: "Human signs, i.e., the words of the language, are not simple associations – they do not directly link a sound to a thing, but pass through the intermediary of meaning, which is an intersubjective reality" (Todorov 1992: 25). Therefore, language refers to reality without being a necessary part of it. This led some scholars to argue that there is no such thing as a language and that language is, at best, a part of something else, for instance, thought or action. We should therefore not overestimate the role of language, some philosophers claimed (Rorty 1992: 371). We better look at what is done with linguistic means. Therefore linguists' work is positioned between the extreme claims that everything finally is language and that nothing can be only language as language is identifiable solely as a part of something else, usually a linguistic action such as a statement or a question. Therefore, the essential part of a linguist's work is to explain how comes that a statement can be made or a question asked (cf. Meyer 1988). This moderate view of language is compatible with the approach to general linguistic questions that dominate this essay. Based on the moderate conviction, the linguist primarily traces the language behind particular languages. Behind these different languages there are sounds and phrase patters that appear under specific circumstances in form of utterances. These utterances make sense to other people, to those who also speak these languages. The linguist therefore does not need to speak many different languages because at the end of the day all speakers speak only one language, the language behind languages that includes such general rules as those mentioned. When he nevertheless knows 'foreign', i.e. other languages, he will observe that they tend to adequately structure linguistic utterances that are patterned in the language behind languages in a more general way. The explanation for it, i.e. the rationale of linguistic diversity is cultural diversity of speakers that emerged due to their discontinuous regional distribution and limited contact. The linguistic diversity has undeniably practical consequences. In the Japanese language no difference is made between human and other animal extremities; there is no linguistic distinction between 'mitt' or 'paw' and 'leg', there is only 'leg', in Japanese 'ashi' that also means 'foot'. Therefore, in Japanese 'leg' also covers the 'paw' of an animal. The distinction exists as a matter of a linguistic principle in many languages, for instance in French where the difference is made between human 'jambe' and animal 'patte'. When speech acts of higher order are created around semantic limitations in the Japanese language, it is difficult to render the ironical switch from leg to paw when talking about a human being. This is a matter of speaking different languages, an advantage as well as a disadvantage. Yet, language is not made of words, at least not alone. We invent words as we go along, with others. For some items, puzzles of reality, we invent words while for others, for example for the unit of 'ten short nails' we do not have any particular names. We could nevertheless imagine that a word 'woog' would represent in the English language such a lexical unit. It would even be practical, especially in professional communication. The foreman could say to his apprentice 'Fetch a woog!' instead of the more cumbersome 'Fetch ten short nails!' Such examples are interesting, yet linguists rather avoid them. The reason for linguists' limited interest in words is that we do not communicate with words, but with speech acts. Even if we do not have a specific word for an identifiable item or an act, we can effectively communicate because language allows for unlimited interactions with sounds, words, and phrases that engender complex units. These interactions may last until understanding is reached. When we in an extreme situation whisper 'water', then we ask for water. The main thing to grasp is the issue of asking to be provided water and not the abstract issue of chemical composition of the mentioned substance. Understanding language includes rules that ensure communication under conditions of syntactic diversity. In French it is possible to say 'Réconcilier Pierre et Jean' or 'Réconcilier Pierre avec Jean'. Both sentences are equally correct and semantically equivalent in French. The same meaning may be found in differently framed utterances. For instance, while aiming at customizing clients a Finnish department store will print on its bills the formula 'Kiitos käynnistä!', i.e. 'Thanks for coming!', while in Swedish it will print 'Välkommen igen' that is closer to the English formulation 'Welcome again!'. The meaning of all three utterances is the same; their particular linguistic forms are different. For linguists, is does not matter much that the utterances are different on their face as long as they mean the same. Moreover, linguistic communication is effective even if our linguistic knowledge is limited. In English, one speaks about 'scooters' also because they 'scoot': 'Here is the bus; you'll have to scoot if you want to get it.' When used as a borrowing from English, e.g. in French 'un scooter', or in Polish 'skuter' the reference to a determined object remains unchanged for all speakers; for a speaker who does not know the English word 'scooter' the original connotation will get lost. Yet, the use of the word is not less effective in French or Polish than it is in English. The above remarks lead us back to the initial statement that language is a sign system. It is constituted like whatever other systems of signs. Operations that are undertaken on language are operations on signs. Constitutive elements of a language sign are: culture that enables different types of meaning to emerge in different languages and logically determined functions such as reference or predication (mentioned already by Bloomfield 1914: 167), and last but not least, reasoning (thoughts) in its linguistic form. Linguistic research into operations on signs may follow the structure of semiotics and focus on syntax, semantics and pragmatics (e.g. interpretation and argumentation). The complex texture that is scrutinized (understood) is the text; it is constituted of speech acts. Last but not least, language is a social phenomenon and a social institution. It primarily serves as a means of communication – there cannot be any private language. Meanwhile, its individual note is rooted in creativity, i.e. the ability to use its underlying structures to create new linguistic forms, speech acts etc. Legal linguistics has to draw consequences from above remarks in order to shape its subject and its method.

6.2.1 True and comprehensive science of language

For legal-linguistic research the decisive question is which scientific conception of language is relevant to legal-linguistic studies. J.L. Austin (1956) invokes in his article *Ifs and Cans* the necessity to establish a 'true and comprehensive science of language'. He asks: "Is it possible that the next century may see the birth, through the joint labours of philosophers, grammarians, and numerous other students of language, of a true and comprehensive science of language?" He has in mind, as always, the role of philosophy in the development of the modern science. Yet, Austin's postulate implies also a dose of criticism on the existing linguistics as it was made by 1956, i.e. in a time when structuralism flourished in Europe and in the US. Meanwhile, one cannot assume that Austin had been ignorant of the development in linguistics although his main interest in linguistic analyses was directed towards other than explicitly linguistic issues, notably the philosophical ones. He will have heard about L. Bloomfield's *Language* and definitely also about some other works that cannot be underestimated by anyone who cares about the development of the theory of language. One could therefore ask what was there in the then-linguistics that led Austin to the contention that it was neither a 'true' nor a 'comprehensive' science of language. Apparently, theories such as structuralism were perceived by Austin as reductionist and therefore only partly true in their assertions about language. One could also ask what means 'true' and what means 'comprehensive' in terms of pragmatics? A negative determination seems easier. In an utterance *'Student sit on bench and reading book' some specialists see an example of an unintelligible sentence because the most fundamental rules of English morphology and syntax were violated there. However, few are the speakers who do not understand that in the above sample a student is apparently sitting on a bench and that he is reading a book. There is a friction between our understanding of the English language and the specialist's opinion. Therefore, a linguistic theory built on such assumptions may have something to offer in terms of science, e.g. the finding that grammatically incorrect utterances exist. Yet, it will not be perceived as 'true' in Austinian terms. It is not 'comprehensive' either as it does not take into consideration the way how speakers may or may not understand grammatically incorrect utterances. Other scholars, e.g. Halsall (1989: 16), stress in Austin's remark the words 'science of language' rather than 'true and comprehensive' that is our point of departure. This apprehension may make things even worse. It would mean that in Austin's politely formulated programmatic question there is an assumption that what was there in linguistics of his time was not science at all.

6.2.2 Historical conceptions of linguistics

History of linguistics is not a playing field for legal linguists. Many perspectives and approaches to language are only of marginal importance for the development of the legal-linguistic paradigm. This may also be the reason why the interdisciplinary dialogue between law and linguistics is so difficult. In antiquity, Panini in his description of Sanskrit treated language as a matter of content, not only of form. Language had for him a material structure that is composed of sounds and sentences that he described. Likewise, parts of speech as well as some overarching structures such as texts that interest us even today have been identified by Denisius of Halicarnassus. In the Middle Ages, the scholastic philosophers were more open to interpretive and argumentative issues in language. They mostly understood them in terms of deciphering of meaning that is already included in linguistic utterances. In the Renaissance, the philosophically founded linguistic thought oscillated around the idea of representativeness of language. Its main interest lies in the relation between the word and the object that the word allegedly represents (Foucault 1966: 93–136). Again, the legal linguist is challenged by this conception of language as she has to ask what objects could actually the legal words represent. Also in the influential *Grammaire Générale et Raisonée* by A. Arnauld and C. Lancelot from 1660 language is perceived as a material entity. For the authors, language has naturally determined sounds, nouns have plural forms naturally, and neutral gender in the Latin language is rationally explicable. All in all, language is an essence that must be described. The 'grammaire générale' represents for them the order of things (Foucault 1966). Meanwhile, the *Grammaire Générale et Raisonée* also introduces into the grammatical analysis the claim of reasonableness. The grammatical analysis has to trace the reasonable aspects of language and it has also to make the linguistic description compatible with the logical analysis. This sort of analysis is mercilessly undertaken in Arnauld's and Lancelot's work and whatever grammatical form is proven to be rational because it always can be explained as a rational formulation of thought. In the 'grammaire générale' grammar corresponds with reason, language corresponds with mind. This view that with contemporary vocabulary could be characterized as essentialist, dominated until modern times where Ferdinand de Saussure made clear that language does not represent or mirror the reality. Subsequently, other linguists and philosophers made plain that language has to be used in order to engender meaning. Other fundamental approaches to language such as comparative linguistics of classical times were not interested in meaning. They focused rather on the origins of languages and on the methods that could prove the common origin of languages that they elucidated with the help of laws of phonetic evolution. Historically, the interest in linguistic studies concerned the origin of languages and their development, i.e. the history of language. It equally concerned the question how language emerged and it also coincided with more detailed insights into the structure of particular languages such as ancient Greek or Sanskrit, their sounds and words. Numerous hypotheses about the origin of particular languages were formulated and languages were divided into families or leagues, depending on the perspective from which this distinction has been undertaken. Microlinguistic perspectives set out numerous differences between languages while macroperspectives stressed their common denominators. Thus, Dutch and German may be perceived as close or remote, depending on the theoretical perspective taken by the analyst. With time passing, these and other languages were described on a more abstract level. Yet, all this meticulous scrutiny belongs to the past, at least as legal linguistics is concerned. In fact, for legal linguistics it is of limited importance.

6.2.3 Contemporary tendencies in linguistics

Subsequent linguistic challenges to law and legal sciences are numerous. The most fundamental struggles between language and law start in the modern times with Ferdinand de Saussure's *Course in General Linguistics* (1916). J.E. Joseph (2012) characterized language in Saussure's conception as "composed of a system of acoustic oppositions (the signifier) matched by social convention to a system of conceptual oppositions (the signified)." In his *Course* Saussure writes without any hidden or malicious hints at law, yet not without consequences for it: "In a language there are only differences without positive terms. Whether we take the signified or the signifier, the language contains neither ideas nor sounds that pre-exist the linguistic system, but only conceptual differences and phonic differences issuing from the system." Saussure's linguistics deals therefore with the signifier in phonology, in morphology and in syntax. Semantics, that would deal with the signified, was in Saussure's view to come later and to complete the picture that started with sounds, words and their order in sentences. Linguistic structuralism that is condensed and portrayed in Saussure's statement seems to block any attempt at co-operation between linguistics and legal sciences. For Saussure, language is indifferent to content or meaning that emerges in it. Meaning emerges outside the structure of language, within the social convention of its use. Language as such, i.e. as a structure, has no meaning. Law, by contrast, is mostly associated with content or meaning. For positivists, law is composed of 'positive terms' that they perceive and study as 'legal concepts'. Law without meaning or with meaning that is structurally external to it is a horrifying idea for most jurists because they approach law through its alleged meaning. Law, for them, contains 'ideas' that are productive for the emergence of 'legal concepts'. For some jurists, these ideas and concepts even clearly pre-exist the law. What links the linguistic-structuralist and the positivist conception is the idea of 'system' because also for the structuralist Saussure language is a system. For most positivists there exists a 'legal system' composed of legal provisions that ground in legal concepts. Yet, this is a weak consolation as Saussure is strict in the application of the term 'system'. Jurists, in turn, have to avoid any formal concept of 'system' because of the semantic indeterminacy of law which even the positivists explicitly or implicitly had to admit. A. Martinet, who followed Saussure's structural approach and who expanded it into functionalism, had been equally strict on meaning that he deemed as external to language (Martinet 1982: 2). Also for him meaning is largely an extralinguistic reality, located in the area between language and the outer world (Kovačec 1982: xiii). In the structural approach to language another fundamental question as to whether semantics might be perceived as structurable developed to a major obstacle for this approach (Mounin 1968: 155). Researchers in the U.S. such as L. Bloomfield and his followers maintained that meaning cannot be grasped scientifically (Mounin 1968: 155). This means apparently that it cannot be grasped within the structuralist approach. For Noam Chomsky, who formulated a theory that is at least partly kindred with Saussure's dichotomy of 'langue' and 'parole', all languages follow the same intrinsic principles. Therefore, our interest in the linguistic diversity is legitimate when the aim at identifying these common principles is kept in mind. Chomsky distinguishes between system (competence) and performance, i.e. the use of language, in approximation to the dichotomy of 'langue' and 'parole'. His theory remains therefore within the structuralist paradigm. Post-structuralist approaches broadened the methodology of the analysis of meaning and created a semantics that claimed the right to be a scientific discipline. The analyses of formal, conceptual and logical structures in language, the discovery of context and of the semantic field are examples of possible answers to the structuralist dilemma concerning structure and meaning (Mounin 1968: 156–166). They have enabled the approximation between linguistics and the legal-linguistic research in the past and they also form the matrix of G. Cornu's *Linguistique juridique*. All these possibilities notwithstanding, the traditional semantic approach appeared as still too narrow and formalistic to both linguists and legal linguists. Semanticians tried to broaden the perspective in that they entered the traditional field of pragmatics. The pragmatists, in turn, moved closer to semantics. These moves created the semantics-pragmatics interface that today constitutes the biotope in which both disciplines survive in an apparent expectation of a friendly merger or a hostile takeover. Tendencies in the contemporary post-structuralist linguistics at the outset of the 21 century can be roughly characterized as aiming at formalization of language and/or describing the social discourse. The first tendency with its multiple streamings, which would not always describe themselves as formal or formalizing, contributes directly or indirectly to the technological development. For many, this technological development is also their finality. On the other hand, the discourse-oriented approaches aim at describing how utterances are made and understood in specific situations and in broader contexts. As a result, all these painful metamorphoses made the application of linguistics in the legal sciences more probable. Thus, constant adjustments of linguistic models are necessary in the legal-linguistic work in order to make them fully operational. These adjustments are also undertaken in order to avoid sterile and pseudo-scientific results. In contemporary linguistic conceptions, especially in those based on pragmatics, content emerges in law as it emerges in language. It is therefore justified to approach law from the linguistic perspective that is aware of this methodological intricacy.

6.3 Specific linguistics for legal sciences

All above remarks have not been made with the aim to disorient existing orientations. Meanwhile, mechanistic application of paradigms of one discipline upon another rarely works. G. Cornu (2005) refers regularly to Saussure in his attempt to lay linguistic foundations for his conception of the legal linguistics. As far as this narrow aim is concerned, Saussure's structuralism may be perceived as a first step towards developing a paradigm for legal linguistics. The second step will be more complicated because Saussure's sign concept is too narrow for the legal-linguistic research. Problems began with Saussure's split between 'langue' and 'parole' that meant for him that 'langue' is an object for scientific research and 'parole' remains a residue of speaker's freedom (cf. Greimas 1977: 87, 110; Baylon 1991: 237). G. Cornu (2005) therefore tacitly expanded Saussure's linguistic matrix and entered the area of discourse as most promising for the legal linguistics. Also Mattila (2012, 2013) expanded his area of interest from legal terminology defined in structuralist terms to communication. Therefore, specific linguistics that adjusts the existing linguistic theory to the needs of the legal linguistics is unavoidable. It can meaningfully use many theoretical prerequisites of general linguistics. For instance, comparative legal linguistics shows how linguistic diversity matters for the constitution and understanding of law all over the planet (cf. Mattila 2013). It reflects the linguistic diversity that it tries to construe in a more general theoretical structure. Furthermore, linguistic understanding in legal discourses reflects general patterns of text comprehension. For instance, non-jurists can meaningfully speak about contracts even if they lack the professional's knowledge of the legal doctrine that describes contracts. This fact is understandable only towards the background of a general theory of linguistic understanding.

6.3.1 Developing a theory about language for law

Traditional and contemporary linguistics teaches the legal linguists a lot about the linguistic face of law. Yet, it also teaches one more disenchanting lesson. The impressive bulk of linguistic experience makes clear that not everything is essential to law and that some linguistic areas and issues matter much more than others. Purely grammatical analysis may therefore not be interesting for a legal linguist. Two sentences that are quite relevant in the context of theoretical grammar, such as: "The police shot the man in the red cap" and "The police shot the man in the right arm" are significant for some grammatically intricate phenomena, yet they are irrelevant to legal linguistics (in: Valeika/Buitkiene 2003: 28). However, an utterance such as 'When were you released from prison?' (in: Valeika/Buitkiene 2003: 132) may acquire an advanced status in the legal-linguistic analysis as a focal point of a legal discourse. Pure syntax is not helpful either. It would be absurd to support a proposition of law with the argument that it has been syntactically well formed. Tribe (2012: 24) spoke in this context of "using the rules of syntax to prove a normative proposition." Syntax can however cause problems. The comma in the Second Amendment to the U.S. Constitution became proverbial in contexts related to syntax in law. The Second Amendment reads, with the comma included, as follows: "A well-regulated militia being necessary to the security of a free State, the right of the people to keep and bear arms shall not be infringed." Its linguistic structure is a challenge to contemporary linguists. The syntax of the sentence is however typical of its time. For instance, the Northwest Ordinance of 1787 says in its Art. 3: "Religion, morality, and knowledge being necessary to good government and happiness of mankind, schools and the means of education shall forever be encouraged." Yet, linguistics is not the only branch of knowledge that causes problems in the area of law. Also philosophy of language, semiotics, rhetoric, literary studies and communication theory have something to teach about law. Among the named disciplines the philosophy of language proposed the most advanced theories about the language of law. John L. Austin's tentative thoughts about the theory of legal language can be reconstructed from his article *A Plea for Excuses* (1956). Austin assumes there that the ordinary language has to be the starting point for any philosophical enquiry, also into legal language. As most linguistic data that is relevant to law is available in the ordinary language, the deadlock that the multifarious ordinary language engenders when law is applied has to be solved. This deadlock is overcome by the creation of a type of specialized language that reduces the contourless variability of ordinary language. This specialized language, that could be called legal language, enables law to function as a social mechanism. The above sketch of the Austinian argument is based on following remarks about ordinary language in his mentioned article: First, when introducing the ordinary language as a focus of philosophical enquiry Austin does not wish to overestimate its importance. He solely posits that the enquiry starts with the ordinary language, yet not necessarily ends with it. Austin says: "...ordinary language has no claim to be the last word, if there is such a thing. It embodies, indeed, something better than the metaphysics of the Stone Age, namely, as was said, the inherited experience and acumen of many generations of men. But then, that acumen has been concentrated primarily upon the practical business of life...Certainly, then, ordinary language is not the last word: in principle it can everywhere be supplemented and improved upon and superseded. Only remember, it is the first word." With this statement Austin opens up the linguistic perspective that can meaningfully include other than ordinary registers. Second, when reflecting upon the multitude of juridical matters he applies this statement as a device to describe law: "In the law a constant stream of actual cases, more novel and more tortuous than the mere imagination could contrive, are brought up for decision – that is, formulae for docketing them must somehow be found. Hence it is necessary first to be careful with, but also to be brutal with, to torture, to fake and to override, ordinary language…" On a simple example he marks the shift from the ordinary to more specific language in terms of law. A statement referring to a fact may be worded as: 'He took her money', yet also 'He robbed her'. Also 'He said Done! as compared with 'He accepted the offer' is illustrative of the same principle. The second statement in both pairs is clearly more explicit in terms of applied legal reasoning than is the first. The second statement is also more expedient in linguistic mechanisms where law is applied. Were the first statement and other such factual utterances dominant in the legal language, law would almost certainly become ineffective as a means of societal regulation. Some such ordinary language with reference to law is illustrative of this process. A speech act (not cited by Austin), such as 'You'll be hearing from my attorney!', that may express threat, is in its ordinary language dress much too vague to function as an efficient regulative social mechanism. Such language may be efficient under given circumstances, yet it is not sufficiently explicit to steer society in more general contexts. Hence, in the light of Austin's argument, legal language is a more appropriate choice because it represents a specialized register that has to become effective to fulfill the task of steering state and society. Interestingly, also L. Bloomfield (1914: 76, 91) observed analogous transformations that involved jurists' linguistic considerations. He referred to a situation of language use where a lawyer "after some consideration of the technical validity of a paper says: Forgery." The use of specialized linguistic register functions here like a shorthand script that also constitutes the context of the speech act as belonging to the legal discourse. This circumstance was however less relevant to Austin. Third, Austin sees that in law the question of diversity of interests is argumentatively omnipresent and law therefore cannot be reduced to a purely rational discourse, at least in the practice of judicial institutions. Law has "a biased interest in life." This biased interest structures speech: "there is the overriding requirement that a decision be reached, and a relatively black or white decision – guilty or not guilty – for the plaintiff or for the defendant." Such a requirement, which is a rule, creates language. Fourth, "there is the general requirement that the charge or action and the pleadings be brought under…procedures that have come in the course of history to be accepted by the Courts." Speaking in procedures does not discourage Austin as these "though fairly numerous, are few and stereotyped in comparison with the accusations and defences of daily life." Speaking in procedures is therefore typical of language, the ordinary and the specialized. Speaking in legal procedures is specific because it depends on institutions. Austin (1975: 28) says in *How to Do Things with Words*: "...on a desert island you may say to me 'Go and pick up wood'; and I may say 'I don't take orders from you' or 'you're not entitled to give me orders' – I do not take orders from you when you try to 'assert your authority' (which I might fall in with but may not) on a desert island, as opposed to the case when you are captain on a ship and therefore genuinely have authority." In sum, institutionally guaranteed values, beliefs, commitments of all sorts make part of the law and its language as does the ordinary language with all its primary imprecision and vagueness. Legal language emerges in order to cope with the linguistic and factual complexity of life that is primarily expressed in ordinary language. Practically speaking, jurists invent legal terminology to cope with this challenge (Austin 1975: 24). Law that is expressed in this way considers life from the perspective of values, beliefs, and commitments that it also conveys. This consideration of life is expressed in performatives such as those described by Austin in *How to Do Things with Words* (1975). Performatives function in procedures that determine the validity of their use (cf. v. Dijk 1978: 16). A speech act of sentencing 'I condemn you to ten years in prison' is valid in law when the context is a trial, the speaker is a judge and the recipient is an accused. Furthermore, it requires regulation (statute or precedent) that would justify the range of the sentence. For Austin, regulation makes part of the linguistic procedures. Austin dealt in *How to Do Things with Words* with numerous legal problems, such as mistakes, mainly from the perspective of the legal doctrine. He might have been influenced at this point by H.L.A. Hart, with whom he also taught a course at Oxford. This specific interest led Austin to deal with conceptual analysis from the point of view of the legal doctrine that impeded progress in the development of his theory. For him, law remained rooted in logic and not in social discourse. One does definitely not exclude the other, yet the results obtained in Austin's analysis show rather the legal doctrine in the light of the speech act theory and logic. 'Discourse' is however also present in Austin's theoretical pondering. J.O. Urmson (1992b: 233) referred to 'areas' in Austin's writings that are in his view "areas of discourse." As could be seen, Austin's approach is only implicitly discursive, as it on its face favors terminological analysis in limited contexts. Also in ideological terms, it is rather affirmative of power structures where people have 'genuine authority' to rule over others. This is how language functions in law according to J.L. Austin. This theory of legal language has been later expanded by John Searle (2011) to a more comprehensive description of legal language as a mechanism of legal discourse. This broad theory of legal language made this book possible.

6.3.2 Choice of language

One more problem is connected with the logical structure of the legal language. Speaking about law is difficult because of the connection between law and power. Many speakers have regularly problems with the choice of appropriate language because they perceive law as something distant, not belonging to their daily matters. Over-officious legal professionals often overburdened their language with all possible attributes of power, while the non-professionals based their language on strategies of either avoiding deference or exaggerated deference. Already Etienne de la Boetie mentioned this phenomenon in his *Discours de la servitude volontaire* (1576). The contrary tendency is represented, for instance, in Dudley Digges's *Unlawfulness of Subjects Taking up Arms against Their Soveraigne, in What Case Soever*, published in London in 1643. Moreover, legal language has rarely used the advantages of the ordinary language and its history is the history of avoidance of ordinary speech (Galdia 2009: 92–95). This regrettable result has apparently its roots in the traditional rhetoric that differentiated several stylistic levels that it connected to specific areas of discursive application. Traditional rhetorical theories identified three levels of style: the grand, the middle, and the plain (cf. Robrieux 2010: 31). Interest in plain language in rhetoric is as late as is the interest in ordinary language in linguistic and philosophical studies. One of the few attempts to use simplified language is the plain language movement. As a result of this movement, which initiated in English-speaking countries, contemporary lawgivers opt for the last rhetorical variety of language. Its relation to ordinary language remains open. Ordinary language also displays another facet of use. Speaking in a way that enables the social identification of the speaker is one of the aspects of language choice in law. For that matter, law can be presented in elevated diction. Law can also be presented in vulgar speech.

6.3.3 Social character of legal language

Since antiquity, language has been perceived predominantly as a social phenomenon. Aristotle in his *Politics* (1253a7, transl. E. Barker, ed. OUP 1995) says: "It is thus clear that man is a political animal, in a higher degree than bees or other gregarious animals. Nature, according to our theory, makes nothing in vain; and man alone of the animals is furnished with the faculty of language. The mere making of sounds serves to indicate pleasure and pain, and is thus a faculty that belongs to animals in general: their nature enables them to attain the point at which they have perceptions of pleasure and pain, and can signify those perceptions to one another. But language serves to declare what is advantageous and what is the reverse, and it is the peculiarity of man, in comparison with other animals, that he alone possesses a perception of good and evil, of the just and the unjust, and other similar qualities; and it is association in these things which makes a family and a city." Thus, humans act in socially relevant ways through language; language and social action are one and inseparable thing. Similarly, according to some ancient Roman sources that, unsurprisingly, have Greek roots, all language emerges in social interaction. For instance, Vitruvius in *De architectura* (Liber II, I, 1) invokes the collective element in language formation: "Homines vetere more ut ferae in silvis et speluncis et nemoribus nascebantur ciboque agresti vescendo vitam exigebant. Interea quondam in loco ab tempestatibus et ventis densae crebritatibus arbores agitate et inter se terentes ramos ignem excitaverunt, et eius flamma vehementi perterriti, qui circa eum locum fuerunt, sunt fugati. Postea re quieta propius accedentes cum animadvertissent commoditatem esse magnam corporibus ad ignis teporem, ligna adicientes et id conservantes alios adducebant et nutu monstrantes ostendebant, quas haberent ex eo utilitates. In eo hominum congressu cum profundebantur aliter e spiritu voces, cotidiana consuetudine vocabula, ut optigerant, constituerunt, deinde significando res saepius in usu ex eventu fari fortuito coeperunt et ita sermones inter se procreaverunt." Also Lucretius in *De rerum natura* (Liber V, verses 1028–1077) stressed the social prerequisites for language constitution: "At uarios linguae sonitus natura subegit/mittere, et utilitas expressit nomina rerum,/non alia longe ratione atque ipsa uidetur/protrahere ad gestum pueros infantia linguae,/cum facit ut digito quae sint praesentia monstrent,/Sentit enim uis quisque suas quoad possit abuti,/...Proinde putare aliquem tum nomina distribuisse/rebus et inde homines didicisse uocabula prima,/desiperest. Nam cur hic posset cuncta notare/uocibus et uarios sonitus emittere linguae,/tempore eodem alii facere id non quisse putentur?/Praeterea si non alii quoque uocibus usi/utilitatis, et unde data est huic prima potestas,/quid uellet facere ut sciret animoque uideret?/Cogere item pluris unus uictosque domare/non poterat, reum ut perdiscere nomina uellent./Nec ratione docere ulla suadereque surdis,/quid sit opus facto, facilest; neque enim paterentur,/nec ratione ulla sibi ferrent amplius auris/uocis inauditos sonitus obtundere frustra,/ Postremo quid in hac mirabile tantoperest re,/si genus humanum, cui uox et lingua uigeret,/pro uario sensu uaria res uoce notaret?..." Clearly, the circumstance that language is a social phenomenon means that it emerges in society. Lucretius rightly asks how one man alone could impose meaning upon others. Language like law emerges in social interaction. It is therefore easy to analyze law like language, as analogies impose themselves (cf. Kirchmann 1938: 24). These images can be contrasted with Augustinus whose *Confessiones* I/8 were quoted also by L. Wittgenstein at the outset of his *Philosophical Investigations*: "cum ipsi (majores homines) appellabant rem aliquam, et cum secundum eam vocem corpus ad aliquid movebant, videbam, et tenebam hoc ab eis vocari rem illam, quod sonabant, cum eam vellent ostendere. Hoc autem eos velle ex motu corporis aperiebatur: tamquam verbis naturalibus omnium gentium, quae fiunt vultu et nutu oculorum, ceterorumque membrorum actu, et sonitu vocis indicante affectionem animi in petendis, habendis, rejiciendis, fugiendisve rebus. Ita verba in variis sententiis locis suis posita, et crebro audita, quarum rerum signa essent, paulatim colligebam, measque iam voluntates, edomito in eis signis ore, per haec enuntiabam." Augustinus's conception of language is static; it equals denotation of conceptual meaning that the child discovers individually by trial and error. But also in this conception there is reference to the social aspect of language acquisition because the child learns the language from others; it does not decipher meaning on its own. When language as such is a socially formed phenomenon, could law emerge outside social boundaries and be, at least partly, an individual creation? Nothing seems to support such an idea. Even if laws had been in history imposed by individuals, they remained a product of complex constitutive social processes that involved many. Similarly, L. Wittgenstein distanced himself from this conception as for him a private language was unimaginable. Also politically, the modern conception of law is resting on consent. This consent cannot come about otherwise than in discursive mechanisms. With this in mind, J. Searle (2011) incorporated rules for emergence of social institutions into language. While taking this step, he closed the debate about the social nature of language and enabled legal linguistics to exist and to flourish.

6.3.4 Language as tongue

Contemporary mainstream legal linguistics perceives the linguistic aspects of law as an intellectual product. It is not interested in biological aspects of sound emission and other neuronal or physiological processes that come about when law is engendered in linguistic form. 'Language' is perceived there in opposition to 'tongue', to its biological component. Meanwhile, the ancients did not make any such strict distinctions. Panini's *Sanskrit Grammar* was mentioned above as one such example of thinking the physical and the mental aspects of language together (cf. 6.2.2). Lucretius in *De rerum natura* (liber V, 1149) speaks about "animi interpres manabat lingua," the language that interprets the mind where 'lingua' clearly means 'tongue', not 'language'. The ancient Romans used the word 'lingua' for the natural organ 'tongue' as well as for the abstract system of signs that constitute meaning, the 'language'. Many modern languages kept up this categorization, for instance Russian, Polish, and Finnish. Other languages occasionally use 'tongue' in the meaning of 'language' as a metaphor. Romance languages complicate the categorization by introducing the sometimes ambiguous differentiation of 'langue' and 'langage' or 'lengua' and 'lenguaje', as do French and Spanish respectively. Historically, these semantic intricacies were the origin of two fundamentally different approaches to language (cf. Vygotskij 1934; Voloshinov 1929). One stressed the mental aspect of speaking and reasoning and neglected the physical components in language and speech. The other described language as a natural phenomenon. Today, both interests in language tend to merge somewhere in an area where interest in language meets interest in mind and consciousness (cf. Searle 2006; Pinker 1997, 1999: 269–287). It this area one could again speak about language as 'lingua' while taking into consideration both the physical and the mental components of speech. Neurosciences and neurolinguistics introduce new knowledge into the linguistics proper (cf. Lakoff 2008). This process will at some point in time change the nature of linguistics. It will certainly elucidate biological prerequisites of speech and meaning formation. It is not yet clarified whether these paradigmatic changes in linguistics will have a bearing on the legal-linguistic research. As shown in the above paragraphs, not all conceptions of language and linguistics are relevant to legal sciences and legal linguistics. Legal linguistics is methodologically capricious when it borrows methods and approaches from the linguistics proper. Probably, this tendency will not be overcome very soon.

Closest to the conception of language as 'tongue' is forensic linguistics. Forensic linguistics involves authorship attribution, language use in libel and defamation cases, analysis of legal documents, courtroom language and some other issues related to written and spoken legal language (cf. Stygall 1994; Du 2004; Rosenhouse 2013: 54). It also regularly deals with issues connected with the physical nature of language. Some phenomena of language construed as tongue, such as prosopagnosia and phonagnosia, play a role in the procedurality of law. Prosopagnosia or faulty identification of offenders by eyewitnesses due to their deficiency to distinguish faces is a challenge to the procedure of testifying that relies on this ability. Testifying in courts occasionally leads to wrong convictions for crimes because witnesses have falsely identified the suspects and they rely on their imaginary recollections. Moreover, some people have problems with recognizing familiar voices on the telephone (phonagnosia). Both prosopagnosia and phonagnosia – dissociation between familiar and unfamiliar voices – may therefore deform the procedure that blindly trusts in human capacities which as a rule are not tested in courts. The named physical features of language play also a role in discursive formations. They are therefore relevant to our pragmatic conception of legal linguistics.

6.3.5 Illegal language – using language and ending in jail

Language use can also be perceived in terms of legality. Perjury is a typical example of language use that is sanctioned by law. The case U.S. v Bronston (cf. Galdia 2009: 390; Tiersma/Solan 2012: 348–353) describes this constellation. The U.S. Supreme Court had to decide whether Bronston's answer, which was on its face truthful, might have been perceived as perjury because it negatively implied another result. The court recognized the institutional requirements for the use of language in court proceedings and acquitted Bronston. Therefore, in terms of colloquial speech Bronston may have lied; yet under the requirements for the institutional use of language he did not commit perjury, even if he was possibly lying. Another decision, which this time led to conviction for manipulative language use, is U.S. v. Liebo (923 F.2d 1308, 8th Cir, 1991). In this case, the court had to decide whether payments for airline tickets used by an official of an African country for private travels in Europe should have been perceived as bribery under the U.S. Foreign Corrupt Practices Act (FCPA). The defendant described payments connected with the tickets as gifts to the foreign official. Yet he could not convince the court with his interpretation. The linguistic classification of a payment as gift, donation, or gratuity alone was not perceived by the court as conclusive in assessing whether it constituted a bribe. However, the court held that intent to pay a bribe could have been inferred from circumstantial evidence that showed the connection between the decisions made by the African country's government and the payments.

6.3.6 Language in other contexts

Language is fundamental not only to law. Many other branches of science, among them also natural sciences, depend on language. This language is often more formalized and can also appear as fully abstract logical form of speech and mind. This is the case in mathematics. Mathematics is the formalized language of science. Science's language is basically the natural (non-formal) language – it is used in cognition via its characteristic feature of being a system of signs. This sign system, which is described in semiotics, can also be formalized; its formalized form is logic. Cognition, thus, can be initiated on the formalized level of the sign system – that is in logic or mathematics – or on the ordinary language level that is the least formalized. The contingency of choice between these levels and some intermediary forms caused confusion among scientists who sometimes claimed that ordinary language cannot be perceived as the basis for cognition in their domains. A. Einstein and L. Wittgenstein also expressed doubts about this matter. Meanwhile, language used in natural sciences can be an instrument of cognition on both ends of the formalization scale as well as on stages between the opposites. In the legal theory it may become important in future attempts towards understanding formal aspects of law.

Law can also be approached from an ethological perspective where animal behavior is perceived as a natural explanation of the emergence of law among humans. Charles Darwin brings in *The Descent of Man* a naturalized narrative about the non-discursive emergence of law. In the chapter "Mental powers of man and the lower animals" he writes: "In the Zoological Gardens, a monkey, which had weak teeth, used to break nuts with a stone; and I was assured by the keepers that after using the stone, he hid it in the straw, and would not let any other monkey touch it. Here, then, we have the idea of property; but this idea is common to every dog with a bone, and to most or all birds with their nests." In fact, Darwin aptly illustrates a phenomenon typical of animal law. This law is however different from the human at least in the aspect of time. While human property rights work in an abstract temporal space, the animal law works in the very moment of its creation, at least in Darwin's examples. It apparently does not even need to be applied, as application presupposes a time distance to the regulated item and this distance cannot be created in the immediate existence of such 'legal rules'. Finally, it is not human law because it is not agreed upon but only unilaterally and immediately imposed. The human concept of property is different from the animal struggle for bones; in its ultimate shape it is discursive. Discursiveness is as a social phenomenon understandable only to humans and applicable only among them. Naturalization of law has therefore limits and Darwin's examples show the differences between the animal 'law' and the human law rather than their resemblances.

6.4 Return to concepts

The first poignant task of the linguistic turn in law would be the action of cleaning law from its metaphysical ideology. A.J. Ayer (1970: 41–58) described the analogous procedures for philosophy in his *Language, Truth and Logic* that appeared in its English original already 1936 (cf. Urmson 1992a: 296). Law and its language, and predominantly its concepts, have been all too long perceived as rooted in an extra-legal natural law that is either true because sanctified by an extra-legal natural power or a divinity or is rooted in the nature of things. As a result of the linguistic turn in law, the level of legitimate and democratic creation of legal concepts is afforded to everyone. For instance, when the concept 'crimes against art' is advocated by an association of citizens, who wish to prohibit damage to works of art worldwide, so it is a legitimate discursive practice in law. It is largely negligible whether national laws in question already know 'crimes committed against art.' The discourse creates concepts that will be used in further discursive practices such as legislative drafting or scholarly research where their further discursive status will be determined. Undoubtedly, what law wants to say depends on the status of concepts used in discourses that relate to it. But the status of concepts in such discourses is never finally determined and this is another fundamental result of the linguistic turn in law. When the concept 'same sex marriage' came up, its legal status in law-related discourses had been low. One could even claim with some dose of social correctness that such a notion did not exist in law. With time, this concept changed radically its status in law-related discourses and entered into the professional legal discourse as a legitimized and in many jurisdictions even as a constitutionally protected legal concept. On the other side, the judicature's right to coin concepts termed as 'technical' such as 'tangible employment action' is not contested. This freedom to create concepts in law is more appealing because it concerns the professionals of law. Yet, also the citizens are professionals of law because they are not only expected to follow it, but first of all to shape it. Another particularly tormenting issue for law is the determination of the linguistic shape of concepts used in law. It concerns the development of a new or a modernized language for the national and the global law. Changes in this respect would also radically transform the professional legal discourse as well as learning and applying law.

6.4.1 Concepts and terms in law

Work on concepts is difficult due to their indeterminate meaning. W. Quine explained this circumstance on his famous gavagai-example (cf. 8.7.6 and Galdia 2009: 235). Concepts and broader conceptions play nevertheless a role in the discourses about law; in some of them they are even dominant. Pragmatics can easily operate with terms because there is no doubt as to their epistemological status. Therefore, when discourses introduce 'concepts' it is worthwhile considering whether one could replace them with 'terms' without modifying the topic. Law is structured around terminology that can be isolated and listed. In modern approaches to law, beginning with H.L.A. Hart, this procedure should be possible even if some objections could come from authors whose ideas would be reformulated. Most of these professional discourses function anyhow in other surroundings than pragmatics or analytical philosophy. They are used here in order to strengthen the linguistic turn in law. Doubtless, those texts, for example

Hart's *Concept of Law*, have also other implications that are less essential to the foundation of a linguistic analysis of legal discourses. Therefore, replacing 'concepts' with 'terms' – where possible – makes the work on discourses methodically easier. Meanwhile, many legal discourses will remain situated in contexts that are explicitly conceptual.

6.4.2 Fundamental concepts

Linguistic creation in law may be more or less central. Some coinages, such as 'rent' or 'lease contract' may be practically important although they are nor particularly demanding in terms of intellectual creation. Some other coinages such as 'contract' or 'intellectual property rights' require more creativity to be coined. Still more, certain linguistic coinages are of fundamental importance for the creation of law with linguistic means. For instance, the linguistic distinction between 'to be' and 'ought to be' is not only central to philosophical questions. It also structures our perspective upon law (cf. Zuleta Puceiro 1981: 9). Occidental law may have emerged as a result of the incremental divide that took place between religious and moral rules on the one side and the legal rules on the other side. This split marks also the birth hour of legal positivism that cultivates the idea of law distinct from morals. In the conceptual split between 'to be' and 'ought to be' moral beliefs are contrasted with factual beliefs. It became clear that moral beliefs are of different nature than beliefs about facts. The naturalistic fallacy that an 'ought to' can be derived from an 'is' is an important distinctive feature of professional thinking about ethics and law. The type of rules is here central, not their content. E. G. Moore is credited for explicitly pointing to this problem in his *Principia Ethica* (1903) where he also coined the term 'naturalistic fallacy'. Earlier, D. Hume in his *Treatise of Human Nature* expressed this view in a pronounced way: "In every system of morality, which I have hitherto met with, I have always remark'd, that the author proceeds for some time in the ordinary way of reasoning...when of a sudden I am surpris'd to find, that instead of the usual copulations of propositions, is, and is not, I meet with no proposition that is not connected with an ought or an ought not. This change is imperceptible, but is, however, of the last consequence. For as this ought or ought not, expresses some new relation or affirmation, 'tis necessary that it shoul'd be observ'd and explain'd; and at the same time that a reason should be given, for what seems altogether inconceivable, how this new relation can be a deduction from others, which are entirely different from it" (cf. III(i)1). To be and ought to be also divide our perspective upon law in two areas, the one of existing legal norms in force and the other of their application in society. The fact that theft happens regularly in department stores – and not only there – does not influence the existence of a legal norm that prohibits and punishes theft. It is an example that norms do not necessarily follow the social facts – normative power of factual situations has limits. Meanwhile, the split into two worlds of legal and social norms may give rise to new discourses about law that may approach the traditional divide critically.

6.4.3 Institutions and concepts

Conceptual constructions, legal institutes and legal doctrines manifest related problems. A. Hamilton, while benefiting from his rhetorical talent, mentions in the *Federalist* the concept of 'government' as a central tenet of the constitution: "It is a singular instance of the capriciousness of the human mind, that, after all the admonitions we have had from experience on this head, there should still be found men who object to the new Constitution for deviating from a principle which has been found the bane of the old, and which is in itself evidently incompatible with the ideas of government; a principle, in short, which, if it is to be executed at all, must substitute the violent and sanguinary agency of the sword to the mild influence of the magistracy" (*Federalist* nr. 15). 'Government' is an essential concept of the constitutional structure; yet it cannot function in isolation. Hamilton links it to law and the legal regulation: "Government implies the power of making laws. It is essential to the idea of a law, that it be attended by a sanction; or, in other words, a penalty or punishment for disobedience. If there be no penalty attached to disobedience, the resolutions or commands which pretend to be laws will, in fact, amount to nothing more than advice or recommendation" (*Federalist* nr. 15). The textual puzzle of the constitution is conceptually reconstructed and concepts are rhetorically linked to each other because the cohesion among them is, in fact, rhetorical.

Another, more recent example of such reconstruction can be found in the public law. J.C.N. Raadschelders (2011) restructured the area of 'public administration' while using conceptual maps that make the links between public administration and other socially relevant institutions better visible. Raadschelders's method can be instrumental in identifying discursive areas as networks where special knowledge both emerges and is required. Meanwhile, he also quotes J.F. Davidson (1961: 851) who questioned the 'conceptual framework' while saying: "Methods become ritual when the analyst concentrates on an elaborate or rigid 'conceptual framework' and limits his interpretive role to the internal structure of the data, as if he believed that only so far as he is able to neutralize his own judgment will his study be scientific and thus, by definition, meaningful." Therefore, discourses can be mapped conceptually within critical discursive procedures and such procedures are also largely used, especially in scientific research. Raadschelders (2011: 49) argues that concepts can only be meaningful when they are related to other concepts. Yet, this is not sufficient to render them meaningful and J.F. Davidson made it clear. The critical element in the discourse is its inherent interpretiveness as a part of discursiveness. Therefore, concepts as such do not say much. They become meaningful when used, it is when interpreted. Raadschelders (2011: 48) is aware of this intricacy and he stresses that the social world is constructed and reconstructed by self-aware individuals. Indeed, the social world is not given within a 'conceptual framework'. When it is constructed and re-constructed, linguistic operations of construction and re-construction take place. In *Legal Linguistics* (Galdia 2009) and also in this book we tried to elucidate these specific operations of construction and re-construction that are in the area of legal discourse called 'legal-linguistic operations'. Furthermore, professional discourses are linked to professional knowledge. In public administration, Raadschelders (2011: 20) with reference to Axelrod (1976) critically identified 'decisions' as characteristic discursive constructs and "smallest possible units" of the discourse. Meanwhile, 'decisions' have been in the past viewed in isolation from the discourse and not as its results. This positivism is still largely present in administration and works such as Raadschelders's may help overcome this conceptual stalemate (cf. Borch 1954; Farmer 1995). Also law as a special discursive area requires professional knowledge. Meanwhile, like public administration or military, law allows also for non-professional discourses. The commingling of professional and non-professional discourses in daily practice engenders law as a discursive phenomenon.

6.4.4 Miranda rights

The interrelation of professional and non-professional discursive patterns is best illustrated on the example of Miranda-rights. The U.S. Supreme Court dealt in Miranda v. Arizona (384 U.S. 436, 86 S. Ct. 1602, 1966) with a question that concerns the emergence of discursive practices. The court reflected upon the meaning of the Fifth Amendment to the U.S. Constitution that says in the here interesting part: "No person shall…be compelled in any criminal case to be a witness against himself…" Meanwhile, as not all U.S. citizens know this protective clause against self-incrimination, the court required that a warning, called subsequently 'Miranda rights', be read to criminal suspects. This procedure includes in its most wide-spread form the following wording: "You have the right to remain silent. Anything you say can and will be used against you in the court of law. You have the right to speak to an attorney and to have an attorney present during the questioning. If you cannot afford a lawyer, one will be provided for you at government expense." The formula uses in its second phrase a rather complex structure composed of two verbs 'can and will be used' that are even more difficult to grasp in spoken language because they follow upon one more verb, namely 'say'. Moreover, the formulation is cumbersome and formalistic. Significantly, in American films that include this procedure as part of the arrest of a criminal suspect only the beginning is clearly identifiable and the rest of the formula is regularly abandoned in an apparent attempt at avoiding a boring scene. Some authorities use a more elaborate formulation: "You have the right to remain silent and refuse to answer questions. Do you understand? Anything you do say may be used against you in a court of law. Do you understand? You have the right to consult an attorney before speaking to the police and to have an attorney present during questioning now or in the future. Do you understand? If you cannot afford an attorney, one will be appointed for you before any questioning if you wish. Do you understand? If you decide to answer questions now without an attorney present, you will still have the right to stop answering at any time until you talk to an attorney. Do you understand? Knowing and understanding your rights as I have explained them to you, are you willing to answer my questions without an attorney present?" An arrested person may be asked to sign a document stating that he/she had been read the Miranda rights. In fact, the formula rather incites the suspect to speak and cooperate (cf. Davis/Leo 2012: 356). Its structure is far from being a warning; its main aim is suggesting to the suspect to co-operate and to speak. Rights that could be perceived as warnings are described formalistically; they make this formula actually redundant. Suspects either understand this sort of procedural rights already and then the formula does not add anything or they do not know their procedural rights and then this sort of explanation of rights cannot help. Regularly, however, statements obtained under violation of the Miranda-procedure can be excluded from evidence at trial. The U.S. Supreme Court reiterated the request for a warning against self-incrimination in its decision Dickerson v. U.S. (530 U.S. 428, 120 S.Ct. 2326, 147 (2000) while saying: "We do not think there is justification for overruling Miranda. Miranda has become embedded in routine police practice to the point where the warnings have become part of our national culture." The Miranda rights entered apparently ino the police jargon as 'Mirandize somebody': "We Mirandized him, he's talking, we'll book him when we're through," as mentioned in J. Lescroat's novel *The Hearing*, p. 24. Meanwhile, police officers in many countries use 'Miranda rights' procedures that are believed to engender legality in actions aiming at depriving citizens of their liberty. In England and Wales the corresponding legal advice to suspects is called 'police caution'. Its text provides as follows: "You do not have to say anything. But it may harm your defence if you do not mention when questioned something which you later rely on in Court. Anything you do say may be given in evidence." The text is structured in a way that suggests to the suspect to speak. The wording of the second sentence is enigmatic; at least some legal training is necessary to construe its bearing in terms of penal procedure. The wording of the previously used caution was simpler: "You do not have to say anything unless you wish to do so, but what you say may be given in evidence." This wording does not encourage speaking; it sounds rather like an upright warning to engage in verbal exchanges with policemen. Pragmatically, it comes closer to the aim of the caution that is to warn. The modernized version of the caution purports to warn, yet its linguistic dress conceals the opposite strategy. While warning against speaking on its face, it implies the recommendation to speak. This recommendation is a forceful argument, introduced by an ambiguous 'but' that might be understood as 'you better speak'. In postmodern times this type of formulation does not surprise; yet caution is called for before taking such a formulation all too literally.

6.4.5 Legalization of concepts

Legal institutions expect all concepts used in their architectural and intellectual frameworks to be institutionally legitimized. An extreme example of such an expectation was brought by *The New Yorker* that quoted in its edition of December 20, 2010 a dialogue from the trial against the poet Josif Brodsky in the Soviet Union in 1964: "Judge: And what is you profession? Brodsky: Poet and translator. Judge: And who told you that you were a poet? Who assigned you that rank? Brodsky: No one. Who assigned me to the human race? Judge: And did you study for this? Brodsky: For what? Judge: To become a poet. Did you try to attend a school where they train…where they teach…Brodsky: I don't think it comes from education." For the Soviet judge, who has professionally moved within the conceptual world that had emerged in a rigid institutional setting, also the concept of a 'poet' must have been institutionalized to be validly applied in a legal proceeding. No institutional sanction, no valid use in law. The judge sentenced Brodsky to six years of internal exile. Literary prototypes of this sort of situations have been developed by Franz Kafka (cf. 7.5.1) and Bruno Schulz. Schulz mentions in his novel *Sanatorium pod klepsydrą* (XL) an investigation by military authorities relating to his protagonist's dream. In the investigation the dream is turned into a legal concept that engenders the dreamer's legal responsibility. This act is exclusively possible due to the institutionalized procedure of investigation that discursively engenders legal consequences such as liability or responsibility. Less confusing are in law rules that prohibit individual concept creation. They may concern the classification of contracts by the parties or rights related to real property. When the parties conclude that one of them conveys the property on a textbook to the other and the other conveys her property on a twenty dollar note, then the parties cannot pretend to have concluded a contract of barter. What the parties have concluded is a sale contract and their linguistic inventiveness remains a pure sophism as they cannot impose upon the legal conceptual framework their own rules for creation of legal concepts. In terms of law, their creation is a manipulation of the legal language.

6.5 Emergence of meaning in law

Words in law have occasionally a different meaning than words in daily use. How is this difference conditioned? Are words in law exposed to the same indeterminacy as are the words in daily speech? Lewis Carroll challenged the professionals of language, linguists and jurists alike, in his *Alice's Adventures in Wonderland* (1865) where he let Humpty Dumpty express the most provocative opinions about language: "When I use a word, Humpty Dumpty said, in rather a scornful tone, it means just what I choose it to mean – neither more nor less. The question is, said Alice, whether you can make words mean so many different things. The question is, said Humpty Dumpty, which is to be master – that's all." Hence, the master of discursive practices legitimizes their semantics and pragmatics. Independently of Humpty Dumpty, J.L. Austin (1975: 14–15) introduced the requirement of institutional qualification for the validity of performatives in law. It seems that the whole legal language is based on this theoretical requirement. Legal language can be effectively used in legal contexts such as trials when speech acts are uttered by the masters of their profession. It means that only prosecutors accuse, only attorneys defend and only judges can sentence the accused (cf. Meyer 2008: 43). None of the involved persons can change their role in the trial although all of them as jurists have the basic legal qualifications that should enable them to perform all the duties of prosecution, defense and judging in a professionally acceptable way. The meaning of language in law is determined along the Humpty Dumpty concept of meaning with numerous variations. First, the semantics of the legal language develops from the inherited linguistic corpus; jurists are not involved in a constant and arbitrary change of meaning in law. Second, the meaning that emerges is a collective product, as the conditions of professional acceptability must be fulfilled for a particular meaning to enter into the language of law. Humpty Dumpty has in mind whimsical and permanent changes of meaning in speech acts. Once uttered, a speech act becomes boring for him and in future he will attribute to his words another meaning. The conditions for the emergence of meaning in law prevent the Humpty Dumpty-rule to triumph in law. This does not mean that exceptions would not exist. Cooter and Ullen (2004: 192) call the American case law relating to the common law concept of consideration 'Humpty Dumpty-jurisprudence'. In their view, the question whether the requirements of consideration are fulfilled in contracts is determined by American courts whimsically and therefore no clear meaning of the concept can be stated as it mutated to a tautology. Thus, a contract is enforceable when it includes consideration and consideration is that circumstance that makes the contract enforceable.

6.5.1 Courts committed to 'ordinary meaning'

Legislators and courts regularly stress that in the application of law the 'ordinary meaning' of words should be favored in controversial cases. American judges also refer to this interpretive strategy that they perceive as binding for their profession. B. Slocum (2012) asked whether American courts really follow this interpretive guideline when applying statutes. He found out that American courts tend to determine the 'possible' rather than the 'ordinary meaning' of texts, mainly due to their methodological deficiencies. Characteristic of this approach in courts is the reference to authoritative dictionaries that are quoted and analyzed in extenso and afterwards abandoned altogether (Galdia 2009: 176–177). This argumentative strategy is related to the argument that courts apply law and nothing more. Judges are apparently embarrassed by the amount of power in their hands and seem to fear that the admitted use of power in law would disqualify them as professionals of law. This, by no means, needs to be so. Power has not necessarily a negative connotation. As already mentioned, M. Foucault perceives the power that is traceable in all social structures, including language, as their typical component. Power is inherent in social institutions. A court decision may illustrate this constellation. In Kasten v. Saint-Gobain Performance Plastics Corp. (131 S. Ct. 1325, U.S. Sup. Ct. 2011) the U.S. Supreme Court had to decide the question whether The Fair Labor Standards Act of 1938 provided protection against measures undertaken by the employer in a situation of an oral complaint made by the employee. The Act contains an antiretaliation provision that forbids discharging or in any other manner discriminating against any employee because such an employee has "filed any complaint or instituted or caused to be instituted any proceeding under or related to (the Act), or has testified or is about to testify in such proceeding, or has served or is about to serve on an industry committee." In casu, the plaintiff made an oral complaint about some technical practices introduced by the defendant and was subsequently discharged. He claimed to be protected by the Act; the defendant contested this allegation and pretended that the Act protects only against written complaints. The court had to deal with the interpretation of the phrase 'filed any complaint' and it had to determine the scope of its application under the Act. In terms of the court, the language of the provision "considered in isolation, may be open to competing interpretations." Some dictionaries consulted by the court connect 'file' with written texts, while others "provide different definitions that permit the use of 'file' in conjunction with oral material." Additionally, the court remarks that some U.S. state statutes also permit 'oral filings'. Furthermore, in times when the Act was debated and passed this linguistic practice existed in some U.S. states. The court then interpreted 'any' in 'any complaint' and decided that it "suggests a broad interpretation." Finally, it decided that 'oral complaints' are covered by the Act due to its goal to protect critical workers against retaliation. The court also recalled the working conditions in 1938 when often illiterate workers 'toiled in factories'. The court decision definitely makes sense towards the background of interests involved in the case. Yet, does it reflect ordinary language use? At least the expression 'file a complaint' may be perceived as typical of ordinary language. It is furthermore imaginable that it could be extended to 'file any complaint' in the ordinary usage. Meanwhile, ordinary language rather connects 'file' with written materials and 'any' in 'any complaint' refers rather to the content and not to the modality of the complaint. It seems therefore that the court followed the ordinary point of view in a situation of a social conflict rather than the ordinary language use. The court itself called the interpretive device used in the case 'flexibility'.

6.5.2 Courts shape 'ordinary language'

Courts' tendency to develop specialized registers for law has been early identified in the legal-linguistic research. Equally interesting is courts' input in the development of ordinary language. The first identifiable process is the transfer of legal terminology from professional discourses into non-professional discourses. Legal terminology enters into the daily discourse and it is with time not perceived by speakers as distinctive any more. The analogous process is known as borrowing of foreign words that at the beginning sound awkward to the ears of speakers who then become accustomed to them. The process of accepting a lexical unit into the ordinary discourse does not mean that its origins are not know or that it is not identified as a borrowing, occasionally also having a synonym in this language. The co-existence of lexical units and their exchange in discourses is frequent and natural. In Commitée Interprofesionel du Vin de Champagne v. Wineworths, Ltd. (2 NZLR 432, 1991) a court in New Zealand had to determine whether the word 'champagne' is perceived in this country as a distinctive word that refers to the specific 'méthode champenoise' of champagne production or whether it is a generic term. The court found out that the word is used in New Zealand as a specific term and not as a generic term that refers to any white sparkling wine as is the case in Australia, U.S. or Canada. Legal language may transform ordinary language into specialized register and by so doing it may even strengthen the use of ephemeral coinages in the ordinary language. This is the case, for instance, with 'crush videos' that as a lexical unit came up in the American subculture related to the cybersphere. Crush videos, which are posted online, feature the torture and killing of helpless animals. In order to combat this practice, the U.S. Congress passed a provision that was subject to judicial review (cf. U.S. v. Stevens, 2009). The U.S. Supreme Court regularly used in its decision the term 'crush video'. As a consequence of the court decision the Animal Crush Video Prohibition Act has been signed into law by U.S. President B. Obama. The legal acts and the court decision have been widely commented in the media. This resulted not only in broadening of the legal language but also in propagating the term 'crush video' over the linguistic barrier of the mainstream speakers who hitherto were neither interested in practices featured in crush videos nor in their linguistic manifestations.

6.5.3 Literal apprehension of meaning

Misguided speakers and some scholars have developed the tendency to approach meaning literally. This means that for them 'red rose' or 'broken contract' refer to a plant with a specific color or to a legal act. Such speakers will be confused when someone says to them 'You are my red rose' or 'This morning my dog broke our contract and therefore he will not get his bone'. In brief, literal apprehension of meaning is an unfortunate device of language use because it conceals meaning rather than to uncover it. It reduces meaning to some, mostly randomly selected meaning varieties that are typical of the speaker's language. Every speaker has own linguistic habits and he tends to speak an idiolect. However, most speakers are also aware of this fact and they realize that other speakers use the language that they speak slightly differently in the same contexts of use. Meanwhile, this linguistic practice is not confusing for most speakers at all. Excepted from this rule are grammarians, purists, and quarrelsome persons. All of them, like the misguided speakers for whom language has one predefined meaning, might call essentialism their intellectual fatherland (cf. 3.6.4). In the legal discourses, the literal apprehension of meaning is not rare. Meanwhile, U.S. courts progressively liberate themselves from the literal apprehension of meaning. This process is illustrated in Golden v. Garafalo (678 F.2d 1139, 2d cir. 1982). There, it was held that the use of 'stock' equals a security transaction due to the mere use of the word. Yet, in Reves v. Ernst and Young (494 U.S. 56, U.S. Sup. Ct 1990) the court applied the family resemblance test in an analogous situation. It means that a simple factor is neither sufficient nor necessary, but that these taken together provide a "Gestalt"-sense (Palmiter 2005: 48) of whatever note involving an investment or a commercial consumer transaction. In law, the literal apprehension of meaning is particularly problematic because language used in the public sphere may create a vast range of meaning varieties and therefore any approach towards meaning formation in public sphere must focus on the apprehension of this vast range of meaning varieties. Is this not the case, then language is not understood properly in judicial institutions. Judges must be particularly aware of the fact that an institutional approach to meaning must be integrative and that it is not limited to 'good language' that they may have assimilated at high school. The theory of indeterminacy of meaning is the device that enables the understanding of this frustrating phenomenon. However, any unbiased approach to linguistic practice provides ample evidence that meaning emerges under conditions of indeterminacy and that it crystallizes in speech acts to what it means. Many judges, however, recognised the problem of meaning formation in law before linguists even thought about the indeterminacy theory of meaning. Justice L. Hand wrote in Commissioner v. National Carbide Co. (1948): "Words are chameleons, which reflect the color of their environment." Justice Blackburn remarked in Allgood v. Blake (1873): "The meaning of words varies according to the circumstances of and concerning which they are used." It has been regularly remarked in literature that jurists were among the pioneers of contemporary understanding of meaning. In terms of linguistic theory, however, they did not make their conceptions explicit enough. This is also one of the reasons why legal linguistics emerged in the vacuum between practically advanced understanding of meaning in the daily work of many jurists and their inability to state their advanced linguistic practices in theoretical terms.

6.5.4 Heirs presumptive and presumptive heirs

Lewis Carroll's *Alice's Adventures in Wonderland* is not the only methodological work on the scope and the limits of the legal language. The inherent and amazingly subversive limits of language are directed against the tendency of some of its users to insist upon a legal language that could be validly formulated once and forever. Yet, language is limited in the sense that it cannot be held on; it is a dynamic tool of communication. Therefore, society that is by necessity opposed to rigidity is supported in its striving for renewal by language that inherently tends to constant, yet regular change. In fact, whatever linguistic unit, when aptly approached, can teach a lesson on legal-linguistic aspects of change. So have the 'heirs presumptive' of some ancient epochs in the history of the common law become in the course of time 'presumptive heirs'. In terms of law, no semantic change accompanied the syntactic transformation that reversed the order in which the adjective and the noun are combined. As a result, the adjective precedes the noun in the more contemporary formulation. Both expressions still refer in equal degree to persons who are heirs, especially to a position of a ruler, only until someone with a stronger right is born. The syntactic difference might therefore seem negligible in law and it might be treated as a pure stylistic variety. It might however also transfer an important message. In terms of language, the syntactic transformation marks an innovation that corresponds with socially relevant linguistic changes that are observed by sociolinguists. These linguistic changes signal the necessity of linguistic reforms in law because language use in socially relevant contexts seems to have evolved. The respective reforms are institutional because the legal language cannot be changed independently of an institutional framework. This is especially the case with legislative acts that are enacted in written form and that cannot be reformulated without parliamentary consent. Sometimes antiquated language or terms no more so valid are set in italics by the editors of legislative compilations. This is another way to signal the necessity of change, i.e. of linguistic reformulation of law. Therefore, 'heirs presumptive' and 'presumptive heirs' do not mean the same although they may refer to the same group of privileged persons.

6.5.5 An attempt to privatize language

In this essay we insist on the social origin and nature of the human language. It means that language is created collectively and that it belongs to all of us. Meanwhile, semantically relevant attempts at privatization of language use are present in daily practice. For instance, a CEO of an American enterprise negotiated a contractual clause that allowed him to unilaterally discontinue his employment contract in case of an "unreasonable interference, in his good faith judgment, by the Board or a substantial stockholder" of the company in carrying out his managerial duties. According to the contract, the CEO would be entitled to the payment of his annual base salary and other benefits for the reminder of the contract that run until his 75th birthday. In fact, his right under the clause would provide him payments totaling 20 million dollars. A shareholder tried to invalidate the clause in a court and asserted that the potentially severe financial penalties would inhibit and deter the Board from exercising its duties (Grimes v. Donald 673 A.2nd 1207, Delaware Supreme Court 1996). The court agreed that the consequences of the 'constructive termination without cause', which the CEO could invoke, would prevent the Board "to some extent" from dismissing him. This circumstance would constitute an impediment to the exercise of rights which the Board is obliged to take seriously because it represents the interests of the shareholders and shall supervise the CEO's activities. On the other side, as any criticism can be perceived as 'unreasonable' the CEO would have the chance to quit the enterprise at whatever moment and enrich himself quite considerably. Meanwhile, the court did not interfere in the freedom of the parties to sign "a rather unusual contract." The court was ready to protect the Board's free decision to sign an unusual contract "unless the facts show that such amounts, compared with the services to be received in exchange, constitute waste or could not otherwise be the product of a valid exercise of business judgment." Facts that clarify the language of the clause and that show how it could easily be misused were perceived by the court as a private matter of the parties. As a result, money proved here to function as a tool that limits the freedom to speak and to act, and the court sanctioned this self-imposed limit. The specific limiting 'extent' that basically prevented the Board from exercising its duties has been in its semantic range abandoned by the court to the CEO's private language use. The court apparently relied on the CEO's ethical commitment to truthful language use and to utilitarian action. While so doing, the court itself transgressed the limits of language as there is no private language. Language means something to all of us, meaning cannot be unilaterally defined. Therefore, language cannot be abandoned to a party. Thus, a clause that was 'unreasonable' because abusive of language and also of freedom to speak and to act, miraculously survived the scrutiny of the Delaware Supreme Court.

6.6 Understandability, vagueness, ambiguity in law

Issues concerning the understandability of legal texts by laypersons and the readability of legal texts are frequently treated in the legal-linguistic research. Connected with these issues are exactness and avoidance of vagueness or ambiguity in legal texts (cf. Solan 2012: 87–99). Some authors, for instance Poscher (2012: 129), distinguish strictly between the two concepts and relate them to indeterminacy. Also plain language initiatives make part of this area related to problems of understanding in legal texts. The main challenge between both areas is rooted in the tensions between attempts at writing in plain language while neglecting the plain law and in reversed procedures. Also Heikki E.S. Mattila (2013: 131, 123) addressed this unfortunate dichotomy of goals. Legal language that emerges in Mattila's perspective is analyzed in his work in contrast to ordinary language. Meanwhile, also plain language claims that are related to ordinary language are taken into consideration, although they do not dominate Mattila's reflection upon linguistic aspects of legal terminology. This is particularly welcome because the plain language movement might have got in many recent legal-linguistic publications a broader coverage than it actually deserves. More often than not, the plain language claims lead to expectations concerning the understandability of law by everyone that can only disillusion their well-intentioned authors. Also Mattila sees limits of such undertakings. His views are particularly valuable as they make plain the politically complex nature of law. Indeed, law is complex, not only linguistically, because it is a social discursive practice that is rooted in the deep structure of society. Many classics of legal theory elucidated already some decades ago the conditions and the contexts of language used in law that they perceived as ideological and clearly not as a simple result of jurists' alleged linguistic clumsiness. Language use in law is therefore mainly an issue of ideology and not of linguistic didactic. In fact, jurists live on their linguistic skills; they are masters of language use. Their skills impress most when they are evaluated from the pragmatic perspective, and Mattila's approach is one more proof of this legal-linguistic constant that was recognized already by the ancient Greek rhetoricians. Meanwhile, Mattila's approach to the issue is conciliatory: plain language attempts make sense within legislative drafting, yet they also have their inherent limits embodied in the reducible yet finally unavoidable complexity of modern law (Mattila 2013: 123, 131). In sum, Mattila's conclusions upon the research agenda of plain language studies may be instrumental in re-adjusting some of its paradigmatic claims. Questions of understanding in law are therefore best positioned between the indeterminacy theory of meaning and the ideological constraints of law.

6.6.1 Plain language and plain law

The most striking feature in the debate about plain language is the interrelation between plain language and plain law. Plain language is best construed in terms of lexical and syntactic simplicity. Following this strategy, the plain language movement within Law and Language obtained already a remarkable simplification of language used in legally relevant contexts, especially in the English-speaking countries. Yet, plain language is a relative notion. A judge wrote in the court opinion Katris v. Carroll (842 N.E. 2d 221 Ill. Ct. App. 2005): "Katris contends, however, that Doherty owed fiduciary duties to the LLC pursuant to section 15–3(g)(3) of the Act. Section 15–3(g)(3) provides: (A) member who pursuant to the operating agreement exercises some or all of the authority of a manager in the management and conduct of the company's business is held to the standards of conduct in subsections (b), (c), (d), and (e) of this Section to the extent that the member exercises the managerial authority vested in a manager by this Act… Looking at the plain language of section 15–3(g)(3) of the Act, Doherty was subject to fiduciary duties if he exercised some or all of the authority of a manager pursuant to the LLC's operating agreement." For the judge, the section of the legal act in question represents plain language, for many non-jurists it may represent hermetically closed legalese. Therefore, the very notion of plain language is largely a question of the perspective taken upon law. Meanwhile, the more relevant question is whether drafting laws in plain language engenders plain law. For instance, Article 15 of the Constitution of Latvia (Satversme) says in its English translation: "The Saeima shall hold its sittings in Riga, and only in extraordinary circumstances may it convene elsewhere." The language in the English translation is understandable without any particular effort. It may therefore be perceived as plain. Yet, the constitutional provision remains nevertheless a mystery when its scope of application is in question. To apply it, one has to know in which extraordinary circumstances the Parliament may assembly outside the capital city. The answer to the interpretive query depends on constitutional law that may include a doctrine about the scope of application of this provision. This may equally well not be the case and then further going interpretation of the provision in the light of the Constitution will be necessary to find out whether in a given case the Parliament may debate elsewhere than in Riga. Another problem concerns the relation between plain language and ordinary language. Ordinary language is not necessarily plain, and the constitutional provision of the Latvian Constitution that was analyzed above illustrates the difference. No one says in ordinary language 'to hold sittings' or 'to convene elsewhere'. One would rather speak about an assembly or Parliament that debates at some other place. Thus, ordinary language does not coincide with plain language, yet it is not necessarily its opposite. Plain language, at least in the perspective of the plain language movement, is based on a drafting technique that deliberately simplifies language. The language developed along such simplifying guidelines is controlled language, like the language proposed for machine translations that was critically approached by some researchers (cf. Mitamura 1999; Sommers 1998). These researchers questioned the possibility of controlled language to function fully like whatever language. What is more, the plain language drafter writes in a language that is not his. He will, as a rule, be a university educated jurist and may even have some general education in other disciplines. Yet, most of the plain language instructions provide for simplification techniques that engender an artificial language that is actually not spoken by anyone. Implied in the instructions is the idea that messages in plain language mainly concern less educated parts of the population. Yet, the language of this part of the population is all but plain. Sociolinguistics shows the complexity of this language that differs from the more elaborate language use in that it is not standard language (cf. Andersson/Trudgill 1991). Yet it is not simple and it is not plain. Therefore, the question whether, for instance, the American 'Miranda rights' should actually reflect the fourth-grade education to be universally comprehensible may not concern the essence of the problem. N. Sevin Goldstein et al. (2012: 307) pointed out the developmental immaturity and aggressivity of juvenile detainees that impedes whatever understanding of written texts, not only legal. Additionally, the attitude of many persons arrested by police is far from respectful towards law and therefore their interest in legal matters is at best limited. Somewhere legislators would have to take note of the inherent social problems of detention and stop the race to the bottom in plain language drafting. Plain language in this sense is closer to controlled language than to ordinary language. Ordinary language is, in turn, the opposite of language for special purposes. Its main advantage is that it is, unlike the plain language, a naturally spoken language. It is used and understood by nearly everyone in society. Drafting in ordinary language is an alternative to plain language. At the same time, it is worthwhile to keep in mind that no variety of language engenders unequivocal meaning in law. Therefore, language used in law will always be subject to interpretation simply because it is language and meaning emerges in it in interpretive speech acts. This regularity of language use in law is irreversible and non-transformative.

6.6.2 Could language in law be circumvented?

Another central challenge to legal linguistics is the claim that language is less central to law than is assumed in the legal-linguistic axiom. The claim that language cannot be 'overlooked' or 'circumvented', that it cannot be 'hintergangen' as expressed in German by Holenstein (1980: 159), that it is 'incontournable' in any social activity, as expressed in French, is present in the general discourse about law. Equally present is the challenging view that language is in socially relevant action actually less important than assumed. Already Charles Darwin in *The Descent of Man* remarked about this issue in the chapter on "Mental Powers of Man and the Lower Animals": "Max Müller gives in italics (*Lectures on Mr. Darwin's Philosophy of Language*, 1873, third lecture) this aphorism: 'There is no thought without words, as little as there are words without thought.' What a strange definition must here be given to the word thought!" J. Searle, unlike many philosophers and linguists before him, distinguished between communicative and cognitive situations where language is helpful although redundant and situations where language is indispensable for social interaction. For Searle, complex social interaction is always dependent on the use of language. This is however not the case in many other communicative situations that are structured in a less complex way. Also P. Strawson (1992: 89) asked: "...where in the world shall we find the relation signified by 'ought'?" Thus, the role of language can be overrated in some areas of its use. In law, it is still insuperable as a conditio sine qua non of meaningful communication. For legal linguistics it seems to be decisive that the discursive and narrative complexity of law could not be rendered or made operational with another tool of communication than language.

6.6.3 Is content in law a linguistic trap?

We spent less and less space in this essay on discussing what the law actually regulates and which solutions to material problems in society it imposes. The reason for this is that our discourse seems to teach us that for law the regulatory content does not matter much. Jurists are specialists in legal argumentation and in other linguistic operations in law. The content of law is not their domain. This circumstance proves fatal in all cases where interpretation of concepts in broader, non-technical contexts becomes necessary. Jurists are not prepared to cope with such challenges. They perform in such cases equally badly or equally well as do other citizens. Only an integration of law as a subject, i.e. its studying and its teaching, into the family of social disciplines may provide a successful remedy for this failure that is rooted in a bad tradition. Already Immanuel Kant in his *Über den Fakultätenstreit* suggested such changes that are still unfulfilled.

While overestimating the regulatory potential of law *The Federalist* (nr. 10) mentions the role of regulation in preserving the status quo of propriety rights in the emerging United States of America: "But the most common and durable source of factions has been the various and unequal distribution of property. Those who hold and those who are without property have ever formed distinct interests in society. Those who are creditors, and those who are debtors, fall under a like discrimination. A landed interest, a manufacturing interest, a mercantile interest, a moneyed interest, with many lesser interests, grow up of necessity in civilized nations, and divide them into different classes, actuated by different sentiments and views. The regulation of these various and interfering interests forms the principal task of modern legislation, and involves the spirit of party and faction in the necessary and ordinary operation of the government." Thus, the modern legislation of 1778 had the task to secure and to protect the given social inequality. James Madison, who is the supposed author of the quoted *Federalist* article, does not explain with even one word why this task falls upon the law. He 'forgets' that law develops within discursive practices in society and that therefore its content is extra-legal and cannot be determined in advance. Meanwhile, for Madison "(T)he diversity in the faculties of men, from which the rights of property originate, is not less an insuperable obstacle to a uniformity of interests. The protection of these faculties is the first object of the government. From the protection of different and unequal faculties of acquiring property, the possession of different degrees and kinds of property immediately results; and from the influence of these on the sentiments and views of the respective proprietors, ensues a division of the society into different interests and parties." All intent towards material change in the subject matter is for Madison sectarian and wicked: "A rage for paper money, for an abolition of debts, for an equal division of property, or for any other improper or wicked project, will be less apt to pervade the whole body of the Union than a particular member of it…" At this point, clearly, the mechanism of law is profoundly misunderstood. It re-emerges however later in the shape of the 'state of law'. It also introduces the idea of 'a strong union' that would be able to prevent "violence in place of law, or the destructive coercion of the sword inplace of the mild and salutary coercion of the magistracy" as noted in *Federalist* (nr. 20) in form of a sudden conclusion.

6.6.4 Another linguistic trap in law and its globalization: the custom

In discourses, terms introduced for social phenomena are not only linguistic references, although they are frequently, especially in positivist approaches, perceived as such. One of such examples of a distorted perception caused by linguistic creation is 'custom', in French 'la coutume'. Researchers into legal history had been interested in tracing the origin of customs with the idea in mind that they represent pure law, a form of societal organization that emerged organically in opposition to imposed statutory law (cf. Gaudemet 2001: 57). Many efforts were spent on this type of research, yet the linguistic form of the customary law was not questioned. In law, where power is exercised with linguistic means, stated custom is someone's custom that appears in its linguistic form of 'our custom'.

The linguistic form traps us as it suggests a preference and a better type of organization. In fact, customs are typologically statutes, only less precisely formulated. They do not represent a 'better law' or a type of law that is 'closer to the people'. Typologically, they are akin to religious laws that also declare to be superior to positive law and pretend to provide better law. Both types of law are alternatives to positive law that use their otherness as an argument legitimizing their raison d'être.

6.7 Legal linguistics as fact in law

From above chapters follows that every jurist is, at least implicitly, a legal linguist. He is a specialist in legal-linguistic operations that make the exercise of law possible. Most important legal-linguistic operations such as legal creativeness, legal interpretation, legal argumentation, legal justification, and legal defining have been mentioned either extensively or at least cursorily in above chapters. Good jurists are masters in the application of skills based on these and related legal-linguistic operations. The problem is that most jurists are not fully aware of the fact that they exercise a profession that is rooted in language. Others still practice their daily legal linguistics in an unsystematic way. Legal linguistics as an academic discipline starts with making explicit the linguistic strategies that jurists use in the exercise of their habitual daily legal-linguistic activities. It makes them discover the legal-linguistic operations more consciously and shows the broader framework of the legal discourse that hosts the legal-linguistic operations. It furthermore breaks down the legal-linguistic operations into simpler structures such as legal speech acts that emerge around legal terms. The truly professional jurist does not only master the legal-linguistic operations perfectly; he is also perfectly aware of their structure, scope, and social relevance.

6.7.1 Legal linguistics as an approach to law

For a jurist to master legal linguistics means primarily being able to use language efficiently in all social contexts relevant to law. These social contexts (situations in which language is used) are mostly institutional (language use in courts, in administrative proceedings, attorney's advice etc). The legal-linguistic skills are therefore closely linked to institutions because legal language does not exist outside contexts that are defined by social institutions such as courts of law. Incidentally, institutions also define these skills as there is no private legal language. Therefore, at least theoretically, the most salient legal-linguistic skill is the ability to use language efficiently under conditions defined by others, i.e. by institutions that impose the rules for its use. Practically, when the improvement of such skills should be reached, some methodical steps must be taken. First, the circumstances of language use must be identified; second, the relevant legal-linguistic skills must be defined and trained. For instance, first cross-examination is identified as a relevant linguistic operation in law; then language use strategies that are most appropriate and efficient in such a context of use are identified and trained with students. Legal-linguistic skills are acquired in numerous such language games. As a matter of fact, in common law countries some of these skills are already trained, yet at random and unsystematically, e.g. in moot courts. In the civil law countries this practical training is even more reduced or does not exist at all. Disappointingly, today, this professional training in legal-linguistic skills takes place only in practical life, haphazardly and superficially. Academic institutions, which should provide legal education, offer sterile legal doctrine instead of professional training in legal-linguistic skills. Consequently, law as a teaching subject is deficient because it does not teach the most essential skills for the practice of law, i.e. the efficient use of the legal language. Legal linguistics addresses this deficiency and provides remedies for these shortcomings that are viewed by ambitious law students rather critically.

What is more, legal linguistics allows linguists, sociologists, philosophers and other representatives of arts and social sciences to approach law from a perspective that is understandable within their frame of reference. It makes plain to them how law is created and how it is applied. When described in terms of legal linguistics, law as a social phenomenon can be integrated into methodological approaches that dominate these branches of knowledge. This is a great progress because the methodology of the traditional subject 'law' is much too particular and hermetical to become accessible to other professions. Therefore, legal linguistics functions also as a bridge between law as an academic discipline and other social disciplines. This shows again how central this branch of knowledge actually is. One more argument strengthens the legal-linguistic approach. All legal theory or jurisprudence is by necessity linguistic because law is a phenomenon that manifests itself in language. The difference between the legal-linguistic approach to law and other theoretical approaches is that legal linguistics as a theory of law is explicitly linguistic while other approaches are implicitly linguistic and focus primarily on other structural features of law such as power or constraint. Occasionally, though, law may also inspire other laws, mostly in comparative perspective that constitutes its further legal and linguistic points of contact. This is an additional perspective that legal linguistics adds to the theoretical research into law. This additional element is also practically relevant because it facilitates the generalization of the legal thought and the shaping of the global law.

Legal linguistics as pragmatic theory of law helps understand the fact that while talking about the law speakers actually make it. Law is not deciphered in statutes or precedents, or developed with a glance at the Constitution. Law, however, does not develop in a vacuum. It is developed with the help of textual sources, be they oral or written. Therefore the pragmatic theory of law should be linguistic. The linguistic component in it enables to embrace law in language, when it is spoken. This act is also theoretically necessary as it shows how law emerges and is applied. Speaking about the law is a performative act because law is made in this speech. Law may be maintained, strengthened, nuanced, modified, or abandoned in this speech. Making law does not, therefore, mean that a totally new proposition of law is introduced by the speaker. The speaker, for instance the judge, who follows a long line of precedents, makes law in the sense that he strengthens the existing content of law. This content is subject to change, yet the judge does not change it. A new interpretation would create a new law based on the unchanged wording of a statutory provision or a line of precedents. In sum, legal linguistics as a pragmatic theory of law is interesting because it makes plain and it canvasses the linguistic operations in law. Many other theoretical approaches to law that are close to it differ from the pragmatically defined legal linguistics because they do not or only partly include the material element of law. This element that is illustrated with the help of legal speech acts is the strength of legal linguistics and a benefit to the general theory of law.

6.7.2 Ptolemaic v. Copernican legal linguistics

Developments in all areas of knowledge regularly lead to paradigmatic changes. Legal linguistics is not an exception in this sense. Accumulated knowledge is in legal linguistics as everywhere else acquired and evaluated in terms of underlying theories. These theories evolve, are abandoned and they are replaced by others. Some knowledge can be integrated in a new paradigm, some cannot. Some knowledge appears to be irrelevant, negligible while some other neglected aspects become decisive in the newly adopted perspective. For instance, all legal linguistics centered around the isolated word, be it a term or a concept, will be viewed sooner or later as a challenge from the perspective of the discursive approaches to the legal language that turn the traditional legal linguistics upside down. Such paradigmatic changes are neither unusual nor are they a danger, although they are often perceived as such. The most striking and challenging example of such a paradigmatic change is the Copernican revolution that radically modified the Ptolemaic system. More specifically, Ptolemy (Claudius

Ptolemeus) founded in his *Almagest* the geocentric system; Copernicus in his work *De revolutionibus orbium celestium,* known better to most contemporary readers as *On the Revolution of the Heavenly Spheres,* re-founded astronomy that he had based on the heliocentric system, and this against all odds. Some scholars, such as Giordano Bruno or Galileo Galilei, had to pay dearly for supporting the revolutionary change in the astronomical paradigm. Institutional resistance to this change that is particularly fascinating as a discursive practice appeared at the end as powerless and the concerned institutions had to give up their violent resistance. The proverbial quote "eppur si muove," attributed sometimes to G. Bruno and sometimes to G. Galilei, also marks the limits of discursive practices and imposes new knowledge on the reason alone that it is knowledge. Legal linguistics is less dramatic. First, no highest sacrifices will ever be demanded from those who deal with this type of research. Occasionally, a researcher may lose her job, yet this is the only socially acceptable limit of academic sanctions against attempts to establish paradigmatic change nowadays. Second, both law and legal linguistics are discursive practices. Astronomy, by contrast, is only partly discursive, partly it is hard facts. Therefore, legal linguistics will remain forever torn between the past and the future paradigmatic constrictions in its teaching and researching. Meanwhile, it is also apparent that supporting whatever Ptolemaic version of it in times of a successfully completed Copernican revolution is not a particularly wise choice. One may bear in mind that the supporters of Ptolemaic teachings in the turbulent times of the paradigmatic change in astronomy might have assured for themselves some material advantages but nothing more than that. The outlook for legal linguistics is, when seen in these terms, rather optimistic.

6.7.3 Legal linguistics as a pragmatic theory of law

When legal linguistics is perceived as a theory of law, the benefits to lawyers are obvious. First of all, a lawyer who reflects upon legal-linguistic issues begins to understand the essence of the activities that she performs, i.e. using language efficiently in legally relevant social contexts. Basically all activities exercised by lawyers are covered by this broad description. Consequently, a lawyer who deals with legal linguistics understands the rules that govern her profession. This is also the main reason why legal linguistics should be integrated into regular curricula for all law students. The reason for this claim is that legal linguistics deals with the most fundamental issues in law, namely with the legal-linguistic operations such as legal argumentation, legal interpretation, legal translation and others, for instance legal defining. Introducing legal linguistics courses at a later stage of legal education supports the view which is skeptically indifferent to legal-linguistic interests as it posits that legal linguistics is a random discipline in law that deals with quixotic and academic questions that may be of interest to some enthusiasts.

6.7.4 Disruptive legal linguistics

Legal-linguistic research is undertaken as a view upon law from the linguistic perspective. Notwithstanding the existing results of this kind of research one could nevertheless (and again) ask whether this perspective is methodologically admissible. In terms of method, one would have to ask whether it makes sense to approach law from the point of view of linguistics. The previous chapters of this book might indicate or even prove that it makes sense. Yet, one more component of the methodological problem has to be considered as well. It can be reduced to a burdensome question: does the existing linguistic descriptive apparatus allow for using it meaningfully in the research that is describing law? Some of the attempts to apply linguistic instruments and matrices upon law may appear as mechanical transfers of one conceptual framework upon another (cf. Greimas 1976, Mattila 2002a, Cao 2004, Galdia 2009). However, results that were obtained in these experiments actually show that at least a quantitative valuation of the descriptive levels is necessary in order to describe the language that is used in law. Legal linguistics concerns theoretically the processes in which meaning emerges in law; all other aspects of legal language are much less important. Therefore, for example, a shift in attention from phonology to semantics or pragmatics is unavoidable in the legal-linguistic research. This result cannot surprise because law unlike syntax or semantics is not a linguistic discipline. It can, like all other areas of knowledge, be approached from the linguistic perspective; yet this is another matter. Also medicine or astronomy can be described in terms of linguistics. This description would manifest the role of language in both disciplines; yet it does not transform them into linguistic disciplines. The linguistic description of medicine or astronomy might, however, show that both disciplines developed at certain stages as discursive practices to the detriment of their experimental nature. Law cannot fall into such a conceptual trap because it is a discursive practice par excellence. It can easily be characterized from the linguistic perspective in its most decisive moments. Insofar it resembles poetry that can equally be described from the linguistic perspective without becoming a linguistic discipline. Earlier linguistic theories were sometimes less and sometimes more confusing for jurists who tried to approach law from the perspective of its alleged content.

6.7.5 Legal semantics and legal pragmatics

Another methodically relevant point is the interrelation of legal semantics and legal pragmatics as both are used in the legal-linguistic research and tend even to dominate it. This is at least the case in this essay. In the background of this interrelation there is the debate about semantics and pragmatics in the general theory of language. The relation between general semantics and general pragmatics has been addressed by many researchers in different ways. Morris (1938: 35) says: "Semantics deals with the relation of signs to…objects which they may or do denote. Pragmatics concerns the relation of signs to their interpreters." Stalnaker (1972: 383) holds: "Syntax studies sentences, semantics studies propositions. Pragmatics is the study of linguistic acts and the contexts in which they are performed. There are two major problems to be solved within pragmatics: first, to define interesting types of speech acts and speech products; second to characterize the features of the speech context which help determine which proposition is expressed by a given sentence… It is a semantic problem to specify the rules for matching sentences of natural language with the propositions that they express. In most cases, however, the rules will not match sentences directly with propositions, but will match sentences with propositions relative to features of the context in which the sentence is used. These contextual features are part of the subject matter of pragmatics." Katz (1977: 14) wrote: "(I) draw the theoretical line between semantic interpretation and pragmatic interpretation by taking the semantic component to properly represent only those aspects of the meaning of the sentence that an ideal speaker-hearer of the language would know in an anonymous letter situation,…(where there is) no clue whatever about the motive, circumstances of transmission, or any factor relevant to understanding the sentence on the basis of its context of utterance." Gazdar (1979: 4–5) mentions: "What we need in addition is some function that tells us about the meaning of utterances…The domain of this pragmatic function is the set of utterances, which are pairs of sentences and contexts, so that for each utterance, our function will return as a value a new context – the context as changed by the sentence uttered…And we can treat the meaning of the utterance as the difference between the original context and the context arrived at by the sentence." Kempson (1988: 139) writes: "Semantics provides a complete account of sentence meaning for the language, by recursively specifying the truth conditions of the sentences of the language…Pragmatics provides an account of how sentences are used in utterances to convey information in context." Most above authors, as pragmatists, stress of course the advantages of the pragmatic enquiry. The authors named above also insisted on strict differentiation between the areas of semiotic exploitation. Meanwhile, some dictionaries are more conciliatory in this respect. The *Oxford Companion to Philosophy* (1995: 709) mentions: "Pragmatics is the study of language which focuses attention on the users and the context of language use rather than on reference, truth, or grammar." The *Cambridge Dictionary of Philosophy* (1995: 588) argues: "Pragmatics studies the use of language in context, and the context-dependence of various aspects of linguistic interpretation…(Its branches include the theory of how) one and the same sentence can express different meanings or propositions from context to context, owing to ambiguity or indexicality or both,…speech act theory, and the theory of conversational implicature." The *Blackwell Companion to Philosophy* (1996: 124) writes: "The distinction between semantics and pragmatics is, roughly, the distinction between the significance conventionally or literally attached to words, and thence to whole sentences, and the further significance that can be worked out, by more general principles, using contextual information." J.C. Gémar (2004: 738–729) writes: "Si l'usage confère sa valeur sémantique première à un mot, c'est le contexte de son emploi, le mot mis en discours, qui en détermine toutefois sa signification réelle. De là l'importance du processus d'interprétation de textes, particulièrement poussé chez les juristes…Ce que presque tous les spécialistes appellent « le langage du droit » posséderait au moins trois éléments fondamentaux analysable dans tous leurs aspects, soit un lexique…une syntaxe…et une sémantique (sens des unités significatives/mots et morphèmes : signifiés) ; ou encore, selon le point de vue (linguistique, sociologique, communicatif, sémiotique, philosophique, littéraire, etc.) une « pragmatique », soit l'étude du langage par l'usage qui en est fait, autrement dit l'étude des phénomènes énonciatifs." F. Recanati (2008) made another attempt to reconcile semantics and pragmatics. He characterized the field in a perspective that unites the philosophy of language and the philosophy of mind that has become also the aim addressed by J. Searle (2006). The unity of both areas of knowledge is however easier to claim than to accomplish. Since the appearance of G. Frege's fundamental works, notions and mental phenomena such as 'denotation', 'connotation', 'proper names', 'reference' and 'utterance' were expected to be better understood in the unitary perspective. This notwithstanding, they were usually dealt with in isolated approaches. Recanati shows that the combination of both perspectives that is undertaken in the Anglo-American tradition of thought can work. Mental representations discussed by Recanati and Searle are particularly important for legal linguistics because most of simple or pre-linguistic representations are not interesting in the area of law. Recanati (2008: 97) advocates the primary role of pragmatics in all unitary undertakings. This perspective seems to be right because the relevance of subjects and issues treated must come from somewhere. He attributes a role to semantics, seen as 'sémantique pragmatique' (Recanati 2008: 98). The 'pragmatic semantics' can contribute to ascertaining the function or the type of use of utterances. Semantics has to become pragmatic because one cannot attribute a context-independent meaning to linguistic utterances (Recanati 2008: 95). Also some approaches developed in France, which were partly described by P. Engel (1994, 2000), show the way that leads beyond the traditional paradigm imposed by G. Frege as speech cannot be limited to utterances and its problems cannot be reduced to the analysis of reference or proper names. In the French philosophical tradition, notions and mental representations were perceived in broader contexts such as discourses. Reference, connotations and proper names become manifest in use and this use is discursive. The integration of this achievement has been however rather weak. This may be also the reason why M. Foucault's works, unlike L. Wittgenstein's writings, were not perceived as belonging to analytic philosophy.

6.8 Dissolution of legal linguistics

Legal linguistics is central to any reflection upon law. Yet, its centrality is a trap. When we reflect upon law from legal-linguistic perspective we actually reflect about the very essence of power. Thus, paradoxically, discovering legal language is discovering an epiphenomenon. Legal language is inherent in law; it is therefore unavoidable in it as a constituent of the legal discourse. Legal linguistics tells us that we have to speak differently about law, to speak like legal linguists or with their help. When the structure of the legal discourse changes, when it becomes linguistic, when jurists began to speak like legal linguists, the legal linguistics ends and disappears as an independent part of reflection about law. G.W.F. Hegel's 'sublation' is a concept that may illustrate this long term process. Legal language may be sublated in 'future law' as the concept of 'family' is sublated in 'civil society' and this further sublated in the 'state' in Hegel's dialectic. The process as such is typical of societal development and should not be perceived as a hindrance for future developments. The 'sublation' has however a dangerous adversary in the shape of the 'deformation' of the legal discourse. Legal discourse that is independent of or parallel to the systematic legal-linguistic reflection is usually profoundly deformed. It produces unjust law and separates law from society. Meanwhile, dissolution of disciplines is not a rare or a dangerous process in science. Legal linguists like many other scholars, for instance those who deal with the comparative law or the conflict of laws in times of emerging global law, work on the destruction of their disciplines. Processes that lead to dissolution of branches of knowledge are long term undertakings. As far as legal linguistics is concerned, its dissolution requires first of all the implementation of some of its main claims. Then, it requires the implementation of a program that is here called the linguistic turn in law. Yet, these times are remote from the time frame of this book.

6.8.1 Is language an epiphenomenon in law?

While speaking about the use of language in legal discourses we constantly and decisively speak about power. And this cannot take anyone by surprise as law is actually another, some might say, a more elegant word for power. In the legal linguistics, we therefore regularly define law as power expressed with the means of language (Galdia 2009: 271). Therefore, when we persistently stress the linguistic aspect of legal discourses we may expose ourselves to criticism that we deal with an epiphenomenon and that we should rather concentrate upon the main issue, i.e. on power and on the social structures that allow some people to dominate others with the help of linguistically expressed law. It would further mean that we should not get involved with intricacies of law that are seen primarily in the perspective of language that is used for its constitution. The legal-linguistic approach may be seen as too cumbersome and much too meticulous to understand some basic matters about law. Is explaining language in law like showing the sun with the lantern? Language and power as an alleged relation are equally metaphysical as are law and language. In law, power is expressed with linguistic means. In other, non-legal contexts power might be expressed differently, without language.

6.8.2 Norming in law

In a legal linguistics conceived as legal pragmatics we will also have to answer the question as to what one is actually further doing with law when discursiveness has been identified as its main characteristic feature. One could think that all legal questions are answered at this moment of the fundamental discovery. And this is also partly true because all theoretical answers to legal queries will include in one way or another the reference to the discursiveness of law. Yet in the further steps of making law its discursiveness will pave the way towards the development of narratives about law. They will display speakers' beliefs, commitments to values and social practices. These narratives can be further exemplified as constituting, for instance, legal norms. The form of communication in which they are developed is the legal discourse. They cannot be developed in other communicative forms because law is rooted in discursiveness. At this point the loop is looped. Therefore, discursiveness, intentionality and norming are closely related phenomena in law. As mentioned, discursiveness in law engenders a particular form of text or narrative that is the norm. Norms are particularly complex texts both in terms of logic and in terms of linguistics. J. Searle (1999: 134) described the way in which the human brain attains the level of consciousness that is necessary to produce such complicated intellectual structures. Norms in law are contextually explicit; it means that there is no doubt ever about the logical and linguistic status of the text as a norm. For instance, the utterance 'No Bill of Attainder or ex post facto Law shall be passed' of Section 9 of the U.S. Constitution is identifiable as a legal provision and not as something else. Likewise, when Art. 2–325(1) of the UCC provides: 'Failure of the buyer seasonably to furnish an agreed letter of credit is a breach of the contract for sale' no other than a legal context of use will be associated with it and the utterance will be clearly identified as providing for a regulation of a situation in law. Norms complicate the life of jurists because they cannot be applied directly or mechanically. In order to become operative, norms must be processed in complex semiotic operations of interpretation in which their meaning emerges. The higher is the abstractness level of a norm the more complex will be their interpretation. Therefore lowering the abstractness of norms might make sense. Legal texts such as *Las Siete Partidas*, which is discussed in this book in another context, have demonstrated that they are well suited for incorporating norms. They make the application of norms by analogy possible. Analogy represents a rather low level of interpretive devices. Overall, procedures of interpretation are not fully elucidated in law. Rationality tests are of course the best procedure to check the quality of propositions about the possible content of legal norms. However, pure rationality does not suffice because competing propositions about the content of law may be rational yet mutually exclusive as to their contents. In such a situation the state of argumentative practices provides the benchmark for further propositional choices.

6.8.3 Systematization in law

Many jurists still perceive the law as a system, or at least as an order. They are committed to the systematization of legal rules as a dominant task of the legal doctrine. In fact, jurists structure the law, its provisions, concepts or precedents in their professional legal discourse. Therefore, the systematization as a legal-linguistic operation structures the professional legal discourse. A challenging constellation has been described by the writer and lawyer H. Fielding in his *Tom Jones* where a person having no other potential heirs as his sister's son intends to appoint his sister's only son as his testamentary heir "which indeed the law, without his interposition, would have done for him." This constellation is frequent in succession law where testamentary heirs are regularly also legal heirs. Overall, this constellation is also frequent in private law where parties decide according to their autonomy within the general framework of law. Very often their decision will coincide with the proposals of the statutory law. One might ask why then the parties make such decisions when they cannot obtain any result other than the one that is already provided for in the law. Additionally, jurists have to ask themselves how to incorporate such legal yet not particularly rational decisions in the structure of law that they aim at describing. For jurists, there is no confusion as they follow the will of the testator and perceive the legal succession order as a default rule. Systematized provisions would therefore have to include the double forms wherever they appear in law. Similarly, A. Hamilton dealt in *The Federalist* (nr. 21) with the possibility of a right that cannot be exercised: "The United States, as now composed, have no powers to exact obedience, or punish disobedience to their resolutions, either by pecuniary mulcts, by a suspension or divestiture of privileges, or by any other constitutional mode. There is no express delegation of authority to them to use force against delinquent members; and if such a right should be ascribed to the federal head, as resulting from the nature of the social compact between the States, it must be by inference and construction, in the face of that part of the second article, by which it is declared: "that each State shall retain every power, jurisdiction, and right, not expressly delegated to the United States in Congress assembled." There is doubtless a striking absurdity in supposing that a right of this kind does not exist, but we are reduced to the dilemma either of embracing this supposition, preposterous as it may seem, or of contravening or explaining away a provision, which has been of late a repeated theme of the eulogies of those who oppose the new Constitution; and the want of which, in that plan, has been the subject of much plausible animadversion and severe criticism." Legal systematization is a legal-linguistic operation that aims at identifying the structure of legal arguments used in discourses. Systematized legal arguments also enable the evaluation of rationality levels reached in legal discourses. As a result of all this intellectual interactions, law evolves and it may even become better.

6.8.4 Linguistic turn and iconic turn in law

In recent years, the interest in the visual aspects of social life has increased in humanities and in social sciences. In the area of legal research the visuality of law has been considered foremost in the semiotic research. There, the question has been raised whether law can be visualized and, if so, whether this visible aspect of it is of any relevance to the subject as such. In the tradition initiated by Umberto Eco's research into architecture many semioticians turned their attention towards the architecture of court houses and arrangements of court halls. Their interpretation of this type of institutional architecture made plain the representative character of these buildings, i.e. the fact that they mark the presence of the state in the social sphere. Some edifices were perceived as intimidating, others, mostly of newer origin, were deemed as sterile like the reasoning that dominates in them. Unlike in other areas of social practice, it might be premature to suppose that the iconic turn would take place also in law and that it would replace the linguistic turn. First, the linguistic turn as a fundamental paradigmatic change in the relation to law did not really take place as of now. Second, law in its claim for rationality as ultimate test in the battle for justice is and must remain a linguistic phenomenon. It is therefore best addressed from the perspective of the legal linguistics. This notwithstanding, it would be difficult to deny the growing tendency in law towards visualization and mediatization. The increasing fluidity of the legal discourse seems to correspond with the visibility of icons that accompany law. The orange jumpsuits of American detainees may say to many people more about American law than a detailed academic analysis of the American penal legislation. There is however a disconcerting moment in the iconic approach to law. Law that appears as an icon, or simply put as an image, is extremely ambiguous like an American detainee seen in his orange jumpsuit. Such an image is emotional and it transfers a message. But which one? Many viewers will decipher many messages in this image. In literature, visual aspects of legally relevant contexts have been occasionally captured with some skill. In Raymond Chandler's *The High Window* (1943) a weapon is almost instinctively presented in a conversation to mark one's position without attempts at threatening the interlocutor: "He stood up with a flash of anger in his pale eyes: Standing there leaning over the desk a little he whipped his right hand up in a neat enough gesture and brought out a small automatic, about .25 calibre, with a walnut grip…The muzzle looked vicious enough pointing at me." In this scene, the risk that the weapon will be used is nearly excluded; yet it is dangerously present because weapons have the tendency to be used. Their very presence or manifestation during non-violent conversations broadens non-verbally the conversational context and refers to the omnipresent yet concealed element of violence in society that Chandler described. Speech and image coincide and form a more coherent structure that displays the legal discourse more fully in Chandler's glimpse of social practice that is relevant to law.

The visible and the linguistic aspects of law have at least one common feature that is their expressiveness. Whenever something is expressed, the law approaches it as speech. Speech is in the American law protected by the First Amendment of the U.S. Constitution. Many other countries also perceive speech as expression of thought, not only the linguistic variety of thought. In the American law, "pictures, graphic design, concept art, sounds, music, stories, and narrative present in video games" are speech in the sense of the First Amendment (cf. C.B.C. Distribution and Marketing, Inc. v. Major League Baseball Advanced Media, LP, 505 F.3d 818, 2007). Expressiveness connects rather than divides the visual and the linguistic elements of law. Therefore, discourses about visual aspects of law are possible and they also take place. They are part of law as a discursive practice. In the extreme ambiguity of the image they challenge the rationality in law. After all, challenging the rationality of law is a justifiable and even helpful enterprise. It should, however, not be confused with the idea that there is no rationality in law. Furthermore, showing how complex is the legal rationality is one thing. Claiming that because of ambiguity and fluidity of the iconic message there is no rationality in law, is another thing. As legal rationality can be engendered only with linguistic means, the iconic challenge remains a trigger point in the legal discourse, not its basis. This interrelation clearly favors the linguistic element over the iconic. It is therefore doubtful whether significant changes could occur in this submission of one semiotic process under another in the future. Also, or even predominantly, in terms of semiotics, law is a quest for rationality in obtaining justice. Would it be redefined in a way that would stress its purely iconic character, it would become uninteresting as a social mechanism that has to fulfill a regulative task in society. Therefore, the linguistic turn is a valuable goal to be envisaged in the legal science and the discourses around it. The iconic turn is welcome, as long as it does not pretend to introduce a post-linguistic period in law.

6.9 Perfect stability of legal science

When viewed from the legal-linguistic perspective, law appears as a largely undefined set of legal-linguistic operations within more complex legal discourses. It seems also that the legal-linguistic operations are valid globally. Everywhere law is shaped and applied with linguistic means. Everywhere propositions about law are advanced and it is asserted in them that a certain content of law is valid and must be enforced. Everywhere law is interpreted according to interpretive guidelines that are in force in particular legal cultures. In sum, legal-linguistic operations such as legal argumentation, legal interpretation, legal translation, legal justification and others are ubiquitous. From the very emergence of law until today they have been instrumental in shaping the institutional understanding of law. There is no reason to assume that this state of affairs would change in future. In this sense, law is stable because its basic structure shaped by the legal-linguistic operations cannot and does not need to be overcome. It could also be that the legal science that tries to understand it in a systematic way is in this sense the only science that does not change. Its fundamental paradigm is based on legal discursiveness and the numerous legal-linguistic operations that enable the formation and the application of law. Notwithstanding other existing and thinkable paradigms of the legal science the legal-linguistic approach proves its amazing stability. Law as a discursive practice is stable in the sense observed by the legal science because of its linguistic basis. Language is equally stable as is law. Like law, it changes some minor elements of its superficial structure while remaining stable as a property of the conscious mind. Legal linguistics makes plain this perfect stability of the legal science. In this sense it is law's most fundamental theory.

Part 7: Legal Narrativity or Law as Literature

7.1 Narrativity of law

Legal discourses rely on narrative materials that in their entirety display all the content-related aspects of legal texts. These aspects were until now only marginally or subliminally mentioned in this book where structural and logical aspects dominated the analysis. Narrativity of law is not less important because discourses are not only practices; they also are practices 'about something'. This something that could be called 'discursive content' cannot be determined arbitrarily. Perception and the more active reception of discursive contents follow rules and rules can be approached in a structured way. The perception of legal discourses is an act of taking into consideration of a legal discourse; it is insignificant in our context as it is rarely creative of further legally relevant contexts. Not much follows therefore from this uninterested perception. The reception of legal discourses equals in most cases the reception of narrative aspects of law because the more abstract discursive features rarely interest the broader public or even the professionals of law. Narrativity concerns the spoken and the written form of legal ontology. In the legal-linguistic research the spoken form is predominantly analyzed in discourse analysis (Anesa 2009, 2012). Furthermore, law is often present in both forms simultaneously, for instance when the accusation act is read in a court by the public prosecutor. After all, law is regularly also received in written form; it is therefore also literature (Galdia 2009: 270). This literary aspect of law has been neglected for quite a long time. Yet, already Mikhail Bakhtin (1981) referred to literality of law in his writings on literary techniques. Bakhtin's 'dialogism' as a method of textual analysis that stresses the interdependence of linguistic inputs smoothly accords with pragmatic demands for taking into consideration the interrelated discursive contributions. Some research has been devoted to Bakhtin's idea of interlaced discourses that are omnipresent in general literature (Bres et al. 2012). For law, this approach has been until now rarely used. Some works on discourse analysis make use of methods close to Bakhtin's 'dialogism'. Narrativity in law in all its interdependent facets may be less evident than in other text types of literature, e.g. in poetry. It is however present as the dominating aspect of perception of written legal discourses and their more active reception. Doubtless, our views about law take shape under the influence of the views of other people and not only at the writing desk. This experience proves Bakhtin's assumption that 'discursive contents' that we produce are largely prefigured in inputs that come from others.

7.1.1 Orality and literacy in law

One may hesitate as to the order in which the topics should be arranged in the heading. Usually, literacy follows orality in social practices (Havelock 1986); in law the relation is somewhat unclear. Orality was the basis for Greek and Roman juridical rhetoric that focused on the actual speaker acting in a court of law rather than a legal writer. Unproblematic are also religious laws. Max Weber (2003) stressed their oral origin, pointing mainly to the Hindu and to the Islamic law. Legal formalism and the memorization of legal formulae in ancient Rome are definitely connected with the oral origins of litigation. M. Weber used as examples the Roman procedures of 'mancipatio' and 'stipulatio' to illustrate how formalism emerged in law. Poetic testimony supports this view. Homer rendered in *Iliad* a pre-legal procedure that was wrought on Achilles's shield (Cantarella 2002). The scene depicted on the shield is described in book XVIII (497). In Samuel Butler's prose translation it goes as follows: "Meanwhile the people were gathered in assembly, for there was a quarrel, and two men were wrangling about the blood-money for a man who had been killed, the one saying before the people that he had paid damages in full, and the other that he had not been paid. Each was trying to make his own case good, and the people took sides, each man backing the side that he had taken; but the heralds kept them back, and the elders sate on their seats of stone in a solemn circle, holding the staves which the heralds had put into their hands. Then they rose and each in his turn gave judgement, and there were two talents laid down, to be given to him whose judgement should be deemed the fairest." In the *Iliad* people are often 'gathered in assembly' to discuss political matters and make political decisions. In such cases, the procedure is limited to some general discursive rules. Certain citizens, the elders and other influential personalities speak and use arguments. Other, less influential participants scream and express their opinions with unstructured noise and gestures without making speeches. Screaming has a specific argumentative value "because it effectively dramatizes the tension among social expectations, group solidarity, and individual freedom," as noticed by Burke (2013: 20) in a non-legal context. Equally, Levine (1988: 195) remarked that in the area of popular culture audiences have been converted "into a collection of people reacting individually rather than collectively." Screaming, moaning, and crying as expressions of primitive legal arguments seem to combine the collective and the individual aspects of speech. Finally, the solution is obtained through the use of emotional and rational arguments. The scene on Achilles's shield displays a more strictly regulated procedure. It differs from the political decision making through its ceremonial order, probably of religious origin. It also includes a more advanced procedure that supports rational decision making and introduces elements of competition for the prize awarded for the best judgment. Meanwhile, under conditions of orality solely a dispute settlement ad hoc comes into question. No explicit and textually coherent legal rules are applied in such a procedure. Only rules of sagesse that the Greeks called μῆτις (metis) can be used for the purpose of a spontaneous dispute settlement. Undoubtedly, therefore, some elements of law or custom will emerge in their oral form first and be fixed in writing only later. Other legal elements may have their origin in literacy. Like in all social practices orality and literacy are interrelated, once a practice emerges either way. The problem has also a technological component. Invention of script and fixing of texts in script enables the emergence of forms typical of written language such as substantivization of verbs and adjectives that for the ancient Greek language originates in Plato's writings. It is also the prerequisite for developments of more complex procedures that cannot be processed by a set of memorized legal or ritual formulae (cf. Vesting 2011). Also more complex syntactic structures that include protasis and apodosis typical of the conditional norm structure of if/then phrases demand for their full development a written form (Bottéro 1992: 127). The technological development engendered also isolated cultural forms such as the style of handwriting. For instance, in English courts an old style of handwriting called *court-hand*, a modification of the Norman style, had been in use from the 16th century until it was abolished by King George II in the 18th century. Law was not simply written, fixed on paper. It was written in a special, 'legal' way. The 'court-hand' is an extreme example that marks the technological borderline between orality and literacy in law. Finally, it could also be that the specific development of law in England and in Scandinavia that differs from the development on the European continent has its roots in the orality of the legal traditions in England and Scandinavia. These oral traditions seem to have been taken more into consideration than the oral legal heritage of the rest of Occidental Europe that has been supplanted by Justinian's codification of law. However, in the legal research most attention has been devoted to written texts. The reason for this particular interest seems to be the assumption that written forms of law are particularly relevant and oral forms are ephemeral and less important for jurists. Meanwhile, putting orally formulated rules into written form is not a magical formula that would engender complete law. Ancient Greeks, ancient Romans and ancient Jews realized in the course of the technological transformation of oral into written rules that written laws do not work without their subsequent oral interpretation (Daube 1949). By so doing, they have intuitively discovered the discursiveness of law.

7.1.2 Written text and intertext

Written texts have some characteristic features that enable their structured apprehension. The most trivial is their textuality, a structural feature analogous to discursiveness. Another such characteristic feature, typical of some of them, is their intertextuality, their textual interrelation. This interrelation means that some texts are written in the way they are actually written because previous texts were written in a specific way and this specific way is reflected in succeeding texts. Text types that are used in law are well established; they are conservative and difficult to modify. A judgment has in a legal culture a strictly normed structure almost like a sonnet. A judge cannot simply modify the structure of his judgment because he has a good idea. In legislation, drafters of legal acts follow stringent patterns that are rarely modernized. Therefore, literary theory and especially comparative literary studies are valuable to the understanding of the textuality and the discursiveness of law. Intertextuality is a constitutive principle of texts. In terms of pragmatics, literature is a discursive practice. Law is perceived by many as exclusively intertextual, as all Occidental law is basically of Roman origin, which means that it is textually a more or less free adaptation of it. Finally, intertextuality in law engenders also a coherent legal language that develops in textual interrelation around legal terms. For the Occidental law, this process of language formation started already in the Roman law where the first statement of the Roman civil law by Quintus Mucius Scevola triggered off an intellectual activity that established the Roman legal science as jurisprudentia (cf. Dozhdev 2003: 2, 6). This science insisted on terminological stability that apparently increased the rationality of the learned discourse about law. On the other side, it could not prevent the evolution of the legal language, because law is, after all, a dynamic discursive practice that cannot be limited to the interpretation of a canon of existing written texts.

Also essayistic law is present, so in M. de Montaigne's *Essays*. Michel de Montaigne in his *Essais* made use of non-doctrinal thinking about law. He says about the task of the judge to shape the law (book 3, chapter 13; cited in original spelling): "Pourtant l'opinion de celuy-là ne me plaist guiere, qui persoit par la multitude des loix brider l'authorité des juges, en leur taillant leurs morceaux: il ne sentoit point qu'il y a autant de liberté et d'estendue à l'interpretation des loix qu'à leur façon...D'autant que nostre esprit ne trouve pas le champ moins spatieux à contreroller le sens d'autruy qu'à representer le sien, et comme s'il y avoit moins d'animosité et d'aspreté à gloser qu'à inventer...Car nous avons en France plus de loix que tout le reste du monde ensemble...et si avons taint laissé à opiner et decider à nos juges, qu'il ne fut jamais liberté si puissante et si licencieuse." In his plea for responsible interpretation of laws by judges Montaigne benefits from the liberty that the literary form of the essay attributes to reasoning. Also the language of the law is approached in this non-doctrinal way: "Pourquoy est-ce que nostre langage commun, si aisé à tout autre usage, devient obscure et non intelligible en contract et testament, et que celuy qui s'exprime si clairement, quoy qu'il die et escrive, ne trouve en cela aucune maniere de se declarer qui ne tombe en doubte et contradiction?" The third book, chapter thirteen of the *Essais* includes numerous such remarks and comments on legally relevant issues. It is a concise treaty on legal method, yet it is free from doctrinal boundaries. It is deplorable that jurists did not use more frequently this literary form of an approach to law apt at competing and even surpassing the textual constraints of the legal doctrine.

7.1.3 Discourse analysis in law

Linguists' interest in the investigation of oral legal discourses seems to have been caused by the observation that language use in these discourses differs significantly from the daily language use. This fundamental finding concerns mostly courtroom discourses (cf. Hoffmann 1983; Ilie 1995; Xu 1998). Therefore, the legal-linguistic discourse analysis comprises foremost the courtroom discourse analysis yet also the analysis of other less formally structured legal discourses. It is clearly dominated by the courtroom speech analysis, especially in the area of penal law. Law, however, is much more than a repressive mechanism of criminal prosecution. The struggle for law in society concerns, as a rule, other than criminal cases. Other areas of public and private law may be more significant to the development of discursive practices in societies. However, it could also be that in terms of their main structural features the non-criminal courtroom discourses do not differ particularly from the criminal courtroom discourses. At least, it seems that the most significant structural feature of language use is ubiquitous in all courtroom settings. Speakers, both professional and non-professional users of language in the legal context, do not speak in courts of law as they used to speak in daily non-professional life. This observation is based on the finding made by Gail Stygall (2012: 370) that "ordinary conversational turn-taking...disappears in a courtroom." This means that speakers cannot simply converse during court proceedings; the accused and his judges cannot just speak with each other whenever they wish and express whatever desires or beliefs. The order of speaking in courtrooms is strictly predetermined and the roles are hierarchical. These roles are played within discursive genres that are predefined in the court procedure. Stygall (2012: 371–380) identified following genres as prefigured in the American legislation: pleas, pleadings, voir dire, opening statements, testimony, and closing arguments. One interesting feature of the legal courtroom discourse is its interdependence relation with the written part of the legal discourse that is expressed in documents. All participants regularly refer in their speeches to the written elements of the discourse. The classical courtroom speech analysis focused primarily on understandability in the courtroom discourse. In the course of more nuanced research, the issue of exercise of power through language use became increasingly important (Stygall 2012: 370). It seems furthermore that the most obtrusive element is not the legal vocabulary but the unusual turns that the oral courtroom discourse imposes upon lay participants. As a remedy for this discursive friction, Stygall (2012: 380) proposed to prepare laypersons better for the participation in courtroom discourses. One could, however, also think about the change of courtroom speech rules that could be more closely aligned with the general discourse of ordinary language. Participation in legal discourses is not limited to adults. A literary prototype of a discourse about law that involves children can be found in Harper Lee's *To Kill a Mockingbird* (1960). When reflecting upon a situation where money is found by two children the author remarks: "Finders were keepers unless title was proven" while simultaneously taking the perspective of a child. Legal language is also used in the novel in a situation where understanding of social practices by a child in a talk with an adult is tested: "Do you know what a compromise is? he asked. Bending the law? No, an agreement reached by mutual concessions." The use of legal language is justified in discussions with children in *To Kill the Mockingbird* because the action concerns a lawyer's family. Yet, it is also significant that the legal language penetrates the private sphere of jurists' biographies, be it only in terms of literary fiction. The described situation of language use is clearly ideal and literary. Yet, it also signals unexplored potentials in contexts connected with the use of legal language. General aspects of participation in legal discourses have been also elucidated with sociological means. Greenhouse (2012: 69) asked whether American public opinion has a bearing upon the decisions of the U.S. Supreme Court. Research that is available about this issue provides somehow ambiguous results. It is generally assumed that there is an influence from the public in particularly spectacular cases such as Roe v. Wade (410 U.S. 113, 1973). Mechanisms of incorporation of public opinion into Supreme Court's decision making processes remain however unclear. Interestingly, Justice William H. Rehnquist mentioned 1986 that "family and friends" rather than "the public at large" would influence judges' views (Greenhouse 2012: 71). Meanwhile, it seems also that the U.S. Supreme Court tries to align itself with the public moral (cf. Rosen 2013). Research available today allows the statement that public opinion has a role to play in the development of the legal discourse about U.S. Supreme Court's decisions.

7.1.4 Proclaiming laws

Legal regulation is nowadays made known through publication. Publication, i.e. making the laws known to everyone who wishes to know them, is a relatively new phenomenon. The Roman law bears witness of a battle about the publication of the *Law of XII Tables*. Furthermore, the Hammurabi Code was perceived by some researchers as the first such publication and was characterized as "the earliest example of a ruler proclaiming publicly to his people an entire body of laws, arranged in orderly groups, so that all men might read and know what was required of them" (in: Horne 1917: 107). Making the written laws accessible is an act that shall legitimize the exercise of power. It may be accompanied by efforts to stabilize power structures and convince the subjects of the righteousness of someone's rule. Hammurabi, who ruled ca. 1792–1750 B.C., says about himself: "Hammurabi is a ruler, who is as a father to his subjects, who holds the words of Marduk in reverence, who has achieved conquests for Marduk over the north and the south, who rejoices the heart of Marduk, his lord, who has bestowed benefits forever and ever on his subjects, and has established order in his land" (in: Horne 1917: 142). It is startling how much effort is spent on shaping the linguistic contour of power that should be perceived by subjects as a natural consequence of things. Hammurabi invokes even future developments to give his compilation of laws the character of eternal law: "In future time, through all coming generations, let the king, who may be in the land, observe the words of righteousness which I have written on my monument..." (in: Horne 1917: 142). Particularly controversial in the research is the text type of Hammurabi's legislation that is traditionally described as a 'code'. For some it displays a commemorative inscription rather than a codification of laws (Bottéro 1992: 156). Finally, access to statutory texts does not equal access to law. Law based on statutory texts is understandable solely within the framework of legal-linguistic operations that make its application possible. Proclaiming laws may be therefore perceived as the first step towards understanding law in force. The search for meaning in law is a discursive process that requires at least the understanding of the most fundamental quality of law that is its discursiveness. Professionals of law acquire other necessary methodical prerequisites for dealing with legal-linguistic operations during their education. Non-professionals of law have to reconstruct these requirements from the linguistic practices of juridical institutions that are, at least partly, open to public enquiry into their modes of functioning.

7.1.5 Stating the law

Law can be perceived and stated in its entirety as a written text. The problems in developing such a texture are known since the attempts to state the Roman law in the *Corpus Iuris Civilis*. The work on the Corpus Iuris commenced as a project of consolidation and ended – as far as we are able to determine – as an exercise in censorship. The Roman law presented in the Corpus Iuris is a fragment that politically might have made sense at the time when it has been developed. The attempt to consolidate law textually also shows the greatest theoretical challenge to stating law as a text, i.e. that legal regulation constantly changes. As an alternative to the legal doctrine the stating of law in written form can only provide interpretive proposals as statements of law. Therefore, the question of what is the law in force is at its bottom purely positivistic as law has always been a dynamic, i.e. constantly evolving discursive practice. Stating law as it is or stating law as of (with reference to a time period) is characteristic of a positivist attitude towards law. Typical of positivist statements are formulations such as: "I have attempted to state the law as at 31st October 1978" or "This book has been written on the basis of the law as it stood on 1 April 2002." Pedantic precision shall in such situations help overcome the intellectual stalemate in stating law that is a dynamic social phenomenon.

Another remarkable written statement of law, this time from medieval Spain, are *Las Siete Partidas* which modified the landscape of European codifications in that they used the local language, in casu the Castillian of Alfonso X el Sabio's period (Mattila 2013: 273–278). The work has been apparently terminated around 1263. Originally it was known as *Libro* (or *Fuero) de las Leyes* and in the following century it had been called *Las Partidas* or *Leyes de Partidas*. They state a law that is a mixture of local customs and the received Roman law. The codification was very influential as it extended not only to the American colonies, but also to parts of Africa and Asia, there especially to the Philippines. In the Americas, it also embraced territories that now make part of the U.S., such as Texas and California. Textually, the law of community property, now widespread in the U.S., has its conceptual origin in the *Partidas*. The textuality of the *Partidas* borders on a full-fledged narrative (cf. Scott/Lobingier 1931). To illustrate, the Law XX, Part I, Title I captured "For What Reason Men Cannot Escape the Operation of the Laws by Saying That They Were Ignorant of Them" provides in the English translation in Scott/Lobingier (1931): "No one can escape the penalties of the laws by saying that he did not know of them, for, since men have to be preserved by them by receiving as well as doing justice, it is reasonable that they should know them and read them, either by acquiring their meaning from those who have read them, or by hearing them discussed in some other way without reading; for men have excuses for many things which happen in this world; but they cannot excuse themselves from sending others in their places to assert their rights in court; and if they should have no one to send, they should communicate with someone of their friends who may happen to be in the place where they are to be judged by the laws, that they too may represent them and argue their cases for them, and they must give them authority to do so. And since by themselves, or by their representatives, or by means of letters, they are able to defend themselves, they cannot avoid doing so by saying that they did not know the laws, and if they should offer such a reason as this it will not avail them." The text of *Las Siete Partidas* is particularly valuable to legal linguistics because it proves that explicit legal language can be practiced. Meanwhile, we have to do with a historical example that cannot be directly considered as a model for possible linguistically explicit legislation that may be of interest today. The *Partidas* as a legal monument remain however a source of inspiration for theoretical attempts at developing linguistically explicit law in the future.

In the long line of legal writers, William Blackstone (1723–1780) is known for having stated the English common law in its supposed entirety for the first time. Since 1753 he was lecturing on the English common law at the Oxford University. His *Commentaries on the Laws of England* (1765–1769) were perceived by some as more synthetic than original, an "able synthesis of the often bewildering doctrines that made up the common law." Surprisingly, his approach is sometimes qualified as analytic, and sometimes as synthetic. One clearly does not exclude the other; meanwhile the question of what had been Blackstone's method in stating the law remains open. Blackstone's treatise had a profound influence in North America. It is said that both A. Hamilton and A. Lincoln studied law from his commentaries and that by this reason Blackstone's commentaries shaped the intent of the framers of the U.S. constitution. Likewise, the American jurist James Kent (1763–1847) developed a synthesis of the U.S. American law in his pioneering and highly respected

Commentaries on American Law that were published in four volumes between 1826 and 1830. In his work Kent treated both state and the federal U.S. law as well as international law. Previously, Charles Viner (1678–1756) published *A General Abridgment of Law and Equity* in 23 volumes that he had compiled during fifty years. The digest based on Henry Rolle's work became popular after an alphabetical index had been supplied to it by Robert Kelham in 1758. Apparently, general statements of law are not read as such, i.e. in their entirety, but rather consulted for clarification of particular questions. Not only therefore, stating the law is a hopeless enterprise because what law is becomes clear in its application. One cannot describe the whole law. The available descriptions of law in force are therefore limited to known cases of its application. The dynamic of development of law makes its statement an unavailing enterprise, as it has to be restated constantly. The statement of law as a text type is therefore not an interesting instrument in acquiring legal knowledge.

Law is regularly also stated orally. Until the internet era, no material was available to analyze this process. Nowadays, recorded lectures on law, which can be viewed on the internet, enable the first determination of the role that oral statements of law play in society or may play in future. Previously, oral statements of law in form of academic courses were limited in their social relevance through the circle of academic hearers. Their influence had indeed limits. Biographers report that the celebrated British legal philosopher, John Austin (1790–1859), author, among others, of *Province of Jurisprudence Determined* and *Lectures on Jurisprudence* had to give up his professorship in jurisprudence at the London University due to the lack of interested students who would enroll in his courses. Instead, Austin's ideas became influential in the written form. Meanwhile, J. Austin had under his sporadic hearers also students such as John Stuart Mill, G.C. Lewis and Lord Romilly. Insofar, his oral statement of law has definitely been efficient.

7.1.6 Restating the Law

The fact that law is expressed in written texts causes textual restatements of the already stated law. This textual type shows best how law determines the choice of text types for its expression. As law allows only for its provisional statement, its restatements will regularly follow suit. So has American law been restated, sometimes subsequently in voluminous restatements, second and third. The individual restatements, such as the *Restatement of Conflict of Laws, Second* or *Restatement of the Law of Agency, Third* have been characterized as codifications of case law. In terms of legal discourse they are also interesting because they lack the formal binding character and are followed by most American judges because of their authoritative character as a professionally pervasive analysis of the American law. They are construed by many American lawyers as a display of the general consensus about the content of the American law. When the work on the restatements started within the American Law Institute in 1923 B.N. Cardozo (1924: 9) described the importance of a restatement of law in following words: "...after all this testing and retesting, it will be something less than a code and something more than a treatise. It will be invested with unique authority, not to command, but to persuade. It will embody a composite thought and speak a composite voice. Universities and bench and bar will have had a part in its creation. I have great faith in the power of such a restatement to unify our law." Within the Roman law, the *Institutions of Justinian*, as a text, are close to the idea of the American restatement. All law commentaries used by their compilators were private legal scholarship; they were accepted as a source or restatement of the Roman law because they were professionally persuasive. It goes without saying that some of them were more persuasive than others, and many were abandoned as they did not find the acceptance within the political class. The consensus idea that they shared with the American restatements is however a double-edge sword; it shows that consensus in law is a consensus of some against others.

7.2 Setting narrative patterns

The most impressive skill in terms of legal narrativity is the ability to set narrative patterns. When such patterns are established, regulative narration will develop in their mould. For instance, U.S. constitutional law is viewed towards the perspective of the 'founding fathers' of the Constitution and of 'colonial patriots' who also had a word to say on it. Furthermore, to perceive A. Lincoln as a 'tyrant' or a 'hero' in legal discourses means to set a narrative pattern. History provides a sufficient number of arguments for taking both stands. More often than not, Lincoln will have in most discourses a 'craggy face'. More habitual textual patterns in law are descriptions of law in patterns of contracts, torts, property and the like. One can observe this textual regularity on the example of the Roman law that represents the first comprehensive discursive practice in the Occidental law. The ancient Roman law as stated in the *Corpus Iuris Civilis* displays a profoundly argumentative structure. The fragments taken from classical texts are contrasted so as to form a broader argument that renders the law in force. The Roman Corpus Iuris Civilis reflects in its form the Byzantine florilegium (cf. Glenn 2010: 18). Other known textual forms of its time of formation are chrestomathy or compilation. Compilations became known, not only in law, mainly under the heading of a 'corpus'. What is more, narrative patterns are also structured institutionally. H. Zehnacker and J.-C. Fredouille (2013: 12) stressed the importance of state archives in ancient Rome that were used as a source of textual reference for the structuring of the public sphere. Analogous institutions existed also in ancient Greece (Saïd et al. 2013: 63). The Roman archives included the official calendar which mentions also days of court activity and the lists of magistrates and consuls. Likewise, *Annales Maximi* listed the most important events in Rome's history. For legal linguistics most interesting are the *Laws of XII Tables* that survived to our day in a modernized form and incompletely. The archive texts had been largely used by legal writers in Rome for accounts on administrative and legal matters. Zhang Qizhi (2004: 77) mentions that in ancient China historians had the task to write down ancient laws: "In the *Records of the Historian* Sima Qian noted the laws and the institutions practiced before the reign of Emperor Wudi of the Han Dynasty." The characteristic feature of narrative patterns is their stability. However, this feature is not limited to legal discourses. Narrativity as a device of text creation is necessarily stable because texts that are structured spontaneously are usually difficult to understand. This holds true particularly of texts used in the public sphere. Therefore, the discovery that legal narratives follow discursive patterns is of limited importance in the area of legal discourse. More important is the way in which legal texts make use of this characteristic feature. One may assume that narrative patterns of legal texts are used as arguments in legal argumentation. Therefore, legal narrativity and legal argumentation are linked to each other like the two sides of a coin.

7.2.1 Contract as narrative

The contract appears in its most advanced narrative form, i.e. in its broadest textuality in Jean-Jacques Rousseau's coinage of the 'social contract'. Rousseau writes in *The Social Contract or Principles of Political Right* (1762): "Each of us puts his person and all his power in common under the supreme direction of the general will, and, in our corporate capacity, we receive each member as an indivisible part of the whole." In Rousseau's view these circumstances are sufficient to institute a contract between all concerned persons. The 'social contract' thus obtained can be perceived as displaying the broadest textual potentiality because it is a pure construct. Unlike in the case of a contract concluded under the private law where parties promise something to each other, Rousseau's 'social contract' lacks any empirical basis. It is a pure literary creation. It causes problems in the shaping of the constitutional law because Western societies simply do not function in the way in which Rousseau described them. Frictions in applications of narratives and concepts like Rousseau's 'social contract' may signal that fiction in law may have limits. The discursive nature of law enables the creation of whatever construction with words, provided the syntactic rules of language are not violated. Meanwhile, the discursiveness seems to be limited on the semiotic level of sign constitution by some social constraints. It means that it is, for instance, possible to legally institute tyranny as the most valuable regime of governance in a state. This is the case because language engenders this type of speech acts without any inherent problems. Meanwhile, the social experience based on historical facts indicates that sooner or later such a rule of constitutional law will cause problems in state and society. At this point the social element manifests itself in the discursiveness of law. In fact, the less a legal fiction corresponds with social reality the less it will be accepted by citizens. It will also cause problems in the linguistic shaping of law because the legal speech acts that would be based on it and that would be developed in relation to it, risk becoming ineffective. This is at least the teaching that might be drawn from the witty yet all too literary idea that Rousseau had introduced into social sciences.

On the other side, one cannot deny that the contract as such is a linguistic creation in law, a legal fiction, because it clearly does not exist materially. In the private law, the concept of contract emerged in the course of generalization of relations between parties that actually and not only hypothetically became involved in exchanges of promises, goods and services (Galdia 2009: 297). Based upon an oral practice, it developed subsequently a written variety of its own existence. Written contracts in private law describe the expectations of the parties. They follow upon the oral part of the negotiation between the parties. Their underlying reference is economical; they focus on the reciprocal flow of value. All these contextual referents are nowadays often put in writing, especially when they are of some importance. Their structure is homogeneous in all legal cultures: identification of parties, recitals, covenants, representations, warranties – and in international contracts – choice of law and jurisdiction clauses, eventually choice of arbitration. Meanwhile, the less formalized the text of the written contract is, the better it may reflect the intentions of the parties. However, some standard documents are regularly used out of fear that courts may judge a particular text as purposefully deflecting from the accepted form and expect there a non-standard message. In contrast, unilateral transactions, such as last wills, may be particularly hostile to standardization as they are perceived as important personal declarations that would be devalued by the use of formalized text types.

Private contracts as narratives are formed towards the background of a fundamental metaphor. It says that there is a contract when the minds of the parties have met. Clearly, this metaphor – even if very broadly interpreted – would impede Rousseau's creation of a 'social contract'. Minds, in the contractual theory of the common law, must correspond really, i.e. in the empirical world of facts. As happens so often with positivist approaches to law, the metaphor becomes problematic at any attempt to apply it. To illustrate, in Marder v. Jennifer Lopez (450 F.3d 445, 2006) the plaintiff sued to obtain additional payments under a copyright-related contract. The plaintiff sold the story of her professional career to a film producer for the sum of 2, 300 dollars. The film producer filmed the screenplay based on this story and obtained one hundred and fifty million dollars in domestic box office receipts. The film, *Flashdance*, was further exploited in media and brought additional profits. The plaintiff wished to participate in the distribution of the generous royalties that her life story had engendered, yet in vain. The contract said as regards the plaintiff that "(she) releases and discharges Paramount Picture Corporation of and from each and every claim, demand, debt, liability, cost and expense of any kind or character which have risen or are based in whole or in part on any matters occurring at any time prior to the date of this Release." In a further clause the release was broadened to embrace claims "arising out of or in any way connected with either directly or indirectly, any and all arrangements in connection with the preparation of screenplay material and the production, filming and exploitation of Flashdance." The release of "each and every claim" broadly formulated in the contract was interpreted by the court as an unconditional transfer of rights to the story. The court admitted that "in the hindsight the agreement appears to be unfair to Marder." The contract would be questionable, so the court further, only if "her consent was obtained by fraud, deception, misrepresentation, duress, or undue influence." The court did not see any reasons to assume such circumstances. The court therefore decided that plaintiff's rights had been validly transferred against payment of the indicated sum. In one more hindsight, there may have been a contract that corresponds with the imagery under the metaphor of parties' minds that must meet to form a contract. It seems, meanwhile, that there is a valid contract between the parties only when one applies this broad metaphor to it. Otherwise, the parties, or at least the plaintiff, seem not to have considered all possible developments in their economical relations. There may be reasons to ask whether this sort of uncertainties may be overcome in law through the use of catch all-formulations that favor the interests of one party. Metaphors like the classical common law formula in contract law do not match to the standards of rational decision making. They would have to be materialized and converted into legal speech acts to form a basis for decision making in courts. Their existence in the legal culture misleads the courts into the application of metaphorical law.

7.2.2 Legal maxims

Legal maxims are a specific text type in law (cf. Stein 1966; Roland/Boyer 1999; Matulewska/Wasielewska 2003). They date at least to the Roman times. A maxim such as 'Where there is no law, there is no freedom' (J. Locke, *Second Treatise of Government*, sec. 57) shows the limits of both. Freedom without law, without rules is none. Law without freedom, i.e. reduced to formal rules is organized oppression. Such law is insufferable, and it risks to be violently overthrown by those who suffer under it. In law, there is the question of justice and not of rules. This means enjoying freedom in democracy. Rules are there to ensure the enjoyment of freedom in democracy. Maxims may be ironical or sarcastic like the Italian 'Le leggi si applicano per il nemico, per il amico si interpretano'. They are, in fact, more typical of other literary texts than of law. It is however occasionally assumed that our law is becoming more and more literary. Let us enjoy it as "(A) lawyer without history or literature is a mechanic, a mere working mason: if he possesses some knowledge of these, he may venture to call himself an architect," so Walter Scott, in *Guy Mannering* (1815, ch. 37). Learned Hand almost poetically stated: "Without law we cannot live; only with it can we ensure the future which by right is ours. The best of men's hopes are enmeshed in its success" (in: *The Spirit of Liberty*, 3rd ed. New York, Alfred A. Knopf, 1960). Benjamin Cardozo is known for many formulations that bear witness to his literary talent. Roscoe Pound is remembered also for the remark: "Law must be stable and yet it cannot stand still," in: *Interpretation of Legal History* (1923). Jerome Frank dealt with: "…law largely vague and variable." This textual heritage seems to encourage the development of literary techniques in the area of law. Richard Weisberg (1992) showed in Law and Literature studies how such attempts at expanding the professional legal language can be made efficient in law.

7.2.3 Humorous use of legal language

Humorous use of legal language complements the ironical and the sarcastic language use. It is however mostly of low quality. It ends up in jokes such as: "Is a lady barrister without her briefs a solicitor?" and the like. The financier, Daniel Drew, is remembered for the humorous formulation that refers to liability for 'naked short sales': "He who sells what isn't his'n, must buy it back or go to pris'n." Also allegories with legal background exist since antiquity. The classical Roman narrative *De erinaceo et vipera* goes as follows: "Erinaceus quidam hieme viperam rogat: Accipe me, o bona, in cavernam tuam, frigore enim vexor. Obtemperat vipera precibus eius eumque angusto loco accipit. Paulo post autem saepe erinacei spinis pungitur, itaque: Relinque – inquit – domum meam et alio demigra, mihi enim et tibi nimis parva est. Cui erinaceus respondet: Mihi placet caverna ista, itaque mihi non est in animo domum tuam relinquere; tu autem, si tibi non placet, alio demigra. Et vipera cogitur domo sua cedere. Periculosum est amicitiam cum eis facere, in quorum potestate erimus." Humorous language use may lead to further going conclusions. So has a French producer of hearing aid promoted his product with a slogan "Everyone has the right to hear." The wit of the advertisement is primarily based on its anchorage in other narrative structures that begin with 'everyone has the right to….' It may aim in its ironical dress at ridiculing legal language. Yet, as most such advertisement language it finally remains unsatisfactorily ambiguous. In another context, Mats Deutschmann (2003) analyzed the British discourse of politeness, especially excuses. It includes also jokes such as the hangman addressing his victim in a polite tone: 'I'm sorry to execute you, Sir!" Politeness in social discourse is a particularly deceiving practice as polite speech acts according to Deutschmann regularly accompany particularly impolite deeds; verbal exculpation is used discursively as a means of social control and is surprisingly often applied by superiors towards their subordinates. Also John L. Austin (1956) in *A Plea for Excuses* sees excuses rather in connection with justification for action and not with regret. Their role in ordinary language seems to be the attempt "to evade responsibility," so says at least Austin. Yet, his essay has no humorous connotations – although it is held in ironical tones – and is therefore not suitable for further discussion at this place.

7.2.4 Assertion of facts as narrative

Originally, asserting or stating facts is a speech act comparable with many other linguistic forms that constitute the discourse such as explaining or describing (Searle 1999: 40). Assertions of facts matter because knowledge cannot develop without them. Problematic has been however the epistemological status of such assertions. Clearly, skepticism about our access to and intelligibility of reality was the main challenging barrier to the meaningful discussion of the valid assertions of facts. To overcome the barrier, we can follow John Searle who maintained that in pragmatic terms "facts are conditions that make statements true, but they are not identical with their linguistic descriptions" (Searle 1999: 22). Thus, our inventing and using words to describe facts does not amount to inventing the facts themselves. Material reality exists independently of our true or false statements about it. Even the perspectivist criticism that insists on our seeing reality from a particular perspective is not really a challenge to the possibility of stating facts. We doubtlessly always state facts from a perspective, and in the legal practice every witness testimony is an illustration of perspectivist speech. Yet, the perspectivist account about facts does not mean that facts are not stated in it but that they are stated from a point of view. This is obvious and also acceptable as a condition of epistemologically valid speech. A claim to state facts from "no point of view" cannot be raised as a counter-argument against the possibility of assertions about facts (Searle 1999: 21). This result is crucial to legal speech acts such as the stating of facts because it allows for speaking about facts in a rational way. It also means that using words to describe facts does not always mean that well-intentioned attempts to state facts linguistically will become accepted. We can furthermore state facts that will not be believed by others, as it happens in many witness testimonies. Philosophically, however, statements of facts are usually analyzed in contextual isolation. The method used in their analysis is logical-conceptual analysis. Meanwhile, in the discourse, fact assertions are contextually embedded in broader textual forms such as the mentioned witness testimony or an accusation act that is read by the public prosecutor in the court of law. What is asserted in such broader textual forms is less easy to analyze than the contextless statements. Fact stating in broader narrative forms is much less researched than other legal-linguistic operations. In legal settings, it is even more complicated because competing or seemingly identical descriptions of facts may be provided to courts. Newmark (1988: 12) remarks in a non-legal context: "Two texts may describe a battle or a riot or a debate, stating the same facts and figures, but the type of language used and even the grammatical structures (passive voice, impersonal verbs often used to disclaim responsibility) in each case may be evidence of different points of view." Newmark's observation applies also to law. In legal documents the description of facts is regularly accompanied by the reference to the context of their assertion, for instance by 'the plaintiff asserts that…'. This type of assertion of facts stresses that the facts provided are the view of one of the parties and that the other party may present another version of facts. They furthermore imply the application of the burden of proof rules for the acceptability of asserted facts in the court procedure. Therefore, in the legal discourse the validity of assertions about facts is exposed to additional tests that determine the truth of assertions in institutionalized procedures.

7.2.5 Writings against the government

Writings against the government constitute another specific narrative type that emerges in legally relevant settings. Such writings usually challenge the politically correct dominant discourse. The text type 'writing against the government' has a long history and is ubiquitous. Berger (1963: 43) writes: "There are even texts from ancient Egypt evincing a profound disenchantment with the political and social order that has acquired the reputation of having been one of the most cohesive in human history." Wang Chong in ancient China wrote dissident text directed against the mainstream Confucianism. Laozi in his daoist doctrine proposed detachment from society. Generally, some discourses about society, its law and government are not welcome in circles that are directly concerned by them. By their opponents the arguments used in these works are called 'interpretive exaggerations' or 'agitation'. These discourses are also known as 'counternarratives'. Tribe (2012: 20) characterizes as counternarratives for the U.S. practice texts that describe the U.S. in terms of 'conquest' and 'self-deception', 'exploitation' and 'decay'. As to their contents, they can be contrasted with "narratives of aspiration and progress" (Tribe 2012: 20), and with affirmative, self-gratulating, and politically correct intellectual contributions. The list of critical writings is rather long, however by far not as long as the list of affirmative contributions. Many of them are preserved because they had appeared in print. Meanwhile, from those preserved the British American Loyalists' writings are even today not easily accessible in the U.S. Henry David Thoreau's *Resistance to Civil Government* and *Walden, or Life in the Woods* are easily accessible and are read even in schools. They had been once perceived as at least mildly subversive reading. Thorstein Veblen's *The Leisure Class* was characterized as a slap in the face of America's industrialists (cf. Berger 1963: 58). Veblen's *The Higher Learning in America* (1918) is for Berger (1963: 206): "one of the most bitter sociological treatises ever written, literally dripping venom on every page, an eloquent testimony to Veblen's savage disillusionment with American university life." W.E.B. DuBois's *The Souls of Black Folk* (1903) or *Black Reconstruction in America: 1860–1880,* first published 1935, had been deemed by some as "antigovernmental socialism" and their author narrowly escaped prison in 1951 (Alger 2010: 983; Lewis 2012: 115). K. Marx's *Capital* and the *Communist Manifesto,* that he co-authored with F. Engels, were perceived as so politically noxious that they were rarely cited in the U.S., although they were eagerly read and broadly known there (cf. Lewis 2012: 107). Also J. Searle ironically called Marx's writings 'subversive' (cf. Searle 1999: 2). The dissident writer M. Bakunin is credited as the co-author of the anarchist *Revolutionary Catechism* (1869). Bakunin wrote in *Principles of Revolution:* "We recognize no other action save destruction though we admit that the forms in which such action will show itself will be exceedingly varied – poison, the knife, the rope, etc." Bakunin's co-author of the *Revolutionary Catechism*, S. Nechaev, contributed to the book's opening paragraphs: "We have an entirely negative plan, which no one can modify – utter destruction." Nowadays, numerous terrorist texts appear on the websites of rebellious organizations. They apparently do not become an issue for the broader public and remain in terms of reception limited to partisans of these organizations. The same concerns A. Hitler's *Mein Kampf* that does not appeal to broader audiences, probably due to dull narration and obscure ideological narrowness. In so far, they share the fate of V. Lenin's revolutionary writings and J. Stalin's voluminous collections of speeches and other intellectual contributions. While no serious interest persists in Hitler's or Stalin's writings, M. Bakunin and S. Nechaev are apparently still read with interest as are K. Marx and F. Engels, at least for their *Communist Manifesto.* Hence, narrative aspects seem to be decisive in anti-governmental writings. Not every one is afraid of such writings. J.C.N. Raadschelders (2011: 147) requested an opening of academic curricula that should include "social commentaries of both left-of-center (in the United States, e.g., Croly, Lippman, Bellah, Nisbet, Bok, etc.) and right-of-center (in the United States, e.g., Bell, Fukuyama, Lasch, Schumpeter, etc.)" Meanwhile, ultraconservative writings continue to flourish in the West, so Robin (2011), and are rarely perceived as anti-governmental while left-wing writings are still held for suspicious readings. C. Robin (2011) analyzed such contributions in the English-speaking world that range from Edmund Burke to Ayn Rand and beyond. All writings that Robin analyzed can be perceived as reactionary in the sense that all of them are more or less explicitly directed against "emancipation of lower orders." These writings persist since the time of reaction against the achievements of the French Revolution; violence and war concepts are broadly functionalized in such works albeit in a dissimulated form. Some of them serve even as programmatic conceptual papers for governments. Both text types, the affirmative-reactionary and the critical, are however relevant to the legal discourse.

7.2.6 Law's true face

The textual interrelation between affirmative and critical writings about law helps understand law in its discursive contexts of emergence and application. Law as a discursive practice is also interdiscursive in the sense that meaning emerges in it in different types of discourses, written and oral, professional and non-professional, literary and media discourses. Attention to the textual interrelations in legal discourses paves the way towards overcoming the isolation in analyzing law. Isolation as method is regularly applied when legal research is reduced to the scrutiny of doctrinal issues in statutes and judgments. In the penal law, the procedure in its part relevant to the accused can be reduced to the question whether the accused is guilty or not. Such questions of 'guilt' are discursively delimited to isolated statements in court decisions, yet life is more complicated. H. Fielding in *Tom Jones* relates the reaction of an acquitted person: "I had now regained my liberty, said the stranger, but I had lost my reputation; for there is a wide difference between the case of a man who is barely acquitted of a crime in a court of justice, and of him who is acquitted in his own heart, and in the opinion of the people. I was conscious of my guilt, and ashamed to look any one in the face; so resolved to leave Oxford the next morning, before the daylight discovered me to the eyes of any beholders." This problem would be described by most legal scholars as extra-legal, not relevant to the trial and its procedure. The literary example shows however that the discursive nature of guilt cannot be limited to a statement in a court judgment. Thus, discourses about law continue long after the court has rendered its formal decision. Law is viewed in them less formally, yet also more personally. As a result, biographies of people are sometimes perturbed by court decisions that on surface are beneficial to them.

7.3 Law is also in the books

Since the classics of the American legal realism discovered and introduced into the legal science the legal reality, i.e. the law as it is practiced at large, reference to the law in the books has been replaced in this sort of legal discourses by reference to the law in action. Doubtless, law's ontology is to be found in its application processes and books about law cannot significantly contribute to this aspect of its existence. The writer and jurist H. Fielding aptly described this challenge in *Tom Jones* (IX, 1): "Neither physic nor law are to be practically known from books. Nay, the farmer, the planter, the gardener, must perfect by experience what he hath acquired the rudiments of by writing." Meanwhile, the act of 'perfecting by experience' seems to presuppose material artifacts that in one way or another relate to law. The writer H. Fielding is definitely aware of the existence of some material rudiments that exist in written form. He will have noticed that enacted statutes, case collections or scholarly writings are artifacts that also shape the legal discourses. Therefore, while law is clearly to be found in action, books provide some knowledge about it. The material written artifacts have at least some significance for the description of the discursiveness of law as a particular social phenomenon. Within the procedure that searches for law, the description of a phenomenon does not mean that the written form is particularly relevant; it states simply the fact that material artifacts abound in law and that they must therefore be considered for its description. In this respect, the problem of the legal science has been that it all too eagerly relied on these written artifacts with relation to law and also all too often confused them with law. Meanwhile, law cannot be reduced to hermeneutics of texts, yet hermeneutics and 'épistémologie' show some features of law that are, rightly or wrongly, systematically invoked in legal discourses. Therefore, it is necessary to scrutinize written texts with reference to law even if law in not really in them but in the social action where legal institutions propel the idle semantic potentiality of texts. The reference to law is to be found in these artifacts on different levels. Court pronouncements display a different degree of reference to law than classical detective stories. Reading strategies related to these texts are adapted to these differing levels of reference to law. Reading is all but a passive process of text consumption. Reading in law is usually even more action oriented that is the reading of other types of texts because it prepares for particular legal action. One can therefore posit that law is definitely also in the books.

7.3.1 Books help jurists more than one would think

Jurists were traditionally rather skeptical about using other literature than the strictly juridical for their professional purposes. Actually only scholarly writings on law have been used in juridical decisions as reference to propositions about valid law. Sometimes also reference to medical literature and some other writings of auxiliary character for courts can be found in judicial opinions. Rarely reference has been made to other works although jurists like other readers read also other books than those that concern their professional activities. General literature, philosophical, historical and political as well as literary fiction are instrumental in clarifying the professional activities of jurists. They propose a cultural agenda that is broader than the juridical prose that in itself is already rather broad as it embraces different text types with different forms of argumentation and narrative elements. As the juridical prose is already so complex, it can be further expanded to comprise all writings that are relevant to law. There is no reason to avoid the broad perspective upon law as part of literature and literature as part of law. P. Berger (1963: 187) mentions: "...a sociologist cannot understand the law who does not recollect the jurisprudence of a certain Queen in *Alice in Wonderland.*" When sociologists cannot allow themselves to skip certain literary products, how could jurists? Law in its written form is definitely a fiction as is the general literary fiction. Because legal fiction and literary fiction are in essence one thing, there is no need to strictly differentiate between them as it is often the case today. In terms of semiotics, law like general literature concerns secondary sign systems. Readers might read them differently as the social role of these writings is different and the legal texts display a different level of sincerity than the general literary fiction (Galdia 2009: 269). This seems to be the only difference between them and the rest of literary fiction. Meanwhile, *The Forsyte Saga* by John Galsworthy (1922) or F. Scott Fitzgerald's *The Great Gatsby* (1926) say more about law than many juridical hornbooks. And it would be hypocritical to pretend that jurists would not know these books.

7.3.2 Founding discourses

Some legal or law-related discourses are more important than others. We are able to evaluate the relevance of law-related discourses from the utilitarian perspective in that we ask which discourses contribute most to the creation of law. The utilitarian perspective is decisive in the valuation test. In fact, some particularly dramatic legal discourses like criminal trials involving capital punishment or divorce procedures that include shared-custody arrangements are of cardinal importance for those immediately concerned, yet of much less value to the development of law. Meanwhile, all discourses constitute law and law is as it is because the valuable and the routine discourses determine its content. The particularly valuable discourses that are placed on the top of the relevance scale lay foundations for other discursive forms in law. This continuity of text types has no determined limits; one text follows hierarchically or chronologically upon another as if it were born of its predecessors. All this is undeniably a metaphor and finally literature. Law is clearly not limited to a sequence of texts like the works of the Russian or French literature that follow chronologically one upon another. For the Russian literature, one may start with Pushkin's efforts to shape a poetic language and contrast these efforts with the achievements of his predecessors and of his successors. For the French literature, one may argue that Proust surpassed Flaubert, and, what is more important in terms of discursiveness, one could posit that Proust wrote as he did because before him Flaubert wrote as is known and Proust had to start where Flaubert stopped in the development of the literary material. Likewise, for law one may claim that its contemporary shape is a result of interrelated literary contributions. Like literature, law is not constructed in a smooth chronological continuum; it evolves in sequences that are structured by founding discourses. With this in mind, Alain Supiot (2005: 21) writes: "Comme tout système dogmatique, le Droit ne se situe pas dans le continuum du temps chronologique, mais dans un temps séquentiel où la loi nouvelle vient tout à la fois réitérer un Discours fondateur et engendrer de nouvelles catégories cognitives." It is therefore necessary for every interpretive work about law to identify these founding discourses and to make clear how they are reflected in subsequent legislative works. The literary theory proceeded in the same way and it identified a set of books, a canon that constitutes the reference for writers and readers of further literary works. In this sense, therefore, one will have to contend that law is very much in the books, that it is largely literature. Only that it is a very special kind of literature. And that it has readers who are particularly active and creative.

Which are the cognitive categories Supiot speaks about? He relates them to the 'dogmatic system' that permeates law at a specific moment of time. It is interesting to note that Supiot does not insist on 'permanent' cognitive categories in law but stresses their doctrinal temporality. As a matter of fact, legal doctrine that wishes to appear in the light of eternal truth constantly changes. This doctrine cannot remain constant due to the dynamic character of law and its language. For the legal linguistics it is important to trace such processes in which cognitive categories emerge or are reshaped. The reason for this interest is that these categories shape the legal language. In fact, the language of law does not depend upon linguistic changes but on shifts in semantics and pragmatics related to existing or emerging social institutions. Supiot concentrated in his anthropological study particularly on 'labor' and showed the impact of categorial changes upon discourse about 'labor' that is also 'work'. Next to this phenomenon he also perceived 'constitutions' as particularly important for the shaping of the legal discourse. In the following paragraphs, this process will be illustrated with narrative samples that emerged in the context of creation of the U.S. Constitution. The results are, however, in no way limited to the U.S. alone and can be generalized.

7.3.3 Constitutions as founding discourses

The symbolically most prominent legal texts are constitutions. They are also perceived as founding myths in law because they constitute symbolical acts such as the establishing of states. It seems that there is basically one underlying linguistic pattern for constitutions. Different constitutional texts all over the world are varieties of the original and generally accepted founding discourse about the most fundamental issues in state and society. Typical of this text type is for example the existence of preambles (Galdia 2009: 259). Meanwhile, it is generally not expected that readers, who are also citizens, would take them all too literally. Most citizens accept the distance between the constitution as a text and the constitutional reality. This strategy of constitutional reception stresses the true nature of constitutions, namely the one of being symbolical creations. They maintain their status as founding discourses even when their factual deficiency is proven. The U.S. Constitution, to use an example, does not mention the right to learning nor the right to education, neither generally nor in any particular context. In a complex society based on skill, and sometimes also on talent, education is essential and citizens are well aware of it. With this in mind, the world's first system of general public education was created in the United States, yet it is not enshrined in the constitution in order to last forever. What is more, the U.S. Constitution does not make clear that citizens have the right to live in safety, knowing that weapons are banned from their immediate surroundings. Some even pretend, and the U.S. Supreme Court sanctions this view, that the U.S. Constitution in its II Amendment guarantees the contrary right, namely the right to accumulating and carrying weapons at will. The nonchalance towards the subject is also palpable in less ambitious literature like detective stories. There, reference is made to weapons as if they were the most ordinary things of daily use in the U.S.: "G. opened the bag and looked inside, put his nose against the opening and smelled the cordite. He recognized the weapon as a North American Arms five-shot revolver, perhaps the smallest commercially made weapon in America. It was most commonly worn as a belt buckle, out in the open, so small it did not seem possible that it could be a real gun. It weighed less than ten ounces and fit easily in the palm of his hand," so J. Lescroart, in *The Hearing*, (New York Penguin, 2001, p. 8). Finally, the tragical destiny of death penalty, that hovers like a scavenger over the American nation and separates it from those who seek social progress, is its most poignant and visible deficiency. It may be only mentioned here as a place holder for all those enigmatic views of jurists for whom the words 'cruel or unusual punishment' in the VIII Amendment to the U.S. Constitution simply mean something else. These and other substantive deficiencies do not impede the U.S. Constitution to function as a symbol of American statehood. Linguistic controversies are even less relevant than the substantive deficiencies that were mentioned. One more semantic problem clarifies the symbolic existence of constitutions. The U.S. Constitution's declared aim is to coin a 'more perfect' union. This expression, although understandable in its historical context of incremental coming closer of the colonies and then of states, challenges the native English-speakers because expressions such as 'very perfect' or 'more perfect' are usually perceived as illogical and therefore not as good English. This constitutional 'bad English' has nevertheless some reasons of existence, as already mentioned. Also *The Federalist* (Nr. 5) provides evidence for the expedient use of a 'perfect' political formation as is manifest from the letter by Queen Anne of 1st July 1706, quoted by Jay: "An entire and perfect union will be the solid foundation of lasting peace: It will secure your religion, liberty, and property; remove the animosities amongst yourselves, and the jealousies and differences betwixt our two kingdoms." This is a description of a perfect union, which the U.S. could not claim to be when its Constitution emerged as a result of a political compromise. Then, against all logic, yet in a symbolically appealing dress, the U.S. could be described by the drafters of the Constitution as forming an entity that strived towards a 'more perfect' union. Significantly, also Christopher Marlowe in his *Faust* (ca. 1589) had been less strict in the use of the term. He lets Valdes encourage Faust to deal with magic: "First I'll instruct thee rudiments,/And then wilt thou be perfecter than I." Indeed, perfection has grades, in life and in law. Other legal-linguistic features of the text are even more relevant to the symbolic character of the U.S. Constitution. More specifically, the U.S. Constitution textually presupposes the existence of the 'United States' that it invokes in its preamble: "We the people of the United States..." and along in the text. It can base itself textually and legally upon the conceptual creation performed in another less commented document, the Articles of Confederation, that also makes part of the American State Papers. In this document the Art. 1 posits: "the style of this Confederacy shall be the United States of America." The 'style' chosen is the type of political organization for the entity created by this provision. As already mentioned, constitutions exist on paper and they also exist in society and society is regularly aware of both forms of their existence. Tribe (2008) distinguishes therefore between constitutional law and the Constitution. This double existence of constitutions has been a challenge for generations of constitutionalists. It is generally admitted that constitutions have a legitimating role to play in formative social processes (Thornhill 2011). The textual analysis of formative documents such as constitutions and pre-constitutional writings shows that constitutions are not only created with words. The analysis makes also plain that words in them are used with a more ambitious goal in mind. Through formative documents new states are created that ground their legitimacy on these documents. This process may seem somehow circular but the creative force of language has its limits. In the area of law, language does not only offer or suggest contents; it is used to create contents that are largely arbitrary because no limits to possible contents can be provided in or by language alone. Social action in formative processes such as emerging of states requires therefore well informed discourses and not only the use of conventional discursive practices that tend conceptually to legitimize the past rather than to expand the boundaries of discursive practices. The emergence of the independent American Republic would not have been possible without content-oriented innovations in the pre-constitutional and constitutional discourses. Furthermore, the United States would not have been formed without the language used in these discourses. Yet, the language alone would not suffice to construct a state. This situation is interesting from the legal-linguistic point of view because it shows both the input of language and its inherent limits.

7.3.4 America in the books

For the United States, the analysis of the emergence of the fundamental lexical units such as 'independent America', 'the United States of America', as well as other related terms and concepts of the public law and the emergence of their discursive components makes sense chronologically, in an approach that proceeds against the legal value of the analyzed documents. Therefore, one may analyze the *Declaration of Independence* with its drafting varieties, and subsequently scrutinize the comments upon the text of the federal *Constitution* known as *The Federalist* or *The Federalist Papers* and finally the *Constitution* itself while bearing in mind that it is the *Constitution* that prevails in terms of law. All three texts testify to the process of conceptualization of American state and society as legal entities. This process becomes epistemologically productive when it is seen in the perspective of an intertextual discourse where political interests and economical antagonisms are incorporated into prevalent legal concepts. Which concepts and which conceptions become dominant in the antagonistic discourse is determined by the economical interests of the most powerful participants. How the concepts are formed and how they become constitutive of fundamental texts and discourses is the matter of discursive practices where diachronical and synchronical text types and their conceptual components provide the material. It is the language that finally shapes and states the law. Language and whatever social and political intentions are inseparable; it is not without reason that recently a diplomatic representation of the U.S. abroad turned to Washington for an instruction in a politically delicate matter with the words: "Please provide language…" (cf. cable text dated November 16, 2005, Paris 7785 txt). What we are willing to say and how we are going to do it are inseparable mental actions. This circumstance will become apparent in the analysis below.

7.3.5 America as favorite in a book

The analysis of independent America provided by Alexis de Tocqueville in *Democracy in America* strengthens this perspective. At this point, the main question would be whether Tocqueville founds or deconstructs the founding discourse about the U.S. American state, society, and its law. Tocqueville's *Democracy in America* (2003: 11) begins in G.E. Bevan's English translation with some astonishing lines: "Of all the novel things which attracted my attention during my stay in the United States, none struck me more forcibly than the equality of social conditions. I had no difficulty in discovering the extraordinary influence this fundamental fact exerts upon the progress of society; it sets up a particular direction to public attitudes, a certain style to the laws, fresh guidelines to governing authorities, and individual habits to those governed." The contemporary reader might wonder that Tocqueville upon arrival in America in 1831 remarks as the first characteristic feature of American society its egalitarian tendency. Doubtless, Tocqueville's observation is in its core neither historically nor sociologically a valid observation. It is legal, and it was made by a jurist. The author has in mind the equality of formal legal status, i.e. absence of differences in this formal status among white inhabitants, and nothing more. Yet, also this feature was far from being assured at that time. Law as a discursive practice is a linguistic construct; the legal author therefore aptly creates a vision of America that interests him personally, because he regards the country from the perspective of the development in France that he deems deficient. Ferguson (2011: 49) commended Tocqueville for providing "a good foundation for understanding how the value of equality helped reinforce the perennial American obsession with racial distinction." This racial distinction is, in discursive terms, a process of emergence of discursive patterns. Ferguson (2011: 47) interprets Tocqueville who showed how "Americans constantly reinvent racial distinctions and invidious race theories in part to resolve the quandary of their national condition, which entails basic equality on one side and a battle for individual distinction or status on the other." Therefore, the 'equality' that Tocqueville found in America could be other than 'legal'. In antiquity, Tacitus proceeded in the same way while writing about Germania – a landscape unknown to him – and implicitly criticizing his native Rome. Sociologically, Tocqueville must have noticed that America at the beginning of the nineteenth century had been all but an egalitarian society. Rather the contrary must have been evident to every visitor or resident. We are far from blaming Tocqueville, as he finally presents the reality he would wish to see. This is the price to pay for the discursive nature of the social element of culture. Therefore, when writing about state, society, or law, the authors can hardly describe such entities because it is their description and many other former and subsequent descriptions that constitute state, society, and law, which compete with theirs. Circularity is another characteristic feature of such discursive formations. Tocqueville continues: "Consequently, as I studied American society, I increasingly viewed this equality of social conditions as the factor which generated all the others and I discovered that it represented a central focus in which all my observations constantly ended." Wherever he starts, Tocqueville always ends up in an imagery of an egalitarian state and society. Likewise, Tocqueville's short essay *Excursion to Lake Oneida* proves not only his literary talents; it also proves that wherever he looks in America he sees France. Tocqueville's *Democracy in America* is in fact a narrative about the missing democracy in France. In America, it has been used as a fundamental description of a missing vision that Tocqueville presented to America and its people. There is nothing wrong with this gift, as conceptions of state, society, or law, are not copyrighted. It therefore also proves interculturality at work. Meanwhile, before Tocqueville could write about America, others had to create it with words.

7.4 Creating a state with words

Next to the term 'constitution' and the narrative that developed around this term also the term 'federalism' is central to the linguistic process of state creation. When the American political system has been formed the term 'federalism' was not in use. Etymologically it derives from the word 'federalist' used abundantly in these times as an adjective and as a noun. The term 'federalism', not to speak about 'dual federalism', is a later coinage. Dual federalism is correlated with dual sovereignty. The school-like definition of it states that it is a form of government in the U.S., in which the federal government and the federal states share powers. Occasionally, also a metaphor of a 'layer cake' is used to portray it. Meanwhile, since 'the triumph of the national idea' this metaphor is not valid any more. The meaning of federalism that interests here is the constitutional principle that recognizes the states' power to make law in areas determined by the U.S. Constitution. This Constitution has literary predecessors that are also its conceptual founding fathers.

The *U.S. Declaration of Independence* was drafted in June 1776 mainly by Thomas Jefferson within a Committee appointed by the Second Continental Congress that also included Benjamin Franklin, John Adams, Roger Sherman, and Robert Livingstone. Th. Jefferson was an experienced drafter who already 1774 published a political pamphlet *A Summary View of the Rights of the British America* were he had argued that America's ties to Britain were voluntary and not irrevocable. The *Declaration of Independence* approved by the deputies on July 4, 1776 differs in some important points from Jefferson's draft. Significantly, Jefferson's reproach directed towards the British monarch that he tolerates and encourages slavery has been removed from the document. The passage reads in Jefferson's manuscript: "He has waged cruel war against human nature itself, violating the most sacred rights of life and liberty in the persons of a distant people who never offended him, captivating and carrying them into slavery in another hemisphere, or to incur miserable death in their transport thither....Determined to keep open a market where men should be bought and sold, he has prostituted his negative for suppressing every legislative attempt to prohibit or to restrain this execrable commerce. And that the assemblage of horrors might want no fact of distinguished die, he is now exciting those very people to rise in arms among us, and to purchase that liberty of which he has deprived them, by murdering the people on whom he also obtruded them: thus paying off former crimes committed against the liberties of one people, with crimes which he urges them to commit against the lives of another." In his *Autobiography* Jefferson quotes the original document as prepared by him and prophetically comments: "As the sentiments of men are known not only by what they receive, but what they reject also, I will state the form of the Declaration as originally reported." The development of the American public law and the civil law are clearly related to the deleted clause on slavery. Another important omission concerns the relation to the British people whom Jefferson blamed in the draft for having supported their monarch: "…and when occasions have been given them, by the regular course of their laws, of removing from their councils the disturbers of our harmony, they have, by their free election, re-established them in power. At this very time too, they are permitting their chief magistrate to send over not only soldiers of our common blood, but Scotch and foreign mercenaries. These facts have given the last stab to agonizing affection, and many spirit bids us to renounce forever these unfeeling brethren. We must endeavour to forget our former love for them, and hold them as we hold the rest of mankind, enemies at war, in peace friends. We might have been a free and great people together; but a communication of grandeur and of freedom, it seems, is below their dignity…" The deputies preferred to focus on criticism concerning the monarch and removed the quoted passage. This editorial measure later enabled the Americans and the British to reshape their relations in that they stressed their historical commonalities. Alliances under international law have been prepared by the prudent formulation that the deputies had favored in the final document. Furthermore, Jefferson writes about the details of communication of the draft to the Congress in his *Autobiography*: "I reported to the House on Friday, the 28th of June, when it was read, and ordered to lie on the table. On Monday, the 1st of July, the House resolved itself into a committee of the whole, and resumed the consideration of the original motion made by the delegates of Virginia…" The further work on Jefferson's draft went on in that it "had been lain on the table by Friday preceding, and on Monday referred to a committee of the whole," as mentioned by Jefferson in his *Autobiography*. In this procedure the words 'to expunge' have been changed into 'to alter', 'unremitting' was changed into 'repeated'; some other changes of the same sort were also undertaken.

The proper declaration of independence in the document so named differs from the text drafted by Jefferson. The act reads in this part so far: "We, therefore, the representatives of the United States of America in General Congress assembled, appealing to the supreme judge of the world for the rectitude of our intentions, do in the name, and by the authority of the good people of these colonies, solemnly publish and declare, that these united colonies are, and of right ought to be free and independent states; that they are absolved from all allegiance to the British crown, and that all political connection between them and the state of Great Britain is, and ought to be, totally dissolved; and that as free and independent states, they have full power to levy war, conclude peace, contract alliances, establish commerce, and to do all other acts and things which independent states may of right do. And for the support of this declaration, with a firm reliance on the protection of divine providence, we mutually pledge to each other our lives, our fortunes, and our sacred honor." The clause refers twice to a divinity, called first 'the supreme judge of the world' and later 'divine providence' as a source of support for the enterprise. The future conception of the United States as a Christian state that is still maintained by some Americans argumentatively relies on this formulation. Furthermore, the clause incorporates R.H. Lee's motion while referring to 'these united Colonies' that 'are and ought to be, free and independent states'. It uses a speech act imperative in reference to the relation with Great Britain which 'is, and ought to be, totally dissolved'. Jefferson proposed the following formulation: "We therefore the representatives of the United States of America in General Congress assembled, do in the name, and by the authority of the good people of these states reject and renounce allegiance and subjection to the kings of Great Britain and all others who may hereafter claim by, through and under them; we utterly dissolve all political connection which may heretofore have subsisted between us and the people or parliament of Great Britain; and finally we do assert and declare these colonies to be free and independent states, and that as free and independent states, they have full power to levy war, conclude peace, contract alliances, establish commerce, and to do all other acts and things which independent states may of right do. And for the support of this declaration, we mutually pledge to each other our lives, our fortunes, and our sacred honor." In Jefferson's proposal there is no reference to divinity; attention is directed to the legal aspect of the declaration where first, it must be made clear that the legal and political ties to Great Britain are dissolved and second, that a representation of citizens called affectionately 'good people' establishes a political body of independent successor states. Jefferson succeeds well in his task although also he falls into an antiquated legalese about possible foreign sovereignty claims of kings and others “by, through, or under them” which could have been omitted. This small text sample illustrates the problem jurists usually have to abandon bad linguistic habits of their profession even if they become aware of them. As is well known, the *Declaration of Independence* affirms an idea introduced by Jefferson that men’s inalienable rights include ‘life, liberty and the pursuit of happiness’. J. Locke, who is the linguistic predecessor of this formulation, wrote in his *Second Treatise on Government* in 1689 “life, liberty and estate” and meant with ‘estate’ acquisition of land. Locke wrote about the willingness to form society and government in chapter IX: “…it is not without reason that he seeks out and is willing to join in society with others who are already united, or have a mind to unite for the mutual preservation of their lives, liberties, and estates, which I call by the general term – property.” Why then the ‘pursuit of happiness’ substitutes in Jefferson’s proposal the equal opportunity to acquire land? G. Wills (1978) proposed a philosophical explanation: “the pursuit of happiness is a phenomenon both obvious and paradoxical. It supplies us with the ground of human right and the goal of human virtue. It is the basic drive of the self, and the only means given for transcending the self…Men in the eighteenth century felt they could become conscious of their freedom only by discovering how they were bound. When they found what they must pursue, they knew they had a *right* to pursue it.” Wills connects the pursuit of happiness to the idea of right that would link it to the text of the *Declaration* that is in its core a legal document. While life and liberty – so one could understand Wills – impose themselves as rights by evidence, property as a general right might be less convincing without entering into an antagonistic discourse about equality in the distribution of property. Jefferson must have been conscious that no consensus was to be obtained about this question at the assembly and had to modify Locke’s philosophical formula that Wills aptly replaced by another.

The declaration of independence as a legal act has, next to the numerous written, also oral components. Already on June 7, 1776, the representative of Virginia, Richard Henry Lee had proposed to the Second Continental Congress that “these united Colonies are, and of a right ought to be, free and independent states.” Lee’s motion marks the revolutionary moment in the creation of the independent state in that it refers to the independence as grounded on a ‘right’. Unsurprisingly, Lee does not further elaborate on the nature of this right. It seems nevertheless to be clear that the Congress did not perceive as sufficient a simple political declaration of independence and the creation of a new state ex nihilo. Likewise, the process of renouncing the legal ties with Britain had been deemed as an inherent but also a mandatory element in the declaration. In terms of writing procedure, the Congress appointed a Committee to draft the declaration on June 11. Lee's resolution was passed on July 2 and the declaration was finally voted on July 4. Later, on August 2, a copy of the declaration on parchment was signed by almost all delegates. Three additional delegates signed the document later. In all, the act of declaring the independence consists of the motion made by the representatives of Virginia that is declared in the assembly by Lee, the decision to have the document of declaration drafted, drafting and communication of the draft, work on the final draft, voting and signing the final draft on July 4, as well as a further signing the parchment on August 2, and also later. In the center stands the vote on July 4 as a legally binding manifestation of intention to create a new state. It is not thinkable in isolation from other actions, previous and following, that ensured that the act of declaration will become effective. The revolutionary element in law lies in the circumstance that a motion contrary to British constitutional law of that time is nevertheless voted. Subsequently, the declaration is accepted as legally binding under international law. The process towards the effectiveness of the legal declaration had been, as is well known, long and bloody. Legally expressed intention reached its effectiveness in a politically structured procedure. Law in splendid isolation of voting, declaring, and signing parchment documents is effective in conceptual terms as a performative speech act. It had to create a state with words. Meanwhile, would events that were to come, have brought results disadvantageous to the American patriots, who were in categories of the British legislation 'rebels', the document would posthaste have fallen into oblivion and the notion 'British America', still used by Jefferson in 1774, might have been operative in the constitutional law to these very days. The performative act had therefore, in order to become effective, to fulfill some additional validity requirements. They depend on the fact that the declaration of independence is a revolutionary act; it means also that it is valid only under a new constitutional law that must prevail in the battle between two competing legal regimes. A regular, non-revolutionary legal declaration that is equally performative does not depend on these requirements because it is made under a legal regime that does not compete with others for validity.

7.4.1 Federalists at work

Among the basic American State Papers, both the *Declaration of Independence* and the *U.S. Constitution* are in terms of the founding discourse rightly positioned in their relation to the papers published and later edited as *The Federalist*.

The Federalist authored by Alexander Hamilton, James Madison, and John Jay is a piece of writing that is argumentative through and through. Its argumentative structure, which owes much if not everything to the Greek and Roman rhetoric and political philosophy of the ancients, makes also use of later scholastic argumentation schemes. This methodological background has been traditionally explained by commentators with reference to the fact that *The Federalist*'s authors were educated according to a curriculum that was based on the ancient classics and practice of the scholastic disputation. The authors did not conceal their intellectual origins and signed their articles with their common pseudonym Publius, apparently also in contradistinction to texts opposing the union of American states that were signed Cato (i.e. the then Governor of New York, De Witt Clinton). Alexander Hamilton, one of the three authors, wrote also immediately upon the publication of the first Cato text two responses to it, signed, not really modestly, with Caesar. The Hamiltonian phrase is in fact Ciceronian rather than Cesarean; yet it may also justify his somehow immoderate choice of the pseudonym because it bears witness to a bold conquest of language: "Among the most formidable of the obstacles which the new Constitution will have to encounter may readily be distinguished the obvious interest of a certain class of men in every State to resist all changes which may hazard a diminution of the power, emolument, and consequence of the offices they hold under the State establishments; and the perverted ambition of another class of men, who will either hope to aggrandise themselves by the confusions of their country, or will flatter themselves with fairer prospects of elevation from the subdivision of the empire into several partial confederacies than from its union under one government" (*Federalist* nr. 1). Publius' classically elaborate arguments are drafted in the mood of 'public good' (*Federalist* nr. 1), allegedly unlike those advanced by the opponents of the new Constitution. Needless to remind that this focus on orator's intention to act in favor of 'public good' in distinction to his opponents who are moved by other reasons is also a typically Cesarean and Ciceronian argument. The Hamiltonian phrase is impressive. It remains meanwhile open whether it has been effective in operating change in the minds of his readers. The syntactic complexity of this florid and Latinate phrase may indicate the contrary result: "Assuming it therefore as an established truth that the several States, in case of disunion, or such combinations of them as might happen to be formed out of the wreck of the general Confederacy, would be subject to those vicissitudes of peace and war, of friendship and enmity with each other, which have fallen to the lot of all neighbouring nations not united under one government, let us enter into a concise detail of some of the consequences that would attend such a situation" (*Federalist* nr. 8). Hamilton's argumentation may appeal not through its rational dispositions but through the repetition of key notions such as 'nations united (or not) under one government'. Within such a linguistic strategy it does not matter much whether the reader actually understands the message in detail. In the contexts of legal texts and texts related to law such a strategy has far-reaching consequences for the composition and for the reception of this type of texts. Finally, on account of the Hamiltonian phrase, another sample related to an appealing issue, namely the increase of real estate prices in case of the economical development is worth noting. Hamilton writes: "Could that which procures a freer vent for the products of the earth, which furnishes new incitements to the cultivation of land, which is the most powerful instrument in increasing the quantity of money in a state – could that, in fine, which is the faithful handmaid of labour and industry, in every shape, fail to augment that article, which is the prolific parent of far the greatest part of the objects upon which they are exerted?" (*Federalist* nr. 12). The Hamiltonian phrase is this time framed in form of a rhetorical question. The banality of money becomes a philosophical issue through the use of language; Hamilton turns it into a philosophy of money. Hamilton will return to the issue later and he will write: "The price of improved land in most parts of the country is much lower than can be accounted for by the quality of waste land at market, and can only be fully explained by that want of private and public confidence which are so alarmingly prevalent among all ranks, and which have a direct tendency to depreciate property of every kind" (*Federalist* nr. 15). This additional remark lays bare the nature of the alleged and addressed problem that is economical, and partly political. The issue of land prices fascinates less when it is depraved of its philosophical status; yet it also makes clear why it is used within the discourse about the constitution. It shows how banal questions such as people's interest in the increase of value of real estate that they own, may become an argument efficiently applied in fundamental discourses about state and society. It holds true provided the appropriate rhetorical apparatus makes them functional in such discourses. The Hamiltonian phrase is, in fact, a dowsing rod for the American political and legal language. Occasionally, pure concepts in impressive syntactic surroundings may not be sufficient to reach the federalists' rhetorical goals. Image-sensitive language must be applied in such cases to make emerging constitutional concepts that are as basic as 'independent America' identifiable and absorbable in the minds of readers. This task had been accomplished against all odds by another occasional contributor to *The Federalist,* Jay, who writes: "It has often given me pleasure to observe, that independent America was not composed of detached and distant territories, but that one connected, fertile, wide-spreading country was the portion of our western sons of liberty. Providence has in a particular manner blessed it with a variety of soils and productions, and watered it with innumerable streams, for the delight and accommodation of its inhabitants. A succession of navigable waters forms a kind of chain around its borders, as if to bind it together; while the noblest rivers in the world, running at convenient distances, present them with highways for the easy communication of friendly aids, and the mutual transportation and exchange of their various commodities. With equal pleasure I have as often taken notice, that Providence has been pleased to give this one connected country to one united people – a people descended from the same ancestors, speaking the same language, professing the same religion, attached to the same principles of government, very similar in their manners and customs, and who, by their joint counsels, arms, and efforts, fighting side by side throughout a long and bloody war, have nobly established general liberty and independence. This country and this people seem to have been made for each other, and it appears as if it was the design of Providence, that an inheritance so proper and convenient for a band of brethren, united to each other by the strongest ties, should never split into a number of unsocial, jealous, and alien sovereignties" (*Federalist* nr. 2). The commonality of rivers and land constitutes in Jay's words a common republic that by necessity must be independent and peopled by one nation that is equally homogenous that the land it already inhabits. The discourse becomes at this point purely fictitious because it is not very probable that anyone of the mentioned inhabitants would be ready to take it at face value. The practice of binding territory and population is here a purely linguistic operation. To declare a union of the territory in terms of law is for Jay therefore only another such linguistic operation. It is however an interesting operation as it is based on a linguistic creation that he had accomplished in the lines above quoted. Thus, the imagery of perfect borders for a happy and homogenous nation enables the discursive emergence of a legal-linguistic operation that creates a social fact. This social fact is, in casu, the American republic.

7.4.2 America for sale

One of the arguments applied by the federalists in order to facilitate the decision of those who hesitated to join the union is the recurring reassurance that the U.S. will be a 'commercial republic'. The classical argument in favor of such a constitutional formation is that commercial republics have an inherent interest in maintaining peace, so *Federalist* nr. 6. However, history does not provide any proof for this assumption. Hamilton sees the problem that he frames with following words: "Is not the love of wealth as domineering and enterprising a passion as that of power or glory?" Hamilton cannot use the term 'greed' in the context of the otherwise positively perceived commercial republic, but he can express a problematic situation that remains unresolved until today. Other fundamental reasons make a state formation that is based on commerce even more suspicious. Already Aristotle expressed in his *Politics* (1280b10) skepticism about such a conception of state. He holds that the purpose of the city is the good life which consists in noble actions – the kind of activity that is worth while in itself. This differentiates his position from those, who like the sophist Lycophron, had seen the city as a device for mutual protection or a kind of commercial alliance. Hamilton does not deal with the Aristotelian idea and avoids criticism on the concept of the commercial republic due to its positive connotation among most of the *Federalist*'s readers. From the perspective of the Aristotelian thought, and not only because of this, the uncritical approach to the idea of commercial republic is deplorable. It is a step back behind the level of the constitutional discourse that was reached by the ancients. It also will have consequences for the development of the constitutional discourse in the future independent America.

7.4.3 Hamilton fails

The Hamiltonian phrase is anchored in the dominating European educational tradition that is followed by the American cultural and political class of his time. It is widespread in literature and a sample from H. Fielding's *Tom Jones* may illustrate this fact as well as the irony that emerged in this epoch around this oratorical form. Fielding writes in book ten, chapter five: "As in the month of June, the damask rose, which chance hath planted among the lilies, with her candid hue mixes his vermilion; or as some playsome heifer in the pleasant month of May diffuses her odoriferous breath over the flowery meadows; or as, in the blooming month of April, the gentle, constant dove, perched on some fair bough, sits mediating on her mate, so looking a hundred charms and breathing as many sweets, her thoughts being fixed on her Tommy, with a heart as good and innocent as her face was beautiful, Sophia (for it was she herself) lay reclining her lovely head on her hand, when her maid entered the room, and, running directly to the bed, cried…" In Fielding's words there is a lot of mockery about the language used by writers such as Hamilton and his companions. This notwithstanding, jurists usually take seriously the tone that dominates the *Federalist* writings and the text of the U.S. Constitution. Indeed, jurists and literary scholars alike perceive the U.S. Constitution as the American master narrative (Chafe 2012: 12; Brooks 2012: 43). It is amazing that an antiquated text that as an artifact defends itself even against well-intentioned penetration with all linguistic means of historical syntax and spelling, dark and overcome formulations and reminiscence of times not always happy or happy only to some Americans, might have obtained such an uncontested place in the American social and legal discourse. The distance between the written text and its modern and highly contested interpretation could not be greater. In order to understand the American constitution one must know what it means before one starts reading. This circumstance, however, does not impede its high status as a text. It might be that the master narrative is constituted by the elements of uncontested authority that prevail notwithstanding its limited textual accessibility. For Brooks (2012: 43) "the U.S. Constitution in many ways takes the place of the texts held to be sacred in other societies." Sacred texts do not need to be read, they are relied upon because they are matters of belief, not matters of knowledge. Tribe (2012: 23) stressed the idea that the understanding of the constitutional discourse as a narrative includes its function as an argumentative text that should persuade the unconvinced. This American textual specificity has its roots in the *Federalist* where the persuasion rather than the statement of law is the main purpose. The idea to read constitutional texts as nonfictional narratives has not been fully explored yet (Galdia 2009: 263). One can assume that it is possible to read meaningfully a constitutional text in order to get acquainted with it, just to see what it says, without any further cognitive interests. This approach is different from the professional reading of constitutional texts that may be studied or re-examined by judges in order to apply them afterwards. These two types of reading are typical of law; they may lead to different sorts of reflection on constitutional and other legal texts. Also interpretive approaches vary according to the sort of reading. Reading just to see what the text says leads to semantic problems of concept or term analysis; professional reading that is caused by the necessity to apply the law leads to more advanced interpretive mechanisms that include creation of meaning. In his treatise on American constitutional law, Tribe (2000: 23–24) argued that "the Constitution provides the basic language through which institutions direct and challenge one another and the society at large and through which the people in turn contest the actions of those institutions." With other words, the constitution provides "the primary language and framework in terms of which we debate our rights" (Tribe 2012: 22) and "it provides a language for challenging its legitimacy" (i.e. the legitimacy of constitutional practice), as stressed by Tribe (2012: 18). Tribe is definitely right in that he posits that the constitutional discourse is centered on the constitutional document, otherwise it would not be identifiable as a legal discourse that relates to the American constitutional law. Other types of discourse about constitutional matters would belong rather to the political discourse where the textual reference does not matter. The discursive challenge to constitutional practice in law also functions with reference to the constitutional document. Without this reference the challenge would be political, not legal. "Reverence to and obedience for" master narratives might be perceived as counterintuitive or socially unproductive (Brooks 2012: 43). What is more, in the U.S., precedents rather than the text of the Constitution are interpreted. Therefore, Levinson (2006) called even for a new convention in the U.S. that would rewrite the American Constitution. Also Tribe (2012: 19) claims that the constitutional interpretation "ultimately rests on acts of imagination." Meanwhile, all advanced methods of text interpretation show that no structural boundaries can prevent a specific interpretation of a text, provided the institutional approval of such an interpretation in case of a legal text can be achieved. Doctorow (2012: 125) refers to a future text of the U.S. Constitution that is based on current experience, a narrative 'C' as a solution to the narrative crisis in the American society: "...the idea of the free citizenry of the red white and blue, along with what we think of as our exceptionalist democracy, may no longer be sustainable. If that is so, we will have written a new American narrative, though, after all, I don't think anyone can know just how it will read." Do we then need constitutional narratives? Brooks (2012: 43) questions this necessity: "Among the many such narratives that Americans regularly call on, one of the most curious is the constitutional narrative – curious because it is not obvious why society should need such explicitly, often technically legal narratives to make sense of itself." Meanwhile, the prudent answer would be rather positive. The discursiveness of law grounds on narrativity that cannot cope without the textuality of law. Law as a social mechanism works easier when it refers to a generally known and pre-formulated set of texts. This holds particularly true when the texts are fixed in written form. These texts bring order into legal-linguistic practices and facilitate the discursive practices in and around the law. Meaning is easier created around such texts. All this procedure of creating meaning would incontestably also work without written nonfictional narratives; yet it would work worse, i.e. less efficiently. Indeed, written artifacts of law are not law's logical prerequisites; meanwhile, they provide a comfortable frame of reference for legal discourses about the meaning of law. Their weak logical status makes them appear as mysterious, magic, or sacred in Brooks' terms. Also linguists ask fundamental question about the importance of linguistic communication for society. Janicki (2010) argues that language as such is actually not a well adapted mechanism for communication because it does not match the complexity and change of our physical, social and mental reality. He supposes that we use language because we lack any better communicative device. In law, traditionally a logically better device could and had been proposed in the project of formalization of the legal language. Meanwhile, as appealing as this idea may appear, formalized legal language with its explicit or implicit logical and mathematical structure will not work in law (Galdia 2009: 63). Therefore, also in future, law will have to rely on natural language as the best existing communicative device. Legal texts that constitute discourses are dominated by conventions and not by logic. Like all such texts they are not really needed, but they play a role in the practice of law. They are useful facilitators.

7.4.4 Consequences for America

What are the consequences of the cognitive category 'founding discourse' introduced by *The Federalist*? Alain Supiot (2005: 262) analyzed the argumentation aiming at the stabilization of the idea that a state is an enterprise and he also pointed the most significant difference between both: "La différence entre l'État et l'entreprise est moins une affaire de structure qu'une question de Référence. L'État est référé à des valeurs qualitatives, supra-patrimoniales; …L'entreprise est référée à des valeurs patrimoniales;…C'est qui rend si effrayante l'idée, aujourd'hui répandue, qu'il faut gérer l'État comme on gère une entreprise…" The argumentative problems that the *Federalist* causes at this point are the consequences of founding a state as a commercial enterprise. *The Federalist* is essential to the understanding of the process in which the American federal state and its constitutional law were shaped. Textually, it is the authoritative interpretation of intentions of the framers of the federal Constitution. Madison's, Hamilton's and Jay's *Federalist* grounds in cognitive categories that are discursive as the whole text is a pleading for the acceptance of the federal Constitution. Its main aim is to make such a text palpable. Its immediate aim had been to persuade the New Yorkers to accept the newly drafted constitution in 1787. The influence of the papers went beyond their immediate aim and placed them among the central works of American political theory. Thomas Jefferson is credited for characterizing them as "the best commentary on the principles of government which ever was written." The papers concentrate on the power-sharing between state and federal authorities and on a conception of a stable federal constitution. In retrospection, one cannot deny their importance for the understanding of the formation process of the American republic. Meanwhile, they are deficient in terms of the discursiveness of law as they reduce constitutional theory to political propaganda.

The American State Papers and *The Federalist* are scarcely thinkable without the works of Locke, Hobbes, Montesquieu, and Rousseau. Hamilton makes in *The Federalist* (nr. 9) an intertextually relevant reference with the intention to reconcile his view with the one expressed by Montesquieu: "The opponents of the plan proposed have, with great assiduity, cited and circulated the observations of Montesquieu on the necessity of contracted territory for a republican government. But they seem not to have been apprised of the sentiments of that great man expressed in another part of his work, nor to have adverted to the consequences of the principle to which they subscribe with such ready acquiescence. When Montesquieu recommends a small extent for republics, the standards he had in view were of dimensions far short of the limits of almost every one of the States..." Hamilton feels the necessity to rhetorically balance his view with Montesquieu in order to increase the acceptance of his proposal to institute a political federation of states on a very large territory. The whole text is an implicit or explicit reference to constitutional and legal theories developed by the classics of the political thought.

The Federalist establishes a notional framework for the discussion of the Constitution. Textually, as a commentary on constitutional law it is interesting, but not controlling any more. Likewise, the Hamiltonian phrase disappears from the discourses step by step and is not perceived as an oratorical ideal nowadays. One may deplore this occurrence. Meanwhile, also as a tool of pervasiveness *The Federalist* largely fails because it does not demonstrate, against all attempts undertaken and against the perfection of the Hamiltonian phrase, the logical necessity to form the union. This had been an impossible enterprise from its inception, a mission that had to fail because law as discursive practice has its limits. Yet, it also has discursive prerequisites. Already Aristotle (*Politics* 1325b33) dealt with the question whether small states are preferable to great ones in terms of organization: "Most people think that the happiness of a city depends on its being great." He showed that discussing the advantages or disadvantages of such societal creation is largely an academic exercise. Aristotelian happiness, efficient state in Hamiltonian thinking, does not depend on size. Discussing structural patterns of the sort finally shifts the focus of state creation upon marginal issues. Likewise, discussing the appropriateness of the driving on the right-hand side of the road or on the left-hand side of the road is equally academic, as no factual state of affairs can prove the appropriateness of the one proposal or of the other. It was therefore not possible to demonstrate in the elaborate rhetorical undertaking of *The Federalist* the factual preponderance of a large union as contrasted with its thinkable alternatives formed around different ideas of smaller regional confederations of American states. In fact, legal operations in law such as concept creation or formation of discourses are rooted in social facts, not in brute facts. The reason for it is, unsurprisingly, that law is a discursive practice. *The Federalist* fails because it attempts at the creation of the union as a brute fact. It pretends that the nature of things, the form of territory and the mindset of people simply impose the creation of a union as a natural necessity. In its failure, therefore, *The Federalist* manifests the limits of discursiveness in law and the limits of law itself. It also underestimates the discursiveness of law that it confuses with brute facts.

Equally, professional interpretive approaches have to adapt to this state of affairs. Interpretive devices such as originalism that emerged in the U.S. Supreme Court and which is supported by the Justices Scalia and Thomas have been counteracted in Justice Breyer's (2010) *Making Our Democracy Work: A Judge's View.* This work is also interesting as the names of the two justices, who advocate originalism in the U.S. Supreme Court, where also Breyer officiates, are not mentioned there. Originalism has its semiotic roots in the intention of the makers and is an interesting and fruitful interpretive method in literary studies. In law, however, it has its limits. We have a justified interest in the meaning Dante Alighieri might have given some of his poetic imagery in his *Divine Comedy* as we might be interested in the view of the founding fathers on certain constitutional principles. Meanwhile, our interest stops with the deciphering of Dante's intention, while the interest in law is inspired by the views of the framers of the Constitution to make further steps in developing democratic state and just society. Therefore, legal originalism cannot be confined to philological studies. Such studies have their own rationale that grounds in epoch-dependent understanding of language, or to say it simply, with the fact that language changes. When we read W. Shakespeare's *Hamlet* we may stumble upon Polonius' complaint that Hamlet is "still harping on my daughter." The use of 'still' may irritate us in this phrase because it makes its sense less precise. We may inquire in secondary literature on Shakespeare where we easily will find out that 'still' in Shakespearean language means 'always'. Therefore, Polonius complains about Hamlet who is always harping on his daughter. The sense of the complaint is now clarified due to the reference to the language use in Shakespeare's times. In *King Lear*, "Th'untended woundings of a father's curse" refer to wounds too deep to be cleaned with a tent, a roll of lint, at least as explained by K. Muir in *The Arden Shakespeare*-edition. The inquiry becomes more complicated in *King Lear* when Shakespeare becomes particularly inventive, for instance in act I, verse 283 where he says "With cadent tears fret channels in her cheeks." The Latinized word 'cadent' in 'cadent tears' means simply 'falling', a meaning that was easily understandable to

Shakespeare's audience that had studied Latin at school. Meanwhile, the word 'cadent' seems to be Shakespeare's individual creation as supposed in the *Arden Shakespeare*-edition. This type of originalism is challenging, and it becomes even more challenging when individual language use cannot be explained at all. Legal originalism is an inquiry different from this sort of philological research, although it may share with it some interest. Modifications of meaning are frequent; deliberative modifications of original meaning in art are even perceived as particularly creative and commendable. In her 2010-adaptation of Shakespeare's *The Tempest* for the cinema J. Taymor switched the gender of protagonists, made a Prospera from Prospero, invented and transposed passages of Shakespeare's play, and deleted others. In law, particularly creative work on legal sources is also possible. Both procedures are however exposed to the test of social acceptability that can be non-professional as well as professional.

7.4.5 Anti-narrativism and law

The usefulness of linguistically stated law in meta-narratives has nevertheless some fundamental opponents. Anti-narrativist tendencies became stronger in the post-modern times that are principally suspicious of meta-narratives. G. Strawson (2004: 448) stressed rather the episodic type of existence that he contrasted with the tendency to construct a diachronic, flawless narrative. For him, "the business of living well… is a completely non-narrative project." This would mean that modern society that aims at 'good life' does not need any overarching ideological terms of reference for its culture, its politics, and its law. Strawson's contention may be right as an empirical result because some people may not need narratives that make sense of things. Some other people do not care about mathematical astronomy; this does not mean that mathematical astronomy is overall useless and that it should be abandoned. Therefore, Strawson's and others' anti-narrativist claims expose themselves to criticism based on naturalistic fallacy. The naturalistic fallacy is based on the assumption that an 'ought to' can be derived from an 'is'. It is an important distinctive feature of the professional thinking about norms. Meanwhile, Strawson's anti-narrativism is a well-founded warning against all attempts to create hermetically closed and pre-defined meta-narratives with universal tendencies that cannot stand the proof of times. This practice is a dangerous experiment in life where "the aspiration to explicit narrative self-articulation" (Strawson 2004: 447) limits possibilities and narrows the intellectual horizon. Strawson (2004: 447) writes about this point more precisely: "My guess is that it almost always does more harm than good – that the (N)arrative tendency to look for story or narrative coherence in one's life is, in general, a gross hindrance to self-understanding." We should therefore not pretend to be able to set up overarching master narratives because we are simply not good enough to do so. Law like life is not a coherent set of texts, or expressed with modern words, a film with a happy end. Examples for the anti-narrative tendencies may however also be misleading. While pointing to the fact that the European Union does not have any master narrative, Donoghue (2012: 5) remarks: "Each member country of the European Union...has agreed to put aside its grand narrative, if it has one – or at least to keep quiet about it – in return for the boon of sharing a political, social, and economic entity – Europe – and, in particular, for the satisfaction of enjoying a vast commercial market and the rules, legal and civic, increasingly prescribed by Brussels...The common understanding of the E.U. is that the imperatives of trade, banking, regulation of borrowing and debt, and other such practices must come first; narratives may be recalled on high, innocent anniversaries." However, this fact may be a sign of lethargy or incapacity to act in Europe rather than the result of a conscious choice against meta-narratives. Europe does not lack narrative skills. Its myths and foundational stories reach down to ancient Greece and Rome where narratives always accompanied the development of states and laws. Yet a myth requires creativity. A myth is not a simple fairy tale; it transfers experience and offers vision. The lack of such narratives in contemporary Europe does not necessarily signal a higher level of reflection upon the social role of meta-narratives but rather the impossibility to create them. Recently attempted overarching narratives such as the failed draft of the European Constitution or the finally adopted *Treaty on the Functioning of the European Union* in its form known as *Treaty of Lisbon* provide rules in the sense mentioned by D. Donoghue. They lack vision, and vision is the structural feature of narratives. This circumstance as such is still no proof for the denial of the cautious role that narratives can play in society and in its law. Law cannot be stated in rules alone. To be intelligible it needs contexts and these contexts are texts. Oral and written sources provided until now a sufficient collection of materials that made law mostly expressed in written rules intelligible to professionals and occasionally to non-professionals as well. Laws without narratives lack authenticity; they are like the E.U. legislation sterile and unappealing. Meanwhile, one cannot exclude that in future a kind of law could emerge that would be less dependent on narrativity. Narrativity in law, i.e. the fact that legal rules are not intelligible per se but require broader contexts to become meaningfully applicable in cases is caused by the structure of the legal rule. This legal rule or norm is expressed formally and abstractly. Another type of rules or norms that would make use of a reformed legal textuality would probably make law less dependent on narrativity. It may also be true that narrativity makes law cumbersome in handling. Whenever a legal problem emerges, complex scrutiny of rules, case law, and other literature of whatever sort becomes necessary because it is not possible to answer legal questions with the formal reference to the text of a legal provision. This legal provision that is traditionally perceived as the basis of a legal rule or norm develops within an inquiry that is a discursive practice. Experimentally, at least, it should be possible to integrate all textual elements that finally enable the proposition of law to emerge. This experiment would include the reformulation of law in terms of its reformed narrativity. Such a reformulation of law could center on principles and standards rather than on systematized provisions. What however cannot be done is the omission of legal discursiveness as law even in an advanced or reformed mode of existence will remain a discursive practice.

More productive and possibly also illuminating within the anti-narrativist debate would be to ask why the U.K. avoids any involvement at accomplishing a constitutional meta-narrative because it is doing it with a declared intent to abstain from such projects. The U.K. has no codified constitution; its political system rests on precedent and 'common sense' as main constitutional arguments (cf. Turpin/Tomkins 2011). It developed as the emanation of the Westminster model concentrating power in a cabinet that rules with the support of the Parliament in contrast to the U.S. system that separates power between the President, the Congress and the Supreme Court. *Everyman's Encyclopaedia* explained the form of the British constitution in 1913 with a mysterious formula: "In Great Britain it is the whole body of the public law, consuetudinary as well as statutory, which has grown up in the process of time, and is continually being modified by the action of the general will as interpreted and expressed by the parliamentary representatives of the nation." Domingo (2010: 67) summed up this conception: "...the British Parliament had been charged with limiting the king's power, as reflected in the expression "King in Parliament," which synthesizes the English constitution's principle of parliamentary sovereignty." The British constitution, so *Everyman's Encyclopaedia* further "came ipso facto into existence" as the realm become centralised. This ipso facto state and informality of the constitution are increasingly perceived as problematic. L. Siedentop (2010) remarks: "Britain's informal, common law constitution is no longer suitable for a society lacking deference and homogeneity that once yielded a coherent political class trusted to defend liberal values, if only out of self-interest. It is now clear that these values were protected by aristocratic 'manners' rather than by formal constitutional principles." The problem has been recognized already by G.W.F. Hegel who in his

Philosophy of History remarked sarcastically in the chapter on *The German World*: "The Parliament governs, although Englishmen are unwilling to allow that such is the case. It is worthy of remark that what has been always regarded as the period of the corruption of the republican people presents itself here; viz., election to seats in Parliament by means of bribery. But this also they call freedom – the power to sell one's vote, and to purchase a seat in Parliament." Britons were aware of the fact that foreign nations copied the Westminster model and that they codified it. Yet, "they retained a sense of superiority – a feeling that the 'virtue' of British society made such arrangements unnecessary" (Siedentop 2010). British constitutionalists still agree that Britain disposes of a fundamental law in the shape of an unwritten constitution; this unwritten British constitution functions through its main theory of constitutionalism. For some this constitutionalism may bring advantages. Clearly, it is difficult to violate constitutional norms when they are textually absent. Textuality is perceived as more and more urgent. A democratic political system that functions under the principle of constitutionalism must be intelligible as it no longer can rely on generally assimilated opinions (cf. Siedentop 2010). Texts instead of aristocratic evasiveness (and in power structures the word 'aristocratic' often conceals untidy practices) turn constitutionalism into a practicable mechanism for the development of discourses that are also legal, and not only political. Additionally, narrative aspects of public discourses such as law can be compared with private discursive practices such as autobiographies or journals. P. Lejeune (1975; 2013) developed a perspective upon such writings called 'récit de soi'. Telling stories about oneself, sometimes exclusively to oneself is an anthropological standing practice. In such texts the individual invents and re-invents itself linguistically and narratively. Through re-reading of such texts the author can reposition himself in time and space, and also gain some distance from his life. Lejeune mentions also a 'journal de la relecture' that can be used for re-writing one's previously stated life experience. Autobiography as 'récit rétrospectif en prose' in the sense developed by Lejeune shapes future life through the narrative retrospective. It is not a coincidence that this type of narrative about one's own life is widespread. Its literary quality varies and most of such writings are not particularly impressive from the point of view of literary technique. Yet, even clumsy narratives structure the reasoning of their authors about their life, past and future. Public discourse is no less dependent on reflection and retrospection. Therefore, narratives about public affairs are useful for its development. This development of social narrative practices about public affairs corresponds with the private discourse about individual life that is equally productive and creative.

7.4.6 How to make discourses of narratives?

Interpretive devices such as the 'stare decisis rule' or interpretive methods such as 'originalism' help create discourses about the meaning of law that the narratives suggest. Discourses may be developed around the argument as to whether an advanced proposition of law is 'sufficiently plausible'. To illustrate, originalism as living constitutionalism transforms amalgams of words into discourses. Orginalist discourse is at least two-fold. First, it may be structured by the allegedly reconstructed subjective intentions of the authors, or second, by the original public meaning. Tribes (2012: 21) remarks about this operativeness of interpretive devices: "This is true to both of us who believe that the Constitution always means just what it originally meant to those who wrote and ratified it – or to the entire country at the time it was enacted – and for those of us who, like me, believe that at least its elastic phrases have an evolving meaning, one that may change with changed circumstances and understandings even though the words of the text itself, and the basic principles they enact, do not change over time." Discourses are based on the "writtenness of the Constitution and its unwritten extensions" that Tribe also calls 'dimensions' (Tribe 2012: 18). Extensions of meaning are typical interpretive practices. For instance, the U.S. Supreme Court in Kyllo v. U.S. (533 U.S. 27 (2001) widens the range of 'unreasonable searches and seizures' beyond physical intrusions and includes also thermal imaging devices that can be used without entering the premises. Tribe is skeptical of post-modern approaches to texts that perceive them as generally semantically undetermined (Tribe 2012: 23). He opposes the radical indeterminacy of meaning approach as "unwelcome". Meanwhile, the choice of interpretive devices is not a matter of political expediency or of good intentions. The choice is determined by philosophical theories of meaning constitution that test the rationality of interpretive devices. In the light of such tests, originalist approaches are not simply clumsy; they are irrational as they pretend to be able to decipher meaning of speech acts from texts without the pragmatic inquiry into their contexts of use. The U.S. Supreme Court opinion Citizens United v. Federal Election Commission, decided 2010 and discussed here in another context, is an example of such a failure. The U.S. Supreme Court mentions the rationale of formerly imposed restrictions on the freedom of speech of corporations in electoral campaigns as: "recognizing a new governmental interest in preventing the corrosive and distorting effects of immense aggregation of (corporate) wealth…that have little or no correlation to the public's support for the corporation's political ideas." However, mindful of its inventive originalism the court that previously identified the risk of unrestricted corporate freedom of speech concludes: "Differential treatment of media corporations and other corporations cannot be squared with the First Amendment, and there is no support for the view that the Amendment's original meaning would permit suppressing media corporations' political speech." Thus, a socially relevant political goal cannot be obtained because the First Amendment in the view of the court's majority does not provide for restrictions in its allegedly reconstructed original sense. Yet, it is impossible to reconstruct the pragmatics of times past. It might have been that 'originally' restrictions of the kind here interesting were not implied in the constitutional provision. Meanwhile, the use is always contemporary, there is, so to say, no theoretical pragmatics. Intentions of people may be reconstructed; intentions in speech acts depend too much on circumstances. What can and often is reconstructed is the semantic change or aspects of pragmatic use. But the quality of times and the momentanous aspects of use cannot be reconstructed. The U.S. Supreme Court has itself recognized the risk to modern society through unlimited freedom of speech exercised by corporations that accumulated substantial wealth that they might spend on support for ideas detrimental to the general interest. Therefore, the use of the term 'corporate freedom of speech' includes today this new semantic and pragmatic requirement of use. And finally, originalism fails, not only because it is unproductive in modern society. Any interpretation operates under the theory of indeterminacy of meaning and no other possibility remains. There are no unambiguous provisions. Provisions that seem unambiguous to us such as the age requirement for eligibility in Art. II of the U.S. Constitution or the rule that each U.S. federal state sends two senators to the U.S. Senate are clear – and not elastic – up to the moment when a case constellation emerges that shows their semantic potentiality and that requires a legally binding decision as to their range. The indeterminacy of meaning makes legal discourses not only possible but also obligatory in law.

Legal discourses may start as small narratives. In H.L.A. Hart's *The Concept of Law* (1961: 8) we read: "At first sight it might seem that the statement that a legal system consists, in general at any rate, of *rules* could hardly be doubted or found difficult to understand. Both those who have found the key to the understanding of law in the notion of orders backed by threats, and those who have found it in its relation to morality or justice, alike speak of law as containing, if not consisting largely of, rules. Yet dissatisfaction, confusion, and uncertainty concerning this seemingly unproblematic notion underlie much of the perplexity about the nature of law. What *are* rules? What does it mean to say that a rule 'exists'? Do courts really apply rules or merely pretend to do so? Once the notion is queried, as it has been especially in the jurisprudence of this century, major divergences in opinion appear." We may call this small narrative a 'discourse about rules'. It presupposes a general understanding that the concept of 'rule' is central to any understanding of law. It does not deny that doubts might exist. Meanwhile, it accepts only certain doubts. The first is the ontological nature of a 'rule'. The second is the rule's metaphysical 'existence'. The third is sociological. It pertains to the suspicion that courts apply their own law that differs from 'rules' as they are stated in the doctrine. No doubt about the alleged centrality of the notion is argumentatively allowed in Hart's narrative. Hart's 'concept of law' grounds in 'rules' and not in language use in law; he cannot accept the necessity to speak about rules in law. It would be for example a solution to the dilemma that he mentions concerning the possibility that courts do not apply rules; that they merely pretend to do so. Yet, Hart's solution is different. Hart (1961: 8) mentions later on: "It is of course true that there are rules of many different types…" Thus, the solution to all dilemmas lies for him in the multitude of rules and not in the use of an unhelpful concept. A lot of freedom is meanwhile allowed within the framework of rules. In another small narrative that may be called 'a story about finding and making law' Hart (1961: 12) writes: "In most important cases there is always a choice. The judge has to choose between alternative meanings to be given to the words of a statute or between rival interpretations of what a precedent 'amounts to'. It is only the tradition that judges 'find' and not 'make' law that conceals this, and presents their decisions as if they were deductions smoothly made from pre-existing rules without intrusion of the judges' choice. Legal rules may have a central core of undisputed meaning, and in some cases it may be difficult to imagine a dispute as to the meaning of the rule braking out." In this narrative that is central to many questions discussed in the legal theory the rule is challenged and defended. Hart admits problems with the application of rules. The 'rule' is saved by the concept of 'undisputed meaning' that Hart could not defend in his work in spite of some examples he gave for its defense or even foundation. In law, there is no 'undisputed meaning' in terms of rules. They may temporarily exist situations where some meaning alternatives are not questioned. Yet their unquestioned existence is only a question of time. Another small narrative concerns 'fiction in law'. Hart (1961: 11) writes from the perspective of some critics of the 'rule': "All that there is, over and above the clear ascertainable facts of group behaviour and predictable reaction to deviation, are our own powerful 'feelings' of compulsion to behave in accordance with the rule and to act against those who do not. We do not recognize these feelings for what they are but imagine that there is something external, some invisible part of the fabric of the universe guiding and controlling us in these activities. We are here in the realm of fiction, which it is said the law has always been connected to. It is only because we adopt this fiction that we can talk solemnly of the government 'of laws not men'." For Hart, this criticism coined by him not without irony is of skeptical nature. It should be, so Hart, further elucidated. Hart (1961: 12) is ready to compromise and admits even: "No doubt the courts so frame their judgments as to give the impression that their decisions are the necessary consequence of predetermined rules whose meaning is fixed and clear." Meanwhile, Hart did not draw the necessary consequences from this criticism that he seems to have shared, at least to some extent. He never elucidated this fundamental critical position that he stated not without literary talent. After all, the concept of 'rule' in law had to be defended at whatever price. Despite all attempts, Hart, skeptical of discursiveness, was not able to escape it in his small narratives.

7.4.7 Importance of fundamental narratives for legal linguistics

The analysis of fundamental classical texts that preceded this remark makes plain that it makes sense to integrate law and literature into legal-linguistic research. The texts that are central to law, state and society create the semantics central to every other form of language used in law. The most striking problem with fundamental texts is the disenchanting attitude that emerges as a product of post-modern thinking which is called by many the incredulity towards meta-narratives. It seems that the more society, or its political class, strives towards establishing fundamental narratives about state and society the less the contemporary society at large cares about these texts. This is particularly visible in the relation to constitutions that are perceived by many citizens as decorative documents. What is more, citizens in many countries do not expect that those texts would be implemented in practice or provide them immediate and enforceable individual rights. Narrativity as a principle of text constitution has always been vulnerable as far as its credibility has been at stake. Many narratives, for instance poems or novels, do not raise any immediate claims to socially relevant credibility. Meanwhile, they may also claim normative validity as standards for further developments of text types such as poems or novels. This structural feature exposes socially relevant legal texts in a situation of skeptical reception of fundamental narrative texts in law to a risk of becoming sterile and empted of applicable content. As a result of this attitude, the fundamental narratives might still be used as textual standards for the development of other fundamental narratives. Yet, their credibility status will not be changed and will remain equally low as the credibility status of their sources of reference. The existence of legally binding, that is formally valid, fundamental narratives in law, which are characterized by diminished credibility as to their actual applicability, complicates the structure of law. One more dynamic component is characteristic of these texts as linguistic constructs. Fundamental narratives shape dominant discourses. The emergence of dominant discourses usually results in emergence of competing discourses that contrast or reposition their key issues and their ideological and emotional components. For instance, female law and the feminist discourse is contrasted and restructured in male law that in turn repositions the discourse in female law. This characteristic feature has been demonstrated here in the scrutiny of male and female law. Further examples of this structural feature abound in all legal cultures. The dominant discourse about the Occidentalization of law in post-Ottoman Turkey has been initiated by Ata Türk's reforms and contrasted by the undercurrent discourse of Islamic law. This undercurrent discourse then influenced the type of Occidental law practised in Turkey and in countries that aligned their law to this dominant discourse. Meanwhile, this dynamic that engenders discourses that are in contrast to dominant discourses is overall a positive feature. It enables the legal discourse to expand and reach its outer logical limits. Doubtless, the readiness to accept this structural feature may also facilitate the emergence of adventurous propositions about the content of law. Yet, this problem is inherent in the structure of law and is, as a rule, taken care of in the institutionalized processes of application of law. In these institutional processes unacceptable propositions about the content of law may be eliminated or in the worst case, they may be accepted and set new standards for its understanding. This somewhat paradoxical result shows that law as an institutional practice is not an enterprise without risk. Meanwhile, it cannot be more rational or more democratic than the society in which it is created and applied.

7.5 Literary law

Law in its most technical sense has never really attracted poets, playwrights or novelists. Explicitly legal themes are rarely an issue for writers. Never a writer committed his artistic work to law as did Lucretius who praised natural sciences in his *De rerum natura*. Historically, classical non-doctrinal texts about law such as Plato's *Laws* are in contemporary categories politics rather than law. Also Augustinus' *De Civitate Dei* develops a political vision of a Christian polis that includes yet is not limited to laws. Thomas of Aquino reflects in his *Summa Theologica* upon discursive aspects of law that are relevant to the contemporary discussion in his *Treatise on Law* (Part 1 of the Second Part of the *Summa Theologica*). After all, the *Summa Theologica* deals with received and revealed law that is pre-determined by a religious institution. Such a conception of law interests today only a minority of jurists. Overall, literature tends to focus more on topics such as power or justice that transgress or circumvent the technicality of law. Paradigmatic for the interest in power and law are Christopher Marlowe's *Tamburlane* (1587–1588) where the 'conqueror of the world' is in his right because he is a great victor and *Cambyses* (1569), attributed to Thomas Preston, that calls to 'punish the guilty'. Both works are typical of literature that tends to understand legal issues towards the background of social life and human condition. Literary works that were written within this paradigm are numerous. Richard Weisberg (1992: 117) spoke therefore in the context of Law and Literature studies of a "self-imploding canon" that would have to incorporate Dostoyevski, Flaubert, Camus, Dickens, Faulkner and many others. Indeed, Law and Literature is not thinkable without F. Dostoyevski's *Crime and Punishment* or *The Brothers Karamazov*, F. Kafka's *The Trial* or A. Camus's *L'étranger*. In positive terms, the first lesson that can be drawn from this circumstance is that dealing with law without taking account of power or justice as constitutive elements of discourses about law does not make much sense. Law deprived of its social extension is a sterile and repugnant enterprise not only for poets. Yet, some exceptions to the general lack of interest of writers towards the technicalities of law are well known and they are not less instructive than the attempt to deal with law in a broader social perspective. By way of example, John Fortescue praised in his *De Laudibus Legum Angliae* (1468–70) the English Constitution and contributed to the formation of the 'national political pride' of the English people. Thomas Elyot in his educational essay *Governour* (1531) admired the Romans' respect for law. Richard Hooker in *The Laws of Ecclesiastical Polity* (1593) argued that the Bible would not provide any strict standards for earthly legislation and that positive laws were susceptible of change. For him, existing laws that were enacted in societies must be obeyed and respected. Hooker's context of law is very broad and was expressed in an admirable language. This English-born writer, who later founded the U.S. state of Connecticut, invokes in one phrase a non-discursive aspect of the conditio humana, and he is doing it with highly elaborate linguistic means: "Now if nature should intermit her course and leave altogether, though it were but for a while, the observation of her own laws; if those principal and mother elements of the world, whereof all things in this lower world are made, should lose the qualities which now they have; if the frame of that heavenly arch erected over our heads should loosen and dissolve itself; if celestial spheres should forget their wonted motions, and by irregular volubility turn themselves any way as it might happen; if the prince of the lights of heaven, which now as a giant doth run his unwearied course, should, as it were through a languishing faintness, begin to stand and to rest himself; if the moon should wander from her beaten way, the times and seasons of the year blend themselves by disordered and confused mixture, the winds breathe out their last gasp, the clouds yield no rain, the earth be defeated of heavenly influence, the fruits of the earth pine away as children at the withered breasts of their mother no longer able to yield them relief – what would become of man himself, whom these things now do all serve?" (in: Thomas Hooker, *Of the Laws of Ecclesiastical Polity*, 1594). William Shakespeare's *The Merchant of Venice* (1596) underwent a profound scrutiny in Law and Literature studies (Weisberg 1992: 94–104). John Fletcher's comedy *The Little French Lawyer* (1619) passed largely unremarked. Thomas Hobbes' *Leviathan* (1651) remains quintessential for every theoretical speculation about law and is discussed in this book at another place. John Lock treated in his essay *Some Thoughts Concerning Education* (1693) in a sober way both the civil law and the common law. In § 186 he wrote about the usefulness of civil law studies for young men: "When he has pretty well digested Tully's *Offices* and added to it Pufendorf's *De officio hominis & civis,* it may be seasonable to set him upon Grotius's *De jure belli & pacis,* or which perhaps is the better of the two, Pufendorf's *De jure naturali & gentium*; wherein he will be instructed in the natural rights of men, and the origins and foundations of society, and the duties resulted from thence. The general part of civil law and history are studies which a gentleman should not bear touch at, but constantly dwell upon and never have done with. A virtuous and well behaved young man that is well versed in the general part of the civil law (which concerns not the chicane of private cases, but the affairs and intercourse of civilized nations in general grounded upon principles of reason), understands Latin well, and can write a good hand, one may turn loose into the world with great assurance that he will find employment and esteem everywhere." Thinking about knowledge in terms of private utility and career is typical of Locke, who unlike Hobbes, avoided all too abstract ideas and ambitious intellectual goals. He does not underestimate intellectual efforts but sets educational goals prudently; not a prince or an academic shall be educated along his guidelines but a successful landowner who will stick with common sense his life long. Locke's guidelines concerning a gentleman's education in common law in § 187 are no more ambitious: "It would be strange to suppose an English gentleman should be ignorant of the law of his country. This, whatever station he is in, is so requisite that from a justice of peace to a minister of state I know no place he can well fill without it. I do not mean the chicane or wrangling and captious part of the law; a gentleman, whose business it is to seek the true measures of right and wrong and not the arts how to avoid doing the one and secure himself in doing the other, ought to be as far from such study of the law as he can concern diligently to apply himself to that wherein he may be serviceable to his country. And to that purpose, I think the right way for a gentleman to study our law, which he does not design for his calling, is to take a view of our English constitution and government in the ancient books of the common law and some more modern writers, who out of them have given an account of this government. And having not a true idea of that, then to read our history and with it join in every king's reign the law then made. This will give an insight into the reason of our statutes, and show the true ground upon which they came to be made and what weight they ought to have." One cannot avoid the impression that for Locke law is not really a subject to be studied by a gentleman. Some general law, international law and a sketch of the constitution would apparently do. It is interesting to recall that England in Locke's time did not have any written constitution that the young gentleman could actually study. The absence of all references to books that should be studied may therefore surprise. Unless one would grasp Locke's advise in negative terms: details of law should rather be avoided in education, unless one wishes to become a jurist. Yet law seems in Locke's conception not to be suitable for a gentleman's occupation because it includes ethically doubtful matters where right and wrong are twisted as it pleases people. And, men who deal with the 'captious part of the law' cannot be gentlemen. That far Locke's main idea about legal education reconstructed for any purposes. Daniel Defoe's *The Adventures of Robinson Crusoe* (1719) had been received as a book about destiny and struggle with nature. This book is commented at another place because the Robinson myth is paradigmatic for the reflection about law. Henry Fielding's *The History of Tom Jones, a Foundling* (1749) may be mentioned here again as a novel including numerous witty remarks about law. As it was written by a judge, it concerns also the technical part of the legal discourse. Meanwhile, *Tom Jones* is clearly not a novel about law. It has been exploited here at many places because it elucidates some allegedly paradoxical aspects of the legal discourse. Among many sarcastic and ironical, yet also convincing remarks about law in Lewis Carroll's *Alice's Adventures in Wonderland* (1865) there is also a lyric that invokes the legal argumentation: "In my youth, said his father, I took to the law,/And argued each case with my wife;/And the muscular strength, which it gave to my jaw/Has lasted the test of my life." Law appears thus as a school for life, in a somehow reversed order of things. This view may also facilitate the understanding of K. Kafka's *The Trial* where life is actually conceived as a legal procedure, in contradistinction to the routinely held view where law is perceived as the formal part of life lived under constraint and life itself is imagined as the residue of freedom that is separated from law. It may be therefore surprising to find such fundamental philosophy in a booklet written primarily for children. Furthermore, Charles Dickens's *The Pickwick Papers* (1836–37), *Bleak House* (1852–53) and *Great Expectations* (1860–61) reflect some legal problems of industrialized England. The last two novels have been analyzed by Richard Weisberg (1992: 34–36) who infers from them the way in which lawyers used to communicate. Also Herman Melville's *Billy Budd, Sailor* (published 1924) has been analyzed by Weisberg (1992, 104–116). R. Weisberg draws one more lesson from legal writings: jurists' work consists in manipulating language. Weisberg (1992: 54) argues: "All great literary lawyers have mastered the art of verbal communication. Storytellers may have otherwise satirized legal jargon, but when they portray successful lawyers, they endow these figures with the ability to control situations through language." In England, John Galsworthy's writings are an illustrative example of this sort of legal-linguistic strategy. J. Galsworthy (1867–1933) was a trained lawyer who was called to the Bar and also remained active as a critic of the English legal system. He authored several literary works with explicit legal focus. The most known is the *Forsite Saga* (1906–1921) that consists of several novels which were often published as a compilation. In the interlude to the *Forsite Saga* that bears the title *Indian Summer of a Forsite,* J. Galsworthy canvasses the limits of law. One of the background figures called by him Old Jolyon, on seeing a visitor who enters upon his land and whom he cannot identify spontaneously thinks: "She's trespassing – I must have a board put on." In fact, the visitor is Irene, one of his preferred relatives, and he is glad about her unexpected visit. Old Jolyon is trapped by predominance of law in all his reflection about life. This law is of mechanistic type and all Forsites prefer it as such and practice it as a tool that protects 'property'. The Forsitian attitude inspired a legal writer, Ulf Jensen (2001: 415), to combine the constitution of the legal concept of property and the ironical treatment of it by Galsworthy in *The Man of Property*. The coinage 'man of property' was also analyzed by L. Valeika and J. Buitkiene in terms of theoretical grammar in the light of grammatical and lexical meaning (2003: 34). *The Man of Property* portrays the lawyer Soames Forsite who embraced law as an overarching worldview. For him, all principles of human action can be derived from this immutable set of rules. Thus, he claims the right to his wife as a matter of property and considers all human relations in terms of property rights. Significantly, though, *The Man of Property* refers through the choice of its motto "You will answer/the slaves are ours" to Shakespeare's *Merchant of Venice* that is another masterpiece based on hypostasized legal claims.

7.5.1 Law neglected by poets

Law like whatever social phenomenon is most strikingly characterized in an artistic expression. Some of such artistic contributions to the broader legal discourse have been mentioned here. At the same time, one has also to maintain that a monumental artistic work that would treat law in an admirative way is still missing. However, a four page long praise of justice and legality in the town of Riga can be found in Basilius Plinius' *Encomium Inclitae Civitatis Rigae Metropolis Livoniae*, printed in Leipzig in 1595. Pathetically and in the style of Renaissance humanists Plinius composed his encomium in elegiac distichs (English translation by Pēteris Cedriņš): "Without the support of reverence and the blessing of Themis,/even the foundation of our common welfare would crumble." He continues: "Truth is the spirit that quickens the soul of the city,/ guiding its citizens to temperance along the path of justice," and characterizes his native town Riga as "Impervious to corruption, beyond reach to the conqueror,/ she stands by her laws, steady in her course." Plinius develops hyperboles of this sort on several pages that finally illustrate wishful thinking rather than social reality in his native town in the 16th century. Meanwhile, the *Encomium* is not only a literary curiosity; as a document it bears witness to the expectations that people in the 16th century had cherished towards judicial institutions. As said, no Lucretius, who had devoted his artistic life to the admiration of natural sciences in his *De rerum natura,* ever existed in the realm of the legal sciences. Never a jurist came close to the achievements of Petronius, Dante, or scholars such as L. Wittgenstein. Even Descartes, who as a trained jurist described in his *Geometry* the fundamentals of analytical geometry in a way that approaches poetical language and where he reached rare clearness, high style and where he proved his commitment to the subject matter, never found any time to deal with law. No legal scholar ever has written a book on law that could compete with Descartes' exposition of analytical geometry in terms of clarity and philosophical depth. Even baldness has been praised, although ironically, in the treatise *Encomium calvitii* by Synesius of Cyrene. Yet, this is not necessarily an obstacle for the legal science. Arguably, also some other disciplines such as dentistry cannot proud themselves to possess any monumental admirative eposes about their subject, in casu the disinterested devotion of dentists to their patients. In sum, no general explicative and aesthetically appealing narrative on law that could explain law in a larger context of human culture and society has ever been handed down in history. Digressions on law are legion in literature; critical remarks are not difficult to find either. Law is present as a largely incidental reference in Robert Frost's poem *The Gift Outright.* This poem reached the status of a political symbol in America and was even read by the poet during the 1961 presidential inauguration ceremony of John F. Kennedy. Frost addresses constitutional issues of formation of the independent American state poetically: "We were withholding from our land of living,/And forthwith found salvation in surrender./Such as we were we gave ourselves outright/(The deed of gift was many deeds of war)/To the land vaguely realizing westward." Finally, possession of the land is for Frost a question of will: "This land was ours before we were the land's." In *The Gift Outright* a complex legal question is expressed in poetical arguments that may be emotionally appealing to Frost's readers. It is however reduced to some images and metaphors that make plain the incidental character of law in the poem. Finally, Frost stresses the will rather than the law in the act of taking possession of the land. The volitive element in power acquisition was seized, although rather naively, by the Hungarian poet János Arany in *The Welsh Bards* (translated into English by Watson Kirkconnel): "Edward the king, the English king,/Bestrides his tawny steed,/'For I will see if Wales,' said he,/'accepts my rule indeed." In the following verses the Welsh will not prove particularly cooperative. More than pure will seems to be necessary to gain power. Yet, laws may not be sufficient either. The American John Greenleaf Whittier (1807–1892) wrote in his *Song of the Negro Boatmen:* "The laws of changeless justice bind/Oppressor with oppressed;/And close as sin and suffering joined/We march to fate abreast." In sum, law is of marginal interest for eminent thinkers and artists. No one reads books on law because they are interesting as books that display an author's particular talent or his intellectual skills. One can read Alan Gardiner's *Egyptian Grammar* simply because it is a great book, even without any particular interest in egyptology. Politics is central to writers, law is boring or oppressive. Is it that jurists are not really committed to law?

7.5.2 Robinson's law

Reflection upon law, both theoretical and practical, is conditioned upon situations in life that may enhance or hinder it. When we ask ourselves what actually is law, we do it amid our standing in society, in an attempt to provide a well- or ill-intentioned contribution to it. When a practical legal problem has to be solved, our position in society incites us to inquire about the content of law, and this inquiry is in our society mostly motivated by the blinkered self-interest. In fact, there is no law without society and only Robinson in Daniel Defoe's *The Adventures of Robinson Crusoe* had no reason to ask himself whether he acted legally while taking possession of parts of the island where he had stranded. He did not think about legal issues because his solitary way of life did not impose any such requirements. The necessity of law re-emerged in his life when the aboriginal Friday appeared. Robinson who was used to hierarchical and patronizing behavioral patterns of his epoch overlooked this circumstance that for us is the context of emergence of law at the moment of societal constitution, i.e. when there is more than one individual actively present (cf. Berger 1963: 38). At this moment the base for our action is re-formulated, also linguistically. Social interaction is a condition of whatever social, linguistically expressed creation in law. Robinson possibly fails because he underestimates law and relies on pre-established power structures that under the circumstances of his life are ineffective. He gives the aboriginal a name, just so and without respecting his will. He also chooses a relatively unusual and ridiculous name; no Englishman of his time would accept it, should he ever happen to be in need of any. Robinson treats the other in a paternalistic way, giving him a name that would fit a foundling discovered by chance on a Friday. Robinson thinks about many issues, and his life on the island gives him occasion to reflect upon many abstract notions of ethics, yet not upon law. We apparently have no natural disposition for thinking about law outside immediate societal contexts. It seems that arts, moon and the stellar bodies impose themselves more or less automatically upon our mind as subjects of discursive or monological pastime reflections, even if we live outside society, by whatever reason. This specific feature of law, the proclivity for the immediate that it imposes as a social phenomenon, has consequences. Law unlike stars is not immediately interesting. Robinson's case illustrates this intricate problem. His societal isolation is connected with limited use of language in solitary surroundings. Numerous Robinson-films show even more impressively than does Defoe's book the fact that Robinson does not speak. In his mute world there is no law, because there is no language. Law is clearly dependent on the level of development of sociolinguistic practices. These linguistic practices are the utmost goal of the theoretical legal analysis.

E.M. Forster (2007: 163) describes in his *Aspects of a Novel*, first published in 1927, Defoe's *Robinson* as "an English book, and only the English could accepted it as adult literature: comforted by feeling that the life of adventure could be led by a man duller than themselves. No gaiety, wit or invention." Indeed, *Robinson* is a boring novel, filled with platitudes and bigoted wisdom. Meanwhile, the story of Robinson – all justified criticism notwithstanding – fascinated generations of readers, and as Forster rightly remarks, it fascinated also adults – we may add – not only the English. There is one first explanation for this general fascination, namely that banality and naivety are ubiquitous and not exclusively English privileges. Meanwhile, this explanation seems too brutal to be true. But there is one more explanation of the role the Robinson myth plays in the heads of adults since now several centuries. Robinson has, as a myth and as a metaphor for a lawless land, much to say about state, society, and law. It has more to say than Daniel Defoe might have assumed and it speaks beyond his author's head and the written text. The fascinating Robinson is outside the book; the book may be actually disregarded and only the myth explored. Karl Marx in the first volume of his *Capital* (1867) mentions Robinson Crusoe in an economical context while entering into polemic with a thesis in David Ricardo's work that he judges anachronistic. Ironically, and not without uncovered malice, he comments upon Robinson's efforts to engender private property and to mark it as such. This requires labor: "Since Robinson Crusoe's experiences are a favourite theme with political economists, let us take a look at him on his island. Moderate though he be, yet some few wants he has to satisfy, and must therefore do a little useful work of various sorts, such as making tools and furniture, taming goats, fishing, and hunting. Of his prayers and the like we take no account, since they are a source of pleasure to him, and he looks upon them as so much recreation. In spite of the variety of his work, he knows that his labour, whatever its form, is but the activity of one and the same Robinson, and consequently of nothing but different modes of human labour." Under the conditions of his life one could assume that Robinson would limit his action to work and the use of its results. Yet, this is not the case. Marx continues: "Necessity itself compels him to apportion his time accurately between his different kinds of work. Whether one kind occupies a greater space in his general activity than another depends on the difficulties, greater or less as the case may be, to be overcome in attaining the useful effect aimed at. This our friend Robinson soon learns by experience, and having rescued a watch, ledger, and pen and ink from the wreck, commences like a true-born Briton, to keep a set of books. His stock-book contains a list of the objects of utility that belong to him, of the operations necessary for their production; and lastly, of the labour time that definite quantities of those objects have, on an average cost him." Thus, Robinson has the propensity to mark objects as belonging to him, in an apparent attempt to establish property rights against all odds. His position to claim property rights is truly uncomfortable in view of his isolation that would transform whatever attempt to contest his alleged property rights to a welcome event. This is a position quintessentially different from that of Jolyon Forsite – mentioned here in another context – who marks property rights as a reaction to alleged attempts of others to claim these rights, which means in his view, to violate them (cf. 7.5). Marx in the above quoted fragment seems to forget that Robinson is half English and half German, so that his pedantry to keep books about everything may be also of German origin. As he 'creates value', he wishes to express this newly created value in a legal act that is a written document. This writ is composed in relation to an unknown reader who may be imagined as a competitor to the goods so created. Marx writes: "All the relations and the objects that form this wealth of his own creation are here so simple and clear as to be intelligible without exertion, ...and yet those relations contain all that is essential to the determination of value. Let us now transport ourselves from Robinson's island bathed in the light to the European middle ages shrouded in darkness." Marx's analysis confirms our assumption that the Robinson narrative becomes interesting only when it is transposed in interpretive acts that allow circumnavigating the intellectual limits of Defoe's literary creation. The results obtained might have evoked some interest in critical readers such as E.M. Forster, yet they were probably overlooked. Thus, a dull book proved fundamental to society and law and it is basic for coherent thinking about both. Significantly, though, *Robinson* is not the only boring book that proved fundamental for our understanding of law.

7.5.3 A stranger's law

In contrast to Defoe's Robinson Crusoe, Albert Camus's *L'étranger* (1942) is a perspicacious analysis of the legal discourse. It takes place in surroundings of an imaginary court proceeding. As so often, it lays bare the characteristic features of this discourse more persuasively than many an analysis of real court proceedings. Camus's approach to legal institutions is based on language analysis or rather its use in a literary work. Camus lets his protagonist and other actors speak about legally relevant issues in an idealistic language that is at any stage characteristic of certain controlling features of the legal language. Camus's protagonist Meursault is accused to have killed a person, is arrested and comes to stand trial. His attorney prepares his defense in a way typical of his profession in that he prepares a narrative about the facts and also about his client's biography. This defense strategy is a legal-linguistic stereotype and it is based on two main ideas: self-defense and emotional confusion or despair experienced after the death of Meursault's mother. This line of defense is not without an outlook to become successful, yet it requires Meursault's support. But Meursault wishes to be defended 'naturally' which means through referring to facts as he sees them in a language that he used to speak. Legal topoi are not interesting for him as long as they do not reflect his 'natural' feelings and speech. Equally, during the interrogation by the investigating judge, who turns out to be a fanatical Catholic, he 'naturally' exposes his atheist views that definitely do not improve his position in the pre-trial investigation. Finally, when interrogated during his trial about the cause that led to the use of the arm and to the death of a person he utters his now proverbial words 'this was because of the sun'. This statement causes laughter in the court room. Meanwhile, it is as true and sincere as is the whole narrative in a book that portrays a linguistic stranger, someone who uses language 'naturally' in circumstances where solely strictly conventional or institutionalized language use is tolerated by society. Under these circumstances Meursault's language is quintessentially inappropriate and therefore he could also be called "an inarticulate victim of the legal system" (Weisberg 1992: 22). All over the narrative, he realizes that his language irritates people as he does not match up to expectations that his interlocutors signal subliminally or even explicitly. Yet, Meursault insists on his right to express himself 'naturally'. His natural language is in fact a simple construct. At the beginning of the novel he, somehow provocatively says: "Today mother has died. Or maybe yesterday, I do not know." In the lines that follow it becomes clear that he does not express indifference about his mother's death, a statement that might estrange some readers from his person. The text makes clear that there is uncertainty in question and not indifference because it is not clear to Meursault when the telegram stating bad news has been sent. The impression of indifference towards the event is due to Meursault's speaking naturally. His natural speaking is idiosyncratic; it is based on a language use device that turns linguistic conventions upside down as is shown in the two initial phrases of the novel. Meursault finally pays with his life for a language use that disregards social conventions for the use of words and that neglects the institutional embeddedness of language used in courts. Unlike Dostoyevsky's Raskolnikov, who as a law student speaks the legal language, Meursault uncompromisingly claims a fundamental right to the use of his language as he used to speak it. In his case, "a kind of 'other' is destroyed by the law" (Weisberg 1992: 44). As no writer before him, Albert Camus has shown in *L'étranger* the outer limits of language use in social settings and the inherent limits to freedom of expression that language as a social phenomenon imposes upon individuals. The legal-linguistic practice of common legal discourse in the real world takes place towards the discursive parameters that were identified by Albert Camus in a literary work. This holds true even if this work only vaguely reflects the legal perspective upon legally relevant data in Meursault's case. In fact, by being explicitly literary and only remotely legal *L'étranger* offers a valid model of the legal language in its most theoretical perspective.

7.5.4 Expanding legal language

Rev. Martin Luther King's speech *I Have a Dream* from 1963 is one more striking example of a complex text that transforms and expands legal language within the discourse about law. The speech became very efficient as means of political action, possibly also due to the conscious amalgamation of strictly legal and other discursive means of linguistic persuasion. Typical of such discursive procedure is the combination of non-legal with legal vocabulary as in: "One hundred years later the life of the Negro is still badly crippled by the manacles of segregation and the chains of discrimination" or "Now is the time to rise from the dark and desolate valley of segregation to the sunlit path of racial justice." The speech is partly drafted in the rhetorical tradition of the 'commercial republic' introduced into the American legal discourse by the authors of *The Federalist*. King, possibly striking an ironical note, continues: "In a sense we've come to our nation's capital to cash a check. When the architects of our Republic wrote the magnificent words of the Constitution and the Declaration of Independence, they were signing a promissory note to which every American was to fall heir. This note was a promise that all men…would be guaranteed the unalienable rights of life, liberty and the pursuit of happiness. It is obvious today that America has defaulted on this promissory note insofar as her citizens of color are concerned. Instead of honoring the sacred obligation, America has given the Negro people a bad check, a check which come back marked "insufficient funds." King combines the noble goals expressed in the notion of human rights that are enshrined in the American State Papers with a reference to commercial practices that are usually, also in the American context, perceived as less noble. He draws conclusions from his extemporary comparison: "But we refuse to believe that the bank of justice is bankrupt. We refuse to believe that there are insufficient funds in the great vaults of opportunity of this nation. So we've come to cash the check, a check that will give us upon demand the riches of freedom and the security of justice." Innovative in the context of his speech are expressions such as 'legitimate discontent' or 'rightful place' that are linguistically not strictly legal, yet by the way of their coinage and context of use pretend to this status: "This sweltering summer of the Negro's legitimate discontent will not pass until there is an invigorating autumn of freedom and equality…" and "In the process of gaining our rightful place we must not be guilty of wrongful deeds." For his sources of inspiration King refers to the 'American dream': "It is a dream deeply rooted in the American dream." Alongside the generously used religious symbolism no further reference to American discursive traditions is explicitly made in the speech. It seems that the religious discourse finally imposes itself upon the juridical and forms an interpretive code for the whole 'dream' where "the glory of the Lord shall be revealed, and all flesh shall see it together." It might have been not the most helpful choice as the essence of the battle for law is not religious oppression but discrimination framed as 'racial'. Therefore, the religious skeleton of the speech seems less fitting in the argumentative context and might have also consequences beyond the political victory of the moment that King doubtlessly achieved during the March on Washington. As central as King's speech is to the universal and the U.S. history and to the history of texts relevant to the shaping of law, it also marks the borderline to universal legal argumentation where arguments seem to have limits that are imposed by universal culture.

7.5.5 Irony in literature about law

Irony seems to dominate descriptions of law and justice in books. It can compete only with emotional expressions of injustice in reference to the application of law in the literature. The English poet, John Keats, wrote 1816 a letter to Gordon Clarke where he ironically made use of the legal style: "To C-C-C-greeting, Whereas I received a Note from the worthy Gentleman Mr. Haydon, to the purport of his not being able to see us on this days Evening, for he hath an order for the Orchestra to see Timon ye Misanthropos, and begging us to excuse the same – it behoves me to make this thing known to you for a manifest Reason – So I rest your Hermit -John Keats" (rendered in: W. Jackson Bates (1966) *John Keats*, New York/Oxford University Press). Another writer, Jonathan Swift made frequent and ironical remarks on law in his *Gulliver's Travels* (1727). He stressed his distance towards law: "I assured his honour, that law was a science wherein I had not much conversed, having little more knowledge of it than what I had obtained by employing advocates, in vain, upon some injustices that had been done me, and by conversing with some others who by the same method had first lost their substance and then left their own country under the mortification of some disappointments, however, I would give him all the satisfaction I was able." This ability at stating the essence of law is expressed by Swift in a sarcastic tone: "I said that those who made profession of this science were exceedingly multiplied…Hence it came to pass that it was found needful to supply that by artifice and cunning, which could not be procured by just and honest methods; the better to bring which about, very many men among us were bred from their youth in the art of proving by words multiplied for the purpose that white was black, and black was white, according as they are paid." Finally, the writer Swift remarks the linguistic component of the whole misfortune: "It is likewise to be observed, that this society hath a peculiar cant or jargon of their own, that no other mortal can understand, and wherein all their laws are written, which they take special care to multiply; whereby they have wholly confounded the very essence of truth and falsehood, of right and wrong; so that it will take thirty years to decide whether the field, left me by my ancestors for six generations, belong to me, or to a stranger three hundred miles off." The legal language is embedded in professional practices that do not make the thing any better: "… they consult precedents, adjourn the cause, from time to time, and in ten, twenty, or thirty years come to an issue." Laurence Sterne in *Tristram Shandy* offers in chapter 15 of the first book a parody of the marriage settlement concerning the protagonist's mother. This parody, that takes several pages, is mainly based on the intricacies of the legal style. It begins as follows: "That the said Walter Shandy, merchant, in consideration of the said intended marriage to be had, and, by God's blessing, to be well and truly solemnized and consummated between the said Walter Shandy and Elizabeth Mollineux aforesaid, and divers other good and valuable causes and considerations him thereunto specially moving, – doth grant, covenant, condescend, consent, conclude, bargain, and fully agree to and with…" It is amazing that the legal language was able to survive such an acerbic and poignant irony. Also T. S. Eliot alluded ironically to law in *The Waste Land*: "Unreal City/Under the brown fog of a winter noon/Mr. Eugenides, the Smyrna merchant/Unshaven, with a pocket full of currants/C.i.f. London: documents at sight,/Asked me in demotic French/To luncheon at the Cannon Street Hotel/ Followed by a weekend at the Metropole." In later editions Eliot felt obliged to comment and explain the verse 'C.i.f. London: documents at sight'. He noted: "The currants were quoted at a price 'carriage and insurance free to London'; and the Bill of Lading etc. were to be handed to the buyer upon the payment of the sight draft." One may hope that Eliot's explanatory note was helpful to his readers who did not enjoy any legal training. Furthermore, Jean Giraudoux in *La guerre de Troie n'aura pas lieu* (1935) remarks ironically: "…que le droit est la plus puissante des écoles de l'imagination." By contrast, irony used by judges in their opinions is less cutting. Justice Coffey writes in Arnhold v. Ocean Atlantic Woodland (284 F. 3d 693 2002): "What a diff'rence a day makes…twenty-four little hours. The only issue before us is whether Ocean Atlantic materially breached the Settlement Agreement by failing to tender $ 7.267 million and close the property by January 25, 2001." The irony in such cases refers to facts rather than to law. In Dayan v. McDonald's Corp., which is more extensively discussed in 5.2.3, the court summarized the evidence provided by witnesses as follows: "Our review of the evidence admits of no doubt; the trial court properly resolved this issue in favor of McDonald's. To characterize the condition of Dayan's restaurants as being in substantial noncompliance with McDonald's QSC standards is a profound understatement. Throughout trial the various witnesses struggled to find the appropriate words to describe the ineffably unsanitary conditions observed in these restaurants…Terms describing the uncleanliness – such as "indescribable," "extremely defective sanitary conditions," "filthy, grimy, cruddy," "deplorable," "significantly unsanitary," "contaminated,"…"disgusting," "abundance of filth," "pig pens," – tell only part of the story. The accuracy of these epithets is supported by voluminous, detailed testimonial evidence which consumed many weeks of trial and thousands of pages of transcript and is also corroborated by over 1,000 photographs admitted in evidence at trial." Irony in the above court decision is well integrated into the evaluation of evidence that is as a speech act determined by formal requirements of trust. The court also uses a strategy that provides maximum security against criticism in that it incorporates ironical remarks into a formally incontestable narrative structure. Finally, irony is turned into ridicule by James Joyce in his *Finnegans Wake* where the 'constitution of the constitutionable as constitutional' turns law into a social joke that is not worth its name. Joyce's transformation marks also the final point of a possible involvement of writers with legal matters.

7.5.6 Crimes witty and funny

In the literary studies, critics tried to come to terms with the phenomenon of 'crime stories' and with the propensity of people towards reading this sort of literature. Julian Symons in his *Bloody Murder* (1972) canvassed the history of written and published 'crime stories'. Already the vocabulary that refers to them is impressive. They are called depending on their characteristic narrative features: 'detective story', 'police novel', 'crime fiction novel', 'thriller', 'detective novel', 'sensational murder story', 'comic crime story' or 'spy story'. This multitude of narrative types incited Symons (1972: 7) to speak ironically about a 'detective crime psychological analytical suspense police story'. Detective stories, so Symons, present a problem, mostly a murder or a theft, that has to be solved by an amateur or professional detective "through processes of deduction." The detection of the criminal is their finality. As Howard Haycraft (1941) put it in *Murder for Pleasure*: "The crime in a detective story is only the means to an end which is – detection." Haycraft characterized this type of literature as "non-serious, entertainment form of literature." In fact, its categorization is the least problem for the research. The most important issue in the research seems to be the elucidation of its social raisons d'être. Symons (1972: 16) remarks: "crime literature offered to its readers for a half century from 1890 onwards …a reassuring world in which those who tried to disturb the established order were always discovered and punished." Meanwhile, at the same epoch thrillers were preferred by lower social strata that had less to lose in case of social change. Subsequently, also crime stories that suggest admiration for the criminal's astuteness emerged in the process of the social evolution. This notwithstanding, readers' interest in crime prevention remains minor in the context of reception of this sort of literature. 'Lawlessness' is even tolerated in them on the part of the detective who primarily enforces the law, be it by unlawful means. Relaxation during the reading is a relevant factor for reader's choices. Such books are in terms of their reception 'enjoyed' by their readers. Their anchorage in 'law and order' ideology is rather formal and mostly reflects prevention of violent crime and omits issues of combating crime types that may be more typical of their readers, such as tax evasion or perjury. Meanwhile, 'false consciousness' can cause interest in 'law and order' literature also in readers who do not have any stakes in the permanence of established societal institutions and do not risk losses due to social disturbances. When criminal aspects central to society are introduced in a novel, it shifts its generic affiliation and becomes general literature. Examples of such processes are Friedrich Dürrenmatt's *The Catastrophe*, *The Quarry*, *The Pledge*, *The Judge and His Hangman* or his play *The Visit*, and Albert Camus's *L'étranger*. All this being said, crime stories, funny and witty or cruel as they may be, are not an unserious literary genre. Their seriousness is established by numbers of readers, among them politicians and statesmen (Symons 1972: 12), judges as well as the rest of the citizenry who are reduced by the system of social stratification to voters. The same conclusion concerns films based on criminal plots. Until now, it has not been clarified how exactly these cultural products contribute to the structure of the legal discourse. It would be however not realistic to assume that they do not have any substantial part in it.

7.5.7 Undesirable class in law

In a non-professional, yet public discourse the 'undesirable class' has a role to play that in texts is marked by abundant vocabulary related to criminality and the tone of reproach that underlies such texts. Let us analyze an excerpt. A French writer of books on British culture, G. Guibillon, after having characterized the unemployed in his *Britannia. A Description of the Home Life and Social Activities of the British People*, Paris, 1948, deals with criminals whom he portrays as an undesirable class: "There is another much less interesting category of unemployed, comprising all those who feel disinclined to any kind of work, and in any cases subsist by dishonest means. This undesirable class includes: innumerable beggars, loafers, vagrants, vagabonds; scamps and rascals of every type; many of whom do not hesitate to resort to larceny, robbery and other felonious means…, e.g. thieves, pickpockets…, burglars…, shop-lifters. Swindlers swindle (cheat) people out of their money by fraudulent schemes; forgers obtain money by forging or counterfeiting documents. Some of these malefactors go to length of murdering their unfortunate victims. The police have a vigilant eye on those jail birds, most of whom, sooner or later, are called to account by the justice of their country" (p. 150). Other texts eagerly establish differences in legal status along the divide line between the desirable and those whom those desirable do not desire. In Art. 4 of the (U.S.) Articles of Confederation doubtful elements – this time they are named paupers, vagabonds, and fugitives – are denied citizenship rights: "The better to secure and perpetuate mutual friendship and intercourse among the people of the different States in this Union, the free inhabitants of each of these States, paupers, vagabonds, and fugitives from justice excepted, shall be entitled to all the privileges and immunities of free citizens in the several States, …" Also the British writer Thomas Carlyle is remembered for his outbursts against law offenders whom he classified as "miserable distorted blockheads, ape-faces, imp-faces, angry dog faces, heavy sullen ox-faces, and the progeny of stupidity, both intellectual and moral." Also historical criminology devoted many efforts to the development of terminology relating to law offenders, for instance 'habitual criminal' who subscribes to 'moral insanity', 'congenital criminal' or 'instinctive criminal' seen in approximation to 'technically insane class', that seems to go beyond the pure epistemological interest in crime. Even today the language of criminology is not free from labelling issues. The legalistic discourse regularly refers to law, so in: "To systematically rid this town of layabouts, we must adopt a special law" (cf. Valeika/Buitkiene 2003: 105). The public discourse developed around this terminological field is close to the legal in its uncompromised linguistic distance to the criminal world that is underscored by the aloofness of the legal style. It is characterized by the relatively rich and differentiated vocabulary that classifies law offenders. Sometimes one may ask why the social class, which refuses those human elements, has such an interest in the developing of minutiously differentiating vocabulary concerning all those undesirable people. The black and white painting of the divided world is less convincing and it suggests rather a more complex structure of society where crime is not necessarily a specialty of the undesirable class. It involves also the leisure class to a non negligible degree.

7.5.8 Literary bridges in legal discourses

Some literary works such as Truman Capote's *In Cold Blood. A True Account of a Multiple Murder and its Consequences* (1965/66) play an equalizing role in the jungle of distinctive genres that constitute legal discourses. It might seem that Capote's novel that was characterized by him as 'nonfiction novel' levels down the difference between the fictional and the factual thus reflecting its author's aesthetic ambitions to create a new genre in the American literature. Capote received even the Edgar Award in 1966 for, as it was somewhat clumsily termed, 'the best fact crime book.' There is something unique about Capote's text that has been cursorily noticed by the British chronicler of the crime novel, Julian Symons, who in his *Bloody Murder* (1972: 225) spent one sole phrase on Capote: "There have been many documentary case histories that read like fiction, among them Truman Capote's *In Cold Blood*." The evasive and laconic conciseness of this phrase in a scholarly book, which explores the history of the genre reaching from the detective story to the crime novel, is revealing. Capote's novel does not harmonize with Agatha Christie's *Hercule Poirot* or Edmund Crispin's *The Moving Toyshop* and other such works that attracted most of Symons' attention as being for him prototypical in their genre. Capote's book is serious and realistic and definitely not a good pastime reading, especially not for American readers. But there is even more in it. Popular reading of the book focused on the thrilling effects that Capote handled with professionalism, although not without some unnecessary showmanship. Yet, the terrifying effect of Capote's *In Cold Blood* is not that much the thriller as such because readers know that the perpetrators will be arrested, tried, and finally hanged. Today, a more adapted reading of the novel focuses on the description of violence in the American society. Capote's main achievement is to have shown the subtly intertwined levels of societal violence in America of his time where the violent means differed from cruel persuasion (Mr Clutter dissuading his daughter from any emotional relations with a Catholic) to the brutal murder on the Clutter family and the ensuing procedures that were far from being a model of due process in a society that pretended to be better than others. Capote showed masterly the process of marginalization of the two protagonists that converts them into criminals in a society where violence is omnipresent and where everyone is attributed his own type of violence in full respect of the rules of social stratification. The religious bigots have their own 'soft' violence, the criminals their 'bloody' violence and the government avails itself of the 'legal' violence. Such a society is truly a nightmare. It seems that Capote was fully aware of his portrayal of this dangerous dimension of the societal structure that through inherent antagonisms produces violence and crime. It seems however also that no direct evidence for such far going intention is documented in the sources related to Capote's book or his other writings. Meanwhile, his zeal and alacrity during the process of writing might indicate a more ambitious enterprise than the mere writing of an innovative thriller. As a text within the legal discourse *In Cold Blood* is not less terrifying. Its base is a short account of the Kansas murder in the New York Times (November 16, 1959, p. 39) that raised Capote's attention. It reads in its entirety: "Wealthy Farmer, 3 of Family Slain. A wealthy wheat farmer, his wife, and their two young children were found shot to death today in their home. They had been killed by shotgun blasts at close range after being bound and gagged. The father, 48-year-old Herbert W. Clutter, was found in the basement with his son, Kenyon, 15. His wife Bonnie, 45, and a daughter, Nancy 15, were in their beds. There were no signs of a struggle and nothing had been stolen. The telephone lines had been cut. 'This is apparently the case of a psychopathic killer,' Sheriff Earl Robinson said. Mr. Clutter was founder of The Kansas Wheat Growers Association. In 1954, President Eisenhower appointed him to the Farm Credit Administration, but he never lived in Washington. The board represents the twelve farm credit districts in the country. Mr. Clutter served from December, 1953 until April, 1957. He declined a reappointment. He was also a local member of the Agriculture Department's Price Stabilization Board and was active with the Great Plains Wheat Growers Association. The Clutter farm and ranch cover almost 1,000 acres in one of the richest wheat areas. Mr. Clutter, his wife and daughter were clad in pajamas. The boy was wearing blue jeans and a T-shirt. The bodies were discovered by two of Nancy's classmates, Susan Kidwell and Nancy Ewalt. Sheriff Robinson said the last reported communication with Mr. Clutter took place last night about 9:30 PM, when the victim called Gerald Van Vleet, his business partner, who lives near by. Mr. Van Vleet said the conversation had concerned the farm and ranch. Two daughters were away. They are Beverly, a student at the University of Kansas, and Mrs. Donald G. Jarchow of Mount Carroll, Illinois." The newspaper note is a rather banal account of a tragical, yet not a seldom case in the American reality. It is therefore not really understandable why it attracted Capote and later also the public at large. After all, it invokes a regular crime scenery and the subsequent events such as investigation and arrest of the suspects are not particularly spectacular. In fact, the perpetrators were arrested on the strength of an inmate's denunciation that turned the investigation into a pure administrative procedure. The case as such is therefore much less interesting than regular crimes that can be elucidated only due to the detectives' professional and devoted work. The only mysterious moment that the newspaper note includes is the absence of a motive as "nothing had been stolen." Yet even this occurrence may be perceived at the initial point of criminal investigations as a relatively minor moment because motives are regularly discovered in the course of the police investigation. Were the crime a deed of a psychopath, the lack of economical or other measurable motive would be irrelevant from the criminal point of view. The newspaper note is as a genre of the legal discourse relatively uninteresting because it states standard facts of a rather typical criminal case, and it limits its range to this sterile statement. Meanwhile, in the Capote-research reference to the extraordinary circumstances of the case is as regular as is the vivid interest of the reading public. However, Capote's book describes the criminal routine rather than an extraordinary criminal case. Capote's literary talent made of a banal newspaper note and of routine criminal investigations a bestseller that is popular and largely admired even almost fifty years after its appearance. And this popularity may accurately give a thrill to his readers as it shows them the impact of the written word. The contrast in appeal between the newspaper note and the novel could not be greater; same facts can be reported differently. Many critics assumed that Capote's text challenged the borderline between fiction and fact and established a new literary genre. This seems however not to have been the case. *In Cold Blood* comes dangerously close to a rhetorically strong factual report that marks the dividing line between factual and fictional legal discourse. The literary techniques and the literary language used by Truman Capote place the book within literary genres half-way on the bridge to extra-literary reality.

7.5.9 Law profoundly misunderstood by a big boy

Literature developed around law and its institutions may easily miss the very essence of law. Charles Lamb surprises readers in his essay *The Old Benchers of the Inner Temple*, which makes part of his collection of writings called *The Essays of Elia* (1823), with a nostalgic or romantic description of the Inns of Law in London. His description is as romantic as it is naïve because it replaces law with reference to venues where it is applied. Lamb's essay is misleading on legal-linguistic terms because it is truly charming and doubtless a pleasure to read. Yet, law and pleasure are rarely associated. For his vision, Lamb appeals to Spencer who also concentrated on the place and not on the action that occurs there: "There when they came, whereas those bricky towers,/The which on Themmes brode aged back doth ride,/Where now the studious lawyers have their bowers,/There whylome wont the Templar knights to bide,/Till they decayd through pride." Romantic vision does not correspond with law, at least for Lamb and for his predecessor Spencer. Meanwhile, Lamb's essay is quoted in the literature with reference to law mainly due to the aphorism "Lawyers, I suppose, were children once." It is for instance quoted as a motto in some editions of Harper Lee's *To Kill a Mockingbird* (1960). To lawyers the aphorism may appeal as being profoundly ambiguous. The context of the phrase makes it however somehow plain: "The artificial fountains of the metropolis are, in like manner, fast vanishing. Most of them are dried up, or bricked over. Yet, where one is left, as in that little green nook behind the South Sea House, what a freshness it gives to the dreary pile! Four little winged marble boys used to play their virgin fancies, spouting out ever fresh streams from their innocent-wanton lips, in the square of Lincoln's Inn, when I was no bigger than they were figured. They are gone, and the spring choked up. The fashion, they tell me, is gone by, and these things are esteemed as childish. Why not then gratify children, by letting them stand? Lawyers, I suppose, were children once. They are awakening images to them at least. Why must everything smack of man, and mannish? Is the world all grown up? Is childhood dead? Or is there not in the bosoms of the wisest and the best some of the child's heart left, to respond to its earliest enchantments?" Lamb's romantic conception of law reduces it to a decoration. Law that is forged in the Inns does not matter; the right perception is the one of aesthetics of the venue that Lamb calls 'spot'. As long as law takes place in appealing surroundings, it is unproblematic. Sometimes, however, the reference to law as it really is spoils the romantic atmosphere. This is the case, for instance, when during a dinner, one of the old benchers, while looking out of the window, observes: "…it was a gloomy day,… Miss Blandy must be hanged by this time, I suppose." This inappropriate conduct causes "embarrassment," as one is not expected to mention reality in a decorum designed to enchant. In Lamb's words, one should not "speak unseasonably." Yet, one can apparently execute or let execute people, as long as one does not mention it too explicitly. Therefore, Lamb's charming portrayal of a venue for law is a major legal-linguistic catastrophe. One cannot misunderstand law more fully than it is the case in the *Old Benchers*. Lamb, however, proves his analytic talent in that he identifies and renders the ambiguity in legal discourses in the immediate surroundings of legal institutions. The legal world and the legal word are perfectly ambiguous and Lamb, partly unconsciously, portrays this characteristic feature of law. The *Old Benchers* are therefore an important contribution to the legal discourse.

7.6 Rendering facts in law

It might be perceived as amazing that among the many complex legal-linguistic operations also the rendering of facts gave rise to heated debates in the area of law. After all, facts are perceived as verifiable under contemporaneous theories or – when they are unverifiable -they are not facts. In law, dealing with facts would therefore be limited to providing evidence according to rules explicitly established for this purpose in the legal procedure. Indeed, the issue would not merit much attention were it not the main obstacle to all fact finding procedures in law: facts are rendered, i.e. expressed in language. The linguistic dress of facts is therefore the main challenge to all dealing with rendering facts in legal settings. Traditionally, jurists tried to avoid the linguistic pitfall and dealt with legally relevant facts as if these facts were simple material artifacts. Positivists' credos professed an almost religious commitment to facts 'as they are'. Illustrative of this intellectual curiosity is G. Guibillon's pledge in the preface to his *Britannia* quoted sporadically in this book. Guibillon writes in 1915 and renders his words unchanged in the later version of his book dating from 1948: "In this work – designed to supply strictly impersonal facts – originality has not been aimed at so much as accuracy, precision, and clearness. As for being accurate, I have made it my rule not to state a single fact unless it is based on my own experience or on the most reliable authority; on the other hand, it has been my endeavour never to sacrifice clearness to conciseness." In Guibillon's remark all ingredients used in the positivist argumentative kitchen are assembled. The first argument is ethical; rendering 'strictly impersonal facts' is for the author a matter of his honor. 'Originality', i.e. a creative element is not totally excluded because it would diminish the author's merit as an author, yet it is subordinated to the noble task of rendering facts. What follows are three elements typical also of positivist legal discourses, 'accuracy', 'precision', and 'clearness'. Guibillon distinguishes between the three elements without going into a detailed analysis. It would be, however, interesting to understand the difference that might or might not exist between these strategic hinges of the fact rendering procedure. Guibillon makes us believe that reporting facts around the narrative axis structured by 'accuracy', 'precision', and 'clearness' shows us the social reality, i.e. the world as it is, especially when this fact rendering is 'strictly impersonal'. He proposes a graph that when aptly filled with 'impersonally' collected data renders or represents social facts. Experience is for him essential in fact rendering; when it is absent 'the most reliable authority' has to be identified and referred to. The weakness of this sort of approaches to facts is rather evident. More dangerous, however, are intermediate approaches that rather conceal their positivist origins.

7.6.1 Presumption and fiction

Both are distinguished by the degree of uncertainty about underlying facts. Presumption, like the presumption of innocence, concerns a situation where the outcome is unclear but will be clarified; fiction establishes a legal status, transforms the real into legal. So can by a means of legal fiction the child born out-of-wedlock be perceived as not related with its biological father, for example in succession law as stated in the now abolished art. 1589 of the German Civil Code (Engisch 2010: 38). Fictions are central to law because they reveal the nature of this phenomenon that is its artificial, created character. Fictions are expedient; they solve a legal problem immediately. F. W. Maitland wrote in his introduction to O. Gierke's *Political Theories of the Middle Ages*: "The corporation is, and must be, the creature of the state, into its nostrils the state must breathe the breath of a fictitious life for otherwise it would be no animated body, but individualistic dust." The state acts accordingly in that it creates corporations in statutes.Through fictions law breaks with nature totally. There is no natural law. The idea of natural law had been one of the biggest illusions cherished by theoretically interested jurists.

7.6.2 Precedents and no end?

Law is materially a collection of provisions and narratives that mainly include court decisions and secondary academic and legal literature. Some legal systems such as the common law of English provenance were traditionally called 'case law' as they mostly consisted of court opinions, i.e. judgments issued by courts. Courts in the common law are bound by the 'stare decisis' doctrine to follow precedents that are opinions in like cases already issued by other courts. They may abstain from taking a precedent into consideration when it does not fit their case. They will then differentiate, i.e. analyze the precedent and explain that the existing case law that on its surface comes close to their case is in fact not applicable. Higher courts may also divert from own precedents in that they overrule them. Distinguishing and overruling are the most important legal operations within the case law. In the civil law of Continental provenance judges are not bound by a doctrine to slavishly follow precedents. Meanwhile, mostly for practical reasons, they will rarely disregard a precedent issued by a higher court in their jurisdiction. However, the number of precedents is constantly growing and the digital technology allows for stockage of complete decisions of every jurisdiction (cf. Danner 2006). Stockage of data is one thing, and their taking into consideration is another. More and more doubts come up as to the physical possibility of jurists to take notice of all precedents that may be interesting for a specific case they deal with. In the case law jurisdictions this state of affairs leads to an unpleasant question as to the fictionality of a law based on precedents. That the case law is based on precedents is visible from the material part of it, i.e. from judgments. The new question is, however, which precedents are used for shaping the court decision. Who can guarantee that all relevant precedents had been studied and taken into consideration? Case law might be nowadays in some cases based on a selection of court decisions; yet this would scarcely harmonize with the proud medieval doctrine of stare decisis. In the civil law countries the growing number of accessible case law is equally a challenge. Nowadays less and less jurists there deny that courts shape law through their decisions (cf. Fischer 2007) and that court decisions constitute law as do provisions collected and systematized in codes. The question however is which decisions actually determine the case law in the civil law countries.

7.6.3 Some precedents value more than others

Some precedents are more valuable than others and those particularly worthy are called 'landmark law'. The landmark law marks breaches in the legal doctrine, turns taken by higher courts, often against their previous decisions. The legal mindset of jurists in case law jurisdictions is largely constituted by landmark law. Every jurist there knows the landmark law cases and has an opinion on them. L. Greenhouse (2012: 77) showed how a U.S. Supreme Court opinion such as Roe v. Wade can be transformed into a symbol. Other leading cases such as Madison v. Marbury or Brown v. Board of Education share this particular semiotic property with Roe v. Wade. It can be assumed that they have been drafted with the intention to create landmark law and that they therefore linguistically reflect this specific role that they intended to play in the formation of the legal discourse.

7.6.4 How to drink coffee?

A German court decided in 2011 that a lady who ordered a cup of coffee in a drive-in and subsequently let it fall on her lap and who was harmed by the hot liquid, had no right to claim damages because she was herself responsible for the harm that occurred to her (cf. Landgericht München, 30 S 3668/11). In the U.S., the temperature of coffee seems to prevail over its taste to most clients. Therefore, coffee is prepared rather hot, and court decisions such as Liebeck v. McDonald's (cf. New Mexico District Court, Bernalillo County, 1994) are consequences of this specific taste. The plaintiff suffered third-degree burns on her legs, groin, and buttocks while taking off the lid of the coffee cup that she purchased form a car via a drive-through window of a McDonald's restaurant in Albuquerque. As she was successful with her complaint that McDonald's did not warn her about the temperature of the coffee served, she finally agreed out of court to accept damages of undisclosed amount, apparently several hundred thousand dollars. According to media reports, McDonald's reduced the temperature at which it sells coffee and placed warnings on the cups. In fact, law steers not only the language use but also actions, which may not be linguistic at all, such as coffee drinking or driving. These actions are relevant to legal linguistics because they make plain the range of social action that law, which is expressed in language, actually regulates. The range of application of legislation expressed linguistically may even concern actions that are predominantly non-linguistic. That far, the result corresponds with the structure of human communication that is only partly linguistic, and partly depends on communicative means that are akin to language. This non-linguistic communication is, as a matter of fact, remotely linguistic in the sense that it does not prohibit linguistic expression in actions, yet it does not necessitate it as a condition sine qua non of these actions.

7.6.5 Doing things in law

Lawyers also regularly have to determine whether people are doing things that correspond with conceptual preconditions of legal actions. One of the standard determinations is 'the doing of business' as an activity that in the American law satisfies the constitutional requirements of due process. As a result, only a party that is 'doing business' in a U.S. state can be sued there, provided – as so often in law – that no exception applies. B. Cardozo coined the term 'doing business in New York' that has been regularly quoted in the American judgments. In Braintech v. Kostiuk (1999) a Canadian court in British Columbia determined that a passive posting on an Internet bulletin board by a Canadian resident, which had been also accessible in Texas, was not equivalent to doing business there because it did not establish any "real and substantial connection" with this foreign state. Meanwhile, the Texas Civil Code deems a non-resident to do business in Texas if he commits a tort there. The Canadian court justified the correctional application of the Texas law in its decision with the reference to procedural efficiency. The recognition of the Texas judgment would lead to a multitude of procedures – so the court – as access to Internet sites is available everywhere. Hence, the Texas Civil Code had to be reinterpreted in the sense that the tort based on the defamation in the Internet had not been committed in Texas, but in British Columbia. British Columbia was therefore the "natural forum" for the litigation between the American and the Canadian parties. The essentialist 'natural' forum emerges in the vicinity of the equally 'natural' doing that the court perceived as a 'real' connection point. The essentialist argumentation is contrary to the concept of law as a discursive practice because 'real' and 'natural' are rather constructed entities. The evidence for this state of affairs is to be found in the argumentation of the same Canadian court that finally referred to the risk of multiplying litigations in case of the recognition that the defamation had been committed at the place where the Internet site had been consulted, it is in Texas. Texas clearly is a real place that would constitute the 'natural' venue for the law suit.

7.7 Real law and literary law

Most parts of the discourse upon law in this book concern the textuality of law in its narrative form. Incrementally, some evidence accumulated that might suggest that next to this form of law that one might call gentle or civilized law also another form of law, the real law may exist. What is worse, the real law may be the realistic form of law, the literary and polished law being only a decoration of a rather rude legal practice. The gentle law would be an epiphenomenon hidden behind the rough mass of power, the real law. The assumption of the existence of the real law that would be separated from the gentle law is not a compliment to all those who are striving towards the improvement of the quality of law. The existence of the real law would mean that all those well-intentioned people actually deal with an epiphenomenon. An epiphenomenon attracts attention yet does not make any difference; something else determines the course of things. In law, the real and not the gentle law would be decisive. Parts of the legal discourse may in fact be without importance for the course of law. Foremost, solipsistic legal science is the best candidate for the epiphenomenal function. Nocera (2012: 45) in an essay on natural sciences stresses solipsism as a danger to scientific thinking. In his view, solipsism impedes science because it "drives one to question whether an external world exists outside the mind. In many ways, the twentieth century was a century of solipsistic science." The solipsistic science was busy with itself. This does not mean that science cannot reflect upon its own structure, it should do it. In fact, many theoreticians of science, and among them most prominently M. Foucault, looked to this issue rather than to the substantial part of the scientific activity. Meanwhile, in the case of law, the focus on metascientific aspects turns the attention from relevant subject matters. For instance, medicine has to deal with real diseases; it cannot concentrate on intellectually impressive yet constructed illnesses. Science in the twenty-first century can, according to Nocera, no longer be solipsistic. This holds true also for the legal science. In a broader perspective upon law, it must expand in terms of method. According to Nocera (2012: 45) solipsistic science "was practiced for the part of society that the scientist lived in and could observe." Globalization of law introduces a correlative into this scientific method because jurists, both theoreticians and practitioners, regularly act in parts of the world in which they do not live. Another correlative is the increasing awareness of discursiveness of law among jurists that protects against falling into the pitfalls of the gentle law. Paradoxically, the reduction on the side of the gentle law would increase the gentleness of the real law. In social sciences, epiphenomenalism is not given once and for all.

Part 8: Ubiquitous Legal Argumentation

8.1 Going over bridges

Dealing with legal argumentation in a broader setting of legal discursiveness makes sense only when argumentation in legally relevant contexts is not limited to specific legal cultures. Therefore, the claim that discursiveness is the most characteristic feature of law stands and falls with its universal nature. With this leading idea in mind, the previous chapters dealt chiefly with diachronic and synchronic formations of legal discourses with the aim to ensure that all of them are deeply rooted in discursiveness. As a result, legal discursiveness emerged as the foundational principle of law notwithstanding some marginal non-linguistic action that accompanies legal discourses. Meanwhile, most analyzed materials represented Occidental law or were related to it. To gain a fuller picture of legal argumentation one has to pass the bridge that leads over the geographical limits of the Occidental law. This passage is however relatively easy and unspectacular in the area of law. In contemporary law, exoticism is rare and romantic expectations of otherness are quickly disappointed. Also comparative linguistics teaches a lesson in evaporating exoticism. For instance, the Chinese word 'liànxí' means 'an exercise' or 'to exercise' and therefore standing in isolation it may mean both (pragmatically however it means almost nothing under such circumstances of use). However, the English word 'exercise' functions exactly the same way. Not only in Chinese, but also in English verbs are nouny and nouns are verby, as pointed out by Karol Janicki. Syntax and semantics, when seen from the pragmatic perspective, also are relatively uniform in all languages, not only in English and in Chinese (cf. Gorelov 1989: 13). Wherever a linguistic phenomenon appears as special, its specialty is only a question of time. Analytical methods help overcome such apparent originality in language. There is no strange or particularly original language that could be perceived as truly different from others. Most advanced linguistic theories enable an approach to language as a uniform phenomenon that displays elements of diversity due to social and geographical factors that are external to its underlying logic. In this sense, law largely resembles language. Also laws or legal orders can be viewed in a general perspective, as laws, notwithstanding their particular legal-linguistic features. Within this framework of reference, legal linguistics deals mainly with the analysis of central linguistic operations in law. Legal argumentation is perceived there as one of the most important legal-linguistic operations (cf. Tannen 2013). The chapter below will show that the assumption of universality of legal argumentation is well founded in legal-linguistic material of non-Occidental origin. Argumentation as a linguistic operation can justly be perceived as ubiquitous. Cultures without language are unknown; languages without the use of argumentative speech acts are not believed to exist. Furthermore, one of the common characteristic features of argumentative speech is the image of universal auditorium that is perceived in the act of argumentation as the recipient of the message (Amossy 2010: 58). In the Occidental world, the discourse about law is relatively coherently structured under two paradox requirements: it must remain Eurocentric and legocentric (cf. Menski 2006). The concept of law is relatively homogenous in the Western philosophical tradition where law is seen in isolation from other social phenomena. However, even under these requirements there is some heterogeneity in the discourse. For instance, when Christian or Jewish conceptions of law (Augustinus, Thomas Aquinas, Old Testament) are included, the uniformity of the legal discourse is challenged. Therefore, the only clear notion of law in the West is the positivist; yet, it is deceiving because it reduces law to a set of pre-determined rules. As soon as the discursive perspective broadens, when, even incidentally, comparative aspects are taken into consideration, the concept of law becomes cumbersome and leads to tensions in the structure of the discourse. This problem is even more visible in comparative law studies. Legal comparatists such as W. Menski (2006) have asked many questions such as: Was there a pre-colonial African law?, Is there African law or African laws?, Are laws of ancient India or China comparable with the Occidental vision of law? Can revealed or religious law be integrated into the contemporary Western legal discourse? Meanwhile, professional legal discourse oftentimes lacks originality because it is still profoundly doctrinary. Werner Menski (2006: 495) dealt with the scholarly representations of Chinese law through the ages. He found out that the discourse about Chinese laws is structured like whatever other professional legal discourse and that it "brings out the familiar dynamic of state law, social norms and value systems throughout Chinese legal history" (Menski 2006: 494). These characteristic features of the descriptive and doctrinary professional legal discourse are also relatively broad; statements about law usually concentrate only on one of the named elements. The most advanced is in this perspective the comparative discourse as it involves the analysis of at least two legal systems. The professional legal discourse tends at best to integrate the elements named by Menski, yet in most cases it will avail itself of a more modest structure. Menski distinguishes between the eurocentric research perspective and the Chinese statements of laws that are sometimes structurally difficult to grasp for Western jurists as the reference to an opinion expressed by van der Sprenkel might suggest (cf. Menski 2006: 495). Also the sinologist Joseph Needham in his *Science and Civilization in China* (1954–2008) may have misunderstood the foundations of the Chinese law in an academic way. F. Oakley (2014: 40) mentions Needham's criticism on China's under-developed natural sciences in the nineteenth century: "For that failure he linked with their prior failure to develop a comparable concept of law imposed upon nature, and that, in turn, with the lack in the dominant Chinese intellectual traditions of any clear notion of a personal, legislating creator-God." Needham underestimates the problem that this creation of law imposed upon nature and upon society of the Western world. Classical Occidental research into the fundamentals of the Chinese civilization, as represented in Needham's writings, manifests paradigmatically a particular type of academic misunderstanding of other cultures. This misunderstanding is due mainly to the overemphasis placed upon the 'otherness' in such approaches. Therefore, stating the law also brings out the fundamental principles of the legal theory that constitute the analyzed texts. They may show that the Chinese jurists perceived the law as playing a minor role in society where it – nevertheless – plays the role of maintaining peace and order like some other mechanisms of social control (cf. Menski 2006: 495). What is more, different opinions have been expressed as to the particular elements of argumentation in different cultures. Perelman and Olbrechts-Tyteca (1970: 43) supposed differences in particular argumentative acts due to differences in culture: "chaque culture, chaque individu a sa propre conception de l'auditoire universel, et l'étude de ces variations serait fort instructive, car elle nous ferait connaître ce que les hommes ont considéré, au cours de l'histoire, comme réel, vrai et objectivement valable." In a literary context, which is related to this thought, R. Kipling, present in these notes already once and represented with a quote that have contributed to his fame yet not to the rise in respect for his views, is widely remembered for another, less offending quote: "East is East and West is West, and never the twain shall meet." This proverbial quote presupposes a borderline between East and West that geographically clearly does not exist. It is possible to walk from Lisbon to Seoul, provided particular interest in such an exercise. The alleged divide is not cultural either as all regional cultures on the Eurasian territory are interrelated. The impression of difference is a question of decorum, both in words and in other more firm artifacts. It can be easily overcome. Meanwhile, S. Huntington (1998) supposed a clash of civilizations mainly because of the very existence of differences. Others, so for instance *The Federalist* (nr. 11), grounded the difference between the continents in different political interests: "The world may politically, as well as geographically be divided into four parts, each having a distinct set of interests. Unhappily for the other three, Europe, by her arms and by her negotiations, by force and by fraud, has, in different degrees, extended her dominion over them all." However, due to the Occidental cultural tradition of text writing, it is difficult to get rid of the divide and establish a more appropriate matrix for legal-linguistic studies. Concededly, the impression of cultural differences has been questioned here only rhetorically, with the help of a digression. This digression cannot be used as a formal proof of cultural affinities. Yet it may function as an efficient tool that lowers our expectations in the research oriented towards the scrutiny of legal-linguistic operations such as the legal argumentation. This concerns particularly regions that are perceived as geographically belonging to Asia where results that would show qualitatively significant differences may be less easy to obtain than has been expected. In all paragraphs that follow this impression of affinity in argumentation will be strengthened. The scrutiny of the question as to possible differences in legal argumentation all over the world requires a step back, a review of the traditional research into this question and the dominant ideological approaches to the globalization of law.

8.1.1 Formation of the notion of law in India

The emergence of a complex concept of law in ancient India, that also comprises or that is dominated by religious and ethical facets, is related to the Hinduistic idea of dharma. Zaehner (1966: 2) relates the word 'dharma' to the Sanskrit root dhṛ that means 'to hold, have or maintain'. Dharma as a word is therefore defined by him as 'the form of things as they are and the power that keeps them as they are and not otherwise'. Like the religious beliefs and rituals in which it is rooted, dharma represents the allegedly pertaining element in society. Zaehner's analysis of the concept formation, that primarily refers to Hinduism as religion and not to Hindu legal culture, is nevertheless essential to the understanding of this concept in the light of the legal culture. Needless to stress that in ancient India no one wished to create an isolated concept of law or a legal culture distinct from religious beliefs and practices of that time. The conception of classical Hinduism as it is reconstructed by scholars (cf. O'Flaherty/Derrett 1978; Flood 1996: 8; Inden 1990) clearly manifests a holistic world view where law, ethics and religion form one and undissoluble entity. Dharma, however, cannot be reduced to a broad ethical and legal concept because it is, as mentioned, fundamentally a religious concept. In it, worldly life and its social values are contrasted with the rejection of worldly life in order to achieve salvation (Flood 1996: 13). Believers may strive for salvation and renounce life and desire prosperity at the same time. Jurists may have their problems with the inner cohesion of biographies conceived in this way. Yet, in order to understand dharma one must think it constantly in its original terms that are religious.

As to its content, dharma is revealed in the sacred writings of *Veda*. Flood (1996: 11, 52) tries to identify a translation of dharma into English and oscillates between 'religion' with incorporation of ideas such as 'truth', 'duty', 'ethics', 'law', 'natural law' or 'principle'. Thus, dharma means all of it at the same time. Practically, dharma refers to the duty of high-caste Hindus in their social position, one's caste in general, and the stage of liege one is at. Dharma provides therefore a set of behavioral rules for every member of the Hindu society. Based on the *Veda*, oral texts have been formulated between the fourth and the eighth century BCE in order to make explicit the Vedic teachings in regards of ritual and law. These texts, *Kalpa Sutras*, are perceived as auxiliary sources, the limbs of veda (vedanga). The *Gautama Dharma Sutra* stresses that the *Veda* is the source of Dharma and all other commenting texts. Thus, the sources of dharma are according to the Dharma Sutras: the revelation in the *Veda* and the tradition (smrti) i.e. remembered texts and good customs of those knowledgeable in the *Veda*. The treaties *Manu Smrti* (*Manava Dharma Sastra*) adds 'what is pleasing to oneself' that can be rendered by 'conscience' (Flood 1996: 53). The Dharma Sutras deal generally with customs and correct human conduct. The Dharma Sastras elaborate on the topics dealt with in the sutras; they are composed in verse unlike the sutras. Sastras give more explanations than the sutras, especially when the sutras remain silent. They also contain more material that can be qualified as explicitly juridical (Poggi 2012: 42). They provide rules for the householder and relate them within the broader cosmic picture. The central texts are *Manu Smrti*, (composed between the second and the third century CE), first translated into English by William Jones and published 1794, *Yajnavalkya Smrti* and *Narada*, probably 320–500 CE, as well as Medhatithi's commentary on *Manu Smrti* (cf. Derrett 1973; 1976–8). These texts contain the universal doctrine of all-encompassing law that, however, has to remain flexible in order to be adaptable to differing circumstances; they were open to a continuous process of interpretation (Flood 1996: 56). Practically, they were used by the Brahmans to decide legal problems. Decisions that were based on them are available today only in form of inscriptions (Flood 1996: 56). Classical texts of Hinduism had been composed and transferred orally. Scholars assume that regularly a period of one thousand years separates the inception of classical Vedic texts and their subsequent fixing in script. Written tradition in India, as far as law in its broader concept is concerned, begins with the inscriptions of King Ashoka's edicts all over the territory of the subcontinent (cf. Woolner 1924; Bloch 1961). These inscriptions refer to dharma in all its areas of application. Some of them are explicitly legal, such as: "It is my desire that there should be uniformity in law and uniformity in sentencing. I even go this far, to grant a three-day stay for those in prison who have been tried and sentenced to death. During this time their relatives can make appeals to have the prisoners' lives spared. If there is none to appeal on their behalf, the prisoners can give gifts in order to make merit for the next world, or observe fasts." The written form may have stabilized the ethical and legal precepts and it might have helped to coin a set of canonical texts that were used as argumentative topoi also in areas relevant to law.

From the inner perspective of Hinduism, dharma appears as fundamental to the ideology of kingship, caste and world renunciation. The last two notions have clearly a social bearing even in today's India. They are nonetheless a local problem that does not contribute to the development of legally relevant narrative structures elsewhere, and especially in East Asia. The central idea of kingdom represented by a king that ruled and judged according to cosmic order (Flood 1996: 59) dominates the dharma. The ideal of kingship is based on king's divinity (cf. Flood 1996: 68). Manu writes: "Because the king is made from particles of these lords of the gods, therefore he surpasses all living beings in brilliant energy, and, like the Sun, he burns eyes and hearts, and no one on earth is able even to look at him. Through his special power he becomes Fire and Wind; he is the Sun and the Moon, and he is (Yama) the King of Justice, he is Kubera (the Lord of wealth) and he is Varuna, and he is great Indra"(in: Manu 7.5–7, Doniger's translation, p. 128). However, the idea of dharma as the essence of the kingship ideology may be important for other regions as well because it has developed in parallel to the European ruler's ideology. For Europe, E. Kantorowicz (1957) has shown the medieval conception of a ruler perceived as a natural person with a mortal body and an immortal body upon which the idea of his sovereignty had been based. The idea of kingship as a given power is related to the passage of time in the social institutions into which one has been born. In this broader Hinduistic narrative conception of life passed as householder and renouncer the legally central idea is the one of immutable belonging to a specific social group that in the Occident is called 'caste' in accordance with the Portuguese linguistic coinage that emerged after the first contacts with Indian society. In India, this regulation of one's passage through social institutions was perceived as a religious matter (cf. Flood 1996: 13) because it was a concept of life and nothing can be more fundamental to believers than their lives. Unlike dharma's founding fathers, Occidental jurists tried to comprehend it within a process of the emergence of legal conceptions. This is, obviously, a methodologically risky undertaking, but it makes clear that dharma is concerned with legitimizing social relationships. This result also legitimizes the risk taking in the legally relevant analysis of the concept.

8.1.2 Argumentation in Bhagavad Gita

In the Hindu religious tradition of Bhagavata (i.e. followers of Bhagavan) the treatise *Bhagavad Gita* (Song of the Lord) has reached a particular popularity, also in the West, since its translation into English in 1785 by Charles Wilkins. As a religious text, it concentrates on the idea of the same, personal and supreme deity (Flood 1996: 124). The Western readers received the text largely out of the religious context and concentrated on the exotic cultural aspects and the intriguing plot of the Gita. The Bhagavad Gita is, nevertheless, also important as a source for the study of ethically and legally relevant argumentation. In this facet one may also see the universalist appeal of the text that belonged to M. Gandhi's preferred readings. The text focuses on the importance of dharma and on the maintaining of social stability and the importance of correct and responsible action while appealing to the devotion to the personal and transcendent Lord. In our context, the last thematic cluster is less important; however, one should not forget that the Gita is in essence a religious text embedded in the internal discourse of Hinduistic traditions. Aspects of the plot, which interest here, concern a dispute between Arjuna and Krishna on the eve of a battle between two tribes. Arjuna's ethical dilemma is whether it is acceptable to fight in the battle and accept the bloodshed that would include also the loss of some of his family members or to renounce and turn back to religious life. Krishna pleads against the ethical and religious ideal of non-violence and urges Arjuna to fulfill his duty as a warrior. Krishna motivates his view with a religious argument: the soul is immortal and therefore Arjuna's fighting or not fighting cannot really affect the reincarnation, a theme essential to a Hindu. Finally, Krishna convinces Arjuna to fight because the war is lawful and should be fought to uphold dharma. The text finally stresses that one's duties must be fulfilled, however with detachment from the results of the action as these belong to God and not to the humans. Through the non-attachment to action the human being will be liberated at death (Flood 1996: 126). Questioning this result, A. Sen (2005: 5) reformulates the ethical dilemma of the text as follows: "The case for doing what one sees as one's duty must be strong, but how can we be indifferent to the consequences that may follow from our doing what we take to be our just duty?" Sen's thought characterizes the most interesting structural feature of discourses that is argumentation. In this context, Werner Menski (2006: 202) points out that the Hindu law strongly emphasizes the rhetoric and practice of plurality and of relative justice and that it displays tolerance almost to the point of selfless extinction. The Hindu law remains according to Menski oftentimes purposely vague; its characteristic feature is the search for appropriateness. Its ideal is an alternative to state-made law, namely an assisted self-control and conscious subordination of personal desires to higher concerns (Menski 2006: 203). The Hindu concept of law is therefore for Menski (2006: 193) social rather than legal. Meanwhile, the textual fluidity that he testifies it (Menski 2006: 221) makes of it a candidate who could contribute argumentatively to the formation of the global law that could be imagined also as a non-state made law. Clearly, its contents that oscillate around personal law for Hindus can be generalized to a lesser degree. Meanwhile, like the Islamic law, the Hindu law is a family of laws rather than a uniform legal doctrine. Doubtless, though, the explicit argumentative note of the Hindu law is worthwhile to be studied and used for the aims of developing future alternatives to the existing law. It is also particularly valuable in the legal-linguistic context as it strengthens the main presupposition of this chapter concerning the ubiquity of legal argumentation.

8.1.3 Sino-Indian argumentative transfers

The relations between the two cultures have a scholarly background. While referring to Tan (1998), Amartya Sen (2005: 161) mentions that circa two hundred Chinese scholars spent long periods of study in India in the first millennium CE. Sen's description begins with Xuanzang and Yi Jing who brought Buddhist manuscripts to China in the seventh century CE after long studies of Sanskrit, Buddhism and also Ayurveda in India. Equally, hundreds of Indian scholars went to China for studies between the first and the seventh century CE (Sen 2005: 161). They concentrated foremost on translating Buddhist scriptures into Chinese, yet they dealt equally with Chinese science, especially with its mathematics (Sen 2005: 161). Overall, their interests rather focused on religious and related matters as the translation of Buddhist scriptures clearly dominates the picture. Yet, the scholars did not artificially limit their interests and dealt with all available knowledge in both countries as the accounts by Faxian, Xuanzand and Yi Jing demonstrate. Thus, the cultural relations were multiple. Sen (2005: 165) criticized therefore the contemporary academia for taking a reductive stance on the issue and for attributing a predominant role to religiosity in interpreting this specific cultural exchange. One may therefore claim that the Sino-Indian cultural contacts might have been generated by Chinese religious interest in Buddhism, yet they were not restricted to religious matters (Sen 2005: 166). The stage of intense exchange took an end in the eleventh century, as no further arrivals are recorded in the Chinese chronicles after 1036 (Sen 2005: 168). Apparently, the strengthening of Confucianism put an end to this cultural exchange. Additionally, Daoist opposition to Buddhism in China of that time is recorded as well. At the same time, the influence of Buddhism diminishes also in India proper (Sen 2005: 168). In secular terms, the religiously focused exchange helped formulate a more general approach to ethical issues, because both cultures had been confronted with heterogeneous and also mutually exclusive views on matters exceeding purely religious interests. (cf. Zhang 2004: 118). Amartya Sen (2005: 171) calls this phenomenon Universalist ethics.

8.1.4 Sino-centric China

The further development of the ethical and legal reasoning that has been received in China can also be reflected from the Chinese point of view. In the past, this view has been traditionally called Sino-centric. Sinologists argued that China had perceived itself in the past as a country of the middle, with its culture being central, at least, to itself. However, the Sino-centric cultural perspective evolved through the reception of Buddhism from India that challenged China's cultural insularity (Sen 2005: 170; Poggi 2012: 215–226). Already the classical author Mouzi (quoted after Sen 2005: 171) in his *Lihao lun* (Disposing of Error) questioned the Sino-centric perspective: "The north polar star is in the center of the Heaven and to the north of man" concluding from it that the land of China is not necessarily situated under the center of Heaven. Buddhism as a cultural phenomenon that emerged outside China has been a challenge to the Sino-centric conception upheld in Taoist-Confucian streamings. The first reaction against it was the attempt at limiting foreign influence upon China. Yet, it did not last and the Chinese legal history is a protocol of cultural exchanges between the Chinese legal culture and others. This attitude also influenced the reception of the Chinese law that beyond East Asia has been perceived as exotic. Even advanced researchers such as Jean Escarra were not able to avoid the stereotype of the Chinese legal exceptionalism. J. Escarra (1936: 3) used as a point of departure for his studies of the Chinese law a philosophical credo: "Dans la mesure où elle est autre chose qu'une fiction, l'opposition traditionnellement établie entre l'Orient et l'Occident ne se rencontre nulle part plus nette que dans le domaine du droit." He admits however that in many other areas of cultural research this opposition is a question of form rather than of matter. It seems that the same applies to law, especially when it is scrutinized in terms of form rather than of content. Escarra himself admits that researchers established parallels between the ancient Greek philosophy and the classical Chinese thinkers. He furthermore acknowledges the intellectual affinity between the Greek sophists and the Chinese legalists (Escarra 1936: 25). Chinese legalists distinguished strictly between the 'government by men' and the 'government by laws'. And Escarra (1936: 31) mentions this circumstance. Yet, he does not mention that Aristotle insisted on exactly the same distinction. Likewise, Th. Hobbes in the conclusions to his *Leviathan* (1651) summarizes his book as having for its aim "to set before men's eyes the mutual relation between protection and obedience; of which the condition of human nature, and the laws divine, both natural and positive, require an inviolable observation." Doubtless, also Confucius could have been held for the author of these lines as they perfectly render his philosophy of state and law. Equally, the Chinese legalists discovered the universality and the objectivity of laws as their main characteristic features (cf. Escarra 1936: 37). At this point they are again in full compliance with Occidental theoretical views upon law, as stated paradigmatically by I. Kant and G.F.W. Hegel. In fact, many academic contributions that are cited by Escarra and that aim at demystifying the law of East Asia allow the conclusion that the classical Chinese law belongs to the universal legal thinking of humankind and is definitely not a curiosity. Meanwhile, in many academic works is has been often described as such. This circumstance manifests once more the importance of discursive mechanisms in law that are responsible for the emergence of meaning also in scientific works.

8.1.5 Lexicology and lexicography

Legal-linguistic research into fundamental legal vocabulary is often possible solely with the help of dictionaries. This holds particularly true for the Chinese legal language as classical works of Chinese ethics that had a bearing upon the emergence of vocabulary, which nowadays can be termed as legal, are not very reliable. Jean Escarra (1936: 3) argued that many classical Chinese works, which became known to posterity in copies of copies, went through a process of emendations and interpolations, if not censorship. They are in this respect comparable with the *Corpus Iuris Civilis* that states the classical Roman law in an abbreviated and modified way, and is therefore all but reliable as a reference tool in the terminological research. J. Escarra (1936: 16–17) preferred therefore terminological researches based on comments in classical dictionaries such as *Shuo wen jie zi* compiled by Xu Shen ca. 100–121 CE. For instance, he demonstrated how the character 'fa' could be explored through the analysis of its composing elements. This method had been in general use in the sinological research. As an approach, however, it has been used less frequently in the research that concerns Occidental law. In the West, dictionaries were the realm of philology. Many Occidental dictionaries have been set up in the Middle Ages to enable the study of Latin and Greek, occasionally also Hebrew. Later on, monolingual dictionaries emerged as inventories of lexical units in a language. Norming of language use has been sometimes less and sometimes more essential in this work. In the Chinese language, the corresponding terms to lexicon or dictionary are *cídiǎn* and *zìdiǎn*, i.e. word or sign norms. Apparently, the original intention behind the lexicographic project has been to set a norm for the specific use of signs and sign combinations into words. The Chinese concept *diǎn* stresses the norming of script use rather than the inventory of signs. The first Chinese dictionary has been *Er Ya* (The Approached Perfection) dating from the second century BCE. As mentioned, the second dictionary, *Shuo wen jie zi* (Explanation of pictograms and characters) was finalized between 100 and 121 by Xu Shen. It introduced a systematic classification of ideograms and the phonetical description of words. Due to the specific approach to law as integral part of ethics or religion in the East Asian tradition no specific legal dictionary has apparently been set up there. Today, work on the Chinese legal vocabulary with the help of commented dictionaries is particularly rewarding because they, unlike most of their Western counterparts, include explicit data about the emergence of characters and lexical units.

8.2 Chinese law in comparative research

Comparative research into the argumentative structures of the Chinese law is exposed to some particularities which seem to be worth mentioning. First of all, the Chinese law can be perceived within its long tradition of internal development. Second, it can be construed in the comparative perspective, mainly due to the influence of the Occidental legal thinking and the Occidental legislation which was crucial to the development of the modern Chinese law. Furthermore, there remains the aspect of socialist law in it (cf. David 1978: 536). Practical interest in the Chinese law is booming in recent times outside China proper. Yet, comparative research into the Chinese law requires that some theoretical questions be addressed as well. The first problem we are confronted with is the knowledge of the Chinese law abroad. This knowledge of the Chinese law as a foreign law is useful when it reaches beyond disparate provisions and embraces the law as an entirety. However, this systematic knowledge of the contemporary Chinese law seems not to be widespread in the Western world. Systematic works on the Chinese law are rare even in China proper and more efforts would be welcome to set up not only databases with the legislation in force but also a legal theory and an analysis of the doctrine and its application in courts. Moreover, only few selected judicial decisions are published in publicly accessible media (Wang 2007: 396). Knowledge about legal precedents is sporadic outside China. This fact does not strengthen the legal certainty in international economical contacts. Doubtless, establishing legal databases is a welcome initiative. However, the knowledge of law (which may be the beginning of a closer emotional relation towards this subject which has been perceived by many as rather sterile) is not limited to the legal provisions. Legal theory and legal doctrine make an essential part of it and should be taken care of (cf. May 1980). It may be added that the emotional character of legal knowledge is not a Chinese invention. Also the classical Roman law had been an enterprise of knowledge of law and it built upon the personal identification of jurists with this law.

8.2.1 Traditional Chinese Law

Chinese scholarship has a long history that is marked by the continuities of cultural tradition and discontinuities that were caused by foreign influence. Foreign influence upon the Chinese scholarship came always from the West; in the remote past it came from its Western neighbor India and much later from the countries of the political and industrialized European West. Continuities and discontinuities in the development of the legal thinking in China can therefore be seen from different perspectives that usually oscillate between perfect isolation of cultural elements that are identified as truly Chinese and perfect interculturalism that questions the possibility to isolate socio-cultural phenomena. Ancient Chinese law is viewed mostly in the perspective of the Confucian doctrine (Fromont 2005: 9). There, ethical aspects of maintaining social harmony were perceived as fundamental to the relations between the state and its citizens, i.e. the Emperor and its subjects as well as between the subjects themselves. The Confucian doctrine, which underlined the necessity to maintain the universal harmony and the necessity to avoid any excessive action and to accept authorities, be it in the family or in higher societal organizations such as the state, has been definitely dominant in the traditional Chinese law and in the legal thinking. It provided conceptual and argumentative patterns in the process where the Chinese law has been formed. However, also other, explicitly legal doctrines existed there as well. Legalism as an explicitly legal doctrine in respect of the Confucian thought, which is in essence ethical, has been considered last among the classical schools of Chinese legal thought (Upham 1990: 83). It has had nevertheless a big influence on the political life of its time (Upham, id.). It can be therefore posited that the tradition of explicit legal thinking has much longer roots in the Chinese culture than sometimes assumed. The mere existence of the legalistic reasoning contradicts the occasionally expressed assumption that the traditional Chinese philosophical reasoning did not distinguish between moral and strictly legal rules and that it construed them as one ideal entity. At least in the legalistic writings, these types of rules were apparently clearly apprehended as different. Another thing is the reaction which the Chinese thinkers of the past developed towards purely legal arguments and rules. These arguments and rules had not been particularly cherished in the past and they may even today not be popular among parts of the population. They have nevertheless – like other rites and rules – accompanied the development of the Chinese society and shaped the structure of the socio-political discourse there. The tradition of legal argumentation is therefore present in the logic of traditional Chinese reasoning as are present there the textual forms typical of law, such as codes.

The traditional Chinese law had been codified in several codes, the most famous being the code of the Tang dynasty (624) and the Ming dynasty (1397). The number of legal codes is impressive in the Chinese history. Their number can be used as one more argument that strengthens the assumption expressed here that issues of legal reasoning, legal argumentation and legal interpretation played always an important role in China and in its law. Insofar, the regularly stressed difference between the Western legal tradition and China in some writings on Chinese law seems smaller than previously believed. It is definitely true that many of the historical codes include primarily penal or administrative regulations and that they may therefore be perceived as different from traditional legal codes of the West. Yet, the Western legal heritage is in fact not much different. Justinian's *Corpus Iuris* includes a voluminous work called *Constitutiones* that reflects the Roman public law. It is much less interesting for contemporary researchers and therefore it is rarely mentioned in the research into Roman law that is dominated by issues related to the private law, its fundamental notions, and its structure. The focus on private law in the research into Roman law distorts the perspective on the Roman codifications that included many other texts than those regularly analyzed by specialists and taught to students. Meanwhile, some concepts of the traditional Chinese law such as the eternal rent ('yong dian quan'), which made part of the old private law, bear witness to the elderly layers of the Chinese law in the proper sense of the word (Sun 2007: 647). They also prove the skills in conceptualization that equal those of the ancient Romans. Remnants of the traditional legal thinking could be probably found in the legal argumentation which is used in the judicial decisions. Taiwan has preserved at least partly the law of the First Chinese Republic (Fromont 2005: 167). Systematic research into this aspect of the Chinese legal culture seems not to exist and contemporary research concentrates rather on isolated text samples (Liao 2012: 404–405). The propensity towards the use of quantitative methods in text analysis further strengthens the trend away from epistemologically relevant conceptual analysis. The textuality and intertextuality of traditional Chinese law in its aspects of conceptual continuity and discontinuity is worth further research. It can be however boldly assumed that more thorough results of this research would not fundamentally question the main thesis of this chapter that posits the ubiquitous character of legal-linguistic operations (cf. Liu 2005; Zhou et al. 2007; Cao 2008; Han 2012).

8.2.2 What is Chinese Law?

This fundamental question is necessary in the context of this chapter because the object of the legal-linguistic comparison must be clearly defined. The Chinese law is definitely the law of the Peoples Republic of China. What role do however Hong Kong, Macao or Taiwan laws play in it? One would have to assume that laws of these entities are well known in China proper, at least by specialists. These laws are different from the mainland Chinese law, but are they less Chinese because of it? Do they influence the legal thinking in China proper? And what shall be done with legal systems influenced, legally or linguistically, by the traditional and modern Chinese law? Traditionally, East Asian countries which developed under the influence of the Confucian philosophy such as Japan, Korea or Vietnam can be counted as belonging to the traditional sphere of Chinese intellectual influence. Furthermore, countries which use predominantly other legal techniques than mainland China like, e.g. Singapore, may also be viewed in this perspective because of linguistic and cultural Chinese influence. Researchers stress also the linguistic particularities in the Chinese language used in mainland China, Taiwan and Hong Kong (cf. Gortych-Michalak/Grzybek 2013: 24). The legislation in force in the People's Republic of China perceives the laws of Hong Kong, Macao and Taiwan as a problem of interlocal law, hence in the perspective of the conflict of laws (Wang 2007: 366). Interestingly, the interlocal conflict cases dominate the judicial decisions on the conflict of law also statistically (Wang ib.). Other than procedural perspectives are apparently not considered in the judicial decisions. Meanwhile, the comparative view upon the region would be more revealing. East Asian legal systems are perceived regularly as closely related to each other. They are even occasionally presented in one volume (cf. Upham

1990). In the narrower perspective, the contemporary development is sometimes described in terms of direct German or American influence without taking into consideration the broader intellectual context (cf. Igarashi 1990). However, the origins of the Japanese legal thinking are different from the Chinese tradition dominated by Confucianism (Kość 2001). The Japanese rules of social conduct emerged in a rural society dominated by the idea of property to land (David 1978: 549). Other aspects were apparently characterized as social or ethical rather than legal and they were solved according to the power balance in society (Fromont 2005: 9). The intellectual unity of East Asian law comes about only due to the spread of the Confucian doctrine in this region. Legal-linguistic operations are the vehicle that enables such interrelated law to emerge and to function.

8.2.3 Reception of foreign law in China

The possibility of transfers of legal regulation and legal concepts from the West is one more indicator of the common discursive structure of law in East and West. No transplants from Occidental law could be efficiently incorporated into it, were the Chinese law a law of different argumentative structure. In fact, the modern Chinese private law of the PRCh is a received law. The influence of the civil law of German and French origin is preponderant there. The decision making process regarding the loans from the German law has been described in all detail in comparative research (Sun 2007). The decision making process that led to the incorporation of foreign law has been apparently influenced by political factors which work to the detriment of the reception of the Western law from Japan, although the received Japanese law would practically be able to contribute more or less the same results than the German law. Yet, preference has been given to direct Western loans. Nevertheless, the likelihood that provisions of the Japanese private law are frequent in the Chinese legislative acts is also worth a serious consideration (Fromont 2005: 173). The comparative legal linguistics could use its methods in order to elucidate such intricacies of emergence of legal systems. J. Escarra (1936) underscored even the necessity to establish a 'legal sinology' in his analysis of the Chinese law in the process of legal Occidentalization. In the preface to his above mentioned work he wrote: "Je souhaite aussi que ces études, élémentaires et dépourvues de caractère scientifique, suggèrent à quelques chercheurs l'idée de créer une véritable 'sinologie juridique'." Escarra combined in his approach to the Chinese law the conceptual frameworks developed by M. Granet (1934) in sinology and by F. Gény in legal theory. Today, numerous are works devoted to the Chinese law in comparative perspective. It seems however that a systematic 'legal sinology' as an established branch of knowledge that scrutinizes the development of the Chinese legal language still does not exist. In this sense, the situation in China does not differ much from the rest of the world. One must however acknowledge the existence of works such as D. Cao's (2004) *Chinese Law. A Language Perspective* that tried to establish a conceptual framework for a 'true and comprehensive' science of the Chinese legal language.

8.2.4 Legal terminology in the reception process

Comparative law studies begin sometimes with the process of emerging of the legal terminology. David (1978: 554) reports that during the Meiji era in Japan (beginning 1868) Japanese terminology has been invented in the process of translation of the European codes into the Japanese language. Terms such as 'kenri' for subjective right and 'gimu' for legal obligation date from this period. However, less interest had been brought towards the existing legal Japanese terminology before the time of the Occidentalization of Japan's legislation (Horie 2010a: 82). An analogous process concerns the Chinese law. Terms such as 'international law' had to be coined to render the concepts hitherto unknown in the traditional law (Zhang 2002: 3). Reception is however often connected with terminological creation. Junwu Pan (2011: 241) mentions that in the Chinese texts on international law the term 'international practice' is used in contexts where regularly 'international custom' appears in other languages. Pan (2011: 241) argues that it has not been yet elucidated whether this specific Chinese terminological coinage introduces a semantically relevant difference into the Chinese texts that deal with international law. Notwithstanding all received law and conceptual implants, the mainland Chinese legislation is a creative institution. The elements of the international contract provided for in the Art. 12 of the Unified Contract Law (UCL) are a good example of this development. They show that the received legal implants are perceived nowadays as a natural element of the modern Chinese society. Therefore, they also can be modified and adapted to the needs of that society.

8.2.5 Application of law

Application of legal provisions is another area in which the specific features of legal culture are most salient. Received legislation may follow in its linguistic form closely the patterns of the original legal acts. Decisive for the legal system is however the way in which those legal acts, which may be even identical with the received versions, are applied in judicial decisions. The same problem is known in the international law. There, the same wording of provisions that were ratified worldwide leads to different interpretive variations and impedes the uniform application of international norms (cf. Mattila 2002b). For instance, the PR of China ratified the United Nations Convention on the International Sale of Goods (CISG). In its application it broadly follows the principle of uniform application as proposed by the convention itself. However, a specific feature of the law of the Peoples Republic of China are the judicial interpretations by the Supreme People's Court which come close to the setting of new positive statutory law (Wang 2007: 364). They may modify the standing international practice. In fact, application of law is, as a cultural phenomenon, partly also extra-legal. It is rooted in social practices of the exercise of power that are often only marginally legal and mostly hard social facts. Elements of legal culture such as solving legal problems 'on the phone' in informal contacts between judges, public prosecutors and political nomenklatura are illustrative of this area where language is used, yet power is exercised. Contemporary China is not a special case in the interface of linguistic and extralinguistic elements that enable law to be applied in social practices. Yet, its example shows the methodological challenges in dealing with language use in legal-linguistic operations.

8.2.6 Intertextuality of Chinese law

It seems appropriate to point out that the comparative legal-linguistic view upon the Chinese law is nowadays best situated in a broader perspective which includes the cultural, the linguistic and the intellectual-doctrinal contexts. Towards this contextual background the Chinese law as a particularly heterogeneous legal system would become better understandable without involving stiff systematic schemes of traditional comparison. Chinese law as the law of the Chinese cultural landscape is broader than its traditional conceptual shape and its received Romano-Germanic elements. Particularly, during the first Republic (1911–1949) the law and the judicial institutions have been formally occidentalized. Five codes covering the traditional legal areas of the Western law have been promulgated between 1927 and 1937 (Fromont 2005: 11). This modern law did not affect the rural China where traditional law continued to govern all relations which would be perceived in the West as legal. The Communist Revolution of 1949 brought doctrinal thought of Soviet origin. This aspect of the law which may be called socialist law manifests itself in several ways. First, the interpretation of legal notions takes place in it towards the background of the Marxist ideology of a communist state. Second, the Government intervenes in social interaction by means of decrees and other administrative decisions which lack the form of statutes and are therefore less accessible to the persons concerned or interested. Third, the Government controls the legal education and the recruitment of judicial personnel. The future will show how stable the elements of the socialist law will be in the evolving socio-political reality of mainland China. Meanwhile, the ideological elements are propelled by legal-linguistic operations that are change-resistant. The intertextuality of the Chinese law is rooted in this quality of discursive social practices.

8.3 Attitudes towards law in Japan

In comparative law, views about Japanese attitudes towards law were explored from the Occidental perspective. They crystallized into a discourse about this subject matter. The dominating idea of this discourse is that many Japanese still nurture the attitude that confrontation in the public sphere should be avoided. It is mentioned that: compared with the U.S., Japan accounts proportionally for about one-fiftieth of the U.S. lawyers; class action or contingency fees are not allowed in Japan; plaintiffs pay to their lawyers a front fee that is relatively high and they pay a non-refundable filing fee to the court; monetary damages are low in Japanese courts; most cases, especially in the business law, are settled in specific procedures. It is however questionable whether the addressed topics correspond with the Japanese discourse about law. When the discourse about law is approached from the legal-linguistic perspective, as is the case in numerous works by M.H. Okawara (1998, 2006, 2012), K. Anderson and Y. Okuda (2007), J. Horie (2010a, 2010b) and many others, it appears that aspects of the content of law and litigation are less central than assumed in numerous publications on Japanese law. Interest towards legal translation, legal narrativity, plain language and emergence of legal terminology (cf. Working Group, 2006) is documented in many research articles and monographs. Issues of discursiveness and legal argumentation play therefore an eminent role in the Japanese law that also in this respect does not differ from many legal traditions that are mentioned in this book.

8.3.1 Ideal of kingdom and Japanese imperial rhetoric

The influence of legal reasoning under the concept of dharma is present also in the traditional Japanese legal thinking. Dharma is a central part of the ideology of Hinduism; it also has its own rhetoric (Flood 1996: 74). An aspect of dharma is the kingdom ideology that appears in a theological dress. The king is the intermediary between the heaven that represents the eternal cosmic law and the people that he rules over of God's grace. If the king acts according to dharma, his kingdom prospers; if he violates dharma principles, his people will suffer (Flood 1996: 70). Overall, it seems that when the aspect of theological revelation in the justification of the idea of kingdom becomes stronger, then also the rhetorical means used to transfer this idea are amplified. Japanese rhetoric in constitutional provisions relating to the role of the emperor shows this interdependence. With the reduction of powers as illustrated by the last example in the paragraph below (cf. 8.3.2) also the rhetorical load of the provision becomes profane, the sacred language loses its role (Galdia 2009: 341). This linguistic transformation marks the central moment in the development of the Japanese legal language. It is closely related to the Occidentalization of Japan's law and to the reception of Occidental textual patterns in the area of law.

8.3.2 Legal-linguistic changes in Japan's Constitutions

The Occidentalization of the Japanese legal language and its law is manifest in text samples from the different Constitutions of Japan which are in terms of language and legal thought typical of the different time periods in which they emerged. They show the relevance of the idea of kingdom in relation to the Japanese Emperor and the legal-linguistic evolution that took place in the course of the past century. The sample of the Constitution dating from 1889 states (cited after Upham 1990: 304): "Art. I The Empire of Japan shall be reigned over and governed by a line of Emperors unbroken for ages eternal…Art. III The Emperor is sacred and inviolable." The text of the Constitution in force from 1908 provides: "A. The prerogatives of the monarch 1.The Ta Ch'ing Emperor will rule supreme over the Ta Ch'ing Empire for one thousand generations in succession and be honored forever." Meanwhile the Constitution of 1947 laconically states: "Art. 1 The Emperor shall be the symbol of the State and of the unity of the people, deriving his position from the will of the people with whom resides sovereign power. Art. 3 The advice and approval of the cabinet shall be required for all acts of the Emperor in matters of State, and the Cabinet shall be responsible therefore. Art. 4 The Emperor shall perform only such acts in matters of State as are provided for in this Constitution and he shall not have powers related to government." The above formulations state also the history of Japanese constitutional law. Legal linguistics as systematic study of language use in law appears in the light of these samples as a rather late reflection of professional skills that were mastered since centuries by legal drafters. Recently, many details of drafting of the Japanese Constitution currently in force were made public. It is known, for instance, that Art. 24 has been drafted by the U.S. interpreter of the team of drafters, Beate Sirota Gordon. It has been opposed by the Japanese negotiators, yet was finally enacted. Art. 24 states: "Marriage shall be based only on the mutual consent of both sexes and it shall be maintained through mutual co-operation with the equal rights of husband and wife as a basis. With regard to choice of spouse, property rights, inheritance, choice of domicile, divorce and other matters pertaining to marriage and the family, laws shall be enacted from the standpoint of individual dignity and the essential equality of sexes."

8.3.3 Conflict resolution mechanisms in Japan

Japan is known for culture-specific alternative conflict resolution mechanisms called 'wakai', 'chusai', and 'chotei'. Wakai is sometimes described in the comparative legal literature as the settlement of a conflict by compromise, chusai as arbitration and chotei as mediation. Wakai involves a judge who, after having discussed the matter with the parties, will prepare the proposal of a compromise solution. Chusai is a technique of dispute resolution by arbitrators appointed by the parties. This technique is however less popular because the imposition of a settlement by a third party cannot restore the harmony between the parties. The most popular method is chotei where the court appoints a mediation committee that mediates between the parties and prepares a report that is registered in the court and acquires the force of a judgment. The mediator usually meets the parties in succession, no face-to-face negotiations take place in order to avoid that negative emotions would come up and be uttered. The traditional Japanese society is rooted in a vertical social hierarchy, especially based on age. In general, young people are expected to respect the older people and value their opinions. A further element of traditional Japanese culture is the emphasis made on 'harmonious relationships' in the society where dissonance should be avoided and peace kept. In terms of concluding contracts, these principles mean that the contract negotiation is a process of building a trusting relationship rather than a pure formation of contractual clauses, which are perceived as minor legal formalities. The mentality formed by these traditional principles of the Japanese culture leads to preference for alternative dispute resolution methods rather than to court litigation that introduces a win/lose situation which would destroy the harmonious relationship between the parties. Today, the process of Occidentalization of Japanese legal culture is advancing and less and less use is made of the traditional methods of avoiding litigation, especially in international settings, where also chusai is used. Therefore, arguments used in regular court procedures become equally relevant as arguments used in less formal conflict resolution mechanisms.

8.3.4 Argumentation in Japanese court decisions

Also Japanese court decisions reflect the universal structure of legal argumentative reasoning. Some translations into English may suggest a scarce use of traditional rhetoric and a tendency towards fact-oriented prose. The court opinion

Min v. Mitsui Bussan K.K. (Tokyo High Court 17 March 1987) can be used as a text sample. The analysis that follows is methodologically risky as it is based upon the translation and not upon the original: "Beginning in August 1973, Plaintiff Min, a Malaysian politician and businessman, conducted negotiations with Mitsui Bussan K.K., a Japanese general trading company (Mitsui), concerning a joint venture project to log and develop a forested area in Indonesia (the Project). Min and the employees of the Lumber Division of Mitsui had several conferences in both Tokyo and Singapore in the course of the negotiations, more than half of the conferences being held in Tokyo. In January 1974, Min and the manager of the Lumber Division reached the following basic understanding at a conference held in Tokyo:

1. For the price of U.S. $ 4,000,000 Mitsui shall purchase from Min 50% of the shares of a certain Brunei corporation which holds a majority of the shares in a certain Indonesian corporation that has lumbering rights in Indonesia.
2. Mitsui shall pay the share purchase price to Min on April 30, 1974.
3. By the end of February 1974, Mitsui and Min shall enter into a basic contract covering the matters necessary for the Project."

Thus far, the wording of the court opinion corresponds perfectly with standards used in Occidental opinions for rendering facts relevant to the legal analysis. The court opinion continues: "After this conference, the Manager sent Min a letter dated January 29, 1974 (the Letter) to confirm these understandings, and on February 6, 1974, Min responded with his own letter, which stated that he accepted the offer made in the Letter. From February 21 to February 27, 1974, Min and the employees in charge at Mitsui held a conference in Singapore at which they completed a draft of the contract between Min and Mitsui for the sale and purchase of the shares in the Brunei corporation and a draft of a basic contract between Min and Mitsui concerning the Project. Min and the employees of Mitsui also agreed that Min should rent an office in Singapore to proceed with the project, and in April 1974 Min began to rent such an office." Also this part reveals textual features characteristic of court opinions all over the world. The court continues: "By the April 30, 1974 deadline, however, Mitsui never signed the draft contracts nor paid to Min the U.S. $ 4,000,000 purchase price for the shares in the Brunei corporation. Instead, Mitsui continued negotiations with Min. In July 1974, Mitsui proposed to Min a loan of U.S. $ 4,000,000, rather than proceeding with the purchase with the Brunei corporation. Mitsui suspended the offer of the loan when Min was arrested and detained by Malaysian authorities in October 1974 under the Public Security Maintenance Regulations (an arrest that Min claims was politically motivated). After Min's arrest, Mitsui maintained contact with representatives of Min, and in July 1975 Mitsui agreed with them that, after Min's release, it would make its best efforts to execute the loan it had suspended. Min was released on January 31, 1976, and requested Mitsui to proceed with the suspended loan. Mitsui refused and in May 1976 told Min that it had no legal obligation to him." In this part the court refers to facts provided by Min that apparently were not verifiable for the court or were contested by the opponent by saying: '…Min claims…' Also this is a technique typically used in Occidental courts. The decision continues: "Min brought suit against Mitsui, raising both contract and tort claims. The District Court rejected Min's contract claims, stating that…the letter should not be regarded as an offer to enter into the alleged Share Purchase Contract. With respect to Min's tort claims, however, the court held in favor of Min, finding that Mitsui was liable to Min for Min's expenses in preparation for the Project and for the attorney's fees. Mitsui appealed the finding of its tort liability." Also this paragraph is rather typical, yet it displays particular politeness and distance from the reported opinions of lower courts. Subsequently, the court begins to present its own view of the situation: "In light of the negotiations towards the conclusion of an agreement, Min came to have a right of expectation of, or interest in, the conclusion of the agreement. Mitsui was thus obligated under the principle of good faith to make efforts to enter into the agreement in order not to infringe upon Min's right or interest. Nonetheless, Mitsui failed to perform its duty and, despite its repeated assurances that it would enter into and perform the agreement, it later reversed its course and concluded that entering into the agreement would be impossible, thereby injuring the said interest of Min." In this paragraph there is no distance to the course of described action. The court seems to speak straight away. And it continues: "In the modern world, the principles of good faith and trust govern not only contractual relationships, but also relationships under private law, and such principles thus apply not only after conclusion of an agreement but also at the stage of preparations toward conclusion of an agreement. In the event that preparation between two parties progresses toward conclusion of an agreement and the first party comes to expect that the agreement will surely be concluded, the second party becomes obligated under the principles of good faith and trust to try to conclude the agreement, in order not to injure the expectation of the first party. Therefore, if the second party, in violation of its obligation, concludes that the agreement is undesirable, it is liable for damages incurred by the first party as the result of its illegal acts." In this paragraph the reference to the 'modern world' is particularly striking. The court has apparently in mind the civil law doctrine of culpa in contrahendo that it will also apply in this case. The court continues: "In this case, we find that the Letter sent by Mitsui and Min's response, to which Mitsui offered no subsequent objection, caused Min to expect that the agreement would be concluded. Mitsui, therefore, should be considered to have become obligated from that time to make good faith efforts, under the principles of good faith and trust, to conclude the agreement. Absent special circumstances that justified suspension of efforts, under the principles of good faith and trust, to conclude the agreement, Mitsui should not have been allowed unilaterally and unconditionally to suspend performance of its obligations. Mitsui should thus be found liable to Min for any damages incurred by Min due to such suspension." The court calls the doctrine of culpa in contrahendo the 'principle of good faith and trust' (provided that the Japanese original also says this more or less literally). The final decision is formulated in a courteous way. Mitsui, which loses the case: '...should not have been allowed...', 'Mitsui should thus be found liable..." The difference between an Occidental and the Japanese decision is thus found in the way how the court formulates its verdict. Truly, one can say in different ways that one of the parties has acted wrongly and that it has to bear consequences of its unlawful action. The Japanese court finds the most polite way to communicate this unpleasant result to the parties.

8.3.5 Samples of Japanese court decisions

Some other samples of Japanese court decisions may indicate differences in the legal argumentation there. However, as long as systematic research into this issue is missing it is difficult to generalize this first impression. The impression of a cultural difference may also result from the English translations, here quoted after Upham (1990: 625). In a divorce case Inoue v. Inoue decided by Japan's Supreme Court Third Petty Bench on Feb. 19, 1952 / 6 Minshuu 110, the court states in the part described as 'Reasons': "As found by the High Court, the Appellee's conduct in pouring water on the Appellant and beating him with a broomstick is truly vulgar and improper. It is obvious however, that the reason for this behavior was the Appellant's sexual relation with S. resulting in her pregnancy." The following sample includes a reflection of ethical nature: "The Appellant reaped what he sowed, as it were the Appellee's behavior as found by the High Court was all excusable and does not constitute a conduct so cruel and humiliating that cohabitation is intolerable as set forth in Art. 813 of the former Civil Code." The precision in fact description is not free from a comical effect, but such formulations can be found all over the world where judges may sometimes underestimate the impression of detailed description of facts upon the readers. In another case concerning the so-called Minamata-disease (mercury poisoning caused by eating fish which was contaminated by effluents from a chemical plant) and state agencies' responsibility for injuries, the court argumentation again seems to differ to a degree from Western patterns: "Re. Kawamoto Teruo (Tokyo High Court 1977, June 14): Whether or not this case constitutes an abuse of the right of public prosecution and should therefore be dismissed will be discussed below." This is a succinct formulation that renders the legal topic relevant to the court opinion. The court continues: "What is distinctive about this case is that the claim of bias which constitutes the essential part of the appeal does not rest on the comparison of the suspects in this case with suspects in another case of the same kind. Instead, the discrimination lies in the manner of dealing with the two parties involved. In other words, there is a so-called assailant's side and a victim's side in a pollution incident. The discrimination in this case is further complicated by the fact that pollution can be called a fatal contradiction in present day society." The analysis of the argumentation of the lower court seems somehow cumbersome and the court seems to avoid the formulation of conclusions that would be expressed all too directly and could thus harm one of the parties. Also here the difference between the Occidental style and the Japanese way lies in the formulation and not in the legal-linguistic operation that is undertaken in law.

8.4 Lex Mundi

Ubiquitous legal argumentation enables the development of a unified global law, a lex mundi or a world law. Constructive linguistic input into the discourse that supports and shapes the global law started early with concepts such as I. Kant's 'lex cosmopoliticum' or the named 'lex mundi' and with some other coinages. These concepts clearly do not exist as isolated creations of terms with the help of language. They are results of discourses about the necessity to overcome the diversity of laws on the planet. The background of these discourses is the goal to achieve 'perpetual peace', a notion that the international law incorporated already centuries ago. Other, less noble aims such as the reduction of purely commercial disadvantages, that in the language of economics are termed 'transaction costs', followed suit. Legal certainty in times of increased international migration is one more such argument in favor of the uniformization of law. National states frequently perceive the emergence and the strengthening of globalized rules as a challenge to their sovereign rights. National states are, as a rule, constituted around dominating political forces that claim the right to leadership on a territory. They use the national law, which they also develop in order to strengthen their dominating role in state and society. They therefore stress in their political discourse the 'nationality' of law and the necessity for law to remain national.

They use this aspect also for federative purposes. What is more, national political elites form global alliances to guarantee their power while paying allegiance to local constituencies. They think globally and act globally, although they recommend to others to think globally and act locally. Moreover, some people are excluded from the processes; they become outcasts (cf. Bauman 2004). This is, in short, the basic discursive structure of the globalization process in law. The argumentation used by national states is purely ideological as no fundamental structural features of law are known that would prevent the approximation or the uniformization of law. Already H.L.A. Hart in his *Concept of Law* (1961: 3) stressed the unifying rather than the dividing features of law: "Most educated people have the idea that the laws in England form some sort of system, and that in France or the United States or Soviet Russia and, indeed, in almost every part of the world which is thought of as a separate 'country' there are legal systems which are broadly similar in structure in spite of important differences." These "important points of similarity" comprised for Hart: "(i) rules forbidding or enjoining certain types of behaviour under penalty; (ii) rules requiring people to compensate those whom they injure in certain ways; (iii) rules specifying what must be done to make wills, contracts or other arrangements which confer rights and create obligations; (iv) courts to determine what rules are and when they have been broken, and to fix the punishment or compensation to be paid; (v) a legislature to make new rules and abolish old ones." Although Hart's approach to law is rule-oriented and our's favors law's discursiveness, his perspective upon law in the world that looks for similarities rather than differences seems to be worth mentioning. Furthermore, J.L. Halpérin (2009: 1) referred to E. Zitelmann's *Die Möglichkeit eines Weltrechts* (1888) for the development of the general doctrinal shape of the global law. Also F. Galgano (2005: 35) perceives legal pluralism as a legal anachronism: "La statualità e la nazionalità del diritto non sono fattori di progresso, bensì di crisi del diritto." Indeed, in all other areas of knowledge the unifying tendency won the competition to shape knowledge. Galgano may be right in his assumption that the reluctance of the legal science to join the globalization process may be a sign of a crisis in law. Likewise, G. Ziccardi-Capaldo (2008) engaged in portraying the ongoing process of legal globalization that she understood as a transformation of the international law. In order to describe the ongoing process she used following criteria: verticality and sharing of decisional processes, legality principles and common global values, integration of legal systems in the direction of global law, and collective guarantees (cf. Ziccardi-Capaldo 2008: xvi). Problems of the descriptive framework of reference were also addressed by M. Delmas-Marty (1998). It seems that the comparative research did not find any fundamental obstacles to legal globalization. Meanwhile, jurists remain divided on this issue.

The discourse about the globalization of law among jurists oscillates between skeptical and enthusiastic approaches (cf. Hargitt 2013: 430–435). In the middle of the spectrum one may identify descriptive positions that elaborate criteria for measuring the progress in the legal globalization process. As can be seen from the above overview, rare are contributions that create principles and rules of the global law. The main reason for this situation seems to be the positivist attitude towards law that reduces jurists' role to so-called systematization of provisions prepared and enacted by others. Thus, the legal profession depraves itself of participation in the process of norm creation and by so doing it risks losing its social relevance in a global reality propelled by rapid change. Also P. Schiff Berman (2012) described the paradigmatic constellation of public discourse about the global law as a discourse between nation-state sovereigntists and international law triumphalists. Gillespie et al. (2012) added to it a review of different perspectives that societies take in approaching legal transfers. These perspectives also include failures of global legal reforms because globalization of law as a contemporary trend in the development of humankind is exposed to countervailing actions of multiple origins (Raadschelders 2011: 216). Some experience may therefore be rather encouraging, as shown by Black and Bell (2011) or Woo and Gallagher for Asia (2011) or by Adamolekun (1999) for Africa. Institutions such as domestic courts play a role in the globalization process that may be impeded or facilitated by their actions (McLaughlin/Powell 2011). Public administration also globalizes in terms of 'conceptual convergence' (Caiden 1994). It means that governments tend to use the same words all over the planet such as: 'bureaucracy, accountability, civil service reform, corruption, management, efficiency, decentralization, welfare state reform' as key terms. Researchers mention also that private law can be harmonized through commercial customs (Frisch/Bhala 1999: 6). Other researchers, so Hofstede (1991: 182) or Aldrich (1979: 22) are skeptical as they stress cultural differences that in their view inhibit convergence. Raadschelders (2011: 217) makes the development dependent on the view people adapt to social reality; they may see it globally or tend to localize differences that impede a global view upon the world. Forced search for identities that are based on cultivation of differences end up in civilizational retrocession. In such processes where ethnic and cultural differences are cultivated against all odds 'apophatic identities' are formed that may lead to unproductive voluntary seclusion or confrontation. Anthropologically, law makes part of the civic identity rather than of a tribal distinction. Culture, with all differences that it may comprise, cannot be an obstacle in structuring or re-structuring the social reality. Humankind's progress has always been based on generalizing change. One may keep in mind that the humankind arrived at a common government of Antarctica while overcoming the small scale perspective and adopting a 'grand design' (Raadschelders 2011: 216, 217). Raadschelders (2011: 216) also stresses the problem of differing application of similar concepts that finally would make legal globalization impossible: "The differences in national culture are not only apparent in how the study is conceptualized and perceived but also in how theory can be applied." Ajani (2005) showed however that the comparative microperspective that focuses on functionality and the comparative macroperspective that focuses on method may be used for the purposes of unification of legal terms notwithstanding their initial functional difference. Legal globalization is therefore a matter of unified method rather than of functional comparison. The method governs the comparison and therefore incongruent legal concepts can be easily turned into perfectly congruent provided the appropriate method has been adopted by the researcher. Argumentatively, law all over the world can always be described as profoundly diverse or as perfectly unified, depending on the method that structures the discourse about the law in the world.

8.4.1 Global law as guiding idea in legal linguistics

Legal linguistics to which this book is a contribution is not a pure theory of law. It has practical goals, and one of them is its possible contribution to the globalization process in law. Many perceive globalization as merely an economical phenomenon. Others, so W. Menski (2006) or H.P. Glenn (2010), deny the possibility of legal globalization because for them law is a part of social and cultural traditions that differ regionally and therefore it cannot be united under one conceptual roof. Fundamental anthropology and political theory may however define these traditions and the possibility of their unification differently. For R. Domingo (2010) the unification of law is not only possible, but also unavoidable. The crisis of the modern national state and the crisis of the international law force the citizenry to reformulate the global body politic and its most efficient mechanism, the law. Globalization in the area of economical, penal and administrative law signals the trend towards the general globalization of law. J. Rawls's works (1993, 1999) in the area of political theory as well as J. Habermas's works (1996) on the transformation of the modern national state provide a theoretical foundation for this process. Domingo calls this law 'global law' or 'derecho global', sometimes also 'ius commune totius orbis', sometimes 'ordo orbis'. Some other terms such as 'iuris ordorum ordo' or 'lex mundi' play the same role in the projects of legal globalization. They refer to the Roman conceptual world where the principles and techniques of the dominant law on the planet had been forged. Domingo (2010: xx) also quotes Harold J. Berman who used the term 'world law'. Berman (1995: 1617) wrote: "The term 'world law' will, I believe, become more and more widely used as humanity moves into a new century, and a new millennium. It will embrace, but not replace, both terms 'international law', introduced by Jeremy Bentham in 1789, and the term 'transnational law' introduced by Philip Jessum in 1956." R. Domingo searches not only for the content but also for the language of this new global law. In respect of the language he remarks: "… the law must serve as an effective catalyst and support for the new supranational language – interpreting it, shaping it, and drawing out its logical consequences" (Domingo 2010: 64). Language capable to express the new global law cannot be enslaved. Domingo (2010: 196) having in mind words such as 'nation' or 'sovereignty' writes about this issue: "The politicization of certain words and their constant political manipulation makes them unusable for the consolidation of the global law." In Rawls's, Habermas's and Domingo's conceptions the globalized law emerges around the 'law of the people' that is a law centered on a person and its rights. At this point Rawls stresses rather the collective aspect and Domingo the individual aspect of the creation of new rights and principles. According to Domingo, this new law does not involve the idea of natural law. Meanwhile, as it is based on the person's dignity and not on the sovereignty of states, it refers to ethics unlike interstate law; "(t)he state by its very nature is coercive; that is to say, it generates its own enforced ethics" (Domingo 2010: 49). However, one may hope that this new law would benefit less from certain religious tendencies that R. Domingo seems to endorse. His generally impressive conception of the new law may discourage all readers who are less committed to the religious ideas of the Catholic doctrine and the institutions in charge of it (cf. Domingo 2010: 49, 164–166, 177–178, 199). Negative religious freedoms, i.e. the freedom not to profess any religion would have to find a place in the edifice constructed by Domingo. Otherwise it can scarcely be perceived as a social progress by those who do not wish to worship god. Domingo's view (2010: 193): "It is the job of religion and ethics, not of the law, to impose on citizens the duty to give God due worship" is at best ambiguous in the respect of negative religious freedom. Law must guarantee the negative religious freedom in society; the question cannot simply be abandoned to society that is expected to take care of non-believers, possibly in the way known from the history of Spain. It is however a consolation that such a project has limited chances to be fulfilled nowadays, notwithstanding some existing currents to the contrary that challenge the general trend. The future global law must therefore guarantee both the positive and the negative religious freedoms and enforce, if need be, protective rights when these claims are jeopardized. Domingo's new global law should not be confused with conceptions that replace the agonizing national states with multinational enterprises as sole agents able to finance and develop the globalized world. The new law is not a 'law of the jungle' but a democratic catalogue of principles universally agreed upon by the people, not by states. The most essential are: freedom, equality, independence and solidarity of peoples, observance of treaties, duty of non intervention, the right to self-defense, and the protection of human rights (cf. Domingo 2010: 42). Its mechanism is one of general 'consent' as described by Held (2005: 12–14). Interestingly, Domingo (2010: 42) questions the necessity of independence in such a law of the cosmopolitan society. At least, it seems to be sure that the principle of justice in which all other principles are anchored remains indispensable to any project of a cosmopolitan political community. Certainly, as a theoretical conception such a project also includes some elements of utopia. Meanwhile, its strong fundaments should be able to support the ongoing detailed processes in the globalizing law. Its fundamental idea is 'justice', the rest is, in the view that is coherent with the main ideas of this book, taken care of in the general operations of law such as argumentation and interpretation that seem ubiquitous. The main material idea of justice and the legal-linguistic operations are the minimal requisites of the new global law. They undeniably correspond with the traditional structural features of law. The difference is in the sincerity. The new global law is the law of people, not of states. It is meant as it is written and it is not a decoration for cynical cryptocracies that oppress the silent majorities. Domingo (2010: 53–97) developed a broad overview over these erosive trends in the modern national state that finally precipitate its decline.

8.4.2 Global law as American law

One of the typical questions asked in relation to the new global law is its possible American structure and content. Domingo (2010: 197) writes about the prospects of the Americanization of the future law that he considers as probable: "In the same way that ius gentium was a Roman law and international law was effectively European, so could global law become an American law. The strategy of the United States is clear: to refuse to play the legal globalization card and establish itself de facto as the true champion of democracy in the world, using American law for this purpose. Everything that is not American law becomes civil law – that is, second-rate law, a non-American law." However, the U.S unlike the U.K., compromised when it ratified the CISG that also includes civil law concepts and a contract structure that does not know the structural element of 'consideration' that is typical of the common law. In more theoretical terms the risk of full Americanization of the global law depends on the approach to pluralism. Further, will this new law be applicable in a global state or within another structure? Some like Shaw (2000) propose the structure of the 'global state' to accommodate the new law. However, this issue that pertains to the traditional political theory, of which it is a prolongation, remains open as the postulate of the universality of the global law may be difficult to reconcile with the doctrine of territoriality of states. Rawls (2005) characterized the challenge in a quote endorsed also by Domingo (2010: 184): "A modern democratic society is characterized not simply by a pluralism of comprehensive religious, philosophical and moral doctrines (…) Political liberalism assumes that, for political purposes, a plurality of reasonable yet incompatible comprehensive doctrines is the normal result of the exercise of human reason within the framework of the free institutions of a constitutional democratic regime." The main challenge to this political and theoretical desideratum is that the incompatible doctrines can coexist when they are also perceived as reasonable. It will probably not suffice that they originate in the human reason as too many ideas have their origin in this structure. Reasonableness of ideas is an issue of rational discourse. When a rational discourse is not possible, there is no reasonable idea. This may appear as not very tolerant, but the global law cannot emerge as an amalgam of everything that the human mind is able to produce. Then the law of the jungle would be more appealing than this sort of pluralism. Meanwhile, the global law remains "the main contribution that legal science can make to humanity" in response to the "irrepressible human desire to organize a global community" (Domingo 2010: 199, 92). It requires therefore a global input during the process of its formation.

8.4.3 Globalization of law in comparative perspective

Comparative law is essentially committed to legal pluralism that is the conditio sine qua non of its existence as an academic discipline. The possibility of a globalization in law is construed there in the perspective of a harmonization or uniformization of legal rules all over the globe (Menski 2006: 16). The chances that the harmonization process would succeed in the near future or at all are perceived in some influential works on comparative law rather skeptically, mostly due to the embeddedness of law in particular legal cultures. Menski (2006: 3) remarks: "It is rather unreal to expect that the whole world would ever follow one rule system, one language and culture, or one law." Glenn (2010: 376) remarks as regards the legal pluralism that it "looks like it will be with us for a long time. It is sustainable, and perhaps there should even be efforts to sustain it." Meanwhile, for Menski (2006: 14, 3) and some others legal pluralism is not good in itself; the same concerns also the legal globalization that as such does not guarantee the end of social conflicts only due to the harmonization of legal rules. Others perceive the co-existence of legal traditions as natural. It seems that the debate about the legal globalization in comparative law concerns mainly the harmonization of legal provisions. Moreover, the shift from "a predominance of authoritative law-making" (Menski 2006: 16) towards a more democratic global law compiled by the citizens of the world is stressed as well (Domingo 2010). Other skeptical and critical voices are quoted and commented by Bauman (2004: 64–65) where especially the democratic deficits of a global law are underscored. The critics warn against a fluid, i.e. not really binding global law concept that blurs the borderline between the legal and the illegal, which it sets up to the benefit of the powerful. Certainly, the acceptance of legal globalization in the global citizenry is bound by conditions and it therefore largely depends on its degree of openness towards change and citizens' commitment to democracy. This attitude in the citizenry can be influenced by the research. When this task is neglected in the research, then someone else will provide the citizens the argumentative framework that they need to make decisions about right or wrong in legal globalization. Therefore, the comparative law should inquire into the prerequisites for acceptance of legal globalization rather than legitimize legal inertia and the status quo in evolving social reality on the planet. Paradoxically though, some researchers even identified an increase in the emergence of differing legal rules all over the world, "a further pluralisation of laws" (Menski 2006: 5). Yet, no tendency towards further diversification of legal interpretation standards or legal argumentation has been observed in the comparative research. Exactly at this point the legal linguistics proposes another view upon the ubiquitous character in that it stresses the globalization of legal-linguistic operations such as legal interpretation or legal argumentation. Legal linguistics is neutral towards the view whether the complete harmonization of rules of existing legal systems should be envisaged as it concerns only the methodological and not the material level of law. This finally does not mean that legal linguists do not have any opinions about the wishful direction in the development of the global law.

8.4.4 What means that laws are different?

A very substantial question in the dialogue between the legal linguistics and the comparative law, as can be seen from the above subsection, regards the alleged or existing differences between laws all over the world. Menski (2006: 26) states:

"Arguments for recognising the inherent plurality of law are well recognised in the theoretical literature on comparative law." The most striking point here is the 'inherent plurality' that apparently cannot be thought away without disintegrating the phenomenon. It would be difficult and also unwise to question the legal plurality in the world (cf. Fenrich et al. 2011). The other thing is to admit that this plurality is inherent in law. Speaking about the law in the abstract does not mean that there is only one law, namely the Occidental law. This speaking comes close to the linguistic perspective upon the plurality of languages that for a linguist makes it possible to speak about the language notwithstanding the differences among some thousands of languages spoken worldwide. Laws can differ as to their source that may be the state or a religion, as to their structure, or the way in which legal transplants from other legal systems are used in them. They, however, seem to have one feature in common. It is not known that a law would be able to cope with social problems without some of the legal-linguistic operations that we are dealing with in this book. Legal linguists can also compare these operations and look at the particular modes and results that are achieved in the particular legal systems. In this sense we can speak about the abstract law as we can speak about language in general while admitting legal and linguistic pluralism on the planet. Several examples may shed some light on this issue. In particular, tendencies towards combining traditional legalism with authoritarian rule are present even today in Asia (Rajah 2012). Rajah mentions as typical of the legal discourse in Singapore the discrepancy between the liberal form and the illiberal content of its law. Law on such occasions is, as observed by Rajah, regularly limited to rigorous observance of legal procedure that is equated with the rule of law. For India, Sarangi et al. (2010) added an analysis of the interrelation of language and politics, especially focusing on the unfolding of this relation in the twentieth century. Meanwhile, in the Islamic law, certain provisions may be perceived as discouraging any attempt at legal globalization. In Kern v. Dynalectron Corp. (577 F. Supp. 1196, N.D. Tex. 1983) a court in Texas had to deal with a complaint of an American pilot who was employed by the defendant to fly helicopters over crowds of Moslems making their pilgrimage to Mecca. Saudi Arabian law prohibits however the entry of non-Moslems to Mecca under penalty of death. As the plaintiff was a Baptist, and he was unwilling to convert to Islam, he could not perform the contract. The defendant offered him a less interesting job, yet he declined the offer. The rest of the lawsuit is not interesting in our context. Striking is the peculiar Saudi Arabian regulation that according to the jurists of this country in based on the Quran. It is doubtful, whether specific regulation of this sort could be surmounted in the legal globalization process in the near future. Other court decisions under the sharia show however parallels in the legal development in the Islamic law and in the Occidental law. They witness to the common rational basis of legal principles. For instance, the sharia has been applied in a way corresponding with secular legal orders in the case Libyan American Oil Comp. v. Government of the Libyan Arab Republic (in: International Law Reports, 1982, vol. 62, p.140). The legal problem in this case concerned the termination of long term concessions to extract and sell petroleum that the plaintiff acquired from the Government of Libya before the military coup of 1969. The new Libyan government nationalized the concessions although the contract provided that it "shall not be altered, except by mutual consent of the parties." The question whether the concessions have been lawfully nationalized has been decided according to Islamic law. The judge held that "the principle of the sanctity of property and contracts, the respect for acquired vested rights, the prohibition of unjust enrichment, the obligation of compensation in cases of expropriation and wrongful damage" made part of the precepts of Islamic law. The judge based his decision on Quran's chapter V, verse 1 that says: "You who believe, perform the contracts" and decided for the plaintiff. The quoted sura corresponds with the Roman legal maxim 'pacta sunt servanda' and the common law principle of the 'sanctity of contracts'. All three maxims in concert form a workable basis for the global law at least in the area mentioned in the above case.

8.4.5 Global law, space law and metalaw

The prolongation of the global law is the space law that as international law covers legal relations beyond this planet. Space law governs the activities in outer space and aims at the peaceful use of outer space, especially in relation to 'space-based resources'. Its terminology is relevant to legal linguistics because its development can be narrowly followed due to the nature of this emerging phenomenon. Meanwhile, a general definition of 'outer space' does not exist, yet specialists agree that 'outer space' begins at the lowest altitude above sea where objects can orbit the Earth. Space law integrates terminology of natural sciences such as 'remote sensing' or 'geostationary orbit', also in exclusively legal terms such as 'geostationary orbit allocation'. Sometimes terminology is less consistent; 'space debris' is also known as 'orbital debris', 'space junk' or 'space waste'. Discursively, space law is dominated by the principle of 'non-appropriation of outer space by any one country'. Some jurists identified a flaw in the construction of the space law that does not cover possible contacts with other 'races' in the outer space. This area of law was labelled 1956 by its inventor Andrew G. Haley 'metalaw'. Its principles have been further developed by E. Fasan (1970). Due to the lack of any immediate need for its application not much research is known in the area of metalaw. It is however interesting as a phenomenon because of its commitment to the principle of legality also in the relations with supposed non-humans. Critically one might note that the metalegal concept of the law for the universe is based on an anthropocentric view that will probably not be understood by 'others' in the outer space. Yet, otherness is anthropologically a question of perspective, as 'others' may develop a more conciliatory view upon legal problems than we are able to construe.

8.4.6 Monolingual law

Linguistic diversity is not particularly problematic in legal linguistics. Unlike natural languages used in everyday communication, the particular legal languages are much less diversified. Their terms have regularly common intellectual roots, mostly of Latin origin (Mattila 2013: 165). Legal-linguistic operations undertaken in them are homogeneous. All are dominated by interpretation and argumentation as complex legal speech acts. Legal languages are therefore studied because of the legal-linguistic operations that constitute their modus vivendi and not because of linguistic or terminological differences that doubtlessly also exist among them. Due to the lack of a unified conceptual system of reference, terminological particularities in legal languages cannot take anyone by surprise. They will be doubtless reduced within the ongoing process of legal globalization. In the global law, that will probably emerge in future, terminological problems that today bother legal comparatists and legal translators will disappear. Legal language will, as a result of these transformations, become unified. Meanwhile, particular problems relative to general linguistic diversity will not disappear (cf. Hargitt 2013: 436–441). Especially problems of text interpretation will remain unchanged. Legal translation will become methodologically more transparent and it will be as complex as translation of medical or technical texts. This means that it will become easier; yet it will still remain a challenging enterprise due to structural differences among natural languages.

8.5 Translation in legal discourses

The above mentioned conception of monolingual law as the main domain of applied legal-linguistic studies is particularly relevant to future generations of legal linguists. Meanwhile, for quite a long time our law will remain multilingual, notwithstanding the processes of legal globalization and regional uniformization related to its principles and rules. As long as these processes are going on, legal translation will have to be discussed in legal-linguistic studies as one of the dominant legal-linguistic operations. It goes also without saying that in areas of law where globalization did not even begin, legal translation remains quintessential in all attempts at understanding law in the comparative perspective. Yet, this is only one aspect of translation in law as an object of the legal-linguistic interest. The other aspect concerns the relation between legal translation and legal discursiveness that is the main issue of this essay. The first point of anchorage here is the fact that legal discourses are or can be translated. Facets of legal discursiveness emerge in them in the perspective of their translatability. All discursive facets in translations have also an institutional background because private translations structurally differ from those made in international organizations or in national public institutions (cf. Borja Albi/Prieto Ramos 2013).This statement may sound evident, yet in the past it caused many problems in the theory of legal translation. The other central point in the reflection about the interrelation between both concepts is the textuality of law. This means that law is created, stated, and applied in texts, where socially relevant commitments and beliefs are omnipresent and where attitudes to texts influence the emergence of meaning. From this assumption follows that it is not without importance what sort of legal texts is actually translated. This result may surprise because the traditional theory of legal translation takes the fact of the very existence of texts in source language for granted. In legal linguistics, this is not the case. It matters for the legal linguist whether the source language text is a death sentence or a human rights convention. It matters furthermore, when the negotiated contract reflects interests of the parties in an equitable way or when its negotiations aim at overreaching one of the parties in the interpreter's presence and with his involvement. The opposite attitude that negates any relation between the translator and the pragmatic quality of the translated texts illustrates misconstrued professionalism. The mentioned examples matter in the context of this essay because also in the area of legal translation the main issue that has to be addressed by the legal linguist is the emergence of meaning. These, in brief, are discursively relevant aspects of legal translation. They will be elucidated in the following paragraphs.

8.5.1 Retrospective upon legal translation

The development of legal linguistics towards an independent discipline that transgresses interdisciplinary boundaries requires an incorporation of methods and approaches of linguistics and legal sciences. Legal linguistics becomes interesting as a scientific discipline when it provides new epistemic insights into law. Interdisciplinary boundaries often lead to a parallel in research attitudes that impedes rather than enables a more advanced dialogue that would be epistemologically valuable. Some researchers call this methodological transformation transdisciplinary. When the research interest is methodically limited to purely linguistic inquiries, it may easily turn all creative efforts into a legal linguistics without law that is a disappointing intellectual enterprise. Some researchers, such as J. Engberg and A.L. Kjaer (2011), have warned against this development. The risk for the future of the discipline can be omitted through integrating some of the methodological approaches used by jurists in the legal doctrine and in the legal theory in their attempt to come to terms with the language use in law. They concern the main issue of legal linguistics, i.e. the institutionalized emergence of meaning in law and some partly related special issues that pertain to legal translation. Many legal-linguistic problems discussed in the area of legal translation are in fact accommodated there purely coincidentally. Very often they represent general lexicological or lexicographical problems. They are discussed as issues of legal translation due to the practical perspective established in the research into legal translation in the course of its development. Legal translation as an area of legal linguistics underwent several stages of paradigmatic change in its relatively short history of systematic development. Meanwhile, the above paragraphs that deal with the legal globalization signal that even more change is to come.

8.5.2 Conceptual interests in legal translation

Classical conceptions of legal linguistics dealt with the specific 'style' that jurists use when speaking or writing and with the particular professional terminology which has been further characterized as the main responsible factor for the emergence of the legal 'style'. Legal terminology then began to overshadow the legal style issue and finally also began to dominate the legal-linguistic research. As this terminology had to be translated and its translation regularly caused problems, the legal translation has established itself in the focus of the researchers dealing with the legal language as one of the central linguistic operations in law. The main translation problem was identified in the struggle between conceptions favoring the idea of impossibility of legal translation and others that opposed the somber view of law as in principle non-translatable (Galdia 2009: 226). It became clear that problems in legal translation are caused by different conception of 'equivalence' used in different approaches. General, ontological conceptions of 'equivalence' automatically lead to the denial of translatability because the source language text appears as different from the target language text; it is not the same text. Why do linguistic versions matter? Let us have a look at the original quote referring to the 'true and comprehensive science of language' from J.L. Austin's *Ifs and Cans* and its French version: "Is it possible that the next century may see the birth, through the joint labours of philosophers, grammarians, and numerous other students of language, of a true and comprehensive science of language?" and "N'est-il possible que le siècle prochain verra la naissance, grâce aux efforts combinés de philosophes, de grammairiens, et de beaucoup d'autres étudiants du langage, d'une science du langage vraie et complete?" (cf. Halsall 1989). Specialists debate since ages about the question whether both text samples can be perceived as equivalent. In fact, communication is a complex semiotic operation and equivalence can be discussed only within the theoretical framework of semiotics as in life nothing is equivalent. Therefore, the less the requirement of sameness is taken into consideration while defining the 'linguistic equivalence', the higher is the chance of success in shaping a method for legal translation. What is searched is the sameness of meaning, not the ontological sameness. Sameness of meaning as semantic 'equality' has been proposed as the most efficient solution to the conceptual trap, also because the very existence of meaningful legal translations could not be neglected, even in a theoretical debate. Skopos-theories stressed the view that translation in law is in principle possible when the aim of translation is well defined (cf. Matulewska 2013: 15–16). As a result, translation strategies had to be made transparent and efficient in order to comply with the requirements of the skopos-theory (cf. Galdia 2013: 78). Today, no-one is lost in translation any more, at least theoretically. It is generally understood that the problem of legal translation is the lack of a common and overarching system of reference for legal concepts. As long as this problem will pertain, the main difficulty in legal translation will remain unchanged. In case of the emergence of a common system of reference, such as the global law, legal translation would become comparable with technical or medical translation. This does not mean that the translation would then become fully unproblematic (cf. 8.4.6). Meanwhile, uniformization of law is largely a political enterprise. Science cannot accomplish this task unilaterally as the validity of the new, proposed law depends on the will of the legislators and not upon the academia. Different linguistically relevant methods may be used in the uniformization and the globalization of law. Morphology of law might provide the map of the common elements which constitute law. It would ensure the conceptual metalanguage of law. Furthermore, alignment of concepts as a method accepts formal grammatical and structural differences of terms. The English 'statute of limitations' and the expression 'statute barred' may be aligned in the common reference system with 'prescription' in the French language. The unified concept will still function differently in English and in French due to syntactical differences between both languages. Yet, it will become translatable. Overall, the conceptualization of legal translation is very advanced when compared with other legal-linguistic operations. Legal linguistics is interested in the generalization of these results, yet some epistemological obstacles to this process must also be taken into consideration. They are discussed in the paragraph below.

8.5.3 Legal translation as guest in legal linguistics

Legal translation as a legal-linguistic operation differs significantly from other central legal-linguistic operations such as legal interpretation or legal argumentation. It emerged as an academic problem due to the necessity to mediate between incongruent legal systems. Likewise, it is connected in its survival strategy with the legal diversity in the world. More generally, one can say that the decrease in legal diversity in the world devalues the place that legal translation takes in legal linguistics. Towards the end of this process the legal translation will become inferior and not interesting. With the progress of legal globalization it will also be losing its leading position among the topics that are relevant to legal linguistics. Another characteristic feature of the legal translation is its dependence upon other legal-linguistic operations such as interpretation or argumentation. This area has however not been sufficiently elucidated in the research. Finally, legal translation is essential to comparative legal linguistics because it signalizes problems in general coherence and consistency of the emerging global legal system. Wherever legal translators encounter problems, legal linguistics and comparatists must see a field for their activity. However, hospitality in legal linguistics finds also its limits in the process of legal globalization. The above stated reasons make the generalization of translatorial studies in the area of legal linguistics less evident.

8.6 Comparative legal linguistics and legal translation

Comparative legal linguistics (cf. Mattila 2002b, 2012, 2013; Engberg 2012: 176) draws the consequences from the problematic fields that are constituted in the mentioned interface between comparative law, conflict of laws and legal translation. First of all, comparative legal linguistics tries to identify the main characteristic features of the language of law that can be used in the globalization of law. The future language of the global law will depend on the findings of comparative legal linguistics. The idea of a uniform legal language is not new. A uniform legal language already existed in Europe in form of the legal Latin of the Roman law and later in the usus modernus Pandectarum. The idea of legal metalanguage has also been discussed in the comparative law. Terms such as contract, offer, and acceptance are ubiquitous; notwithstanding the incongruent conceptual structures of the respective parts of the legal systems. The main task of the comparative legal linguistics is to assist the international legislators in the process of the coinage of this new language. The analysis of legal discourse shows that problems of contemporary legal language are mostly caused by inadequate language use strategies by participants in legal discourses. Furthermore, some researchers stressed that comparative law is a method for legal translation (cf. Galdia 2003). Others perceived it rather as an aid. Comparative law explains why legal translations from Finnish into Swedish are perceived as relatively easy although both languages are genetically not related, and legal translations from French into English are regularly challenging although both languages are rather close to each other, at least when compared with those formerly named. The same phenomenon is observable within the EU law where there is only one legal system of reference that delimits translatorial choices. Thus, the EU law leads away from the problems of legal translation to the problem of institutionalized meaning emergence in law. Last but not least, the method of translating into ordinary language remains unexplored. Yet also there problems of differentiation between concepts belonging to the ordinary language and those belonging to the specialized register have not been solved. For instance, in the Berlin Agreement, now out of force, the German term 'Verbindung' suggests ties such as connections, e.g. train connections while 'Bindung', a knot, marks linguistically a stronger bond. Both convey varying degrees of intensity and were so understood by the negotiators of the Agreement. In the method of comparative legal linguistics such communicative situations are not sufficiently elucidated. Within the comparative legal linguistics, legal translation appears in a broader context. It allows for the generalization of the translatorial experience within the project of legal globalization. From the above remarks also follows that the link to law in legal translation must be maintained.

8.6.1 Legal methods in legal translation

Legal translation can also be used as a litmus paper in the area of comparative law, conflict of laws, and legal informatics. The incongruity of legal terminology and legal languages in general led to the emergence of numerous problems in these three areas. Comparative law and conflict of laws owe their existence to legal and linguistic diversity and legal informatics has to bear the consequences of this double diversity. One of the main issues in the legal translation is the role that methods of comparative law and conflict of laws play in it. As mentioned, some scholars pretend that legal translation is a form of legal comparison. Some ponder over the role of the method of characterization/classification or qualification applied in the area of the conflict of laws in professional legal translation. It is a traditional method used by legal comparatists to deal with incongruent legal concepts. In fact, characterization is not a specific operation in law because all areas of knowledge are based on conceptual classifications in one way or another (Scott 1979: 9). However, in most areas of knowledge, with the exception of law, reference systems are largely homogenous. E. Bartin (1897) argued therefore that the characterization problem in law is unsolvable. Meanwhile, when a Spanish legal term such as 'gananciales' becomes problematic in the moment of application of the Spanish law in a foreign country, its linguistic manifestation seems to be secondary. Within the conflict of laws, the main methodological question would be whether 'gananciales' – claimed by a widow – conceptually represent family law or inheritance law. The further application of law depends upon this determination. The question as of how to call 'gananciales' in another language is methodologically indifferent in the process of characterization. It is dominated by the question of the applicability of a set of rules in a situation when two domestic legal systems compete for being applied. Furthermore, is the right to dower in divorce in connection with the Islamic law a contractual claim or a claim based on family law? Still further, is the French 'fiducie' tantamount to 'trust' and this to the Islamic 'waqf'? 'Parental consent to marry' or 'statute of frauds' are additional examples of situations where characterization is necessary in order to choose the applicable law. All too eagerly jurists may tend to assume that language or linguistic transformation does not play any important role in the characterization process. In the common law, the identification of the 'cause of action' is even singled out as the characteristic feature of the characterization procedure (Scott 1979: 9). Meanwhile, the civil law doctrine stresses the notional equivalence of two systematically incompatible legal notions. Could both be achieved through an intellectual operation that is extra-linguistic? Within the operation of the choice of law the linguistic factor manifests itself more in the characterization than in the device called 'connecting factor'. Moreover, which adaptation processes take place before the legal translator translates 'biens' as 'goods'? Translatorial strategies display therefore a structural similarity with the characterization problem. These unsolved and partly unsolvable questions show the limits of legal translation under the constraints of the mentioned double incongruity. Under the given circumstances, at least theoretically, legal translation cannot become any better (cf. Husa 2011). It clearly has its inherent limits. Only the globalization of law will bring the solution to the intricate problems that manifest themselves at the interface of comparative law, conflict of law methodology and the methods and strategies known in translation studies (Galdia 2013). In the meantime, a more advanced project of the legal thesaurus that would incorporate the meta-language of law would be helpful. It would also pave the way towards a less troubled shift within the legal globalization process. This idea seems to be essential because the transition period will be rather extensive.

8.6.2 Literality of translation

Comparative law may offer also new insights into the problem of literal translation. Since the beginning of modern translation studies the stress in the methodology of translation has been to combat the idea of literal translation as the right methodology for translating legal texts. The view that the correct legal translation must be literally close to the original emerged among jurists probably because of the necessity to test the correctness of translations. Literal translation is easy to check when its correctness is at stake. It is sufficient to open the dictionary and compare the words of the translation with the entries in a dictionary. For the translator, it provides the insurance against aggressive and incompetent criticism. The translator can, while using the same text, easily convince the critics that the translation is right, because an authoritative dictionary provides for the correspondence of terms used in her translation. It is amazing that generations of users of translated texts had been convinced that the best translator is the one who comes as close as possible to the literal course of the translated text. In the classical theory of translation that begins with the theological reasoning on the quality of translated biblical texts, the opposite view seems to have been preponderant. There, theologians such as St. Augustin, and later also F. Schleiermacher, M. Buber and F. Rosenzweig as well as Eugene Nida stressed the necessity to render the sense of the translated biblical texts (cf. also Sandrini 2011: 1095–1096). They accepted as unavoidable that the equivalence that is produced is the one of meaning, and not of the context of meaning. Meanwhile, and also somehow paradoxically, translated texts including legal texts, are largely literal translations. It is therefore necessary to avoid theoretical orthodoxy in legal translation studies. For instance, the German term 'Polizeistaat' corresponds literally with the English 'police state'. The Russian term 'policejskoje gosudarstvo' equally means 'police state' in English. One would be able to quote numerous such examples where legal terms and not only terms, but entire syntagmas or sentences can be translated literally without any objection. The method of translating by identifying and transforming the subject-predicate-object structure of the source text into subject-predicate-object structure of the target text is used with much success, although it is rarely admitted by translators. For instance, the European Convention on Human Rights (EHRC) says in Art. 6 of the English text: 'civil rights and obligations' and in the Swedish translation it says 'civila rättigheter och skyldigheter'. It is difficult to say what the convention actually means with 'civil rights and obligations' and the French translation saying 'droits et obligations de caractère civil' is not particularly helpful in this respect (Koivu 2008: 148). Therefore the translator strategically avoids the problem and translates literally into Swedish. When the source text is semantically inexplicit, the literal translation imposes itself as the best translatorial strategy. Inexplicit originals engender inexplicit translations. Clearly, the pragmatic approach enables literal translation where it is appropriate. Meanwhile, when the French policeman asks for the ID-card while referring to 'papers': 'Papiers, s'il vous plait', the Spanish policeman will almost certainly ask for 'documents': 'Documentación, por favor'. Therefore, legal translation does not mean the avoidance of literal correspondence of words. It means that the literal correspondence of words cannot be used as a translation strategy when the sense would be impaired. Languages are close to each other. Therefore, they will to a large extent coincide in many respects. This is not a reason for anxiety and the legal translation is not unprofessional only because it is close to the translated original. A related issue will be also discussed in 8.7.2.

8.6.3 Commitment to translated message

The communicative role of the interpreter is equally redefined in the discourses about the legal translation. Interestingly and increasingly, especially in business interpretation cases, parties require interpreters' personal commitment to the message that is interpreted (Clegg, 2010). Traditionally, the interpreter has been a foreigner to the transaction negotiated by the parties as he has been expected to preserve distance towards the parties and the message. This distance is also stressed by working conditions, where interpreters sit in booths and may be even invisible to the parties that use their services. This may for some have the advantage to prevent that parties look at the interpreter instead of facing each other. Yet, distance and commitment to grammatical exactness of the target language text may not always be appreciated. Occasionally, interpreters' aloofness is made responsible for failures in contract negotiations (Clegg, 2010). Garbled communication is caused by the situation where "there is none of the give and the take of chatting freely in your own language" (Clegg, 2010). Increasingly, therefore, it is required that the interpreter joins the parties and works with them on the negotiation; of course, this technique is feasible only when the interpreter belongs to the entity where she interprets. This is the case when the interpreter's services are for instance used in discussions among different subsidies of an international corporation, where the common language does not exist. Therefore, it seems important to brief the interpreter before a meeting about its essentials and goals. It is, however, also important to prepare parties to use the services of interpreters and to describe the intricacies of translated communication to which they would have to adapt. Historically, it has been perceived as an achievement by translators and interpreters that they were not made responsible for the content of messages they interpret. These messages may include, especially in areas related to the penal law, perjuries, slander, or offence of whatever sort. It may be that in changing communicative contexts the question of responsibility would have to be addressed again, although from a different perspective. The procedures of awareness raising and of accountability of translators would also include mandatory indications of translators' names and the names of their supervisors on all official legal acts that have been translated.

8.6.4 Translation mistakes

It is difficult to address translation mistakes within the discursive frame of reference. Structurally, language used in social discourses does not integrate 'errors'. It may at best refer to them as to terms that create some social discourses. Generally, social discursive practices do not concern the truth of social developments; they are based exclusively on linguistic practices that engender all necessary contents for social developments in whatever area. Therefore, strictly speaking, 'errors' do not exist in discourses. Instead, one would have to speak of better or worse adapted or convincing propositions. This may also be the reason why standards for determination of translation mistakes are difficult to set up. Meaning can be translated with different words and syntactic structures in an adequate way from one language to another. Different translation proposals may be equivalent; some may be stylistically more suitable than others, especially in the translation of legal acts or judgments. The traditional methodological approach to discovery of translation mistakes is the test for discovery of translation language. Meanwhile, those who identify translation language in the target text often also admire the translation skills visible in the analyzed text. Avoiding translation language is an enormously challenging enterprise. However, some legal translations are clearly erroneous. This means that multilingual discourse can suffer under requirements of equivalence that are not necessarily discursive in essence. Especially, the skopos-theory shows limits of attempts to transform multilingual discourses, foremost the legal. The more appropriate device that may help to cope with semantic requirements in discourse transformations are translatorial strategies and standards.

8.6.5 Faux amis identified

Also faux amis such as 'consideration' of the common law became less noxious when the context of the use of legal terms is taken into account. A faux ami exists exclusively in terms of an isolated semantic analysis of a concept such as 'consideration'. In discursive contexts, the problem disappears because its meaning emerges in an interplay of words that excludes abstractly construed propositions. For example, it is plainly understandable that in: 'A few states provide that contracts made under seal cannot be challenged for lack of consideration' or 'The courts do not inquire into the adequacy of consideration,' 'consideration' is meant in the legal sense of the term. It means something of value that is a result of bargain among the contracting parties. It clearly cannot mean the 'consideration' of ordinary parlance because the sentence would become absurd when this meaning variety would be substituted. No speaker would need to engage in such substitution tests because there is no doubt about the meaning variety of the linguistic unit that is meant. Faux amis are a problem of linguistic appropriateness rather than a legal-linguistic issue. When the Spanish 'Es una ofensa' is translated into English with 'It's an offense' instead of 'It's an insult' so it is clearly not a correct translation. The main reason for this judgment is that pragmatically 'ofensa' does not correspond with 'offense' in English, although some parallel contexts of use could probably be identified. In terms of legal philosophy, differences between 'rule of law', 'Rechtsstaat' and 'état de droit' may also become relevant (Grote 1999). This particularity notwithstanding, in professional translation all three terms can be used as equivalent in most contexts.

8.7 Pragmatic quantities and qualities

Quantity and quality are interrelated, so Hegel; quantity tends to be transformed into quality. One of the hypotheses advanced here is the ubiquitous existence of discursive forms in law. Ubiquitous in terms of quantity does not mean ubiquitous in terms of quality. Mattila (2006: 153) mentions that in the common law jurisdictions the Latin term 'amicus curiae' is regularly used while it is unknown in civil law countries, although it is understandable there. The consequence of this finding is that it can be assumed that Latin legal terminology is basically present in law of whatever provenance, either directly and visibly or indirectly and less visibly, and in different quantity. The Roman element in the French 'prescription' is more visible that in the Japanese 'giru' that is not less rooted in the Roman legal thinking. Interestingly, E. Rabel was quoted by J. Husa (2008: 98) with following words: "Hidden behind apparent dissimilarity, there are fundamental likenesses, suggesting international cooperation, though of course not necessarily unification." Legal translation reflects this particularity of legal diversity. On the other side, it also displays a striking similarity with language that functions all over the world with amazing diversity of utterances that is rooted in a restricted set of speech acts applicable to all languages, notwithstanding their diversity. Legal linguistics makes translators aware of this particularity of transformations of legal language that are not limited to translation, yet include also mechanisms which come close to translation. Such mechanisms are mainly used in the conflict of laws and in the comparative law and they include foreign notional implants and legal-linguistic characterization of foreign legal terms. Therefore, legal translation as a legal-linguistic operation is embedded in a set of other transformative mechanisms of law that are in one way or another dependant on language.

8.7.1 Strategies in legal translation

Main transformative mechanisms in the legal translation concern legal speech acts. In our context, a long list of legal speech acts comes to mind: acceptation, accord, accusation, adhesion, affirmation, favorable and unfavorable appreciation, approbation, assurances, and menace. Relatively rare are in legal contexts: admiration, indifference, impatience, hesitation, hope, regret. Legal speech acts, although presumably ubiquitous in qualitative terms, are distributed quantitatively in a less proportional manner. 'Accusation' or 'decision' will be more frequent than 'discouragement' or 'tristess'. The legal speech act of regret occurs relatively often in American judgments and much less in European court decisions. In Gnazzo v. G.D. Searle (973 F2d 136, 1992) the judge remarks: "We are sympathetic to Gnazzo's situation and mindful that the unavoidable result we reach in this case is harsh. Nevertheless, we are equally aware that it is within the Connecticut General Assembly's constitutional authority to decide when claims for injury are to be brought. Where a plaintiff has failed to comply with this requirement, a court may not entertain the suit." In Dementas v. Estate of Tallas (764 F2d 628, 1988 Utah App. Lexis 174) while speaking about the requirement of consideration in a contract the judge mentions: "This rule can surely work unfair results and has accordingly been criticized. We acknowledge, as have other courts in disregarding contracts for lack of consideration, that appellant will probably remain convinced he should be paid. Nevertheless he failed to meet the burden of proof, and this court will not find a contract where one has not been proved to exist." The structure of regret emerges as a threefold construction: First the sympathy with the losing party is expressed, then the law is described and finally, it is stressed that law has to be applied and that the losing party did not fulfill the legal requirements. This regret is therefore somehow circular as the court regrets that the party with which it sympathizes or pretends to do so did not follow the law and therefore the court, which is on its side, finally has to take a disadvantageous decision to its favorite. 'Admiration' is perceptible in Hoffman v. Capital Cities (33 F. Supp. 2d 867, 1999). The judge writes in his findings of facts: "Plaintiff, Dustin Hoffman, is a highly successful and recognizable motion picture actor. For the past thirty years he has appeared in scores of motion pictures and has received numerous honors, including six Academy Award nominations and two Academy Awards. He has also been nominated and has been awarded a Golden Globe Award and an Emmy Award for his work. It can be said that Mr. Hoffman is truly one our country's living treasures, joining the ranks of an exclusive handful of motion picture talent." Needless to mention, Dustin Hoffman won the suit, yet he lost the appeal that followed. Legal linguistics is interested in identifying the relevant legal speech acts and it also should support legal translators in developing translatorial strategies and devices that enable their appropriate transformation in legal discourses.

8.7.2 Institutional emergence of meaning in legal translation

The focus upon the legal terminology in the legal linguistics and in the theory of legal translation may lead to the false conclusion that while translating we replace some words by some others. In fact, translating is not based on words or lexicology as language does not consist solely of words. The bricks of the translation are the speech acts which must be rendered in the target language. This is equally evident in literature as it is in law. Examples borrowed from the UN Convention on the International Sale of Goods (CISG) may illustrate this procedure. The Art. 25 of the convention deals with the breach of contract. Its wording in English, French and German reads in the official translation with the emphasis added as follows:

Art. 25 A breach of contract committed by one of the parties is **fundamental** if it results in such detriment to the other party as **substantially** to deprive him of what he is entitled to expect under the contract, unless the party in breach did not foresee and a reasonable person of the same kind in the same circumstances would not have foreseen such a result.

Art. 25 Une contravention au contrat commise par l'une des parties est **essentielle** lorsqu'elle cause à l'autre partie un préjudice tel qu'elle la prive **substantiellement** de ce que celle-ci était en droit d'attendre du contrat, à moins que la partie en défaut n'ait pas prévu un tel résultat et qu'une personne raisonnable de même qualité placée dans la même situation ne l'aurait pas prévu non plus.

Art. 25 Eine von einer Partei begangene Vertragsverletzung ist **wesentlich**, wenn sie für die andere Partei solchen Nachteil zur Folge hat, dass ihr im **wesentlichen** entgeht, was sie nach dem Vertrag hätte erwarten dürfen, es sei denn, dass die vertragsbrüchige Partei diese Folge nicht vorausgesehen hat und eine vernünftige Person der gleichen Art diese Folge unter den gleichen Umständen auch nicht vorausgesehen hätte.

In the above text, lexical units corresponding to the terms *fundamental* and *substantial* have been emphasized by bold print. It would be however vain to discuss here the possible differences between *fundamental, substantial* and eventually also *essential*, and favor one to the detriment of others. Loewe (1989: 11) argues that the choice of the terminological equivalents in Art. 25 does not influence its meaning, especially when compared with the German variety that uses one and the same word to render *fundamental* and *substantial*, namely *wesentlich* and the Spanish translation that follows the French dichotomy of *essentielle* and *substantielle* by writing accordingly *esencial* and *substancialmente*. The sense of the translator's work is to render the meaning of the speech act concerning some circumstances of the breach of the contract. An intersection between sentence and utterance must be reflected, but the utterance remains the dominating force in the determination of the speech act (Stolze 2005: 125). Moreover, an isolated lexicological analysis would not help the translator, because the application of general terms upon a contract is a matter of interpretation. There, the difference may or may not matter, as the breach of the contract depends upon the circumstances of the case and not upon the preformulated meaning of a word in a specific language. The translator's task is to focus on the difference that may matter. As an example, it can be assumed that the difference between the English and the German versions where the party is perceived as being of male gender *he* in the English text or of female gender *sie* in the German text would not matter for the meaning of the legal speech act that constitutes the Art. 25 of the CISG. Legal speech acts manifest themselves in the application of linguistically determined legal norms. Only in the dynamic of the application process words acquire their proper meaning. Therefore, the possible difference between *fundamental, substantial* and *essential* becomes interesting when they are used. The Art. 17 of the Warsaw Convention treated in this book already in Part 1 illustrates the same problem. There, no artificial or isolated difference needs to be established between the French and the English meaning of 'accident' because the meaning of 'accident' is established by the courts in the act of application of the article due to legal-linguistic and not due to purely linguistic criteria. In the translation, when the words are not confronted with facts that may constitute a breach of contract, i.e. while being idle, their use may be well founded (Strawson 1992: 4; 6). Idle speech acts are typical of law. An idle speech act adapts its meaning according to the circumstances of use that confine the legal translation in terms of best possible translation that the translator would be able to achieve.

8.7.3 Façade translated

Legal theoreticians such as Alf Ross, Aulis Aarnio, Ernst Rabel and others referred to the fact that court decisions in one way or another may be façades, that real reasons for the decisions are frequently not mentioned in them. What is more, the real reasons are replaced by formal reasoning that is inadequate with the subject matter. What is translated or translatable in such cases? The extreme case of façade translation is a challenge to the very substance of law. Further, a translator may be able to establish the perfect terminological equivalence in the translation of a capital punishment sentence. Yet in what practice does he actually engage? Is he still translating law? Until now, these issues have not been dealt with in translatorial theories. The principle of translatorial professionalism seemed to exclude any reasoning upon translators' professional or ethical responsibility for contents of texts that they translate. In terms of these approaches, translators deal with texts, not with their contents. They are therefore responsible solely for the quality of texts, and not for the quality of their contents. Meanwhile, in times where social activities become more and more complex, and where even enterprises speak about their 'social responsibility', these aspects could be integrated into the general theory of translation. They are particularly interesting in our context because they seem to have their origin in discursive practices. Thus, discursive practices in law influence also professional standards and they form our views about professional skills and practices.

8.7.4 Understandability of translated law

Understanding is perceived as the hermeneutical prerequisite for translation. Translation strategies have from their very beginning of the reflection upon the translation process struggled with the challenge that a text should be first understood and only then translated. Yet, understanding is a misleading concept. In the sentence: 'This medicine reduces mucous production in the gut' understanding is at least twofold. In this sentence nothing is particularly difficult for the translator to understand. Yet, this understanding is one of the sentence, not of the discursive embedding. The sentence does not indicate whether it is actually a good thing that the mucous production is reduced or whether it is an adverse effect of the drug. And this also is understanding. The double level structure of understanding complicates the translation theory. It seems that controlling the first level of sentence understanding would be sufficient for the translatorial practice. Some related problems are often overcome in practice through 'subject-predicate-object translation' that is also called here 'literal translation'. When the second level understanding of the text cannot be achieved, the legal translator follows the first level translation and identifies the subject, the object, and the predicate that she renders in the target language. Literal translation as a strategy is equally old and also regularly used to-day (cf. 8.6.2). This type of translation may be criticized as unprofessional, yet it becomes understandable as a discursive practice.

8.7.5 Argumentation in translation

The position of an interpreter or a translator in discourses, written, or oral, had all too long been perceived as neutral. Admittedly, the transfer has rarely been perceived as automatic and the creative moment has been admitted within the framework of equivalence. This equivalence did not interfere with the neutrality credo subscribed to by the translators. Meanwhile, equivalence is translator-made in the sense that the translator decides about the facets of meaning that will be transferred. The choice survives in the translated text as argumentation in defense of the strategical choice made by the translator. The translator is not neutral towards her task. Some researchers (Newmark 1988, Ladmiral 1979) assumed already in times of structuralist approaches to translation that the translator "reviews the criteria for the various options before he makes his choice of translation strategy" (Newmark 1988: 8). Earlier, Jean-René Ladmiral called on a theory of action: "La traduction appelle une théorie en act" having in mind these multiple and badly researched processes of choice. Coinages invented or used by legal translators such as 'same sex marriage' or the French 'marriage pour tous' are definitely not neutral in semantic terms. They are embedded in socially relevant discursive practices.

8.7.6 Philosophical (theoretical) translatability

Analytical philosophers' interest in language also raised the theoretical interest in the problem of translatability. Towards the background of the indeterminacy theory of meaning research focused on the issue of meaning transfer between languages. Quine's 'gavagai'-example refers to the situation where an English speaker meets an aboriginal who says 'gavagai' to him while pointing at a rabbit that runs across the field. This 'gavagai' is clearly undetermined to someone who does not speak the language as it could mean many things. It might mean 'Look, a rabbit' or 'Let us hunt this rabbit' and many other things. It almost certainly denotes something, but what? It also connotes attitudes of speakers that differ when they consider rabbits as particularly tasteful animals when grilled and served with salad or when they consider them as sacred animals. The ambiguity of reference cannot be overcome in this frozen picture of a situation limited to one act of verbal and non-verbal reference. B. Rolf (1986: 32) aptly characterized this problem with following words: "The evidence for meaning will depend on the behaviour of language users and there is no other fact of the matter that can settle truth or falsity of interpretations or translations. Behaviouristic evidence is scarce, however. Therefore, the interpreter/translator must to a large extent construct what he claims to be a translation without any correspondence to past, present, or future behavioural facts." The analytical philosophers have asked whether this transfer of meaning from one language to another is possible at all and if so, what is actually transferred. Quine (1976) addressed the issue of meaning and translation in his *Word and Object* where he also coined the term 'radical translation'. The radical translation deals, as does the linguistic theory of translation, with the adequacy of meaning transfer between the source and the target texts. This transfer relation is dealt with in both theories under the common notion of 'equivalence'. The difference between both lies in the postulate raised by the theory of radical translation to reflect upon the theoretical prerequisites of one's own work. One more approach, namely the conception of 'idleness of concepts' developed by Peter Strawson (1992) is closely connected with the approaches to legal translation. Strawson's 'idleness of concepts' covers a semantic problem known since antiquity. Concepts such as 'freedom', 'democracy', or 'time' seem to be clear as long as no description of their content is claimed by somebody who, as a rule will not be satisfied with the description provided by the proponent. Legal language that is translated is an institutional phenomenon. Meaning in it is therefore established discursively and finally by competent authorities, mostly courts of law. This has profound consequences for the legal translation.

8.7.7 Levels of non-translatability

Problems of translatability may become clearer in the confrontation with an unusual text. James Joyce's novel *Finnegans Wake* has been perceived as untranslatable. The reason for this paradoxical state of affairs seems to be Joyce's highly inventive vocabulary that emerged along the lines of Standard English. Joyce's language reminds of the English language without really being it. It is as if the innovative language would follow upon an explicit version of Standard English that is hidden. Apparently, the text would first need to be deciphered, before it is translated. Therefore, the work as such is in a way readable and understandable. This holds true as long as one is not asked to explain every word in the text. This is a very specific understanding that owes its structure to specific constitution of meaning in Joyce's text. It could nevertheless be that our daily understanding comes close to this pattern. Who can claim to understand a text fully? What is a text's full meaning? Isn't it that we regularly decipher texts? Technically, deciphering requires the reference text in a language that is known. Alternatively, it requires a language that is close to the text that should be deciphered. Would only written texts in Ukrainian exist without the language as such being known to us, one may readily assume that we could decipher them via Russian and Polish as closest languages to Ukrainian. The process of deciphering the Rosetta stone, that is a classical example of the technique of deciphering unknown languages, reminds of this procedure. Meanwhile, when D. Davidson (2001: 186) speaks about translatability from 'Saturnian' into English and from 'Plutonian' into 'Saturnian'', yet not from 'Plutonian' into English, we may assume that one of the sign systems concerned is not a language. Thus, the levels of untranslatability may be different and they are determined discursively.

8.7.8 Readability of translated law

Readability is occasionally reduced to composition of sentences. Simple sentences are recommended in guidelines for drafters of legislative texts and legal translators. 'The cat that is on the mat is very fat' is opposed as potentially confusing for the citizens at large. Instead, its propositional content is split in two: 'The cat is on the mat. The cat is very fat.' and this solution is perceived as a model formulation of contemporary democratic legislation. Translation includes also transformations of the source text in terms of its readability. This holds particularly true when the source text is written in a drafting tradition based on traditional legalese and the target language favors plain language. Conflicting drafting strategies should rather be solved in the light favorable to target language readers. Translator's skill is also responsible for striking the right balance between the two standards. No mechanistic rules can replace translator's choices in this area. Translators as professionals of legal language set readability standards also in legal texts. Therefore, they should not hesitate to apply the knowledge they have acquired about the structure and the reception of written texts to the legal texts that they translate. This is particularly true in circumstances where recipients and clients may be less aware than translators of the procedural intricacies of text reception.

In this sense, legal translators are also pioneers of the idea of a modern, explicitly stated law. Such law, when translated according to legal-linguistic standards of explicitly stated law, ensures the readability of the target text.

8.8 Repositioning legal translation

Recent developments in the legal linguistics enable the repositioning of this legal-linguistic research items within the spectrum of legal-linguistic concepts, operations and methods. The re-assessment of legal translation is partly also a disillusionment. Translation is a transformation. Yet, unlike in its mathematical prototype, meaning is transferred in accordance with the interpreter's understanding and not absolutely. This is so because – at least in the light of pragmatic theories of translation – meaning cannot be transferred automatically without interference of the semiotical level of transfer where the translated signs are restructured around the axis prefigured by the theoretical approach adopted by the translator. Practically not less important for the translation as a discursive operation is the emergence of global English that diminishes the scope of applications of the theory of legal translation as speakers increasingly use the global English in international commercial and other contacts. They use and develop this language spontaneously and their former English teachers would have been scared by the results that come about in these creative and spontaneous processes. Whatever the opinions of specialists of the English composition, this group of speakers, and middle-size enterprises are leading there, will not be interested in the services of professional legal translators and rather cope on their own as long as no particular problems emerge. A Czech and a Finnish small or middle size enterprises will in negotiating and in drafting commercial contracts between them tend to avoid linguistic intermediaries and come to terms without foreign help, mostly because of costs. This development is relevant because the particular interest in linguistics towards translation as a linguistic operation arose due to the increasing number of international contacts that potentiated the number of translated texts. With the diminishing interest in translation also the theory of translation will be repositioned and possibly refocus upon translation of texts belonging to the higher levels of culture.

8.8.1 Discursive interest in translation

Discursiveness of law covers also the discursiveness of legal translations. Every translation, at least ideally, contributes to the emergence of new law as it displays legal language in a perspective that differs from the language used in the domestic laws. Translated law has an impact upon jurists' views about structure and language of law and it also suggests them a perspective that is rooted in the legal-linguistic conception that is described in this book. The discursive component in legal translation studies can be situated in its aspect directed towards improving the quality of law. Translation problems indicate, as a rule, problems of inter-systemic coherence that are particularly important in the process of legal globalization or in the shaping of the EU law. Predilection for certain term borrowings (cf. Coendet 2012) or avoidance of foreign implants are further such discursive contributions to law from the legal translation. Meanwhile, in other chapters of this book innovative strategies in monolingual settings have been identified and also scrutinized. They have proven to be equally innovative and creative as linguistic coinages developed within translatorial strategies. This result means that creativeness in legal discourses is not necessarily a phenomenon typical of legal translation. Other legal-linguistic operations engender creative language in equal degree also in monolingual surroundings. Legal translation is therefore linked discursively to most of the issues discussed in this book in one way or another.

8.8.2 Quality of language and quality of law

When we stress the importance of language in law, we should not forget that the decisive issue in legal discourses is the quality of law that is engendered by language. However, the stress on language in translation of legal speech acts may lead to the misunderstanding that legal translation foremost concerns language. In fact, legal translation is undertaken with the goal to transmit the law in the language, not the language. Legal linguistics contributes to better law in statutes and court decisions. Global and uniform law in regional settings is an area where legal translation helps identify the relevant issues in legal-comparative work. Doubtless, the legal translation as one of the central legal-linguistic operations can contribute to the increase in quality of law. Further work on translatorial strategies should therefore integrate also the aspects of quality of law, which may become easily overlooked in translatorial perspectives that are focused on language. New professionalism in legal translation is based on the idea that a good legal translation is the one that serves and engenders better law.

8.9 Lessons learned from legal translation

Before the legal translation disappears from the collection of legal-linguistic operations that constitute the legal linguistics, it should be evaluated as to its impact upon the legal science and linguistics. It seems that for both disciplines the most important lesson is the increase in the level of rational perception of law. The confrontation with incongruence of legal systems prevents the emergence of noxious phenomena such as petrification of law as well as orthodox legal doctrine, and finally it annihilates essentialist conceptions of law that dominated professional legal reasoning in the past centuries and that survive in the contemporary legal science in form of legal positivism. In linguistics, it constitutes an interesting parallel to the mystery of linguistic diversity. Not much can be said to the defense of legal diversity. Arguments in favor of linguistic diversity are more convincing, at least at this stage of the civilizational development, as cultures are translatable into each other under skopos-theoretical constraints. This means that they gain something in the translation process but also suffer losses. For instance, a Japanese haiku poem is translatable into Latvian under the angle of its specific poetic structure (metrics, prosody), imagery, or literal meaning. These angles cannot, due to diversity of natural languages, be fully adjusted. This is only one of reasons against linguistic uniformization of the planet, at least at the stage of cultural globalization that has been hitherto achieved. The globalization of law, that is a sluggish process, has better chances to succeed in the future. The general structure of the global communicational landscape represented by an amalgam of global English and regional languages is therefore the best formula for our time.

Part 9: Discursive Perspectives and New Horizons

9.1 Legal discourse identified

The retrospective upon the results obtained in the above chapters of the book may appear disenchanting. One would at this place rather expect comprehensive results that would make law clearer and easier to apply. However, the preceding pages do not necessarily make the understanding of law and the application of the understood law any easier. Actually, rather the contrary seems to be the case. Law appears in the light of the preceding pages as amazingly simple in its logical form and immensely complex in its linguistic formation and application. This result may seem a regress, a cumbersome and incoherent vision of law. Meanwhile, coherence as a legitimate expectation in every branch of knowledge is also a legitimate benchmark for whatever is asserted as a theoretical explanation of law. At least, our social world undeniably includes law. It is also undeniable that our understanding of law has been perceived as particularly problematic. It is time, therefore, to draw the first substantial conclusion from the above chapters and paragraphs that document the complexity of law while referring to its logical simplicity. It is worthwhile to bear in mind that when approaching the legal discourse at the beginning of this essay no particular attempts have been made to prove its existence and boundaries. Both issues were largely presupposed and taken for granted. At this initial stage of argument the legal discourse appeared therefore as an amalgam of textual contributions with reference to law that had been or are currently expressed by all interested persons who wish to contribute to it. This preliminary description might not have been the worst possible because there is at least some sociological evidence for its content. Everyone will agree that people, professionals of law and non-professionals alike, regularly engage in discursive practices about the content of the valid or the future law. They may do it deliberately, because they are interested in the process of shaping law or they may participate in these discourses under pressure because they became involved in actions where law is applied against their interests. This group of discourses reflects other discourses: Parliaments enact laws that are supported or criticized by the citizenry. Politicians claim merit for their input in the shaping of new law. Legal scholars comment or acclaim the results of the application of law in higher courts. All these situations are discursive and their existence can be taken for granted without any field work or evidence based on it. Meanwhile, one fundamental question persists. When all this discursive material is reflected in the rear-view mirror, can it simply be described as a unity only because it is perceived as one image? This risk is typical of any analysis of discursive materials. M. Foucault (1969: 99) warned against such precipitate steps when he described the discourse that consists of a 'dispersion d'éléments': "Or cette dispersion… peut être décrite dans sa singularité si on est capable de déterminer les règles spécifiques selon lesquelles ont été formés objects, énonciations, concepts, options théoriques: si unité il y a, elle n'est point dans la cohérance visible…" The preliminary results of the above analyses of discursive materials lead into the calamitous situation described by Foucault. In a way, there is a discourse but it is created by heterogeneous elements that make it appear as consisting of dispersed, unconnected elements. What could provide for a visible coherence? As mentioned, it would be easy to propose the content of the discourse itself that is the law as a textual referent that would guarantee the visible coherence in the legal discourse. This idea imposes itself the more so as the subject who speaks can be almost automatically eliminated as a unifying device. For his part, Foucault (1969: 46) considers the possibility to reach coherence by addressing the totality of its elements, "…peut être en considérant l'ensemble des énoncés…" Finally, Foucault (1969: 78) warns against such a simplification: "Tout à l'heure, on a montré que ce n'était ni par les "mots" ni par les "choses" qu'il fallait définir le régime des objects propres à une formation discursive." Clearly, there are still too many dispersed and heterogeneous elements in the characterization of the legal discourse that contradict its alleged coherence. Also therefore the reference to law as the least common denominator would not do. Meanwhile, the search for a visible coherence can also lead into a trap. Foucault (1969: 99) identified this situation and solved the paradox in a question that he abundantly commented: "Comment affirmer qu'on a bien individualisé des ensembles discursives?" This is an important question that refers to the beginning of every work on discourses that may be perceived as legal, political, medical etc. Foucault spent much time on commenting this discursive feature and he suggested that in case of an alleged dispersion of elements that threatens the coherence of the described discourse we simply might have identified or individualized another set of discursive practices. It means that in case where the legal discourse described on the preceding pages is something different from what has been expected, the result is by no means incoherent. Simply, the legal discourse as a result of the analysis differs from the initial assumption of what it actually is or might be. Foucault is right with his solution. Were he wrong, the legal discourse as described above with reference to textual samples could not be accepted as such. And this would be a result deadly to any theory. It would namely mean that something clearly is and at the same time cannot be. Foucault realized this risk and he explained with impressive clearness why such a result that identifies or individualizes a discourse as composed of elements that might be perceived as dispersed, is coherent and justified. Indeed, the legal discourse as described in previous chapters differs from the idea that many interested or less interested participants in discursive practices might have had about its structure. This discourse is not limited to the analysis of the concept of the legal norm and its application by judges. It appears as a much more complex textual structure that in all its complexity can nevertheless be perceived as a unity based on specific rules. This unity will emerge in discursive practices such as the interpretation. There is apparently no other proof for the existence of legal discourses than the interpretive. In social sciences interpretive methods are not perceived as weak evidence due to the discursive nature of phenomena that are scrutinized there. We can therefore continue to speak meaningfully about the legal discourse because its existence has been sufficiently proven here with interpretive methods.

9.1.1 Discursive multiplicity further expanded

Michel Foucault encourages the view upon the discourse that is not timidly limited by any apparent conceptual prerequisites. In fact, the legal discourse is clearly more than a set of professionally acceptable assertions about the propositions of law. It is actually fully incomprehensible in such a limited form. In this limited view might also ground the divide between the traditional legal doctrine and the positivist legal theory. When the positivist legal theory is committed to the legal discourse that is limited to the structure of the legal norm, then it cannot contribute in any substantial way to the extra-theoretical positivist legal doctrine that perceives law as a matter of fact. This intricate situation was identified in the analysis of many court decisions and legal problems in the above chapters. Meanwhile, M. Foucault also teaches another important truth that is relevant to the legal science. In his view, there is absolutely no reason to fear the expansion of conceptual boundaries of a branch of knowledge. It will not fall apart simply because it is approached in a broader conceptual perspective. For him, the contrary is actually the case. Therefore, when law is approached from the perspective of a pragmatically founded legal linguistics it can, as a result of epistemological changes that such analysis may provoke, be easier understood and applied. The mentioned impression that may suggest the contrary is therefore misleading. The gap between the theoretical reflection upon law and the activities aiming at shaping and applying law tends to diminish in this perspective. The unity of reflection upon law and application of law comes closer and the price paid for the operation is modest. Some adjustment in teaching, forming and applying law would suffice to match up to this expanded, yet not really new characterization of the legal discourse. Jurists are used to a more limited version of the legal discourse and its expanded version may therefore appear to them as cumbersome. This misperception can easily be surmounted. The legal discourse that has been described here is close to the social reality and the daily experience of people. An example may facilitate the acceptance of the conception of the legal discourse as proposed here. In many civil law countries the doctrine of the sources of law excludes court precedents. Jurists, of course, know that all judges study precedents, especially those issued by the higher courts. Judges all over the world will hesitate to render decisions that are contrary to the decisions rendered by higher courts of their jurisdiction. They will therefore, as a rule, follow the precedents that are for them one of the most important sources of law. At the same time, their commitment to precedents will be denied by the legal doctrine in the name of the freedom of the judicial decision. Clearly, judges in the common law and in the civil law jurisdictions apply only law. Yet, this law has for them mainly the form given by the higher courts of their jurisdictions. It would be difficult to deny this finding. Meanwhile, legal linguistics as an interdisciplinary theory of law is not bound by the legal doctrine. It takes the legal doctrine independently into consideration and can sometimes propose better solutions for the application of law. Perceiving the legal precedent as a source of law in civil law countries is one of such proposals. Providing further linguistically founded guidelines for the work on precedents would be another. As this example illustrates, it is actually easier to work as a legal professional within the framework of the expanded legal discourse because it is less fictitious than the limited legal discourse proposed by the positivist legal doctrine and the positivist legal theory. It has the further advantage that it is not really new. It reflects the discourse in which jurists and non-jurists communicate daily, although they identify differently the boundaries of the linguistic activity that they exercise. This leads to tensions in relations with non-professionals of law because legal non-professionals construe such situations as exposures to unknown and mysterious mechanisms in which they can only lose. Legal professionals may feel equally unsatisfied in situations in which they are perceived as linguistic oppressors, especially when they are not ready to endorse such negative roles. They may not wish to exercise a profession that has a bad renown. The solution proposed here, that has been encouraged by M. Foucault and not only by him, is a theoretical answer to many practical questions. It has therefore a bearing on the daily exercise in the institutions dealing with law in its immediate and more remote surroundings. It is namely clear that this legal discourse sets requirements for the participation in it that cannot be fulfilled within the traditional positivist approaches to law. Social sciences will have to integrate the legal science and contribute to the discourse with equal responsibility. As a result, the dispersed elements of the legal discourse will also become less disconnected. Law, shaped and spoken, will look somewhat differently. Yet, it will remain law. After all these possible transformations, killers and fraudsters will presumably still end up in prison, even if the legal discourse will more consciously reflect the totality of its dispersed elements.

9.1.2 Discursive multiplicity regulated

Another traditional textual evidence for the existence of discourses is the interrelation that can be traced in the discursive materials (cf. van Dijk 1980: 22). As shown above in many case analyses, the dispersed elements of the legal discourse are intertwined. When these interrelations are discovered, the legal discourse becomes fully operative, i.e. it enables the understanding and the application of law. M. Foucault (1969: 100) made a remark concerning these interrelations: "...quant on parle d'un système de formation, on n'entend pas seulement la juxtaposition, la coexistence ou l'interaction d'éléments hétérogènes (institutions, techniques, groupes sociaux, organisations perceptives, rapports entre des discours divers) mais leurs mise en relation – et sous une forme bien déterminée – par la pratique discursive." It is therefore less interesting to discover that the legal discourse is complex; it is decisive to discover how the interrelation among its elements develops within the discursive practice. It is fundamental because meaning emerges in this situation. It is relatively easy to show that different propositions of law may be related to the same concept. It is more important and also more difficult to show which proposition of law actually wins in the competition. The strategies of inclusion and exclusion of the propositions about the valid law are multiple. All of them are part of the complex speech act of legal interpretation. Foucault (1969: 100) introduces one more essential facet of discourse that is important for law. He stresses that at the stage of competition, which in this essay concerns the propositions of law, the concepts are actually formed. This aspect is decisive for the legal-linguistic approach because it enables to integrate a large part of the learned discourse about law that concerns the creation of legal concepts. In this learned discourse concepts are introduced as a result of free imagination of legal professionals. Theoretically, it is still badly explained why these and not other concepts have emerged in the legal discourse and why they became central to law in a specific epoch. These concepts were not introduced into law simply because someone has had a good idea. In certain epochs certain concepts are coined and certain theories are perceived as valid and sufficient. And this is not a coincidence, either. The understanding of the legal discourse includes the understanding of such intricate and often also undercover processes. Unfortunately, jurists never really liked to talk about them. They might have feared the complexity of the issue or have suspected a political element being in play. As in the affirmative and in the positivist tradition of dealing with law, politics had been prudently perceived as extra- or pre-legal, the discussion of the legal-linguistic strategies that make legal concepts emerge and subsist in law was neglected. As a result, the isolated legal rule dominated the limited positivist legal discourse. The interest in discursive practices in which legal discourses came about was banned from the legal research and it was marginalized as unprofessional. Today, legal-linguistic methods can be instrumental in overcoming this artificial barrier. Finally, the reconstruction of the legal discourse means also the reconstruction of all formative discursive practices and Foucault rightly insists on this point while characterizing the structure of the general discourse. Interpretive discursive practices, when aptly applied, can engender structuring effects. With their help, the multiplicity of discourses can be further regulated; the discourse can be tamed and ordered. What could be the practical results of such discursive reconstructions?

9.2 Law based on regulative principles

Legal discourses, both the professional and the non-professional, manifest a complexity that regularly gives rise to discontent. On the other side, rare are those who could imagine a radical simplification of the existing structures of law that would significantly reduce this complexity. Is there an alternative to this type of law that regularly also engenders discontent of professionals and of non-professionals? One could think about a merger of the ancient Greek creative and the Roman systematizing approaches to law that could converge into a law based on regulative principles and not on explicit rules. Other legal traditions, mostly those based on religion and natural law developed a view parallel to this one. Yet, in those traditions law is perceived as revealed in a broad framework of traditional ethical beliefs. In the Occidental tradition, law is perceived as being made by people. It is therefore discursively of a different sort than the natural or religious laws. A law without statutes and precedents would function as a primary discursive practice. Legal discourses would be reduced to the emergence and the interpretation of those regulative principles. Case law would have an illustrative and not a binding character, statutory law or codes would not exist. Such a modified law may have advantages, especially because it is always up to date and because it reflects the struggle for values in society at the given moment. It would be discursively explicit. The discursively explicit type of law would also be better suited for the whole world as it allows for adjustments that may be needed in the ongoing cultural evolution. This vision is as of now purely theoretical and also largely speculative. More realistic appears therefore the vision of law that is closely rooted in its textuality as the dominating and most visible feature of its discursiveness. This law will remain for a long time linked to standards applied in written texts that are developed in specialised languages. Drafting laws along these standards will practically also remain one of the most common legal-linguistic operations. It is essential to legal linguistics to expand these standards and to demonstrate that progress is possible in this area that is perceived by many jurists as arcane and irremediable.

9.2.1 Would laws be drafted differently?

The expanded boundaries of the legal discourse prepare new ground for the drafting of laws. In the deliberation about the future law more elements will be taken into account. The increased awareness that law emerges in discursive practices facilitates its drafting. Its future drafters will be better aware of this principle and laws that will have to be applied will also be drafted towards the background of this simple thought. The main task for the drafters will be to reflect upon the potential applicability of laws by other professionals of law. The schematic use of linguistic forms that remain unchanged in decades will be overcome. As a result, and for the first time in history, laws would say what they mean. All these ambitious steps require however some changes in line with the legal-linguistic findings. It would be necessary to expand the notion of 'plain language' that dominates the current legal-linguistic discussion and to explore the possibilities of the use of ordinary language in law. Furthermore, explicitness in the use of language, i.e. saying what one means would become a fundamental principle of legislation. This would be truly a Copernican revolution of legislative practices. Meanwhile, law would remain law and its interpretation would still be necessary. The interpretive devices that would be implemented would coincide with those used in the practice of the ordinary language. Jurists would not be exposed any more to interpretive practices that turn the meaning of words they know from daily practice into their contrary. Such a law would be a fascinating and a noble practice. Its study would remain a challenge, yet it could also become a pleasure. One cannot exclude that a new Lucretius appreciative of its intellectual depth and ethical cleanliness could desire to commit all his poetical talents to the chant and the praise of such a law.

9.2.2 Judgments as intellectual contributions

Would the activity of judges that interests the legal linguist change significantly? Would court decisions be written differently? Doubtless, writing court opinions has always been perceived as a demanding activity. One may see critically the positivist argumentation in the decisions of courts, yet one cannot deny that the development of such arguments in writing demands skills. The traditional court decision constitutes therefore an advanced linguistic practice. This holds even truer for the modern times where the written justification of the decisions taken by courts of law is mandatory in most cases and in most jurisdictions. Strategies used for drafting of this written input into the legal discourse have been multiple. Some judges favored schematic forms for their judgments and filled a pre-formulated conceptual skeleton with words. Others elaborated more freely on the law and on its connection with the case they had to decide. As the accessibility to court decisions increases in many jurisdictions, judges will have to ask whether they can accept the given standards that shape their decisions and that they sign with their names and make public. 'Public' means nowadays potentially accessible to millions of readers all over the world on the internet. This is an unusual circumstance as by now most public documents of daily bearing were drafted for limited distribution that comprised the immediately concerned parties and some other, mostly professional readers. The only exception was the landmark law that often has been also written with the idea in mind that landmark law was written. This practice will almost certainly be modified in future. Meanwhile, do we overburden judges when we demand from them to write judgments that could be taken for intellectual contributions? The legal discourse that was described in the above parts of this essay is so complex and constituted of so many disparate elements that the judicial decision must include also other elements than those purely intellectual, so a possible point of criticism against our request. With other words: the choice among the thinkable propositions of law is simply too big to be handled in a purely intellectual operation. In the pragmatist tradition, it has been claimed that when we are faced with a genuine choice about what to believe, and where evidence does not decide the matter, we are free to decide it however we want. As William James (1907: 129) puts it in his famous quote in his *Pragmatism. A New Name for Some Old Ways of Thinking*: "…our passional nature not only lawfully may, but must, decide an option between propositions, whenever it is a genuine option that cannot by its nature be decided on intellectual grounds." Meanwhile, this situation does not mean anarchy or arbitrariness. There may exist situations that are 'genuine options', yet most situations in which propositions of law are to be elucidated are not genuine because they emerge within complex and intertwined discourses. In law, there are no situations that could not be decided 'on intellectual grounds' and where passion alone would lead towards a decision. The discursiveness of law provides the basis for the intellectual activity that rightfully aims at understanding law. In discourses that emerge under the conditions described in above chapters no other grounds than the intellectual are wishful or even thinkable in order to cope with the propositions of law. W. James's remark is however important because it makes plain the process of the theoretical or anthropologically relevant emergence of law. It marks the point in which law emerges as a discursive and not as another practice. Wherever one looks in law, its discursiveness appears as its most salient feature. Meanwhile, it would be premature to ask whether the choice of discursiveness – as it might be reconstructed in legal anthropology – refers to the situation of a 'genuine choice'. It seems that in law, which is a social phenomenon, no such situation actually existed. Where there was society, there had been laws and these laws were stated and applied as expressed in language. Discursiveness of law is therefore not a matter of choice. Law is a purely intellectual product that is accessible in its entirety intellectually within complex discursive practices. This situation opens many doors for judges and all others who wish to state the law of their epoch. As judges are the main contributors to these specific writings about law, they may profit most from the fact that law is a discursive practice and not something else. The request that judgments have to be formed as intellectual contributions to the legal discourse is therefore fully justified.

9.2.3 Can jurists contribute more than discourses to law?

This question concerns the generalized expectation that jurists would know the law and not only words. This knowledge could be described as encompassing the material part of law. As a matter of fact, law has a substantial part, i.e. it regulates issues. For instance, driving may be allowed on the left-hand side of the road or on the right-hand side of the road. Law will also, as a rule, determine the appropriate time limits for filing claims in courts. Law will say whether a country shall be a republic or a monarchy. Law will say whether prostitution is allowed in a country or whether theft will be punished with more or less than two years of prison. Law clearly regulates, yet this regulation, as relevant as it may be in a case, is not decisive. In all above examples the regulation could have easily taken another shape. It seems therefore to be largely contingent and ephemeral. The German jurist Julius von Kirchmann wrote in his booklet *Die Wertlosigkeit der Jurisprudenz als Wissenschaft* (1938: 37) about this challenging structural feature of law: "Indem die Wissenschaft das Zufällige zu ihrem Gegenstand macht, wird sie selbst zur Zufälligkeit; drei berichtigende Worte des Gesetzgebers und ganze Bibliotheken werden zu Makulatur." Kirchmann stressed the ephemeral and incidental character of legal regulation that may evolve at whatever moment due to unforeseeable or capricious legislative initiatives. Kirchmann's view is in line with the most ancient epistemological doctrines rendered by Aristotle in the first book of his *Metaphysics* (987a). Aristotle writes about the Heraclitean doctrine: "…all sensible things are ever in a state of flux and there is no knowledge about them." Indeed, constant change does not facilitate theory formation. This holds particularly true in the area of law where attention is mostly focused on material aspects of regulation. Therefore, regulation perceived as a matter of fact will not do. Legal regulation emerges and is applied in legal-linguistic operations that were exhaustively discussed in previous chapters. What is more, Kirchmann (1938: 33) positions positive law, as it is understood by the legal positivists, between the law and the legal science. He stresses that law exists independently of the legal science (Kirchmann 1938: 22). Both aspects are helpful in the understanding of regulation. In the positivist conception it is the content of law, something related to law. Kirchmann calls therefore the positive law a middle stage between law and the legal science. This law can definitely exist without the legal science. Law's further existence under such circumstances would however become difficult because it, as a discursive practice, needs an explicit theory of its discursiveness in order to be applied in a rational way. Legislative regulation is therefore largely secondary to law, and Kirchmann rightly warned against too much attention to this feature of law in the legal science. Therefore, regulation can survive in the theory of law as propositional content of legal speech acts. This is a different form of existence than the one proposed by the positivist view upon regulation. In it, regulation is understood as a matter of fact that pertains at representing law. Law is therefore a matter of regulation and regulation is its reference. Jurists are specialists in speaking about this regulation, i.e. about the validity of propositions of law uttered as legal speech acts in legal discourses. The legal theory, and especially the legal linguistics, keeps an eye on the regulation while concentrating on other, more relevant legal-linguistic operations in law. Central at this point is the question whether legal regulation is in essence a linguistic phenomenon. Does it resemble the Morning Star? One cannot deny that legal regulation is centered on linguistic creation. Meanwhile, as far as its content is concerned, jurists will never be able to answer the question whether the most appropriate speed limit for driving in towns is fifty kilometres per hour. Knowing this speed limit that is enacted in the legislation is part of their professional knowledge, yet it is rudimentary to other relevant professional skills that make jurists of them. One could also ask more generally whether jurists are qualified to determine these matters, or more precisely, whether they are qualified better than others to determine them? This seems not to be the case. Jurists are trained in the use of argumentative procedures. In this sense they have acquired the procedural knowledge and they are qualified to apply techniques related to drafting laws and applying statutes and precedents in a way that suits best society at large. As far as the subject matter itself is concerned, they do not know it any better than other citizens. Therefore, jurists' professional role in the area of law is limited by the discursiveness of the phenomenon. It is not necessarily a disadvantage because jurists are specialists in the linguistic application of law that is the practical consequence of the fact that law is a discursive phenomenon. This specific professional skill guarantees them also an advanced position in all legal matters that are perceived in this essay as the application of legal regulation in legal-linguistic operations. As of now, jurists are irreplaceable in this area of their particular professional competence.

9.3 Sense of law

Law is frequently underestimated in science and society. In science, it is held for the realm of those less original and less courageous. Unlike in other social sciences, scholars who deal with law are rarely quoted as great thinkers or creators of schools of thought or of new approaches to social phenomena. Jurists overall are deemed to be prudent, which means cowardly. Particularly painful is the work in the area of law in societies where law does not matter much. Jurists, both legal scholars as well as practitioners, are degraded there to the role of decorative puppets and alibi researchers. There is no Nobel Prize for achievements in legal sciences. Students, also law students, regularly complain that the subject law is boring. Some advanced students even argue that nothing can be done about it because law is simply, in its very essence and irremediably, a boring matter. It is studied to enter the civil service or private legal practice in order to ensure good life, which means prosperity, security and social influence. Academic reflection does not matter under such crude conditions. In society, law as a mechanism is often met with skepticism. Its rigidity and backward orientation are criticized. Both points of criticism are not necessarily compulsive as more creative and critical approaches to law are possible and examples of such creativeness in law can be named. When society does not care about right and wrong and when it does not care about procedures that would provide means for shaping discourses about right and wrong, not much can be done against it from the side of jurists. Educational institutions would have to convince the citizens that law, i.e. the state of law or the future global legal governance are better suited to find solutions to societal problems than other mechanisms. These mechanisms, when abandoned, will sooner or later take the shape of arbitrariness, anarchy or violence. Some citizens might wrongly assume that they could gain something under such circumstances. Meanwhile, experience teaches that arbitrary rule or open violence as regulative ideas in society benefit only a few, and this usually for a relatively short period of time. What is more, language is a reliable tool in the context of legal-linguistic construction of sense. This holds true notwithstanding the indeterminacy of meaning and the ambiguity of whatever sort. It holds even true when meaning is associated with sense, as is the case in the English language. Are meaning and sense comparable with freedom and liberty? And if this is the case, why does the English language maintain a double lexical structure along centuries? The double structure of English lexis marks the socially distinctive speech. Typical examples of such speech are doublets such as: 'She came too early' and 'She arrived prematurely' that are perceived as semantically equivalent, yet stylistically different. It follows from the above that the language of law does not need to be plain or simple. Some complexity in its structures provides potential for legal creativeness. Sense or meaning of law that emerge in legal-linguistic discourses depends on this complexity.

9.3.1 Axiological elements in legal discourses

Legal discourses encountered here as amalgams of interrelated legal signs do not exist in a vacuum. They are embedded in dynamic power structures that cause constant changes in the regulation of state and society that are implemented with legal instruments. The power in question is not a primitive and overwhelming physical dominance, although it can also be this. Power in law is the discursive element that endorses social values that are introduced into the legal discourse. This legal discourse is not simply there; it makes the application of law, i.e. the enforcement of the dominant social values possible. The legal discourse is therefore an axiological discourse. Even if the social discourse sometimes tends to appear in a formal shape, it is always the result of axiological choices. Likewise, the preference for the discussion of formal questions of law in courts is also a result of such axiological choices. Similarly, the preference in the bureaucracy for quantitative arguments against qualitative arguments is one another such axiological choice. Still further, an Italian legal maxim says 'Giustizia è uguale per tutti'. The lofty maxim of a 'Justice that is equal for everyone' decorates the walls of all Italian courtrooms. Daily experience shows that socially underprivileged parties pay a tribute under this maxim. What is with the privileged? Are they treated better? Elites are privileged when they act as elites. Acting against elites excludes privileged members and exposes them to sanctions that overweigh those applied to mainstream citizens. – Habent sua fata sententiae. – The axiological elements of law increase the complexity of the legal discourse; yet they guarantee also that it can be instrumental in steering and inspiring society. Society masters perfectly the discursive devices that are necessary for the development of an explicitly value-oriented and discursive law. John Searle (2006) characterized the axiological element in the discourse as deontic. It is for him an unavoidable component of speech acts that require speaker's commitment to truth. This commitment is the feature that "enables language to form the foundation of human society in general." Searle integrates axiology into language use as for him using language without the commitment to truth does not make much sense. Furthermore, it would be uninteresting to study such language use and its importance for society. Finally, the axiology of law that is understood in the broader sense introduced by J. Searle and supported all along the lines of this essay also shows that the legal discourse is best positioned and understood in the focus of all interested branches of science, and mainly the social sciences. Liberated from the isolation caused by the long negligence of many jurists interested in and co-responsible for its development, the legal discourse appears as a chance for the modern society. The above pages have hopefully shown that the legal discourse is an interesting offer that history has made to modern society. It would be unwise to decline this offer.

9.3.2 Law with a human face

The analysis of the discursiveness of law and of particular legal discourses has consequences for social practices that relate to law. Law as a social mechanism will be generally accepted when it will reflect the idea of democracy. John Rawls's *Theory of Justice* aptly states the trend towards equality present at least in the Occidental democracies. Legal discourse is all too often used to circumvent the fundamental concepts that frame democracy. The tension that emerges cannot be resolved with purely discursive means. The problem jurists have is that they are not specialists in the content of law; they master law in terms of its discursiveness. As a consequence of the use of language in legal discourses, participatory democratic rights must be strengthened and direct democracy enhanced. As long as knowledge of doctrinary law will be used as a mechanism of social selection between those who govern and those who are governed, no realistic democratic participation comes into question. The future may bring the shift of attention from adjudication to the legislative process. It may also modify participatory rights that today are at best discursively turned into consultations (Fishkin 2009). Fishkin combines in his approach deliberative democracy and public consultation that he perceives as progress in the shaping of the discursive matrix. 'Consultation', that Fishkin traces down to ancient Athens, is a discursive text type that stresses participation. This participation includes creating and applying laws with linguistic means. Parts of this book may suggest how both tasks could be accomplished in line with requirements that rules for the use of language impose upon speakers. In particular, prohibitive use of doctrinary hermetic language in law must be limited, if necessary by law. Explicit language should be preferred to plain language. There are many examples of plain legal language that represent also the worst possible law, such as a section of the General Statute of Massachusetts from mid-nineteenth century providing that "No child under 12 years of age shall be employed in any manufacturing establishment more than 10 hours in one day." In literature, Albert Camus's *L'étranger* marks the outer limits of plain legal language that is in his case pure horror: "Je n'en ai pas eu le temps parce que le président m'a dit dans une forme bizarre que j'aurais la tête tranchée sur une place publique au nom du peuple français." Legal linguistics can therefore contend that law with a human face is linguistically explicit.

9.4 New horizons

Despite the above enthusiastic lines that show the usefulness of law for society, one must be aware of the fact that an outlook in law is always difficult. Law does not develop independently of societies. In fact, it is their most efficient mechanism that enables their development. Contemporary law is therefore not a necessary evil in society and it is not a default mechanism that is used when other devices that steer society cannot work. Society needs law and it is constituted by law not because humans are wicked and unreasonable but because society develops within a dynamic system of discursive practices that engender rules. It is therefore unproductive to claim the abolition of law; more persuasive are attempts at improving the quality of law. What is more, tendencies towards developing a global law in the form of an overarching regulation applicable all over the planet will definitely modify our views upon law in future. Today one can only predict that also the future law will be a discursive social practice based on legal-linguistic operations. It can be further assumed that this law will be better understood by professionals and non-professionals in terms of its inherent discursiveness. However, one cannot say whether it will be a better law in the sense of the claims regularly repeated along the lines of this essay. A broader and more literary approach to the question as advocated in this essay may therefore be helpful. A broader or broadened legal discourse transgresses artificial conceptual borders that impede its further development. It is also more ambitious than the strictly professional doctrinal discourse because it also includes a vision of law in society. This circumstance might therefore justify the pathos and the febrility of the last chapter that aims at reaching the conceptual horizons of the future law. Preliminary work for this chapter has been done in some of the above paragraphs that explicitly deal with legal-linguistic methodology. Also literary methods and some 'higher levels of culture' have been abundantly explored in the above chapters in order to find a better methodological approach to law. Their sense in the general argument has been to illustrate the range of the legal discourses that fundamentally depend on written and spoken word used in other, non-legal social and cultural practices. They include less advanced and not really impressive legal discourses of daily life and some more advanced discourses that are called here literary in contradistinction to other professional discourses about law that are engendered by jurists in their daily professional activities. In the above chapters not much has been said about daily discourses about law where law is treated rather sweepingly. The reason for this shortcoming is mainly that these discourses have proven less productive in processes where law is developed and that their role is mostly limited to issues of acceptability of law that is made by others. They are rarely creative discourses and they differ in this sense from more advanced discourses called here literary discourses. These discourses provide more explicit visions about law than the purely evaluative daily discourses. They are therefore more interesting objects of study in a legal-linguistic analysis. Yet, could literary visions become dominant in law?

9.4.1 Relevance of historical matrix

At least historically, multiple classic, scholastic and humanist strains in the political reasoning were used as linguistic matrices for the creation of law. They could have been also used differently because texts, also literary texts, have a meaning potential that manifests itself in interpretive acts. Some of these linguistic matrices may disappoint as shown in some of the examples analyzed above and below. They may however also engender useful notional fields in which a better law could function. A better law needs a better society, where good life is fairly defined and conditions of happiness determined. Numerous attempts were undertaken to reach these goals, they range from pure descriptions to utopian visions. Meanwhile, in all such visions the linguistic creation is central. Yet, utopian visions may be deceiving. The most explicit of such deceiving visions is Thomas More's *Utopia*. Its author, himself a lawyer, proposes in his *Utopia*, first published 1516, an alternative to the existing state. Before him Plato in *The Republic* and *Laws*, later Aristotle, mainly in his *Politics*, Augustinus in *De Civitate Dei*, Hooker in *On the Laws of Ecclesiastical Polity* and others developed discourses about the better state that were constructed as radical alternatives to the existing social practice. They can be therefore construed as political projects. More's discourse on the ideal commonwealth is particularly ambiguous as a political project due to its limited innovativeness. In fact, it does not attract the reader in the least. The other previously mentioned proposals attract even less, therefore one could ask why they are actually until our own days used in educational institutions as alternative descriptions of better societies. The discursive approach to law is here the part of the answer. All of these visions have a trait in common that is linguistically relevant. They develop concepts that are matrices for more advanced discursive practices about the state, society and the mechanism that structures them, the law. They invent the 'eudaimonia', 'eunomia', and 'autarchy' as requirements for further notional perfectionism. Indeed, further categories and subcategories of the linguistic-political discourse are developed until today. Th. More attempts in his lawyerly Latin a description of a no-place as an alternative or model for places he knows. His utopia, ambiguous in terms and contents, discourages more than it attracts. Liberty is arbitrarily limited there; wars are waged if expedient. The disservice to the public expectation is perfectly rendered in More's *Utopia*. Requirements for alternative notions may be linguistically fulfilled, the contents that they produce are disenchanting. This is the critical result that can be reached with the help of the discursive approach to law. In fact, Th. More proposes an obscure alternative and deprives his readers of dreams about a better future. One could also ask whether this lack of readiness to give the future a chance is the result of his legal education. What is more, the lack of seriousness surprises in a legal author. After all, the unserious trait shows *Utopia*'s real face: it is an academic joke, a piece of science fiction suitable as pastime lecture for rulers, not to be read by the ruled. Its primary perfect reader is however the Renaissance humanist who might have taken pleasure in detecting the hidden classical sources of More's ideas and enjoy his Greek-based composition of neologisms. Meanwhile, lack of seriousness and responsibility in dealing with public affairs only strengthens and legitimizes the societal status quo. Th. More as a writer of the establishment clearly obstructed with his caustic book the reformist tendencies in society of his time. He turned the dream of a better future into a satire. In its structural cynicism there is irresponsibility that in turn catches the author as responsible for obstructing a democratic discourse about law. Th. More in the initial part of his *Utopia* mentioned a seemingly neglected question, namely where to find Utopia in the New World? This question will not be answered in his book because his project remains utopian. For his readers, the impression emerges that there is nowhere to go. And this conclusion might have been intended by the author. Yet, all this disappointing reading experience can finally be neglected as *Utopia* like all other utopian visions about societal and legal alternatives survive as bearers of anti-essentialist discursive practices. Apparently, also the literary approach to law makes sense and even bad and manipulative books may be valuable to attempts at shaping a better future.

Another prominent author of More's times, Nicolo Machiavelli, probably makes the right step in the right direction with *Il Principe*, written before More's *Utopia* in 1513, yet published much later, in 1532. He dissociates himself from most of the speculative projects of his learned predecessors and analyzes the power structures. In point of fact, Machiavelli regrets the boundaries put upon his work by the political practice. His *Discorsi* manifest his commitment to an ethical concept of society and of man that cannot materialize under the circumstances of practical life that he had experienced. What is more, Machiavelli's *Il Principe* is serious. Cynicism that dominates its textuality is the cynicism of the world, not Machiavelli's. Machiavelli attracts less than More because he does not develop visions and only presents the ugly face of power. He also develops language needed for the description of processes that enable to gain and maintain power. Notions such as 'necessità', 'virtù', 'fortuna', and 'qualità dei tempi' became essential to any reflection about this complicated and largely intransparent process which leads individuals to power. In this process individuals do many things; for us it is essential that they also or even mainly speak on their way to power. For Machiavelli whatever those speakers do, is actually rather negative. Others, mostly modern writers such as M. Foucault, did not always assume that the exercise of power is by its nature a negative thing. After all, M. Foucault's work, which has been used in many chapters of this essay, would not emerge without such surgical dissections of state and society that may be received by readers as dark and hopeless visions. Also Hobbes's *Leviathan* supports such readers' attitudes in that it equips them with language of hopelessness in confrontation with social reality of their time. It is not a pastime reading for the ruled either. Yet work on legal aspects of literary visions does not need to be a pleasant task. Reading and writing about law is often unpleasant and irritating. The reason for this discomforting experience is that law is a social discursive practice. Individual involvement in such a practice can only be contributive, which means creative within limits. One can write a *Hamlet* alone, yet even an intellectually insignificant piece of law such as a road code imposes upon those who create it formal and institutional requirements that could not be further complicated.

Nowadays, a social order is construed as utopian when it is imagined as self-controlled by individuals. W. Menski (2006: 203) mentions such an order in a context different from ours within a higher (cosmic) superstructure of the Hindu law. The main idea there is to surpass state-made law. And indeed, the idea that humans would agree on a (global) legal order that they would also respect as a matter of principle is the main utopia in the law of our time. A modern theologist, H. Küng (1997) developed such a vision that is close to R. Domingo's (2010) more juridical project of the future global law. Justice theories such as J. Rawls's and R. Dworkin's theory of law show prerequisites for this type of new or newer society. R. Dworkin (2006) insisted on dealing with regulation within a broad exegesis of law and included comments on matters of regulation such as abortion, race, euthanasia, death penalty and the like. More strikingly, the crime novel author, Raymond Chandler, wrote about law in *The High Window* (1943): "The law, whatever it is, is a matter of give-and-take…Like most other things." And indeed, legal utopias are mostly formulated in realistic terms. They do not promise a paradise, and are therefore within their limits less literary than literary utopias. Similarly, American utopian projects were less literary but they have been also rendered in literature. Born Americans and those who came to the country via Ellis Island had cherished expectations regarding the future. It may sound exaggerated when one would claim that they had expectations concerning law, constitutional, penal and other. Even the most inveterate jurists will rarely emigrate in the aim to enjoy a legal system that corresponds with their programmatic visions. Yet, at the bottom of all expectations, expressed or implicit, they are residues of order according to which people not only live but they live with other people. Some people may not be aware of this bottom line prerequisite, while others may be it. In fact, the very result of this merger of born Americans and others in the U.S. is also the result of being aware of this prerequisite or not being it. Somewhere, there is also a point in social life where everyone is called upon and everyone is responsible. Responsibility for law, it goes without saying, can be claimed only within individual options that underlie the human condition. Also in East Asia, that developed outside the classical Greek political discourse, the evolution of the language of the political and the legal thought transgresses Confucius' academic and sterile state loyalty in Wang Chong's writings. One can therefore assume that new utopias about law will emerge in future.

9.4.2 New Utopia

Narratives, competing and complementary, about the future of society and its law are necessary. They would provide the narrative texture for arguments about the future law in society that aims at its reorganization. The seek and hide in the adventure around the law is typical of dealing with law that is not a private fantasy but the product of an ongoing social discourse. Elements of such utopian project are included in many existing works. R. Dworkin will be remembered as a legal writer who insisted upon 'human dignity' as a notional prerequisite for any creative work on law. Others stressed 'human rights', collective and individual. 'Participative democracy', 'decent argumentation', 'partnership democracy', 'governments' equal concern for citizens' or 'self-government' are linguistic creations upon which projects for the legal future such as the global law could be based. Such projects require competent writers and readers willful to take such writings seriously. Countertendencies to such projects have also been identified. Hannah Arendt remarked about the relation between discursiveness and meaning in the academic discourse in *The Human Condition* (1998: 3–4): "The reason why it may be wise to distrust the political judgment of scientists qua scientists is not primarily their lack of 'character'… but precisely the fact that they move in a world where speech has lost its power. And whatever men do or know or experience can make sense only to the extent that it can be spoken about." Therefore, discursiveness of law as its most distinctive feature can become truly productive only in surroundings where discursiveness matters.

9.4.3 On providing unsolicited advice

The entire preceding essay is also meant as a piece of advice. Such an approach is frequently questioned, as for many law is an enterprise that starts late, after the legislator has said his last word. Criticism on legal writers seems therefore to be unavoidable, as the subject 'law' had long been perceived as an internal matter of rulers or states. Legal and other critical writers exposed themselves to criticism for entering a reserved domain, where they actually were not welcome. Parts of this criticism may be anticipated in the lines below. T. Todorov (1992: 249) writes: "…It is the exiled person who today best incarnates, though warping it from its original meaning, the ideal of Hugh of St. Victor, who formulated it this way in the twelfth century: The man who finds his country sweet is only a raw beginner; the man for whom each country is as his own is already strong; but only the man for whom the whole world is as foreign country is perfect." For the source of his citation Todorov refers to Erich Auerbach's *Philologie und Weltliteratur*, rendered in *Gesammelte Aufsätze zur romanischen*

Philologie (Bern: Franke, 1967). Significantly, also Edward Said refers to this source in his *Orientalism*. Exile as territory is not necessarily a place for which one cherishes – or as some may claim – is obliged to cherish the feeling of profound gratitude for having been admitted. It does not prevent the exiled from reflection, a benevolent activity when compared with much other action undertaken by men. Auerbach in Turkey, Todorov in France and Said in the U.S., all reflect under such imposed conditions. Their advice to society is sober, yet not without well concealed emotion. It is based on commitment to some very general, simple and understandable aspirations. Why can advice be expounded under such conditions of territorial limitations? The answer is rather simple. Commitment to values, especially those most fundamental, is not linked to a passport one has in one's pocket. Therefore, also unsolicited advice has its raison d'être in societies.

9.4.4 State without law and law without state

The *Longman Dictionary of Contemporary English* explains the use of 'consist in' with reference to the phrase "True freedom consists in the absence of laws." The phrase represents the social discourse that is skeptical of state and law. Many intellectual efforts have been spent in the past on the propositional content of this phrase. William Godwin forged even an ideology known as anarchism, while his wife Mary Wollstonecraft in *Vindication of the Rights of Woman* (1792) required equal rights for both genders. Today, the anarchistic idea is present mostly in marginal social circles. Meanwhile, absence of state and law is invoked by Roberto Saviano in his essay *Gomorra* (2006). Saviano mentions that absence of state does not mean absence of organization and structure. In Southern Italy the state of law is replaced by the camorra; rules that govern this organization are strict. Interestingly, it is not referred to as 'camorra' by its members and associates. They used to speak about 'il sistema' rather than 'la camorra'. They are, like some other criminals, inclined to use respectful language and also expect respectable attitudes from their interlocutors. In such settings, written founding myths are rare. Mafiotic structures are rather inspired by action films as visuality and not literality appeals more to simplistic organizational structures and gangster audiences. Saviano's *Gomorra* shows a world without state and law and it corresponds in this sense with Hobbes's *Leviathan* that tried to show the consequences of this absence that do not mean absence of rule or rule-related language. At the first sight it seems that both state and law are inseparable. It may generally be so, yet both state and law evolve with time.

9.4.5 Missing language in absent discourses

All above remarks encourage to ask one more principal question: why the contemporary society, which socially and culturally represents an advanced civilization, still cultivates a form of law that is firmly rooted in past centuries? Modern forms of communication as well as the techniques used in the sale of goods and services all over the planet reached a level of interconnection unimaginable even several decades ago. Law, however, relies on its status of dependence on institutions that are in terms of the modern democratic state at best indirectly legitimized. This circumstance leads inevitably to constraints in discursive practices. The main problem with language use in such institutions is, as shown on above pages, the procedural limitation of language use. This linguistic barrier engenders specialized language that is used as a vehicle for the development of professional legal argumentation and that favors those who use this language. Law is meanwhile a stable mechanism because it, as a discursive practice, processes utterances within legal-linguistic operations that are not accidental. The struggle for law takes place in discourses that are also struggles for language. One can assume that legal discourses evolve in terms of their narrativity sluggishly because language that could transport them is missing. Traditional legal institutions discourage the use of ordinary language that would be the sole reliable vehicle for such modern advanced discourses. It would engender, in contrast to the professional legal argumentation, a type of legal argumentation that would reflect the societal values more fully. That language and narration are interrelated also in terms of the narrative subject matter has been also shown in the above chapters. It can be therefore argued that speakers have at their disposal a broad linguistic competence to shape legal discourses. As was demonstrated above, they are able to use language efficiently even in the most extreme situations such as the execution of a death penalty judgment. Hickock's speaking (cf. 3.3.4) in a dramatic situation where a linguistic convention is missing, is a striking example of such a communicative behavior. However, some communicative strategies strengthen linguistic comportment that favors passive participation in legally relevant contexts. A perfect illustration of such an archetype can be found – as so often – in literature. Stendhal's novel *Le Rouge et le Noir* (1830) ends badly for its protagonist, Julien Sorel. He is condemned to death and during the trial he allows himself a critical remark that was rare in Stendhal's time. Julien criticizes the composition of the jury as socially biased against him: "Voilà mon crime, messieurs, et il sera puni avec d'autant plus de sévérité, que, dans le fait, je ne suis point jugé par mes pairs. Je ne vois point sur les bancs des jurés quelque paysan enrichi, mais uniquement des bourgeois indignés..." So far, Stendhal's text encourages participatory strategies in legal discourses. However, the situation changes when Julien is condemned to death. In the chapters that precede his condemnation and even after it Julien reflects and speaks a lot. His execution however is a mute scene. Language is absent in it, as for Stendhal such a context is apparently non-discursive, which means that there is no language that could be meaningfully used in it. In the novel, he quotes Jean de Rotrou's tragicomedy *Venceslas* (1647) that favors a mechanistic approach to extreme life situations in legal contexts. For Rotrou an execution is a non-linguistic, mechanical act: "Ladislas:..Mon âme est toute prête./ Le roi, père de Ladislas: L'échafaud l'est aussi; portez-y votre tête." This scene suggests Julien to remain silent during his execution. Therefore, Julien speaks only in his inner forum: "Allons, tout va bien, se dit-il, je ne manque point de courage." His 'tout va bien' definitely cannot reflect his particular situation, as nothing worse than that what is going to happen could actually happen to him. Yet, this 'tout va bien' fits perfectly the mechanistic structure of the execution as a scenery prepared by others. It is also rendered in the novel from the point of view of those complacent others: "Jamais cette tête n'avait été aussi poétique qu'au moment où elle allait tomber...Tout se passa simplement, convenablement, et de sa part sans aucune affectation." Unfortunately, in legal and in other texts one will be able to find numerous such linguistic strategies that suggest to citizens passive and opportunistic behavior in situations where the application of law is contrary even to their most vital interests. As this strategy is purely linguistic, it is not particularly difficult to eliminate it from contemporary discursive practices. Lack of innovative discourses in the area of law is therefore caused by the lack of appropriate language or rather by the lack of interest for the ordinary language that would perfectly function under the conditions of legal discourses in advanced modern societies (cf. Mead 1964: 242). Social history of humankind seems however to indicate that such periods of stagnation are transitory. Finally, a breakthrough follows upon epochs that favor and cherish institutions committed to the yesterday.

9.5 Law is in the air

The legal discourse shows that legally relevant contexts of law must be marked rather broadly. Therefore, our imagination and search for new sources of law cannot be limited to legal precedents or statutory provisions. Neither the landmark law nor the perfect statutory articles can render law in its entirety. It seems that whatever cultural artifact can become a source of law. Such sources can be more or less literary. The least literary may be monuments such as the Statue of Liberty. The Statue of Liberty is a present. Since 1886 it decorates the New York Harbor. This present developed to a symbol, primarily of democracy. Frédéric Auguste Bartholdi gave its 33 meters high statue the name *La Liberté éclairant le monde*. This is the key to the torch she holds. Light here is definitely not meant as a purely physical phenomenon. Some time ago, the Statue of Liberty turned green as a result of the corrosion of copper metal that constitutes it physically. Restoration of its surface ended 1986. Also law, like society that is constitutive of it, may be exposed to corrosion. History seems to teach that restoration always follows suit. Equally, or even more so, the statue seems to symbolize the U.S., i.e. America in a more popular parlance. This symbolic force is so strong that even a distortion like Franz Kafka's description of the statue in his *Amerika* on its first page as holding a sword, cannot weaken its impact on other minds. As a present, the statue may not oblige to anything; yet, as a symbol it does. While being also a symbol, it is a double-edge sword because it can be turned into visionary literature as shown in Kafka's case. Kafka's literary experiment marks the outer limits of the literary project as it apparently also signals the potential to fail when truth is construed in photographic terms. This is the modern version of a utopia about state and law that also fails. Sadly, from its very outset, American state papers lagged behind the discursive expectations that many people have cherished. The U.S. Constitution and *The Federalist* that were analyzed in the above chapters represent all but visions that could attract modern citizens. The French *Declaration of Rights of Man and Citizen* – another present to the world at large, this time fixed in writing, hence less visible and maybe also less influential because of it – sets up slightly higher standards. Yet also these standards seem to have been forgotten. Literature seems not to work as a vehicle of law. Thus, the generous donors may have offered a Trojan horse to the citizens at large. Another, less generous parent – mother England – offered the common law. Was this present a poisonous fruit? Had England been a perfect step-mother? The backwards oriented common law in its inherited shape did not encourage further efforts. Finally, the society disappointed its own people who like F. Scott Fitzgerald portrayed the diminishing trust in the American dream. For some, like those with African-American forefathers, there have never been any. Still others, such as Tennessee Williams turned away from this type of society where heroes fail, so at least in his *Cat on a Hot Tin Roof* or *The Glass Menagerie*. R. Dworkin in *Is Democracy Possible Here?* suggests what is to be done. J. Rawls prepared the framework for this practical reasoning. J. Searle explained how language shapes the social reality. T. Todorov looked back at its origins that appear less edifying than many textbook authors would wish. N. Chomsky added a more critical view upon the present situation. The list of visionary proposals is long and some of them have been scrutinized on above pages. Also Raymond Chandler, referred to in previous chapters, wrote in *The High Window* (1943) with unusual depth for a crime novel author: "We stared at each other, with that inner hostility that had been there from the first. After a moment I pushed my chair back and went over to the french windows. I opened the screen and stepped out on the porch. The night was all around, soft and quiet. The white moonlight was cold and clear, like the justice we dream of but don't find." Why should it be impossible to find it? The legal discourse includes even today sufficient material that could be used in approaching this goal that not only crime novel authors perceive as essential to the human race. Indeed more than literature is necessary to make law. Doubtless, though, language is unavoidable in law because it shapes social reality. Yet it does not provide visions automatically. Also the political discourse develops slogans and formulas that are perceived as linguistically innovative (Innerwinkel 2009). It is open whether these linguistic creations may be instrumental in obtaining other goals than the electional. Open and wise discourses are necessary to shape law.

Language can be used in law with admirable force. This force is not only linguistic, as it also conveys contents that are fundamental to discursive patterns that shape societies. Written legal texts bear witness to this theoretical prerequisite: *The Declaration of Rights of Man and Citizen* (1789) states in its first article: "Les hommes naissent et demeurent libres et égaux en droits. Les distinctions sociales ne peuvent être fondées que sur l'utilité commune." The English translation of this article says: "Men are born, and always continue, free and equal in respect of their rights. Civil distinctions, therefore, can be founded only on public utility." It is a visionary and a perfect formulation of a discursive frame of reference that is wishful in the modern world. It remains however also legalistic, especially in the English translation where the human beings are characterized as "free and equal in respect of their rights." This 'in respect of' establishes an inexplicit discursive relation between the citizens and their rights where they are not simply free and equal, but free and equal 'in respect of' an undefined position that is their right. One could not express the idea of 'equality before law' more confusingly. Meanwhile, M.L. King quoted in his *I Have a Dream* the sober statement of the *Declaration of Independence* (1776) "We hold these truths to be self-evident, that all men are created equal…" Regularly one may have the impression that it is difficult to express the equality of all human beings in legal discourses and this difficulty has reasons. The discourse about law is a struggle for law. It relies upon the well-established principle that Liberty enjoyed in Democracy is Justice. To fill this formula with words that would enable its application is the task of the discourse that shapes the law. Philosophers and poets would be most fond of such a law!

Bibliography

The bibliography includes only secondary literature. Reference to sources from which solely examples or other text samples were taken is provided in the main text. Likewise, reference to classical texts of philosophy or jurisprudence can be found in the main text only.

Aarnio, A. (1987): The Rational as Reasonable: A Treatise on Legal Justification (Dordrecht: Reidel).

Aarnio, A. (1989): Laintulkinnan teoria (Porvoo et al.: W. Söderström).

Aarnio, A. (2012): Remembrance – Legal Theory in the Shadow of G.H. von Wright, in: Rechtstheorie, vol. 43, nr. 1, pp. 1–18.

Adamolekun, L. (ed.) (1999): Public Administration in Africa: Main Issues and Selected Country Studies (Boulder: Westview Press).

Ajani, G. (2005): Sistemi Giuridici Comparati. Lezioni e Materiali (Torino: G. Giappichelli Ed.).

Akmajian, A., Demers, R.A., et al. (2001): Linguistics. An Introduction to Language and Communication, 5th ed. (Cambridge/London: MIT Press).

Alchourrón, C., Bulygin, E. (1971): Normative Systems (Vienna/New York: Springer Verlag).

Aldrich, H.E. (1979): Organizations and Environments (Upper Saddle River: Prentice Hall).

Alexy, R. (1983): Theorie der juristischen Argumentation. Die Theorie des rationalen Diskurses als Theorie der juristischen Begründung (Frankfurt: stw).

Alexy, R. (1986): Theorie der Grundrechte (Frankfurt: stw).

Alexy, R. (1995): Recht, Vernunft, Diskurs. Studien zur Rechtsphilosophie. (Frankfurt: stw).

Alger, J.R. (2010): From Desegregation to Diversity and Beyond: Our Evolving Legal Conversation on Race and Higher Education, in: The Journal of College and University Law, vol. 36, nr. 3, pp. 983–1001.

Amossy, R. (2010): L'argumentation dans le discours, 3d ed. (Paris: Colin).

Andell, v. P., Bourcier, D. (2009): Sérendipité (L'Act Mem: Chambery).

Anderson, K., Okuda, Y. (2007): Translation of Japan's Private International Law: Act on the General Rules of the Application of Laws, in: Yearbook of Private International Law 8/2007.

Andersson, L., Trudgill, P. (1991): Bad Language (Oxford: Blackwell).

Anesa, P. (2009): Courtroom Discourses. An Analysis of the Westerfield Jury Trial. (Verona: Università degli Studi di Verona) Unpublished PhD-thesis available online.

Anesa, P. (2012): Jury Trials and the Popularization of Legal Language. A Discourse Analytical Approach (Bern/Berlin/Bruxelles et al.: P. Lang).

Arendt, H. (1998): The Human Condition, 2nd ed. (Chicago/London: University of Chicago Press).

Asimow, P., Mader, S. (2013): Law and Popular Culture. A Course Book, 2nd ed. (New York: P. Lang).

Atienza, M. (1991): Las razones del Derecho. Teorías de la argumentación jurídica (Lima: Palestra).

Atienza, M. (2011): El derecho como argumentación. Concepciones de la argumentación, 5 ed. (Barcelona: Ariel).

Austin, J.L. (1956): Ifs and Cans, Proceedings of the British Academy; reprinted in:

Austin, J.L. (1970) Philosophical Papers, Oxford: Oxford University Press, pp. 205–232.

Austin, J.L. (1956/7): A Plea for Excuses, in: Proceedings of the Aristotelian Society, vol. LVII, pp. 1–29.

Austin, J.L. (1975): How to Do Things with Words, 2nd ed. (Oxford/New York: Oxford University Press).

Axelrod, R. (1976): The Structure of Decision: The Cognitive Maps of Political Elites (Princeton: Princeton University Press).

Ayer, A.J. (1970): Sprache, Wahrheit und Logik (Stuttgart: Reclam), Engl. orig. Language, Truth and Logic (1936).

Bakhtin, M. (1981): The Dialogic Imagination: Four Essays, ed. by M. Holmquist (Austin: University of Texas Press).

Bartin, E. (1897): De l'impossibilité d'arriver à une solution définitive de conflicts de lois, in : Journal de droit international, vol. 24.

Bauman, Z. (2004): Wasted Lives. Modernity and its Outcasts (Oxford: polity).

Bautro, E. (1933): Idea antytetyki prawniczej (Szkic pragmatyczny) (Lwów).

Bautro, E. (1934): De iurisprudentia symbolica, vol. 1, Prolegomena do logistyki prawniczej (Lwów).

Bautro, E. (1935): Idea lingwistyki i semantyki prawniczej (Lwów: Dom Książki Polskiej).

Baylon, Ch. (1991): Sociolinguistique. Société, langue et discours (Paris: Nathan Université).

Beer, G. (2014): Excerpts from The Waves by Virginia Woolf, in: Daedalus, vol. 143, nr.1, pp. 54–63.

Bejan, A., Zane, J.P. (2012): Design in Nature. How the Constructal Law Governs Evolution in Biology, Physics, Technology, and Social Organizations (New York/London: Doubleday).

Benkler, Y. (2011): WikiLeaks and the Protect-IP Act: A New Public-Private Threat to the Internet Commons, in: Daedalus, vol. 140, nr. 4, pp. 154–164.

Bennett R.W. (2012): Constitutional Interpretation, in: Tiersma, P.M., Solan, L.M. (eds.): The Oxford Handbook of Language and Law (Oxford: Oxford University Press) pp. 114–127.

Berger, P.L. (1963): Invitation to Sociology. A Humanistic Perspective (Harmondsworth/New York: Penguin).

Berman, H.J. (1974): The Interaction of Law and Religion (Nashville/New York: Abingdon Press).

Berman, H.J. (1995): World Law, in: Fordham International Law Journal, 18/1995.

Berring, R.C. (2000): Legal Information and the Search for Cognitive Authority, in: California Law Review, vol. 88, pp. 1673–1708.

Bix, B.H. (2012): Legal Interpretation and the Philosophy of Language, in: Tiersma, P.M., Solan, L.M., The Oxford Handbook of Language and Law (Oxford: Oxford University Press) pp. 145–155.

Black, E.A., Bell, G.F. (2011): Law and Legal Institutions of Asia. Traditions, Adaptations and Innovations (Cambridge: Cambridge University Press).

Black, O. (2012): Agreements. A Philosophical and Legal Study (Cambridge: Cambridge University Press).

Bloch, J. (1961): Les inscriptions d'Asoka (Paris: Les Belles Lettres).

Bloomfield, L. (1914): An Introduction to the Study of Language (London: G. Bell & Sons/New York: Henry Holt & Co.).

Bloomfield, L. (1961/1984): Language (Chicago/London: Chicago University Press).

Borch, v. H. (1954): Obrigkeit und Widerstand. Zur politischen Soziologie des Beamtentums (Tübingen: Mohr).

Borja Albi, A., Prieto Ramos, F. (eds.) (2013): Legal Translation in Context. Professional Issues and Prospects (Oxford: P. Lang).

Bottéro, J. (1992): Mesopotamia. Writing, Reasoning, and the Gods (Chicago: University of Chicago Press).

Brandom, R.B. (2000): Articulating Reasons. An Introduction into Inferentialism (Cambridge/London: Harvard University Press).

Bres, J., Nowakowska, A., Sarale, J.M., Sarrazin, S. (2012): Dialogisme: langue, discours (Bruxelles, Bern et al.: P. Lang).

Breyer, S. (2010): Making Our Democracy Work: A Judge's View (New York: Vintage Press).

Brooks, P. (2001): Troubling Confessions. Speaking Guilt in Law and Literature (Chicago: Chicago University Press).

Brooks, P. (2012): Narratives of the Constitutional Covenant, in: Daedalus, vol. 141, nr. 1, pp. 43–51.

Bülow, E. (1986): Strafandrohungsformeln und ihr magisches Potential, in: Lange-Seidl, A. (ed.) Zeichen und Magie (Tübingen: Stauffenburg Verlag) pp. 93–107.

Burke, P. (2013): The Screamers, in: Daedalus, vol. 142, nr. 4, pp. 11–23.

Burket, R.E. (2010): The Construction and Transmission of Law Enforcement Discourse as the Dominant Discourse on Serial Killing in the U.S., in: Heine, C., Engberg, J. (eds.): Reconceptualizing LSP. Online proceedings of the XVII European LSP Symposium 2009 (Aarhus).

Caiden, G.E. (1994): Globalizing the Theory and the Practice of Public Administration, in: Garcia-Zamor, J.C. and Khator, R (eds.) Public Administration in the Global Village (Westport: Praeger Publishers) pp. 45–59.

Cantarella, E. (2002): Dispute settlement in Homer once again on the shield of Achilles, in: Blachos, G. (ed.): Droits antiques et société. Mélanges en l'honneur Panayotis D. Dimakis (Athens: Sakkoulas) pp.147–166.

Cao, D. (2004): Chinese Law. A Language Perspective (Aldershot: Ashgate).

Cao, D. (2007): Translating Law (Clevedon: Multilingual Matters).

Cao, D. (2008): Is the Chinese Legal Language More Ambiguous and Vaguer?, in: Wagner, A., Cacciaguidi-Fahy, S. (eds.), Obscurity and Clarity in Law. Prospects and Challenges (Aldershot: Ashgate).

Cardozo, B.N. (1924): The Growth of the Law (New Haven: Yale University Press).

Chafe, W.H. (2012): The American Narrative: Is There One and What Is It?, in: Daedalus, vol. 141, nr. 1, pp. 11–17.

Cheshire, C. (2011): Online Trust, Trustworthiness or Assurance?, in: Daedalus, vol. 140, nr. 4, pp. 49–58.

Chierichetti, L. (2010): Discursos del derecho y discursos sobre el derecho: aspectos intertextuales, in: Chierichetti, L., Garofalo, G. (eds.): Lengua y Derecho: líneas de investigación interdisciplinaria (Bern/Berlin/Bruxelles: P. Lang).

Christmann, H.H. (1983): Das Französische der Gegenwart, in: Hausmann. F.J. (ed.), Die französische Sprache von heute (Darmstadt: Wissenschaftliche Buchgesellschaft).

Clegg, A. (2010): A Matter of Interpretation, in: Financial Times, February 2, 2010.

Clegg, S.R. (1989): Frameworks of Power (London: Thousand Oaks).

Coendet, T. (2012): Rechtsvergleichende Argumentation. Phänomenologie der *Veranderung* im rechtlichen Diskurs (Tübingen: Mohr Siebeck).

Connell, M.A. (2010): Race and Higher Education: The Tortuous Journey Toward Desegregation, in: The Journal of College and University Law, vol. 36. nr. 3, pp. 945–982.

Cooper, J.M. (1990): Political Animals and Civic Friendship, in: Patzig, G. (ed.), Aristoteles' Politik (Göttingen: Vandenhoek & Ruprecht).

Corder, S.P. (1977): Introducing Applied Linguistics (New York: Penguin Books).

Cornu, G. (2005): Linguistique juridique, 3rd ed. (Paris: Montchrestien).

Cownie, F. (2004): Legal Academics: Culture and Identities (Oxford: Hart).

Craig, B. (2013): Cyberlaw. The Law of the Internet and Information Technology (Boston: Pearson).

Crain, C. (2010): Tea and Antipathy. Did principle or pragmatism start the American Revolution?, in: The New Yorker, Dec 20, 2010, pp. 132–138.

Cutter, R., Ulen, T. (2004): Law and Economics, 4th ed. (Boston/San Francisco: Pearson).

Dahl, R.A. (1957): The Concept of Power, in: Behavioral Studies, vol. 2, pp. 201–215.

Danner, R.A. (2006): Legal Information and the Development of American Law: Writings on the Form and Structure of the Published Law, in: Law Library Journal, vol. 99 (2), pp. 193–227.

Dasgupta, P., Singh, R., Ford, A. (2005): After Etymology: Towards a Substantivist Linguistics (Munich: Lincom).

David, R. (1978): Grands systèmes du droit contemporains, 7th ed. (Paris: Dalloz).

Davidson, J.F. (1961): Political Science and Political Action, in: American Political Science Review, 55 (4), pp. 851–860.

Davidson, D. (2001): Inquiries into Truth and Interpretation (Oxford: Clarendon Press).

Davis, D., Leo, R.A. (2012): Interrogation through Pragmatic Implication: Stikking to the Letter of Law while Violating its Intents, in: Tiersma, P.M., Solan, L.M. (eds.): The Oxford Handbook of Language and Law (Oxford: Oxford University Press) pp. 354–366.

Daube, D. (1949): Rabbinic Methods of Interpretation and Hellenistic Rhetoric, in: HUCA, pp. 239–264.

Daube, D. (1969): Roman Law: Linguistic, Social, and Philosophical Aspects (New York: Columbia University Press).

Delmas-Marty, M. (1998): Trois défis pour un droit mondial (Paris: Seuil).

Derrett, J.D. (1973): Dharmasutras and Juridical Literature. History of Indian Literatures, fasc. I. (Wiesbaden: Otto Harrassowitz).

Derrett, J.D. (1976–8): Essays in Classical and Modern Hindu Law, 4 vols. (Leiden: Brill).

Derrida, J. (2002): Without Alibi (Stanford: Stanford University Press).

Deutschmann, M. (2003): Apologising in British English (Umeå: Umeå Universitet).

Dickinson, J. (1927): Administrative Justice and the Supremacy of Law in the United States (Cambridge: Harvard University Press).

Dijk, van, T.A. (1978): Taal en handelen. Een interdisciplinaire inleiding in de pragmatik (Muiderberg: Coutinho).

Dijk, van, T.A. (1980): Textwissenschaft. Eine interdisziplinäre Einführung (Tübingen: Niemeyer).

Doctorow, E.L. (2012): Narrative C, in: Daedalus, vol. 141, nr. 1, pp. 118–125.

Domingo, R. (2010): The New Global Law (Cambridge: Cambridge University Press).

Doniger, W. (1991): The Laws of Manu (Harmondsworth: Penguin).

Donoghue, D. (2012): Introduction to 'On the American Narrative', in: Daedalus, vol. 141, nr. 1, pp. 5–10.

Dozhdev, D.V. (2003): Rimskoye častnoye pravo, 2d ed. (Moskva: Norma).

Droste, F.G. (1972): The Grammar of Traffic Regulation, in: semiotica, vol. 5, pp. 257–262.

Du, J. (2004): Forensic Linguistics (Shanghai: Foreign Language Education Press).

Duffy, H. (2012): The 'War on Terror' and the Framework of International Law, 2nd ed. (Cambridge: Cambridge University Press).

Durston, G. (2007): Victims and Viragos. Metropolitan Women, Crime and the Eighteenth-Century Justice System (Bury St. Edmunds: arima).

Dworkin, R. (1977): Taking Rights Seriously (London: Duckworth).

Dworkin, R. (1991): Law's Empire (London: Fontana Press).

Dworkin, R. (2006): Is Democracy Possible Here? Principles for a New Political Debate (Princeton: Princeton University Press).

Early, G. (2011): The Two Worlds of Race Revisited: Meditation on Race in the Age of Obama, in: Daedalus, vol. 140, nr. 1, pp. 11–27.

Eco, U. (1968/2008): La struttura assente. La ricerca semiotica e il metodo strutturale (Milano: Bompiani).

Eco, U. (1990): I limiti dell'interpretazione (Bologna: Bompiani).

Eco, U. (2004): Interpretazione e sovrainterpretazione (Bologna: Bompiani).

Eemeren, van, F., Grootendorst, R. (2011): Una teoría sistemática de la argumentación (Buenos Aires: Editorial Biblos).

Engberg, J. (2007): Vom Vorgriff auf das Ungreifbare. (Schein?-)Präzision, unvermeidliche und erstrebte Vagheit in der Gesetzesredaktion, in: Lötscher, A., Nussbaumer, M. (eds.) Denken wie ein Philosoph und schreiben wie ein Bauer. Sprache, mir der ein Staat zu machen ist (Zurich: Schultheiss) pp. 67–82.

Engberg, J., Kjaer, A.L. (2011): Approaches to Language and the Law – Some Introductory Notes, in: Hermes – Journal of Language and Communication Studies, nr. 46, pp. 7–10.

Engberg, J. (2012): Word Meaning and the Problem of the Globalized Legal Order, in: Tiersma, P.M., Solan, L.M. (eds.): The Oxford Handbook of Language and Law (Oxford: Oxford University Press) pp. 175–186.

Engel, P. (1994): Introduction à la philosophie de l'esprit (Paris: Editions de la découverte).

Engel, P. (ed.) (2000): Précis de la philosophie analytique (Paris: puf).

Engisch, K. (2010): Einführung in das juristische Denken, 11th ed. (Stuttgart: Kohlhammer).

Escarra, J. (1936): Le droit chinois. Conception générale, aperçu historique (Beijing: Henri Vetch).

Fairclough, N. (1992): Discourse and Social Change (Cambridge: Polity Press).

Farmer, D.J. (1995): The Language of Public Administration: Bureaucracy, Modernity, and Postmodernity (Tuscaloosa: University of Alabama Press).

Fasan, E. (1990): Relations with Alien Intelligences: The Scientific Basis of Metalaw (Berlin: Berlin Verlag).

Fenrich, J., Galizzi, P., Higgins, P. (eds.) (2011): The Future of African Customary Law (Cambridge: Cambridge University Press).

Ferguson, J.B. (2011): Freedom, Equality, Race, in: Daedalus, vol. 140, nr. 1, Race in the Age of Obama, vol. 1, pp. 44–52.

Ferreira Acuña, A.V. (2011): La realización de quejas en la conversación femenina y masculina. Diferencias y semejanzas en el habla cotidiana de las mujeres y los hombres (Munich: Lincom).

Fischer. C. (2007): Topoi verdeckter Rechtsfortbildung im Zivilrecht (Tübingen: Mohr Siebeck).

Fischer, F., Forester, J. (1993): Editor's Introduction, in: Fischer, F. Forester, J. (eds.) The Argumentative Turn in Policy Analysis and Planning (London: UCL Press) pp. 1–20.

Fishkin, J. (2009): When the People Speak. Deliberative Democracy and Public Consultation (Oxford: Oxford University Press).

Flood, G. (1996): An Introduction to Hinduism (Cambridge: Cambridge University Press).

Fontanille, J. (1998): Sémiotique du Discours (Limoges: PULIM).

Forster, E.M. (2007): Aspects of the Novel (London/New York: Penguin).

Forsythe, D.P. (2011): The Politics of Prisoner Abuse. The United States and Enemy Prisoners after 9/11 (Cambridge: Cambridge University Press).

Foucault, M. (1966): Les mots et les choses. Une archéologie des sciences humaines (Paris: Gallimard).

Foucault, M. (1969): L'archéologie du savoir (Paris: Gallimard).

Frisch, D., Bhala, R. (1999): Global Business Law. Principles and Practice (Durham: Carolina Academic Press).

Fromont, M. (2005): Grands systèmes de droit étrangers, 5. ed. (Paris: Dalloz).

Fukuda-Parr, S. (ed.) (2004): Rapport mondial sur le développement humain 2004. La liberté culturelle dans un monde diversifié (Paris: Economica).

Furberg, M. (1986): On Reading the Law, in: Peczenik, A. (ed.) Meaning, Interpretation, and the Law (Tampere: A-Tieto), pp. 62–75.

Gabstone, W.A. (2013): The Common Good: Theoretical Content, Practical Utility, in: Daedalus 142 (2), pp. 9–14.

Galdia, M. (2003): Comparative Law and Legal Translation, in: The European Legal Forum, vol. 1-2003, pp. 1–4.

Galdia, M. (2009): Legal Linguistics (Frankfurt/New York: P. Lang).

Galdia, M. (2013): Strategies and Tools for Legal Translation, in: Comparative Legilinguistics. International Journal for Legal Communication, vol. 15, pp. 77–94.

Galgano, F. (2005): La globalizzazione nello specchio del diritto (Bologna: Il Mulino).

Gaudemet, J. (2001): Les naissances du droit. Le temps, le pouvoir et la science au service du droit, 3rd ed. (Paris: Montchrestien).

Gazdar, G. (1979): Pragmatics: Implicature, Presupposition and Logical Form (New York: Academic Press).

Geary, D. (2011): Racial Liberalism, the Moynihan Report & the Daedalus Project on "The Negro American", in: Daedalus, vol. 140, nr. 1, pp. 53–66.

Gémar, J.C. (2004): Traduire le langage du droit, in: Übersetzung Translation Traduction, Kittel, H., et al. (eds.), vol. 1 (Berlin: Walter de Gruyter).

Giannoni, D. S. (2005): 'Any dispute shall be settled by arbitration.' A Study of Vagueness in International Model Arbitration Clauses, in: Bhatia, V.K., Engberg, J., Gotti, M., Heller, D. (eds.), Vagueness in Normative Texts (Bern: P. Lang) pp. 227–253.

Giannoni, D.S. (2010): Mapping Academic Values in the Disciplines. A Corpus-Based Approach (Frankfurt/New York: P. Lang).

Gibson, J.L. (2012a): Being Free in Obama's America: Racial Differences in Perceptions of Constraints on Political Action, in: Daedalus, vol. 141, nr. 4, pp. 114–129.

Gibson, J.L. (2012b): Electing Judges: The Surprising Effects of Campaigning on Judicial Legitimacy (Chicago: Chicago University Press).

Gillespie, J., Nicholson, P. (2012): Law and Development and the Global Discourses of Legal Transfers (Cambridge: Cambridge University Press).

Glenn, H.P. (2010): Legal Traditions of the World: Sustainable Diversity in Law, 4th ed. (New York/Oxford: Oxford University Press).

Golanski, A. (2002): Linguistics in Law, in: Albany Law Review, vol. 66, pp. 61–121.

Goodrich, P. (1987): Legal Discourse: Studies in Linguistics, Rhetoric and Legal Analysis (London: Macmillan Press).

Gorelov, B.I. (1989): Teoreticheskaya grammatika kitajskogo iazyka (Moskva: Prosvjeshtchenje).

Gortych-Michalak, K., Grzybek, J. (2013): Polysemic Terms in Chinese-German-Greek and Polish Legal Language. A Comparative Study, in: Comparative Legilinguistics. International Journal for Legal Communication, vol. 15, pp. 19–32.

Gotti, M. (2008): Investigating Specialized Discourse, 3rd ed. (Bern/Berlin/Brussels: P. Lang).

Gotti, M., Williams C. (eds.) (2010): Legal Discourse across Languages and Cultures (Frankfurt/New York: P.Lang).

Gottweis, H. (1998): Governing Molecules. The Discursive Politics of Genetic Engineering in Europe and the United States (Cambridge/London: MIT Press).

Grabowski, A. (1999): Judicial Argumentation and Pragmatics (Kraków: Księgarnia Akademicka).

Granet, M. (1934): La pensée chinoise (Paris: Alban Michel).

Greenhouse, L. (2012): Public Opinion & the Supreme Court: The Puzzling Case of Abortion, in: Daedalus, vol. 141, nr. 4, pp. 69–82.

Gregg, B. (2012): Human Rights as Social Construction (Cambridge: Cambridge University Press).

Greimas, A.J. (1976): Analyse sémiotique d'un discours juridique. La loi commerciale sur les societés, in: Sémiotique et sciences sociales, pp. 79–128.

Greimas, A.J. (1977): Der wissenschaftliche Diskurs in den Sozialwissenschaften, in: Zima, P.V. (ed.) Textsemiotik als Ideologiekritik (Frankfurt a.M.: Suhrkamp).

Grote, R. (1999): Rule of Law, Rechtsstaat and État de droit, in: C. Stark (ed.), Constitutionalism, Universalism, and Democracy – A Comparative Analysis (Baden-Baden: Nomos) pp. 269–306.

Guilfoyle, D. (2011): Shipping Interdiction and the Law of the Sea (Cambridge: Cambridge University Press).

Habermas, J. (1988): Theorie des kommunikativen Handelns, vol. 1 and 2 (Frankfurt/M.: Suhrkamp).

Habermas, J. (1992): Faktizität und Geltung (Frankfurt a.M.: Suhrkamp).

Habermas, J. (1996): Die Einbeziehung des Anderen (Frankfurt a.M.: Suhrkamp).

Hajer, M.A. (1995): The politics of environmental discourse, ecological modernization and the policy process (Oxford: Clarendon Press).

Haley, A.G. (1956): Space Law and Metalaw – A Synoptic View, in: Harvard Law Record 23, Nov. 8, 1956.

Halpérin, J.L. (2009): Profils de mondialisations du droit (Paris: Dalloz).

Halsall, A.W. (1989): La Rhétorique en 1990, in: Texte, vol. 8/9, pp. 5–18.

Hammer, L.M. (2007): A Foucauldian Approach to International Law. Descriptive Thoughts for Normative Issues (Aldershot: Ashgate).

Han, Z. (2012): Legal Communication of Chinese Judiciary. A Discourse-based View (Bern/Berlin/Bruxelles et al.: P. Lang).

Hare, R.M. (1952): The Language of Morals (Oxford: Clarendon Press).

Hargitt, S. (2013): What Could be Gained in Translation: Legal Language and Lawyer-Linguists in Globalized World, in: Indiana Journal of Global Legal Studies, vol. 20, pp. 425–447.

Hart, H.L.A. (1948): The Ascription of Responsibility and Rights, in: A. Flew (ed.) (1963): Essays on Logic and Language (Oxford: Oxford University Press), pp. 145–166.

Hart, H.L.A. (1961): The Concept of Law (Oxford: Clarendon Press).

Havelock, E.A. (1986): The Muse Learns to Write. Reflections on Orality and Literacy form Antiquity to the Present (New Haven/London: Yale University Press).

Haycraft, H. (1941): Murder for Pleasure: the Life and Times of the Detective Story (New York: Biblo and Tannen).

Held, D. (2005): Principles of Cosmopolitan Order, in: Brock, G., Brighouse, H. (eds.) The Political Philosophy of Cosmopolitanism (Cambridge/New York: Cambridge University Press).

Henriques, D.B. (2011): The Wizard of Lies. Bernie Madoff and the Death of Trust (New York: Time Books).

Héritier, F. (2011): Interview in Le Figaro Magazine, July 2, 2011, pp. 109–110.

Hoffmann, L. (1983): Kommunikation vor Gericht (Tübingen: Narr).

Hofstede, G. (1991): Cultures and Organizations: Software of the Mind (New York: McGraw-Hill).

Holenstein, E. (1980): Von der Hintergehbarkeit der Sprache. Kognitive Unterlagen der Sprache. Anhang: Zwei Vorträge von Roman Jakobson (Frankfurt a.M.: Suhrkamp).

Holloway, K.F.C. (2014): Legal Fictions: Constituting Race, Composing Literature (Durham: Duke University Press).

Hong, P. (1999): Zhongguo gudai falü mingzhu tiyao (Hangzhou: Zhejiang renmin chubanshe).

Honoré, T. (2002): Ulpian. Pioneer of Human Rights (Oxford: Oxford University Press).

Horie, Y. (2010a): The Roots of Japanese Legal Terminology, in: Comparative Legilinguistics. International Journal for Legal Communication, vol. 4/2010, pp. 79–90.

Horie, Y. (2010b): Divorce Proceedings Differences in Polish and Japanese Law for Purposes of Legal Translation, in: Legilingwistyka Porównawcza, vol. 3/2010, pp. 23–35.

Horne, Ch. F. (1917): The Sacred Books and Early Literature of the East, vol. 1 Babylonia and Assyria (New York/London: Parke, Austin & Lipscomb, Inc.).

Howarth, D. (1995): Discourse Theory, in: Marsh, D., Stoker, G. (eds.), Theory and Methods in Political Science (London: Macmillan Press) pp.115–133.

Huang, Y. (2007): Pragmatics (Oxford: Oxford University Press).

Huntington, S.P. (1998): The Clash of Civilizations and the Remaking of World Order (London: Touchstone Books).

Husa, J. (2008): Funktionalistisen oikeusvertailun perinne ja oikeuskielen kääntäminen - Ernst Rabel ja oikeuskieli fasadina, in: Foley, R. et al. (eds.): Kielen ja oikeuden kohtaamisia. Heikki E.S. Mattilan juhlakirja, (Helsinki: Talentum), pp. 89–104.

Husa, J. (2011): Review of M. Galdia's Legal Linguistics, in: Maastricht Journal of European and Comparative Law, vol.18: 3, pp. 336–341.

Hutton, Ch. (2009): Language, Meaning and the Law (Edinbourgh: Edinbourgh University Press).

Igarashi, K. (1990): Einführung in das japanische Recht (Darmstadt: Wissenschaftliche Buchgesellschaft).

Ilie, C. (1995): The Validity of Rhetorical Questions as Arguments in the Courtroom, in: van Eemeren, F.H., Grootendorst, J.A. et al. (eds.): Special Fields and Cases. Proceedings of the Third International ISSA Conference on Argumentation, (Amsterdam: SICSAT), pp. 73–88.

Inden, R. (1990): Imagining India (Oxford/Cambridge: Blackwells).

Innerwinkler, S. (2010): Sprachliche Innovation im politischen Diskurs. Eine Analyse ausgewählter Beispiele aus dem politischen Diskurs zwischen 2000 und 2006 in Österreich (Frankfurt/Berlin: P. Lang).

Innis, R.E. (ed.) (1985): Semiotics. An Introductory Anthology (Bloomington: Indiana University Press).

Jackson, B. (1985): Semiotics and Legal Theory (London: Routledge).

Jackson, S., Scott, J. (1980): Structure of Conversational Argument: Pragmatic Issues for the Enthymeme, in: The Quarterly Journal of Speech, vol. 66, pp. 251–265.

Janicki, K. (2002): Against essentialism: Toward language awareness (Munich: Lincom).

Janicki, K. (2006): Language Misconceived: Arguing for Applied Cognitive Sociolinguistics (Mahwah: Lawrence Erlbaum Associates).

Janicki, K. (2010): Confusing Discourse (Basingstoke: Palgrave Macmillan).

Jensen, U. (2001): Fast egendom, in: Strömholm, S. (ed.) Svensk rätt – en översikt (Iustus förlag: Uppsala) pp. 415–434.

Joas, H. (2011): Die Sakralität der Person. Eine neue Genealogie der Menschenrechte (Berlin: Suhrkamp Verlag).

Jopek-Bosiacka, A. (2006): Przekład prawny i sądowy (Warszawa: Wydawnictwo Naukowe PWN).

Joseph, J.E. (2012): Saussure (Oxford: Oxford University Press).

Kaag, J.J. (2009): Pragmatism and the lessons of experience, in: Daedalus, vol. 138, nr. 1, pp. 63–72.

Kangas, U. (1991): Ihmisen nimi. Nimenmääräytymisen oikeudelliset rajat (Helsinki: Lakimiesliiton kustannus).

Kantorowicz, E.H. (1957): The King's Two Bodies (Princeton: Princeton University Press).

Katz, J.J. (1977): Propositional Structure and Illocutionary Force (New York: Crowell).

Kempson, R.M. (1988): Mental Representations. The Interface between Language and Reality (Cambridge: Cambridge University Press).

Kerber, L.K. (2012): Why Diamonds Really are a Girl's Best Friend: Another American Narrative, in: Daedalus, vol. 141, nr. 1, pp. 89–100.

Kirchmann, von, J. (1938): Die Wertlosigkeit der Jurisprudenz als Wissenschaft (Stuttgart/Berlin: Kohlhammer).

Koivu, V. (2008): Yksi sopimus – monta tulkintaa: kansainvälisen sopimuksen eri kieliversioiden soveltamisen aiheuttamat kielelliset haasteet, in: Foley, R., Salmi-Tolonen, T. et al., Kielen ja oikeuden kohtaamisia, Heikki E.S. Mattilan juhlakirja (Helsinki: Talentum), pp. 141–155.

Kopytko, R. (2002): Review of K. Janicki's Against essentialism: Toward language awareness, in: Language in Society (2002), vol. 31, pp. 128–131.

Kość, A. (2001): Filozoficzne podstawy prawa japońskiego w perspektywie historycznej (Lublin: KUL).

Kovačec, A. (1982): Funkcionalizam Andréa Martineta u okviru strukturalne lingvistike, in: Martinet, A. (1982), Osnove opće lingvistike (GZH: BibliotekaTeka) pp. v–xiii.

Krasner, S. (1999): Sovereignty: Organized Hypocrisy (Princeton: Princeton University Press).

Kubánek, M., Klabal, O. (2012): Plain or Archaic: The New Czech Civil Code Going Against the Flow, in: Comparative Legilinguistics. International Journal for Legal Communication, vol. 12, pp. 7–17.

Kuhn, T.S. (1973): The Structure of Scientific Revolutions (Chicago: University of Chicago Press).

Kullmann, W. (1991): Man as a Political Animal in Aristotle, in: Keyt, D., Miller, F. (eds.), A Companion to Aristotle's Politics (Oxford: Oxford University Press) pp. 94–117.

Küng, H. (1997): A Global Ethics for Global Politics and Economy (Oxford: Oxford University Press).

Kuźmicz, K. (2009): Wpływ filozofii Immanuela Kanta na poglądy filozoficznoprawne Eugeniusza Bautro, in: Miscellanea Historico-Iuridica, vol. 7, pp. 95–120.

Laclau, E., Mouffe, Ch. (1985): Hegemony and Socialist Strategy. Towards a Radical Democratic Politics (London/New York: Verso).

Ladmiral, J.-R. (1979): Traduire: théorèmes pour la traduction (Paris: Payot).

Lakoff, G. (1987): Women, Fire, and Dangerous Things: What Categories Reveal about the Mind (Chicago: Chicago University Press).

Lakoff, G. (2008): The Neural Theory of Metaphor, in: R.W. Gibbs, Jr. (ed.): The Cambridge Handbook of Metaphor and Thought (Cambridge: Cambridge University Press) pp. 17–38.

Laugier, S., Plaud, S. (eds.) (2011): Lectures de la philosophie analytique (Paris: ellipses).

Lejeune, P. (1975): Le Pacte autobiographique (Paris: Seuil).

Lejeune, P. (2013): Autogenèses. Les brouillons de soi (Paris: Seuil).

Levine, L.W. (1988): Highbrow/Lowbrow: The Emergence of Cultural Hierarchy in America (Cambridge: Harvard University Press).

Levinson, S.C. (1983): Pragmatics (Cambridge: Cambridge University Press).

Levinson, S. (2006): Our Undemocratic Constitution: Where the Constitution Goes Wrong (And How We the People Can Correct It) (New York: Oxford University Press).

Lewis, D.L. (2012): Exceptionalism's Exceptions: The Changing American Narrative, in: Daedalus, vol. 141, nr. 1, pp. 101–117.

Liao, M. (2012): Courtroom Discourse in China, in: Tiersma, P.M., Solan, L.M. (eds.): The Oxford Handbook of Language and Law (Oxford: Oxford University Press) pp. 395–407.

Liu, W. (2005): Illocutionary and Perlocutionary Acts in Chinese Judge's Attached Discourse (unpublished presentation at 7th IAFL Conference, Cardiff University).

Locke, J.L. (2011): Eavesdropping: An Intimate History (Oxford: Oxford University Press).

Loewe, R. (1989): Internationales Kaufrecht (Wien: Manzsche Verlags- und Universitätsbuchhandlung).

Londras, de, F. (2011): Detention in the 'War on Terror'. Can Human Rights Fight Back? (Cambridge: Cambridge University Press).

Luhmann, N. (1993): Das Recht der Gesellschaft (Frankfurt a.M.: Suhrkamp).

Maccoby, H. (1989): Judaism in the First Century (London: Sheldon Press).

Macedo de, S. (1985): Das funções lógicas ás funções jurídicas, in: Revista Brasileira de Filosofia, vol. xxxiv, pp. 84–87.

Martinet, A. (1982): Osnove opće lingvistike (GZH: BibliotekaTeka).

Marx, G.T. (2011): 'Cough a Little upon Entering': Some Reflections on the History of Surreptitious Spectatorship, in: Surveillance and Society, vol. 9, nr. 1/2, pp. 248–256.

Mattila, H.E.S. (2002a): Towards the Science of Legal Linguistics, in: Mattila, H.E.S. (ed.) The Development of Legal Language (Helsinki: Kauppakaaari).

Mattila, H.E.S. (2002b): Les matériaux non finnois dans l'interprétation jurdique en Finlande, in: Sacco, R. (ed.): L'interprétation des textes juridiques rédigés dans plus d'une langue (Torino: L'Harmattan Italia) pp. 151–182.

Mattila, H.E.S. (2006): Comparative Legal Linguistics (Aldershot: Ashgate).

Mattila, H.E.S. (2012): Jurilinguistique comparée. Langage du droit, latin et langues modern (Cowansville: Blais).

Mattila, H.E.S. (2013): Comparative Legal Linguistics. Language of Law, Latin and Modern Lingua Francas. 2nd ed. (Aldershot: Ashgate).

Matulewska, A., Wasielewska, M. (2003): Latin Maxims and Expressions in English, Estonian and Polish. Legal Language in the Aspect of Translation, in: Investigationes Linguisticae, vol. X, pp. 1–18.

Matulewska, A. (2010): Legal Linguistics No Longer Neglected: Review of Legal Linguistics by Marcus Galdia, in: Comparative Legilinguistics. International Journal for Legal Communication 4/2010, pp. 109–112.

Matulewska, A. (2013): Legilinguistic Translatology. A Parametric Approach to Legal Translation (Bern/Berlin/Bruxelles et al.: P. Lang).

Maturana, H., Varela, F.J. (1980): Autopoiesis and Cognition (Dordrecht: Kluwer).

May, R. (1980): Problematik chinesischen Rechtsverständnisses, in: Archiv für Rechts- und Staatsphilosophie, vol. LXVI/2, pp. 193–205.

McGuinness, B. (1991): Der Löwe spricht…und wir können ihn nicht verstehen. Zu Wittgensteins hundertstem Geburtstag, in: B. McGuinness, J. Habermas et al., Der Löwe spricht…und wir können ihn nicht verstehen (Frankfurt a.M.: Suhrkamp) pp. 7–19.

McLaughlin, S., Powell, E.J. (2011): Domestic Law Goes Global (Cambridge: Cambridge University Press).

Mead, G.H. (1934): Mind, Self and Society (Chicago: Chicago University Press).

Mead, M. (1964): Anthropology (Princeton/Toronto: Nostrand).

Mellinkoff, D. (1963): The Language of the Law (Boston/Toronto: Little, Brown & Co.).

Menski, W. (2006): Comparative Law in a Global Context. The Legal Systems of Asia and Africa, 2nd ed. (Cambridge: Cambridge University Press).

Meyer, M. (1988): Questions and Questioning (Berlin/New York: Walter de Gruyter).

Meyer, M. (2008): Principia Rhetorica. Une théorie générale de l'argumentation (Paris: Fayard).

Mitamura, T. (1999): Controlled Language for Multilingual Machine Translation, in: Proceedings of MT Summit VII, Singapore.

Moore, B. (1983): Privacy: Studies in Social and Cultural History (Armonk: Sharpe).

Morawski, L. (1988): Argumentacje, racjonalność prawa i postępowanie dowodowe (Toruń: Uniwersytet M. Kopernika).

Morris, C.W. (1938): Foundations of the Theory of Sign, in: Neurath, O., Carnap, R., Morris, C. (eds.): International Encyclopedia of Unified Science (Chicago: University of Chicago Press) pp. 77–138.

Morris, Ch. W. (1971): Writings on the General Theory of Signs (The Hague: Mouton).

Mounin, G. (1968): La linguistique (Paris: Seghers).

Moyn, S. (2012): The Last Utopia. Human Rights in History (Harvard: Harvard University Press).

Mulder, J.W.F., Rastall, P. (2005): Ontological Questions in Linguistics (Munich: Lincom).

Muller, K. (2000): The Effect of the Accusatorial System on the Child Witness, in: Child Abuse Research in South Africa, vol. 1, pp. 13–23.

Newmark, P. (1988): A Textbook of Translation (New York/London: Prentice Hall).

Nocera, D.G. (2012): Can We Progress From Solipsistic Science to Frugal Innovation?, in: Daedalus, vol.141, nr. 3, pp. 45–52.

Nöth, W. (1975): Semiotik. Eine Einführung mit Beispielen für Reklameanalysen (Tübingen: Niemeyer).

Núñez, R. (2008): Conceptual Metaphor, Human Condition, and the Nature of Mathematics, in: Gibbs, R.W. (ed.), The Cambridge Handbook of Metaphor and Thought (Cambridge: Cambridge University Press), pp. 339–362.

Oakley, F. (2014): Politics & Eternity, in: Daedalus, vol. 143, nr. 1, pp. 35–45.

O'Flaherty, W.D., Derrett, J.D.M. (1978): The Concept of Duty in Southeast Asia (New Delhi: Vikas).

Okawara, M.H. (1998): The Comprehensibility of Japanese Legal Language of the Penal Code, in: Chiiki Seisaku Kenkyu, vol. 1/2, pp. 197–206.

Okawara, M.H. (2006): A Linguistic Analysis of Some Japanese Trademark Cases (unpublished PhD-thesis, University of Sidney) available online.

Okawara, M.H. (2012): Courtroom Discourse in Japan's New Judicial Order, in: Tiersma, P.M., Solan, L.M. (eds.): The Oxford Handbook of Language and Law (Oxford: Oxford University Press) pp. 381–394.

Olivekrona, K. (1969): Det rättsliga språket och verkligheten (Lund: Ekstrands Trykeri).

Paglieri, F., Castelfranchi, C. (2009): Self-argumentation: On a neglected function of internal discourse, in: Capone, A. (ed.): Perspectives on Language Use and Pragmatics (Munich: Lincom).

Palmiter, A.R. (2005): Securities Regulation (New York: Aspen).

Pan, J. (2011): Chinese Philosophy and International Law, in: Asian Journal of International Law, vol. 1, pp. 233–248.

Peczenik, A. (ed.) (1986): Meaning, Interpretation and the Law (Tampere: A-Tieto).

Peirce, Ch. S. (1931–35, 1958–60): Collected Papers of Charles Sanders Peirce, vol. 1–8 (Cambridge: Harvard University Press).

Peirce, Ch. S. (1963): Charles S. Peirce's Letters to Lady Welby, E.C. Lieb (ed.) (New Haven: Whitock's).

Perelman, C., Olbrechts-Tyteca, L. (1970): Traité de l'argumentation. La nouvelle rhétorique (Bruxelles: Éditions de l'université de Bruxelles).

Pinker, S. (1997): How the Mind Works (London/New York: Penguin).

Pinker, S. (1999): Words and Rules. The Ingredients of Language, 3rd ed. (London: Weidenfeld & Nicolson).

Plantin, C. (2011): Les bonnes raisons des émotions. Principes et méthode pour l'étude du discours émotionné (Bern, Berlin & al: P. Lang).

Poggi, C. (2012): Le Sanskrit souffle et lumière. Voyage au cœur de la langue sacrée de l'Inde (Paris: Almora).

Poscher, R. (2012): Ambiguity and Vagueness in Legal Interpretation, in: Tiersma, P.M., Solan, L.M. (eds.): The Oxford Handbook of Language and Law (Oxford: Oxford University Press) pp. 128–155.

Posner, R. A. (1990): Cardozo. A Study in Reputation (Chicago/London: Chicago University Press).

Quine, W.V. (1980): Wort und Gegenstand, Engl. Orig. Word and Object (1976), 10th ed. (Stuttgart: Reclam).

Raadschelders, J.C.N. (2011): Public Administration. The Interdisciplinary Study of Government (Oxford: Oxford University Press).

Rajah, J. (2012): Authoritarian Rule of Law. Legislation, Discourse and Legitimacy in Singapore (Cambridge: Cambridge University Press).

Rastall, P. (2006): The Power of Speech (Munich: Lincom).

Rawls, J. (1971): Theory of Justice (Harvard: Harvard University Press).

Rawls, J. (1993): The Law of Peoples, in: Collected Papers (ed. Freeman, S.) (Cambridge: Harvard University Press) pp. 529–564.

Rawls, J. (1999): The Law of Peoples, with the Idea of Public Reason Revisited (Cambridge: Harvard University Press).

Rawls, J. (2005): Political Liberalism (New York: Columbia University Press).

Recanati, F. (2008): Philosophie du language (et de l'esprit) (Paris: Gallimard).

Rienzer, M. (2011): Interkulturelle Kommunikation im Asylverfahren (Frankfurt a.M./Berlin: Lang).

Robin, C. (2011): The Reactionary Mind. Conservatism from Edmund Burke to Sarah Palin (Oxford: Oxford University Press).

Robrieux, J.J. (2010): Rhétorique et argumentation, 3rd ed. (Paris: Armand Colin).

Roland, H., Boyer, L. (1992): Adages du droit français, 3rd ed. (Paris: Litec).

Rolf, B. (1986): The Logic of Verifying Interpretations, in: A. Peczenik (ed.) Meaning, Interpretation and the Law (Tampere: A-Tieto) pp. 30–61.

Rommerskirchen, J. (2011): Prekäre Kommunikation: Die Vernehmung in der multikulturellen Gesellschaft (Wiesbaden: VS Verlag).

Rorty, R.M. (ed.) (1992): The Linguistic Turn (Chicago/London: University of Chicago Press).

Rosen, J. (2013): Can the Judicial Branch be a Steward in a Polarized Democracy, in: Daedalus 142 (2), pp. 25–35.

Rosenhouse, J. (2013): General and Local Issues in Forensic Linguistics: Arabic as a Case Study, in: Comparative Legilinguistics. International Journal for Legal Communication, vol. 15, pp. 53–63.

Rosnow, R., Fine, G.A. (1976): Rumor and Gossip: The Social Psychology of Hearsay (Amsterdam: North Holland Elsevier).

Ross, A. (1958): On Law and Justice (London: Stevens).

Said, E. (1979): Orientalism (New York: Vintage).

Saïd, S., Trédé, M., Le Boulluec, A. (2013): Histoire de la littérature grecque, 3rd ed. (Paris: puf).

Sandrini, P. (2011): Translationswissenschaft, in: Reinalter, H., Brenner, P. (eds.): Lexikon der Geisteswissenschaften. Sachbegriffe-Disziplinen-Personen (Wien: Böhlau).

Sandywell, B. (2011): Dictionary of Visual Discourse. A Dialectical Lexicon of Terms (Aldershot: Ashgate).

Sarangi, A. (ed.) (2010): Language and Politics in India (Oxford: Oxford University Press).

Saussure, de, F. (1967): Grundfragen der allgemeinen Sprachwissenschaft (Berlin: Walter de Gruyter).

Savellos, E.E., Galvin, R.F. (2001): Reasoning and the Law: the Elements (Boston: Wadsworth).

Savigny, von, E. (1983): Zum Begriff der Sprache. Konvention, Bedeutung, Zeichen (Stuttgart: Reclam).

Schaff, A. (1962): Introduction to Semantics (New York: Springer).

Schane, S. (2012): Contract Formation as a Speech Act, in: Tiersma, P.M., Solan, L.M. (eds.): The Oxford Handbook of Language and Law (Oxford: Oxford University Press) pp. 100–113.

Schiff Berman, P. (2012): Global Legal Pluralism. A Jurisprudence of Law beyond Borders (Cambridge: Cambridge University Press).

Schmid, von, J.J. (1946): Wijsbegeerte van het recht, 3rd ed. (Den Haag: N.V. Servire).

Scott, S.P., Lobingier, Ch. (ed./trans.) (1931): Las Siete Partidas (New York: Commerce Clearing House).

Scott, A.W. (1979): Private International Law. Conflict of Laws, 2nd ed. (Plymouth: Macdonald & Evans).

Searle, J. (1999): Mind, Language and Society. Doing Philosophy in the Real World (London: Weidenfeld & Nicolson).

Searle, J. (2006): What is Language: Some Preliminary Remarks, in: Abel, G. (ed.) Kreativität. XX Deutscher Kongress für Philosophie (Hamburg: Felix Meiner Verlag).

Searle, J. (2007): Freedom and Neurobiology: Reflections on Free Will, Language and Political Power (New York: Columbia University Press).

Searle, J. (2011): Die Konstruktion der gesellschaftlichen Wirklichkeit. Zur Ontologie sozialer Tatsachen (Frankfurt: Suhrkamp); Engl. orig.: The Construction of Social Reality (2005).

Searle, J. (2012): Making the Social World. The Structure of Human Civilization (Oxford: Oxford University Press).

Sen, A. (2005): The Argumentative Indian. Writings on Indian History, Culture and Identity (Picador: New York).

Sevin Goldstein, N.E., Messenheimer Kelly, S. et al. (2012): Potential Impact of Juvenile Suspects' Linguistic Abilities on Miranda Understanding and Appreciation, in: Tiersma, P.M., Solan, L.M. (eds.): The Oxford Handbook of Language and Law (Oxford: Oxford University Press) pp. 299–311.

Shaw, M. (2000): Theory of the Global State (Cambridge/New York, Cambridge University Press).

Shelby, T. (2011): Justice & Racial Conciliation: Two Visions, in: Daedalus, vol. 140, nr. 1, pp. 95–107.

Shuy, R.W. (2012): The Language of Perjury Cases (Oxford: Oxford University Press).

Siedentop, L. (2010): Britain needs much more than voting reform, in: Financial Times, May 31, 2010.

Siltala, R. (2011): Law, Truth, and Reason. A Treatise on Legal Argumentation (Dordrecht: Springer).

Slocum, B.G. (2012): Linguistics and 'Ordinary Meaning' Determinations, in: Statute Law Review, vol. 33 (1) pp. 39–83.

Skuczyński, P. (2013): The Status of Legal Ethics (Frankfurt am Main: P. Lang).

Smart, J.J.C. (1961): Free Will, Praise and Blame, in: Mind, vol. LXX, pp. 291–306.

Solan, L.M. (2012): Linguistic Issues in Statutory Interpretation, in: Tiersma, P.M., Solan, L.M. (eds.): The Oxford Handbook of Language and Law (Oxford: Oxford University Press) pp. 87–99.

Sommers, H.L. (1998): Machine translation, applications, in: Baker, M. (ed.): Routledge Encyclopedia of Translation Studies (London/New York: Routledge).

Sperber, D., Wilson, D. (2008): A Deflationary Account of Metaphors, in: Gibbs, R.W. (ed.), The Cambridge Handbook of Metaphor and Thought (Cambridge: Cambridge University Press) pp. 84–105.

Stalley, R.F. (2009): Introduction to Aristotle's Politics, in: Aristotle, Politics (Oxford: Oxford University Press) pp. vii–xlvii.

Stalnaker, R.C. (1972): Pragmatics, in: Davidson, D., Harman, G. (eds.): Semantics of Natural Language (Dordrecht: Reidel) pp. 380–397.

Stein, P. (1966): Regulae Iuris. From Juristic Rules to Legal Maxims (Edinburgh: Edinburgh University Press).

Stolze, R. (2005): Übersetzungstheorien. Eine Einführung (Tübingen: Narr).

Stone, G.R. (2013): The Supreme Court in the 21st Century, in: Daedalus, vol. 142, nr. 2, pp. 36–45.

Strawson, G. (2004): Against Narrativity, in: Ratio 17/4, pp. 431–449.

Strawson, P. (1992): Analysis and Metaphysics (Oxford: Oxford University Press).

Studnicki, F. (1964): Traffic Signs, in: Semiotica vol. 2, pp. 151–172.

Stygall, G. (1994): Trial Language (Philadelphia: J. Benjamins Publishing Comp.).

Stygall, G. (2012): Discourse in the US Courtroom, in: Tiersma, P.M., Solan, L.M. (eds.): The Oxford Handbook of Language and Law (Oxford: Oxford University Press) pp. 369–380.

Sun, X. (2007): Die Rezeption der westlichen Zivilrechtswissenschaft und ihre Auswirkung im modernen China, in: Rabels Zeitschrift, vol. 71, pp. 644–662.

Supiot, A. (2005): Homo juridicus. Essai sur la fonction anthropologique du Droit (Paris: Seuil).

Symons, J. (1972): Bloody Murder. From the Detective Story to the Crime Novel: A History (Harmondsworth: Penguin).

Szabó, M., Varga, Cs. (eds.) (2000): Jog és nyelv (Budapest: Tempus).

Tan, Y.S. (1998): Sino-Indian Culture (Calcutta: Visva Bharati).

Tannen, D. (2013): The Argument Culture, in: Daedalus, vol. 142, nr. 2, pp. 177–184.

Thornhill, C. (2011): A Sociology of Constitutions. Constitutions and State Legitimacy in Historical-Sociological Perspective (Cambridge: Cambridge University Press).

Tiersma, P.M. (1999): Legal Language (Chicago/London: University of Chicago Press).

Tiersma, P.M. (2005): Categorical Lists in the Law, in: Bhatia, V.K., Engberg, J., Gotti, M., Heller, D. (eds.), Vagueness in Normative Texts (Bern: Peter Lang) pp. 109–130.

Tiersma, P.M., Solan, L.M. (2012): The Language of Crime, in: Tiersma, P.M., Solan, L.M. (eds.): The Oxford Handbook of Language and Law (Oxford: Oxford University Press) pp. 340–353.

Tishkov, V. (2003): Rekviem po etnosu (Moskva: Nauka).

Tocqueville, de, A. (2003): Democracy in America (Penguin: London/New York).

Todorov, T. (1992): The Conquest of America. The Question of the Other (New York: Harper Perennial).

Tokarev, V. (2010): Spory o sushchnosti prava v diskurse pravoporjadka, in: Comparative Legilinguistics. International Journal for Legal Communication, vol. 4/2010, pp. 99–107.

Toobin, J. (2008): The Nine. Inside the Secret World of the Supreme Court (New York: Doubleday).

Toobin, J. (2010): Annals of Law. Without a Paddle, in: The New Yorker, September 27, 2010, pp. 34–41.

Toulmin, E.S. (1958): The Uses of Argument (Cambridge: Cambridge University Press).

Tribe, L.H. (2000): American Constitutional Law, 3d ed. (Mineola: Foundation Press).

Tribe, L.H. (2008): The Invisible Constitution (Oxford: Oxford University Press).

Tribe, L.H. (2012): America's Constitutional Narrative, in: Daedalus, vol. 141, nr. 1, pp. 18–42.

Turpin, C., Tomkins, A. (2011): British Government and the Constitution. Text and Materials, 7th ed. (Cambridge: Cambridge University Press).

Upham, F.K. (1990): Introduction into East Asian Legal Systems (Boston: Boston College Law School).

Urmson, J.O. (1992a): The History of Philosophical Analysis, in: Rorty, R.M. (ed.), The Linguistic Turn. Essays in Philosophical Method (Chicago/London: University of Chicago Press) pp. 295–301.

Urmson, J.O. (1992b): J.L. Austin, in: Rorty, R.M.(ed.), The Linguistic Turn. Essays in Philosophical Method (Chicago/London: University of Chicago Press) pp. 232–238.

Vaidhyanathan, S. (2001): Copyrights and Copywrongs. The Rise of Intellectual Property and How It Threatens Creativity (New York/London: New York University Press).

Valeika, L., Buitkiene, J. (2003): An Introductory Course in Theoretical English Grammar (Vilnius: Vilnius Pedagogical University).

Vels, K. (2004): Trade Restrictions on Animal Welfare Grounds in the European Union, RGSL Working Papers no. 18 (Riga: RGSL).

Vesting, T. (2011): Die Medien des Rechts: Schrift (Weilerwist: Velbrück).

Viehweg, T. (1954): Topik und Jurisprudenz (München: C.H. Beck).

Vinnai, E. (2010): A jogi nyelv nyelvészeti megközelítése, in: Publicationes Universitatis Miskolciensis. Sectio Juridica et Politica, Miskolc, vol. 28/2010, pp. 145–171.

Vinnai, E. (2011): Nyelvhasználat a jogi eljárásban. Unpublished PhD-thesis at University of Miskolc (available online).

Visconti, J. (ed.) (2010): Lingua e diritto. Livelli di analisi (Milano: Edizioni universitarie di Lettere Economia Diritto).

Vlachopoulos, S. (2011): Wie viel Kreativität vertragen Rechtstexte?, in: Zybatow, L.N., Petrova, A., Ustaszewski, M. (eds.): Translation Studies: Old and New Types of Translation in Theory and Praxis (Frankfurt a.M./Berlin: P. Lang).

Vogel, F. (2012): Linguistik rechtlicher Normgenese. Theorie der Rechtsnormdiskursivität am Beispiel der Online-Durchsuchung (Berlin: De Gruyter).

Voloshinov, V.N. (1929/1975): Marxismus und Sprachphilosophie (Frankfurt a.M.: Ullstein).

Vygotskij, L.S. (1934/1964): Denken und Sprechen (Frankfurt a.M.: Fischer).

Wang, B. (2007): Neue Entwicklungen im IPR der VR China, in: IPRax 2007, vol. 4, pp. 363–369.

Wang, C. (2011): Lunheng. Balance des discours (Paris: Les Belles Lettres).

Warren, S., Brandeis, L. (1890): The Right to Privacy, in: Harvard Law Review 4/1890, pp. 193–220.

Weber, M. (2003): Hindouisme et bouddhisme (Paris: Champs-Flammarion).

Weinberger, O., Weinberger, C. (1979): Logik, Semantik, Hermeneutik (München: Beck).

Weisberg, R. (1992): Poethics and Other Strategies of Law and Literature (New York: Columbia University Press).

Wesel, U. (2006): Geschichte des Rechts. Von den Frühformen bis zur Gegenwart, 3rd ed. (München: Beck).

Westin, W. (1967): Privacy and Freedom (New York: Atheneum).

White, J.B. (1985): Heracles' Bow (Madison: University of Wisconsin).

White, L. (2010): Fifty Years of Academic Freedom Jurisprudence, in: The Journal of College and University Law, vol. 36, nr. 3, pp. 791–842.

Williams, M. (2001): Problems of Knowledge (Oxford: Oxford University Press).

Wills, G. (1978): Inventing America: Jefferson's Declaration of Independence (New York: Houghton Mifflin).

Wilsher, D. (2011): Immigration Detention. Law, History, Politics (Cambridge: Cambridge University Press).

Wilson, F. (2003): The Courtesan's Revenge: Harriett Wilson, the Woman who Blackmailed the King (London: Faber and Faber).

Winter, S.L. (2008): What Is the "Color" of Law, in: R.W. Gibbs, Jr., The Cambridge Handbook of Metaphor and Thought, (Cambridge: Cambridge University Press) pp. 363–379.

Woo, M.Y.K., Gallagher, M.E. (2011): Chinese Justice. Civil Dispute Resolution in Contemporary China (Cambridge: Cambridge University Press).

Woolner, A.C. (1924): Asoka Text and Glossary, vol. I–II (Calcutta: Punjab University Oriental Publications).

Working Group, Cabinet Secretariat (2006): Hôrei yôgo nichi-ei hyôjun taiyaku jisho. Japanese-English Legal Terms Standard Bilingual Dictionary (available online).

Xu, W.Y. (1998): The Court Records of O.J. Simpson Trial (Beijing: Publishing House of Law).

Zaehner, R.C. (1966): Hinduism (Oxford: Oxford University Press).

Zehnacker, H., Fredouille, J.C. (2013): Littérature latine, 2nd ed. (Paris: puf).

Zhang, N. (2002): Guoji fa yuanli (Theory of International Law) (Beijing: Zhongguo Zheng Fa Daxue).

Zhang, Q. (2004): Traditional Chinese Culture (Beijing: Foreign Languages Press).

Zhou, Q., Wang, J., Su, J. (eds.) (2007): Yuyan yu falü yanjiu de xin shiye. Language and Law in a New Perspective (Beijing: Law Press China).

Ziccardi Capaldo, G. (2008): The Pillars of Global Law (Aldershot: Ashgate).

Zitelmann, E. (1888): Die Möglichkeit eines Weltrechts (München/Leipzig: Duncker & Humblot).

Zuleta Puceiro, E. (1981): Paradigma dogmatico y ciencia del derecho (Madrid: Editoriales de Derecho Reunidas).

Index of names

Names of classical thinkers of Antiquity and the Middle Ages are not included in this index.

Index of matters

In the main texts many of the terms listed below are collocated with "legal" due to the context of their use. In the list, however, the attribute "legal" had been omitted in most cases for practical reasons.